An Introduction to Physical Science

Custom Edition
Louisiana State University Shreveport

Thirteenth Edition

James T. Shipman | Jerry D. Wilson | Charles A. Higgins, Jr.

Australia • Brazil • Japan • Korea • Mexico • Singapore • Spain • United Kingdom • United States

CENGAGE
Learning®

An Introduction to Physical Science: Custom Edition, Louisiana State University Shreveport, Thirteenth Edition

Senior Manager, Student Engagement:

Linda deStefano

Janey Moeller

Manager, Student Engagement:

Julie Dierig

Marketing Manager:

Rachael Kloos

Manager, Production Editorial:

Kim Fry

Manager, Intellectual Property Project Manager:

Brian Methe

Senior Manager, Production and Manufacturing:

Donna M. Brown

Manager, Production:

Terri Daley

An Introduction to Physical Science, Thirteenth Edition
James T. Shipman | Jerry D. Wilson | Charles A. Higgins, Jr.

© 2013 Cengage Learning. All rights reserved.

For product information and technology assistance, contact us at
Cengage Learning Customer & Sales Support, 1-800-354-9706

For permission to use material from this text or product,
submit all requests online at **cengage.com/permissions**
Further permissions questions can be emailed to
permissionrequest@cengage.com

This book contains select works from existing Cengage Learning resources and was produced by Cengage Learning Custom Solutions for collegiate use. As such, those adopting and/or contributing to this work are responsible for editorial content accuracy, continuity and completeness.

Compilation © 2014 Cengage Learning

ISBN-13: 9781305026667

ISBN-10: 1305026667

WCN: 01-100-101

Cengage Learning

5191 Natorp Boulevard
Mason, Ohio 45040
USA

Cengage Learning is a leading provider of customized learning solutions with office locations around the globe, including Singapore, the United Kingdom, Australia, Mexico, Brazil, and Japan. Locate your local office at:
international.cengage.com/region.

Cengage Learning products are represented in Canada by Nelson Education, Ltd.
For your lifelong learning solutions, visit **www.cengage.com/custom.**
Visit our corporate website at **www.cengage.com.**

Printed in the United States of America

Contents

Preface

Science and technology are the driving forces of change in our world today. They have created a revolution in all aspects of our lives, including communication, transportation, medical care, the environment, and education. Because the world is rapidly being transformed, it is important that today's students advance their knowledge of science. While increasing their understanding of the principles of science, students must also know how science is conducted, and when, where, and to what it is applied. Equipped with this knowledge, they can better adapt to their environment and make informed decisions that ultimately affect their lives and the lives of others.

The primary goal of the thirteenth edition of *An Introduction to Physical Science* is in keeping with that of previous editions: to stimulate students' interest in science and to build a solid foundation of general knowledge in the physical sciences. Additionally, we continue to present the content in such a way that students develop the critical reasoning and problem-solving skills that are needed in our ever-changing technological world.

An *Introduction to Physical Science,* Thirteenth Edition, as for previous editions, is intended for an introductory course for college nonscience majors. The five divisions of physical science are covered: physics, chemistry, astronomy, meteorology, and geology. Each division of physical science is discussed in the context of real-world examples. The textbook is readily adaptable to either a one- or two-semester course, or a two- to three-quarter course, allowing the instructor to select topics of his or her choice.

Approach

One of the outstanding features of this textbook continues to be its emphasis on fundamental concepts. These concepts are built on as we progress through the chapters. For example, Chapter 1, which introduces the concepts of measurement, is followed by chapters on the basic topics of physics: motion, force, energy, heat, wave motion, electricity and magnetism, atomic physics, and nuclear physics. This foundation in physics is useful in developing the principles of chemistry, astronomy, meteorology, and geology in the chapters that follow. We hope that this will lead to more students choosing careers in the sciences, engineering, and mathematics.

Organizational Updates in the Thirteenth Edition

The thirteenth edition of *An Introduction to Physical Science* retains its 24-chapter format. There have been several organizational changes in chapter order and title. Each chapter has several new Conceptual Questions and Answers features. These highlight not only important material but important nonmathematical concepts as well. A short section, Chapter 10.8, Elementary Particles, has been added so students may be familiar with items often heard in the news, such as quarks, the Large Hadron Collider (LHC), the Higgs boson (the God particle), and antimatter.

Chapter 13.5 has been expanded slightly, incorporating an example and exercises to emphasize the importance of Avogadro's number. Chapter 14 is reorganized slightly by adding section 14.6, Biochemistry, which groups all the information about biological materials together as they relate to chemistry.

Chapters 16 and 17 have updated sections because of the 2006 reorganization of solar system bodies by the International Astronomical Union (IAU), as well as new discoveries and classifications of objects beyond Neptune. These are section 16.6, The Dwarf Planets, and section 17.5, Moons of the Dwarf Planets. Also, the title of section 17.6 has been changed to Small Solar-System Bodies to conform to the new definition. Section 18.7, Cosmology, has been reorganized and updated slightly to incorporate the new findings regarding dark matter and dark energy. Chapters 16, 17, and 18 each have several new photos from the Hubble Space Telescope.

Chapters 19 and 20 have been updated to include recent tornado outbreaks, hurricanes, pollution, and global warming.

Chapters 21 and 22 retain their organization to provide a top-down discussion of geologic processes. The largest scale processes are presented first and work towards smaller ones. For example, the Earth's interior, continental drift, and plate tectonics are introduced in Chapter 21, and smaller-scale rock and mineral formations are discussed in Chapter 22. Finally, Chapter 24 retains its emphasis on the use of the scientific method to define the absolute geologic time scale and the age of the Earth.

Math Coverage and Support

Each discipline is treated both descriptively and quantitatively. To make the thirteenth edition user-friendly for students who are not mathematically inclined, we continue to introduce concepts to be treated mathematically as follows. First, the concept is defined, as briefly as possible, using words. The definition is then presented, where applicable, as an equation in word form. And, finally, the concept is expressed in symbolic notation.

The level of mathematics in the textbook continues to be no greater than that of general high school math. Appendixes I though VII provide a review of the math skills needed to deal with the mathematical exercises in this textbook. It may be helpful for students to begin their study by reading through these seven appendixes. This will help identify and remediate any mathematical weaknesses and thereby build confidence and ability for working the mathematical exercises in the textbook. Practice Exercises for mathematical concepts and skills appear in Cengage Learning's CourseMate.

Assistance is also offered to students by means of in-text worked *Examples* and follow-up *Confidence Exercises* (with answers at the end of the book). However, the relative emphasis, whether descriptive or quantitative, is left to the discretion of the instructor. To those who wish to emphasize a descriptive approach, the *Exercises* may be omitted, and the other end-of-chapter sections may be used for assignments.

Outstanding Pedagogical Features
in the Thirteenth Edition

▶ New to the thirteenth edition are chapter Conceptual Questions and Answers. Conceptual in nature (no mathematics), the questions are designed to pique student interest in associated chapter material—and answers are given. A few example questions (see text for answers):
- At night, a glass windowpane acts as a mirror when viewed from inside a lighted room. Why isn't it a mirror during the day?
- Why do wet clothes or water spots on clothes appear to be a darker color? Does the color change?
- Microwave glass oven doors have a metal mesh with holes. What is the purpose of this?
- We have a periodic table of elements. Why not a periodic table of compounds?
- Why do onions make you cry?
- Why is NO_2 called "laughing gas"?
- Does it ever get too cold to snow?
- Will the Sun turn into a black hole?
- What is one global Earth process we have studied that drives the rock cycle?

▶ Each chapter begins with a list of *Facts*—a brief description of interesting, pertinent, and user-friendly items regarding concepts and topics to be covered in the chapter.

▶ Each section begins with *Preview Questions* that ask about principles and concepts that should be learned in studying the section. The questions are also designed to introduce important topics to pique the curiosity of the student.

▶ Each section ends with *Did You Learn?* statements that remind and emphasize the answers to the *Preview Questions* and important section topics that should have been noted.

▶ The acclaimed *Highlight* feature has been retained, in detailed features of pertinent chapter topics.

▶ All worked-out *Examples* within a chapter give step-by-step solutions and are followed by related *Confidence Exercises* that give students immediate practice in solving that specific type of problem. *Answers to Confidence Exercises* may be found at the back of the book, so students can judge immediately their degree of comprehension.

▶ Nine *Appendixes* and a back-of-the-book *Glossary* of all chapter Key Terms and other associated terms are included to further aid student learning.

End-of-Chapter Features

For the thirteenth edition, the end-of-chapter material continues to include important features in the following order:

1. *Key Terms* that summarize the important boldface chapter terms, all of which are defined in the back-of-the-book *Glossary*.
2. Matching Questions following the *Key Terms* are designed to test students' ability to match an appropriate statement with each key term. For immediate feedback, answers to these questions are provided at the back of the book.
3. *Multiple-Choice Questions* follow the *Matching Questions*. The questions are keyed to the appropriate chapter section should the student need help, and the answers are given at the back of the book.
4. Next come *Fill-in-the-Blank Questions*. These questions are keyed to the appropriate chapter section should the student need help, and the answers are given at the back of the book.
5. *Short-Answer Questions* test students' knowledge of important concepts by section.
6. Following the *Short-Answer Questions* section is a colorful, associative *Visual Connection* of chapter terms. The answers to the *Visual Connection* can be found at the back of the book.
7. Next is the *Applying Your Knowledge* section. These questions involve conceptual and practical applications of material covered in the chapter and everyday topics relevant to the subject matter and challenge the student to apply the concepts learned.
8. When the chapter contains mathematical equations, a list of *Important Equations* is given as a helpful review tool for students and for quick reference when needed in working Exercises.
9. The *Exercises* section follows, but only for those chapters with mathematical content. As in previous editions, these exercises are *paired,* with the answer being provided to the first exercise (odd number) of each pair.
10. *On the Web* is the last end-of-chapter feature that challenges students to answer questions related to concepts discussed in each chapter. This feature is available and integrated with the textbook at: **www.cengagebrain.com/shop/ISBN/9781133104094** and also within CourseMate. It includes suggested answers and recommended hot-linked websites.

Design, Photo, and Illustration Program

Recognizing that many students are visual learners, we have increased the visual appeal and accessibility of this edition with new and more color photos and an updated art program.

Complete Text Support Package

CourseMate with eBook Interested in a simple way to complement your text and course content with study and practice materials? Cengage Learning's CourseMate brings course concepts to life with interactive learning, study, and exam preparation tools that support the printed textbook. Watch student comprehension soar as your class works with the printed textbook and the textbook-specific website.

CourseMate goes beyond the book to deliver what you need!

Enhanced WebAssign for Shipman, Wilson, Higgins's *An Introduction to Physical Science* **13th Edition** Exclusively from Cengage Learning, Enhanced WebAssign® combines the exceptional mathematics, physics, and astronomy content that you know and love with the most powerful online homework solution, WebAssign. Enhanced WebAssign engages students with immediate feedback and an interactive eBook, helping students to develop a deeper conceptual understanding of their subject matter. Online assignments can be built by selecting from hundreds of text-specific problems or supplemented with problems from any Cengage Learning textbook.

Enhanced WebAssign includes the Cengage YouBook: an engaging and customizable new eBook that lets you tailor the textbook to fit your course and connect with your students. You can remove and rearrange chapters in the table of contents and tailor assigned readings that match your syllabus exactly. Powerful editing tools let you change as much as you'd like–or leave it just like it is. You can highlight key passages or add sticky notes to pages to comment on a concept in the reading, and then share any of these individual notes and highlights with your students, or keep them personal. You can also edit narrative content in the textbook by adding a text box or striking out text. With a handy link tool, you can drop in an icon at any point in the eBook that lets you link to your own lecture notes, audio summaries, video lectures, or other files on a personal website or anywhere on the web. A simple YouTube widget lets you easily find and embed videos from YouTube directly into eBook pages.

The Cengage YouBook helps students go beyond just reading the textbook. Students can also highlight the text, add their own notes, and bookmark the text. Animations and videos play right on the page at the point of learning so that they're not speed bumps to reading but true enhancements.

WebTutor Rich with content for your physical sciences course, this Web-based teaching and learning tool integrates with your school's learning management system and includes course management, study/mastery, and communication tools. A wealth of student learning activities includes animations, quizzing, and flashcards. Chapter-based practice quizzes offer immediate feedback and link to the interactive eBook so students can focus their efforts where they need to. Reduce your preparation time with a fully customizable test bank and PowerPoint lectures. Use WebTutor™ to provide virtual office hours, post your syllabus, and track student progress—all directly from your learning management system.

PowerLecture for Shipman, Wilson, Higgins's *An Introduction To Physical Science,* **13th Edition** This DVD provides the instructor with dynamic media tools for teaching. This dual-platform digital library and presentation tool provides text art, photos, and tables in a variety of easily exportable electronic formats. This enhanced DVD also contains animations to supplement your lectures, as well as lecture outlines. In addition, you can customize your presentations by importing your personal lecture slides or any other material you choose. Microsoft® PowerPoint® lecture slides and figures from the book are also included on this DVD. Turn your lectures into an interactive learning environment that promotes conceptual understanding with "clicker" content. With these slides you can pose text-specific questions to a large group, gather results, and display students' answers seamlessly. Using Diploma, instructors have all of the tools they need to create, author/edit, customize, and deliver multiple types of tests. Instructors can import questions directly from the test bank, create their own questions, or edit existing algorithmic questions, all within Diploma's powerful electronic platform.

Acknowledgments

We wish to thank our colleagues and students for the many contributions they continue to make to this textbook through correspondence, questionnaires, and classroom testing of the material. We would also like to thank all those who have helped us greatly in shaping this text over the years and especially the following reviewers of this thirteenth edition:

Jennifer Cash, South Carolina State University

Richard Holland, Southeastern Illinois College

Mark Holycross, Spartanburg Methodist College

Trecia Markes, University of Nebraska—Kearney

Eric C. Martell, Millikin University

Robert Mason, Illinois Eastern Community College

Edgar Newman, Coastal Carolina University

Michael J. O'Shea, Kansas State University

Kendra Sibbernsen, Metropolitan Community College

Todd Vaccaro, Francis Marion University

While they are not official reviewers for the book, we would like to acknowledge the contributions to the chemistry chapters by Lynn Deanhardt, Lander University, and Allison Wind, Middle Tennessee State University.

We are grateful to those individuals and organizations who contributed photographs, illustrations, and other information used in the text. We are also indebted to the Cengage Learning staff and several others for their dedicated and conscientious efforts in the production of *An Introduction to Physical Science*. We especially would like to thank Mary Finch, Publisher, Physical Sciences; Charles Hartford, Publisher, Astronomy and Physics; Brandi Kirksey, Development Editor; Margaret Pinette, Development Editor; Brendan Killion, Editorial Assistant; Cathy Brooks, Senior Content Project Manager; Jack Cooney, Marketing Manager; and Cate Barr, Senior Art Director.

As in previous editions, we continue to welcome comments from students and instructors of physical science and invite you to send us your impressions and suggestions.

About the Authors

James T. Shipman passed away July 10, 2009. (See descriptive note on Jim below.)

Jerry D. Wilson received his physics degrees from: B.S., Ohio University; M.S., Union College (Schenectady, NY); and Ph.D., Ohio University. He is one of the original authors of the first edition of *An Introduction to Physical Science,* published nationally in 1971, and has several physics textbooks to his credit. Wilson is currently Emeritus Professor of Physics at Lander University, Greenwood, SC. Email: *jwilson@greenwood.net*

Charles A. (Chuck) Higgins received his B.S. degree in physics from the University of Alabama in Huntsville, and his M.S. and Ph.D. degrees in astronomy from the University of Florida in 1996. Areas of interest and research include planetary radio astronomy, astronomy education, and public outreach. He is currently an Associate Professor in the Department of Physics and Astronomy at Middle Tennessee State University in Murfreesboro, Tennessee. Email: *chiggins@mtsu.edu*

A note about our coauthor, James T. Shipman, who passed away July 10, 2009, at the age of 90. Jim initiated the first of three sections of *An Introduction to Physical Science* in the late 1960s. He wrote the first physics section and collaborated with Jerry L. Adams on the second section, modern physics and chemistry. Being elected chair of a large physics department at Ohio University and his time limited, he asked Jerry D. Wilson and Jack Baker to write the third meteorology and geology section. The textbook was published locally until the national publication by D.C. Heath and Co. in 1971. Jim contributed directly to nine editions until his retirement but continued to revise the accompanying laboratory manual with Clyde Baker. He will be missed and fondly remembered.

A note about a previous coauthor, *Aaron W. Todd.* Aaron passed away April 5th, 2007, after a valiant battle against brain cancer. His contributions to five editions of *An Introduction to Physical Science* were many and appreciated. His input and friendship are greatly missed.

Measurement

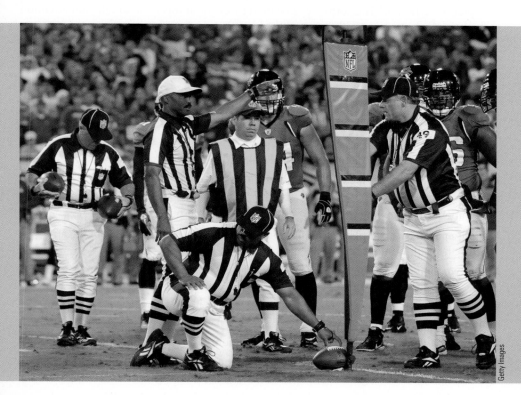

It is a capital mistake to theorize before one has data. Insensibly one begins to twist the facts to suit the theories, instead of the theories to suit the facts.

•

Sherlock Holmes
(Arthur Conan Doyle,
1859–1930)

< Bring in the chain for a measurement. First and 10!

S cience is concerned with the description and understanding of our environment. A first step in understanding our environment is to measure and describe the physical world. Over the centuries, humans have developed increasingly sophisticated methods of measurement, and scientists make use of the most advanced of these.

We are continually making measurements in our daily lives. Watches and clocks are used to measure the time it takes for events to take place. A census is taken every 10 years to determine (measure) the population. Money, calories, and the days and years of our lives are counted.

It was once thought that all things could be measured with exact certainty, but as smaller and smaller objects were measured, it became evident that the act of

PHYSICS FACTS

▶ Tradition holds that in the twelfth century, King Henry I of England decreed that 1 yard should be the distance from his royal nose to the thumb of his outstretched arm. (Had King Henry's arm been 3.37 inches longer, the yard and the meter would have been equal in length.)

▶ The abbreviation for the pound, lb, comes from the Latin word *libra,* which was a Roman unit of weight approximately equal to 1 pound. The word *pound* comes from the Latin *pondero,* meaning "to weigh." Libra is also a sign of the zodiac, symbolized by a set of scales (used for weight measurement).

Chapter Outline

measuring distorted the measurement. This uncertainty in making measurements of the very small is discussed in more detail in Chapter 9.5. (Note that "Chapter 9.5" means "Chapter 9, Section 5." This format will be used throughout this book to call your attention to further information in another part of the book.)

Measurement is crucial to understanding our physical environment, but first let's discuss the physical sciences and the methods of scientific investigation.

1.1   The Physical Sciences

Preview Questions*

● What are the two major divisions of natural science?
● What are the five major divisions of physical science?

Think about the following:

▶ *Hung up.* A basketball player leaping up to make a shot seems to "hang" in the air before he slam-dunks a basketball.

▶ *Spot you one.* Driving in the summer, you may see what looks like water or a "wet spot" on the road ahead, but you never get to it.

▶ *All stuck up.* The professor rubs a balloon on his sweater and touches it to the ceiling, and the balloon stays there.

▶ *Mighty small.* There are pictures of individual atoms.

▶ *It doesn't add up.* Exactly 100 cc of ethanol alcohol is mixed with exactly 100 cc of water, and the resulting mixture is less than 200 cc.

▶ *Get in line.* There won't be a total solar eclipse visible from the United States until 2017, but there will be six or more visible elsewhere before then.

▶ *Dark Moon.* The dark side of the Moon isn't dark all the time.

▶ *A bolt from the blue.* You don't have to be in a thunderstorm for lightning to strike.

▶ *No blow.* One continent has no hurricanes, and a particular latitude has none either.

▶ *All shook up.* An earthquake with a magnitude of 8.0 on the Richter scale is not twice as energetic as one with a magnitude of 4.0 (but about a million times more).

▶ *Keep an eye on the sky.* There is evidence that a meteorite caused dinosaurs to become extinct.

Would you like to know how or why such things occur, or how they are known? All these statements are explained in this book. Most people are curious about such topics, and explanations of these and many other phenomena are obtained through scientific observations. The above statements pertain to physical science, but there are several other branches of science as well.

Science (from the Latin *scientia,* meaning "knowledge") may be defined as an organized body of knowledge about the natural universe and the processes by which that knowledge is acquired and tested. In general, there are *social sciences,* which deal with human society and individual relationships, and *natural sciences,* which investigate the natural universe. In turn, the natural sciences are divided into the *biological sciences* (sometimes called *life sciences*), which are concerned with the study of living matter, and the *physical sciences,* which involve the study of nonliving matter.

---

*Preview Questions are listed at the beginning of each section. The answers to these questions are found in the related Did You Learn at the end of the section.

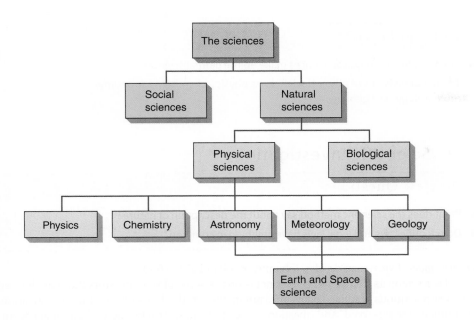

Figure 1.1 The Major Physical Sciences
A diagram showing the five major physical sciences and how they fit into the various divisions of the sciences. (See text for discussion.)

This book introduces the various disciplines of physical science, the theories and laws fundamental to each, some of the history of their development, and the effect each has on our lives. Physical science is classified into five major divisions (● Fig. 1.1):

Physics, the most fundamental of the divisions, is concerned with the basic principles and concepts of matter and energy.

Chemistry deals with the composition, structure, and reactions of matter.

Astronomy is the study of the universe, which is the totality of all matter, energy, space, and time.

Meteorology is the study of the atmosphere, from the surface of the Earth to where it ends in outer space.

Geology is the science of the planet Earth: its composition, structure, processes, and history.

(The last three physical sciences are sometimes combined as *Earth and Space Science.*)

Physics is considered the most fundamental of these divisions because each of the other disciplines applies the principles and concepts of matter and energy to its own particular focus. Therefore, our study of physical science starts with physics (Chapters 1–10); then moves on to chemistry (Chapters 11–14), astronomy (Chapters 15–18), and meteorology (Chapters 19 and 20); and ends with geology (Chapters 21–24).

This exploration will enrich your knowledge of the physical sciences and give you perspective on how science has grown throughout the course of human history; how science influences the world we live in today; and how it is employed through *technology* (the application of scientific knowledge for practical purposes).

Although the earliest humans had no sophisticated means to make measurements, they did have curiosity about the world around them, along with a compelling need to survive in a harsh environment that resulted in the making of tools and the harnessing of fire. The desire to understand the movement of the stars, the passing of the seasons, and the hope of predicting the weather by using the clues of the wind and the clouds grew out of such curiosity and all were addressed by observations of the Earth and sky.

Indeed, observation forms the basis of all scientific knowledge, even in the modern world. Scientific knowledge is cumulative, and if our predecessors had not asked questions and made observations, our own knowledge of the physical sciences would be far less extensive. Each new discovery yields the possibility for more.

1.2   Scientific Investigation

Preview Questions

● What does the scientific method say about the description of nature?

● Do scientific laws and legal laws have anything in common?

Theory guides. Experiment decides. Johannes Kepler (1571–1630)

Today's scientists do not jump to conclusions as some of our ancestors did, which often led to superstitious results. Today, measurements are the basis of scientific investigation. Phenomena are observed, and questions arise about how or why these phenomena occur. These questions are investigated by the **scientific method.**

The scientific method can be broken down into the following elements:

1. *Observations* and *measurements* (quantitative data).

2. *Hypothesis.* A possible explanation for the observations; in other words, a tentative answer or an educated guess.

3. *Experiments.* The testing of a hypothesis under controlled conditions to see whether the test results confirm the hypothetical assumptions, can be duplicated, and are consistent. If not, more observations and measurements may be needed.

4. *Theory.* If a hypothesis passes enough experimental tests and generates new predictions that also prove correct, then it takes on the status of a theory, a well-tested explanation of observed natural phenomena. (Even theories may be debated by scientists until experimental evidence decides the debate. If a theory does not withstand continued experimentation, then it must be modified, rejected, or replaced by a new theory.)

5. *Law.* If a theory withstands the test of many well-designed, valid experiments and there is great regularity in the results, then that theory may be accepted by scientists as a *law.* A law is a concise statement in words or mathematical equations that describes a fundamental relationship of nature. Scientific laws are somewhat analogous to legal laws, which may be repealed or modified if inconsistencies are later discovered. Unlike legal laws, scientific laws are meant to describe, not regulate.

The bottom line on the scientific method is that no hypothesis, theory, or law of nature is valid unless its predictions are in agreement with experimental (quantitative measurement) results. See ● Fig. 1.2 for a flowchart representing the scientific method.

The **Highlight: The "Face" on Mars**, which follows, illustrates the need for the scientific method.

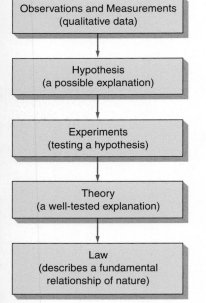

Figure 1.2 The Scientific Method A flowchart showing the elements of the scientific method. If experiments show that a hypothesis is not consistent with the facts, more observations and measurements may be needed.

*Did You Learn? notes are listed at the end of each section and relate to the Preview Questions at the beginning of each section.

1.3 The Senses

Preview Questions

- Which two senses give us the most information about our environment?
- How may our senses be enhanced?

Our environment stimulates our senses, either directly or indirectly. The five senses (sight, hearing, touch, taste, and smell) make it possible for us to know about our environment. Therefore, the senses are vitally important in studying and understanding the physical world.

Most information about our environment comes through sight. Hearing ranks second in supplying the brain with information about the external world. Touch, taste, and smell, although important, rank well below sight and hearing in providing environmental information.

All the senses have limitations. For example, the unaided eye cannot see the vast majority of stars and galaxies. We cannot immediately distinguish the visible stars of our galaxy from the planets of our solar system, which all appear as points of light. The limitations

Highlight The "Face" on Mars

In 1976, NASA's *Viking 1* spacecraft was orbiting Mars. When snapping photos, the spacecraft captured the shadowy likeness of an enormous head, 2 miles from end to end and located in a region of Mars called Cydonia (Fig. 1a).

The surprise among the mission controllers at NASA was quickly tempered as planetary scientists decided that the "face" was just another Martian mesa, a geologic landform common in the Cydonia region. When NASA released the photo to the public a few days later, the caption noted a "huge rock formation . . . which resembles a human head . . . formed by shadows giving the illusion of eyes, nose, and mouth." NASA scientists thought that the photo would attract the public's attention to its Mars mission, and indeed it did!

The "face" on Mars became a sensation, appearing in newspapers (particularly tabloids), in books, and on TV talk shows. Some people thought that it was evidence of life on Mars, either at present or in the past, or perhaps that it was the result of a visit to the planet by aliens. As for NASA's contention that the "face" could be entirely explained as a combination of a natural landform and unusual lighting conditions, howls arose from some of the public about "cover-up" and "conspiracy." Other people, with a more developed scientific attitude, gave provisional acceptance to NASA's conclusion, realizing that extraordinary claims (witty aliens) need extraordinary proof.

Twenty-two years later, in 1998, the *Mars Global Surveyor* (MGS) mission reached Mars, and its camera snapped a picture of the "face" 10 times sharper than the 1976 *Viking* photo. Thousands waited for the image to appear on NASA's website. The photo revealed a natural landform, not an alien monument. However, the image was taken through wispy clouds, and some people were still not convinced that the object was just a plain old mesa.

Not until 2001 did the MGS camera again pass over the object. This time there were no clouds, and the high-resolution picture was clearly that of a mesa similar to those common in the Cydonia region and the American West (Fig. 1b).

Why would so many articles and books be written extolling the alien origin of the "face"? Perhaps many authors were trading on the gullibility and ignorance of part of our population to line their own pockets or to gain attention. If so, the best ways to deal with similar situations in the future would be to improve the standard of education among the general public and to emphasize the importance of a well-developed scientific method.

Most of the information for this Highlight came from Tony Phillips, "Unmasking the Face on Mars," NASA, May 24, 2001.

(a)

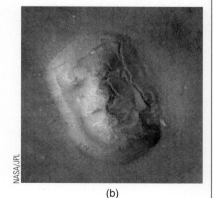

(b)

Figure 1 The Face on Mars
(a) In 1976, at the low resolution of the *Viking I* camera, the appearance of a sculpted face can be seen. (b) In 2001, at the high resolution of the *Mars Global Surveyor* camera, the object is seen to be a common mesa.

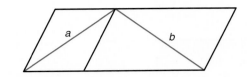

(a) Is the diagonal line *b* longer than the diagonal line *a*?

(b) Are the horizontal lines parallel or do they slope?

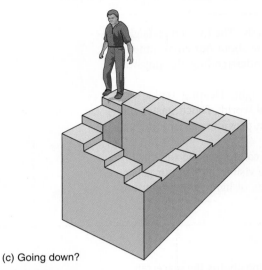

(c) Going down?

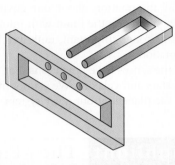

(d) Is something dimensionally wrong here?

Figure 1.3 Some Optical Illusions
We can be deceived by what we see. Answer the questions under the drawings.

of the senses can be reduced by using measuring instruments such as microscopes and telescopes. Other examples of limitations are our temperature sense of touch being limited to a range of hotness and coldness before injury and our hearing being limited to a certain frequency range (Chapter 6.4).

Not only do the senses have limitations, but they also can be deceived, thus providing false information about our environment. For example, perceived sight information may not always be a true representation of the facts because the brain can be fooled. There are many well-known optical illusions, such as those shown in ● Fig. 1.3. Some people may be quite convinced that what they see in such drawings actually exists as they perceive it. However, we can generally eliminate deception by using instruments. For example, the use of rulers to answer the questions in Fig. 1.3a and b.

Did You Learn?

● Sight and hearing give us the greatest amount of information about our environment.

● The limitations of the senses can be reduced by using instruments such as microscopes and telescopes.

1.4 Standard Units and Systems of Units

Preview Questions

● What is a standard unit?

● What are the standards units of length, mass, and time in the SI?

To describe nature, we make measurements and express these measurements in terms of the magnitudes of units. Units enable us to describe things in a concrete way, that is, numerically. Suppose that you are given the following directions to find the way to cam-

NOTRE SIGNALISATION ROUTIÈRE EST **MÉTRIQUE**
OUR TRAFFIC SIGNS ARE **METRIC**
MAXIMUM 55 → MAXIMUM 90
km/h

Pascal Quittemelle/Stock Boston

Figure 1.4 A Mostly Metric World
This Canadian sign warns drivers that the metric system is in use. Notice the differences in the magnitudes of the speed limit. You'd better not go 90 mi/h.

pus when you first arrive in town: "Keep going on this street for a few blocks, turn left at a traffic light, go a little ways, and you're there." Certainly some units or numbers would be helpful.

Many objects and phenomena can be described in terms of the *fundamental* physical quantities of length, mass, and time (*fundamental* because they are the most basic quantities or properties we can imagine). In fact, the topics of *mechanics*—the study of motion and force—covered in the first few chapters of this book require *only* these physical quantities. Another fundamental quantity, electric charge, will be discussed in Chapter 8. For now, let's focus on the units of length, mass, and time.

To measure these fundamental quantities, we compare them with a reference, or standard, that is taken to be a standard unit. That is, a **standard unit** is a fixed and reproducible value for the purpose of taking accurate measurements. Traditionally, a government or international body establishes a standard unit.

A group of standard units and their combinations is called a **system of units**. Two major systems of units in use today are the **metric system** and the **British system**. The latter is used primarily in the United States but is gradually being replaced in favor of in favor of the metric system, which is used throughout most of the world (● Fig. 1.4). The United States is the only major country that has not gone completely metric.

Length

The description of space might refer to a location or to the size of an object (amount of space occupied). To measure these properties, we use the fundamental quantity of **length**, the measurement of space in any direction.

Space has three dimensions, each of which can be measured in terms of length. The three dimensions are easily seen by considering a rectangular object such as a bathtub (● Fig. 1.5). It has length, width, and height, but each dimension is actually a length. The dimensions of space are commonly represented by a three-dimensional Cartesian coordinate system (named in honor of French mathematician René Descartes, 1596–1650, who developed the system).

The standard unit of length in the metric system is the **meter** (m), from the Greek *metron*, "to measure." It was defined originally as one ten-millionth of the distance from the Earth's equator to the geographic North Pole (● Fig. 1.6a). A portion of the meridian between Dunkirk, France, and Barcelona, Spain, was measured to determine the meter length, and

Figure 1.5 Space Has Three Dimensions
(a) The bathtub has dimensions of length (*l*), width (*w*), and height (*h*), but all are actually measurements of length. (b) The dimensions of space are commonly represented by a three-dimensional Cartesian coordinate system (*x, y, z*) with the origin as the reference point.

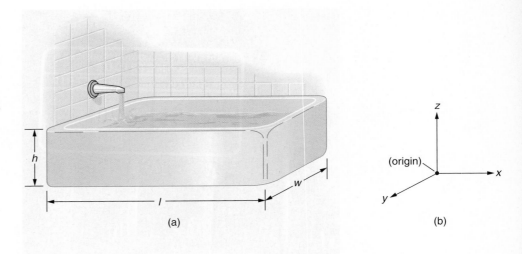

that unit was first adopted in France in the 1790s. One meter is slightly longer than 1 yard, as illustrated in Fig. 1.6b.

From 1889 to 1960, the standard meter was defined as the length of a platinum–iridium bar kept at the International Bureau of Weights and Measures in Paris, France. However, the stability of the bar was questioned (for example, length variations occur with temperature changes), so new standards were adopted in 1960 and again in 1983. The current definition links the meter to the speed of light in a vacuum, as illustrated in Fig. 1.6c. Light travels at a speed of 299,792,458 meters/second (usually listed as 3.00×10^8 m/s). So, by definition, 1 meter is the distance light travels in 1/299,792,458 of a second.

The standard unit of length in the British system is the *foot,* which historically was referenced to the human foot. As noted in the Physics Facts at the beginning of this chapter, King Henry I used his arm to define the yard. Other early units commonly were referenced to parts of the body. For example, the *hand* is a unit that even today is used in measuring the heights of horses (1 hand is 4 in.).

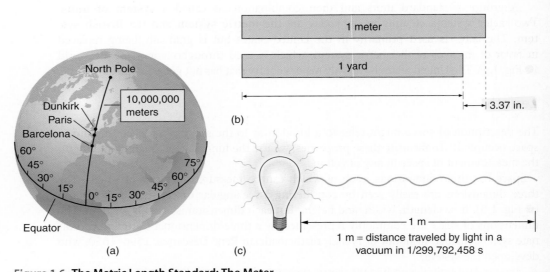

Figure 1.6 The Metric Length Standard: The Meter
(a) The meter was originally defined such that the distance from the North Pole to the equator would be 10 million meters. (b) One meter is a little longer than one yard, about 3.4 in. longer (not to scale). (c) The meter is now defined by the distance light travels in a vacuum in a small fraction of a second.

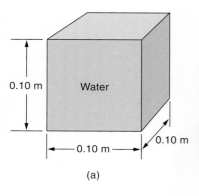

(a)   (b)

Figure 1.7 The Metric Mass Standard: The Kilogram
(a) The kilogram was originally defined in terms of a specific volume of water, that of a cube 0.10 m on a side (at 4°C, the temperature at which water has its maximum density). As such, the mass standard was associated with the length standard. (b) Prototype kilogram number 20 is the U.S. standard unit of mass. The prototype is a platinum–iridium cylinder 39 mm in diameter and 39 mm high.

National Institute of Standards and Technology

Mass

Mass is the amount of matter an object contains. The more massive an object, the more matter it contains. (More precise definitions of mass in terms of force and acceleration, and in terms of gravity, will be discussed in Chapter 3.)

The standard metric unit of mass is the **kilogram** (kg). Originally, this amount of matter was related to length and was defined as the amount of water in a cubic container 0.10 m, or 10 cm, on a side (● Fig. 1.7a). However, for convenience, the mass standard was referenced to a material standard (an artifact or a human-made object). Currently, the kilogram is defined to be the mass of a cylinder of platinum–iridium kept at the International Bureau of Weights and Measures in Paris. The U.S. prototype (copy) is kept at the National Institute of Standards and Technology (NIST) in Washington, D.C. (Fig. 1.7b).

This standard is based on an artifact rather than on a natural phenomenon. Even though the cylinder is kept under controlled conditions, its mass is subject to slight changes because of contamination and loss from surface cleaning. A property of nature, by definition, is always the same and in theory can be measured anywhere. Scientists have yet to agree on an appropriate fundamental constant, such as the speed of light for the meter, on which to base the kilogram.

The unit of mass in the British system is the *slug,* a rarely used unit. We will not use this unit in our study because a quantity of matter in the British system is expressed in terms of weight on the surface of the Earth and in units of pounds. (The British system is sometimes said to be a gravitational system.) Unfortunately, weight is not a *fundamental* quantity, and its use often gives rise to confusion. Of course, a fundamental quantity should be the same and not change. However, weight is the gravitational attraction on an object by a celestial body, and this attraction is different for different celestial bodies. (The gravitational attraction of a body depends on its mass).

For example, on the less massive Moon, the gravitational attraction is $\frac{1}{6}$ that on the Earth, so an object on the Moon weighs $\frac{1}{6}$ less than on the Earth. For example, a suited astronaut who weighs 300 pounds on the Earth will weigh $\frac{1}{6}$ that amount, or 50 pounds, on the Moon, but the astronaut's mass will be the same (● Fig. 1.8).

A fundamental quantity does not change at different locations. The astronaut has the same mass, or quantity of matter, wherever he or she is. As will be learned in Chapter 3.3, mass and weight are related, but they are not the same. For now, keep in mind that *mass, not weight, is the fundamental quantity.*

Time

Each of us has an idea of what time is, but when asked to define it, you may have to ponder a bit.

Some terms often used when referring to time are *duration, period,* and *interval.* A common descriptive definition is that **time** is the continuous, forward flow of events. Without

Figure 1.8 Mass Is the Fundamental Quantity
The weight of an astronaut on the Moon is $\frac{1}{6}$ the astronaut's weight on the Earth, but the astronaut's mass is the same in any location.

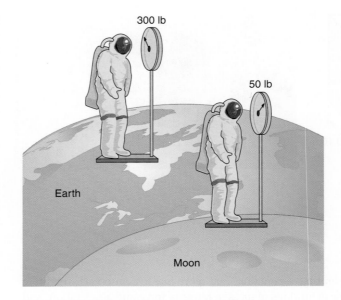

Figure 1.9 Time and Events
Events mark intervals of time. Here, at the New York City Marathon, after starting out (beginning event), a runner crosses the finish line (end event) in a time of 2 hours, 12 minutes, and 38 seconds.

events or happenings of some sort, there would be no perceived time (● Fig. 1.9). The mind has no innate awareness of time, only an awareness of events taking place in time. In other words, we do not perceive time as such, only events that mark locations in time, similar to marks on a meterstick indicating length intervals.

Note that time has only one direction—forward. Time has never been observed to run backward. That would be like watching a film run backward in a projector.

Conceptual Question and Answer

Time and Time Again

Q. What is time?

A. Time is a difficult concept to define. The common definition that *time is the continuous, forward flow of events* is more of an observation that a definition.

Others have thought about time. Marcus Aurelius, the Roman emperor and philosopher, wrote:

Time is a strong river of passing events, and strong is its current.

St. Augustine pondered this question, too:

What is time? If no one asks me, I know; if I want to explain it to a questioner, I do not know.

The Mad Hatter in Lewis Carroll's *Alice in Wonderland* thought he knew time:

If you know time as well as I do, you wouldn't talk about wasting it. It's him. . . . Now, if you only kept on good terms with him, he'd do almost anything you liked with the clock. For instance, suppose it were nine o'clock in the morning, just time to begin lessons; you'd only have to whisper a hint to Time, and around goes the clock in a twinkling: Half past one, time for dinner.

A safe answer is: *Time is a fundamental property or concept.* This definition masks our ignorance, and physics goes on from there, using the concept to describe and explain what we observe.

Time and space seem to be linked. In fact, time is sometimes considered a fourth dimension, along with the other three dimensions of space. If something exists in space, it also must exist in time. But for our discussion, space and time will be regarded as separate quantities.

Fortunately, the standard unit of time is the same in both the metric and British systems: the **second**. The second was originally defined in terms of observations of the Sun, as a certain fraction of a solar day (● Fig. 1.10a).

In 1967, an atomic standard was adopted. The second was defined in terms of the radiation frequency of the cesium-133 atom. This "atomic clock" used a beam of cesium atoms to maintain our time standard with a variation of about 1 second in 300 years (Fig. 1.10b). In 1999, another cesium-133 clock was adopted. This atomic "fountain clock," as its name implies, uses a fountain of cesium atoms (Fig. 1.10c). The variation of this timepiece is within 1 second per 100 million years.

NIST is currently working on a "quantum logic" clock that makes use of the oscillations of a single ion of aluminum. It is expected to not gain or lose more than 1 second in about 3.7 billion years!

The standard units for length, mass, and time in the metric system give rise to an acronym, the **mks** system. The letters *mks* stand for *meter, kilogram,* and *second.* They are also standard units for a modernized version of the metric system, called the International System of Units (abbreviated **SI,** from the French *Système International d'Unités).*

When more applicable, smaller units than those standard in the mks system may be used. Although the mks system is the *standard* system, the smaller *cgs system* is sometimes used, where *cgs* stands for *centimeter, gram,* and *second.* For comparison, the units for length, mass, and time for the various systems are listed in ● Table 1.1.

Table 1.1 Units of Length, Mass, and Time for the Metric and British Systems of Measurement

Fundamental Quantity	Metric		British
	SI or mks	*cgs*	
Length	meter (m)	centimeter (cm)	foot (ft)
Mass	kilogram (kg)	gram (g)	slug
Time	second (s)	second (s)	second (s)

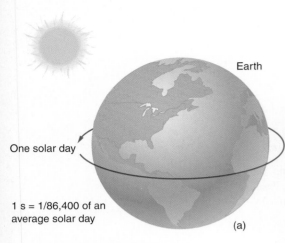

One solar day

1 s = 1/86,400 of an
average solar day

(a)

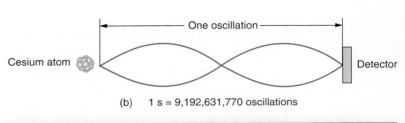

Cesium atom

One oscillation

Detector

(b)   1 s = 9,192,631,770 oscillations

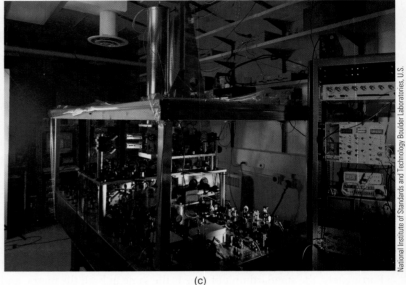

(c)

National Institute of Standards and Technology Boulder Laboratories, U.S.

Figure 1.10 A Second of Time
(a) The second was defined originally in terms of a fraction of the average solar day. (b) One second is currently defined in terms of the frequency of radiation emitted from the cesium atom. (c) A clock? Yes, the National Institute of Standards and Technology (NIST) "fountain" cesium atomic clock. Such a clock provides the time standard for the United States.

Did You Learn?

● A standard unit is a fixed and reproducible value for accurate measurements.

● The SI standard units for length, mass, and time are the meter, kilogram, and second, respectively.

1.5   More on the Metric System

Preview Questions

● What are the four most common metric prefixes?

● What is the difference between a cubic centimeter (cm^3) and a milliliter (mL)?

The SI was established in 1960 to make comprehension and the exchange of ideas among the people of different nations as simple as possible. It now contains seven base units: the meter (m), the kilogram (kg), the second (s), the ampere (A) to measure the flow of electric charge, the kelvin (K) to measure temperature, the mole (mol) to measure the amount of a substance, and the candela (cd) to measure luminous intensity. A definition of each of these units is given in Appendix I. However, we will be concerned with only the first three of these units for several chapters.

One major advantage of the metric system is that it is a decimal (base-10) system. The British system is a duodecimal (base-12) system, as in 12 inches equals a foot. The base-10 system allows easy expression and conversion to larger and smaller units. A series of *metric prefixes* is used to express the multiples of 10, but you will only need to know a few common ones:

mega- (M)   1,000,000 (million, 10^6)
kilo- (k)   1000 (thousand, 10^3)
centi- (c) $\frac{1}{100} = 0.01$ (hundredth, 10^{-2})
milli- (m) $\frac{1}{1000} = 0.001$ (thousandth, 10^{-3})

Examples of the relationships of these prefixes follow.

1 meter is equal to 100 centimeters (cm) or 1000 millimeters (mm).
1 kilogram is equal to 1000 grams (g).
1 millisecond (ms) is equal to 0.001 second (s).
1 megabyte (Mb) is equal to a million bytes.
(See ● Table 1.2 for more metric prefixes.)

You are familiar with another base-10 system: our currency. A cent is $\frac{1}{100}$ of a dollar, or a centidollar. A dime is $\frac{1}{10}$ of a dollar, or a decidollar. Tax assessments and school bond levies are sometimes given in mills. Although not as common as a cent, a mill is $\frac{1}{1000}$ of a dollar, or a millidollar.

As using factors of 10 demonstrates, the decimal metric system makes it much simpler to convert from one unit to another than in the British system. For example, it is easy to see that 1 kilometer is 1000 meters and 1 meter is 100 centimeters. In the British system, though, 1 mile is 5280 feet and 1 foot is 12 inches, making this system unwieldy compared with the metric system.

Some nonstandard metric units are in use. One of the most common is a unit of fluid volume or capacity. Recall that the kilogram was originally defined as the mass of a cube of water 0.10 m, or 10 cm, on a side (Fig. 1.7a). This volume was defined to be a **liter** (L). Hence, 1 L has a volume of 10 cm × 10 cm × 10 cm = 1000 cm^3 (cubic centimeters, sometimes abbreviated as cc, particularly in chemistry and biology). Because 1 L is 1000 cm^3 and 1 kg of water is 1000 g, it follows that 1 cm^3 of water has a mass of 1 g. Also, because 1 L contains 1000 milliliters (mL), 1 cm^3 is the same volume as 1 mL (● Fig. 1.11).*

Table 1.2 Some Metric Prefixes

Prefix	Symbol	Example: meter (m)	Pronunciation
giga- (billion)	G	Gm (gigameter, 1,000,000,000 m or 10^9 m)*	JIG-a (*jig* as in *jiggle, a* as in *about*)
mega- (million)	M	Mm (megameter, 1,000,000 m or 10^6 m)	MEG-a (as in *megaphone*)
kilo- (thousand)	k	km (kilometer, 1000 m or 10^3 m)	KIL-o (as in *kilowatt*)
hecto- hundred)	h	hm (hectometer, 100 m or 10^2 m)	HEK-to (*heck-toe*)
deka- (ten)	da	dam (dekameter, 10 m or 10^1 m)	DEK-a (*deck* plus *a* as in *about*)
		meter (m)	
deci- (one-tenth)	d	dm (decimeter, 0.10 m or 10^{-1} m)	DES-I (as in *decimal*)
centi- (one-hundredth)	c	cm (centimeter, 0.01 m or 10^{-2} m)	SENT-i (as in *sentimental*)
milli- (one-thousandth)	m	mm (millimeter, 0.001 m or 10^{-3} m)	MIL-li (as in *military*)
micro- (one-millionth)	μ	μm (micrometer, 0.000001 m or 10^{-6} m)	MI-kro (as in *microphone*)
nano- (one-billionth)	n	nm (nanometer, 0.000000001 m or 10^{-9} m)[†]	NAN-oh (*an* as in *annual*)

*Powers-of-10, or scientific, notation (10^x) is often used instead of decimals. If you are not familiar with this notation, or if you need to review it, see Appendix VI.

[†]You will be hearing more about nano- in terms of *nanotechnology,* which is any technology on the nanometer scale. To get an idea of this size, a human hair is about 50,000 nm across, and it takes 10 hydrogen atoms in a line to make 1 nanometer.

---

*The liter is sometimes abbreviated with a lowercase "ell" (l) as in ml, but a capital "ell" (L) is preferred so that the abbreviation is less likely to be confused with the numeral one (1). In type, 1 L is much clearer than 1 l.

Figure 1.11 Mass and Volume (the Liter)
(a) The kilogram was originally related to length. The mass of the quantity of water in a cubic container 10 cm on a side was taken to be 1 kg. As a result, 1 cm³ of water has a mass of 1 g. The volume of the container was defined to be 1 liter (L), and 1 cm³ = 1 mL. (b) One liter is slightly larger than 1 quart.

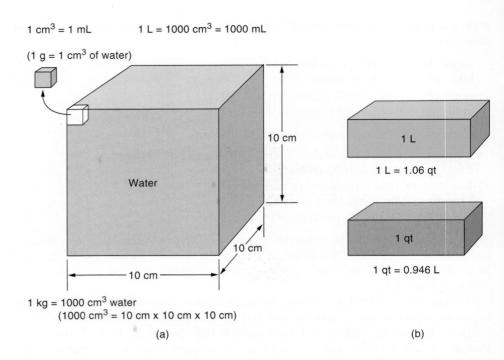

(a)   (b)

You may wonder why a nonstandard volume such as the liter is used when the standard metric volume would use the standard meter length, a cube 1 m on a side. This volume is rather large, but it too is used to define a unit of mass. The mass of a quantity of water in a cubic container 1 m on a side (1 m³) is taken to be a *metric ton* (or *tonne*) and is a relatively large mass. One cubic meter contains 1000 L (can you show this?), so 1 m³ of water = 1000 kg = 1 metric ton.

The liter is now used commonly for soft drinks and other liquids, having taken the place of the quart. One liter is a little larger than 1 quart: 1 L = 1.06 qt (● Fig. 1.12).

Figure 1.12 Liter and Quart
(a) The liter of drink on the right contains a little more liquid than 1 quart of milk. (b) One quart is equivalent to 946 mL, or slightly smaller than 1 liter (1 L = 1.06 qt).

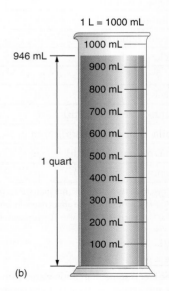

(a)   (b)

Did You Learn?

- The most common metric prefixes are mega- (M, 10^6), kilo- (k, 10^3), centi- (c, 10^{-2}), and milli- (m, 10^{-3}).

- From the definition of the liter, the volumes of 1 cubic centimeter (cm^3) and 1 milliliter (mL) are the same.

1.6　Derived Units and Conversion Factors

Preview Questions

- What are derived units?

- How can you tell which is longer, 1 kilometer or 1 mile?

Derived Units

How are most physical quantities generally described using *only* the three basic units of length, mass, and time? We use **derived units**, which are multiples or combinations of units. The various derived units will become evident to you during the course of your study. Some examples of derived units follow.

Derived Quantity	Unit
Area (length)^2	m^2, cm^2, ft^2, etc.
Volume (length)^3	m^3, cm^3, ft^3, etc.
Speed (length/time)	m/s, cm/s, ft/s, etc.

Let's focus on a particular quantity with derived units, density, which involves mass and volume.

The **density** of a substance reflects the compactness of the matter or mass of a substance. In more formal language, *density,* commonly represented by the lowercase Greek letter rho (ρ), is the amount of mass located in a definite volume, or simply the mass per volume.

$$\text{density} = \frac{\text{mass}}{\text{volume}} = \frac{\text{mass}}{(\text{length})^3}$$

or

$$\rho = \frac{m}{V} \qquad \qquad 1.1$$

Thus, if sample A has a mass of 20 kg that occupies a volume of 5.0 m^3, then it has a density of 20 kg/5.0 m^3 = 4.0 kg/m^3. If sample B has a mass of 20 kg that occupies a volume of 4.0 m^3, then it has a density of 20 kg/4.0 m^3 = 5.0 kg/m^3. So sample B is denser (has greater density) and its mass is more compact than sample A.

Also, if mass is distributed uniformly throughout a volume, then the density will be constant. Such would not be the case for the pillow in ● Fig. 1.13.

Although the standard units of density are kg/m^3, it is often convenient to use g/cm^3 (grams per cubic centimeter) for more manageable numbers. For example, by our original definition, 1 L (1000 cm^3) of water has a mass of 1 kg (1000 g), so water has a density of $\rho = m/V$ = 1000 g/1000 cm^3 = 1.0 g/cm^3. If density is expressed in units of grams per cubic centimeter, then the density of a substance can be easily compared with that of water. For example, a rock with a density of 3.3 g/cm^3 is 3.3 times as dense as water. Iron has a density of 7.9 g/cm^3, and the Earth as a whole has an average density of 5.5 g/cm^3. The planet Saturn, with an average density of 0.69 g/cm^3, is less dense than water.

Richard Megna/Fundamental Photographs, NYC

Figure 1.13 Mass, Volume, and Density
Both the weight and the pillow have the same mass, but they have very different volumes and hence have different densities. The metal weight is much denser than the pillow. If the mass of the metal were distributed uniformly throughout its volume (homogeneous), then the density would be constant. This distribution would not be the case for the pillow, and an average density would be expressed.

EXAMPLE 1.1   Determining Density

Density can be useful in identifying substances. For example, suppose a chemist had a sample of solid material that is determined to have a mass of 452 g and a volume of 20.0 cm³. What is the density of the substance?

Solution

Density is easily computed using Eq. 1.1:

$$\rho = \frac{m}{V} = \frac{452 \text{ g}}{20.0 \text{ cm}^3} = 22.6 \text{ g/cm}^3$$

This density is quite large, and by looking up the known densities of substances, the chemist would suspect that the material is the chemical element osmium, the densest of all elements. (Gold has a density of 19.3 g/cm³, and silver has a density of 10.5 g/cm³.)

Confidence Exercise 1.1

A sample of gold has the same mass as that of the osmium sample in Example 1.1. Which would have the greater volume? Show by comparing the volume of the gold with that of the osmium. (The density of gold is given in Example 1.1.)

The answers to Confidence Exercises may be found at the back of the book.

Densities of liquids such as blood and alcohol can be measured by means of a *hydrometer,* which is a weighted glass bulb that floats in the liquid (● Fig. 1.14). The higher the bulb floats, the greater the density of the liquid.

When a medical technologist checks a sample of urine, one test he or she performs is for density. For a healthy person, urine has a density of 1.015 to 1.030 g/cm³; it consists mostly of water and dissolved salts. When the density is greater or less than this normal range, the urine may have an excess or deficiency of dissolved salts, usually caused by an illness.

A hydrometer is also used to test the antifreeze in a car radiator. The closer the density of the radiator liquid is to 1.00 g/cm³, the closer the antifreeze and water solution is to being pure water, and more antifreeze may be needed. The hydrometer is usually calibrated in degrees rather than density and indicates the temperature to which the amount of antifreeze will protect the radiator.

Finally, when a combination of units becomes complicated, it is often given a name of its own. For example, as discussed in Chapter 3.3, the SI unit of force is the newton, which in terms of standard units is*

$$\text{newton (N)} = \text{kg} \cdot \text{m/s}^2$$

It is easier to talk about a newton (N) than about a kg·m/s². As you might guess, the newton unit is named in honor of Sir Isaac Newton. The abbreviation of a unit named after an individual is capitalized, but the unit name itself is not: newton (N). We will encounter other such units during the course of our study.

Conversion Factors

Often we want to convert units within one system or from one system to another. For example, how many feet are there in 3 yards? The immediate answer would be 9 feet, because it is commonly known that there are 3 feet per yard. Sometimes, though, we may want to make comparisons of units between the metric and the British systems. In general, to convert units, a **conversion factor** is used. Such a factor relates one unit to another. Some convenient conversion factors are listed on the inside back cover of this book. For instance,

$$1 \text{ in.} = 2.54 \text{ cm}$$

---

*The centered dot means that the quantities for these units are multiplied.

Figure 1.14 Measuring Liquid Density
A hydrometer is used to measure the density of a liquid. The denser the liquid, the higher the hydrometer floats. The density can be read from the calibrated stem.

Edward Kinsman/Photo Researchers, Inc.

Although it is commonly written in equation form, this expression is really an *equivalence statement;* that is, 1 in. has an equivalent length of 2.54 cm. (To be a true equation, the expression must have the same magnitudes and units or dimensions on both sides.) However, in the process of expressing a quantity in different units, a conversion relationship in ratio or factor form is used:

$$\frac{1 \text{ in.}}{2.54 \text{ cm}} \quad \text{or} \quad \frac{2.54 \text{ cm}}{1 \text{ in.}}$$

For example, suppose you are 5 ft 5 in., or 65.0 in., tall, and you want to express your height in centimeters. Then

$$65.0 \text{ in.} \times \frac{2.54 \text{ cm}}{1 \text{ in.}} = 165 \text{ cm}$$

Note that the in. units cancel and the cm unit is left on both sides of the equation, which is now a true equation, $65.0 \times 2.54 \text{ cm} = 165 \text{ cm}$ (equal on both sides). In the initial example of converting units in the same system, 3 yd to feet, a conversion factor was actually used in the form:

$$3 \text{ yd} \times \frac{3 \text{ ft}}{1 \text{ yd}} = 9 \text{ ft}$$

where 3 ft/1 yd, or 3 ft per yard. In this case, because the conversion is so common, the mathematics can be done mentally.

The steps may be summarized as follows:

Steps for Converting from One Unit to Another

Step 1

Use a conversion factor, a ratio that may be obtained from an equivalence statement. (Often it is necessary to look up these factors or statements in a table; see the inside back cover of this book.)

Step 2

Choose the appropriate form of conversion factor (or factors) so that the unwanted units cancel.

Step 3

Check to see that the units cancel and that you are left with the desired unit. Then perform the multiplication or division of the numerical quantities. Here is an example done in stepwise form.

EXAMPLE 1.2   Conversion Factors: One-Step Conversion

The length of a football field is 100 yards. In constructing a football field in Europe, the specifications have to be given in metric units. How long is a football field in meters?

Solution

Question: 100 yd is equivalent to how many meters? That is, 100 yd = ? m.

Step 1

There is a convenient, direct equivalence statement between yards and meters given inside the back cover of the textbook under Length:

$$1 \text{ yd} = 0.914 \text{ m}$$

The two possible conversion factor ratios are

$$\frac{1 \text{ yd}}{0.914 \text{ m}} \quad \text{or} \quad \frac{0.914 \text{ m}}{\text{yd}} \quad \text{(conversion factors)}$$

For convenience, the number 1 is commonly left out of the denominator of the second conversion factor; that is, we write 0.914 m/yd instead of 0.914 m/1 yd.

Step 2

The second form of this conversion factor, 0.914 m/yd, would allow the yd unit to be canceled. (Here yd is the unwanted unit in the denominator of the ratio.)

Step 3

Checking this unit cancellation and performing the operation yields

$$100 \ \cancel{yd} \times \frac{0.914 \text{ m}}{\cancel{yd}} = 91.4 \text{ m}$$

Confidence Exercise 1.2

In a football game, you often hear the expression "first and 10" (yards). How would you express this measurement in meters to a friend from Europe?

The answers to Confidence Exercises may be found at the back of the book.

As the use of the metric system in the United States expands, unit conversions and the ability to do such conversions will become increasingly important. Automobile speedometers showing speeds in both miles per hour (mi/h) and kilometers per hour (km/h) are common. Also, road signs comparing speeds can be seen. Some are designed to help drivers with metric conversion (● Fig. 1.15).

In some instances, more than one conversion factor may be used, as in Example 1.3.

EXAMPLE 1.3   Conversion Factors: Multistep Conver

A computer printer has a width of 18 in. What is its width in meters?

Solution

Question: How many meters are there in 18 inches? 18 in. = ? m. Suppose you didn't know and couldn't look up the conversion factor for inches to meters but remembered that 1 in. = 2.54 cm (which is a good length equivalence statement to remember between the British and metric systems). Then, using this information and another well-known equivalence statement, 1 m = 100 cm, you could do the multiple conversion as follows:

inches × centimeters × meters

$$18 \ \cancel{in.} \times \frac{2.54 \ \cancel{cm}}{\cancel{in.}} \times \frac{1 \text{ m}}{100 \ \cancel{cm}} = 0.46 \text{ m}$$

Figure 1.15 Unit Conversions
(a) The speedometers of automobiles may be calibrated in both British and metric units. The term mph is a common, nonstandard abbreviation for miles per hour; the standard abbreviation is mi/h. Note that 60 mi/h is about 100 km/h. (b) Road signs in Canada, which went metric, are designed to help drivers with the conversion, particularly U.S. drivers going into Canada. Notice the highlighted letters in Think*m*etric.

(a)

(b)

Highlight Is Unit Conversion Important? It Sure Is.

In 1999, the *Mars Climate Orbiter* spacecraft reached its destination after having flown 670 million km (415 million mi) over a 9.5-month period (Fig. 1). As the spacecraft was to go into orbit around the red planet, contact between it and personnel on the Earth was lost, and the *Orbiter* was never heard from again.

What happened? Investigations showed that the loss of the *Orbiter* was primarily a problem of unit conversion, or a lack thereof. At Lockheed Martin Astronautics, which built the spacecraft, engineers calculated the navigational information in British units. When flight control at NASA's Jet Propulsion Laboratory received the data, it was assumed that the information was in metric units, as called for in the mission specifications.

Unit conversions were not made, and as a result, the *Orbiter* approached Mars at a far lower altitude than planned. It either burned up in the Martian atmosphere or crashed to the planet's surface. Because of a lack of unit conversion, a $125 million spacecraft was lost on the red planet, causing more than a few red faces.

This incident underscores the importance of using appropriate units, making correct conversions, and working consistently in the same system of units.

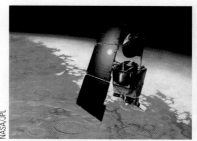

Figure 1 An Artist's Conception of the *Mars Climate Orbiter*

Notice that the units cancel correctly.

Let's check this result directly with the equivalence statement 1 m = 39.4 in.

$$18 \text{ in.} \times \frac{1 \text{ m}}{39.4 \text{ in.}} = 0.46 \text{ m}$$

Confidence Exercise 1.3

How many seconds are there in 1 day? (Use multiple conversion factors, starting with 24 h/day.)

Equivalence statements that are not dimensionally or physically correct are sometimes used; an example is 1 lb = 2.2 kg. This equivalence statement may be used to determine the weight of an object in pounds, given its mass in kilograms. It means that 1 kg is *equivalent* to 2.2 lb; that is, a 1-kg *mass* has a *weight* of 2.2 lb. For example, a person with a mass of 60 kg ("kilos") would have a weight in pounds of 60 kg × 2.2 lb/kg = 132 lb.

For an example of the kind of problem that can result from the concurrent use of both the British and metric systems, see the **Highlight: Is Unit Conversion Important? It Sure Is.**

Did You Learn?

● Derived units are multiples or combination of units. For example, density ρ = kg/m³.

● Looking at the equivalence statements (inside back cover) 1 mi = 1.61 km and 1 km = 0.62 mi, it can be seen that 1 mi is longer than 1 km.

1.7   Significant Figures

Preview Questions

● What is the purpose of significant figures?

● Why are mathematical results rounded?

Figure 1.16 Significant Figures and Insignificant Figures
Performing the division operation of 6.8/1.67 on a calculator with a floating decimal point gives many figures. However, most of these figures are insignificant, and the result should be rounded to the proper number of significant figures, which is two. (See text for further explanation.)

When working with quantities, hand calculators are often used to do mathematical operations. Suppose in an exercise you divided 6.8 cm by 1.67 cm and got the result shown in ● Fig. 1.16. Would you report 4.0718563? Hopefully not—your instructor might get upset.

The reporting problem is solved by using what are called **significant figures** (or *significant digits*), a method of expressing measured numbers properly. This method involves the accuracy of measurement and mathematical operations.

Note that in the multiplication example, 6.8 cm has two figures or digits and 1.67 has three. These figures are significant because they indicate a magnitude read from some measurement instrument. In general, more digits in a measurement implies more accuracy or the greater fineness of the scale of the measurement instrument. That is, the smaller the scale (or the more divisions), the more numbers you can read, resulting in a better measurement. The 1.67-cm reading is more accurate because it has one more digit than 6.8 cm.

The number of significant figures in 6.8 cm and 1.67 cm is rather evident, but some confusion may arise when a quantity contains one or more zeros. For example, how many significant figures does the quantity 0.0254 have? The answer is three. Zeros at the beginning of a number are not significant, but merely locate the decimal point. Internal or end zeros are significant; for example, 104.6 and 3705.0 have four and five significant figures, respectively. (An end or "trailing" zero must have a decimal point associated with it. The zero in 3260 would not be considered significant.)

However, a mathematical operation cannot give you a better "reading" or more significant figures than your original quantities. Thus, as general rules,

1. When multiplying and dividing quantities, leave as many significant figures in the answer as there are in the quantity with the least number of significant figures.

2. When adding or subtracting quantities, leave the same number of decimal places in the answer as there are in the quantity with the least number of significant places.*

Applying the first rule to the example in Fig. 1.16 indicates that the result of the division should have two significant figures (abbreviated s.f.). Hence, rounding the result:

$$6.8 \text{ cm}/1.67 \text{ cm} = 4.1$$

↑	↑
limiting term has 2 s.f.	**4.0718563 is rounded to 4.1 (2 s.f.)**

If the numbers were to be added, then, by the addition rule,

6.8 cm (least number of decimal places)

+ 1.67 cm

8.47 cm → 8.5 cm (final answer rounded to one decimal place)

Clearly, it is necessary to round numbers to obtain the proper number of significant figures. The following rules will be used to do this.

Rules for Rounding

1. If the first digit on the right to be dropped is less than 5, then leave the preceding digit as is.

2. If the first digit to be dropped is 5 or greater, then increase the preceding digit by one.

EXAMPLE 1.4   Rounding Numbers

Round each of the following:
(a) 26.142 to three significant figures.
The 4 is the first digit to be removed and is less than 5. Then, by rule 1,

$$26.142 \rightarrow 26.1$$

---

*See Appendix VII for more on significant figures.

(b) 10.063 to three significant figures.

The 6 is the first digit to be removed. (Here, the zeros on each side of the decimal point are significant because they are internal and have digits on both sides. Then, by rule 2,

$$10.063 \rightarrow 10.1$$

(c) 0.09970 to two significant figures.

In this case, the first nondigit to be removed is the 7. (The zeros to the immediate left and right of the decimal point are not significant but merely serve to locate the decimal point.) Because 7 is greater than 5, by rule 2,

$$0.0997 \rightarrow 0.10$$

(d) The result of the product of the measured numbers 5.0×356.

Performing the multiplication,

$$5.0 \times 356 = 1780$$

Because the result should have only two significant figures, as limited by the quantity 5.0, we round

$$1780 \rightarrow 1800$$

A problem may exist here. Standing alone, it might not be known whether the "trailing" zeros in the 1800 result are significant or not. This problem may be remedied by using *powers-of-ten (scientific) notation*. The 1800 may be equivalently written as

$$1800 = 1.8 \times 10^3$$

and there is no doubt that there are two significant figures. See Appendix VI if you are not familiar with powers-of-ten notation. More information on this notation usage is given in the next chapter.

Confidence Exercise 1.4

Multiply 2.55 by 3.14 on a calculator and report the result in the proper number of significant figures.

Did You Learn?

- Significant figures are a method of expressing measured numbers properly.
- A mathematical result is rounded so as to express the proper number of significant figures.

KEY TERMS

1. science (1.1)
2. scientific method (1.2)
3. standard unit (1.4)
4. system of units
5. metric system
6. British system
7. length
8. meter
9. mass
10. kilogram
11. time
12. second
13. mks
14. SI
15. mega- (1.5)
16. kilo-
17. centi-
18. milli-
19. liter
20. derived units (1.6)
21. density
22. conversion factor
23. significant figures (1.7)

MATCHING

For each of the following items, fill in the number of the appropriate Key Term from the preceding list. Compare your answers with those at the back of the book.

a. _____ The most widely used system of units

b. _____ One-hundredth

c. _____ Method of properly expressing measured numbers

d. _____ The measurement of space in any direction

e. _____ The relationship of one unit to another

f. _____ Thousand

g. _____ Standard unit of mass

h. _____ A valid theory of nature must be in agreement with experimental results.

i. _____ Defined in terms of the radiation frequency of a cesium atom

j. _____ An organized body of knowledge about the natural universe

k. _____ The amount of matter an object contains

l. _____ A group of standard units and their combinations

m. _____ One-thousandth

n. _____ A system of units that is slowly being phased out

o. _____ The continuous forward flowing of events

p. _____ A fixed and reproducible value for making measurements

q. _____ Multiples and combinations of standard units

r. _____ Defined in terms of the speed of light

s. _____ Million

t. _____ Modernized version of the metric system

u. _____ Compactness of matter

v. _____ Acronym for metric standard units

w. _____ $V = 10 \text{ cm} \times 10 \text{ cm} \times 10 \text{ cm}$

MULTIPLE CHOICE

Compare your answers with those at the back of the book.

1. Which is the most fundamental of the physical sciences? (1.1)
   (a) astronomy   (b) chemistry   (c) physics   (d) meteorology

2. Which one of the following is a concise statement about a fundamental relationship in nature? (1.2)
   (a) hypothesis   (b) law   (c) theory   (d) experiment

3. Which human sense is first in supplying the most information about the external world? (1.3)
   (a) touch   (b) taste   (c) sight   (d) hearing

4. Which is the standard unit of mass in the metric system? (1.4)
   (a) gram   (b) kilogram   (c) slug   (d) pound

5. Which one of the following is *not* a fundamental quantity? (1.4)
   (a) length   (b) weight   (c) mass   (d) time

6. Which metric prefix means "one-thousandth"? (1.5)
   (a) centi-   (b) milli-   (c) mega-   (d) kilo-

7. Which metric prefix means "thousand"? (1.5)
   (a) centi-   (b) milli-   (c) mega-   (d) kilo-

8. Which of the following metric prefixes is the smallest? (1.5)
   (a) micro-   (b) centi-   (c) nano-   (d) milli-

9. How many base units are there in the SI? (1.5)
   (a) four   (b) five   (c) six   (d) seven

10. Which combination of units expresses density? (1.6)
    (a) mass/(time)³   (b) mass/(kg)³
    (c) mass/(length)³   (d) mass/m²

11. What is the expression 1 in. = 2.54 cm properly called? (1.6)
    (a) equation   (b) conversion factor
    (c) SI factor   (d) equivalence statement

12. A student measures the length and width of a rectangle to be 49.4 cm and 0.590 cm, respectively. Wanting to find the area (in cm²) of this rectangle, the student multiplies on a calculator and obtains a result of 2.9146. The area should be reported as ___. (1.7)
    (a) 2914.6 cm²   (b) 2915 cm²
    (c) 2.9×10^3 cm²   (d) 2.91×10^2 cm²

13. Which of the following numbers has the greatest number of significant figures? (1.6)
    (a) 103.07   (b) 124.5   (c) 0.09914   (d) 5.048×10^5

FILL IN THE BLANK

Compare your answers with those at the back of the book.

1. The natural sciences, in which scientists study the natural universe, are divided into physical and ___ sciences. (1.1)

2. A(n) ___ is used to test a hypothesis. (1.2)

3. According to the ___, no hypothesis or theory of nature is valid unless its predictions are in agreement with experimental results. (1.2)

4. Most information about our environment reaches us through the sense of ___. (1.3)

5. All the human senses have ___. (1.3)

6. One liter is slightly ___ than 1 quart. (1.4)

7. One yard is slightly ___ than 1 meter. (1.4)

8. Unlike mass, weight is not a(n) ___ property. (1.4)

9. The standard unit of ___ is the same in all measurement systems. (1.4)

10. The metric prefix *mega-* means ___. (1.5)

11. A common nonstandard metric unit of fluid volume or capacity is the ___. (1.5)

12. If A is denser than B, then A contains more ___ per unit volume. (1.6)

SHORT ANSWER

What is the first step in understanding our environment?

1.1 The Physical Sciences

1. What is the definition of *science?*
2. What are the five major divisions of physical science?

1.2 Scientific Investigation

3. What is the first element of the scientific method?
4. Which generally comes first in solving problems, hypothesis or experiment?
5. What is the difference between a law and a theory?
6. What does the controversy over the "face" on Mars illustrate?

1.3 The Senses

7. How do the five senses rank in importance in yielding information about our environment?
8. The senses cannot be completely relied on. Why?
9. Answer the questions that accompany ● Fig. 1.17.

1.4 Standard Units and Systems of Units

10. Why are some quantities called "fundamental"?
11. A standard unit must have what characteristics?
12. What makes up a system of units?
13. For a given speed limit, would the numerical value be greater in mi/h or in km/h?
14. Is the United States officially on the metric system? Explain.
15. Initially, how many metric standard units were referenced to artifacts? How many are still referenced to artifacts?
16. Which is a fundamental property, weight or mass? Why?
17. Explain the acronyms mks, SI, and cgs.

1.5 More on the Metric System

18. What are the metric prefixes for million and millionth?
19. What are the four most common metric prefixes?
20. What is a metric ton, and how is it defined?
21. What is the standard unit of volume in the SI?

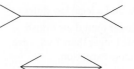

(a) Is the upper horizontal line longer?

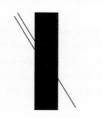

(c) With which of the upper lines does the line on the right connect?

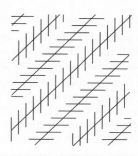

(b) Are the diagonal lines parallel?

Figure 1.17 Seeing Is Believing
See Short-Answer Question 10.

1.6 Derived Units and Conversion Factors

22. How many standard units are generally used to describe the mechanics of nature?
23. What does density describe?
24. In general, when a derived unit becomes complicated (involves too many standard units), what is done?
25. Is an equivalence statement a true equation? Explain.
26. In Fig. 1.15a, the abbreviation mph. is used. Is this a correct abbreviation? Why might it be confusing to some people? (*Hint: miles, meters.*)

1.7 Significant Figures

27. Why are significant figures used?
28. How are significant figures obtained?
29. If you multiplied 9874 m by 36 m, how many significant figures should you report in your answer?

VISUAL CONNECTION

Visualize the connections and give answers for the blanks. Compare your answers with those at the back of the book.

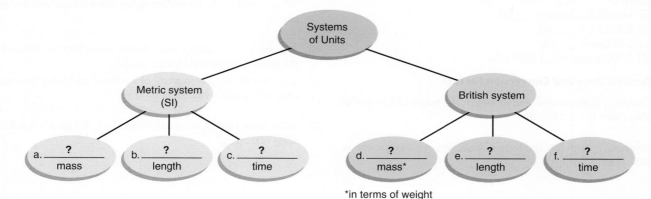

*in terms of weight

APPLYING YOUR KNOWLEDGE

1. Give two ways in which a scientific law and a legal law differ.

2. In general, common metric units are larger than their British counterparts; for example, 1 m is a little longer than 1 yd. Give two other examples, as well as one notable exception.

3. In the original definition of the kilogram as a volume of water, it was specified that the water be at its maximum density, which occurs at 4°C (39°F). Why? What would be the effect if another temperature were used? (*Hint*: See the Highlight: Freezing from the Top Down in Chapter 5.2.)

4. Suppose you could buy a quart of a soft drink and a liter of the soft drink at the same price. Which would you choose, and why?

5. In the opening scenes of the movie *Raiders of the Lost Ark,* Indiana Jones tries to remove a gold idol from a booby-trapped pedestal. He replaces the idol with a bag of sand of approximately the same volume. (Density of gold = 19.32 g/cm³ and density of sand ≈ 2 g/cm³.)
   (a) Did he have a reasonable chance of not activating the booby trap? Explain.
   (b) In a later scene, he and an unscrupulous guide play catch with the idol. Assume that the volume of the idol is about 1.0 L. If it were solid gold, then what mass would the idol have? Do you think playing catch with it is plausible?

6. Currently, the tallest building in the world is the Burj Khalifa (with 160 stories) in Dubai, United Arab Emirates, which is 828 m tall. Previously, the tallest was the Taipei 101 skyscraper (with 101 floors) in Taiwan, which is 508 m tall. A friend wants you to describe the process by which you could find how much taller, in feet, the Burj is compared with the Taipei 101. What would you tell him?

IMPORTANT EQUATION

density: $\rho = \dfrac{m}{V}$ (1.1)

EXERCISES

1.5 More on the Metric System

1. What is your height in meters?
   Answer: varies with person (5.0 ft = 1.5 m)

2. What is your height in centimeters?

3. What is the volume of a liter in cubic millimeters?
   Answer: 1,000,000 or 106 mm³

4. Show that 1 cubic meter contains 1000 L.

5. Water is sold in half-liter bottles. What is the mass, in kilograms and in grams, of the water in such a full bottle?
   Answer: 0.50 kg, 500 g

6. A rectangular container measuring 10 cm × 20 cm × 25 cm is filled with water. What is the mass of this volume of water in kilograms and in grams?

7. Write the following quantities in standard units.
   (a) 0.55 Ms   (c) 12 mg
   (b) 2.8 km   (d) 100 cm
   Answer: (a) 550,000 s (b) 2800 m (c) 0.000012 kg (d) 1 m

8. Fill in the blanks with the correct numbers for the metric prefixes.
   (a) 40,000,000 bytes = ___ Mb
   (b) 0.5722 L = ___ mL
   (c) 540.0 m = ___ cm
   (d) 5,500 bucks = ___ kilobucks

1.6 Derived Units and Conversion Factors

9. Compute, in centimeters and in meters, the height of a basketball player who is 6 ft 5 in. tall.
   Answer: 196 cm, 1.96 m

10. Compute, in both feet and inches, the height of a woman who is 165 cm tall.

11. In Fig 1.15b, is the conversion on the sign exact? Justify your answer.
   Answer: Yes

12. If we changed our speed limit signs to metric, what would probably replace (a) 55 mi/h and (b) 65 mi/h?

13. Is the following statement reasonable? (Justify your answer.) It took 300 L of gasoline to fill up the car's tank.
   Answer: No, 300 L is about 300 qt, or 75 gal.

14. Is the following statement reasonable? (Justify your answer.) The area of a dorm room is 49 m².

15. Referring to number 6 in Applying Your Knowledge, how much shorter in feet is the Taipei 101 than the Burj Khalifa?
   Answer: 1050 ft

16. The new Hoover Dam Bridge connecting Arizona and Nevada opened in October 2010 (● Fig. 1.18). It is the highest and longest arched concrete bridge in the Western Hemisphere, rising 890 ft above the Colorado River and extending 1900 ft in length. What are these dimensions in meters?

17. A popular saying is "Give him an inch, and he'll take a mile.". What would be the equivalent saying using comparable metric units?
   Answer: "Give him a centimeter and he'll take a kilometer."

18. A metric ton is 1000 kg, and a British ton is 2000 lb. Which has the greater weight and by how much?

19. Compute the density in g/cm³ of a piece of metal that has a mass of 0.500 kg and a volume of 63 cm³.
   Answer: 7.9 g/cm³ (the density of iron)

20. What is the volume of a piece of iron (ρ = 7.9 g/cm³) that has a mass of 0.50 kg?

Figure 1.19 **How Many Significant Figures?**
See Exercise 26.

23. Round the following numbers to three significant figures.
    (a) 0.9986   (c) 0.01789
    (b) 7384.38   (d) 47.645

    Answer: (a) 0.999 (b) 7380 or 7.38 × 10³ (c) 0.0179 (d) 47.6

24. Round the following numbers to four significant figures.
    (a) 3.1415926   (c) 483.5960
    (b) 0.00690745   (d) 0.0234973

25. What is the result of (3.15 m × 1.53 m)/0.78 m with the proper number of significant figures?

    Answer: 6.2 m

26. The calculator result of multiplying 2.15 × π is shown in
    ● Fig. 1.19. Round the result to the proper number of significant figures.

Figure 1.18 **High and Wide**
An aerial view of the new four-lane Hoover Dam Bridge between Arizona and Nevada with the Colorado River beneath (as seen from behind the dam). See Exercise 16.

1.7 Significant Figures

21. Round the following numbers to two significant figures.
    (a) 7.66   (c) 9438
    (b) 0.00208   (d) 0.000344

    Answer: (a) 7.7 (b) 0.0021 (c) 9400 or 94 × 10² (d) 0.00034

22. Round the following numbers to three significant figures.
    (a) 0.009995   (c) 0.010599
    (b) 644.73   (d) 8429.55

ON THE WEB

1. Method to the Madness

Outline the three steps of problem solving as presented in this textbook. Visit the student website for this textbook at **www
.cengagebrain.com/shop/ISBN/1133104096** to verify your answers.

2. The Measurement of Time

How fast is the new optical clock? What is the basis of atomic clocks? How does the NIST compact atomic clock differ from the atomic clock? What effect might atomic clocks have on your life? Explore answers to these questions on the student website at **www.cengagebrain.com/
shop/ISBN/1133104096.**

Give me matter and motion, and I will construct the universe.

•

René Descartes
(1596–1650)

Strobe lighting captures a >
bullet tearing through a card at
about 900 m/s (about 2000 mi/h)

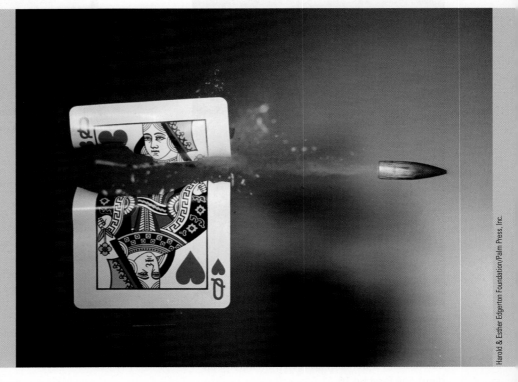

Harold & Esther Edgerton Foundation/Palm Press, Inc.

PHYSICS FACTS

▶ It takes 8.33 minutes for light to travel from the Sun to the Earth. (See Example 2.2.)

▶ Electrical signals between your brain and muscles travel at about 435 km/h (270 mi/h).

▶ A bullet from a high-powered rifle travels at a speed of about 2900 km/h (1800 mi/h).

▶ NASA's X43A uncrewed jet flew at a speed of 7700 km/h (4800 mi/h), faster than a speeding bullet.

▶ Nothing can exceed the speed of light (in vacuum), 3.0×10^8 m/s (186,000 mi/s).

▶ *Velocity* comes from the Latin *velocitas,* meaning "swiftness."

▶ *Acceleration* comes from the Latin *accelerare,* meaning "hasten."

H aving been introduced to measurement and units, you are ready to begin your study of physics. **Physics,** the most fundamental physical science, is concerned with the basic principles and concepts that describe the workings of the universe. It deals with matter, motion, force, and energy.

There are various areas of physics:

▶ *Classical mechanics* is the study of the motion of objects moving at relatively low speeds.

▶ *Waves and sound* is the study of wave motion and its application to sound.

▶ *Thermodynamics* is the study of temperature, heat, and thermal processes.

▶ *Electromagnetism* is the study of electricity and magnetism.

Chapter Outline

▶ *Optics* is the study of the properties of light, mirrors, and lenses.

▶ *Quantum mechanics* is the study of the behavior of particles on the microscopic and submicroscopic levels.

▶ *Atomic and nuclear physics* is the study of the properties of atoms and nuclei.

▶ *Relativity* is the study of objects traveling at speeds approaching the speed of light.

We will delve into all of these areas, except relativity, and begin with classical mechanics and the study of motion.

Motion is everywhere. Students walk to class. You drive to the store. Birds fly. The wind blows the trees. Rivers flow. Even the continents slowly drift. On a larger scale, the Earth rotates on its axis; the Moon revolves around the Earth, which revolves around the Sun; the Sun moves in its galaxy; and the galaxies move with respect to one another.

This chapter focuses on describing motion and on defining and discussing terms such as *speed*, *velocity*, and *acceleration*. These concepts will be considered without the forces that produce motion. The discussion of forces is reserved for Chapter 3.

[*Note:* If you are not familiar with powers-of-10 notation (scientific notation) or if you need a math review, then see the appropriate sections in the Appendix.]

2.1   Defining Motion

Preview Questions

● What is needed to designate a position?

● What is motion?

The term **position** refers to the location of an object. To designate the position of an object, a *reference point* and a *measurement scale* are needed. For example, the entrance to campus is 1.6 km (1 mi) from the *intersection* with a particular traffic light. The book is 15 cm from the *corner* of the table. The Cartesian coordinates of the point on a graph are $(x, y) = (2.0$ cm, 3.0 cm$)$. Here the reference point is the *origin* of the coordinate system (Chapter 1.4).

If an object changes position, we say that motion has occurred. That is, an object is in **motion** when it is undergoing a continuous change in position.

Consider an automobile traveling on a straight highway. The motion of the automobile may or may not be occurring at a constant rate. In either case, the motion is described by using the fundamental units of *length* and *time*.

The description of motion by length and time is evident in running. For example, as shown in ● Fig. 2.1, the cheetah runs a certain distance at full speed in the shortest possible time. Combining length and time to give the *time rate of change of position* is the basis of describing motion in terms of speed and velocity, as discussed in the following section.

Did You Learn?

● To designate a position or location, both a reference point and a measurement scale are needed.

● Motion involves a continuous change of position.

2.2   Speed and Velocity

Preview Questions

● Between two points, which may be greater in magnitude, distance or displacement?

● What is the difference between speed and velocity?

Figure 2.1 Motion

Motion is described in terms of time and distance. Here, a running cheetah appears to be trying to run a distance in the shortest time possible. The cheetah is the fastest of all land animals, capable of reaching speeds of up to 113 km/h, or 70 mi/h. (The slowest land creature is the snail, which can move at a speed of 0.05 km/h, or 0.03 mi/h.)

Steve Umland/The Image Works

The terms *speed* and *velocity* are often used interchangeably; however, in physical science, they have different distinct meanings. Speed is a *scalar* quantity, and velocity is a *vector* quantity. Let's distinguish between scalars and vectors now, because other terms will fall into these categories during the course of our study. The distinction is simple.

A **scalar** quantity (or a *scalar*, for short) has only magnitude (numerical value and unit of measurement). For example, you may be traveling in a car at 90 km/h (about 55 mi/h). Your speed is a scalar quantity; the magnitude has the numerical value of 90 and unit of measurement km/h.

A **vector** quantity has magnitude *and* direction. For example, suppose you are traveling at 90 km/h *north*. This describes your velocity, which is a vector quantity because it consists of magnitude *plus* direction. By including direction, a vector quantity (or a *vector*, for short) gives more information than a scalar quantity. No direction is associated with a scalar quantity.

Vectors may be graphically represented by arrows (● Fig. 2.2). The length of a vector arrow is proportional to the magnitude and may be drawn to scale. The arrowhead indicates the direction of the vector. Notice in Fig. 2.2 that the red car has a negative velocity vector, $-v_c$, that is equal in magnitude (length of arrow) but opposite in direction, to the positive velocity vector, $+v_c$, for the blue car. The velocity vector for the man, v_m, is shorter than the vectors for the cars because he is moving more slowly in the positive (+) direction. (The + sign is often omitted as being understood.)

Speed

Now let's look more closely at speed and velocity, which are basic quantities used in the description of motion. The **average speed** of an object is the total distance traveled divided by the time spent in traveling the total distance. **Distance** (d) is the actual length of the path that is traveled. In equation form,

Figure 2.2 Vectors

Vectors may be graphically represented by arrows. The length of a vector arrow is proportional to the magnitude of the quantity it represents, and the arrowhead indicates the direction. (See text for description.)

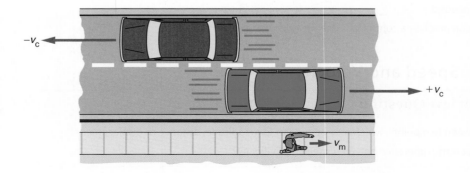

$$\text{average speed} = \frac{\text{distance traveled}}{\text{time to travel the distance}}$$

$$\bar{v} = \frac{d}{t} \qquad \qquad \text{2.1}$$

where the bar over the symbol ($\bar{v}$, "vee-bar") indicates that it is an average value.

Note that length d and time t are *intervals*. They are sometimes written Δd and Δt to indicate explicitly that they are intervals ($\Delta d / \Delta t$). The Δ (Greek delta) means "change in" or "difference in." For example, $\Delta t = t - t_o$, where t_o and t are the original (or initial) and final times (on a clock), respectively. If $t_o = 0$, then $\Delta t = t$. Speed has the standard units of meters per second (m/s) or feet per second (ft/s)—length/time. Other common nonstandard units are mi/h and km/h.

Taken over a time interval, speed is an average. This concept is somewhat analogous to an average class grade. Average speed gives only a general description of motion. During a long time interval like that of a car trip, you may speed up, slow down, and even stop. The average speed, however, is a single value that represents the average rate of motion for the entire trip.

The description of motion can be made more specific by taking smaller time intervals such as a few seconds or even an instant. The speed of an object at any instant of time may be quite different from its average speed, and it gives a more accurate description of the motion. In this case, we have an instantaneous speed.

The **instantaneous speed** of an object is its speed at that instant of time (Δt becoming extremely small). A common example of nearly instantaneous speed is the speed registered on an automobile speedometer (● Fig. 2.3). This value is the speed at which the automobile is traveling at that moment, or instantaneously.

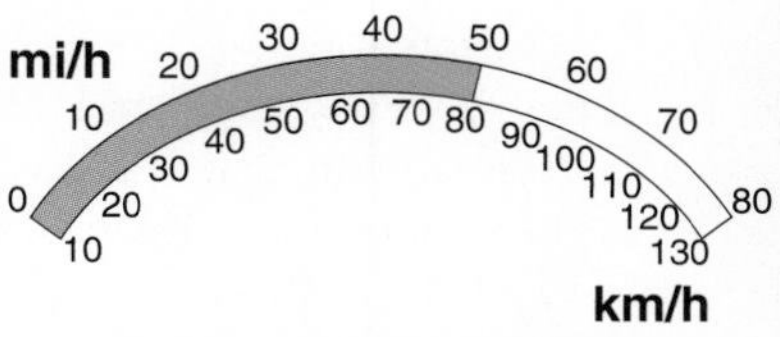

Velocity

Now let's look at describing motion with velocity. Velocity is similar to speed, *but* a direction is involved. **Average velocity** is the displacement divided by the total travel time. **Displacement** is the straight-line distance between the initial and final positions, with direction toward the final position, and is a vector quantity (● Fig. 2.4).

For straight-line motion in one direction, speed and velocity have something in common. Their magnitudes are the same because the lengths of the distance and the displacement are the same. The distinction between them in this case is that a direction must be specified for the velocity.

As you might guess, there is also **instantaneous velocity**, which is the velocity at any instant of time. For example, a car's instantaneous speedometer reading and the direction

Figure 2.3 Instantaneous Speed
The speed on an automobile speedometer is a practical example of instantaneous speed, or the speed of the car at a particular instant. Here it is 80 km/h, or 50 mi/h.

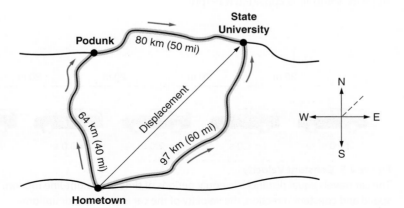

Figure 2.4 Displacement and Distance
Displacement is a vector quantity and is the straight-line distance between two points (initial and final), plus direction. In traveling from Hometown to State University, the displacement would be so many kilometers NE (northeast). Distance is a scalar quantity and is the actual path length traveled. Different routes have different distances. Two routes are shown in the figure, with distances of 97 km and 144 km (64 km + 80 km = 144 km).

in which it is traveling at that instant give the car's instantaneous velocity. Of course, the speed and direction of the car may and usually do change. This motion is then *accelerated motion*, which is discussed in the following section.

If the velocity is *constant*, or *uniform*, then there are no such changes. Suppose an airplane is flying at a constant speed of 320 km/h (200 mi/h) directly eastward. Then the airplane has a constant velocity and flies in a straight line. (Why?)

For this special case, you should be able to convince yourself that the constant velocity and the average velocity are the same ($\bar{v} = v$). By analogy, think about everyone in your class getting the same (constant) test score. How do the class average and the individual scores compare under these circumstances?

A car traveling with a constant velocity is shown in ● Fig. 2.5. Examples 2.1 through 2.3 illustrate the use of speed and velocity.

EXAMPLE 2.1   Finding Speed and Velocity

Describe the motion (speed and velocity) of the car in Fig. 2.5.

Solution

Step 1

The data are taken from the figure.
Given: $d = 80$ m and $t = 4.0$ s
(The car travels 80 m in 4.0 s.)

Step 2

Wanted: Speed and velocity. The units of the data are standard.

Step 3

The car has a constant (uniform) speed and travels 20 m each second. When a speed is constant, it is equal to the average speed; that is, $v = \bar{v}$. (Why?) Calculating the average speed using Eq. 2.1 yields

$$\bar{v} = \frac{d}{t} = \frac{80 \text{ m}}{40 \text{ s}} = 20 \text{ m/s}$$

If the motion is in one direction (straight-line motion), then the car's velocity is also constant and is 20 m/s *in the direction of the motion*.

Confidence Exercise 2.1

How far would the car in Example 2.1 travel in 10 s?
The answers to Confidence Exercises may be found at the back of the book.

Example 2.1 was worked in stepwise fashion, as suggested in the approach to problem solving in Appendix II. This stepwise approach will be used in the first example in early chapters as a reminder. Thereafter, examples generally will be worked directly, unless a stepwise solution is considered helpful.

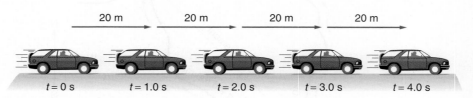

| 20 m | 20 m | 20 m | 20 m |

| $t = 0$ s | $t = 1.0$ s | $t = 2.0$ s | $t = 3.0$ s | $t = 4.0$ s |

Figure 2.5 Constant Velocity
The car travels equal distances in equal periods of time in straight-line motion. With constant speed and constant direction, the velocity of the car is constant, or uniform.

EXAMPLE 2.2 Finding the Time It Takes for Sunlight to Reach the Earth

The speed of light in space (vacuum) is $c = 3.00 \times 10^8$ m/s. (The speed of light is given the special symbol c.) How many seconds does it take light from the Sun to reach the Earth if the distance from the Sun to the Earth is 1.50×10^8 km?

Solution

Given: $v = c = 3.00 \times 10^8$ m/s, $d = 1.5 \times 10^8$ km. Converting the distance to meters (the standard unit) yields

$$d = 1.50 \times 10^8 \, \cancel{km} \left(\frac{10^3 \, m}{\cancel{km}} \right) = 1.50 \times 10^{11} \, m$$

Wanted: t (time for light to travel from the Sun)
Rearranging Eq. 2.1 for the unknown t, we have $t = d/v$, where the bar over the v is omitted because the speed is constant, and $\bar{v} = v$. Then

$$t = \frac{d}{v} = \frac{1.50 \times 10^{11} \, m}{3.00 \times 10^8 \, m/s}$$

$$= 5.00 \times 10^2 \, s = 500 \, s$$

From this example, it can be seen that although light travels very rapidly, it still takes 500 seconds, or 8.33 minutes, to reach the Earth after leaving the Sun (● Fig. 2.6). Again we are working with a constant speed and velocity (straight-line motion).

Confidence Exercise 2.2

A communications satellite is in a circular orbit about the Earth at an an altitude of 3.56 $\times 10^4$ km. How many seconds does it take a signal from the satellite to reach a television receiving station? (Radio signals travel at the speed of light, 3.00×10^8 m/s.)*
    The answers to Confidence Exercises may be found at the back of the book.

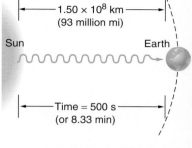

Figure 2.6 Traveling at the Speed of Light
Although light travels at a speed of 3.00×10^8 m/s, it still takes more than 8 minutes for light from the Sun to reach the Earth. (See Example 2.2.)

EXAMPLE 2.3 Finding the Orbital Speed of the Earth

What is the average speed of the Earth in miles per hour as it makes one revolution about the Sun? (Consider the Earth's orbit to be circular.)

Solution

Our planet revolves once around the Sun in an approximately circular orbit in a time of 1 year. The distance it travels in one revolution is the circumference of this circular orbit. (The orbit is actually slightly elliptical, as discussed in Chapter 16.1.)
    The circumference of a circle is given by $2\pi r$, where r is the radius of the orbit. In this case, r is taken to be 93.0 million miles (9.30×10^7 mi), which is the mean distance of the Earth from the Sun (see Fig. 2.6). The time it takes to travel this distance is 1 year, or about 365 days.
    Putting these data into Eq. 2.1 and multiplying the time by 24 h/day to convert to hours gives

$$\bar{v} = \frac{d}{t} = \frac{2\pi r}{t} = \frac{2(3.14)(9.30 \times 10^7 \, mi)}{365 \, \cancel{days} \, (24 \, h/\cancel{day})}$$

$$= 6.67 \times 10^4 \, mi/h \, (\text{or about } 18.5 \, mi/s)$$

---

*The greatest speed that has been achieved *on* the Earth is Mach 9.6 (9.6 times the speed of sound; see Chapter 6.4), which is about 7000 mi/h (1.9 ft/s) or 11,000 km/h (3.1 km/s). This speed record was set by NASA's X43A, an experimental, pilotless, scram-jet-powered aircraft.

You are traveling through space with the Earth at this speed. In 1 second (the time it takes to say, "one-thousand-one"), you travel 18.5 mi (about 30 km). That's pretty fast!

Confidence Exercise 2.3

What is the average speed in mi/h of a person at the equator as a result of the Earth's rotation? (Take the radius of the Earth to be $R_E = 4000$ mi.)

The solution to Example 2.3 shows that the Earth *and all of us on it* are traveling through space at a speed of 66,700 mi/h (or 18.5 mi/s). Even though this speed is exceedingly large and relatively constant, we do not sense this great speed visually because of the small relative motions (apparent motions) of the stars and because our atmosphere moves along with the Earth (which is a good thing). Think about how you know you are in motion when traveling in a perfectly smooth-riding and quiet car. You see trees and other fixed objects "moving" in relative motion.

Also, there is no sensing of any change in velocity if the change is small. Changes in motion can be sensed if they are appreciable. Think about being in a smooth-riding car and being blindfolded. Minor changes in velocity would go unnoticed, but you would be able to tell if the car suddenly sped up, slowed down, or went around a sharp curve, all of which are changes in velocity. A change in velocity is called an *acceleration*, the topic of the following sections.

Did You Learn?

- Distance (actual path length) is always greater than or equal to the magnitude of displacement (straight-line distance).
- Speed is a scalar (magnitude), and velocity is a vector (magnitude and direction).

2.3   Acceleration

Preview Questions

- What motional changes produce an acceleration?
- Is a negative acceleration ($-a$) necessarily a deceleration?

When you are riding in a car on a straight interstate highway and the speed is suddenly increased—say, from 20 m/s to 30 m/s (45 mi/h to 56 mi/h)—you feel as though you are being forced back against the seat. If the car then whips around a circular cloverleaf, you feel forced to the outside of the circle. These experiences result from changes in velocity.

Because velocity is a vector quantity, with both magnitude and direction, a change in velocity involves either or both of these factors. Therefore, an acceleration may result from (1) a change in *speed* (magnitude), (2) a change in *direction*, or (3) a change in *both speed and direction.* When any of these changes occur, an object is accelerating. Examples are (1) a car speeding up (or slowing down) while traveling in a straight line, (2) a car rounding a curve at a constant speed, and (3) a car speeding up (or slowing down) while rounding a curve.

Acceleration is defined as *the time rate of change of velocity*. Taking the symbol Δ (delta) to mean "change in," the equation for **average acceleration** ($\bar{a}$) can be written as

$$\text{average acceleration} = \frac{\text{change in velocity}}{\text{time for change to occur}}$$

$$\bar{a} = \frac{\Delta v}{\Delta t} = \frac{v_f - v_o}{t}$$

2.2

The change in velocity (Δv) is the final velocity v_f minus the original velocity v_o. Also, the interval Δt is commonly written as t ($\Delta t = t - t_o = t$), with t_o taken to be zero (starting the clock at zero, and t is understood to be an interval).

The units of acceleration in the SI are meters per second per second, (m/s)/s, or meters per second squared, m/s². These units may be confusing at first. Keep in mind that an acceleration is a measure of a *change* in velocity during a given time period.

Consider a constant acceleration of 9.8 m/s². This value means that the velocity changes by 9.8 m/s *each* second. Thus, for straight-line motion, as the number of seconds increases, the velocity goes from 0 to 9.8 m/s during the first second, to 19.6 m/s (that is, 9.8 m/s + 9.8 m/s) during the second second, to 29.4 m/s (that is, 19.6 m/s + 9.8 m/s) during the third second, and so forth, adding 9.8 m/s each second. This sequence is illustrated in ● Fig. 2.7 for an object that falls with a constant acceleration of 9.8 m/s². Because the velocity increases, the distance traveled by the falling object each second also increases, but *not* uniformly.

Our discussion will be limited to such constant accelerations. For a constant acceleration, $\bar{a} = a$ (we omit the overbar because the average acceleration is equal to the constant value). Equation 2.2 may be rearranged to give an expression for the final velocity of an object in terms of its original velocity, time, and constant acceleration (a):

$$v_f - v_o = at$$

or

$$v_f = v_o + at \qquad\qquad 2.3$$

This Equation 2.3 is useful for working problems in which the quantities a, v_o, and t are all known and v_f is wanted. If the original velocity $v_o = 0$, then

$$v_f = at \qquad\qquad 2.3a$$

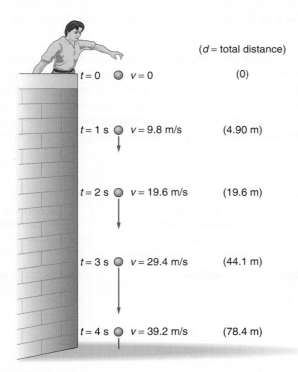

(d = total distance)

$t = 0$ ⚫ $v = 0$ (0)

$t = 1$ s ⚫ $v = 9.8$ m/s   (4.90 m)

$t = 2$ s ⚫ $v = 19.6$ m/s   (19.6 m)

$t = 3$ s ⚫ $v = 29.4$ m/s   (44.1 m)

$t = 4$ s ⚫ $v = 39.2$ m/s   (78.4 m)

Figure 2.7 Constant Acceleration
For an object with a constant downward acceleration of 9.8 m/s², its velocity increases 9.8 m/s each second. The increasing lengths of the velocity arrows indicate the increasing velocity of the ball. The distances do not increase uniformly. (The distances of fall are obviously not to scale.)

It should be noted that the use of Eq. 2.3 requires a *constant* acceleration, one for which the velocity changes uniformly.

EXAMPLE 2.4   Finding Acceleration

A race car starting from rest accelerates uniformly along a straight track, reaching a speed of 90 km/h in 7.0 s. What is the magnitude of the acceleration of the car in m/s²?

Solution

Let's work this example stepwise for clarity.

Step 1

Given: $v_o = 0$, $v_f = 90$ km/h, $t = 7.0$ s
(Because the car is initially at rest, $v_o = 0$.)

Step 2

Wanted: a (acceleration in m/s²)
Because the acceleration is wanted in m/s², 90 km/h is converted to m/s using the conversion factor from the inside back cover of this book:

$$v_f = 90 \ \cancel{km/h} \left(\frac{0.278 \text{ m/s}}{\cancel{km/h}} \right) = 25 \text{ m/s}$$

Step 3

The acceleration may be calculated using Eq. 2.2:

$$a = \frac{v_f - v_o}{t} = \frac{25 \text{ m/s} - 0}{7.0 \text{ s}} = 3.6 \text{ m/s}^2$$

Confidence Exercise 2.4

If the car in the preceding example continues to accelerate at the same rate for an additional 3.0 s, what will be the magnitude of its velocity in m/s at the end of this time?

Because velocity is a vector quantity, acceleration is also a vector quantity. For an object in straight-line motion, the acceleration (vector) may be in the same direction as the velocity (vector), as in Example 2.4, *or* the acceleration may be in the direction opposite the velocity (● Fig. 2.8). In the first instance, the acceleration causes the object to speed up and the velocity increases. If the velocity and acceleration are in opposite directions, however, then the acceleration slows the object and the velocity decreases, which is sometimes called a *deceleration*.*

Figure 2.8 Acceleration and Deceleration
When the acceleration is in the same direction as the velocity of an object in straight-line motion, the speed increases. When the acceleration is in the opposite direction of the velocity (beginning at the vertical dashed line), there is a deceleration and the speed decreases.

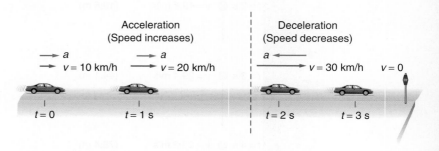

Acceleration
(Speed increases)

a
$v = 10$ km/h
$t = 0$

a
$v = 20$ km/h
$t = 1$ s

Deceleration
(Speed decreases)

a
$v = 30$ km/h
$t = 2$ s

$v = 0$
$t = 3$ s

---

*Note that a deceleration is *not* necessarily a negative acceleration $(-a)$. If the motion is in the negative direction $(-v)$ and the velocity and the acceleration are in the *same* direction, then the object speeds up; that is, its velocity increases in the negative direction.

Conceptual Question and Answer

Putting the Pedal to the Metal

Q. Why is the gas pedal of an automobile commonly called the "accelerator"? What might the brake pedal be called? How about the steering wheel?

A. When you push down on the gas pedal or accelerator, the car speeds up (increasing magnitude of velocity), but when you let up on the accelerator, the car slows down or decelerates.

Putting on the brakes would produce an even greater deceleration, so perhaps the brake pedal should be called a "decelerator." An acceleration results from a change in the velocity's magnitude and/or direction. Technically, then, the steering wheel might also be called an "accelerator," since it changes a speeding car's direction.

In general, we will consider only constant, or uniform, accelerations. A special constant acceleration is associated with the acceleration of falling objects. The **acceleration due to gravity** at the Earth's surface is directed downward and is denoted by the letter g. Its magnitude in SI units is

$$g = 9.80 \text{ m/s}^2$$

This value corresponds to 980 cm/s^2, or about 32 ft/s^2.

The acceleration due to gravity varies slightly depending on such factors as distance from the equator (latitude) and altitude. However, the variations are very small, and for our purposes, g will be taken to be the same everywhere on or near the Earth's surface.

Italian physicist Galileo Galilei (1564–1642), commonly known just as Galileo, was one of the first scientists to assert that all objects fall with the same acceleration. Of course, this assertion assumes that frictional effects are negligible. To exclude frictional and any other effects, the term *free fall* is used. Objects in motion solely under the influence of gravity are said to be in **free fall**. One can illustrate the validity of this statement experimentally by dropping a small mass, such as a coin, and a larger mass, such as a ball, at the same time from the same height. They will both hit the floor, as best as can be judged, at the same time (negligible air resistance). Legend has it that Galileo himself performed such experiments. (See the **Highlight: Galileo and the Leaning Tower of Pisa.**) More modern demonstrations are shown in ● Fig. 2.9.

On the Moon, there is no atmosphere, so there is no air resistance. In 1971, while on the lunar surface, astronaut David Scott dropped a feather and a hammer simultaneously. They

Figure 2.9 Free Fall and Air Resistance
(a) When dropped simultaneously from the same height, a feather falls more slowly than a coin because of air resistance. But when both objects are dropped in an evacuated container with a good partial vacuum, where air resistance is negligible, the feather and the coin fall together with a constant acceleration. (b) An actual demonstration with multiflash photography: An apple and a feather are released simultaneously through a trap door into a large vacuum chamber, and they fall together, almost. Because the chamber has a partial vacuum, there is still some air resistance. (How can you tell?)

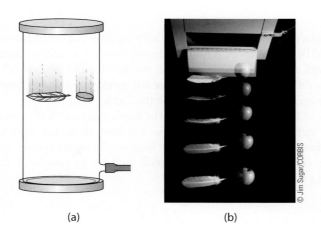

© Jim Sugar/CORBIS

(a)   (b)

Highlight   Galileo and the Leaning Tower of Pisa

One of Galileo's greatest contributions to science was his emphasis on experimentation, a basic part of the scientific method (Chapter 1.2). See Fig. 1. However, it is not certain whether he actually carried out a now-famous experiment. There is a popular story that Galileo dropped stones or cannonballs of different masses from the top of the Tower of Pisa to determine experimentally whether objects fall with the same acceleration (Fig. 2).

Galileo did indeed question Aristotle's view that objects fell because of their "earthiness" and that the heavier, or more earthy, an object, the faster it would fall in seeking its "natural" place toward the center of the Earth. His ideas are evident in the following excerpts from his writings.*

> *How ridiculous is this opinion of Aristotle is clearer than light. Who ever would believe, for example, that . . . if two stones were flung at the same moment from a high tower, one stone twice the size of the other, . . . that when the smaller was half-way down the larger had already reached the ground?*

> *And Aristotle says that "an iron ball of one hundred pounds falling a height of one hundred cubits reaches the ground before a one-pound ball has fallen a single cubit." I say that they arrive at the same time.*

Although Galileo refers to a *high tower*, the Tower of Pisa is not mentioned in his writings, and there is no independent record of such an experiment. Fact or fiction? No one really knows. What we do know is that all freely falling objects near the Earth's surface fall with the same acceleration.

Figure 1 Galileo Galilei (1564–1642)
The motion of objects was one of Galileo's many scientific inquiries.

The Granger Collection, NYC

Figure 2 Free Fall
All freely falling objects near the Earth's surface have the same constant acceleration. Galileo is alleged to have proved this by dropping cannonballs or stones of different masses from the Tower of Pisa. Over short distances, the air resistance can be neglected, so objects dropped at the same time will strike the ground together.

*From L. Cooper, *Aristotle, Galileo, and the Tower of Pisa* (Ithaca, NY: Cornell University Press, 1935).

both hit the surface of the Moon at the same time because neither the feather nor the hammer was slowed by air resistance. This experiment shows that Galileo's assertion applies on the Moon as well as on the Earth. Of course, on the Moon all objects fall at a slower rate than do objects on the Earth's surface because the acceleration due to gravity on the Moon is only $\frac{1}{6}$ of the acceleration due to gravity on the Earth.

The velocity of a freely falling object on the Earth increases 9.80 m/s each second, so its magnitude increases uniformly with time, but how about the distance covered each second? The distance covered is not uniform because the object speeds up. The distance a dropped object ($v_o = 0$) travels downward with time can be computed from the equation $d = \frac{1}{2}at^2$, with g substituted for a.

$$d = \tfrac{1}{2}gt^2$$

2.4

EXAMPLE 2.5   **Finding How Far a Dropped Object Falls**

A ball is dropped from the top of a tall building. Assuming free fall, how far does the ball fall in 1.50 s?

Solution

With $t = 1.50$ s, the distance is given by Eq. 2.4, where it is known that $g = 9.80$ m/s^2.

$$d = \tfrac{1}{2}gt^2 = \tfrac{1}{2}(9.80 \text{ m/s}^2)(1.50 \text{ s})^2 = 11.0 \text{ m}$$

Confidence Exercise 2.5

What is the speed of the ball 1.50 s after it is dropped?

Review Fig. 2.7 for the distances and velocities of a falling object with time. Note that the increase in distance is directly proportional to the time squared ($d \propto t^2$, Eq. 2.4), and the increase in velocity is directly proportional to time ($v_f \propto t$, Eq. 2.3a).

Using these equations, it can be shown that at the end of the third second ($t = 3.00$ s), the object has fallen 44.1 m, which is about the height of a 10-story building. It is falling at a speed of 29.4 m/s, which is about 65 mi/h. Pretty fast. Look out below!

When an object is thrown straight upward, it slows down while traveling. (The velocity decreases 9.80 m/s each second.) In this case, the velocity and acceleration are in opposite directions, and there is a deceleration (● Fig. 2.10). The object slows down (its velocity decreases) until it stops *instantaneously* at its maximum height. Then it starts to fall downward as though it had been dropped from that height. The travel time downward to the original starting position is the same as the travel time upward.

The object returns to its starting point with the same speed it had initially upward. For example, if an object is thrown upward with an initial speed of 29.4 m/s, it will return to the starting point with a speed of 29.4 m/s. You should be able to conclude that it will travel 3.00 s upward, to a maximum height of 44.1 m, and return to its starting point in another 3.00 s.

The preceding numbers reflect free-fall motion, but air resistance generally retards or slows the motion. For a good example of air resistance, consider skydiving, jumping out of an airplane and falling toward the Earth (with a parachute). Before the parachute opens,

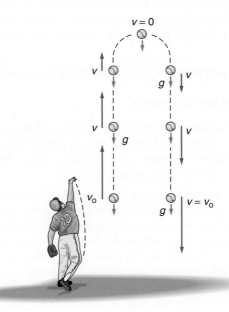

Figure 2.10 Up and Down
An object projected straight upward slows down because the acceleration due to gravity is in the opposite direction of the velocity, and the object stops ($v = 0$) for an instant at its maximum height. Note the blue acceleration arrow at $v = 0$. That is $a \neq 0$. Gravity still acts and $a = g$. The ball then accelerates downward, returning to the starting point with a velocity equal in magnitude and opposite in direction to the initial velocity, $-v_o$. (The downward path is displaced to the right in the figure for clarity.)

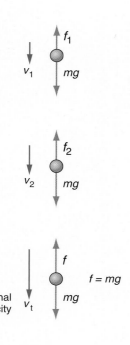

(a)

Figure 2.11 Air Resistance and Terminal Velocity
(a) As the velocity of a falling object increases, so does the upward force f of air resistance. At a certain velocity, called the *terminal velocity*, the force f is equal to the weight of the object (mg). The object then falls with a constant velocity. (b) Skydivers assume a "spread-eagle" position to increase air resistance and reach terminal velocity more quickly, allowing for a greater time of fall.

(b)

Getty Images

the falling skydiver is said to be in "free fall," but it is not free fall by our definition. Here, there is air resistance, which skydivers use to their advantage.

Air resistance is the result of a moving object colliding with air molecules. Therefore, air resistance (considered a type of friction) depends on an object's size and shape, as well as on its speed. The larger the object (or the more downward area exposed) and the faster it moves, the more collisions and the more air resistance there will be. As a skydiver accelerates downward, his or her speed increases, as does the air resistance. At some point, the upward air resistance balances the downward weight of the diver and the acceleration goes to zero. The skydiver then falls with a constant velocity, which is called the **terminal velocity**, v_t (● Fig. 2.11a).

Wanting to maximize the time of fall, skydivers assume a "spread-eagle" position to provide greater surface area and maximize the air resistance (Fig. 2.11b). The air resistance then builds up faster and terminal velocity is reached sooner, giving the skydiver more fall time. This position is putting air resistance to use. The magnitude of a skydiver's terminal velocity during a fall is reached at about 200 km/h (125 mi/h).

Conceptual Question and Answer

And the Winner Is . . .

Q. Suppose two metal balls of different materials, but the same size and shape, were dropped simultaneously from a high-altitude balloon. Let one ball be more massive (heavier) than the other. Which ball will strike the ground first, or would they hit at the same time?

A. Here air resistance is a factor. As the falling balls gain speed, the upward air resistance would increase the same on each (same size and shape). However, when the air resistance is sufficient to balance the weight of the lighter ball, it would reach terminal velocity and cease to accelerate.

The magnitude of this air resistance does not balance the weight of the heavier ball, which would continue to accelerate downward until it reached its greater terminal velocity. So, the heavier ball would be ahead of the lighter ball and falling faster, reaching the ground first.

Did You Learn?

- Acceleration results from a change in velocity, which may result from a change in magnitude, a change in direction, or both.
- A negative acceleration ($-a$) will speed up an object with a negative velocity ($-v$).

2.4   Acceleration in Uniform Circular Motion

Preview Questions

- What is needed for uniform circular motion?
- For an object in uniform circular motion, are both the speed and the velocity constant?

An object in *uniform* circular motion has a constant speed. A car goes around a circular track at a uniform speed of 90 km/h (about 55 mi/h). However, the velocity of the car is *not* constant because the direction is continuously changing, giving rise to a change in velocity and an acceleration.

This acceleration cannot be in the direction of the instantaneous motion or velocity, because otherwise the object would speed up and the motion would not be uniform. In what direction, then, is the acceleration? Because the object must continually change *direction* to maintain a circular path, the acceleration is actually perpendicular, or at a right angle, to the velocity vector.

Consider a car traveling in uniform circular motion, as illustrated in ● Fig. 2.12. At any point, the instantaneous velocity is *tangential* to the curve (at an angle of 90° to a radial line at that point). After a short time, the velocity vector has changed (in direction). The change in velocity (Δv) is given by a vector triangle, as illustrated in the figure.

This change is an average over a time interval Δt, but notice how the Δv vector generally points inward toward the center of the circle. For instantaneous measurement, this generalization is true, so for an object in uniform circular motion, the acceleration is toward the center of the circle. This acceleration is called **centripetal acceleration**.

Even when traveling at a constant (tangential) speed, an object in uniform circular motion must have an inward acceleration. For a car, this acceleration is supplied by friction on the tires. When a car hits an icy spot on a curved road, it may slide outward if the centripetal acceleration is not great enough to keep it in a circular path.

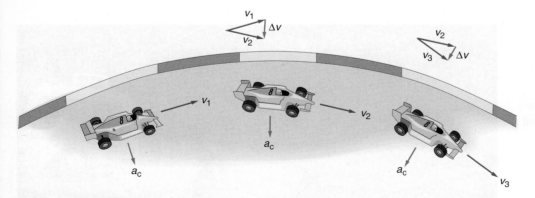

Figure 2.12 Centripetal Acceleration
A car traveling with a constant speed on a circular track is accelerating because its velocity is changing (direction change). This acceleration is toward the center of the circular path and is called *centripetal* ("center-seeking") *acceleration.*

In general, whenever an object moves in a circle of radius r with a constant speed v, the magnitude of the centripetal acceleration a_c in terms of tangential speed is given by the equation

$$\text{centripetal acceleration} = \frac{(\text{speed})^2}{\text{radius}}$$

$$a_c = \frac{v^2}{r} \qquad\qquad 2.5$$

The centripetal acceleration increases as the square of the speed. That is, when the speed is doubled, the acceleration increases by a factor of 4. Also, the smaller the radius, the greater the centripetal acceleration needed to keep an object in circular motion for a given speed.

EXAMPLE 2.6   Finding Centripetal Acceleration

Determine the magnitude of the centripetal acceleration of a car going 12 m/s (about 27 mi/h) on a circular cloverleaf with a radius of 50 m (● Fig. 2.13).

Solution

Given: $v = 12$ m/s, $r = 50$ m

The centripetal acceleration is given by Eq. 2.5:

$$a_c = \frac{v^2}{r} = \frac{(12\ \text{m/s})^2}{50\ \text{m}}$$

$$= 2.9\ \text{m/s}^2$$

The value of 2.9 m/s^2 is about 30% of the acceleration due to gravity, $g = 9.8$ m/s^2, and is a fairly large acceleration.

Confidence Exercise 2.6

Using the result of Example 2.3, compute the centripetal acceleration in m/s^2 of the Earth in its nearly circular orbit about the Sun ($r = 1.5 \times 10^{11}$ m).

Did You Learn?

- A centripetal (center-seeking) acceleration is needed for uniform circular motion.

- In uniform circular motion, there is a change in velocity (direction), but the tangential speed is constant.

Figure 2.13 Frictional Centripetal Acceleration

The inward acceleration necessary for a vehicle to go around a level curve is supplied by friction on the tires. On a banked curve, some of the acceleration is supplied by the inward component of the acceleration due to gravity.

Farrell Grehan/Photo Researchers, Inc.

2.5   Projectile Motion

Preview Questions

- Neglecting air resistance, why would a ball projected horizontally and another ball dropped at the same time from the same initial height hit the ground together?

- On what does the range of a projectile depend? (Neglect air resistance.)

Another common motion in two dimensions is that of an object thrown or projected by some means. For example, the motion of a thrown ball or a golf ball driven off a tee is called **projectile motion**. A special case of projectile motion is that of an object projected horizontally, or parallel, to a level surface. Suppose a ball is projected horizontally, while at the same time another ball is dropped from the same height (● Fig. 2.14a). You might be surprised that both balls hit the ground at the same time (neglecting air resistance). An object thrown horizontally will fall at the same rate as an object that is dropped (both fall with acceleration g). The velocity in the horizontal direction does not affect the velocity and acceleration in the vertical direction.

The multiflash photo in Fig. 2.14b shows a dropped ball and one projected horizontally at the same time. Notice that the balls fall vertically together as the projected ball moves to the right. Neglecting air resistance, a horizontally projected object essentially travels in a horizontal direction with a constant velocity (no acceleration in that direction) while falling vertically under the influence of gravity. The resulting path is a curved arc, as shown in Fig. 2.14. Occasionally, a sports announcer claims that a hard-throwing quarterback can throw a football so many yards "on a line," meaning a straight line. This statement, of course, must be false. All objects thrown horizontally begin to fall as soon as they leave the thrower's hand.

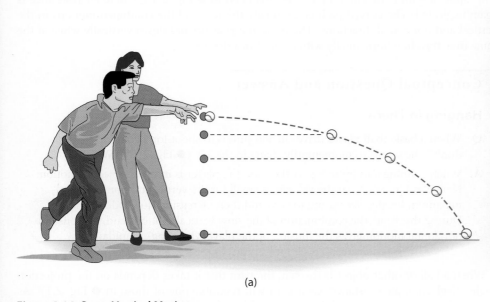

(a)

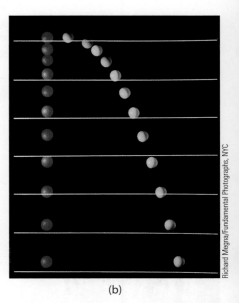

(b)

Richard Megna/Fundamental Photographs, NYC

Figure 2.14 Same Vertical Motions
(a) When one ball is thrown horizontally and another ball is dropped simultaneously from the same height, both will hit the ground at the same time (with air resistance neglected), because the vertical motions are the same. (Diagram not to scale.) (b) A multiflash photograph of two balls, one of which was projected horizontally at the same time the other ball was dropped. Notice from the horizontal lines that both balls fall vertically at the same rate.

Figure 2.15 Projectile Motion
(a) The curved path of a projectile is a result of the combined motions in the vertical and horizontal directions. As the ball goes up and down, it travels to the right. The combined effect is a curved path. (b) Neglecting air resistance, the projected football has the same horizontal velocity (v_x) throughout its flight, but its vertical velocity (v_y) changes in the same way as that of an object thrown upward.

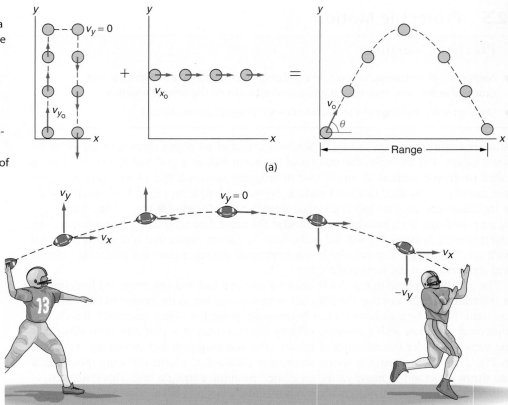

(a)

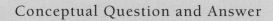

(b)

If an object is projected at an angle θ (lowercase Greek theta) to the horizontal, then it will follow a symmetric curved path, as illustrated in ● Fig. 2.15, where air resistance is again neglected. The curved path is essentially the result of the combined motions in the vertical and horizontal directions. The projectile goes up and down vertically while at the same time traveling horizontally with a constant velocity.

Conceptual Question and Answer

Hanging in There

Q. When a basketball player drives in and jumps to shoot for a goal (or "slam dunk"), he seems to momentarily "hang in the air" (● Fig. 2.16). Why?

A. When running and jumping for the shot, the player is in near projectile motion. Notice in Fig. 2.10 that the velocity is small for the vertical motion near the maximum height, decreasing to zero and then increasing slowly downward. During this time, the combination of the slow vertical motions and the constant horizontal motion gives the illusion of the player "hanging" in midair.

When a ball or other object is thrown, the path that it takes depends on the projection angle. Neglecting air resistance, each path will resemble one of those in ● Fig. 2.17. As shown, the *range*, or horizontal distance the object travels, is maximum when the object is projected at an angle of 45° relative to level ground. Notice in the figure that for a given initial speed, projections at complementary angles (angles that add up to 90°)—for example, 30° and 60°—have the same range as long as there is no air resistance.

With little or no air resistance, projectiles have symmetric paths, but when a ball or object is thrown or hit hard, air resistance comes into effect. In such a case, the projectile

Figure 2.16 Hanging in There
Carmelo Anthony seems to "hang" in the air at the top of his "projectile" jump path. (See text for description.)

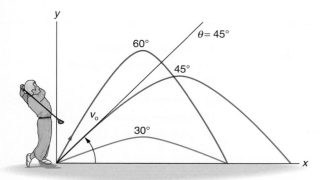

Figure 2.17 Maximum Range
A projectile's maximum range on a horizontal plane is achieved
with a projection angle of 45° (in the absence of air resistance).
Projectiles with the same initial speed and projection angles
the same amount above and below 45° have the same range,
as shown here for 30° and 60°.

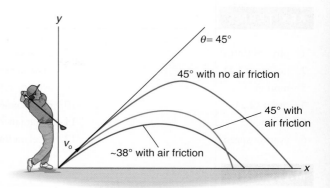

Figure 2.18 Effects of Air Resistance on Projectiles
Long football passes, hard-hit baseballs, and driven golf balls
follow trajectories similar to those shown here. Frictional air
resistance reduces the range.

Figure 2.19 Going for the Distance
Because of air resistance, the athlete
hurls the javelin at an angle of less
than 45° for maximum range.

path is no longer symmetric and resembles one of those shown in ● Fig. 2.18. Air resistance reduces the velocity of the projectile, particularly in the horizontal direction. As a result, the maximum range occurs at an angle less than 45°.

Athletes such as football quarterbacks and baseball players are aware of the best angle at which to throw to get the maximum distance. A good golfing drive also depends on the angle at which the ball is hit. Of course, in most of these instances there are other considerations, such as spin. The angle of throw is also a consideration in track and field events such as discus and javelin throwing. ● Figure 2.19 shows an athlete hurling a javelin at an angle of less than 45° in order to achieve the maximum distance.

Did You Learn?

- A horizontally projected ball and another ball dropped from the same height have the same downward motion because the vertical acceleration (g) is the same (neglecting air resistance).

- The range of a projectile depends on the initial velocity and angle of projection (neglecting air resistance).

KEY TERMS

1. physics (intro)
2. position (2.1)
3. motion
4. scalar (2.2)
5. vector
6. average speed
7. distance
8. instantaneous speed
9. average velocity
10. displacement
11. instantaneous velocity
12. acceleration (2.3)
13. average acceleration
14. acceleration due to gravity
15. free fall
16. terminal velocity
17. centripetal acceleration (2.4)
18. projectile motion (2.5)

MATCHING

For each of the following items, fill in the number of the appropriate Key Term from the preceding list. Compare your answers with those at the back of the book.

a. _____ Displacement/travel time
b. _____ Has magnitude only
c. _____ Velocity at an instant of time
d. _____ Directed toward the center of circular motion
e. _____ Actual path length
f. _____ Straight-line directed distance
g. _____ A continuous change of position
h. _____ Time rate of change of velocity
i. _____ Has magnitude and direction

j. _____ Motion solely under the influence of gravity
k. _____ Motion of a thrown object
l. _____ Speed at an instant of time
m. _____ The location of an object
n. _____ 9.8 m/s^2
o. _____ Distance traveled/travel time
p. _____ The most fundamental of the physical sciences
q. _____ Difference between final and initial velocities divided by time
r. _____ Zero acceleration in free fall

MULTIPLE CHOICE

Compare your answers with those at the back of the book.

1. What is necessary to designate a position? (2.1)
    (a) fundamental units   (b) motion
    (c) a direction   (d) a reference point

2. Which one of the following describes an object in motion? (2.1)
    (a) A period of time has passed.
    (b) Its position is known.
    (c) It is continuously changing position.
    (d) It has reached its final position.

3. Which one of the following is always true about the magnitude of a displacement? (2.2)
    (a) It is greater than the distance traveled.
    (b) It is equal to the distance traveled.
    (c) It is less than the distance traveled.
    (d) It is less than or equal to the distance traveled.

4. Distance is to displacement as ____. (2.2)
    (a) centimeters is to meters   (b) a vector is to a scalar
    (c) speed is to velocity   (d) distance is to time

5. Acceleration may result from what? (2.3)
    (a) an increase in speed
    (b) a decrease in speed
    (c) a change in direction
    (d) all of the preceding

6. For a constant linear acceleration, what changes uniformly? (2.3)
    (a) acceleration
    (b) velocity
    (c) distance
    (d) displacement

7. Which one of the following is true for a deceleration? (2.3)
    (a) The velocity remains constant.
    (b) The acceleration is negative.
    (c) The acceleration is in the direction opposite to the velocity.
    (d) The acceleration is zero.

8. Which is true for an object in free fall? (2.3)
    (a) It has frictional effects.
    (b) It has a constant velocity.
    (c) It has a constant displacement.
    (d) It increases in distance proportionally to t^2.

9. If the speed of an object in uniform circular motion is tripled and the radial distance remains constant, then the magnitude of the centripetal acceleration increases by what factor? (2.4)
    (a) 2   (b) 3   (c) 4   (d) 9

10. Neglecting air resistance, which of the following is true for a ball thrown at an angle θ to the horizontal? (2.5)
    (a) It has a constant velocity in the $+x$ direction.
    (b) It has a constant acceleration in the $-y$ direction.
    (c) It has a changing velocity in the $+y$ direction.
    (d) All of the preceding are true.

11. In the absence of air resistance, a projectile launched at an angle of 28° above the horizontal will have the same range as a projectile launched at which of the following angles? (2.5)
    (a) 45°   (b) 57°   (c) 62°   (d) $180° - 33° = 147°$

12. A football is thrown on a long pass. Compared to the ball's initial horizontal velocity, the velocity at the highest point is ____. (2.5)
    (a) greater   (b) less   (c) the same

FILL IN THE BLANK

Compare your answers with those at the back of the book.

1. An object is in motion when it undergoes a continuous change of ___. (2.1)
2. Speed is a(n) ___ quantity. (2.2)
3. Velocity is a(n) ___ quantity. (2.2)
4. ___ is the actual path length. (2.2)
5. A car's speedometer reads instantaneous ___. (2.2)
6. Speed and direction do not change for a(n) ___ velocity. (2.2)
7. The distance traveled by a dropped object increases with ___. (2.3)
8. Objects in motion solely under the influence of gravity are said to be in ___. (2.3)
9. The metric units associated with acceleration are ___. (2.3)
10. An object in uniform circular motion has a constant ___. (2.4)
11. If the speed of one object in uniform circular motion is two times that of another such object (same radius), then its centripetal acceleration is ___ times greater. (2.4)
12. Neglecting air resistance, a horizontally thrown object and an object dropped from the same height fall with the same constant ___. (2.5)

SHORT ANSWER

1. What area of physics involves the study of objects moving at relatively low speeds?

2.1 Defining Motion

2. What is necessary to designate the position of an object?
3. How are position and motion related?

2.2 Speed and Velocity

4. Distinguish between scalar and vector quantities.
5. Distinguish between distance and displacement. How are these quantities associated with speed and velocity?
6. How is average speed analogous to an average class grade?
7. A jogger jogs two blocks directly north.
   (a) How do the jogger's average speed and the magnitude of the average velocity compare?
   (b) If the jogger's return trip follows the same path, then how do average speed and magnitude of the average velocity compare for the total trip?

2.3 Acceleration

8. What changes when there is acceleration? Give an example.
9. The gas pedal of a car is commonly referred to as the accelerator. Would this term be appropriate for (a) the clutch in a stick-shift car? (b) the gears in a stick-shift car? Explain.
10. Does a negative acceleration always mean that an object is slowing down? Explain.
11. A ball is dropped. Assuming free fall, what is its initial speed? What is its initial acceleration? What is the final acceleration?
12. A vertically projected object has zero velocity at its maximum height, but the acceleration is not zero. What would be implied if the acceleration were zero?

2.4 Acceleration in Uniform Circular Motion

13. Can a car be moving at a constant speed of 60 km/h and still be accelerating? Explain.
14. What does the term *centripetal* mean?
15. Are we accelerating as a consequence of the Earth spinning on its axis? Explain.
16. What is the direction of the acceleration vector of a person on the spinning Earth if the person is (a) at the equator? (b) at some other latitude? (c) at the poles?

2.5 Projectile Motion

17. For projectile motion, what quantities are constant? (Neglect air resistance.)
18. How do the motions of horizontal projections with the same initial speed compare on the Earth and on the Moon?
19. On what does the range of a projectile depend?
20. Can a baseball pitcher throw a fastball in a straight, horizontal line? Why or why not?
21. Figure 2.14(b) shows a multiflash photograph of one ball dropped from rest and, at the same time, another ball projected horizontally from the same height. The two hit the floor at the same time. Explain.
22. Taking into account air resistance, how do you throw a ball to get the maximum range? Why?

VISUAL CONNECTION

Visualize the connections and give answers for the blanks. Compare your answers with those at the back of the book.

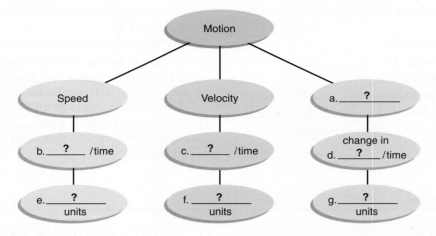

APPLYING YOUR KNOWLEDGE

1. Do highway speed limit signs refer to average speeds or to instantaneous speeds? Explain.

2. (a) If we are moving at a high speed as the Earth revolves about the Sun (18.5 m/s, Example 2.3), then why don't we generally feel this motion? (b) Similarly, we are traveling through space because of the Earth's rotation (1000 mi/h at the equator, Confidence Exercise 2.3). We don't generally feel this motion either, but we do easily sense it otherwise. How?

3. What is the direction of the acceleration vector of a person on the spinning Earth if the person is (a) at the equator? (b) at some other latitude? (c) at the poles?

4. Is an object projected vertically upward in free fall? Explain.

5. A student sees her physical science professor approaching on the sidewalk that runs by her dorm. She gets a water balloon and waits. When the professor is 2.0 s from being directly under her window 11 m above the sidewalk, she drops the balloon. You finish the story.

6. How would (a) an updraft affect a skydiver in reaching terminal velocity? (b) a downdraft?

7. A skydiver uses a parachute to slow the landing speed. Parachutes generally have a hole in the top. Why? Wouldn't air going through the hole deter the slowing?

8. Tractor-trailer rigs often have an airfoil on top of the cab, as shown in ● Fig. 2.20. What is the purpose of this airfoil?

Figure 2.20 Air Foil
See Question 8 in Applying Your Knowledge.

Dean Fox/SuperStock

IMPORTANT EQUATIONS

Average Speed: $\bar{v} = \dfrac{d}{t}$ (2.1)

Acceleration: $\bar{a} = \dfrac{\Delta v}{t} = \dfrac{v_f - v_o}{t}$ (2.2)

$$v_f = v_o + at \qquad \text{(constant acceleration)} \qquad (2.3)$$
or with $v_o = 0$,
$$v_f = at \qquad (2.3a)$$

Distance Traveled by a Dropped Object: $d = \frac{1}{2}gt^2$ (2.4)

Centripetal Acceleration: $a_c = \dfrac{v^2}{r}$ (2.5)

EXERCISES

2.2 Speed and Velocity

1. A gardener walks in a flower garden as illustrated in ● Fig. 2.21. What distance does the gardener travel?

   Answer: 7 m

2. What is the gardener's displacement (Fig. 2.21)? Give a general direction, such as south or west. (*Hint:* Think of a 3-4-5 triangle, Pythagorean theorem.)

3. At a track meet, a runner runs the 100-m dash in 12 s. What was the runner's average speed?

   Answer: 8.3 m/s

4. A jogger jogs around a circular track with a diameter of 300 m in 10 minutes. What was the jogger's average speed in m/s?

5. A space probe on the surface of Mars sends a radio signal back to the Earth, a distance of 7.86×10^7 km. Radio waves travel at the speed of light (3.00×10^8 m/s). How many seconds does it take the signal to reach the Earth?

   Answer: 2.62×10^2 s

6. A group of college students eager to get to Florida on a spring break drove the 750-mi trip with only minimum stops. They computed their average speed for the trip to be 55.0 mi/h. How many hours did the trip take?

7. A student drives the 100-mi trip back to campus after spring break and travels with an average speed of 52 mi/h for 1 hour and 30 minutes for the first part of the trip.
   (a) What distance was traveled during this time?
   (b) Traffic gets heavier, and the last part of the trip takes another half-hour. What was the average speed during this leg of the trip?
   (c) Find the average speed for the total trip.

   Answer: (a) 78 mi (b) 44 mi/h (c) 50 mi/h

8. Joe Cool drives to see his girlfriend who attends another college.
   (a) The 130-km trip takes 2.0 h. What was the average speed for the trip?
   (b) The return trip over the same route takes 3.0 h because of heavy traffic. What is the average speed for the return trip?
   (c) What is the average speed for the entire trip?

9. An airplane flying directly eastward at a constant speed travels 300 km in 2.0 h.
   (a) What is the average velocity of the plane?
   (b) What is its instantaneous velocity?

   Answer: (a) 150 km/h, east (b) same

10. A race car traveling northward on a straight, level track at a constant speed travels 0.750 km in 20.0 s. The return trip over the same track is made in 25.0 s.
    (a) What is the average velocity of the car in m/s for the first leg of the run?
    (b) What is the average velocity for the total trip?

2.3 Acceleration

11. A sprinter starting from rest on a straight, level track is able to achieve a speed of 12 m/s in 6.0 s. What is the sprinter's average acceleration?

    Answer: 2.0 m/s²

12. Modern oil tankers weigh more than a half-million tons and have lengths of up to one-fourth mile. Such massive ships require a distance of 5.0 km (about 3.0 mi) and a time of 20 min to come to a stop from a top speed of 30 km/h.

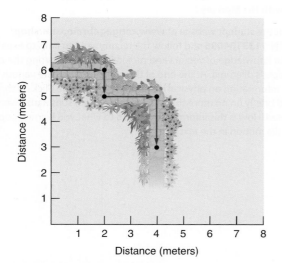

Figure 2.21   A Walk through the Garden
See Exercises 1 and 2.

(a) What is the magnitude of such a ship's average acceleration in m/s^2 in coming to a stop?

(b) What is the magnitude of the ship's average velocity in m/s? Comment on the potential of a tanker running aground.

13. A motorboat starting from rest travels in a straight line on a lake.

(a) If the boat achieves a speed of 8.0 m/s in 10 s, what is the boat's average acceleration?

(b) Then, in 5.0 more seconds, the boat's speed is 12 m/s. What is the boat's average acceleration for the total time?

Answer: (a) 0.80 m/s^2 in the direction of motion (b) same

14. A car travels on a straight, level road.

(a) Starting from rest, the car is going 44 ft/s (30 mi/h) at the end of 5.0 s. What is the car's average acceleration in ft/s^2?

(b) In 4.0 more seconds, the car is going 88 ft/s (60 mi/h). What is the car's average acceleration for this time period?

(c) The car then slows to 66 ft/s (45 mi/h) in 3.0 s. What is the average acceleration for this time period?

(d) What is the overall average acceleration for the total time? (Note these convenient British unit conversions: 60 mi/h = 88 ft/s, 45 mi/h = 66 ft/s, and 30 mi/h = 44 ft/s.)

15. A ball is dropped from the top of an 80-m-high building. Does the ball reach the ground in 4.0 s? (See Figure 2.7.)

Answer: No, it falls only 78 m in 4.0 s.

16. What speed does the ball in Exercise 15 have in falling 3.5 s?

17. Figure 1.18 (Chapter 1) shows the Hoover Dam Bridge over the Colorado River at a height of 271 m. If a heavy object is dropped from the bridge, how much time passes before the object makes a splash?

Answer: 7.4 s

18. A student drops an object out the window of the top floor of a high-rise dormitory.

(a) Neglecting air resistance, how fast is the object traveling when it strikes the ground at the end of 3.0 s? Express the speed in mi/h for a familiar comparison. Can things dropped from high places be dangerous to people below?

(b) How far, in meters, does the object fall during the 3.0 s? Comment on how many floors the dormitory probably has.

2.4 Acceleration in Uniform Circular Motion

19. A person drives a car around a circular, level cloverleaf with a radius of 70 m at a uniform speed of 10 m/s.

(a) What is the acceleration of the car?

(b) Compare this answer with the acceleration due to gravity as a percentage. Would you be able to sense the car's acceleration if you were riding in it?

Answer: (a) 1.4 m/s^2, toward the center (b) 14%, yes

20. A race car goes around a circular, level track with a diameter of 1.00 km at a constant speed of 90.0 km/h. What is the car's centripetal acceleration in m/s^2?

2.5 Projectile Motion

21. If you drop an object from a height of 1.5 m, it will hit the ground in 0.55 s. If you throw a baseball horizontally with an initial speed of 30 m/s from the same height, how long will it take the ball to hit the ground? (Neglect air resistance.)

Answer: 0.55 s

22. A golfer on a level fairway hits a ball at an angle of 42° to the horizontal that travels 100 yd before striking the ground. He then hits another ball from the same spot with the same speed, but at a different angle. This ball also travels 100 yd. At what angle was the second ball hit? (Neglect air resistance.)

ON THE WEB

1. Galileo and the Leaning Tower of Pisa

The Highlight: Galileo and the Leaning Tower of Pisa talks about Galileo and the "experiments" that he may or may not have conducted. Follow the recommended links on the student website at **www.cengagebrain.com/shop/ISBN/1133104096** to perform simulations of three experiments. After you are finished, note what you found out about gravity.

2. Vectors and Projectiles: Can You Help the Zookeeper with His Monkey?

Visit the student website at **www.cengagebrain.com/shop/ISBN/1133104096** and follow the recommended links to expand your knowledge of vectors and projectiles by considering the zookeeper's dilemma. At the end of the online exercise are various links for information on physical descriptions of motion. Click on the links and briefly (in no more than a sentence or two) summarize what was stated. How is this information related to what you learned about projectile motion in the text?

Force and Motion

Syracuse Newspapers/Li-Hua Lan/The Image Works

The whole burden of philosophy seems to consist of this—from the phenomena of motions to investigate the forces of nature, and from these forces to explain the other phenomena. [Physics was once called natural philosophy.]

•

Sir Isaac Newton
(1642–1727)

< A force is needed to produce a change in motion, as the pusher well knows.

In Chapter 2 the description of motion was discussed but not the cause of motion. What, then, causes motion? You might say a push causes something to start moving or to speed up or slow down, but in more scientific terms, the push is the application of a *force*. In this chapter we will go one step further and study force *and* motion. The discussion will consider Newton's three laws of motion, his law of universal gravitation, and later the laws of conservation of linear and angular momentum, making it a very legal sounding chapter with all these laws. In Chapter 3.6 buoyant force is considered. Will an object float or sink?

During the sixteenth and seventeenth centuries, a "scientific revolution" occurred. The theories of motion, which were handed down from the Greeks for almost 2000 years, were reexamined and changed. Galileo (1564–1642) was one

PHYSICS FACTS

▶ "If I have seen further [than certain other men] it is by standing upon the shoulders of giants." Isaac Newton, in a letter to Robert Hooke, February 5, 1675, in reference to work in physics and astronomy done by Galileo and Kepler.

Chapter Outline

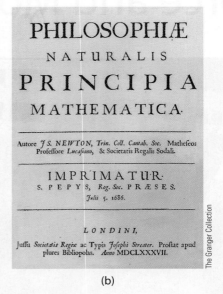

(a)   (b)

Figure 3.1 The Man and the Book
(a) Sir Isaac Newton (1642–1727). (b) The title page from the *Principia.* Can you read the Roman numerals at the bottom of the page that give the year of publication?

of the first scientists to experiment on moving objects. It remained for Sir Isaac Newton, who was born the year Galileo died, to devise the laws of motion and explain the phenomena of moving objects on the Earth and the motions of planets and other celestial bodies.

Newton was only 25 years old when he formulated most of his discoveries in mathematics and mechanics. His book *Mathematical Principles of Natural Philosophy* (commonly referred to as the *Principia*) was published in Latin in 1687 when he was 45. It is considered by many to be the most important publication in the history of physics and certainly established Newton as one of the greatest scientists of all time. (See ● Fig. 3.1.)

3.1   Force and Net Force

Preview Questions

● Does a force always produce motion?

● What is the condition for motion when more than one force acts?

First let's look at the meaning of force. It is easy to give examples of forces, but how would you define a force? A force is defined in terms of what it does, and as you know from experience, a force can produce changes in motion. A force can set a stationary object into motion. It can also speed up or slow down a moving object, or it can change the direction of the motion. In other words, a force can produce a *change in velocity* (speed and/or direction) or an *acceleration*. Therefore, an observed change in motion, including motion starting from rest, is evidence of a force, which leads to the following definition: A **force** is a vector quantity capable of producing motion or a change in motion, that is, a change in velocity or an acceleration (Chapter 2.3).

The word *capable* here is significant. A force may act on an object, but its capability to produce a change in motion may be balanced or canceled by one or more other forces. The net effect is then zero. Thus, a force does not *necessarily* produce a change in motion. It follows, though, that if a force acts *alone*, then the object on which it acts will exhibit a change in velocity, or an acceleration.

(a)   (b)

Figure 3.2 Balanced and Unbalanced Forces
(a) When two applied forces are equal in magnitude and acting in opposite directions, they are said be *balanced*, and there is no net force and no motion if the system is initially at rest. (b) When F_2 is greater than F_1, there is an *unbalanced*, or net force to the right, and motion occurs.

To take into account the application of more than one force on an object, we speak of an **unbalanced** or **net force**. To understand the difference between balanced and unbalanced forces, consider the tug of war shown in ● Fig. 3.2a. Forces are applied, but there is no motion. The forces in this case are balanced; they are equal in magnitude and opposite in direction. In effect, the forces cancel each other, and the net force is zero because the forces are "balanced." Motion occurs when the forces are *unbalanced*, when they are not equal and there is a *net* force F_{net} to the right, and motion occurs (Fig. 3.2b).

Because forces have directions as well as magnitudes, they are *vector* quantities. Several forces may act on an object, but for there to be a change in velocity or for an acceleration to occur, there must be an unbalanced, or net, force. With this understanding, let's next take a look at both force and motion.

Did You Learn?

● A single or net applied force can produce an acceleration.

● When more than one force acts, a net or unbalanced force is needed to produce a change in velocity or an acceleration.

3.2 Newton's First Law of Motion

Preview Questions

● If you were moving with a constant velocity in deep space, how far would you travel?

● How can the inertias of objects be compared?

Long before the time of Galileo and Newton, scientists had asked themselves, "What is the natural state of motion?" The early Greek scientist Aristotle had presented a theory that prevailed for almost 20 centuries after his death. According to this theory, an object required a force in order to remain in motion. The natural state of an object was one of rest, with the exception of celestial bodies, which were naturally in motion. It is easily observed that moving objects such as a rolling ball tend to slow down and come to rest, so a natural state of being at rest must have seemed logical to Aristotle.

Galileo studied motion using a ball rolling down an inclined plane onto a level surface. The smoother he made the surface, the farther the ball would roll (● Fig. 3.3). He reasoned that if a very long surface could be made perfectly smooth, there would be nothing to stop the ball, so it would continue to slide in the absence of friction indefinitely or until

Figure 3.3 Motion without Resistance
If the level surface could be made perfectly smooth, then how far would the ball travel?

something stopped it. Thus, contrary to Aristotle, Galileo concluded that objects could *naturally* remain in motion rather than coming to rest.

Newton also recognized this phenomenon, and Galileo's result is incorporated in **Newton's first law of motion**:

An object will remain at rest or in uniform motion in a straight line unless acted on by an external, unbalanced force.

Uniform motion in a straight line means that the velocity is constant. An object at rest has a constant velocity of zero. An *external* force is an applied force, one applied on or to the object or system. There are also internal forces. For example, suppose the object is an automobile and you are a passenger traveling inside. You can push (apply a force) on the floor or the dashboard, but this has no effect on the car's velocity because your push is an internal force.

Because of the ever-present forces of friction and gravity on the Earth, it is difficult to observe an object in a state of uniform motion, but in free space, where there is no friction and negligible gravitational attraction, an object initially in motion maintains a constant velocity. For example, after being projected on its way, an interplanetary spacecraft approximates this condition quite well. Upon going out of the solar system where there is negligible gravitational influence, as two *Voyager* spacecraft have done (Chapter 16.6), a spacecraft will travel with a constant velocity until an external, unbalanced force alters this velocity.

Motion and Inertia

Galileo also introduced another important concept. It appeared that objects had a property of maintaining a state of motion; there was a resistance to changes in motion. Similarly, if an object was at rest, it seemed to "want" to remain at rest. Galileo called this property *inertia*. **Inertia** is the natural tendency of an object to remain in a state of rest or in uniform motion in a straight line.

Newton went one step further and related the concept of inertia to something that could be measured: mass. **Mass** is a measure of inertia. The greater the mass of an object, the greater its inertia, and vice versa.

To help understand the relationship between mass and inertia, suppose you horizontally pushed two different people on swings initially at rest, one of them a very large man and the other a small child (● Fig. 3.4a). You would quickly find that it was more difficult to get the adult moving; there would be a noticeable difference in the resistance to a change in motion between the man and the child. Also, once you got them swinging and then tried to stop their motions, you would notice a difference in the resistance to a change in motion again. Being more massive, the man has greater inertia and a greater resistance to a change in motion.*

Another example of inertia is shown in Fig. 3.4b. The stack of coins has inertia and resists being moved when at rest. If the paper is jerked quickly, then the inertia of the coins

---

*A suggested inertia example: When you enter a supermarket with an empty shopping cart, the cart is easy to maneuver, but when you leave with a full cart, making changes in motion (speed and direction) requires much greater effort even though the cart rolls freely with little friction. (Courtesy of Dr. Philip Blanco, Grossmont College.)

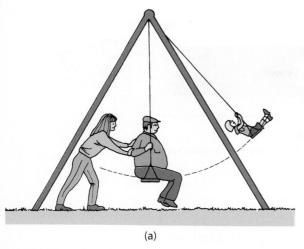
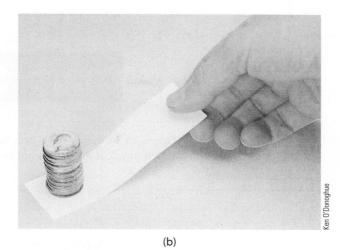

(a)   (b)

Figure 3.4 Mass and Inertia
(a) An external, applied force is necessary to set an object in motion. The man has more mass and more inertia than the child and hence has more resistance to motion. (b) Because of inertia, it is possible to remove the paper strip from beneath the stack of quarters without toppling it, by giving the paper a quick jerk. Try it.

will prevent them from toppling. You may have pulled a magazine from the bottom of a stack with a similar action.

Because of the relationship between motion and inertia, Newton's first law is sometimes called the *law of inertia*. This law can be used to describe some of the observed effects in everyday life. For example, suppose you were in the front seat of a car traveling at a high speed down a straight road and the driver suddenly put on the brakes for an emergency stop. What would happen, according to Newton's first law, if you were not wearing a seat belt? The friction on the seat of your pants would not be enough to change your motion appreciably, so you'd keep on moving while the car was coming to a stop. The next external, unbalanced force you'd experience would not be pleasant. Newton's first law makes a good case for buckling up.

Conceptual Question and Answer

You Go Your Way, I'll Go Mine

Q. An air-bubble level on a surface, as illustrated in ● Fig. 3.5, is given an applied horizontal force toward the left. Which way does the bubble move?

A. Some might say the bubble stays behind and "moves" to the right, but it actually moves to the left in the direction of the force. The incorrect answer arises because we are used to observing the bubble instead of the liquid. The bubble is chiefly air, which has little mass or inertia, and readily moves. The correct answer is explained by Newton's first law. Because of inertia, the liquid resists motion and "piles up" toward the rear of the level, forcing the bubble forward. Think about giving a stationary pan of water on a table a push. What happens to the water?

Did You Learn?

● An object in uniform motion would travel in a straight line until acted upon by some external unbalanced force, so in free space with negligible gravity an object would travel indefinitely.

● Objects' relative inertias can be compared by their masses.

Figure 3.5 Pushing a Level on a Table
Which way does the bubble go? See the Conceptual Question and Answer.

3.3 Newton's Second Law of Motion

Preview Questions

- How are force and motion related?
- Which is generally greater, static friction or kinetic friction?

In our initial study of motion (Chapter 2), acceleration was defined as the time rate of the change of velocity ($\Delta v/\Delta t$). However, nothing was said about what *causes* acceleration, only that a change in velocity was required to have an acceleration. So, what causes an acceleration? The answer follows from Newton's first law: *If an external, unbalanced force is required to produce a change in velocity*, then an external, unbalanced force causes an *acceleration*.

Newton was aware of this result, but he went further and also related acceleration to inertia or mass. Because inertia is the tendency not to undergo a *change* in motion, a reasonable assumption is that the greater the inertia or mass of an object, the smaller the change in motion or velocity (acceleration) when a force is applied. Such insight was typical of Newton in his many contributions to science.

Summarizing

1. The acceleration produced by an unbalanced force acting on an object (or mass) is directly proportional to the magnitude of the force ($a \propto F$) and in the direction of the force (the $\propto$ symbol is a proportionality sign). In other words, the greater the unbalanced force, the greater the acceleration.

2. The acceleration of an object being acted on by an unbalanced force is inversely proportional to the mass of the object ($a \propto 1/m$). That is, for a given unbalanced force, the greater the mass of an object, the smaller the acceleration.

Combining these effects of force and mass on acceleration gives

$$\text{acceleration} = \frac{\text{unbalanced force}}{\text{mass}}$$

When appropriate units are used, the effects of force and mass on acceleration can be written in equation form as $a = F/m$. Or, as commonly written in terms of force in magnitude form, we have **Newton's second law of motion**:

$$\text{force} = \text{mass} \times \text{acceleration}$$
$$F = ma \qquad\qquad\qquad 3.1$$

These relationships are illustrated in ● Fig. 3.6. Note that if the force acting on a mass is doubled, then the acceleration doubles (direct proportion, $a \propto F$). However, if the same

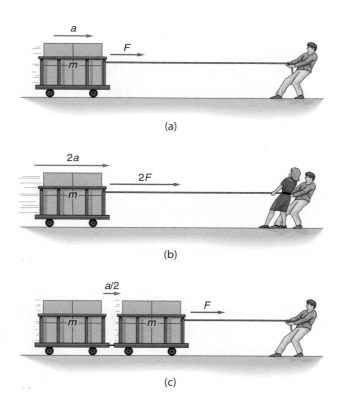

Figure 3.6 **Force, Mass, and Acceleration**
(a) An unbalanced force *F* acting on a mass *m* produces an acceleration *a*. (b) If the mass remains the same and the force is doubled, then the acceleration is doubled. (c) If the mass is doubled and the force remains the same, then the acceleration is reduced by one-half. The friction of the cars is neglected in all cases.

force is applied to twice as much mass, the acceleration is one-half as great (inverse proportion, $a \propto 1/m$).

Notice from Fig. 3.6 that the mass *m* is the *total* mass of the system or all the mass that is accelerated. A system may be two or more separate masses, as will be seen in Example 3.1. Also, *F* is the net, or unbalanced, force, which may be the vector sum of two or more forces. Unless otherwise stated, a general reference to force means an *unbalanced* force.

In the SI metric system, the unit of force is appropriately called the **newton** (abbreviated N), This is a derived unit. The standard unit equivalent may be seen from Eq. 3.1 by putting it in standard units: force = mass × acceleration = kg × m/s^2 = kg·m/s^2 = N.

In the British system, the unit of force is the *pound* (lb). This unit also has derived units of mass multiplied by acceleration (ft/s^2). The unit of mass is the *slug*, which is rarely used and will not be employed in this textbook. Recall that the British system is a gravitational or force system and that in this system, objects are weighed in pounds (force). As will be seen shortly, *weight* is a force and is expressed in newtons (N) in the SI and in pounds (lb) in the British system. If you are familiar with the story that Newton gained insight by observing (or being struck by) a falling apple while meditating on the concept of gravity, it is easy to remember that an average-size apple weighs about 1 newton (● Fig. 3.7).

Example 3.1 uses $F = ma$ to illustrate that *F* is the unbalanced or net force and *m* is the total mass.

EXAMPLE 3.1   Finding Acceleration with Two Applied Forces

Forces are applied to blocks connected by a string and resting on a frictionless surface, as illustrated in ● Fig. 3.8. If the mass of each block is 1.0 kg and the mass of the string is negligible, then what is the acceleration of the system?

Solution

Step 1
Given: $m_1 = 1.0$ kg, $F_1 = -5.0$ N (left, negative direction)
           $m_2 = 1.0$ kg, $F_2 = +8.0$ N (right, positive direction)
Keep in mind that force (*F*) is a vector with direction, here + or −.

Figure 3.7 **About a Newton**
An average-size apple weighs about 1 newton (or 0.225 lb).

Figure 3.8 $F = ma$
Net force and total mass. (See
Example 3.1.)

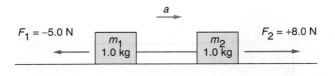

Step 2

Wanted: a (acceleration)
(The units are standard in the metric system.)

Step 3

The acceleration may be calculated using Eq. 3.1, $F = ma$, or $a = F/m$. Note, however, that F is the unbalanced (net) force, which in this case is the vector sum of the forces. Effectively, F_1 cancels part of F_2, and there is a net force $F_{net} = F_2 + F_1 = 8.0 \text{ N} - 5.0 \text{ N}$ in the direction of F_2. The total mass of the system being accelerated is $m = m_1 + m_2$. Hence, we have an acceleration in the direction of the net force (to the right).

$$a = \frac{F}{m} = \frac{F_{net}}{m_1 + m_2} = \frac{8.0 \text{ N} - 5.0 \text{ N}}{1.0 \text{ kg} + 1.0 \text{ kg}} = \frac{3.0 \text{ N}}{2.0 \text{ kg}} = 1.5 \text{ m/s}^2$$

Question: What would be the case if the surface were not frictionless? Answer: There would be another (frictional) force in the direction of F_1 opposing the motion.

Confidence Exercise 3.1

Given the same conditions as in Example 3.1, suppose $F_1 = -9.0$ N and $F_2 = 6.0$ N in magnitude. What would be the acceleration of the system in this case?
    The answers to Confidence Exercises may be found at the back of the book.

Because Newton's second law is so general, it can be used to analyze many situations. A dynamic example is *centripetal force*. Recall from Chapter 2.4 that the centripetal acceleration for uniform circular motion is given by $a_c = v^2/r$ (Eq. 2.5). The magnitude of the centripetal force that supplies such an acceleration is given by Newton's second law, $F = ma_c = mv^2/r$.

Mass and Weight

This is a good place to make a clear distinction between mass and weight. As learned previously, *mass* is the amount of matter an object contains (it is also a measure of inertia). **Weight** is related to the force of gravity (related to the gravitational force acting on a mass or object). The quantities are related, and Newton's second law clearly shows this relationship.
    On the surface of the Earth, where the acceleration due to gravity is relatively constant ($g = 9.80 \text{ m/s}^2$), the weight w on an object with a mass m is given by

weight = mass × acceleration due to gravity

$$w = mg \qquad\qquad 3.2$$

Note that this equation is a special case of $F = ma$ where different symbols, w and g, have been used for force and acceleration.

Conceptual Question and Answer

Fundamental is Fundamental

Q. Is weight a fundamental quantity?

A. No, and here's why. A fundamental quantity is constant or has the same value no matter where it is measured. In general, a physical object always has the same amount of matter, so it has a constant mass. The weight of an object, on the other hand, may differ, depending on the value of the acceleration due to gravity, g.

    For example, on the surface of the Moon, the acceleration due to gravity (g_M) is one-sixth the acceleration due to gravity on the surface of the Earth [$g_M = g/6 = (9.8 \text{ m/s}^2)/6 = 1.6 \text{ m/s}^2$], because of the Moon's mass and size. (See Chapter 3.5.) Thus, an object will have the *same* mass on the Moon as on the Earth, but its weight will be *different*. Mass, not weight, is the fundamental quantity. (A review of an important item from Chapter 1.4. See Fig. 1.8.)

EXAMPLE 3.2   Computing Weight

What is the weight (in newtons) of a 1.0-kg mass on (a) the Earth and (b) the Moon?

Solution

(a) Using Eq. 3.2 and the Earth's $g = 9.8 \text{ m/s}^2$,

$$w = mg = (1.0 \text{ kg})(9.8 \text{ m/s}^2) = 9.8 \text{ N}$$

(b) On the Moon, where $g_M = g/6 = 1.6 \text{ m/s}^2$,

$$w = mg_M = (1.0 \text{ kg})(1.6 \text{ m/s}^2) = 1.6 \text{ N}$$

Although the mass is the same in both cases, the weights are different because of different g's.

Confidence Exercise 3.2

On the surface of Mars, the acceleration due to gravity is 0.39 times that on the Earth. What would a kilogram weigh in newtons on Mars?

    The answers to Confidence Exercises may be found at the back of the book.

An unknown mass or object may be "weighed" on a scale. The scale can be calibrated in mass units (kilograms or grams) or in weight units (newtons or pounds). See ● Fig. 3.9. In Europe, weight is expressed in terms of mass. People "weigh" themselves in kilograms or "kilos."

Finally, an object in free fall has an unbalanced force of $F = w = mg$ acting on it (downward).* Why, then, do objects in free fall all descend at the same rate, as stated in the last chapter? Even Aristotle thought a heavy object would fall faster than a lighter one. Newton's laws explain.

Suppose two objects were in free fall, one having twice the mass of the other, as illustrated in ● Fig. 3.10. According to Newton's second law, the more massive object would have two times the weight, or gravitational force of attraction. By Newton's first law, however, the more massive object has twice the inertia, so it needs *twice the force to fall at the same rate*.

---

*Recall from Chapter 2.3 that an object falling solely under the influence of gravity (no air resistance) is said to be in *free fall*.

Figure 3.9 Mass and Weight
A mass of 1.0 kg suspended on a scale calibrated in newtons shows the weight to be 9.8 N, which is equivalent to 2.2 lb.

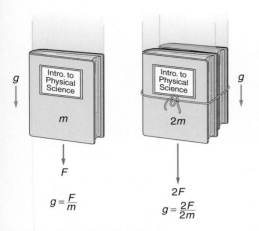

$$g = \frac{F}{m}$$

$$g = \frac{2F}{2m}$$

Figure 3.10 Acceleration Due to Gravity
The acceleration due to gravity is independent of the mass of a freely falling object. Thus the acceleration is the same for all such falling objects. An object with two times the mass of another has twice the gravitational force acting on it, but it also has twice the inertia and so falls at the same rate.

Friction

The force of friction is commonplace in our everyday lives. Without it, we would not be able to walk (our feet would slip), pick things up, and so on. **Friction** is the ever-present resistance to relative motion that occurs whenever two materials are in contact with each other, whether they are solids, liquids, or gases. In some instances, we want to increase friction by, for example, putting sand on an icy road or sidewalk to improve traction. In other instances, it is desired to reduce friction. Moving machine parts are lubricated to allow them to move freely, thereby reducing wear and the expenditure of energy. Automobiles would not run without friction-reducing oils and greases. With friction, energy is generally lost in the form of heat.

This section is concerned with friction between solid surfaces. (Air friction or resistance was discussed in Chapter 2.3.) All surfaces, no matter how smooth they appear or feel, are microscopically rough. It was originally thought that friction between solids arose from an interlocking of surface irregularities, or high and low spots, but research has shown that friction between contacting surfaces (particularly metals) is due to local adhesion. When surfaces are pressed together, local bonding or welding occurs in a few small patches. To overcome this local adhesion, a force great enough to pull apart the bonded regions must be applied.

Friction is characterized by a force of friction that opposes an applied force. Between solid surfaces, friction is generally classified into two types: static friction and sliding (or kinetic) friction.* *Static friction* occurs when the frictional force is sufficient to prevent relative motion between surfaces. Suppose you want to slide a filing cabinet across the floor. You push on it, but it doesn't move. The force of static friction between the bottom of the cabinet and the floor is opposite and at least equal to your applied force, so there is no motion; it is a static condition.

To get the job done, you push harder, but still the cabinet does not move. This indicates that the static frictional force increased when you increased the applied force. Increasing the applied force even more, you finally get the cabinet moving, but there is still a great deal of resistance—called kinetic friction—between the cabinet bottom and the floor. *Kinetic (or sliding) friction* occurs when there is a relative sliding motion between the surfaces in contact. You may notice that it is easier to keep the cabinet sliding than it is to get it moving. This is because sliding friction is generally less than the maximum static friction.

As you might imagine, the frictional force depends on how hard the surfaces are pressed together, which usually depends on the weight of an object on a surface. Because contacting surfaces can be of various materials, *coefficients of friction*—coefficients of static friction and coefficients of kinetic friction—are used to characterize particular situations. ● Table 3.1 lists some approximate values of these for various materials. The coefficient of static fric-

Table 3.1 Approximate Values for Coefficients of Static and Kinetic Friction between Certain Surfaces

Friction between Materials	μ_s	μ_k
Aluminum on aluminum	1.90	1.40
Aluminum on steel	0.61	0.47
Teflon on steel	0.04	0.04
Rubber on concrete		
dry	1.20	0.85
wet	0.80	0.60
Wood on wood	0.58	0.40
Lubricated ball bearings	< 0.01	< 0.01

*There is also rolling friction, such as occurs between a train wheel and a rail. This type of friction is difficult to analyze and will not be discussed here.

tion, μ_s, is proportional to the maximum applied force needed to just overcome static friction. The coefficient of kinetic friction, μ_k, is proportional to the applied force necessary to keep an object moving (at a constant velocity). Notice that $\mu_s > \mu_k$, which reflects that it takes more force to get an object moving than it does to keep it moving.

Did You Learn?

- According to Newton's second law, an external net force will produce a change in velocity or an acceleration.

- The maximum force of static friction is generally greater than the force of kinetic friction. It takes less force to keep an object moving than to get it going.

3.4 Newton's Third Law of Motion

Preview Questions

- What's the difference between an action and a reaction?
- Is the net force of Newton's third-law force pair equal to zero?

Newton's third law of motion is of great physical significance. We commonly think of single forces, but Newton recognized that it is *impossible* to have a single force. He observed that in the application of a force there is always a mutual reaction, so forces always occur in pairs. As Newton illustrated, "If you press a stone with your finger, the finger is also pressed upon by the stone." Another example is when you ride in a car that is braked to a quick stop. If you push against your seat belt, your seat belt pushes against you. This is Newton's third law in action.

Newton's third law of motion is sometimes called the *law of action and reaction*. **Newton's third law of motion** states the following:

For every action there is an equal and opposite reaction.

In this statement, the words *action* and *reaction* refer to forces. The law is also stated another way:

For every force there is an equal and opposite force.

A more descriptive statement would be the following:

Whenever one object exerts a force on a second object, the second object exerts an equal and opposite force on the first object.

Expressed in equation form, Newton's third law may be written as

$$\text{action} = \text{opposite reaction}$$
$$F_1 = -F_2 \qquad\qquad 3.3$$

where

$$F_1 = \text{force exerted on object 1 by object 2}$$
$$-F_2 = \text{force exerted on object 2 by object 1}$$

The negative sign in Eq. 3.3 indicates that F_2 is in the opposite direction from F_1.

Jet propulsion is an example of Newton's third law. In the case of a rocket, the exhaust gas is accelerated from the rocket, and the rocket accelerates in the opposite direction (● Fig. 3.11a). A common misconception is that on launch the exhaust gas pushes against the launch pad to accelerate the rocket. If this were true, then there would be no space travel because there is nothing to push against in space. The correct explanation is one of action (gas being forced backward by the rocket) and reaction (the rocket being propelled forward by the escaping gas). The gas (or gas particles) exerts a force on the rocket, and

(a)

(b)

Figure 3.11 Newton's Third Law in Action
(a) The rocket and exhaust gas exert equal and opposite forces on each other and so are accelerated in opposite directions. (b) The equal and opposite forces are obvious here. Notice the distortion of both the tennis ball and the racquet.

the rocket exerts a force on the gas. The equal and opposite actions of Newton's third law should be evident in Fig. 3.11b.

Let's take a look at the third law in terms of the second law ($F = ma$). Writing Eq. 3.3 in the form

$$F_1 = -F_2$$

or

$$m_1 a_1 = -m_2 a_2$$

shows that if m_2 is much greater than m_1, then a_1 is much greater than a_2.

Consider dropping a book on the floor. As the book falls, it has a force acting on it (the Earth's gravity) that causes it to accelerate. What is the equal and opposite force? It is the force of the book's gravitational pull on the Earth. Technically, the Earth accelerates upward to meet the book. However, because our planet's mass is so huge compared with the book's mass, the Earth's acceleration is so minuscule it cannot be detected.

An important distinction to keep in mind is that <u>Newton's third law relates two equal and opposite forces that act on two *separate* objects</u>. <u>Newton's second law concerns how forces acting on a *single* object cause an acceleration.</u> If two forces acting on a single object are equal and opposite, there will be no net force and no acceleration, but these forces are *not* the third-law force pair. (Why?)

Let's look at one more example that illustrates the application of Newton's laws. Imagine that you are a passenger in a car traveling down a straight road and entering a circular curve at a constant speed. As you know, there must be a centripetal force to provide the centripetal acceleration necessary to negotiate the curve (Chapter 2.4). This force is supplied by friction on the tires, and the magnitude of this frictional force (f) is given by $f = ma_c = mv^2/r$. Should the frictional force not be great enough—say, if you hit an icy spot (reduced friction)—the car would slide outward because the centripetal force would not be great enough to keep the car in a circular path (● Fig. 3.12).

You have no doubt experienced a lack of centripetal force when going around a curve in a car and have had a feeling of being "thrown" outward. Riding in the car before entering the curve, you tend to go in a straight line in accordance with Newton's first law. As the car makes the turn, you continue to maintain your straight-line motion until the car turns "into you."

It may feel that you are being thrown outward toward the door, but actually the door is coming toward you because the car is turning, and when the door gets to you, it exerts a force on you that supplies the centripetal force needed to cause you to go around the curve with the car. The friction on the seat of your pants is not enough to do this, but if you are buckled up, then the requisite force may be supplied by a seat belt instead of the door.

Another practical application involving Newton's laws is discussed in the **Highlight: The Automobile Air Bag**.

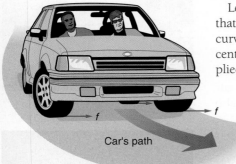

Figure 3.12 Newton's First Law in Action
Friction supplies the centripetal force necessary for the car to negotiate the curve. When a car goes around a sharp curve or corner, the people in it tend to have the sensation of being thrown outward as the car rounds the curve, but that is not so. See the text for a description.

Did You Learn?

● A reaction is an equal, but opposite, force to an action force.

● The equal and opposite force pair of Newton's third law do not cancel each other as they act on different objects.

3.5 Newton's Law of Gravitation

Preview Questions

● What keeps the Moon in orbit around the Earth?

● Are astronauts seen floating in the International Space Station really weightless?

Highlight   The Automobile Air Bag

A major automobile safety feature is the air bag. As noted earlier, seat belts restrain you so that you don't keep going per Newton's first law when the car comes to a sudden stop. Where, though, does the air bag come in, and what is its principle?

When a car has a head-on collision with another vehicle or hits an immovable object such as a tree, it stops almost instantaneously. Even with seat belts, the impact of a head-on collision could be such that seat belts might not restrain a person completely and injuries could occur.

Enter the automobile air bag. This balloon-like bag inflates automatically on hard impact and cushions the driver. Front air bags are mounted in the center of the steering wheel on the driver's side and in the dashboard on the passenger side.

The air bag tends to increase the contact time in stopping a person, thereby reducing the impact force, as compared with the force experienced when hitting the dashboard or steering column (Fig. 1). Also, the impact force is spread over a large general area and not applied to certain parts of the body, as in the case of seat belts.

You might wonder what causes an air bag to inflate and what inflates it. Keep in mind that to do any good, the inflation must occur in a fraction of a second, a shorter time than the time between the driver's reaction and collision contact. The air bag's inflation is initiated by an electronic sensing unit. This unit contains sensors that detect rapid decelerations such as those that occur in high-impact collisions. The sensors have threshold settings so that normal hard braking does not activate them.

Sensing an impact, a control unit sends an electric current to an igniter in the air-bag system that sets off a chemical explosion. The gases (mostly nitrogen) rapidly inflate the thin nylon bag. The total process of sensing to complete inflation takes about 30 milliseconds, or 0.030 second. Pretty fast, and that's a good thing, too! A car's occupant hits the air bag about 50 milliseconds after a collision. (For more on the chemical explosion, see the Highlight: The Chemistry of Air Bags in Chapter 13.2.)

In a front-end collision, a car's battery and alternator are among the first things to go, so an air bag's sensing unit is equipped with its own electrical power source. Such front automobile air bags offer protection only for front-end collisions, in which the car's occupants are thrown forward (excuse me, *continue to travel forward,* per Newton's first law).

Automobile side air bags are also available to protect occupants from side-impact collisions, which account for 30% of all accidents. Side air bags must be engineered to deploy much more quickly than those that protect from front-end collisions because only a few inches of door separate the occupant from the colliding vehicle. Side air bags are mounted in the doors, in the roof (from which they deploy downward), and in seat backs (from which they deploy toward the door).

Unfortunately, injuries and deaths have resulted from the deployment of front air bags. An air bag is not a soft, fluffy pillow. When activated, it deploys at speeds of up to 320 km/h (200 mi/h) and could hit a person close by with enough force to cause severe injury and even death. Adults are advised to sit at least 25 cm (10 in.) from the air-bag cover. Seats should be adjusted to allow for the proper safety distance. Probably the most serious concern is associated with children. Children may get close to the dashboard if they are not buckled in or are not buckled in securely. Another dangerous practice is using a rear-facing child seat in the front passenger seat. On deployment, the air bag could force the child into the back of the front seat, causing injury.

The next generation of "smart" air bags will be designed to sense the severity of an accident and inflate accordingly, as well as to base the inflation on the weight of the occupant. For example, if the sensors detect the small weight of a child in the passenger seat, the air bag won't deploy.

Specific problems may exist, but air bags save many lives. Even if your car is equipped with air bags, *always* remember to buckle up. (Maybe we should make that Newton's "fourth law of motion.")

(a)

(b)

Figure 1 Softening the Impact (a) Automobile air bags tend to increase the contact time, thereby reducing the impact force, (b) compared with hitting the dashboard, windshield, or steering column.

Having gained a basic understanding of forces, let's take a look at a common fundamental force of nature—gravity. Gravity is a fundamental force because we do not know what causes it and can only observe and describe its effects. Gravity is associated with mass and causes the mutual attraction of mass particles.

The law describing the gravitational force of attraction between two particles was formulated by Newton from his studies on planetary motion. Known as **Newton's law of universal gravitation** (universal because it is believed that gravity acts everywhere in the universe), this law may be stated as follows:

> Every particle in the universe attracts every other particle with a force that is directly proportional to the product of their masses and inversely proportional to the square of the distance between them.

Suppose the masses of two particles are designated as m_1 and m_2, and the distance between them is r (● Fig. 3.13a). Then the statement of the law is written in symbol form as

$$F \propto \frac{m_1 m_2}{r^2}$$

where $\propto$ is a proportionality sign. Notice in the figure that F_1 and F_2 are equal and opposite; they are a mutual interaction *and* a third-law force pair.

When an appropriate constant (of proportionality) is inserted, the equation form of Newton's law of universal gravitation is

$$F = \frac{G m_1 m_2}{r^2} \qquad\qquad 3.4$$

where **G** is the universal gravitational constant and has a value of $G = 6.67 \times 10^{-11}$ N·m²/kg².

The gravitational force between two masses is said to have an infinite range. That is, the only way for the force to approach zero is for the masses to be separated by a distance approaching infinity $r \to \infty$. (You can't escape gravity.)

An object is made up of a lot of point particles, so the gravitational force on an object is the vector sum of all the particle forces. This computation can be quite complicated, but one simple and convenient case is a homogeneous sphere.* In this case, the net force acts as though all the mass were concentrated at the center of the sphere, and the separation distance for the mutual interaction with another object is measured from there. If it is assumed that the Earth, other planets, and the Sun are spheres with uniform mass distributions, then to a reasonable approximation the law of gravitation can be applied to such bodies (Fig. 3.13b).

In using such an approximation, your weight (the gravitational attraction of the Earth on your mass, m) is computed as though all the mass of the Earth, M_E, were concentrated at its center, and the distance between the masses is the radius of the Earth, R_E. That is, $w = mg = G m M_E / R_E^2$.

Figure 3.13 Newton's Law of Gravitation
(a) Two particles attract each other gravitationally, and the magnitude of the forces is given by Newton's law of gravitation. The forces are equal and opposite: Newton's third-law force pair. (b) For a homogeneous or uniform sphere, the force acts as though all the mass of the sphere were concentrated as a particle at its center.

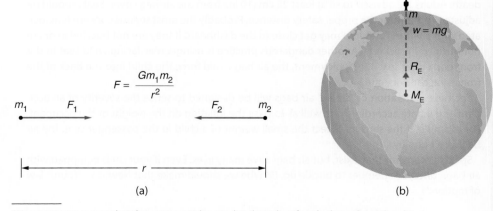

$$F = \frac{G m_1 m_2}{r^2}$$

m_1 F_1 → ← F_2 m_2

r

(a)

m
$w = mg$
R_E
M_E

(b)

*_____
Homogeneous means that the mass particles are distributed uniformly throughout the object.

In Eq. 3.4, as *r* increases, the force of gravity becomes less. Hence, gravity and the acceleration due to gravity become less with altitude above the Earth.

Conceptual Question and Answer

A Lot of Mass

Q. If you look inside the back cover of this book, you will find the mass of the Earth is listed as 6.0×10^{24} kg. How could the Earth be "weighed" or "massed"?

A. It would take some big scales, and of course isn't possible. Like many quantities in physics, values are gained indirectly. If you look at the previous equation for your weight on the surface of the Earth using Newton's law of gravitation, then you will note that the *m*'s cancel and you are left with $g = GM_E/R_E^2$. With a little mathematical manipulation, the mass of the Earth is given by $M_E = gR_E^2/G$. The values of g, G, and R_E are known. (The circumference of the Earth was measured in the first century BCE, from which the radius R_E was calculated.) So, plug in the numbers and you have the mass of the Earth.

Newton used his law of gravitation and second law of motion to show that gravity supplies the centripetal acceleration and force required for the Moon to move in its nearly circular orbit about the Earth, but he did not know or experimentally measure the value of G. This very small value was measured some 70 years after Newton's death by the English scientist Henry Cavendish, who used a very delicate balance to measure the force between two masses.

When an object is dropped, the force of gravity is made evident by the acceleration of the falling object, but if there is a gravitational force of attraction between every two objects, why don't you feel the attraction between yourself and this textbook? (No pun intended.) Indeed there *is* a force of attraction between you and this textbook, but it is so small that you don't notice it. Gravitational forces can be very small, as illustrated in Example 3.3.

EXAMPLE 3.3   Applying Newton's Law of Gravitation

Two objects with masses of 1.0 kg and 2.0 kg are 1.0 m apart (● Fig. 3.14). What is the magnitude of the gravitational force between these masses?

Solution

The magnitude of the force is given by Eq. 3.4:

$$F = \frac{Gm_1m_2}{r^2}$$

$$= \frac{(6.67 \times 10^{-11}\,\text{N} \cdot \text{m}^2/\text{kg}^2)(1.0\,\text{kg})(2.0\,\text{kg})}{(1.0\,\text{m})^2}$$

$$= 1.3 \times 10^{-10}\,\text{N}$$

This number is very, very small. A grain of sand would weigh more. For an appreciable gravitational force to exist between two masses, at least one of the masses must be relatively large (see Fig. 3.14).

Confidence Exercise 3.3

If the distance between the two masses in Fig. 3.14 were tripled, by what factor would the mutual gravitational force change? (*Hint:* Use a ratio.)

With regard to astronauts in space, we hear the (incorrect) terms *zero g* and *weightlessness* (● Fig. 3.15). These terms are not true descriptions. *Microgravity* and *apparent*

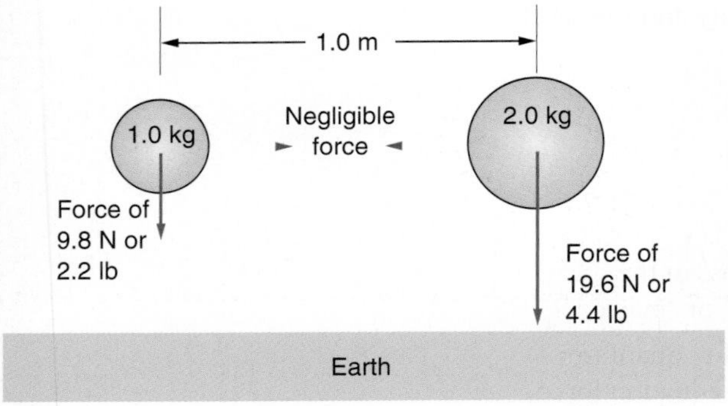

← 1.0 m →

1.0 kg   Negligible
              ► force ◄   **2.0 kg**

Force of
9.8 N or
2.2 lb

Force of
19.6 N or
4.4 lb

Earth

Figure 3.14 The Amount of Mass Makes a Difference
A 1.0-kg mass and a 2.0-kg mass separated by a distance of 1.0 m have a negligible mutual gravitational attraction (about 10^{-10} N). However, because the Earth's mass is quite large, the masses are attracted to the Earth with forces of 9.8 N and 19.6 N, respectively. These forces are the weights of the masses.

NASA/Johnson Space Center

Figure 3.15 Floating Around
Astronauts in a space shuttle orbiting the Earth are said to "float" around because of "zero *g*" or "weightlessness." Actually, the gravitational attraction of objects keeps them in orbit with the spacecraft. Because gravity is acting, by definition an astronaut has weight. Here, astronaut pilot Susan L. Still enters data into an onboard computer.

weightlessness are more applicable terms. Gravity certainly acts on an astronaut in an orbiting spacecraft to provide the necessary centripetal force. Without gravity, the spacecraft (and astronaut) would not remain in orbit but instead would fly off tangentially in a straight line (analogous to swinging a ball on a string about your head and the string breaks). Because gravity is acting, the astronaut by definition has weight.

The reason an astronaut floats in the spacecraft and feels "weightless" is that the spacecraft and the astronaut are both "falling" toward the Earth. Imagine yourself in a freely falling elevator standing on a scale. The scale would read zero because it is falling just as fast as you are. You are not weightless, however, and *g* is not zero, as you would discover upon reaching the bottom of the elevator shaft.

Did You Learn?

● The gravitational attraction between the Earth and the Moon supplies the necessary centripetal force to keep the Moon in its orbit around the Earth.

● By definition, astronauts in an Earth-orbiting spacecraft are not "weightless." Gravity acts on them, so they have weight.

3.6 Archimedes' Principle and Buoyancy

Preview Questions

● What is the magnitude of the buoyant force on an object in a fluid?

● What determines if an object will float or sink in water?

Let's take a look at another common force associated with fluids. (Unlike solids, fluids can "flow," so liquids and gases are fluids.) Objects float in fluids because they are buoyant or are buoyed up. For example, if you immerse a cork in water and release it, the cork will be buoyed up to the surface and remain there. From your knowledge of forces, you know that such motion requires an upward net force. For an object to come to the surface, there must be an upward force acting on it that is greater than the downward force of its weight. When the object is floating, these forces must balance each other, and we say the object is in *equilibrium* (zero net force).

The upward force resulting from an object being wholly or partially immersed in a fluid is called the **buoyant force**. The nature of this force is summed up by **Archimedes' principle**:*

> An object immersed wholly or partially in a fluid experiences a buoyant force equal in magnitude to the weight of the *volume of fluid* that is displaced.

We can see from Archimedes' principle that the buoyant force depends on the weight of the volume of fluid displaced. Whether an object will sink or float depends on the density of the object (ρ_o) relative to that of the fluid (ρ_f). There are three conditions to consider:

▶ An object will float in a fluid if its average density is less than the density of the fluid ($\rho_o < \rho_f$).

▶ An object will sink if its average density is greater than the density of the fluid ($\rho_o > \rho_f$).

▶ An object will be in equilibrium at any submerged depth in a fluid if the average density of the object and the density of the fluid are equal ($\rho_o = \rho_f$).

(Average density implies that the object does not have a uniform mass, that is, that it has more mass in one area than another.) An example of the application of the first condition is shown in ● Fig. 3.16.

These three conditions also apply to a fluid within a fluid, provided that the two are immiscible (do not mix). For example, you might think cream is "heavier" than skim milk, but that's not so. Cream floats on milk, so it is less dense.

Figure 3.16 Fluid Buoyancy
The air is a fluid in which objects, such as this dirigible, float. Because of the helium gas inside, the average density of the blimp is less than that of the surrounding air. The weight of the volume of air displaced is greater than the weight of the blimp, so the blimp floats, supported by a buoyant force. (The ship is powered so that it can maneuver and change altitude.) It is sometimes said that helium is "lighter" than air, but it is more accurate to say that helium is *less dense* than air.

Conceptual Question and Answer

Float the Boat

Q. A 1.0-lb piece of iron or steel readily sinks in water, yet ocean liners made of iron and steel weigh thousands of tons and float. Why?

A. Because an ocean liner floats, its average density must be less than that of seawater. An ocean liner is made of iron and steel, but overall most of its volume is occupied by air. Thus, its average density is less than that of seawater. Displacing a huge volume of water, it floats. Similarly, the human body has air-filled spaces, so most of us float in water.

In some instances the overall density is purposefully varied to change the depth. For example, a submarine submerges by flooding its tanks with seawater (called "taking on ballast"). This flooding increases the sub's average density, and it sinks and dives. (Propulsion power enables it to maneuver.) When the sub is to surface, water is pumped out of the tanks. The average density becomes less than that of the surrounding seawater, and up it goes.

When an object floats, some of it is submerged, displacing enough volume so that the buoyant force equals the weight force. The volume submerged depends on the weight of the object. In some instances the submerged volume can be appreciable. For example, the

---

*Archimedes (287–212 BCE), a Greek scholar, was given the task of determining whether a gold crown made for the king was pure gold or contained a quantity of some other metal. Legend has it that the solution to the problem came to Archimedes while he was in the bathtub. It is said that he was so excited he jumped out of the tub and ran through the streets of the city (unclothed) shouting, "Eureka! Eureka!" (Greek for "I have found it!")

Ralph A. Clevenger/CORBIS

Figure 3.17 The Tip of the Iceberg
The majority of a floating iceberg is beneath the water, as illustrated here. Approximately 90% of its bulk is submerged. The displacement of water by the submerged portion gives rise to a buoyant force that equals the iceberg's weight.

submerged volume of an iceberg is on the order of 90% (● Fig. 3.17). Thus, the 10% that remains above water is "only the tip of the iceberg."

Another important property of liquids is discussed in the **Highlight: Surface Tension, Water Striders, and Soap Bubbles**.

Did You Learn?

● The buoyant force is equal in magnitude to the weight of the volume of fluid an object displaces.

● An object with an average density greater than 1.0 g/cm^3 (the density of water) will sink in water; if it is less than 1.0 g/cm^3, then the object will float.

3.7   Momentum

Preview Questions

● When is the linear momentum of a system conserved?

● What gives rise to a change in angular momentum?

Another important quantity in the description of motion is *momentum*. This term is commonly used; for example, it is said that a sports team has a lot of momentum or has lost its momentum. Let's see what momentum means scientifically. There are two types of momentum: linear and angular.

Linear Momentum

Stopping a speeding bullet is difficult because it has a high velocity. Stopping a slowly moving oil tanker is difficult because it has a large mass. In general, the product of mass and velocity is called **linear momentum**, the magnitude of which is

$$\text{linear momentum} = \text{mass} \times \text{velocity}$$
$$p = mv \qquad\qquad 3.5$$

where v is the instantaneous velocity.

Because velocity is a vector, momentum is also a vector with the same direction as the velocity. Both mass and velocity are involved in momentum. A small car and a large truck both traveling at 50 km/h in the same direction have the same velocity, but the truck has more momentum because it has a much larger mass. For a system of masses, the linear momentum of the system is found by adding the linear momentum vectors of all the individual masses.

The linear momentum of a system is important because if there are no external unbalanced forces, then the linear momentum of the system is *conserved*; it does not change with time. In other words, with no unbalanced forces, no acceleration occurs, so there is no change in velocity and no change in momentum. This property makes linear momentum extremely important in analyzing the motion of various systems. The **law of conservation of linear momentum** may be stated as follows:

The total linear momentum of an isolated system remains the same if there is no external, unbalanced force acting on the system.

Even though the internal conditions of a system may change, the vector sum of the momenta remains constant.

$$\text{total final momentum} = \text{total initial momentum}$$
or
$$P_f = P_i$$
where
$$P = p_1 + p_2 + p_3 + \dots \qquad\qquad 3.6$$
$$\text{(sum of individual momentum vectors)}$$

Highlight Surface Tension, Water Striders, and Soap Bubbles

Have you ever noticed how drops of water bead up on a clean kitchen surface or on a newly waxed car? What causes this beading? The answer is tension. The molecules of a liquid exert a small attractive force on one another (due to an asymmetry of electrical charge; see Chapter 12). Within a liquid, any molecule is completely surrounded by other molecules, and the net force is zero (Fig. 1). For molecules at the surface, however, there is no attractive force acting on them from above the surface. As a result, net forces act on molecules of the surface layer due to the attraction of neighboring molecules just below the surface. The inward pull on the surface molecules causes the surface of a liquid to contract, giving rise to what is called *surface tension*.

If a sewing needle is carefully placed on the surface of a bowl of water, the surface acts like an elastic membrane because of surface tension. There is a slight depression in the surface, and molecular forces along the depression act at an angle to the surface (Fig. 2). The vertical component of these forces balances the weight (*mg*) of the needle, and it "floats" on the surface. Similarly, surface tension supports the weight of a water strider on water.

The net effect of surface tension is to make the surface area of a liquid as small as possible. A volume of liquid tends to assume the shape that has the least surface area. As a result, drops of water and soap bubbles have spherical shapes because a sphere has the smallest surface area for a given volume (Fig. 3). In forming a drop or a bubble, surface tension pulls the molecules together to minimize the surface area.

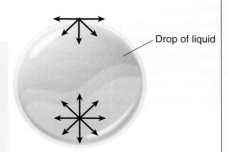

Figure 1 Surface Tension
The net force on a molecule in the interior of a liquid is zero because the molecule is surrounded by other molecules. At the surface, though, there are no molecules above, and an inward force thus acts on a molecule due to the attractive forces of the neighboring molecules just below the surface. This gives rise to surface tension.

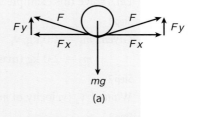

Figure 3 Surface Tension at Work
Because of surface tension, soap bubbles assume the shape of a sphere to minimize the surface area. Beads of water on a newly waxed car also assume spherical shapes.

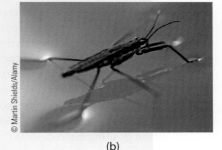

(b)

Figure 2 Walk on Water
(a) A light object, such as a needle, forms a depression in the liquid, and the surface area acts like a stretched membrane, with the weight (*mg*) of the object supported by the upward components of the surface tension. (b) Some insects, such as water striders, can walk on water because of surface tension, as you might walk on a large trampoline. Notice the depressions in the liquid's surface where the legs touch it.

Suppose you are standing in a boat near the shore, and you and the boat are the system (● Fig. 3.18). Let the boat be stationary, so the total linear momentum of the system is zero (no motion for you or the boat, so zero linear momentum). On jumping toward the shore, you will notice immediately that the boat moves in the opposite direction. The boat moves because the force you exerted in jumping is an *internal* force. Thus, the total linear momentum of the system is conserved and must remain zero (water resistance neglected). You have momentum in one direction, and to cancel this vectorially so that the total momentum remains zero, the boat must have an equal and opposite momentum. Remember that momentum is a vector quantity, and momentum vectors can add to zero.

Figure 3.18 Conservation of Linear Momentum
When the system is at rest, the total momentum of the system (man and boat) is zero. When the man jumps toward the shore (an internal force), the boat moves in the opposite direction, conserving linear momentum.

Man jumps forward

Boat moves backward

EXAMPLE 3.4   Applying the Conservation of Linear Momentum

Two masses at rest on a frictionless surface have a compressed spring between them but are held together by a light string (● Fig. 3.19). The string is burned, and the masses fly apart. If m_1 has a velocity $v_1 = 1.8$ m/s (to the right), then what is the velocity of m_2?

Solution

Let's solve this example stepwise for clarity.

Step 1

Given: $m_1 = 1.0$ kg, $v_1 = 1.8$ m/s (positive, to the right)
$\quad\quad\quad m_2 = 2.0$ kg (masses from figure)

Step 2

Wanted: v_2 (velocity of m_2)

Step 3

Reasoning: The total momentum of the system is initially zero ($P_i = 0$) before the string is burned. (The reason for releasing the masses in this manner is to ensure that no external forces are applied as there might be if the masses were held together with hands.)

The spring is part of the system and so applies an *internal* force to each of the masses. Hence, the linear momentum is conserved. After leaving the spring, the moving masses have nonzero momenta, and the total momentum of the system is $P_f = p_1 + p_2$. (The spring is assumed to be motionless.)

With the total linear momentum being conserved (no unbalanced *external* forces acting), using Eq. 3.6,

$$P_f = P_i$$

or

$$p_1 + p_2 = 0$$

Rearranging gives

$$p_1 = -p_2$$

which tells us that the momenta are equal and opposite. Then, in terms of mv,

$$m_1 v_1 = -m_2 v_2$$

Solving for v_2 yields

$$v_2 = -\frac{m_1 v_1}{m_2} = -\frac{(1.0 \text{ kg})(1.8 \text{ m/s})}{2.0 \text{ kg}} = -0.90 \text{ m/s}$$

to the left in Fig. 3.19, because v_1 was taken to be positive to the right.

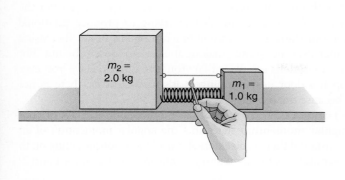

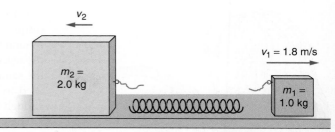

Figure 3.19 An Internal Force and Conservation of Linear Momentum When the string is burned, the compressed spring applies an internal force to the system. See Example 3.4.

Confidence Exercise 3.4

Suppose you were not given the values of the masses but only that $m_1 = m$ and $m_2 = 3m$. What could you say about the velocities in this case?

Earlier we looked at the jet propulsion of rockets in terms of Newton's third law. This phenomenon can also be explained in terms of linear momentum. The burning of the rocket fuel gives energy by which *internal* work is done and hence internal forces act. As a result, the exhaust gas goes out the back of the rocket with momentum in that direction, and the rocket goes in the opposite direction to conserve linear momentum. Here the many, many exhaust gas molecules have small masses and large velocities, whereas the rocket has a large mass and a relatively small velocity.

You can demonstrate this rocket effect by blowing up a balloon and letting it go. The air comes out the back and the balloon is "jet" propelled, but without a guidance system, the balloon zigzags wildly.

Angular Momentum

Another important quantity Newton found to be conserved is angular momentum. Angular momentum arises when objects go in paths around a center of motion or axis of rotation. Consider a comet going around the Sun in an elliptical orbit, as illustrated in ● Fig. 3.20. The magnitude of **angular momentum** (L) is given by

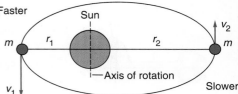

Figure 3.20 Angular Momentum The angular momentum of a comet going around the Sun in an elliptical orbit is given at the two opposite points in the orbit by mv_1r_1 and mv_2r_2. Angular momentum is conserved in this case, and $mv_1r_1 = mv_2r_2$. As the comet comes closer to the Sun, the radial distance r decreases, so the speed v must increase. Similarly, the speed decreases when r increases. Thus, a comet moves fastest when it is closest to the Sun and slowest when it is farthest from the Sun, which is also true for the Earth. (The orbit here is exaggerated to show radial differences.)

> angular momentum = mass × velocity × object distance from axis of rotation
>
> or $\qquad\qquad L = mvr$ $\qquad\qquad$ 3.7

An external, unbalanced force can change the linear momentum. Similarly, angular momentum can be changed by an external, unbalanced (net) *torque*. Such a torque gives rise to a twisting or rotational effect. Basically, a force produces linear motion, and a torque produces rotational motion. For example, in ● Fig. 3.21, a net torque on the steering wheel is produced by two equal and opposite forces acting on different parts of the wheel. These forces give rise to two torques, resulting in a net torque that causes the steering wheel to turn or rotate. (Would there be a net torque [and rotation] if both forces were upward?)

Note that these forces are at a distance r (called the *lever arm*) from the center of motion or axis of rotation. When r and F vectors are perpendicular, the magnitude of the **torque** (τ, Greek tau) is given by

> torque = force × lever arm
>
> $\qquad\qquad \tau = Fr$ $\qquad\qquad$ 3.8

with the units N · m.

Torque varies with r, so for a given force, the greater r is, the greater the torque. You have probably used this fact in trying to produce rotational motion to loosen something, such as a bolt or a nut (● Fig. 3.22). Increasing the lever arm r increases the torque, making it easier to loosen the nut. For the same reason, doorknobs are placed far from the hinges. Have you ever tried to push open a door near the hinges? It's very difficult; there is not enough torque because the lever arm is too short.

There is also a conservation law for angular momentum. The **law of conservation of angular momentum** states that the angular momentum of an object remains constant if there is no external, unbalanced torque acting on it. That is, the magnitudes of the angular momenta are equal at times 1 and 2:

$$L_1 = L_2$$

or

$$m_1 v_1 r_1 = m_2 v_2 r_2 \qquad 3.9$$

where the subscripts 1 and 2 denote the angular momentum of the object at different times.

In our example of a comet, the angular momentum mvr remains the same because the gravitational attraction is internal to the system. As the comet gets closer to the Sun, r decreases, so the speed v increases. For this reason, a comet moves more rapidly when it is closer to the Sun than when it is farther away (see Fig. 3.20). Comet orbits are highly elliptical, so they move at very different speeds in different parts of their orbits. Planets have relatively less elliptical orbits but do move with different speeds.

Figure 3.21 Torque
A torque is a twisting action that produces rotational motion or a change in rotational motion. Torque is analogous to a force producing linear motion or a change in linear motion. The forces F_1 and F_2 supply the torque.

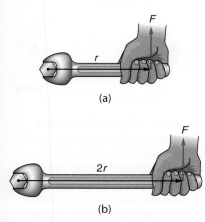

Figure 3.22 Torque and Lever Arm
(a) Torque varies with the length of the lever arm r. (b) When the length of the lever arm is doubled for a given force, the torque is doubled. Thus, by using a longer wrench, more torque can be applied to a bolt or nut.

EXAMPLE 3.5   Applying the Conservation of Angular Momentum

In its orbit at the farthest point from the Sun, a certain comet is 900 million miles away and traveling at 6000 mi/h. What is its speed at its closest point to the Sun at a distance of 30 million miles?

Solution

We are given v_2, r_2, and r_1, so v_1 can be calculated (Eq. 3.9):

$$mv_1 r_1 = mv_2 r_2$$
$$v_1 r_1 = v_2 r_2$$

or

$$v_1 = \frac{v_2 r_2}{r_1}$$

$$= \frac{(6.0 \times 10^3 \text{ mi/h})(900 \times 10^6 \text{ mi})}{30 \times 10^6 \text{ mi}}$$

$$= 1.8 \times 10^5 \text{ mi/h, or } 180{,}000 \text{ mi/h}$$

Thus, the comet moves much more rapidly when it is close to the Sun than when it is far away.

Confidence Exercise 3.5

The Earth's orbit about the Sun is not quite circular. At its closest approach, our planet is 1.47×10^8 km from the Sun, and at its farthest point, it is 1.52×10^8 km from the Sun. At which of these points does the Earth have the greater orbital speed and by what factor? (*Hint:* Use a ratio.)

Another example of the conservation of angular momentum is demonstrated in ● Fig. 3.23. Ice-skaters use the principle to spin faster. The skater extends both arms and perhaps one leg and obtains a slow rotation. Then, drawing the arms in and above the head (making r smaller), the skater achieves greater angular velocity and a more rapid spin because of the decrease in the radial distance of the mass.

(a)

(b)

Figure 3.23 Conservation of Angular Momentum: Ice-Skater Spin
(a) An ice-skater starts with a slow rotation, keeping the arms and a leg extended. (b) When the skater stands and draws the arms inward and above the head, the average radial distance of mass decreases and the angular velocity increases to conserve angular momentum, producing a rapid spin.

Angular momentum also affects the operation of helicopters. What would happen when a helicopter with a single rotor tried to get airborne? To conserve angular momentum, the body of the helicopter would have to rotate in the direction opposite that of the rotor. To prevent such rotation, large helicopters have two oppositely rotating rotors (● Fig. 3.24a). Smaller helicopters instead have small "antitorque" rotors on the tail (Fig. 3.24b). These rotors are like small airplane propellers that provide a torque to counteract the rotation of the helicopter body.

Did You Learn?

● Linear momentum is conserved when there is no external, unbalanced force acting on the system.

● An external, unbalanced torque causes a change in angular momentum.

(a)

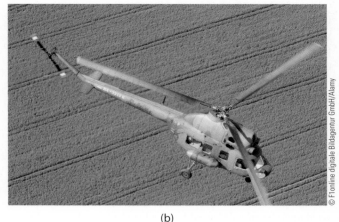

(b)

Figure 3.24 Conservation of Angular Momentum in Action
(a) Large helicopters have two overhead rotors that rotate in opposite directions to balance the angular momentum. (b) Small helicopters with one overhead rotor have an "antitorque" tail rotor to balance the angular momentum and prevent rotation of the helicopter body.

KEY TERMS

1. force (3.1)
2. unbalanced, or net, force
3. Newton's first law of motion (3.2)
4. inertia
5. mass
6. Newton's second law of motion (3.3)
7. newton
8. weight
9. friction
10. Newton's third law of motion (3.4)
11. Newton's law of universal gravitation (3.5)
12. G
13. buoyant force (3.6)
14. Archimedes' principle
15. linear momentum (3.7)
16. law of conservation of linear momentum
17. angular momentum
18. torque
19. law of conservation of angular momentum

MATCHING

For each of the following items, fill in the number of the appropriate Key Term from the preceding list. Compare your answers with those at the back of the book.

a. _____ Law of inertia

b. _____ Changes angular momentum

c. _____ mg

d. _____ Required for an object to float

e. _____ mvr

f. _____ Tendency of an object to remain at rest or in uniform, straight-line motion

g. _____ Mass × velocity

h. _____ F = ma

i. _____ Conservation law requiring the absence of an unbalanced torque

j. _____ Action and reaction

k. _____ Capable of producing motion or a change in motion

l. _____ Universal constant

m. _____ SI unit of force

n. _____ Resistance to relative motion

o. _____ A nonzero vector sum of forces

p. _____ Occurs in the absence of an unbalanced force

q. _____ Describes the force of gravity

r. _____ A measure of inertia

s. _____ Gives the magnitude of the buoyant force

MULTIPLE CHOICE

Compare your answers with those at the back of the book.

1. Mass is related to an object's ___. (3.1)
   (a) weight
   (b) inertia
   (c) density
   (d) all of the preceding

2. What is a possible state of an object in the absence of a net force? (3.2)
   (a) at rest
   (b) constant speed
   (c) zero acceleration
   (d) all of the preceding

3. What term refers to the tendency of an object to remain at rest or in uniform, straight-line motion? (3.2)
   (a) mass
   (b) force
   (c) inertia
   (d) external force

4. What is necessary for a change in velocity? (3.3)
   (a) inertia
   (b) an unbalanced force
   (c) a zero net force
   (d) a change in direction

5. According to Newton's second law of motion, when an object is acted upon by an unbalanced force, what can be said about the acceleration? (3.3)
   (a) It is inversely proportional to the object's mass.
   (b) It is zero.
   (c) It is inversely proportional to the net force.
   (d) It is independent of mass.

6. A net force ___.
   (a) can produce motion
   (b) is a scalar quantity
   (c) is capable of producing a change in velocity
   (d) both (a) and (c)

7. For every action force, there is which of the following? (3.4)
   (a) a net force
   (b) a friction force
   (c) an unbalanced force
   (d) an equal and opposite force

8. Which is true of the force pair of Newton's third law? (3.4)
   (a) The two forces never produce an acceleration.
   (b) The two forces act on different objects.
   (c) The two forces always cancel each other.
   (d) The two forces are in the same direction.

9. Which is true about the acceleration due to gravity? (3.5)
   (a) It is a universal constant.
   (b) It is a fundamental property.
   (c) It decreases with increasing altitude.
   (d) It is different for different objects in free fall.

10. What is true about the constant *G*? (3.5)
    - (a) It is a very small quantity.
    - (b) It is a force.
    - (c) It is the same as *g*.
    - (d) It decreases with altitude.

11. A child's toy floats in a swimming pool. The buoyant force exerted on the toy depends on the volume of ___. (3.6)
    - (a) water in the pool
    - (b) the pool
    - (c) the water displaced
    - (d) the toy under water

12. If a submerged object displaces an amount of liquid with a weight less than its own, when the object is released, it will ___. (3.6)
    - (a) sink
    - (b) remain submerged in equilibrium
    - (c) float
    - (d) pop up out of the surface

13. If a submerged object displaces a volume of liquid of greater weight than its own and is then released, what will the object do?
    - (a) sink
    - (b) rise to the surface and float
    - (c) remain at its submerged position

14. A change in linear momentum requires which of the following? (3.7)
    - (a) a change in velocity
    - (b) an unbalanced force
    - (c) an acceleration
    - (d) all of these

15. Angular momentum is conserved in the absence of which of the following? (3.7)
    - (a) inertia
    - (b) gravity
    - (c) a net torque
    - (d) linear momentum

FILL IN THE BLANK

Compare your answers with those at the back of the book.

1. A force is a quantity that is ___ of producing motion or a change in motion. (3.1)

2. Forces are ___ quantities. (3.1)

3. Galileo concluded that objects ___ (could/could not) remain in motion without a net force. (3.2)

4. An object will *not* remain at rest or in uniform, straight-line motion if acted upon by a(n) ___ force. (3.2)

5. The inertia of an object is related to its ___. (3.2)

6. According to Newton's second law, an object's acceleration is ___ proportional to its mass. (3.3)

7. The newton unit of force is equal to ___ in standard units. (3.3)

8. The coefficient of ___ friction is generally greater than the coefficient of ___ friction. (3.3)

9. Newton's third-law force pair acts on ___ objects. (3.4)

10. The universal gravitational constant is believed to be constant ___. (3.5)

11. An object will sink in a fluid if its average density is ___ than that of the fluid. (3.7)

12. Milk is ___ dense than the cream that floats on top. (3.7)

13. The total linear momentum is *not* conserved if there is a(n) ___ force acting on the system. (3.7)

14. The angular momentum of an object is *not* conserved if the object is acted upon by unbalanced ___. (3.7)

SHORT ANSWER

3.1 Force and Net Force

1. Does a force always produce motion? Explain.

2. Distinguish between a net force and an unbalanced force.

3.2 Newton's First Law of Motion

3. Consider a child holding a helium balloon in a closed car at rest. What would the child observe the balloon to do when the car (a) accelerates from rest and (b) brakes to a stop? (The balloon does not touch the roof of the car.)

4. An old party trick is to pull a tablecloth out from under dishes and glasses on a table. Explain how this trick is done without pulling the dishes and glasses with the cloth.

5. To tighten the loose head of a hammer, the base of the handle is sometimes struck on a hard surface (● Fig. 3.25). Explain the physics behind this maneuver.

6. When a paper towel is torn from a roll on a rack, a jerking motion tears the towel better than a slow pull. Why? Does this method work better when the roll is large or when it is small and near the end? Explain.

3.3 Newton's Second Law of Motion

7. Describe the relationship between (a) force and acceleration, and (b) mass and acceleration.

Figure 3.25 Make It Tight
See Short-Answer Question 5.

8. Can an object be at rest if forces are being applied to it? Explain.

9. If no forces are acting on an object, can the object be in motion? Explain.

10. What is the unbalanced force acting on a moving car with a constant velocity of 25 m/s (56 mi/h)?

11. The coefficient of kinetic friction is generally less than than the coefficient of static friction, Why?

12. A 10-lb rock and a 1-lb rock are dropped simultaneously from the same height.
    (a) Some say that because the 10-lb rock has 10 times as much force acting on it as the 1-lb rock, it should reach the ground first. Do you agree?
    (b) Describe the situation if the rocks were dropped by an astronaut on the Moon.

3.4 Newton's Third Law of Motion

13. When a rocket blasts off, is it the fiery exhaust gases "pushing against" the launch pad that cause the rocket to lift off? Explain.

14. There is an equal and opposite reaction for every force. Explain how an object can be accelerated when the vector sum of these forces is zero.

15. Suppose your physical science textbook is lying on a table. How many forces are acting on it? (Neglect air pressure.)

16. Explain the kick of a rifle in terms of Newton's third law. Do the masses of the gun and the bullet make a difference?

3.5 Newton's Law of Gravitation

17. Show that the universal gravitational constant G has units of $N \cdot m^2/kg^2$.

18. The gravitational force is said to have an infinite range. What does that mean?

19. Explain why the acceleration due to gravity on the surface of the Moon is one-sixth that of the acceleration due to gravity on the Earth's surface.

20. An astronaut has a mass of 70 kg when measured on the Earth. What is her weight in deep space far from any celestial object? What is her mass there?

21. Is "zero g" possible? Explain.

3.6 Archimedes' Principle and Buoyancy

22. In Chapter 1.6 in the discussion of the hydrometer, it is stated: "The higher the bulb floats, the greater the density of the liquid." Why is this? (See Fig. 1.14.)

23. What is a major consideration in constructing a life jacket that will keep a person afloat?

24. As learned in Chapter 1.5, 1 L of water has a mass of 1 kg. A thin, closed plastic bag (negligible weight) with 1 L of water in it is lowered into a lake by means of a string and submerged. When fully submerged, how much force would you have to exert on the string to prevent the bag from sinking more?

25. A large piece of iron with a volume of 0.25 m³ is lowered into a lake by means of a rope until it is just completely submerged. It is found that the support on the rope is less than when the iron is in air. How does the support vary as the iron is lowered more?

26. Is it easier for a large person to float in a lake than a small person? Explain.

27. Why must a helium balloon be held with a string?

3.7 Momentum

28. What are the units of linear momentum?

29. Explain how the conservation of linear momentum follows directly from Newton's first law of motion.

30. In Example 3.4 there are external forces acting on the masses. (a) Identify these forces. (b) Why is the linear momentum still conserved?

31. When a high diver in a swimming event springs from the diving board and "tucks in," a rapid spin results. Why?

VISUAL CONNECTION

Visualize the connections and give answers for the blanks. Compare your answers with those at the back of the book.

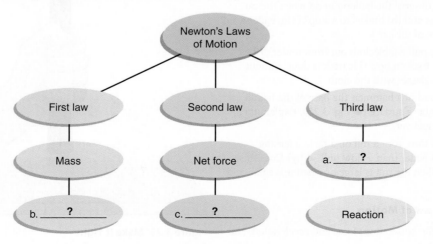

APPLYING YOUR KNOWLEDGE

1. Astronauts walking on the Moon are seen "bounding" rather than walking normally. Why?

2. A person places a bathroom scale in the center of the floor and stands on the scale with his arms at his sides (● Fig. 3.26a). If he keeps his arms *rigid* and quickly raises them over his head (Fig. 3.26b), he notices the scale reading increases as he brings his arms upward. Why? Then, with his arms over his head (Fig. 3.26c), he quickly lowers his arms to his side. How does the scale reading change and why? (Try it yourself.)

3. Using Eq. 3.4 show that the acceleration due to gravity is given by:

$$g = GM_E/R_E^2 \quad (g \text{ on the Earth's surface})$$

where M_E is the mass of the Earth and R_E its radius (Fig. 3.13b) Note that g is independent of *m*, so it is the same for all objects on the surface of the Earth. (If you are adventurous, plug in the values of G, M_E, and R_E from the back cover of the book and see what you get for *g*.) Why is the value of *g* less on the surface of the Moon?

4. People can easily float in the Great Salt Lake in Utah and in the Dead Sea in Israel and Jordan. Why?

5. In a washing machine, water is extracted from clothes by a rapidly spinning drum (● Fig. 3.27). Explain the physics behind this process.

6. When you push on a heavy swinging door to go into a store, why is it harder to push the door open if you mistakenly push on the side closer to the hinges?

7. When unable to loosen the lug nut on an automobile tire, a mechanic may put a piece of pipe on the handle of the tire wrench so as to extend its length. How does that help?

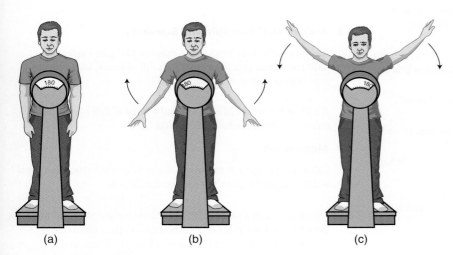

(a)   (b)   (c)

Figure 3.26 Up and Down
A quick way to gain or lose weight. See Applying Your Knowledge Question 2.

Figure 3.27 Get the Water Out
See Applying Your Knowledge Question 5.

IMPORTANT EQUATIONS

Newton's Second Law: $\quad F = ma \quad$ (3.1)

for weight: $w = mg \quad$ (3.2)

Newton's Third Law: $F_1 = -F_2 \quad$ (3.3)

Newton's Law of Gravitation: $F = \dfrac{Gm_1m_2}{r^2} \quad$ (3.4)

(Universal gravitational constant: $G = 6.67 \times 10^{-11}$ N·m²/kg²)

Linear Momentum: $p = mv \quad$ (3.5)

Conservation of Linear Momentum:

$$P_f = P_i$$

where $P = p_1 + p_2 + p_3 + \ldots \quad$ (3.6)

Angular Momentum: $L = mvr \quad$ (3.7)

Torque: $\tau = Fr \quad$ (3.8)

Conservation of Angular Momentum:

$$L_1 = L_2$$
$$m_1v_1r_1 = m_2v_2r_2 \quad (3.9)$$

EXERCISES

3.1 Force and Net Force

1. What is the net force of a 5.0-N force and an 8.0-N force acting on an object for each of the following conditions?
    (a) The forces act in opposite directions.
    (b) The forces act in the same direction.
    Answer: (a) 3.0 N, (b) 13 N

2. A horizontal force of 250 N is applied to a stationary wooden box in one direction, and a 600-N horizontal force is applied in the opposite direction. What additional force is needed for the box to remain stationary?

3.3 Newton's Second Law of Motion

3. Determine the net force necessary to give an object with a mass of 3.0 kg an acceleration of 5.0 m/s^2.
    Answer: 15 N

4. A force of 2.1 N is exerted on a 7.0-g rifle bullet. What is the bullet's acceleration?

5. A 1000-kg automobile is pulled by a horizontal tow line with a net force of 950 N. What is the acceleration of the auto? (Neglect friction.)
    Answer: 0.95 m/s^2

6. A constant net force of 1500 N gives a toy rocket an acceleration of 2.5 m/s^2. What is the mass of the rocket?

7. What is the weight in newtons of a 6.0-kg package of nails?
    Answer: 59 N

8. What is the force in newtons acting on a 4.0-kg package of nails that falls off a roof and is on its way to the ground?

9. (a) What is the weight in newtons of a 120-lb person? (b) What is your weight in newtons?
    Answer: (a) 534 N (b) Answers will vary

10. What is the weight in newtons of a 250-g package of breakfast cereal?

3.5 Newton's Law of Gravitation

11. Two 3.0-kg physical science textbooks on a bookshelf are 0.15 m apart. What is the magnitude of the gravitational attraction between the books?
    Answer: 2.7 × 10^{-8} N

12. (a) What is the force of gravity between two 1000-kg cars separated by a distance of 25 m on an interstate highway? (b) How does this force compare with the weight of a car?

13. How would the force of gravity between two masses be affected if the separation distance between them were (a) doubled? (b) decreased by one-half?
    Answer: (a) $F_2 = F_1/4$ (b) $F_2 = 4F_1$

14. The separation distance between two 1.0-kg masses is (a) decreased by two-thirds and (b) increased by a factor of 3. How is the mutual gravitational force affected in each case?

15. (a) Determine the weight on the Moon of a person whose weight on the Earth is 180 lb. (b) What would be your weight on the Moon?
    Answer: (a) 30 lb (b) Answers will vary.

16. Suppose an astronaut has landed on Mars. Fully equipped, the astronaut has a mass of 125 kg, and when the astronaut gets on a scale, the reading is 49 N. What is the acceleration due to gravity on Mars?

3.6 Archimedes' Principle and Buoyancy

17. A child's cubic play block has a mass of 120 g and sides of 5.00 cm. When placed in a bathtub full of water, will the cube sink or float? (*Hint*: See Chapter 1.6.)
    Answer: float, p = 0.96 g/cm^3

18. A ball with a radius of 8.00 cm and a mass of 600 g is thrown into a lake. Will the ball sink or float?

3.7 Momentum

19. Calculate the linear momentum of a pickup truck that has a mass of 1000 kg and is traveling eastward at 20 m/s.
    Answer: 2.0 × 10^4 kg · m/s, east

20. A small car with a mass of 900 kg travels northward at 30 m/s. Does the car have more or less momentum than the truck in Exercise 19, and how much more or less? (Is direction a factor in this exercise?)

21. Two ice-skaters stand together as illustrated in ● Fig. 3.28. They "push off" and travel directly away from each other, the boy with a velocity of 0.50 m/s to the left. If the boy weighs 735 N and the

Figure 3.28 Pushing Off
See Exercises 21 and 22.

(a) Before

0.50 m/s ⟵   ⟶ ?

(b) After

girl weighs 490 N, what is the girl's velocity after they push off? (Consider the ice to be frictionless.)

22. For the couple in Fig. 3.28, suppose you were told that the girl's mass was three-fourths that of the boy's mass. What would be the girl's velocity in this case?

23. A comet goes around the Sun in an elliptical orbit. At its farthest point, 600 million miles from the Sun, it is traveling with a speed

of 15,000 mi/h. How fast is it traveling at its closest approach to the Sun, at a distance of 100 million miles?

24. An asteroid in an elliptical orbit about the Sun travels at 1.2×10^6 m/s at perihelion (the point of closest approach) at a distance of 2.0×10^8 km from the Sun. How fast is it traveling at aphelion (the farthest point), which is 8.0×10^8 km from the Sun?

ON THE WEB

1. Newton's First Law of Motion

How many "laws of motion" did Sir Isaac Newton propose? What is Newton's first law of motion (and what is it sometimes called)? What do the two parts of the law predict? How does the law apply to your own life? Name at least two ways in which understanding this law can help keep you safe. To see this law in motion, go to the student website for this text at **www.cengagebrain.com/shop/ISBN/1133104096**.

2. Newton's Law of Gravitation

Follow the recommended links on the student website at **www.cengagebrain.com/shop/ISBN/1133104096** to explore antigravity further by creating an antigravity environment. How is this subject related to what you have learned in the text about Newton's law of gravitation?

CHAPTER 4

Work and Energy

> *I like work; it fascinates me. I can sit and look at it for hours.*
>
> •
>
> Jerome K. Jerome
> (1859–1927)

Courtesy Cedar Point Amusement Park/Resort, Sandusky Ohio

A lot of work going up, and a lot of energy at the top. The roller coaster at Cedar Point Amusement Park in Sandusky, Ohio, is shown here. The roller coaster reaches speeds of 120 miles per hour within 4 seconds.

PHYSICS FACTS

- *Kinetic* comes from the Greek *kinein*, meaning "to move."

- *Energy* comes from the Greek *energeia*, meaning "activity."

- The United States has about 5% of the world's population and consumes about 26% of the world's energy supply.

- Muscles are used to propel the human body by turning stored (potential) energy into motion (kinetic energy).

- The human body operates within the limits of the conservation of total energy. The sum of dietary input energy minus the energy expended in the work of daily activities, internal activities, and system heat losses equals zero.

The commonly used terms *work* and *energy* have general meanings for most people. For example, work is done to accomplish some task or job. To get the work done, energy is expended. Hence, work and energy are related. After a day's work, one is usually tired and requires rest and food to regain one's energy.

The scientific meaning of work is quite different from the common meaning. A student standing and holding an overloaded book bag is technically doing no work, yet he or she will feel tired after a time. Why does the student do no work? As will be learned in this chapter, mechanical work involves force *and* motion.

Energy, one of the cornerstones of science, is more difficult to define. Matter and energy make up the universe. Matter is easily understood; in general, we can touch

Chapter Outline

it and feel it. Energy is not actually tangible; it is a concept. We are aware of energy only when it is being used or transformed, such as when it is used to do work. For this reason, energy is sometimes described as stored work.

Our main source of energy is the Sun, which constantly radiates enormous amounts of energy into space. Only a small portion of this energy is received by the Earth, where much of it goes into sustaining plant and animal life. On the Earth, energy exists in various forms, including chemical, electrical, nuclear, and gravitational energies. However, energy may be classified more generally as either *kinetic energy* or *potential energy*. Read on.

4.1 Work

Preview Questions

- Is work a vector quantity? In other words, does it need a direction associated with it?
- What are the units of work?

Mechanically, work involves force and motion. One can apply a force all day long, but if there is no motion, then there is technically no work. The work done by a *constant force F* is defined as follows:

The **work** done by a constant force F acting on an object is the product of the magnitude of the force (or parallel component of the force) and the parallel distance d through which the object moves while the force is applied.

In equation form,

$$\text{work} = \text{force} \times \text{parallel distance}$$
$$W = Fd \tag{4.1}$$

In this form, it is easy to see that work involves motion. If $d = 0$, then the object has not moved and no work is done.

Figures 4.1 and 4.2 illustrate the difference between the application of force without work resulting and the application of force that results in work. In ● Fig. 4.1, a force is being applied to the wall, but no work is done because the wall doesn't move. After a while the man may become quite tired, but no mechanical work is done. ● Figure 4.2 shows an object being moved through a distance d by an applied force F. Note that the force and the directed distance are parallel to each other and that the force F acts through the parallel distance d. The work is then the product of the force and distance, $W = Fd$.

Another important consideration is shown in ● Fig. 4.3. When the force and the distance are not parallel to each other, only a component or part of the force acts through the parallel distance. When a lawn mower is pushed at an angle to the horizontal, only the component of the force that is parallel to the level lawn (horizontal component F_h) moves through a parallel distance and does work ($W = F_h d$). The vertical component of the force (F_v) does no work because this part of the force does not act through a distance. It only tends to push the lawn mower against the ground.

Work is a *scalar* quantity. Both force and parallel distance (actually, displacement) have directions associated with them, but their product, work, does not. Work is expressed only as a magnitude (a number with proper units). There is no direction associated with it.

Because work is the product of force and distance, the units of work are those of force times length ($W = Fd$). The SI unit of work is thus the newton-meter (N·m, force × length). This unit combination is given the special name **joule** (abbreviated J and pronounced "jool") in honor of nineteenth-century English scientist James Prescott Joule, whose research concerned work and heat.

Figure 4.1 No Work Done
A force is applied to the wall, but no work is done because there is no motion ($d = 0$).

$W = Fd = 0$

F

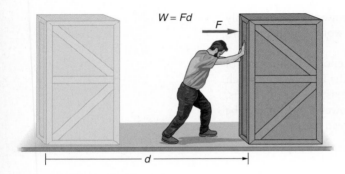

Figure 4.2 Work Being Done
An applied constant force *F* acts through a parallel distance *d*.
When the force and the displacement are in the same direction,
the amount of work equals the force times the distance the object
moves, $W = Fd$.

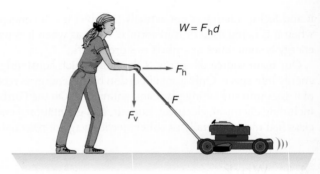

Figure 4.3 Work and No Work
Only the horizontal component F_h does work because only it
is in the direction of the motion. The vertical component F_v
does no work because $d = 0$ in that direction.

One joule is the amount of work done by a force of 1 N acting through a distance of
1 m. Similarly, the unit of force multiplied by length in the British system is the pound-foot.
However, English units are commonly listed in the reverse order, and work is expressed
in **foot-pound** (ft · lb) units. A force of 1 lb acting through a distance of 1 ft does 1 ft · lb of
work. The units of work are summarized in ● Table 4.1.

When doing work, you apply a force and feel the other part of Newton's third-law force
pair acting against you. Therefore, we say that work is done *against* something, such as
work against gravity or friction. When something is lifted, a force must be applied to overcome the force of gravity (as expressedw by an object's weight $w = mg$), so work is done
against gravity. This work is given by $W = Fd = wh = mgh$, where *h* is the height to which
the object was lifted.

Similarly, work is done *against* friction. Friction opposes motion. Hence, to move something on a surface in a real situation, you must apply a force. In doing so, you do work
against friction. As illustrated in ● Fig. 4.4a, if an object is moved with a constant velocity,
then the applied force *F* is equal and opposite to the frictional force *f* (zero net force on the
block and no acceleration). The work done by the applied force against friction is $W = Fd$.

Notice in Fig. 4.4(a) that the frictional force acts through the distance and therefore
does work. The frictional force and the displacement are in opposite directions. Taking
right to be positive and expressing directions by plus and minus signs, we have $+d$ and
$-f$. The work done by the frictional force is then $-fd = -W$; that is, it is negative work.
The negative frictional work is equal to the positive work done by the applied force, so the
total work is zero, $W_t = Fd - fd = 0$. Otherwise, there would be net work and an energy
transfer such that the block would not move with a constant velocity. If the applied force
were removed, then the block would slow down (decrease in energy) and eventually stop
because of frictional work.

When walking, there must be friction between our feet and the floor; otherwise, we
would slip. In this case, though, no work is done against friction because the frictional
force prevents the foot from slipping (Fig. 4.4b). No motion of the foot, no work. Of
course, other (muscle) forces do work because in walking there is motion. It is interesting

Table 4.1 Work Units (Energy Units)		
System	Force × Distance Units $W = F \times d$	Special or Common Name
SI	newton × meter (N · m)	joule (J)
British	pound × foot	foot-pound (ft · lb)

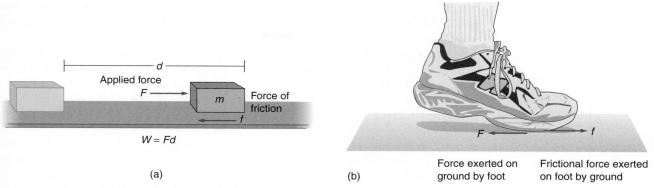

Figure 4.4 Work and No Work Done Against Friction
(a) The mass is moved to the right with a constant velocity by a force *F*, which is equal and oppo-site to the frictional force *f*. (b) When you are walking, there is friction between your feet and the floor. This example is a static case, and the frictional force prevents the foot from moving or slipping. No motion, no work.

to note in Fig. 4.4b that to walk forward, one exerts a backward force on the floor. The frictional force is in the direction of the walking motion and opposes the motion (slipping) of the foot on the ground.

Did You Learn?

- Work is a scalar quantity. Both force and parallel distance (actually, displacement) have directions associated with them, but their product, work, does not.

- Work = $F \times d$ and so has the units newton-meter (N · m), which is called a joule (J).

4.2   Kinetic Energy and Potential Energy

Preview Questions

- By what process is energy transferred from one object to another?
- To find the difference in gravitational potential energies, the difference in heights is taken. What is taken to find the difference in kinetic energies?

When work is done on an object, what happens? When work is done against gravity, an object's height is changed, and when work is done against friction, heat is produced. Note that in these examples some physical quantity changes when work is done.

The concept of energy helps unify all the possible changes. Basically, when work is done there is a change in energy, and the amount of work done is equal to the change in energy. But what is energy? Energy is somewhat difficult to define because it is abstract. Like force, it is a concept: easier to describe in terms of what it can do rather than in terms of what it is.

Energy, one of the most fundamental concepts in science, may be described as a prop-erty possessed by an object or system (a group of objects). **Energy** is the ability to do work; that is, an object or system that possesses energy has the ability or capability to do work. That is how the notion of energy as stored work arises. When work is done by a system, the amount of energy of the system decreases. Conversely, when work is done on a system, the system gains energy. (Remember, however, that not all the energy possessed by a sys-tem may be available to do work.)

Hence, <u>work is the process by which energy is transferred from one object or system to another.</u> An object with energy can do work on another object and give it energy. That being the case, it should not surprise you to learn that work and energy have the same units. In the SI, energy is measured in joules, as is work. Also, both work and energy are scalar quantities, so no direction is associated with them.

Energy occurs in many forms—chemical energy, heat energy, and so on (Chapter 4.5). Here the focus will be on *mechanical energy*, which has two fundamental forms: *kinetic energy* and *potential energy*.

Kinetic Energy

As noted previously, when a constant net force acts and work is done on an object, the object's velocity changes. This can be seen by using equations from Chapter 2, where $d = \frac{1}{2}at^2$ and $v = at$. Then, with work given by $W = Fd$ and with $F = ma$, we have

$$W = Fd = mad$$
$$= ma(\tfrac{1}{2}at^2) = \tfrac{1}{2}m(at)^2$$
$$= \tfrac{1}{2}mv^2$$

This amount of work is now *energy of motion*, and it is defined as *kinetic energy*.

Kinetic energy is the energy an object possesses because of its motion, or simply stated, it is the energy of motion. The amount of kinetic energy an object has when traveling with a velocity v is given by*

$$\text{kinetic energy} = \tfrac{1}{2} \times \text{mass} \times (\text{velocity})^2$$
$$E_k = \tfrac{1}{2}mv^2 \qquad\qquad\qquad \textbf{4.2}$$

As an example of the relationship between work and kinetic energy, consider a pitcher throwing a baseball (● Fig. 4.5). The amount of work required to accelerate a baseball from rest to a speed v is equal to the baseball's kinetic energy, $\frac{1}{2}mv^2$.

Suppose work is done on a moving object. Because the object is moving, it already has some kinetic energy, and *the work done goes into changing the kinetic energy*. Hence,

$$\text{work} = \text{change in kinetic energy}$$
$$W = \Delta E_k = E_{k_2} - E_{k_1} = \tfrac{1}{2}mv_2^2 - \tfrac{1}{2}mv_1^2 \qquad\qquad \textbf{4.3}$$

If an object is initially at rest ($v_1 = 0$), then the change in kinetic energy is equal to the kinetic energy of the object. Also keep in mind that to find the change in kinetic energy, you must first find the kinetic energy for each velocity and then subtract, *not* find the change or difference in velocities and then compute to find the change in kinetic energy.

EXAMPLE 4.1   Finding the Change in Kinetic Energy

A 1.0-kg ball is fired from a cannon. What is the change in the ball's kinetic energy when it accelerates from 4.0 m/s to 8.0 m/s?

Solution

Given: $m = 1.0$ kg and $v_1 = 4.0$ m/s
$\qquad\qquad\qquad\qquad v_2 = 8.0$ m/s

Equation 4.3 can be used directly to compute the change in kinetic energy. Notice that the kinetic energy is calculated for each velocity.

$$\Delta E_k = E_{k_2} - E_{k_1} = \tfrac{1}{2}mv_2^2 - \tfrac{1}{2}mv_1^2$$
$$= \tfrac{1}{2}(1.0\ \text{kg})(8.0\ \text{m/s})^2 - \tfrac{1}{2}(1.0\ \text{kg})(4.0\ \text{m/s})^2$$
$$= 32\ \text{J} - 8.0\ \text{J} = 24\ \text{J}$$

---

*Although velocity is a vector, the product of $v \times v$, or v^2, gives a scalar, so kinetic energy is a scalar quantity. Either instantaneous velocity (magnitude) or speed may be used to determine kinetic energy.

Figure 4.5 Work and Energy
The work necessary to increase the velocity of a mass is equal to the increase in kinetic energy; here it is that of the thrown ball. (It is assumed that no energy is lost to friction, that is, converted to heat.)

Confidence Exercise 4.1

In working the preceding example, suppose a student first subtracts the velocities and says $\Delta E_k = \frac{1}{2} m(v_2 - v_1)^2$. What would the answer be, and would it be correct? Explain and show your work.

The answers to Confidence Exercises may be found at the back of the book.

Work is done in getting a stationary object moving, and the object then has kinetic energy. Suppose you wanted to stop a moving object such as an automobile. Work must be done here, too, and the amount of work needed to stop the automobile is equal to its change in kinetic energy. The work is generally supplied by brake friction.

In bringing an automobile to a stop, we are sometimes concerned about the braking distance, which is the distance the car travels after the brakes are applied. On a level road the work done to stop a moving car is equal to the braking force (f) times the braking distance ($W = fd$). As has been noted, the required work is equal to the kinetic energy of the car ($fd = \frac{1}{2} mv^2$). Assuming that the braking force is constant, the braking distance is directly proportional to the square of the velocity ($d \propto v^2$).

Squaring the velocity makes a big difference in the braking distances for different speeds. For example, if the speed is doubled, then the braking distance is increased by a factor of 4. (What happens to the braking distance if the speed is tripled?)

This concept of braking distance explains why school zones have relatively low speed limits, commonly 32 km/h (20 mi/h). The braking distance of a car traveling at this speed is about 8.0 m (26 ft). For a car traveling twice the speed, 64 km/h (40 mi/h), the braking distance is four times that distance, or 4×8.0 m = 32 m (105 ft). See ● Fig. 4.6. The driver's reaction time is also a consideration. This simple calculation shows that if a driver exceeds the speed limit in a school zone, then he or she may not be able to stop in time to avoid hitting a child who darts into the street. Remember v^2 the next time you are driving through a school zone.

Figure 4.6 Energy and Braking Distance
Given a constant braking force, if the braking distance of a car traveling 32 km/h (20 mi/h) is 8.0 m (26 ft), then for a car traveling twice as fast, or 64 km/h (40 mi/h), the braking distance is four times greater, or 32 m (105 ft), that is, $d \propto v^2$.

Potential Energy

An object doesn't have to be in motion to have energy. It also may have energy by virtue of where it is. **Potential energy** is the energy an object has because of its position or location, or more simply, it is the energy of position. Work is done in changing the position of an object; hence, there is a change in energy.

For example, when an object is lifted at a slow constant velocity, there is no net force on it because it is not accelerating. The weight mg of the object acts downward, and there is an equal and opposite upward force. The distance parallel to the applied upward force is the height h to which the

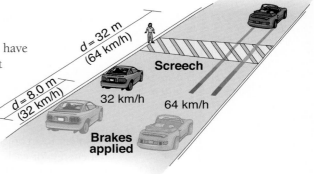

Figure 4.7 Work Against Gravity
In lifting weights (*mg*) to a height *h*, a weight lifter applies an upward lifting force *F*. The work done in lifting the weights is *mgh*. While standing there with the weights overhead, is the weight lifter doing any work?

object is lifted (● Fig. 4.7). Thus, the *work done against gravity* is, in equation form,

$$\text{work} = \text{weight} \times \text{height}$$
$$W = mgh \qquad \qquad \textbf{4.4}$$
$$(W = Fd)$$

Suppose you lift a 1.0-kg book from the floor to a tabletop 1.0 m high. The amount of work done in lifting the book is

$$W = mgh$$
$$= (1.0 \text{ kg})(9.8 \text{ m/s}^2)(1.0 \text{ m}) = 9.8 \text{ J}$$

With work being done, the energy of the book changes (increases), and the book on the table has energy and the ability to do work because of its height or position. This energy is called **gravitational potential energy.** If the book were allowed to fall back to the floor, it could do work; for example, it could crush something.

As another example, the water stored behind a dam has potential energy because of its position. This gravitational potential energy is used to generate electrical energy. Also, when walking up stairs to a classroom, you are doing work. On the upper floor you have more gravitational potential energy than does a person on the lower floor. (Call down and tell the person so.)

The gravitational potential energy E_p is equal to the work done, and this is equal to the weight of the object multiplied by the height (Eq. 4.4). That is,

$$\text{gravitational potential energy} = \text{weight} \times \text{height}$$
$$E_p = mgh \qquad \qquad \textbf{4.5}$$

When work is done by or against gravity, the potential energy changes, and

$$\text{work} = \text{change in potential energy}$$
$$= E_{p_2} - E_{p_1}$$
$$= mgh_2 - mgh_1$$
$$= mg(h_2 - h_1)$$
$$= mg\,\Delta h$$

Similar to an object having kinetic energy for a particular velocity, an object has a potential energy for each particular height or position. When work is done there is a *change* in position, so the (Δh) is really a height *difference*. The *h* in Eqs. 4.4 and. 4.5 is also a height difference, with $h_1 = 0$.

The value of the gravitational potential energy at a particular position depends on the reference point or the reference or zero point from which the height is measured. Near the surface of the Earth, where the acceleration due to gravity (g) is relatively constant, the designation of the zero position or height is arbitrary. Any point will do. Using an arbitrary zero point is like using a point other than the zero mark on a meterstick to measure length (● Fig. 4.8). This practice may give rise to negative positions, such as the minus ($-$) positions on a Cartesian graph.

Heights (actually, displacements or directed lengths) may be positive or negative relative to the zero reference point. However, note that the height *difference*, or change in the potential energy between two positions, is the same in any case. For example, in Fig. 4.8 the top ball is at a height of $h = y_2 - y_1 = 50$ cm $- 0$ cm $= 50$ cm according to the scale on the left, and $h = 100$ cm $- 50$ cm $= 50$ cm according to the meterstick on the right. Basically, you can't change a length or height by just changing scales.

A negative ($-$) h gives a *negative* potential energy. A negative potential energy is analogous to a position in a hole or a well shaft because we usually designate $h = 0$ at the Earth's surface. Negative energy "wells" will be important in the discussion of atomic theory in Chapter 9.3.

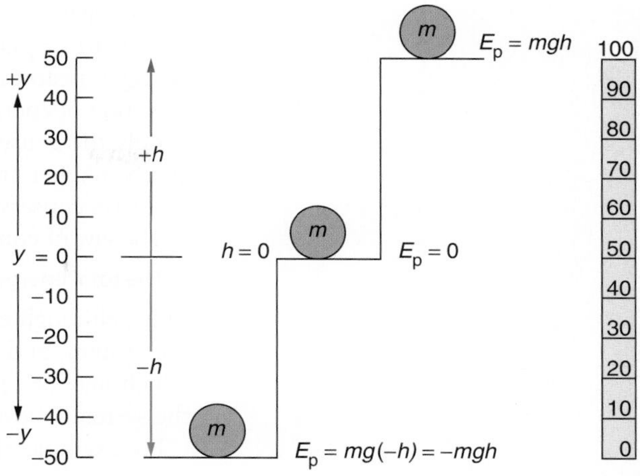

Figure 4.8 Reference Point
The reference point for measuring height is arbitrary. For example, the zero reference point may be that on a Cartesian axis (*left*) or that at one end of the meterstick (*right*). For positions below the chosen zero reference point on the Cartesian *y*-axis, the potential energy is negative because of negative displacement. However, the potential-energy values measured from the zero end of the meterstick would be positive. The important point is that the energy *differences* are the same for any reference.

Conceptual Question and Answer

Double Zero

Q. A fellow student tells you that she has both zero kinetic energy and zero gravitational potential energy. Is this possible?

A. Yes. If she is sitting motionless ($v = 0$), then her kinetic energy is zero. The value of the gravitational potential energy depends on the reference or zero point. If this point is taken at the student's position ($h = 0$), then she will have both zero kinetic and potential energies. (Some work would change the situation.)

There are other types of potential energy besides gravitational. For example, when a spring is compressed or stretched, work is done (against the spring force) and the spring has potential energy as a result of the change in length (position). Also, work is done when a bowstring is drawn back. The bow and the bowstring bend and acquire potential energy. This potential energy is capable of doing work on an arrow, thus producing motion and kinetic energy. Note again that work is a process of transferring energy.

Did You Learn?

● Energy is the ability or capability to do work, and work is the process by which energy is transferred from one object to another.

● To find the difference in kinetic energies, the difference in the squares of the velocity is taken, $\Delta E = \frac{1}{2}m(v_2^2 - v_1^2)$, *not* the difference in velocities squared $(v_2 - v_1)^2$.

4.3 Conservation of Energy

Preview Questions

● Overall, can energy be created or destroyed?
● What is the difference between total energy and mechanical energy?

Energy may change from one form to another and does so without a net loss or net gain. That is to say, energy is *conserved*, and the total amount remains constant. The study of energy transformations has led to one of the most basic scientific principles, the law of conservation of energy. Although the meaning is the same, the *law of conservation of energy* (or simply the conservation of energy) can be stated in different ways. For example, "energy can be neither created nor destroyed" and "in changing from one form to another, energy is always conserved." are both ways of stating this law.

The law of **conservation of total energy** may also be conveniently stated as follows:

The total energy of an isolated system remains constant.

Thus, although energy may be changed from one form to another, energy is not lost from the system, and so it is conserved. A *system* is something enclosed within boundaries, which may be real or imaginary, and *isolated* means that nothing from the outside affects the system (and vice versa).

For example, the students in a classroom might be considered a system. They may move around in the room, but if no one leaves or enters, then the number of students is conserved (the "law of conservation of students"). It is sometimes said that the total energy of the universe is conserved, which is true. The universe is the largest system of which we can think, and all the energy that has ever been in the universe is still there somewhere in some form or other.

To simplify the understanding of the conservation of energy, we often consider *ideal* systems in which the energy is in only two forms, kinetic and potential. In this case, there is **conservation of mechanical energy**, which may be written in equation form as

$$\text{initial energy} = \text{final energy}$$
$$(E_k + E_p)_1 = (E_k + E_p)_2$$
$$(\tfrac{1}{2}mv^2 + mgh)_1 = (\tfrac{1}{2}mv^2 + mgh)_2 \qquad \textbf{4.6}$$

where the subscripts indicate the energy at different times. There are initial (subscript 1) and final (subscript 2) times. Here it is assumed that no energy is lost in the form of heat because of frictional effects (or any other cause). This unrealistic situation is nevertheless instructive in helping us understand the conservation of energy.

EXAMPLE 4.2   Finding Kinetic and Potential Energies

A 0.10-kg stone is dropped from a height of 10.0 m. What will be the kinetic and potential energies of the stone at the heights indicated in ● Fig. 4.9? (Neglect air resistance.)

Solution

With no frictional losses, by the conservation of mechanical energy the total energy ($E_T = E_{k+} E_p$) will be the same at all heights above the ground. When the stone is released, the total energy is all potential energy ($E_T = E_p$) because $v = 0$ and $E_k = 0$.

At any height h, the potential energy will be $E_p = mgh$. Thus, the potential energies at the heights of 10 m, 7.0 m, 3.0 m, and 0 m are

$$h = 10 \text{ m}: E_p = mgh = (0.10 \text{ kg})(9.8 \text{ m/s}^2)(10.0 \text{ m}) = 9.8 \text{ J}$$
$$h = 7.0 \text{ m}: E_p = mgh = (0.10 \text{ kg})(9.8 \text{ m/s}^2)(7.0 \text{ m}) = 6.9 \text{ J}$$
$$h = 3.0 \text{ m}: E_p = mgh = (0.10 \text{ kg})(9.8 \text{ m/s}^2)(3.0 \text{ m}) = 2.9 \text{ J}$$
$$h = 0 \text{ m}: E_p = mgh = (0.10 \text{ kg})(9.8 \text{ m/s}^2)(0 \text{ m}) = 0 \text{ J}$$

Because the total mechanical energy is conserved, or constant, the kinetic energy (E_k) at any point can be found from the equation $E_T = E_k + E_p$. That is, $E_k = E_T - E_p = 9.8 \text{ J} - E_p$ because the total energy is all potential energy at the 10-m height. ($E_T = E_p = 9.8$ J. Check to see whether the equation gives $E_k = 0$ at the release height.) A summary of the results is given in ● Table 4.2.

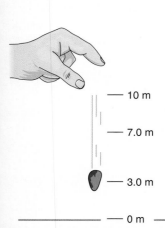

— 10 m

— 7.0 m

— 3.0 m

— 0 m

Figure 4.9 Changing Kinetic and Potential Energies
See Example 4.2.

Table 4.2 Energy Summary for Example 4.2

Height (m)	E_T (J)	E_p (J)	E_k (J)	v (m/s)
10.0	9.8	9.8	0	0
7.0	9.8	6.9	2.9	7.7
3.0	9.8	2.9	6.9	12
0	9.8	0	9.8	14
(decreases)	(constant)	(decreases)	(increases)	(increases)

Confidence Exercise 4.2

Find the kinetic energy of the stone in the preceding example when it has fallen 5.0 m. The answers to Confidence Exercises may be found at the back of the book.

Note from Table 4.2 that as the stone falls, the potential energy becomes less (decreasing h) and the kinetic energy becomes greater (increasing v). Potential energy is converted into kinetic energy. Just before the stone hits the ground ($h = 0$), all the energy is kinetic, and the velocity is a maximum.

This relationship can be used to compute the magnitude of the velocity, or the speed, of a falling object released from rest. The potential energy lost is $mg\Delta h$, where Δh is the change or decrease in height measured *from the release point down*. This is converted into kinetic energy, $\frac{1}{2} mv^2$. By the conservation of mechanical energy, these quantities are equal:

$$\tfrac{1}{2} mv^2 = mg\,\Delta h$$

Then, canceling the m's and solving for v, *the speed of a dropped object after it has fallen a distance h from the point of release is*

$$v = \sqrt{2g\,\Delta h} \qquad\qquad 4.7$$

This equation was used to compute the v's in Table 4.2. For example, at a height of 3.0 m, $\Delta h = 10.0 \text{ m} - 3.0 \text{ m} = 7.0 \text{ m}$ (a decrease of 7.0 m), and

$$v = \sqrt{2g\Delta h} = \sqrt{2(9.8 \text{ m/s}^2)(7.0 \text{ m})} = 12 \text{ m/s}$$

Conceptual Question and Answer

The Race Is On

Q. They're off! Two identical balls are released simultaneously from the same height on individual tracks as shown in ● Fig. 4.10. Which ball will reach the end of its track first (or do they arrive together)?

A. The Track B ball finishes first and wins the race. Obviously, the B ball has a longer distance to travel, so how can this be? Although the B ball must travel farther, it gains greater speed by giving up potential energy for kinetic energy on the downslope, which allows it to cover a greater distance in a shorter time. The B ball has a greater average speed on both the lower downslope and upslope of the track, and so it pulls ahead of the Track A ball and gets to the finish line first. (On the upslope, ball B is decelerating, but it is still traveling faster than ball A.)

Question: Are their speeds the same at the finish line? *Hint:* Look at their overall changes in potential energies. Did you get it? Note that the balls overall have the same decrease in height. Hence, they have the same decrease in potential energy and the same increase in kinetic energy, and they arrive at the finish line with the same speed.

Figure 4.10 The Race Is On
Two identical balls are released simultaneously from the same height on individual tracks. Which ball will reach the end of its track first? (See Conceptual Question and Answer.)

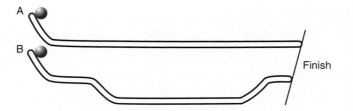

Did You Learn?

● In changing energy from one form to another, the total energy is always conserved.

● Total energy is all the energy of an isolated system, which may be of any form. Mechanical energy is that of an ideal system having only kinetic and potential energies.

4.4 Power

Preview Questions

● What is the difference in the operations of a 2-hp motor and a 1-hp motor?

● Electric bills from power companies charge for so many kilowatt-hours (kWh). What are we paying for?

When a family moves into a second-floor apartment, a lot of work is done in carrying their belongings up the stairs. In fact, each time the steps are climbed, the movers must not only carry up the furniture, boxes, and so on, but they also raise their own weights.

If the movers do all the work in 3 hours, then they will not have worked as rapidly as if the job had been done in 2 hours. The same amount of work would have been done in each case, but there's something different: the *time rate* at which the work is done.

To express how fast work is done, the concept of power is used. **Power** is the time rate of doing work. Power is calculated by dividing the work done by the time required to do the work. In equation form,

$$\text{power} = \frac{\text{work}}{\text{time}}$$

or

$$P = \frac{W}{t} \qquad\qquad 4.8$$

Because work is the product of force and distance ($W = Fd$), power also may be written in terms of these quantities:

$$\text{power} = \frac{\text{force} \times \text{distance}}{\text{time}}$$

$$P = \frac{Fd}{t} \qquad\qquad 4.9$$

In the SI, work is measured in joules, so power (W/t) has the units of joules per second (J/s). This unit is given the special name **watt** (W) after James Watt, a Scottish engineer who developed an improved steam engine, and 1 W = 1 J/s (● Fig. 4.11).

Light bulbs are rated in watts such as a 100-W bulb, which means that the bulb uses 100 J of electrical energy each second (100 W = 100 J/s). You have been introduced to several SI units in a short time. For convenience, they are summarized in ● Table 4.3.

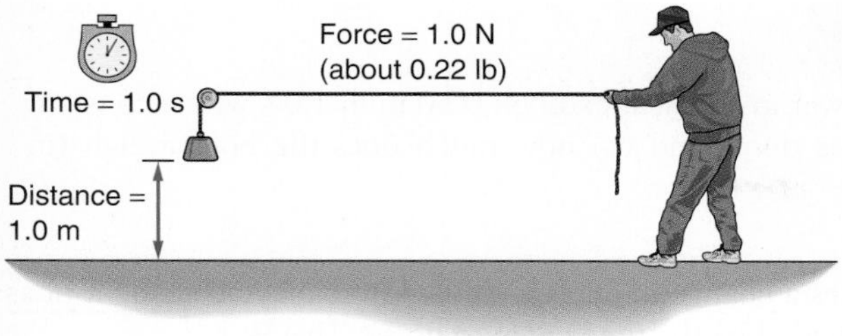

Figure 4.11 The Watt
In applying a force of 1.0 N to raise a mass a distance of 1.0 m, the amount of work done (*Fd*) is 1.0 J. If this work is done in a time of 1.0 s, then the power, or time rate of doing work, is 1.0 W. ($P = W/t = 1.0$ J/1.0 s = 1.0 W)

Table 4.3 SI Units of Force, Work, Energy, and Power

Quantity	Unit	Symbol	Equivalent Units
Force	newton	N	$kg \cdot m/s^2$
Work	joule	J	$N \cdot m$
Energy	joule	J	$N \cdot m$
Power	watt	W	J/s

One should be careful not to be confused by the two meanings of the capital letter W. In the equation $P = W/t$, the (italic) *W* stands for work. In the statement $P = 25$ W, the (roman) W stands for watts. In equations, letters that stand for variable quantities are in italic type, whereas letters used as abbreviations for units are in regular (roman) type.

In the British system, the unit of work is the foot-pound and the unit of power is the foot-pound per second (ft·lb/s). Technically, by equation form the unit of work ($W = Fd$) would be pound-foot. However, this is the same unit as torque (Chapter 3.7, $\tau = Fr$, pound-foot), so to distinguish, work is written foot-pound.

A larger unit, the **horsepower** (hp), is commonly used to rate the power of motors and engines, and

$$1 \text{ horsepower (hp)} = 550 \text{ ft} \cdot \text{lb/s} = 746 \text{ W}$$

The horsepower unit was originated by James Watt, after whom the SI unit of power is named. In the 1700s horses were used in coal mines to bring coal to the surface and to power water pumps. In trying to sell his improved steam engine to replace horses, Watt cleverly rated the engines in horsepower to compare the rates at which work could be done by an engine and by an average horse.

The greater the power of an engine or motor, the faster it can do work; that is, it can do more work in a given time. For instance, a 2-hp motor can do twice as much work as a 1-hp motor in the same amount of time, or a 2-hp motor can do the same amount of work as a 1-hp motor in half the time.

Example 4.3 shows how power is calculated.

EXAMPLE 4.3 Calculating Power

A constant force of 150 N is used to push a student's stalled motorcycle 10 m along a flat road in 20 s. Calculate the power expended in watts.

Solution

First we list the given data and what is to be found in symbol form:

Given: $F = 150$ N   *Wanted:* P (power)
$d = 10$ m
$t = 20$ s

Equation 4.9 can be used to find the power with the work expressed explicitly as *Fd*:

$$P = \frac{W}{t} = \frac{Fd}{t} = \frac{(150 \text{ N})(10 \text{ m})}{20 \text{ s}} = 75 \text{ W}$$

Notice that the units are consistent, $N \cdot m/s = J/s = W$. The given units are all SI, so the answer will have the SI unit of power, the watt.

Figure 4.12 Energy Consumption
Electrical energy is consumed as the motor of the grinder does work and turns the grinding wheel. Notice the flying sparks and that the operator wisely is wearing a face shield rather than just goggles, as the sign in the background suggests. An electric *power* company is actually charging for *energy* in units of kilowatt-hours (kWh).

Bob Daemmrich/The Image Works

Confidence Exercise 4.3

A student expends 7.5 W of power in lifting a textbook 0.50 m in 1.0 s with a constant velocity. (a) How much work is done, and (b) how much does the book weigh (in newtons)?

As we have seen, work produces a change in energy. Thus power may be thought of as energy produced or consumed divided by the time taken to do so. That is,

$$\text{power} = \frac{\text{energy produced or consumed}}{\text{time taken}}$$

or

$$P = \frac{E}{t} \qquad \qquad 4.10$$

Rearranging the equation yields

$$E = Pt \qquad \qquad 4.10a$$

Equation 4.10a is useful in computing the amount of electrical energy consumed in the home. Because energy is power times time ($P \times t$), it has units of watt-second (W·s). Using the larger units of kilowatt (kW) and hour (h) gives the larger unit of **kilowatt-hour** (kWh).

When paying the power company for electricity, in what units are you charged? That is, what do you pay for? If you check an electric bill, you will find that the bill is for so many kilowatt-hours (kWh). Hence, people actually pay the power company for the amount of energy consumed, which is used to do work (● Fig. 4.12). Example 4.4 illustrates how the energy consumed can be calculated when the power rating is known.

EXAMPLE 4.4   Computing Energy Consumed

A 1.0-hp electric motor runs for 10 hours. How much energy is consumed (in kilowatt-hours)?

Solution

Given: $P = 1.0$ hp   *Wanted:* E (energy in kWh)
            $t = 10$ h

Note that the time is given in hours, which is what is wanted, but the power needs to be converted to kilowatts. With 1 hp = 746 W, we have

$$1.0 \text{ hp} = 746 \text{ W } (1 \text{ kW}/1000 \text{ W}) = 0.746 \text{ kW}$$
$$= 0.75 \text{ kW (rounding)}$$

Then, using Eq. 4.10a,

$$E = Pt = (0.75 \text{ kW})(10 \text{ h}) = 7.5 \text{ kWh}$$

This is the electrical energy consumed when the motor is running (doing work).

We often complain about our electric bills. In the United States, the cost of electricity ranges from about 7¢ to 17¢ per kWh, depending on location. Thus, running the motor for 10 hours at a rate of 12¢ per kWh costs 90¢. That's pretty cheap for 10 hours of work output. (Electrical energy is discussed further in Chapter 8.2.)

Confidence Exercise 4.4

A household uses 2.00 kW of power each day for 1 month (30 days). If the charge for electricity is 8¢ per kWh, how much is the electric bill for the month?

Conceptual Question and Answer

Payment for Power

Q. Some factory workers are paid by the hour. Others are paid on a piecework basis (paid according to the number of pieces or items they process or produce.) Is there a power consideration in either of these methods of payment?

A. For hourly payment, there is little consideration for worker incentive or power consumed. A worker gets paid no matter how much work or power is expended. For piecework, on the other hand, the more work done in a given time or the more power expended, the more items produced and the greater the pay.

Did You Learn?

● A 2-hp engine can do twice as much work as a 1-hp engine in the same time, or the same amount of work in half the time.

● The kilowatt-hour (kWh) is a unit of energy ($E = Pt$).

4.5 Forms of Energy and Consumption

Preview Questions

● How many common forms of energy are there, and what are they?

● What are the two leading fuels consumed in the United States, and which is used more in the generation of electricity?

Forms of Energy

We commonly talk about various *forms* of energy such as chemical energy and electrical energy. Many forms of energy exist, but the main unifying concept is the conservation of energy. Energy cannot be created or destroyed, but it can change from one form to another.

In considering the conservation of energy to its fullest, there has to be an accounting for *all* the energy. Consider a swinging pendulum. The kinetic and potential energies of the pendulum bob change at each point in the swing. Ideally, the *sum* of the kinetic and potential energies—the total mechanical energy—would remain constant at each point in the swing and the pendulum would swing indefinitely.

In the real world, however, the pendulum will eventually come to a stop. Where did the energy go? Of course, friction is involved. In most practical situations, the kinetic and potential energies of objects eventually end up as heat. *Heat*, or *thermal energy*, will be examined at some length in Chapter 5.2, but for now let's just say that heat is transferred energy that becomes associated with kinetic and potential energies on a molecular level.

We have already studied *gravitational potential energy*. The gravitational potential energy of water is used to generate electricity in hydroelectric plants. Electricity may be described in terms of electrical force and *electrical energy* (Chapter 8.2). This energy is associated with the motions of electric charges (electric currents). It is electrical energy that runs numerous appliances and machines that do work for us.

Electrical forces hold or bond atoms and molecules together, and there is potential energy in these bonds. When fuel is burned (a chemical reaction), a rearrangement of the electrons and atoms in the fuel occurs, and energy—*chemical energy*—is released. Our

Table 4.4	Common Forms of Energy
Chemical energy	
Electrical energy	
Gravitational (potential) energy	
Nuclear energy	
Radiant (electromagnetic) energy	
Thermal energy	

main fossil fuels (wood, coal, petroleum, and natural gas) are indirectly the result of the Sun's energy. This *radiant energy*, or light from the Sun, is electromagnetic radiation. When electrically charged particles are accelerated, electromagnetic waves are "radiated" (Chapter 6.3). Visible light, radio waves, TV waves, and microwaves are examples of electromagnetic waves.

A more recent entry into the energy sweepstakes is *nuclear energy*. Nuclear energy is the source of the Sun's energy. Fundamental nuclear forces are involved, and the rearrangement of nuclear particles to form different nuclei results in the release of energy as some of the mass of the nuclei is converted into energy. In this case mass is considered to be a form of energy (Chapter 10). See ● Table 4.4 for a summary of the common forms of energy.

As we go about our daily lives, each of us is constantly using and giving off energy from body heat. The source of this energy is food (● Fig. 4.13). An average adult radiates heat energy at about the same rate as a 100-W light bulb. This explains why it can become uncomfortably warm in a crowded room. In winter extra clothing helps keep our body heat from escaping. In summer the evaporation of perspiration helps remove heat and cool our bodies.

The commercial sources of energy on a national scale are mainly coal, oil (petroleum), and natural gas. Nuclear and hydroelectric energies are about the only other significant commercial sources. ● Figure 4.14 shows the current percentage of energy supplied by each of these resources. Over one-half of the oil consumption in the United States comes from imported oil. The United States does have large reserves of coal, but there are some pollution problems with this resource (see Chapter 20.4). Even so, it is the major energy source for the generation of electricity (● Fig. 4.15).

Perhaps you're wondering where all this energy goes and who consumes it. ● Figure 4.16 gives a general breakdown of energy use by economic sector.

Energy Consumption

All these forms of energy go into satisfying a growing demand. Although the United States has less than 5% of the world's population, it accounts for approximately 26% of the world's annual energy consumption of fossil fuels: coal, oil, and natural gas. With increasing world population (now about 7 billion), there is an ever-increasing demand for energy. Where will it come from?

Of course, fossil fuels and nuclear processes will continue to be used, but increasing use gives rise to pollution and environmental concerns. Fossil fuels contribute to greenhouse gases and possible global warming (Chapter 20.5). Nuclear reactors do not have gaseous

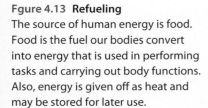

Fgure 4.13 Refueling
The source of human energy is food. Food is the fuel our bodies convert into energy that is used in performing tasks and carrying out body functions. Also, energy is given off as heat and may be stored for later use.

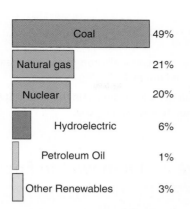

Oil — 37%
Natural gas — 24%
Coal — 23%
Nuclear — 8.5%
Renewables* — 7.5%

Figure 4.14 Comparative Fuel Consumption
The bar graph shows the approximate relative percentages of current fuel consumption in the United States.

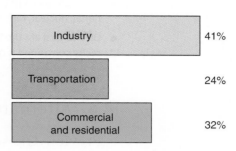

Coal — 49%
Natural gas — 21%
Nuclear — 20%
Hydroelectric — 6%
Petroleum Oil — 1%
Other Renewables — 3%

Figure 4.15 Fuels for Electrical Generation
The bar graph shows the relative percentages of fuels used for generating electricity in the United States.

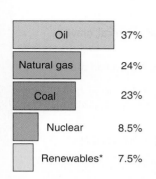

Industry — 41%
Transportation — 24%
Commercial and residential — 32%

Figure 4.16 Energy Consumption by Sector
The bar graph shows the relative consumption of energy by three main sectors of the United States economy.

*Renewables (hydro, biofuels, solar, and wind).

emissions, but nuclear wastes are a problem. (See the Chapter 10.7 Highlight: Nuclear Power and Waste Disposal.)

Research is being done on so-called alternative or renewable fuels and energy sources, which would be nonpolluting supplements to our energy supply. These sources will be addressed in the next section. Before then, however, let's consider a relatively new and potential alternative *form* of "fossil" fuel in the **Highlight: Ice That Burns**.

Highlight Ice That Burns

A frozen substance, *methane hydrate*, is described as "ice that burns" (Fig. 1). Found under the ocean floors and below polar regions, methane hydrate is a crystalline form of natural gas and water. (Methane is the major constituent of natural gas.) Methane hydrate resembles ice, but it burns if ignited. Until recently, it was looked upon as a nuisance because it sometimes plugged natural gas lines in polar regions.

Now this frozen gas–water combination is the focus of research and exploration. Methane hydrate occupies as much as 50% of the space between sediment particles in samples obtained by exploratory drilling. It has been estimated that the energy locked in methane hydrate amounts to twice the global reserves of conventional sources (coal, oil, and natural gas).

Methane hydrate may be an energy source in the future, but for now, there are many problems to solve, such as finding and drilling into deposits of methane hydrate and separating the methane from the water. Care must be taken to ensure that methane does not escape into the atmosphere. Methane, a "greenhouse" gas, is 10 times more effective than carbon dioxide in causing climate warming (Chapter 20.5).

Leibniz-Institute of Marine Sciences at Kiel University, Germany, Dr. Jens Greinert

Figure 1 Burning Ice
Found under the ocean floors and below polar regions, methane hydrate is a crystalline form of natural gas and water. It resembles ice and will burn if ignited.

4.6   Alternative and Renewable Energy Sources

Preview Questions

● What is the difference between alternative and renewable energy sources?

● Why are solar power and wind power somewhat unreliable?

Fossil fuels will be our main source of energy for some time. However, fossil-fuel combustion contributes to pollution and possible climate change: greenhouse gases and global warming (Chapter 20.5). The amount of fossil fuels is limited. They will be depleted someday. For example, it is estimated that at our present rate of consumption, known world oil reserves will last perhaps only 50 years.

Let's distinguish between alternative energy and renewable energy. **Alternative energy sources** are energy sources that are not based on the burning of fossil fuels and nuclear processes. **Renewable energy sources** are energy sources from natural processes that are constantly replenished. In large part these energy sources overlap. It is estimated that they account for about 7–8% of the energy consumption in the United States. See whether you would classify each of the following as alternative or renewable energy sources or as both.

▶ *Hydropower* Hydropower is used widely to produce electricity (● Fig. 4.17). We would like to increase this production because falling water generates electricity cleanly and efficiently. However, most of the best sites for dams have already been developed. There are over 2000 hydroelectric dams in the United States. The damming of rivers usually results in the loss of agricultural land and alters ecosystems.

▶ *Wind power* Wind applications have been used for centuries. If you drive north from Los Angeles into the desert, you will suddenly come upon acres and acres of windmills

Figure 4.17   Grand Coulee Dam
The potential energy of dammed water can be used to generate electricity. Shown here, the Grand Coulee Dam across the Columbia River in Washington state is the largest facility in the United States producing hydroelectric power and the fifth largest in the world.

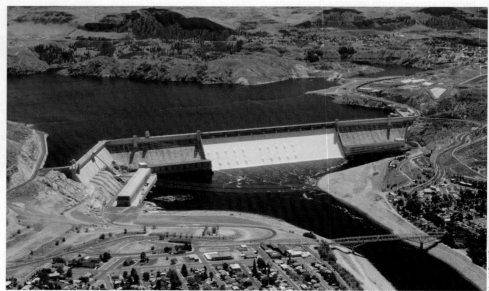

Harald Sund/Getty Images

Figure 4.18 Wind Energy
Wind turbines in Tehachapi Pass, California, generate electricity using the desert wind.

(● Fig. 4.18). Windmills for pumping water were once common on American farms. There have been significant advances in wind technology, and modern wind turbines, as shown in Fig. 4.18, generate electricity directly. The wind is free and nonpolluting. However, the limited availability of sites with sufficient wind (at least 20 km/h or 12 mi/h) prevents widespread development of wind power. And the wind does not blow continuously.

One projected solution is a wind farm of floating wind turbines offshore in the ocean. This technology requires the development of an undersea power cable network to bring the electricity ashore.

▶ *Solar power* The Sun is our major source of energy and one of the most promising sources of energy for the future. Solar power is currently put to use, but more can be done. Solar heating and cooling systems are used in some homes and businesses, and other technologies focus on concentrating solar radiation for energy production.

One of the most environmentally promising solar applications is the photovoltaic cell (or photocell, for short). These cells convert sunlight directly into electricity (● Fig. 4.19).

Figure 4.19 Solar Energy
Photocells convert solar energy directly into electrical energy. (a) Solar panels at the Nellis Air Force Base near Las Vegas, Nevada. Occupying 140 acres, 70,000 solar panels use a solar-tracking system for greater capacity. (b) The world's largest solar farm is in southern Spain. The farm consists of 120,000 solar panels occupying 247 acres.

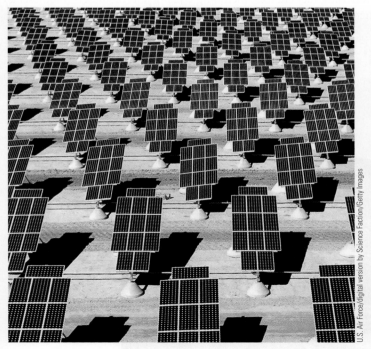

(a)

(b)

The light meter used in photography is a photocell, and photocell arrays are used on Earth satellites. Efficiency has been a problem with photocells, but advanced technology has boosted it to about 30–35%. Even so, electricity from photocells costs approximately 30¢ per kWh, which is not economically competitive with electricity produced from fossil fuels (on average, 10¢ to 12¢ per kWh). Photocell arrays could be put on the roofs of buildings to reduce the need for additional land, but electrical backup systems would be needed because the photocells could be used only during the daylight hours. Like windmills, photocell energy production depends on the weather. And clouds would reduce its efficiency.

Perhaps we will one day learn to mimic the Sun and produce energy by nuclear fusion. You'll learn more about nuclear fusion in Chapter 10.

▶ *Geothermal* Geothermal hotspots and volcanic features can be found around the world (Chapter 22.4). The Earth's interior is hot, and heat is energy. At the surface, geysers and hot springs are evidence of this extreme heat. Steam from geysers in California and Italy are used to generate electricity (● Fig. 4.20). In Iceland, water from hot springs is used to heat the capital of Reykjavik. Work is being done on geothermal systems that pump hot water into underground hotspots and then use the resulting steam to generate electricity. Such systems are relatively inefficient and costly.

▶ *Tides* Unlike the weather problems with wind and solar energy production, tidal energy production is steady, reliable, and predictable. There is constant water motion and thus a constant energy source. In France, electrical power is generated by strong tides going in and out of the Rance River. Underwater generators are planned to take advantage of the tide going in and out. Surface generators are also being developed to take advantage of surface wave action (● Fig. 4.21).

▶ *Biofuels* Because of the agricultural capacity of the United States, large amounts of corn can be produced, from which ethanol (an alcohol) is made. A mixture of gasoline and ethanol, called "gasohol," is used to run cars. Ethanol is advertised as reducing air pollution (less carbon dioxide) when mixed and burned with gasoline. Some pollution is reduced, but there are still emissions. Also, there is the disposal of waste by-products from the ethanol production to consider, and more fossil-fuel energy is actually used in ethanol production than the use of ethanol saves.

In some places a variety of biofuels are available. ● Fig. 4.22 shows a filling station in San Diego, CA advertising fuel choices, including ethanol and biodiesel. (Biodiesel is typically made by chemically reacting vegetable oil with an alcohol).

Figure 4.20 The Geysers
Located 72 miles north of San Francisco, the "Geysers" is a naturally occurring steam field reservoir below the Earth's surface used to generate electricity. As the largest complex of geothermal power plants in the world, the net generation capacity is enough to provide electricity for 750,000 homes.

Figure 4.21 Wave-Action Electrical Generation
The Aguçadoura wave in Peru converts the energy of ocean surface waves into electrical power. The snake-like structures float in the water, where they arc and bend, forcing oil to be pumped through high-pressure motors that in turn drive electrical generators. The power is then transferred to shore. (Underwater turbines generators also take advantage of the in-and-out motions of ocean water due to the daily rise and fall of tides.)

Figure 4.22 Take Your Choice
A sign advertising gasoline (3 grades), ethanol, diesel, biodiesel, natural gas, and propane at a San Diego (CA) filling station.

Work is being done on algae-based biofuels. Algae are organisms that grow in aquatic environments. A green layer of algae is commonly seen on ponds in the summer. Algae use photosynthesis (Chapter 19.1) to produce energy for rapid growth and can double in weight several times on a sunny day. As part of the photosynthesis process, algae produce oils which can be harvested as biofuels.

▶ *Biomass* Biomass is any organic matter available on a renewable basis. It includes agricultural crops, wood and wood wastes, animal wastes, municipal wastes, and aquatic plants. Processed and capable of being burned, biomass constitutes a source of energy, some of which can be used in transportation fuels or chemicals.

For other energy topics, see the **Highlight: Hybrids and Hydrogen**.

In addition to alternative energy resources, emphasis is placed on using our available energy more efficiently. Appliances come with Energy Guide labels that compare energy costs or usage. Also, there are more efficient light sources. Compact fluorescent bulbs are coming into increasing use (● Fig. 4.23a). The common incandescent bulbs are relatively inefficient, producing most of the radiation in the infrared region, whereas fluorescent light is more in the visible region. There is some environmental concern because fluorescent lamps and bulbs contain mercury, which is potentially environmentally hazardous (see Chapter 23.3). Compact bulbs use less energy (watts or energy per time) and last up to 5 years, saving not only energy but replacement costs.

More recently, light-emitting diode, or LED, bulbs have been introduced (Fig. 4.23b). The common little Christmas tree lights are LEDs. These bulbs use just 12 W to produce the same amount of light as a 60-W incandescent bulb, an 80% savings of energy. LED bulbs are reported to last 25 times as long as an incandescent bulb and have no mercury. However, they are much more expensive. LEDs are also becoming common in flashlights and automobile headlights.

(a)

(b)

Figure 4.23 More Efficient Lightning
(a) A compact fluorescent light (CFL) bulb. Note that the 15-W CFL is as efficient as a 60-W incandescent bulb. (b) For even more efficiency and longer life, LED (light emitting diode) bulbs are coming into use.

Highlight   Hybrids and Hydrogen

Automobiles have been powered primarily by gasoline combustion for 100 years or so. With concerns about petroleum (gasoline) supply and environmental pollution (Chapter 20.4), alternative power sources are being sought. You have probably heard about electric cars that are powered by batteries. However, these cars have a limited range, an average of 120 km (75 mi), before the batteries need to be recharged. Recharging requires the generation of electricity, which can be polluting.

Two top candidates that offer some improvement are *hybrid cars* and an *alternative fuel engine* that uses hydrogen as a fuel. First let's look at the gasoline–electric hybrid car, which is a combination of a gasoline-powered car and an electric car. These hybrids are becoming increasingly common.

A hybrid car has a small gasoline engine and an electric motor that assists the engine when accelerating. The electric motor is powered by batteries that are recharged when the car is running on gasoline. For more efficiency (and less pollution), the engine temporarily shuts off when stopped in traffic and restarts automatically when put back in gear. The electric motor can also assist the car in slowing. The combo hybrid saves fuel in getting more miles per gallon (mpg) of gasoline. Now, all-electric cars are on the market.

Hydrogen (derived from Greek words meaning "maker of water") is the most abundant element in the universe. It is the third most abundant on the Earth's surface, where it is found primarily in water and organic compounds. There are vast quantities of hydrogen in the water of the oceans, rivers, lakes, polar ice caps, and atmosphere (humidity). Hydrogen is produced from sources such as natural gas, methanol, and water. A common chemistry lab experiment is the electrolysis of water. When an electric current is supplied to platinum plates in water (H_2O), hydrogen gas (H_2) is formed at one plate and oxygen (O_2) at the other.

Hydrogen is used in fuel cells, which work somewhat like a battery. A fuel cell, though, does not run down or need recharging. As long as hydrogen is supplied, a fuel cell produces electricity (which can power an automobile) and heat. We will not go into the details of the operation of a fuel cell. Suffice it to say that just as electricity can be used in the electrolysis process described above to separate water into hydrogen and oxygen, electricity is *produced* when hydrogen and oxygen are combined in a fuel cell (hydrogen fuel and oxygen from the air). Fuel cells combine hydrogen and oxygen without combustion to yield water, heat, and electricity with no pollution.

Automobiles with fuel-cell engines have been built, but it will probably be some time before they become commonplace. One problem is the large-scale distribution of hydrogen fuel (Fig. 1). Hydrogen is normally a gas, but when compressed it liquefies, and the very cold liquid hydrogen can be pumped. As you can imagine, adding liquid-hydrogen pumps to filling stations would be very costly. Another concern is that hydrogen is very flammable (as is gasoline). Even so, hydrogen is as safe for transport, storage, and use as many other fuels. There is, however, a historical reluctance to use hydrogen known as the *Hindenburg syndrome*. Check out Chapter 11.6 to see why.

Figure 1 Fill It Up . . . with Hydrogen
Automobiles with fuel-cell engines have been built, but a major problem for commercial use is the distribution of hydrogen fuel. Imagine the enormous task of adding liquid-hydrogen pumps to filling stations.

Henning Bock/Bransch

Did You Learn?

- Alternative energy sources are those not based on fossil fuels and nuclear processes; biofuels are an example. Renewable energy sources are those that cannot be exhausted; solar and wind are examples.

- Solar power (sunlight) varies because of weather conditions and seasonal changes. Wind power varies because the wind does not blow continuously.

KEY TERMS

1. work (4.1)
2. joule
3. foot-pound
4. energy (4.2)
5. kinetic energy
6. potential energy
7. gravitational potential energy
8. conservation of total energy (4.3)
9. conservation of mechanical energy
10. power (4.4)
11. watt
12. horsepower
13. kilowatt-hour
14. alternative energy sources (4.6)
15. renewable energy sources

MATCHING

For each of the following items, fill in the number of the appropriate Key Word from the preceding list. Compare your answers with those at the back of the book.

a. _____ The ability to do work
b. _____ Time rate of doing work
c. _____ SI unit of energy
d. _____ British unit of power
e. _____ Equal to work done against gravity
f. _____ Energy of position
g. _____ A process of transferring energy
h. _____ British unit of work

i. _____ Energy sources that cannot be exhausted
j. _____ SI unit of power
k. _____ $E_k + E_p$ = a constant
l. _____ Energy of motion
m. _____ Unit of electrical energy
n. _____ Requires an isolated system
o. _____ Energy sources other than fossil fuels and nuclear reactions

MULTIPLE CHOICE

Compare your answers with those at the back of the book.

1. Work is done on an object when it is (4.1)
   (a) moved
   (b) stationary
   (c) acted on by a balanced force
   (d) none of the preceding

2. Which of the following is a unit of work? (4.1)
   (a) W   (b) J·s   (c) N/s   (d) N·m

3. What is the SI unit of energy? (4.2)
   (a) ft·lb   (b) newton   (c) watt   (d) joule

4. Which of the following objects has the greatest kinetic energy? (4.2)
   (a) an object with a mass of $4m$ and a velocity of v
   (b) an object with a mass of $3m$ and a velocity of $2v$
   (c) an object with a mass of $2m$ and a velocity of $3v$
   (d) an object with a mass of m and a velocity of $4v$

5. When negative work is done on a moving object, its kinetic energy (4.2)
   (a) increases   (b) decreases   (c) remains constant

6. The reference point for gravitational potential energy may be which of the following? (4.2)
   (a) zero   (b) negative
   (c) positive   (d) all of the preceding

7. When the height of an object is changed, the gravitational potential energy (4.2)
   (a) increases
   (b) decreases
   (c) depends on the reference point
   (d) remains constant

8. Energy *cannot* be ___ .
   (a) created   (b) conserved
   (c) transferred   (d) in more than one form

9. On which of the following does the speed of a falling object depend? (4.3)
   (a) mass   (b) $\sqrt{\Delta h}$
   (c) $\frac{1}{2}mv^2$ (d) parallel distance

10. Power is expressed by which of the following units? (4.4)
    (a) J/s   (b) N·m   (c) W·s   (d) W/m

11. If one motor has three times as much power as another, then the less powerful motor ___ . (4.4)
    (a) can do the same work in three times the time
    (b) can do the same work in the same time
    (c) can do the same work in one-third the time
    (d) can never do the same work as the larger motor

12. In the United States, which one of the following sectors consumes the most energy? (4.5)
    (a) residential   (b) commercial
    (c) industry   (d) transportation

13. Which one of the following would not be classified as a total alternative fuel source? (4.6)
    (a) photocells   (b) gasohol   (c) windmills   (d) wood

14. Which of the following renewable energy sources currently produces the most energy?
    (a) wind power
    (b) solar power
    (c) hydropower
    (d) tidal power

FILL IN THE BLANK

Compare your answers with those at the back of the book.

1. Work is equal to the force times the ___ distance through which the force acts. (4.1)
2. Work is a ___ quantity. (4.1)
3. The unit N · m is given the special name of ___ . (4.1)
4. When energy is transferred from one object to another, ___ is done. (4.2)
5. Mechanical energy consists of ___ and potential energy. (4.2)
6. The stopping distance of an automobile on a level road depends on the ___ of the speed. (4.2)

7. Work is a process of ___ energy. (4.2)
8. The total energy of a(n) ___ system remains constant. (4.3)
9. Power is the time rate of doing ___ . (4.4)
10. A horsepower is equal to about ___ kW. (4.4)
11. The kilowatt-hour (kWh) is a unit of ___ . (4.4)
12. In the United States, ___ is the most consumed fuel in generating electricity. (4.5)
13. Renewable energy sources cannot be ___ . (4.6)
14. Gasohol is gasoline mixed with ___ . (4.6)

SHORT ANSWER

4.1 Work

1. What is required to do work?
2. Do all forces do work? Explain.
3. How much work is required to lift a bucket of water from a well?
4. A weight lifter holds 900 N (about 200 lb) over his head. Is he doing work on the weights? Did he do any work on the weights? Explain.
5. For the situation in Fig. 4.4a, if the applied force is removed, then the frictional force will continue to do work, so there is an energy transfer. Explain this transfer.

4.2 Kinetic Energy and Potential Energy

6. Car B is traveling twice as fast as car A, but car A has three times the mass of car B. Which car has the greater kinetic energy?
7. Why are water towers very tall structures and often placed on high elevations?
8. If the speed of a moving object is doubled, how many times more work is required to bring it to rest?
9. A book sits on a library shelf 1.5 m above the floor. One friend tells you the book's total mechanical energy is zero, and another says it is not. Who is correct? Explain.
10. (a) A car traveling at a constant speed on a level road rolls up an incline until it stops. Assuming no frictional losses, comment on how far up the hill the car will roll.
    (b) Suppose the car rolls back down the hill. Again, assuming no frictional losses, comment on the speed of the car at the bottom of the hill.
11. An object is said to have a negative potential energy. Because it is preferable not to work with negative numbers, how can you change the value of the object's potential energy without moving the object?

4.3 Conservation of Energy

12. Distinguish between total energy and mechanical energy.
13. A ball is dropped from a height at which it has 50 J of potential energy. How much kinetic energy does the ball have just before hitting the ground?
14. When is total energy conserved? When is mechanical energy conserved?

15. A simple pendulum as shown in ● Fig. 4.24 oscillates back and forth. Use the letter designations in the figure to identify the pendulum's position(s) for the following conditions. (There may be more than one answer. Consider the pendulum to be ideal with no energy losses.)
    (a) Position(s) of instantaneous rest ___
    (b) Position(s) of maximum velocity ___
    (c) Position(s) of maximum E_k ___
    (d) Position(s) of maximum E_p ___
    (e) Position(s) of minimum E_k ___
    (f) Position(s) of minimum E_p ___
    (g) Position(s) after which E_k increases ___
    (h) Position(s) after which E_p increases ___
    (i) Position(s) after which E_k decreases ___
    (j) Position(s) after which E_p decreases ___
16. Two students throw identical snowballs from the same height, both snowballs having the same initial speed v_o (● Fig. 4.25). Which snowball has the greater speed on striking the level ground at the bottom of the slope? Justify your answer using energy considerations.
17. A mass suspended on a spring is pulled down and released. It oscillates up and down as illustrated in ● Fig. 4.26. Assuming the total energy to be conserved, use the letter designations to

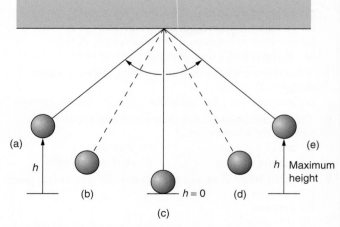

Figure 4.24 The Simple Pendulum and Energy
See Short-Answer Question 15.

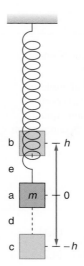

Figure 4.26 Energy Transformation
See Short-Answer Question 17.

Figure 4.25 Away They Go!
See Short-Answer Question 16.

identify the spring's position(s) as listed in Question 15. (There may be more than one answer.)

18. When you throw an object into the air, is its return speed just before hitting your hand the same as its initial speed? (Neglect air resistance.) Explain by applying the conservation of mechanical energy.

4.4 Power

19. (a) What is the SI unit of power?
    (b) Show that in terms of fundamental units, the units of power are $kg \cdot m^2/s^3$.

20. Persons A and B do the same job, but person B takes longer. Who does the greater amount of work? Who is more "powerful"?

21. What does a greater power rating mean in terms of (a) the amount of work that can be done in a given time and (b) how fast a given amount of work can be done?

22. What do we pay the electric company for, power or energy? In what units?

23. A 100-W light bulb uses how much more energy than a 60-W light bulb?

4.5 Forms of Energy and Consumption

24. Which fuel is consumed the most in the United States?

25. Which fuel is used the most in the generation of electricity in the United States?

26. On average, how much energy do you radiate each second?

27. List some different general forms of energy (other than kinetic energy and potential energy).

4.6 Alternative and Renewable Energy Sources

28. What are two examples of alternative energy sources?

29. What are two examples of renewable energy sources?

30. Which two renewable energy sources are affected by the weather?

VISUAL CONNECTION

Visualize the connections and give answers for the blanks. Compare your answers with those at the back of the book.

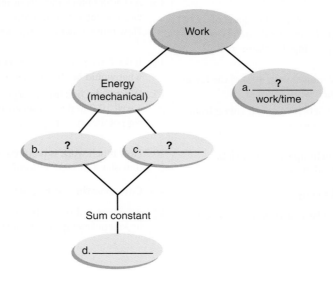

APPLYING YOUR KNOWLEDGE

1. A fellow student tells you that she has both zero kinetic energy and zero potential energy. Is this possible? Explain.

2. Two identical stones are thrown from the top of a tall building. Stone 1 is thrown vertically downward with an initial speed v, and stone 2 is thrown vertically upward with the same initial speed. Neglecting air resistance, how do their speeds compare on hitting the ground?

3. A person on a trampoline can go higher with each bounce. How is this possible? Is there a maximum height to which the person can go?

4. With which of our five senses can we detect energy?

5. What are three common ways to "save" electricity to reduce electric bills?

IMPORTANT EQUATIONS

Work: $W = Fd$ (4.1)

Kinetic Energy: $E_k = \frac{1}{2} mv^2$ (4.2)

and work: $W = \Delta E_k = E_{k_2} - E_{k_1}$

$\qquad\qquad = \frac{1}{2} mv_2^2 - \frac{1}{2} mv_1^2$ (4.3)

Potential Energy (Gravitational): $E_p = mgh$ (4.4)

Conservation of Mechanical Energy:

$\qquad (E_k + E_p)_1 = (E_k + E_p)_2$

or $\left(\frac{1}{2} mv^2 + mgh\right)_1 = \left(\frac{1}{2} mv^2 + mgh\right)_2$ (4.6)

Speed and Height (from rest): $v = \sqrt{2g\,\Delta h}$ (4.7)

Power: $P = \dfrac{W}{t} = \dfrac{Fd}{t}$ (4.8–4.9)

(or, in terms of energy, $P = \dfrac{E}{t}$ and $E = Pt$) (4.10)

EXERCISES

4.1 Work

1. A worker pushes horizontally on a large crate with a force of 250 N, and the crate is moved 3.0 m. How much work was done?

   Answer: 750 J

2. While rearranging a dorm room, a student does 400 J of work in moving a desk 2.0 m. What was the magnitude of the applied horizontal force?

3. A 5.0-"kilo" bag of sugar is on a counter. How much work is required to put the bag on a shelf a distance of 0.45 m above the counter?

   Answer: 22 J

4. How much work is required to lift a 4.0-kg concrete block to a height of 2.0 m?

5. A man pushes a lawn mower on a level lawn with a force of 200 N. If 40% of this force is directed downward, then how much work is done by the man in pushing the mower 6.0 m?

   Answer: 7.2×10^2 J

6. If the man in Exercise 5 pushes the mower with 40% of the force directed horizontally, then how much work is done?

7. How much work does gravity do on a 0.150-kg ball falling from a height of 10.0 m? (Neglect air resistance.)

   Answer: 14.7 J

8. A student throws the same ball straight upward to a height of 7.50 m. How much work did the student do?

4.2 Kinetic Energy and Potential Energy

9. (a) What is the kinetic energy in joules of a 1000-kg automobile traveling at 90 km/h?

   (b) How much work would have to be done to bring a 1000-kg automobile traveling at 90 km/h to a stop?

   Answer: (a) 3.1×10^5 J (b) same

10. A 60-kg student traveling in a car with a constant velocity has a kinetic energy of 1.2×10^4 J. What is the speedometer reading of the car in km/h?

11. What is the kinetic energy of a 20-kg dog that is running at a speed of 9.0 m/s (about 20 mi/h)?

    Answer: 8.1×10^2 J

12. Which has more kinetic energy, a 0.0020-kg bullet traveling at 400 m/s or a (6.4×10^7)-kg ocean liner traveling at 10 m/s (20 knots)? Justify your answer.

13. A 0.50-kg block initially at rest on a frictionless, horizontal surface is acted upon by a force of 8.0 N for a distance of 4.0 m. How much kinetic energy does the block gain?

    Answer: 32 J

14. If the force in Exercise 13 had acted for a distance of 8.0 m, then what would be the block's velocity?

15. What is the potential energy of a 3.00-kg object at the bottom of a well 10.0 m deep as measured from ground level? Explain the sign of the answer.

    Answer: −294 J

16. How much work is required to lift a 3.00-kg object from the bottom of a well 10.0 m deep?

4.3 Conservation of Energy

17. An object is dropped from a height of 12 m. At what height will its kinetic energy and its potential energy be equal?

    Answer: 6.0 m

18. A 1.0-kg rock is dropped from a height of 6.0 m. At what height is the rock's kinetic energy twice its potential energy?

19. A sled and rider with a combined weight of 60 kg are at rest on the top of a hill 12 m high.
    (a) What is their total energy at the top of the hill?
    (b) Assuming there is no friction, what would the total energy be on sliding halfway down the hill?

    Answer: (a) 7.1×10^3 J (b) same

20. A 30.0-kg child starting from rest slides down a water slide with a vertical height of 10.0 m. What is the child's speed (a) halfway down the slide's vertical distance and (b) three-fourths of the way down? (Neglect friction.)

4.4 Power

21. If the man in Exercise 5 pushes the lawn mower 6.0 m in 10 s, how much power does he expend?

    Answer: 72 W

22. If the man in Exercise 5 expended 60 W of power in pushing the mower 6.0 m, how much time is spent in pushing the mower this distance?

23. A student who weighs 556 N climbs a stairway (vertical height of 4.0 m) in 25 s.
    (a) How much work is done?
    (b) What is the power output of the student?

    Answer: (a) 2.2×10^3 J (b) 89 W

24. A 125-lb student races up stairs with a vertical height of 4.0 m in 5.0 s to get to a class on the second floor. How much power in watts does the student expend in doing work against gravity?

25. On a particular day, the following appliances are used for the times indicated: a 1600-W coffee maker, 10 min, and a 1100-W microwave oven, 4.0 min. With these power requirements, find how much it costs to use these appliances at an electrical cost of 8¢ per kWh.

    Answer: 3¢

26. A microwave oven has a power requirement of 1250 W. A frozen dinner requires 4.0 min to heat on full power.
    (a) How much electrical energy (in kWh) is used?
    (b) If the cost of electricity is 12¢ per kWh, then how much does it cost to heat the dinner?

ON THE WEB

1. Forms and Sources of Energy: To Conserve or Not to Conserve

If energy can be neither created nor destroyed, why is there discussion about energy conservation? Where do the fossil fuels—coal, oil, and natural gas—come from? Why is the loss of these energy sources problematic? How can we conserve these sources of energy? Follow the recommended links on our student website at **www.cengage brain.com/shop/ISBN/1133104096** to discover more about "The Energy Story" and to answer the questions above.

2. Clean Energy

What is renewable energy? Why is it important? Why is energy efficiency important? What does "clean energy" have to do with you? From our student website at **www.cengagebrain.com/shop/ISBN/1133104096**, visit the Clean Energy site to answer these questions.

CHAPTER

5

Temperature and Heat

If you can't stand the heat, stay out of the kitchen.

•

Harry S. Truman
(1884–1972)

Molten steel being poured at a >
steel mill.

Mark Joseph/Getty Images

PHYSICS FACTS

▶ Daniel Gabriel Fahrenheit
(1686–1736), a German instrument maker, constructed the
first alcohol thermometer
(1709) and the first mercury
thermometer (1714). Fahrenheit used temperatures of 0°
and 96° for reference points.
The freezing and boiling points
of water were then measured
to be 32°F and 212°F.

▶ Anders Celsius (1701–1744), a
Swedish astronomer, invented
the Celsius temperature scale
with a 100° interval between
the freezing and boiling points
of water (0°C and 100°C).
Celsius' original scale was
reversed, 100°C (freezing) and
0°C (boiling), but it was later
changed.

▶ The Golden Gate Bridge across
San Francisco Bay varies in
length about 1 m (3.3 ft)

Both *temperature* and *heat* are commonly used terms when referring to hotness or coldness, but they are not the same thing. They have different and distinct meanings, as we will discover in this chapter. The concepts of temperature and heat play an important part in our daily lives. We like hot coffee and cold ice cream. We heat (or cool—remove heat from) our living and working spaces to adjust the temperature to body comfort. The daily temperature forecast is an important part of a weather report. How cold or how hot it will be affects the clothes we wear and the plans we make.

How the Sun provides heat to the Earth will be discussed in detail in Chapter 19.2. The heat balance between various parts of the Earth and its atmosphere gives rise to wind, rain, and other weather phenomena. On a cosmic scale, the temperature

Chapter Outline

of various stars gives clues to their ages and to the origin of the universe. More locally, the study of temperature and heat will enable the many phenomena that occur in our environment to be explained.

5.1 Temperature

Preview Questions

● We talk about temperature, but what does it physically represent?

● Are there any limits on the lowest and highest temperatures?

Temperature tells us whether something is hot or cold. That is, temperature is a *relative* measure, or indication, of hotness or coldness. For example, if water in one cup has a higher temperature than water in another cup, then we know the water in the first cup is hotter, but it would be colder than a cup of water with an even higher temperature. Thus, hot and cold are *relative* terms; that is, they are comparisons.

On the molecular level, temperature depends on the kinetic energy of the molecules of a substance. The molecules of all substances are in constant motion. This observation is true even for solids, in which the molecules are held together by intermolecular forces that are sometimes likened to springs. The molecules move back and forth about their equilibrium positions.

In general, the greater the temperature of a substance, the greater the motion of its molecules. On this basis, we say that **temperature** is a measure of the average kinetic energy of the molecules of a substance.

Humans have temperature perception in the sense of touch, but this perception is unreliable and may vary a great deal among different people. Our sense of touch doesn't enable us to measure temperature accurately or quantitatively. The quantitative measurement of temperature may be accomplished through the use of a thermometer. A thermometer is an instrument that uses the physical properties of materials to determine temperature accurately. The temperature-dependent property most commonly used to measure temperature is thermal expansion. Nearly all substances expand with increasing temperature and contract with decreasing temperature.

The change in length or volume of a substance is quite small, but the effects of thermal expansion can be made evident by using special arrangements. For example, a bimetallic strip is made of pieces of different metals bonded together (● Fig. 5.1). When it is heated, one metal expands more than the other and the strip bends toward the metal with the smaller thermal expansion. As illustrated in Fig. 5.1, the strip can be calibrated with a scale to measure temperature. Bimetallic strips in the form of a coil or helix are used in dial-type thermometers and thermostats.

The most common type of thermometer is the *liquid-in-glass thermometer*, with which you are no doubt familiar. It consists of a glass bulb on a glass stem with a capillary bore and a sealed upper end. A liquid in the bulb (usually mercury, or alcohol colored with a red dye to make it visible) expands on heating, forcing a column of liquid up the capillary tube. The glass also expands, but the liquid expands much more.*

Thermometers are calibrated so that numerical values can be assigned to different temperatures. The calibration requires two reference, or fixed, points and a choice of unit. By analogy, think of constructing a stick to measure length. You need two marks, or reference points, and then you divide the interval between the marks into sections or units. For example, you might use 100 units between the reference marks to calibrate the length of a meter in centimeters.

Two common reference points for a temperature scale are the ice and steam points of water. The *ice point* is the temperature of a mixture of ice and water at normal atmospheric

---

*There are a variety of thermometers. One digital type monitors the infrared radiation in the ear, which is proportional to the body temperature.

Figure 5.1 Bimetallic Strip and Thermal Expansion
(a) and (b) Because of different degrees of thermal expansion, a bimetallic strip of two different metals bends when heated. The degree of deflection of the strip is proportional to the temperature, and a calibrated scale could be added for temperature readings. Such a scale is shown but not calibrated. (c) Bimetallic coils are used as shown here. An indicator arrow is attached directly to the coil. See also Figure 5.21.

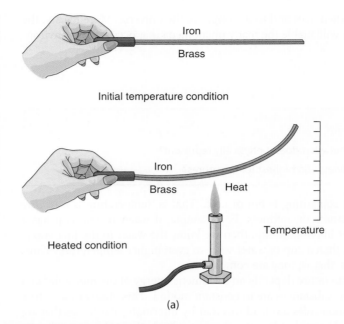

(a)

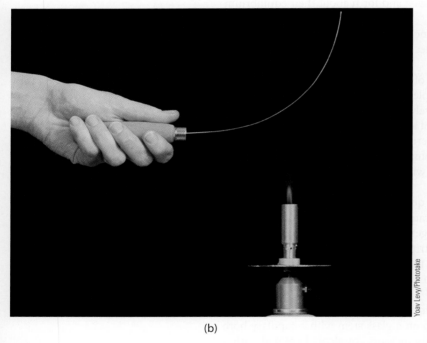

(b)

(c)

pressure. The *steam point* is the temperature at which pure water boils at normal atmospheric pressure. The ice point and the steam point are commonly called the *freezing point* and the *boiling point*, respectively.

Two familiar temperature scales are the Fahrenheit and Celsius scales (● Fig. 5.2). The **Fahrenheit scale** has an ice point of 32° (read "32 degrees") and a steam point of 212°. The interval between the ice point and the steam point is evenly divided into 180 units, and each unit is called a *degree*. Thus, a *degree Fahrenheit*, abbreviated °F, is $\frac{1}{180}$ of the temperature change between the ice point and the steam point.

The **Celsius scale** is based on an ice point of 0° and a steam point of 100°, and there are 100 equal units or divisions between these points. So, a *degree Celsius*, abbreviated °C, is $\frac{1}{100}$ of the temperature change between the ice point and the steam point. Thus, a degree

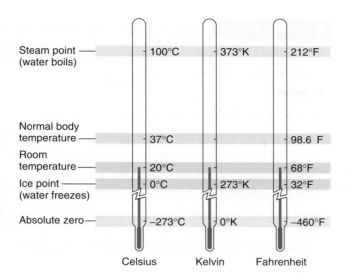

Steam point — (water boils)   100°C   373°K   212°F

Normal body temperature —   37°C   98.6 F

Room temperature —   20°C   68°F

Ice point — (water freezes)   0°C   273°K   32°F

Absolute zero —   −273°C   0°K   −460°F

Celsius   Kelvin   Fahrenheit

Figure 5.2 Temperature Scales
The common temperature scales are the Fahrenheit and Celsius scales. They have 180-degree and 100-degree intervals, respectively, between the ice and steam points. A third scale, the Kelvin (absolute) scale, is used primarily in scientific work. The unit or interval on the absolute Kelvin scale is the kelvin (K). This scale takes zero as the lower limit of temperature, or absolute zero (0 K).

Celsius is 1.8 times (almost twice) as large as a degree Fahrenheit (100°C and 180°F for the same temperature interval). The Celsius temperature scale is used predominantly in "metric countries" and hence throughout most of the world (Chapter 1.4).

There is no known upper limit of temperature, but there is a lower limit. It is about −273°C (actually −273.15°C), or −460°F, and is called *absolute zero*. Another temperature scale, the **Kelvin scale**, has its zero temperature at this absolute limit (see Fig. 5.2).* It is sometimes called the *absolute temperature scale*. The unit on the Kelvin scale is the **kelvin**, abbreviated K (*not* °K), and is the same size as a degree Celsius. Because the Kelvin scale has absolute zero as its lowest reading, it can have no negative temperatures.

Since the kelvin and the degree Celsius are equal intervals, it is easy to convert from the Celsius scale to the Kelvin scale: simply add 273 to the Celsius temperature. In equation form,

$$T_K = T_C + 273 \quad \text{(Celsius } T_C \text{ to Kelvin } T_K) \qquad 5.1$$

As examples, a temperature of 0°C equals 273 K, and a Celsius temperature of 27°C is equal to 300 K: $T_K = T_C + 273 = 27 + 273 = 300$ K.

Converting from Fahrenheit to Celsius and vice versa is also quite easy. The equations for these conversions are

$$T_F = \tfrac{9}{5}T_C + 32 \qquad 5.2a$$

or $$T_F = 1.8T_C + 32$$

(Celsius T_C to Fahrenheit T_F)

and $$T_C = \tfrac{5}{9}(T_F - 32) \qquad 5.2b$$

(Fahrenheit T_F to Celsius T_C)

or $$T_C = \frac{T_F - 32}{1.8}$$

The two equations in 5.2a and 5.2b are the same; they are just different arrangements for scale conversion.

As examples, try converting 100°C and 32°F to their equivalent temperatures on the other scales. (You already know the answers.) Remember that on these scales there are negative temperatures, whereas there are no negative values on the Kelvin scale.

---

*The Kelvin scale is named for Lord Kelvin (William Thomson, 1824–1907), the British physicist who developed it.

EXAMPLE 5.1   Converting Temperatures between Scales

The normal human body temperature is usually taken as 98.6°F. What is the equivalent temperature on the Celsius scale?

Solution

With $T_F = 98.6°F$ and using Eq. 5.2b to find T_C,

$$T_C = \tfrac{5}{9}(T_F - 32) = \tfrac{5}{9}(98.6 - 32) = \tfrac{5}{9}(66.6) = 37.0°C$$

So, on the Celsius scale, normal body temperature is 37.0°C (a nice, round number).

Confidence Exercise 5.1

Show that a temperature of −40° is the same on both the Fahrenheit and the Celsius scales.

   Answers to Confidence Exercises may be found at the back of the book.

   In converting temperatures between Celsius and Fahrenheit, it is sometimes difficult to remember whether one multiplies by 9/5 or by 5/9 and whether one adds or subtracts 32. Keep the following in mind. When going from T_C to T_F, you get a larger number (for example, 100°C to 212°F), so the larger fraction, 9/5, is used. (This reflects that a degree Celsius is larger than a degree Fahrenheit.) Similarly, in going from T_F to T_C, a smaller number is obtained (for example, 212°F to 100°C), so the smaller fraction, 5/9, is used.

   There is another convenient conversion procedure that eliminates the 32 question you might care to use knowing the 9/5 and 5/9 distinction. Try this method:

   Celsius to Fahrenheit: T_C + 40, multiply by 9/5, subtract 40 (= T_F)

   Fahrenheit to Celsius: T_F + 40, multiply by 5/9, subtract 40 (= T_C)

(Remember the sequence: add 40, multiply, subtract 40.)

For example, converting $T_C = 100°C$ to T_F (where 9/5 is used to convert to a larger number):

$$100° + 40 = 140 \times (9/5) = 252 - 40 = 212°F.$$

Conceptual Question and Answer

The Easy Approximation

Q. In most countries temperatures are given in Celsius. Is there a simple way to convert these temperatures to Fahrenheit without using the regular conversion equation and a calculator?

A. A quick way to do Celsius to Fahrenheit conversions for ambient temperatures is to use an approximation of Eq. 5.2a ($T_F = 1.8T_C + 32$) that you can do in your head. This is, $T_F \approx 2T_C + 30$ (increasing $1.8T_C$ to $2T_C$ and decreasing 32 to 30). That is, double the Celsius temperature and add 30. For example, for 20°C we have $T_F \approx 2(20) + 30 = 70°F$. This answer is not exactly 68°F, but it is close enough to give you an idea of the Fahrenheit temperature. (Remember this simple conversion on your next trip abroad.)

Did You Learn?

● Temperature is a measure of the average kinetic energy of the molecules of a substance.

● There is no known upper limit to temperature, and the lower limit is absolute zero (0 K, −273°C, or −460°F).

5.2 Heat

Preview Questions

- Why is heat called "energy in transit"?
- Most substances contract with decreasing temperature. Is this true for water?

We commonly describe heat as a form of energy. However, this definition can be made more descriptive. The molecules of a substance may vibrate back and forth, rotate, or move from place to place. They have kinetic energy. As stated previously, the average kinetic energy of the molecules of a substance is related to its temperature. For example, if an object has a high temperature, the average kinetic energy of the molecules is relatively high. (The molecules move relatively faster.) In kinetic theory of gases (Chapter 5.6), the kinetic energy is actually the average *translational* kinetic energy of the molecules. (Translation means that the molecule moves linearly as a whole.)

For a diatomic gas, however, besides having translational "temperature" kinetic energy, the molecules may also have kinetic energy due to vibrations and rotations. This kinetic energy is associated with the vibrations or rotational modes of the atoms within molecules and the molecular bonds, which simplistically may be thought of as "springs." There is also potential energy due to intramolecular interactions of the bond "springs" in stretching and compressing. The total energy (sum of kinetic plus potential) is called the *internal energy*.

When heat is transferred from one body to another, we often say that heat "flows" from a region of higher temperature to a region of lower temperature.* Actually, **heat** is the net energy transferred from one object to another because of a temperature difference. In other words, heat is energy in transit because of a temperature difference. When heat is added to a body, its internal energy increases. Some of the transferred energy may go into the translational kinetic energy of the molecules, which is manifested as a temperature increase, and some may go into the kinetic-potential energy of the internal energy.

Because heat is energy, it has the SI unit of joule (J), but a common and traditional unit for measuring heat energy is the calorie. A **calorie** (cal) is defined as the amount of heat necessary to raise one *gram* of pure water by one Celsius degree at normal atmospheric pressure. In terms of the SI energy unit,

$$1 \text{ cal} = 4.186 \text{ J } (\approx 4.2 \text{ J})$$

The calorie just defined is not the same as the one used when discussing diets and nutrition. This is the kilocalorie (kcal), and 1 kcal is equal to 1000 cal. A **kilocalorie** is the amount of heat necessary to raise the temperature of one *kilogram* of water one Celsius degree. A food calorie (Cal) is equal to 1 kcal and is commonly written with a capital C to avoid confusion. We sometimes refer to a "big" (kilogram) Calorie and a "little" (gram) calorie to make this distinction.

1 food Calorie = 1000 calories (1 kcal)

1 food Calorie = 4186 joules ($\approx$ 4.2 kJ)

Food Calories indicate the amount of energy produced when a given amount of the particular food is completely burned.

The unit of heat in the British system is the British thermal unit (Btu). One **Btu** is the amount of heat necessary to raise one *pound* of water one Fahrenheit degree at normal atmospheric pressure. Air conditioners and heating systems are commonly rated in Btu's. These ratings are actually the Btu's removed or supplied per hour. If food energies were rated in Btu's instead of Calories (kcal), then the values would be greater. Because 1 kcal is about 4 Btu, a 100-Cal soft drink would have 400 Btu.

As we saw in the measurement of temperature, one effect of heating a material is expansion. As a general rule, nearly all matter—solids, liquids, and gases—expands when heated

---

*Heat was once thought to be a fluid called "caloric," and fluids flow.

Highlight   Freezing from the Top Down

As a general rule, a substance expands when heated and contracts when cooled. An important exception to this rule is water. A volume of water does contract when cooled, to a point (about 4°C). When cooled from 4°C to 0°C, however, a volume of water *expands*. Another way of looking at it is in terms of density ($\rho = m/V$, Chapter 1.6). This behavior is illustrated in Fig. 1. As a volume of water is cooled to 4°C, its density increases (its volume decreases), but from 4°C to 0°C, the density decreases (the volume increases). Hence, water has its maximum density at 4°C (actually 3.98°C).

The reason for this unique behavior is molecular structure. When water freezes, the water molecules bond together in an open hexagonal (six-sided) structure, as evident in (six-sided) snowflakes (Fig. 2). The open space in the molecular structure explains why ice is less dense than water and therefore floats (see Chapter 3.6). Again, this property is nearly unique to water. The solids of almost all substances are denser than their liquids.

Water has its maximum density at 4°C, which explains why lakes freeze from the top down. Most of the cooling takes place at the top open surface. As the temperature of the top layer of water is cooled toward 4°C, the cooler water at the surface is denser than the water below and the cooler water sinks to the bottom. This process takes place until 4°C is reached. Below 4°C, the surface layer is less dense than the water below and so remains on top, where it freezes at 0°C.

Thus, because of water's very unusual properties in terms of density versus temperature, lakes freeze from the top down. If the water thermally contracted and the density increased all the way to 0°C, then the coldest layer would be on the bottom and freezing would begin there. Think of what that would mean to aquatic life, let alone ice-skating.

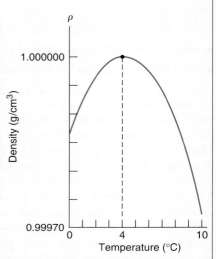

Figure 1 Strange Behavior
As is true of most substances, the volume of a quantity of water decreases (and its density increases) with decreasing temperature, but in the case of water, that is true only down to 4°C. Below this temperature, the volume increases slightly. With a minimum volume at 4°C, the density of water is a maximum at this temperature and decreases at lower temperatures.

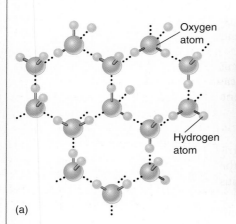

Oxygen atom

Hydrogen atom

(a)

(b)

Leslie B Bohm/iStockphoto.com

Figure 2 Structure of Ice
(a) An illustration of the open hexagonal (six-sided) molecular structure of ice. (b) Six-sided snowflakes.

and contracts (negative expansion) when cooled. *The most important exception to this rule is water in the temperature range near its freezing point.* When water is frozen, it expands. That is, ice at 0°C occupies a larger volume than the same mass of water at 0°C. The underlying reason is hydrogen bonding (Chapter 12.6), which leads to some interesting environmental effects as discussed in the **Highlight: Freezing from the Top Down.**

The change in length or volume of a substance as a result of heat and temperature changes is a major factor in the design and construction of items ranging from steel bridges and automobiles to watches and dental cements. The cracks in some highways are designed so that the concrete will not buckle as it expands in the summer heat. Expansion joints are designed into bridges for the same reason (● Fig. 5.3). The Golden Gate Bridge across San Francisco Bay varies in length by about 1 m (3.3 ft) between summer and winter.

Heat expansion characteristics of metals are used to control such things as the flow of water in car radiators and the flow of heat in homes through the operation of metallic thermostats (see Fig. 5.21). Electronic thermostats are now coming into common use.

(a)   (b)

Figure 5.3 Thermal-Expansion Joints
(a) Expansion joints are built into bridges and connecting roadways to allow for the expansion and contraction of the steel girders caused by the addition and removal of heat. Were the girders allowed to come into contact when expanding, serious damage could result. (b) Thermal expansion causes the Golden Gate Bridge in San Francisco to vary over 1 m (3.3 ft) in length between summer and winter. (The "Golden" Gate is actually orange vermilion in color.)

Did You Learn?

● Heat is the net energy transfer from one object to another because of a temperature difference.

● In general, water contracts on cooling, but from 4°C to 0°C, it expands.

5.3 Specific Heat and Latent Heat

Preview Questions

● What is specific about specific heat?

● Why is latent heat referred to as "hidden" heat?

Specific Heat

Heat and temperature, although different, are intimately related. When heat is added to a substance, the temperature generally increases. For example, suppose you added equal amounts of heat to equal masses of iron and aluminum. How do you think their temperatures would change? You might be surprised to find that if the temperature of the iron increased by 100°C, then the corresponding temperature change in the aluminum would be only 48°C. You would have to add more than twice the amount of heat to the aluminum to get the same temperature change as for an equal mass of iron.

This result reflects that the internal forces of the materials are different (different inter-molecular "springs," so to speak). In iron, more of the energy goes into translational kinetic energy than into intramolecular potential energy, so the iron has a higher temperature. (Both have the same change in internal energy.)

This difference is expressed in terms of specific heat. The **specific heat** of a substance is the amount of heat necessary to raise the temperature of one kilogram of the substance one Celsius degree.

By definition, 1 kcal is the amount of heat that raises the temperature of 1 kg of water 1°C, so it follows that water has a specific heat of 1.00 kcal/kg·°C (that is, 1.00 kcal per kilogram per degree Celsius). For ice and steam, the specific heats are nearly equal, about 0.50 kcal/kg·°C. Other substances require different amounts of heat to raise the temperature of 1 kg of the substance by 1°C. A specific heat is *specific* to a particular substance.

The SI units of specific heat are J/kg·°C, but kcal is sometimes used for energy, kcal/kg·°C. We will work in both kcal and J. (The latter is generally preferred, but the larger kcal unit makes the specific heat values smaller and more manageable mathematically, particularly for water.) The specific heats of a few common substances are given in ● Table 5.1.

The greater the specific heat of a substance, the greater the amount of heat necessary to raise the temperature per unit mass. Put another way, the greater the specific heat of a substance, the greater its capacity for heat (given equal masses and temperature change). In fact, the full technical name for specific heat is *specific heat capacity*. With regard to the previous example of aluminum and iron, note in Table 5.1 that the specific heat of aluminum is slightly greater than twice that of iron. Hence, for equal masses, it takes a little more than twice as much heat to raise the temperature of aluminum as to raise the temperature of iron.

We often say that certain materials "hold their heat" because such materials have relatively high specific heats. Since it takes more heat per unit mass to raise their temperatures, or "heat them up," they have more stored energy, as is sometimes painfully evident when one eats a baked potato or cheese on a pizza. Other food and pizza toppings and crust may have cooled, but you still might burn your mouth. This is because water, which has one of the highest specific heats, makes up large portions of both potato and cheese.

Water has one of the highest specific heats and so can store more heat energy for a given temperature change. Because of this, water is used in solar energy applications. Solar energy is collected during the day and is used to heat water, which can store more energy than most liquids without getting overly hot. At night, the warm water may be pumped through a home to heat it. The high specific heat of water also has a moderating effect on temperature around bodies of water, such as large lakes.

Table 5.1 Specific Heats of Some Common Substances

Substance	Specific Heat (20°C)	
	kcal/kg·°C	J/kg·°C
Air (0°C, 1 atm)	0.24	1000
Alcohol (ethyl)	0.60	2510
Aluminum	0.22	920
Copper	0.092	385
Ice	0.50	2100
Iron	0.105	440
Mercury	0.033	138
Steam (at 1 atm)	0.50	2100
Water (liquid)	1.00	4186
Wood (average)	0.40	1700

The specific heat, or the amount of heat necessary to change the temperature of a given amount of a substance, depends on three factors: the mass (m), the specific heat (designated by c), and the temperature change (ΔT). In equation form,

$$\text{amount of heat to change temperature} = \text{mass} \times \text{specific heat} \times \text{temperature change}$$

or

$$H = mc\,\Delta T \qquad\qquad 5.3$$

Equation 5.3 applies when heat is added to (or removed from, $-\Delta T$, negative ΔT) a substance and it does *not* undergo a phase change (such as changing from a solid to a liquid). When heat is added to, or removed from, a substance that is changing phase, the temperature does not change and a different equation, which will be presented shortly, must be used.

EXAMPLE 5.2   Using Specific Heat

How much heat in kcal does it take to heat 80 kg of bathwater from 12°C (about 54°F) to 42°C (about 108°F)?

Solution

Step 1

Given: $m = 80$ kg

$\qquad \Delta T = 42°C - 12°C = 30°C$

$\qquad\quad c = 1.00$ kcal/kg·°C (for water, known)

Step 2

Wanted: H (heat)

(The units are consistent, and the answer will come out in kilocalories. If the specific heat c were expressed in units of J/kg·°C, then the answer would be in joules.)

Step 3

The amount of heat required may be computed directly from Eq. 5.3:

$H = mc\,\Delta T = (80\text{ kg})(1.00\text{ kcal/kg}\cdot°C)(30°C) = 2.4 \times 10^3$ kcal

Let's get an idea how much it costs to heat the bathwater electrically. Each kilocalorie corresponds to 0.00116 kWh (kilowatt-hour; recall from Chapter 4.4 that we pay for electrical energy in these units). Hence, this amount of heat in kWh is

$$H = 2.4 \times 10^3 \text{ kcal} \left(\frac{0.00116 \text{ kWh}}{\text{kcal}} \right) = 2.8 \text{ kWh}$$

At 10¢ per kWh, the cost of the electricity to heat the bathwater is 2.8 kWh × 10¢/kWh = 28¢. For four people each taking a similar bath each day for 1 month (30 days), it would cost 4 × 30 × $0.28 = $33.60 to heat the water.

Confidence Exercise 5.2

A liter of water at room temperature (20°C) is placed in a refrigerator with a temperature of 5°C. How much heat in kcal must be removed from the water for it to reach the refrigerator temperature?

Answers to Confidence Exercises may be found at the back of the book.

Latent Heat

Substances in our environment are normally classified as solids, liquids, or gases. These forms are called *phases of matter*. When heat is added to (or removed from) a substance, it may undergo a change of phase. For example, when water is heated sufficiently, it boils and changes to steam, and when enough heat is removed, water changes to ice.

Water changes to steam at a temperature of 100°C (or 212°F) under normal atmospheric pressure. If heat is added to a quantity of water at 100°C, it continues to boil as the liquid is converted into gas, but the temperature remains constant. Here is a case of adding heat to a substance without a resulting temperature change. Where does the energy go? The heat associated with a phase change is called **latent heat** (*latent* means "hidden"). Latent heat is sometimes called hidden heat because it is not reflected by a temperature change.

On a molecular level, when a substance goes from a liquid to a gas, work must be done to break the intermolecular bonds and separate the molecules. The molecules of a gas are farther apart than the molecules in a liquid, relatively speaking. Hence, during such a phase change, the heat energy must go into the work of separating the molecules and not into increasing the molecular kinetic energy, which would increase the temperature. (Phase changes are discussed in more detail in Chapter 5.5.)

Referring to ● Fig. 5.4, let's go through the process of heating a substance (water in the figure) and changing phases from solid to liquid to gas. In the lower left-hand corner, the substance is represented in the solid phase. As heat is added, the temperature rises. When point *A* is reached, adding more heat does *not* change the temperature (horizontal line, constant temperature). Instead, the heat energy goes into changing the solid into a liquid. The amount of heat necessary to change 1 kg of a solid into a liquid at the same temperature is called the *latent heat of fusion* of the substance. In Fig. 5.4 this heat is simply the amount of heat necessary to go from point *A* to point *B* (assuming 1 kg of the substance).

When point *B* has been reached, the substance is all liquid. The temperature of the substance at which this change from solid to liquid takes place is known as the *melting point* (or *freezing point* when going from liquid to solid). After point *B*, further heating again causes a rise in temperature. As heat is added, the temperature continues to rise until point *C* is reached.

Figure 5.4 Graph of Temperature versus Heat for Water
The solid, liquid, and gas phases are ice, water, and steam, as shown over the sloping graph lines. During a phase change (*A* to *B* and *C* to *D*) heat is added, but the temperature does not change. Also, the two phases exist together.

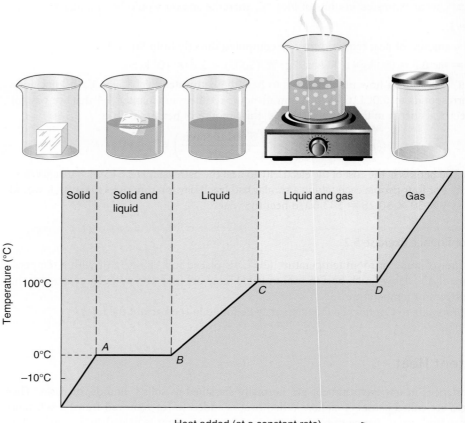

From point B to point C, the substance is in the liquid phase. When point C is reached, adding more heat does *not* change the temperature. The added heat now goes into changing the liquid into a gas. The amount of heat necessary to change one kilogram of a liquid into a gas is called the *latent heat of vaporization* of the substance. In Fig. 5.4 it is the amount of heat necessary to go from point C to point D.

When point D has been reached, the substance is all in the gaseous phase. The temperature of the substance at which this change from liquid to gas phase occurs is known as the *boiling point* (or *condensation point* when going from a gas to a liquid). After point D is reached, further heating again causes a rise in the temperature (superheated steam for water).

In some instances a substance can change directly from the solid to the gaseous phase. This change is called *sublimation*. Examples include dry ice (solid carbon dioxide, CO_2), mothballs, and solid air fresheners. The reverse process of changing directly from the gaseous to the solid phase is called *deposition*. The formation of frost is an example (Chapter 20.1). The processes of phase changes are illustrated in ● Fig. 5.5.

The temperature of a body rises as heat is added only when the substance is not undergoing a change in phase. When heat is added to ice at 0°C, the ice melts without a change in its temperature. The more ice there is, the more heat is needed to melt it. In general, the heat required to change a solid into a liquid at the melting point can be found by multiplying the mass of the substance by its latent heat of fusion. Thus, we may write

$$\text{heat needed to melt a substance} = \text{mass} \times \text{latent heat of fusion}$$

or

$$H = mL_f \qquad\qquad 5.4$$

Similarly, at the boiling point, the amount of heat necessary to change a mass of liquid into a gas can be written as

$$\text{heat needed to boil a substance} = \text{mass} \times \text{latent heat of vaporization}$$

or

$$H = mL_v \qquad\qquad 5.5$$

For water, the latent heat of fusion (L_f) and the latent heat of vaporization (L_v) are

$$L_f = 80 \text{ kcal/kg} = 3.35 \times 10^5 \text{ J/kg}$$

$$L_v = 540 \text{ kcal/kg} = 2.26 \times 10^6 \text{ J/kg}$$

These values are rather large numbers compared with the specific heats. Note that it takes 80 times as much heat energy (latent heat) to melt 1 kg of ice at 0°C as to raise the temperature of 1 kg of water by 1°C (specific heat). Similarly, changing 1 kg of water to steam at 100°C takes 540 times as much energy as raising its temperature by 1°C (definition of kcal). Also note that it takes almost seven times as much energy to change 1 kg of water at 100°C to steam as it takes to change 1 kg of ice at 0°C to water.

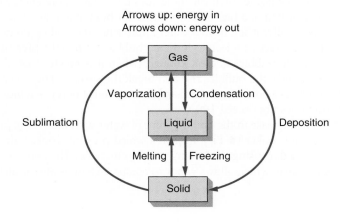

Figure 5.5 Phase Changes
This diagram illustrates the various phase changes for solids, liquids, and gases. See text for description.

| Table 5.2 | Temperatures of Phase Changes and Latent Heats for Some Substances (normal atmospheric pressure) |

Substance	Latent Heat of Fusion, L_f (kcal/kg)	Melting Point	Latent Heat of Vaporization, L_v (kcal/kg)	Boiling Point
Alcohol, ethyl	25	−114°C	204	78°C
Helium*	—	—	377	−269°C
Lead	5.9	328°C	207	1744°C
Mercury	2.8	−39°C	65	357°C
Nitrogen	6.1	−210°C	48	−196°C
Water	80	0°C	540	100°C

*Not a solid at 1 atm pressure; melting point −272°C at 26 atm.

See ● Table 5.2 for the latent heats and the boiling and melting points of some other substances.

EXAMPLE 5.3   Using Latent Heat

Calculate the amount of heat necessary to change 0.20 kg of ice at 0°C into water at 10°C.

Solution

The total heat necessary is found in two steps: ice melting at 0°C and water warming from 0°C to 10°C.

$$H = H_{\text{melt ice}} + H_{\text{change } T}$$
$$= mL_f + mc\,\Delta T$$
$$= (0.20 \text{ kg})(80 \text{ kcal/kg}) + (0.20 \text{ kg})(1.00 \text{ kcal/kg} \cdot °C)(10°C − 0°C)$$
$$= 18 \text{ kcal}$$

Confidence Exercise 5.3

How much heat must be removed from 0.20 kg of water at 10°C to form ice at 0°C? (Show your calculations.)

Pressure has an effect on the boiling point of water. The boiling point increases with increasing pressure as would be expected. *Boiling* is the process by which energetic molecules escape from a liquid. This energy is gained from heating. If the pressure is greater above the liquid, then the molecules must have more energy to escape, and the liquid has to be heated to a higher temperature for boiling to take place.

Normally, when heated water approaches the boiling point in an open container, pockets of energetic molecules form gas bubbles. When the pressure due to the molecular activity in the bubbles is great enough (when it is greater than the pressure on the surface of the liquid), the bubbles rise and break the surface. The water is then boiling. In this sense boiling is a cooling mechanism for the water. Energy is removed, and the water's temperature does not exceed 100°C.

The increase in the boiling point of water with increasing pressure is the principle of the pressure cooker (● Fig. 5.6). In a sealed pressure cooker, the pressure above the liquid is increased, causing the boiling point to increase. The extra pressure is regulated by a pressure valve, which allows vapor to escape. (There is also a safety valve in the lid in case the pressure valve gets stuck.) Hence, the water content of the cooker boils at a temperature greater than 100°C, and the cooking time is reduced.

At mountain altitudes, the boiling point of water may be several degrees lower than at sea level. For example, at the top of Pikes Peak (elevation 4300 m, or 14,000 ft), the atmospheric pressure is reduced to the point where water boils at about 86°C rather than at 100°C. Pressure cookers come in handy at high altitudes, especially if you want to eat on time. It is interesting that cake mixes designed for use at high altitudes contain less baking powder than those used at or near sea level. The baking powder supplies gas to "raise" a cake. If normal cake mixes were used at high altitudes, then the cake would rise too much and could explode.

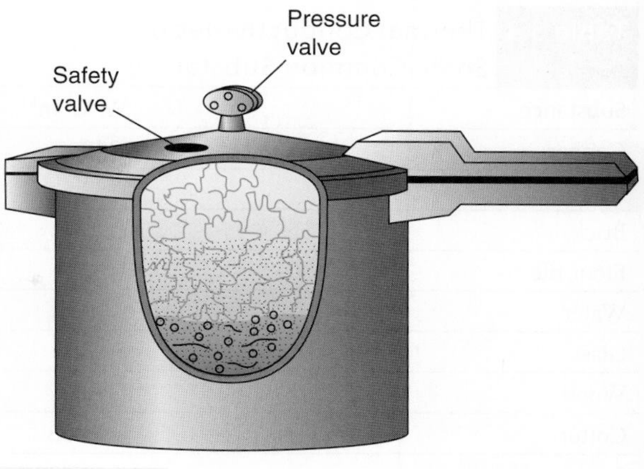

Figure 5.6 The Pressure Cooker
Because of the increased pressure in the cooker, the boiling point of water is raised and food cooks faster at the higher temperature.

Conceptual Question and Answer

Under Pressure

Q. Automobile engine cooling systems operate under pressure. What is the purpose of this pressurizing?

A. Under pressure, the boiling point of the water coolant is raised and the engine can operate at a higher temperature, which makes it more efficient in removing heat. (Never remove a radiator cap immediately after turning off a hot engine. Why?)

Finally, let's consider a type of phase change that is important to our personal lives. *Evaporation* is a relatively slow phase change of a liquid to a gas, which is a major cooling (heat removal) mechanism of our bodies. When hot, we perspire, and the evaporation of perspiration has a cooling effect because energy is lost. This cooling effect of evaporation is quite noticeable on the bare skin when one gets out of a bath or shower or has a rubdown with alcohol.

The comforting evaporation of perspiration is promoted by moving air. When you are perspiring and standing in front of a blowing electric fan, you might be tempted to say that the air is cool, but it is the same temperature as the other air in the room. The motion of the air promotes evaporation by carrying away molecules (and energy) and thus has a cooling effect.

On the other hand, air can hold only so much moisture at a given temperature. The amount of moisture in the air is commonly expressed in terms of *relative humidity* (Chapter 19.3). When it is quite humid, there is little evaporation of perspiration and we feel hot.

Did You Learn?

● Different amounts of heat are required to raise the temperature of 1 kg of a substance 1°C. Specific heat is substance specific (varies with substance).

● Latent heat is associated with a phase change, and there is no change in temperature when heat is added (seemingly "hidden").

5.4 Heat Transfer

Preview Questions

● What are the three methods of heat transfer?

● Which type of heat transfer involves mass transfer?

Table 5.3 Thermal Conductivities of Some Common Substances

Substance	W/°C · m*
Copper	390
Iron	80
Brick	3.5
Floor tile	0.7
Water	0.6
Glass	0.4
Wood	0.2
Cotton	0.08
Styrofoam	0.033
Air	0.026
Vacuum	0

*W/°C = (J/s)/°C is the rate of heat flow per temperature difference, where W represents the watt. The length unit (m) comes from considering the dimensions (area and thickness) of the conductor.

Because heat is energy in transit as a result of a temperature difference, how the transfer is done is an important consideration. Heat transfer is accomplished by three methods: conduction, convection, and radiation.

Conduction is the transfer of heat by molecular collisions. The kinetic energy of molecules is transferred from one molecule to another through collisions. How well a substance conducts heat depends on its molecular bonding. Solids, especially metals, are generally the best thermal conductors.

In addition to undergoing molecular collisions, metals contain a large number of "free" (not permanently bound) electrons that can move around. These electrons contribute significantly to heat transfer, or thermal conductivity. (These electrons also contribute to electrical current; see Chapter 8.1.) The *thermal conductivity* of a substance is a measure of its ability to conduct heat. As shown in ● Table 5.3, metals have relatively high thermal conductivities.

In general, liquids and gases are relatively poor thermal conductors. Liquids are better conductors than gases because their molecules are closer together and consequently collide more often. Gases are relatively poor conductors because their molecules are farther apart, so conductive collisions do not occur as often. Substances that are poor thermal conductors are sometimes referred to as *thermal insulators*.

Cooking pots and pans are made of metals so that heat will be readily conducted to the foods inside. Looking at Table 5.3, you can see why some cooking pots have copper bottoms; they provide better thermal conductivity (heat transfer) and faster cooking. Most pot holders, on the other hand, are made of cloth, which is a poor thermal conductor for obvious reasons. Many solids, such as cloth, wood, and plastic foam (Styrofoam), are porous and have large numbers of air (gas) spaces that add to their poor conductivity. For example, foam coolers depend on this property, as does the fiberglass insulation used in the walls and attics of our homes.

Conceptual Question and Answer

Hug the Rug

Q. In a bedroom with a tile or vinyl floor (common in dorms), when you rise and shine and your bare feet hit the floor, you might remark, "Oh, that floor is cold!" A throw rug is often used to prevent this discomfort. How does this help, when the rug and floor are in contact all night and are at the same temperature?

A. The rug and floor are at the same temperature, but their thermal conductivities are different. A tile floor *feels* colder because it conducts heat from the feet faster. See Table 5.3 for the conductivities of cotton (rug) and tile. To be more accurate, you should say, "Oh, that floor has a high thermal conductivity!"

Convection is the transfer of heat by the movement of a substance, or mass, from one place to another. The movement of heated air or water is an example. Many homes are heated by convection (movement of hot air). In a forced-air system, air is heated at the furnace and circulated throughout the house by way of metal ducts. When the air temperature has dropped, it passes through a cold-air return on its way back to the furnace to be reheated and recirculated (● Fig. 5.7).

The warm-air vents in a room are usually in the floor (under windows). Cold-air return ducts are in the floor too, but on opposite sides of a room. The warm air entering the room rises (being "lighter," or less dense, and therefore buoyant). As a result, cooler air is forced toward the floor and convection cycles that promote even heating are set up in the room. Heat is distributed in the Earth's atmosphere (Chapter 19.4) in a manner similar to the transfer of heat by convection currents set up in a room.

The transfer of heat by convection and conduction requires a material medium for the process to take place. The heat from the Sun is transmitted through the vacuum of space and this occurs by radiation. **Radiation** is the process of transferring energy by means of electromagnetic waves (Chapter 6.3). Electromagnetic waves carry energy and can travel through a vacuum. These waves include visible light, infrared, and ultraviolet radiations.

Another example of heat transfer by radiation occurs in an open fire or a fireplace. The warmth of the fire can be felt on exposed skin, yet air is a poor conductor. Moreover, the air warmed by the fire is rising (by convection and and most goes up the chimney in a fireplace). Therefore, the only mechanism for appreciable heat transfer via a fireplace is radiation. The three methods of heat transfer are illustrated in ● Fig. 5.8.

In general, dark objects are good absorbers of radiation, whereas light-colored objects are poor absorbers and good reflectors. For this reason, we commonly wear light-colored clothing in summer to be cooler. In winter, we generally wear dark-colored clothes to take advantage of the absorption of solar radiation.

A device that involves all three methods of heat transfer is the thermos bottle, which is used to keep liquids either hot or cold (● Fig. 5.9). Actually, knowledge of the methods of heat transfer is used to *minimize* the transfer in this case. The space between the double glass walls of the bottle is partially evacuated and then sealed. Glass is a relatively poor conductor, and any heat conducted through a wall (from the outside in or the inside out) will encounter a partial vacuum, an even greater thermal insulator. This vacuum also reduces heat transfer from one glass wall to the other by convection. Finally, the inner surface of the glass bottle is silvered for reflection to prevent heat transfer through the glass by radiation. Thus, a hot (or cold) drink in the bottle remains hot (or cold) for some time.

Did You Learn?

● Heat may be transferred by conduction, convection, or radiation.

● Convection is the transfer of heat by the movement of a substance, or mass, from one place to another.

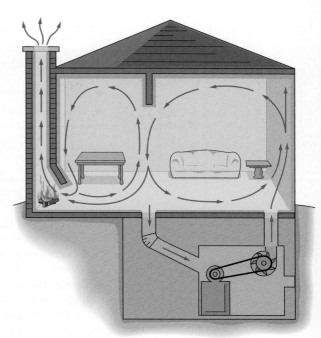

Figure 5.7 Convection Cycles
In a forced-air heating system, warm air is blown into a room. The warm air rises, the cold air descends, and a convection cycle is set up that promotes heat distribution. Some of the cold air returns to the furnace for heating and recycling. Note that a great deal of heat is lost up the chimney of the fireplace.

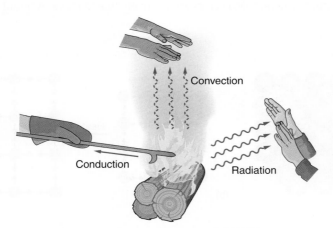

Figure 5.8 Conduction, Convection, and Radiation
The gloved hand is warmed by conduction. Above, the hands are warmed by the convection of the rising hot air (and some radiation). To the right, the hands are warmed by radiation.

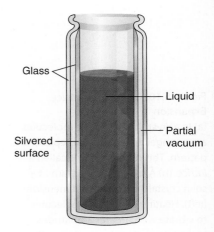

Figure 5.9 A Vacuum Bottle
A vacuum thermos bottle is designed to keep hot drinks hot and cold drinks cold. The bottle usually has a stopper and protective case, which are not shown. (See text for description.)

5.5   Phases of Matter

Preview Questions

● What are the three common phases of matter?

● How are the three phases of matter defined in terms of shape and volume?

As learned in Chapter 5.3, the addition (or removal) of heat can cause a substance to change phase. The three common **phases of matter** are solid, liquid, and gas. All substances exist in each phase at some temperature and pressure. At normal room temperature and atmospheric pressure, a substance will be in one of the three phases. For instance, at room temperature, oxygen is a gas, water is a liquid, and copper is a solid.*

The principal distinguishing features of solids, liquids, and gases are easier to understand if we look at the phases from a *molecular* point of view. Most substances are made up of very small particles called *molecules*, which are chemical combinations of atoms (see Chapter 11.3). For example, two hydrogen atoms attached to an oxygen atom form a water molecule, H_2O.

A solid has relatively fixed molecules and a definite shape and volume. In a *crystalline* solid, the molecules are arranged in a particular repeating pattern. This orderly arrangement of molecules is called a *lattice*. ● Figure 5.10(a) illustrates a lattice structure in three dimensions. The molecules (represented by small circles in the figure) are bound to one another by electrical forces.

Upon heating, the molecules gain kinetic energy and vibrate about their equilibrium positions in the lattice. The more heat that is added, the greater the vibrations become. Thus, the molecules move farther apart, and as shown diagrammatically in Fig. 5.10b, the solid expands.

When the melting point of a solid is reached, additional energy (the latent heat of fusion, 80 kcal/kg for water) breaks apart the bonds that hold the molecules in place. As bonds break, holes are produced in the lattice and nearby molecules can move toward the holes. As more and more holes are produced, the lattice becomes significantly distorted and the solid becomes a liquid.

Solids that lack an ordered molecular structure are said to be *amorphous*. Examples are glass and asphalt. They do not melt at definite temperatures but do gradually soften when heated.

● Figure 5.11 illustrates an arrangement of the molecules in a liquid. A liquid has only a slight, if any, lattice structure. Molecules are relatively free to move. A liquid is an arrange-

Figure 5.10 Crystalline Lattice Expansion
(a) In a crystalline solid the molecules are arranged in a particular repeating pattern. This orderly array is called a *lattice*. (b) A schematic diagram of a solid crystal lattice in two dimensions (left). Heating causes the molecules to vibrate with greater amplitudes in the lattice, thereby increasing the volume of the solid (right). The arrows represent the molecular bonds, and the drawing is obviously not to scale.

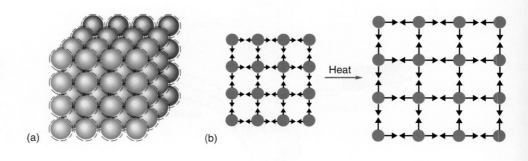

(a)   (b)

*Solids, liquids, and gases are sometimes referred to as states of matter rather than phases of matter. Thermodynamically, however, the *state* of a quantity of matter is a particular condition defined by certain variables such as, for a gas, pressure (*p*), volume (*V*), and temperature (*T*). See Chapter 5.6. Thus, a quantity of gas can have many states. The term *phases of matter* is preferred and is used here to avoid confusion.

ment of molecules that may move and assume the shape of the container. A liquid has a definite volume but no definite shape.

When a liquid is heated, the individual molecules gain kinetic energy. The result is that the liquid expands. When the boiling point is reached, the heat energy is sufficient to break the molecules completely apart from one another. The latent heat of vaporization is the heat per kilogram necessary to free the molecules completely from one another. Because the electrical forces holding the different molecules together are quite strong, the latent heat of vaporization is fairly large (540 kcal/kg for water). When the molecules are completely free from one another, the gaseous phase is reached.

A gas is made up of rapidly moving molecules and assumes the size and shape of its container; a gas has no definite shape or volume. The molecules exert little or no force on one another except when they collide. The distance between molecules in a gas is quite large compared with the size of the molecules (● Fig. 5.12). The pressure, volume, and temperature of a gas are closely related, as will be seen in the next section.

Continued heating of a gas causes the molecules to move more and more rapidly. Eventually, at ultrahigh temperatures the molecules and atoms are ripped apart by collisions with one another. Inside hot stars such as our Sun, atoms and molecules do not exist and another phase of matter, called a plasma, occurs (no relationship to blood plasma). A plasma is a hot gas of electrically charged particles.

Although plasma is not generally listed as a common phase of matter, there are plasmas all around. One of them—a dense plasma that surrounds the Earth in a layer of the atmosphere called the *ionosphere* (Chapter 19.1)—is *literally* all around. Plasmas exist in the paths of lightning strikes, where the air is heated up to 30,000°C (54,000°F), and in neon and fluorescent lamps. Another phase of matter has been reported—a Bose-Einstein condensate. Jagadis Chandra Bose was an Indian physicist who, with Albert Einstein, predicted the theoretical possibility of the existence of this phase in the 1920s.

By extreme cooling of atoms, a condensate is formed that has completely different properties from all other phases of matter. This extreme cooling was first accomplished in 1995, but this new phase of matter isn't very common. Most recently, rubidium atoms had to be cooled to less than 170 billionths of a degree above absolute zero before condensation occurred.

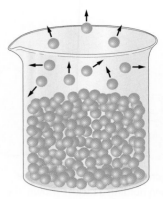

Figure 5.11 Liquids and Molecules This illustration depicts the arrangement of molecules in a liquid. The molecules are packed closely together and form only a slight lattice structure. Some surface molecules may acquire enough energy through collisions to break free of the liquid. This process is called *evaporation*. When a liquid is heated and surface molecules break free from the boiling liquid, it is called *vaporization*.

Did You Learn?

● The three common phases of matter are solid, liquid, and gas.

● A solid has a definite shape and volume. A liquid has a volume but no definite shape. A gas has no definite shape or volume.

5.6 The Kinetic Theory of Gases

Preview Questions

● In the ideal gas law, pressure is directly proportional to what temperature?

● In kinetic theory, how are the temperature and molecular speed of a gas related?

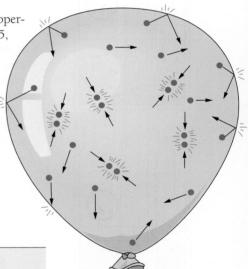

Figure 5.12 Gases and Molecules Gas molecules, on average, are relatively far apart. They move randomly at high speeds, colliding with one another and the walls of the container. The force of their collisions with the container walls causes pressure on the walls.

Unlike solids and liquids, gases take up the entire volume and shape of any enclosing container and are easily compressed. Gas pressure rises as the temperature increases, and gases *diffuse* (travel) slowly into the air when their containers are opened. These observations and others led to a model called the *kinetic theory of gases*.

The **kinetic theory** describes a gas as consisting of molecules moving independently in all directions at high speeds; the higher the temperature, the higher the average speed. The molecules collide with one another and with the walls of the container. The distance between molecules is, on average, large compared to the size of the molecules themselves. Theoretically, an *ideal gas* (or *perfect gas*) is one in which the molecules are point particles

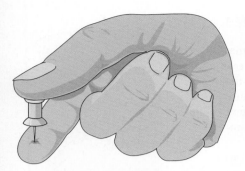

Figure 5.13 Force and Pressure
When holding a tack as shown, the thumb and the finger experience equal forces (Newton's third law). However, at the sharp end of the tack, the area is smaller and the pressure is greater. It can hurt you if you apply enough force. (Ouch!)

(have no size at all) and interact only by collision. A *real gas* behaves somewhat like an ideal gas unless it is under so much pressure that the space between its molecules becomes small relative to the size of the molecules or unless the temperature drops to the point at which attractions among the molecules can be significant.

Each molecular collision with a wall exerts only a tiny force. However, the frequent collisions of billions of gas molecules with the wall exert a steady average force per unit area, or pressure, on the wall. **Pressure** is defined as the force per unit area, $p = F/A$. ● Figure 5.13 illustrates how these three quantities are related.

The SI unit of pressure is newtons per square meter, or N/m^2 (force per area), which is called *a pascal* (Pa) in honor of Blaise Pascal, a seventeenth-century French scientist who was one of the first to develop the concept of pressure.

In the British system, the unit of pressure is pound per inches squared (lb/in^2). A nonstandard unit of pressure used when dealing with gases is the *atmosphere* (atm), where 1 atm is the atmospheric pressure at sea level and 0°C (1.01×10^5 Pa, or 14.7 lb/in^2).

Pressure and Number of Molecules

To see how pressure (p), volume (V), *Kelvin temperature* (T), and number of molecules (N) are related, let's examine the effect of each of V, T, and N on pressure (p) when the other two are held constant.

If the temperature and volume (T and V) are held constant for a gas, then pressure is directly proportional to the number of gas molecules present: $p \propto N$ (● Fig. 5.14). It is logical that the greater the number of molecules, the greater the number of collisions with the sides of the container.

Pressure and Kelvin Temperature

If the volume and number of molecules (V and N) are held constant for a gas, pressure is directly proportional to the Kelvin temperature: $p \propto T$ (● Fig. 5.15). As T increases, the molecules move faster and strike the container walls harder and more frequently. No wonder the pressure increases.

Be aware that many accidental deaths have resulted from lack of knowledge of how pressure builds up in a closed container when it is heated. An explosion can result. A discarded spray can is a good example of such a dangerous container.

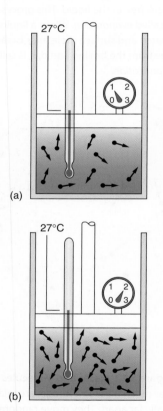

Figure 5.14 Pressure and Number of Molecules
In both containers the temperature and volume are constant. However, in the container in (b), there are twice as many molecules as in the container in (a). This causes the pressure to be twice as great, as indicated on the gauge. (The more molecules, the more collisions and the greater the pressure.)

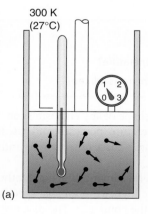
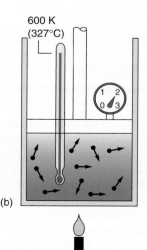

Burner

Figure 5.15 Pressure and Kelvin Temperatures
In both containers the number of molecules and the volume are constant. However, the gas in (b) has been heated to twice the Kelvin temperature of that in (a), that is, to 600 K (327°C) versus 300 K (27°C). This temperature causes the pressure to be twice as great as shown on the gauge (the higher the temperature, the greater the kinetic energy, the more collisions, and the greater the pressure).

Pressure and Volume

If the number of molecules and the Kelvin temperature (N and T) are held constant for a gas, then pressure and volume are found to be inversely proportional: $p \propto 1/V$ (● Fig. 5.16). As the volume decreases, the molecules do not have so far to travel and have a smaller surface area to hit. It is logical that they exert more pressure (more force per unit area) than they did before. This relationship was recognized in 1662 by Robert Boyle (Chapter 11.2) and is called *Boyle's law.*

The Ideal Gas Law

Summarizing the factors affecting the pressure of a confined gas, we find that pressure (p) is directly proportional to the number of molecules (N) and to the Kelvin temperature (T) and inversely proportional to the volume (V); that is,

$$p \propto \frac{NT}{V} \qquad\qquad 5.6$$

This proportion can be used to make a useful equation for a given amount of gas (N is constant). In this case the relationship $p \propto T/V$ applies at any time, and we may write the **ideal gas law** in ratio form as

$$\frac{p_2}{p_1} = \left(\frac{V_1}{V_2}\right)\left(\frac{T_2}{T_1}\right)$$

(N, number of molecules, constant)   5.7

where the subscripts indicate conditions at different times. Examples of some gas law relationships are shown in ● Fig. 5.17.

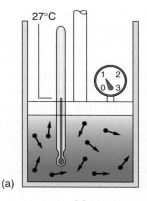

27°C

(a)

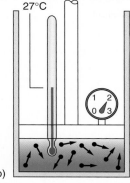

27°C

(b)

Figure 5.16 Pressure and Volume
In both containers the temperature and the number of molecules are constant, but the container in (b) has only half the volume of the container in (a). This difference causes the pressure to be twice as great as shown on the gauge (same average kinetic energy but less distance to travel, on average, in a smaller volume, so more collisions).

EXAMPLE 5.4   Changing Conditions

A closed, rigid container holds a particular amount of gas that behaves like an ideal gas. If the gas is initially at a pressure of 1.80×10^6 Pa at room temperature (20°C), then what will be the pressure when the gas is heated to 40°C? (See Fig. 5.15.)

Solution

Let's work this example in steps for clarity.

Step 1

Given: $V_1 = V_2$ (rigid container)

$p_1 = 1.80 \times 10^6$ Pa (or N/m²)

$T_1 = 20°C + 273 = 293$ K

$T_2 = 40°C + 273 = 313$ K

The temperatures here were converted to kelvins. This step is a *must* when the ideal gas law is used.

Step 2

Wanted: p_2 (new pressure)

Step 3

Equation 5.7 may be used directly. Because $V_1 = V_2$, the volumes cancel, and

$$p_2 = \left(\frac{T_2}{T_1}\right)p_1 = \left(\frac{313\ \text{K}}{293\ \text{K}}\right)(1.80 \times 10^6\ \text{Pa})$$

$$= 1.92 \times 10^6\ \text{Pa}$$

The pressure increases, as would be expected, because $p \propto T$.

Figure 5.17 Up They Go!
(top) In a cold climate with low temperatures, the pressure in the weather balloon is low and is increased by adding more gas, $p \propto N$ (number of molecules), as the penguins watch. (bottom) For a hot-air balloon, the balloon is inflated and a flame is used to heat the air in the balloon, which increases the temperature and results in increased pressure and volume. The increased volume makes the air less dense and buoyant in the surrounding cooler air.

Confidence Exercise 5.4

Suppose the initial pressure of the gas in this example doubled. What would be the final temperature in kelvins in this case?

Some applications of the ideal gas law are given in the **Highlight: Hot Gases: Aerosol Cans and Popcorn.**

Did You Learn?

- The temperature used in the ideal gas law is the Kelvin or absolute temperature.
- In the kinetic theory, the higher the temperature of a gas, the greater the average speed of the molecules.

Highlight   Hot Gases: Aerosol Cans and Popcorn

Suppose a trapped gas (constant volume) is heated. What happens? As the temperature of the gas increases, its molecules become more active and collide with the walls of the container more frequently, and the pressure increases. This process may be seen from the ideal gas law in the form $p \propto NT/V$ (Eq. 5.6), which tells us that with the number of molecules (N) and the volume (V) constant, the pressure (p) will change in direct proportion to the change in Kelvin temperature (T). That is,

$$p \propto T$$

Continued heating and temperature increase may cause the gas pressure to build up to the point at which the container is ruptured or explodes. This situation could be dangerous, and warnings to this effect are printed on aerosol can labels (Fig. 1a).

A more beneficial hot-gas explosion occurs when we make popcorn. When heated, moisture inside the popcorn kernel is vaporized and trapped therein. Continued heating raises the gas (steam) pressure until it becomes great enough to rupture the kernel (Fig. 1b). This "explosion" causes the cornstarch inside to expand up to 40 times its original size. (Butter and salt, anyone?)

Another example of using hot gases appeared in the Highlight: The Automobile Air Bag, in Chapter 3.5. Here, a chemical explosion occurred, and the rapidly expanding hot gas inflated the automobile air bag. Could you analyze this situation in terms of the ideal gas law?

(a)   (b)

Figure 1 Hot Gases
Hot gases can be dangerous in some situations (a), but beneficial in others (b). (See text for description.)

5.7   Thermodynamics

Preview Questions

- What is the basis of the first law of thermodynamics?
- What is the difference between a heat engine and a heat pump?

The term **thermodynamics** means "the dynamics of heat," and its study includes the production of heat, the flow of heat, and the conversion of heat to work. Heat energy is used either directly or indirectly to do most of the work that is performed in everyday life. The operation of heat engines, such as internal-combustion engines, is based on the laws of thermodynamics. These laws are important because of the relationships among heat energy, work, and the directions in which thermodynamic processes may occur.

First Law of Thermodynamics

Because one aspect of thermodynamics is concerned with heat energy transfer, accounting for the energy involved in a thermodynamic process is important. This accounting is done by the principle of the conservation of energy, which states that energy can be neither created nor destroyed. The first law of thermodynamics is simply the principle of conservation of energy applied to thermodynamic processes.

Suppose some heat (H) is added to a system. Where does it go? One possibility is that it goes into increasing the system's internal energy (ΔE_i). Another possibility is that it results in work (W) being done by the system. Or both possibilities could occur. Thus, heat added to a closed system goes into the internal energy of the system, into doing work, or both.

For example, consider heating an inflated balloon. As heat is added to the system (the balloon and the air inside), the temperature increases and the system expands. The temperature of the air inside the balloon increases because some of the heat goes into the internal energy of the air. The gas does work in expanding the balloon (work done by the system).

The **first law of thermodynamics**, which expresses this and other such energy balances, may be written in general as follows:

heat added to (or removed from) a system	=	change in internal energy of the system	+	work done by (or on) the system	

or in equation form

$$H = \Delta E_i + W \qquad\qquad 5.8$$

For this equation, a positive value of heat ($+H$) means that heat is *added to* the system, and a positive value of work ($+W$) means that work is *done by* the system (as in the case of the heated balloon). Negative values indicate the opposite conditions.

Heat Engines

Another good example of the first law is the heat engine. A **heat engine** is a device that converts heat into work. Many types of heat engines exist: gasoline engines on lawn mowers and in cars, diesel engines in trucks, and steam engines in old-time locomotives. They all operate on the same principle. Heat input (for example, from the combustion of fuel) goes into doing useful work, but some of the input energy is lost or wasted.

Thermodynamics is concerned not with the components of an engine, but rather with its general operation. A heat engine may be represented schematically as illustrated in ● Fig. 5.18.

A heat engine operates between a high-temperature reservoir and a low-temperature reservoir. These reservoirs are systems from which heat can be readily absorbed and to which heat can be readily expelled. In the process, the engine uses some of the input energy to do work. Notice that the widths of the heat and work paths in the figure are in keeping with the conservation of energy. Actual heat engines usually operate in cycles.

Second Law of Thermodynamics

The first law of thermodynamics is concerned with the conservation of energy. As long as the energy check sheet is balanced, the first law is satisfied. Suppose a hot body at 100°C and a colder body at room temperature (20°C) are placed in contact and heat flows from the colder body to the hotter body. The energy is easily accounted for and the first law is satisfied. but something is physically wrong. Heat does not spontaneously flow from a colder body to a hotter body (● Fig. 5.19). That would be like

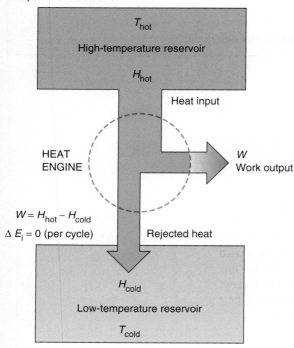

Figure 5.18 Schematic Diagram of a Heat Engine
A heat engine takes heat, H_{hot} from a high-temperature reservoir, converts some into useful work, W, and rejects the remainder, H_{cold}, to a low-temperature reservoir.

T_{hot}

High-temperature reservoir

H_{hot}

Heat input

HEAT ENGINE

W
Work output

$W = H_{hot} - H_{cold}$
$\Delta E_i = 0$ (per cycle)

Rejected heat

H_{cold}

Low-temperature reservoir

T_{cold}

heat flowing up a "temperature hill," a situation analogous to a ball spontaneously rolling *up* a hill.

Something more than the first law is needed to describe a thermodynamic process. As you might have guessed, it is the direction of the process or whether or not something actually occurs. The **second law of thermodynamics** specifies what can and what cannot happen thermodynamically. This law can be stated in several ways, depending on the situation. A common statement of the second law as applied to our preceding example of heat flow is as follows:

> **It is impossible for heat to flow spontaneously from a colder body to a hotter body.**

Another statement of the second law applies to heat engines. Suppose a heat engine operated in such a way that *all* the heat input was converted into work. Such an engine doesn't violate the first law, but it would have a thermal efficiency of 100%, which has never been observed. Then, the second law as applied to heat engines may be stated as follows:

> **No heat engine operating in a cycle can convert thermal energy completely into work.**

Third Law of Thermodynamics

Another law is associated with absolute zero (Chapter 5.1). Absolute zero (0 K) is the lower limit of temperature. The temperature of absolute zero cannot be attained physically because to do so would require virtually all the heat to be taken from an object. Therefore,

> **It is impossible to attain a temperature of absolute zero.**

This law is sometimes called the **third law of thermodynamics**.

Scientists try to get close to absolute zero. In one attempt, the temperature of a sodium gas was cooled to below 1 nK (nanokelvin, or one-billionth, 10^{-9}, of a kelvin), setting a record.

The third law has still never been violated experimentally. It becomes more difficult to lower the temperature of a material (to pump heat from it) the closer the temperature gets to absolute zero. The difficulty increases with each step to the point at which an infinite amount of work would be required to reach the very bottom of the temperature scale.

Conceptual Question and Answer

Common Descriptions

Q. Do the following statements have any general association with the laws of thermodynamics? (a) You can't get something for nothing. (b) You can't even break even. (c) You can't sink that low.

A. (a) First law. Energy cannot be created (or destroyed). (b) Second law. Thermal energy cannot convert completely into work. (c) Third law. Absolute zero cannot be reached.

Heat Pumps

The second law of thermodynamics states that heat will not flow *spontaneously* from a colder body to a hotter body, or up a "temperature hill," so to speak. The analogy of a ball spontaneously rolling up a hill was used. Of course, we can get a ball to roll up a hill by applying a force and doing work on it. Similarly, heat will flow up the "temperature hill" when work is done. This is the principle of a heat pump.

A **heat pump** is a device that uses work input to transfer heat from a low-temperature reservoir to a high-temperature reservoir (● Fig. 5.20). Work input is required to "pump" heat from a low-temperature reservoir to a high-temperature reservoir. Theoretically, a heat pump is the reverse of a heat engine.

A refrigerator is an example of a heat pump. Heat is transferred from the inside volume of a refrigerator to the outside by the compressor doing work on a gas (by the expenditure of electrical energy). The heat is transferred to the room (high-temperature reservoir). Similarly, an automobile air conditioner transfers heat from the inside of a car to the outside.

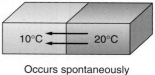

Occurs spontaneously

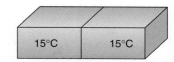

Thermal equilibrium at a later time

(a)

Does *not* occur spontaneously

(b)

Figure 5.19 Heat Flow
(a) When objects are in thermal contact, heat flows spontaneously from a hotter object to a colder object until both objects are at the same temperature, or come to thermal equilibrium. (b) Heat never flows spontaneously from a colder object to a hotter one. That is, a cold object never spontaneously gets colder when placed in thermal contact with a warm object.

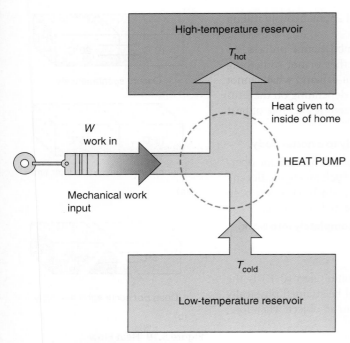

Figure 5.20 Schematic Diagram of a Heat Pump
Work input is necessary to pump heat from a low-temperature reservoir to a high-temperature reservoir—for example, a refrigerator. The inside volume of the refrigerator (low-temperature reservoir) is kept cool by pumping heat into the room (high-temperature reservoir). The pumping requires work input. Notice that the widths of the heat and work paths are in keeping with the conservation of energy.

The "heat pumps" used for home heating and cooling are aptly named. In summer they operate as air conditioners by pumping air from the inside (low-temperature reservoir) to the outside (high-temperature reservoir). In winter heat is extracted from the outside air or from water in a reservoir such as a well or a system of underground coils (low-temperature reservoir) and pumped inside the home (high-temperature reservoir) for heating. In the United States, heat pumps are used extensively in the South where the climate is mild. On very cold days, an auxiliary heating unit in the heat pump (generally an electric heater) is used to supply extra heat when needed.

A heat pump is generally more expensive than a regular furnace, but it has long-term advantages. For example, it has no associated fuel costs (other than the cost of the electricity to supply the work input) because it takes heat from the air.

Entropy

You may have heard the term *entropy* and wondered what it means. **Entropy** is a mathematical quantity; thermodynamically speaking, its change tells whether or not a process can take place naturally. Hence, entropy is associated with the second law.

In terms of entropy, the second law of thermodynamics can be stated as follows:

The entropy of an isolated system never decreases.

To facilitate understanding this idea, entropy is sometimes expressed as a measure of the disorder of a system. When heat is added to an object, its entropy increases because the added energy increases the disordered motion of the molecules. As a natural process takes place, the disorder increases. For example, when a solid melts, its molecules are freer to move in a random motion in the liquid phase than in the solid phase. Similarly, when evaporation takes place, the result is greater disorder and increased entropy.

Systems that are left to themselves (isolated systems) tend to become more and more disordered, but never the reverse. By analogy, a student's dormitory room or room at home naturally becomes disordered, never the reverse. Of course, the room can be cleaned and items put in order, and in this case the entropy *of the room system* decreases. To put things back in order, someone must expend energy resulting in a greater overall entropy increase than the room's entropy decrease. Another statement of the second law is:

The total entropy of the universe increases in every natural process.

This statement has long-term implications. Heat naturally flows from a region of higher temperature to one of lower temperature. In terms of order, heat energy is more "orderly" when it is concentrated. When transferred naturally to a region of lower temperature, it is "spread out" or more "disorderly," and the entropy increases. Hence, the universe—the stars and the galaxies—eventually should cool down to a final common temperature when the entropy of the universe has reached a maximum. This possible fate, billions of years from now, is sometimes referred to as the "heat death" of the universe.

Did You Learn?

- The first law of thermodynamics is the principle of conservation of energy applied to thermodynamic processes.

- A heat engine converts heat to work. A heat pump uses work to transfer heat from a low-temperature reservoir to a high-temperature reservoir. (A refrigerator is an example.)

KEY TERMS

1. temperature (5.1)
2. Fahrenheit scale
3. Celsius scale
4. Kelvin scale
5. kelvin
6. heat (5.2)
7. calorie
8. kilocalorie
9. Btu

10. specific heat (5.3)
11. latent heat
12. conduction (5.4)
13. convection
14. radiation
15. phases of matter (5.5)
16. kinetic theory (5.6)
17. pressure
18. ideal gas law

19. thermodynamics (5.7)
20. first law of thermodynamics
21. heat engine
22. second law of thermodynamics
23. third law of thermodynamics
24. heat pump
25. entropy

MATCHING

For each of the following items, fill in the number of the appropriate Key Word from the preceding list. Compare your answers with those at the back of the book.

a. _____ Water has one of the highest
b. _____ Food Calorie
c. _____ Transfer of heat by electromagnetic waves
d. _____ Can never attain absolute zero
e. _____ Transfer of heat by molecular collisions
f. _____ A measure of average molecular kinetic energy
g. _____ Solid, liquid, and gas
h. _____ Never decreases in an isolated system
i. _____ Scale based on absolute zero
j. _____ Heat associated with a phase change
k. _____ Common temperature scale in the United States
l. _____ Describes gases in terms of moving molecules
m. _____ Raises the temperature of one gram of water one Celsius degree

n. _____ Same size as a degree Celsius
o. _____ Transfer of heat by mass movement
p. _____ Thermodynamic conservation of energy
q. _____ $p \propto NT/V$
r. _____ Common temperature scale worldwide
s. _____ Uses work to transfer heat to a high-temperature reservoir
t. _____ Raises the temperature of one pound of water one Fahrenheit degree
u. _____ Force per unit area
v. _____ Tells what can and what cannot happen thermodynamically
w. _____ Energy transferred because of temperature difference
x. _____ The dynamics of heat
y. _____ Converts heat into work

MULTIPLE CHOICE

Compare your answers with those at the back of the book.

1. Temperature is _____ . (5.1)
   (a) a measure of heat
   (b) a relative measure of hotness and coldness
   (c) internal energy in transit
   (d) both (b) and (c)

2. Which unit of the following is smaller? (5.2)
   (a) a degree Fahrenheit
   (b) a kelvin
   (c) a degree Celsius

3. Which of the following is the largest unit of heat energy? (5.2)
   (a) kilocalorie   (b) calorie   (c) joule   (d) Btu

4. The specific heat of substance A is 10 times that of substance B. If equal amounts of heat are added to equal masses of the substances, then the temperature increase of substance A would be _____ . (5.3)
   (a) the same as that of B   (b) 10 times that of B
   (c) one-tenth that of B   (d) none of the preceding

5. Which of the following methods of heat transfer generally involves mass movement? (5.4)
   (a) conduction   (b) convection   (c) radiation

6. The heat we get from the Sun is transferred through space by which process? (5.4)
   (a) conduction   (b) convection
   (c) radiation   (d) all of the preceding

7. In which of the following is intermolecular bonding greatest? (5.5)
   (a) solids   (b) liquids   (c) gases

8. Which of the following has a definite volume but no definite shape? (5.5)
   (a) solid   (b) liquid   (c) gas   (d) plasma

9. Pressure is defined as (5.6)
   (a) force   (b) force times area
   (c) area divided by force   (d) force divided by area

10. When we use the ideal gas law, the temperature must be in which of the following units? (5.6)
    (a) °C   (b) °F   (c) K

11. When heat is added to a system, it goes into which of the following? (5.7)
    (a) doing work only
    (b) adding to the internal energy only
    (c) doing work, increasing the internal energy, or both

12. The direction of a natural process is indicated by which of the following? (5.7)
    (a) conservation of energy
    (b) change in entropy
    (c) thermal efficiency
    (d) specific heat

FILL IN THE BLANK

Compare your answers with those at the back of the book.

1. When a bimetallic strip is heated, it bends toward the metal with the ___ thermal expansion. (5.1)

2. A ___ difference is necessary for net heat transfer. (5.2)

3. The food Calorie is equal to ___ calories. (5.2)

4. From the equation $H = mc\,\Delta T$, it can be seen that the SI units of specific heat are ___. (5.3)

5. The latent heat of vaporization for water is almost ___ times as great as its latent heat of fusion. (5.3)

6. The boiling point of water may be increased by increasing ___. (5.3)

7. Electrons contribute significantly to the ___ heat transfer process in metals. (5.4)

8. The ___ phase of matter has no definite shape, and no definite volume. (5.4)

9. Pressure is defined as force per ___. (5.5)

10. In the ideal gas law, pressure is ___ proportional to volume. (5.5)

11. The second law of thermodynamics essentially gives the ___ of a process. (5.7)

12. The household refrigerator is a heat ___. (5.7)

SHORT ANSWER

5.1 Temperature

1. When the temperature changes during the day, which scale, Fahrenheit or Celsius, will have the greater degree change?

2. On which temperature scale would a temperature change of 10 degrees be the largest?

3. The two common liquids used in liquid-in-glass thermometers are alcohol (ethanol) and mercury, which have melting points and boiling points of −114°C, 79°C and −39°C, 357°C, respectively. Would either one of these thermometers be better for low-temperature or high-temperature measurements?

4. An older type of thermostat used in furnace and heat pump control is shown in ● Fig. 5.21. The glass vial tilts back and forth so that electrical contacts are made via the mercury (an electrically conducting liquid metal), and the furnace or heat pump is turned off and on. Explain why the vial tilts back and forth. (Newer thermostats are electronic.)

5.2 Heat

5. Heat may be thought of as the "middleman" of energy. Why?

6. When one drinking glass is stuck inside another, an old trick to unstick them is to put water in one of them and run water of a different temperature on the outside of the other. Which water should be hot, and which water should be cold?

7. Heat always flows from a high-temperature body in contact with one with a low temperature. Does heat always flow from a body with more internal energy to one with less internal energy? (*Hint*: Think about dropping a hot BB into a tub of water.)

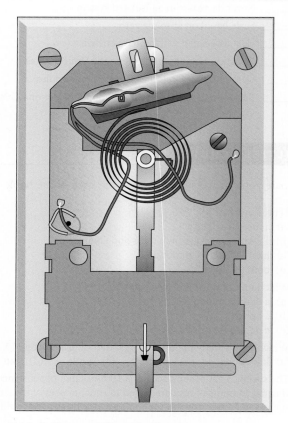

Figure 5.21 An Exposed View of a Thermostat
See Short-Answer Question 4.

Figure 5.22 A Cold Warning
See Short-Answer Question 15.

Figure 5.23 Keeping Warm
See Short-Answer Question 16.

5.3 Specific Heat and Latent Heat

8. What does the specific heat of a substance tell you when you compare it with the specific heat of another substance?

9. When eating a piece of hot apple pie, you may find that the crust is only warm but the apple filling burns your mouth. Why?

10. If equal amounts of heat are added to two containers of water and the resultant temperature change of the water in one container is twice that of the water in the other container, then what can you say about the quantities of water in the containers?

11. When you exhale outdoors on a cold day, you can "see your breath." Why?

12. Compare the SI units of specific heat and latent heat and explain any differences.

5.4 Heat Transfer

13. Give two examples each of good thermal conductors and good thermal insulators. In general, what makes a substance a conductor or an insulator?

14. Which would feel colder on your bare feet, a tile floor or a wooden floor (at the same temperature)? (*Hint*: See Table 5.3.)

15. Highway road signs give warnings, as shown in ● Fig. 5.22. Why would a bridge freeze or ice before the road?

16. Thermal underwear is made to fit loosely. (● Fig. 5.23). What is the purpose of this?

5.5 Phases of Matter

17. What determines the phase of a substance?

18. Give descriptions of a solid, a liquid, and a gas in terms of shape and volume.

19. Name the processes of going (a) from a solid to a gas and (b) from a gas to a solid.

5.6 The Kinetic Theory of Gases

20. How does the kinetic theory describe a gas?

21. What is meant by an *ideal* gas?

22. When does the behavior of a real gas approximate that of an ideal gas?

23. On the molecular level, what causes gas pressure?

24. In terms of kinetic theory, explain why a basketball stays inflated.

5.7 Thermodynamics

25. An inflated balloon is put in a refrigerator, and it shrinks. How does the first law of thermodynamics apply to this case?

26. What does the first law of thermodynamics tell you about a thermodynamic process? What does the second law tell you?

27. Explain the following statements in terms of the laws of thermodynamics.
    (a) Energy can be neither created nor destroyed.
    (b) Entropy can be created but not destroyed.

28. Why can't entropy be destroyed?

29. What can be said about the total entropy of the universe? Why is it true?

30. Can absolute zero be attained? Explain.

31. According to the ideal gas law, what would be the pressure of a gas at absolute zero?

VISUAL CONNECTION

Visualize the connections and give answers for the blanks. Compare your answers with those at the back of the book.

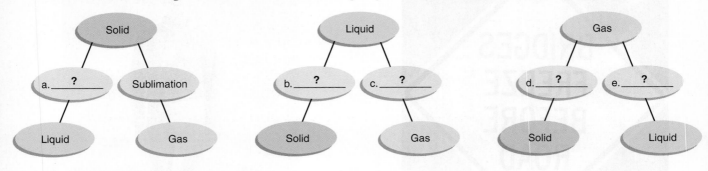

APPLYING YOUR KNOWLEDGE

1. When someone leaves an outside door open on a cold, still day, it is often said that the person is letting in cold air. If so, how? (*Hint*: Think of convection.)

2. Why are steam burns more severe than hot water burns? (Consider the same mass of steam and hot water.)

3. Your automobile has a "radiator" as part of its cooling system. Is radiation the only method of heat transfer in this system? Explain.

4. When a thermometer is inserted into hot water, the mercury or alcohol is sometimes observed to fall slightly before it rises. Why?

5. Could the Earth be considered a heat engine? Explain.

6. When you freeze ice cubes in a tray, there is a decrease in entropy because there is more order in the crystalline lattice of the ice than in the water you started with. Are you violating the second law? Explain.

7. In the Conceptual Question and Answer in Chapter 5.1, an approximation for Celsius to Fahrenheit conversion was given: $T_F \sim 2T_C + 30$. What might be an approximation equation for Fahrenheit to Celsius conversion?

IMPORTANT EQUATIONS

Kelvin–Celsius Conversion:

$$T_K = T_C + 273 \tag{5.1}$$

Fahrenheit–Celsius Conversion:

$$T_F = \tfrac{9}{5}T_C + 32 \qquad \text{(or } T_F = 1.8T_C + 32) \tag{5.2a}$$

$$T_C = \tfrac{9}{5}(T_F - 32) \qquad [\text{or } T_C = (T_F - 32)/1.8] \tag{5.2b}$$

Celsius to Fahrenheit: $T_C + 40$, multiply by 9/5, subtract 40.
Fahrenheit to Celsius: $T_F + 40$, multiply by 5/9, subtract 40.

(Remember: add, multiply, subtract.)

Specific Heat: $H = mc\,\Delta T$ $\qquad$ (5.3)

$$c_{\text{water}} = 1.00 \text{ kcal/kg} \cdot {}^{\circ}\text{C}$$

$$c_{\text{ice}} = c_{\text{steam}} = 0.50 \text{ kcal/kg} \cdot {}^{\circ}\text{C}$$

Latent Heat: $H = mL$ $\qquad$ (5.4–5.5)

$$\text{(water) } L_f = 80 \text{ kcal/kg}$$

$$L_v = 540 \text{ kcal/kg}$$

Changing Conditions for a Gas (Ideal Gas Law):

$$p \propto \frac{NT}{V} \tag{5.6}$$

Ideal Gas Law:

$$\frac{p_2}{p_1} = \left(\frac{V_1}{V_2}\right)\left(\frac{T_2}{T_1}\right) \tag{5.7}$$

First Law of Thermodynamics: $H = \Delta E_i + W$ $\qquad$ (5.8)

EXERCISES

(Assume temperatures in the Exercises to be exact numbers.)

5.1 Temperature

1. While in Europe, a tourist hears on the radio that the temperature that day will reach a high of 17°C. What is this temperature on the Fahrenheit scale?

Answer: 63°F

2. Which is the lower temperature: (a) 245°C or 245°F? (b) 200°C or 375°F?

3. Normal room temperature is about 68°F. What is the equivalent temperature on the Celsius scale?

Answer: 20°C

4. A person running a fever has a temperature of 39.4°C. What is this temperature on the Fahrenheit scale?

5. Researchers in the Antarctic measure the temperature to be −40°F. What is this temperature (a) on the Celsius scale? (b) on the Kelvin scale?

Answer: (a) −40°C (b) 233 K

6. The temperature of outer space is about 3 K. What is this temperature on (a) the Celsius scale? (b) on the Fahrenheit scale?

5.2 Heat

7. A college student produces about 100 kcal of heat per hour on the average. What is the rate of energy production in joules?

Answer: 420 kJ

8. How many kilocalories of heat does an expenditure of 250 kJ produce?

9. A pound of body fat stores an amount of chemical energy equivalent to 3500 Cal. When sleeping, the average adult burns or expends about 0.45 Cal/h for every pound of body weight. How many Calories would a 150-lb person burn during 8 hours of sleep?

Answer: 540 Cal (kcal)

10. How long would the person have to sleep continuously to lose 1 lb of body fat?

11. On a brisk walk, a person burns about 325 Cal/h. At this rate, how many hours of brisk walking would it take to lose 1 lb of body fat? (See Exercise 9.)

Answer: 10.8 h

12. If the brisk walk were done at 4.0 mi/h, how far would a person have to walk to burn off 1 lb of body fat?

5.3 Specific Heat and Latent Heat

13. How much heat in kcal must be added to 0.50 kg of water at room temperature (20°C) to raise its temperature to 30°C?

Answer: 5.0 kcal

14. How much heat in joules is needed to raise the temperature of 1.0 L of water from 0°C to 100°C? (*Hint:* Recall the original definition of the liter.)

15. (a) How much energy is necessary to heat 1.0 kg of water from room temperature (20°C) to its boiling point? (Assume no energy loss.)

(b) If electrical energy were used, how much would it cost at 12¢ per kWh?

Answer: (a) 80 kcal (b) 1.1¢

16. Equal amounts of heat are added to equal masses of aluminum and copper at the same initial temperature. Which metal will have the higher final temperature, and how much greater will that temperature change be than the temperature change of the other metal?

17. How much heat is necessary to change 500 g of ice at −10°C to water at 20°C?

Answer: 52.5 kcal

18. A quantity of steam (300 g) at 110°C is condensed, and the resulting water is frozen into ice at 0°C. How much heat was removed?

5.6 The Kinetic Theory of Gases

19. A sample of neon gas has its volume quadrupled and its temperature held constant. What will be the new pressure relative to the initial pressure?

Answer: $p_2 = p_1/4$

20. A fire breaks out and increases the Kelvin temperature of a cylinder of compressed gas by a factor of 1.2. What is the final pressure of the gas relative to its initial pressure?

21. A cylinder of gas is at room temperature (20°C). The air conditioner breaks down, and the temperature rises to 40°C. What is the new pressure of the gas relative to its initial pressure?

Answer: $p_2 = 1.07p_1$

22. A cylinder of gas at room temperature has a pressure p_1. To what temperature in degrees Celsius would the temperature have to be increased for the pressure to be $1.5p_1$?

23. A quantity of gas in a piston cylinder has a volume of 0.500 m³ and a pressure of 200 Pa. The piston compresses the gas to 0.150 m³ in an isothermal (constant-temperature) process. What is the final pressure of the gas?

Answer: 667 Pa

24. If the gas in Exercise 23 is initially at room temperature (20°C) and is heated in an isobaric (constant-pressure) process, then what will be the temperature of the gas in degrees Celsius when it has expanded to a volume of 0.700 m³?

ON THE WEB

1. To the Boiling Point

What happens to the temperature of water when it is boiling? Find out! Follow the recommended links on the student website at **www.cengagebrain.com/shop/ISBN/1133104096** to carry out an experiment in latent heat. You must be careful to take necessary safety precautions when performing this experiment.

2. Thermodynamic Equilibrium

Perform a series of thermodynamic experiments to give you some hands-on experience. How can you use this information in your daily life? How could you use this information to design a product to sell to the consuming public? What would that product be, and how would it work? Follow the recommended links on the student website at **www.cengagebrain.com/shop/ISBN/1133104096** to get started.

Waves and Sound

*You can't just cut out
the perfect wave and
take it home with you.
It's constantly moving
all the time.*

•

Jimi Hendrix
(1942–1970)

Ride the wave! Surfers ride the
wave of a breaking surf. >

Rick Doyle/CORBIS

T he word *wave* brings to mind different things for different people. Probably most would associate it with ocean waves (a big one is shown in the
opening photo) or their smaller relatives, those on the surface of a lake
or pond. Others might think of sound waves or light waves. Music is made up of
sound waves, and we see beautiful rainbows because of light waves.

Indeed, waves are all around us, and understanding their properties is essen-
tial to describing our physical environment. Our eyes and ears are the two main
wave-detecting devices that link us to our world (Chapter 1.3). This and the next
chapter explore the important roles that waves play in our lives.

Chapter Outline

6.1 Waves and Energy Propagation

Preview Questions

● What causes waves, and how and what do they propagate?

● Is matter propagated by waves?

PHYSICS FACTS *cont.*

▶ The visible part of the outer ear is called the *pinna* or ear flap. Many animals move the ear flap to focus their hearing in a certain direction. Humans cannot do so, although some humans can wiggle their ears.

Since beginning the study of energy, much has been said about its forms, its relationship to work, and its conservation. It was learned that heat is energy in transit because of a temperature difference, but the transfer and *propagation* of energy in matter are not limited to temperature differences. In many common cases such as a disturbance in water, energy is propagated in media as **waves**.

For example, when a stone is thrown into a still pond or when you dive into a swimming pool, there is a disturbance. In such instances, water waves propagate outward, propagating energy from the disturbance source (● Fig. 6.1). When you are swimming in a lake and a high-speed boat goes by a short distance away, waves propagate the energy of the boat's disturbance of the water toward you, and when they hit you, it is clear that the waves have energy. Wind can also generate wave disturbances on a lake or pond. This transfer of energy is called *wave motion*. As a wave propagates outward from a disturbance, energy is transmitted from one particle to another in the medium.

In general, only energy, not matter, is transferred by waves. When you are fishing and water waves come toward and reach your floating bobber, the bobber bobs up and down but generally stays in the same place (unless there is a current). Only energy is propagated, not matter (the water or the bobber).

A similar situation can occur in a solid. For example, during an earthquake a disturbance takes place because of a slippage along a fault, and the energy is transmitted through the Earth by waves (Chapter 21.5). Again, the disturbance is a transfer of energy, not of matter. On a more local scale, suppose someone is playing loud music in an adjacent closed room. You can hear sound, so wave energy must propagate through the wall.

We know that waves propagate in gases, with air being the most common example. Disturbances give rise to sound waves such as an explosion, which produces a shock wave, or a vibrating guitar string, which produces continuous waves (● Fig. 6.2). Another common source of sound waves—a whistle—is also shown in Fig. 6.2.

Richard Megna/Fundamental Photographs, NYC

Figure 6.1 Waves and Energy
Waves propagate energy outward from disturbances.

Steel or nylon string

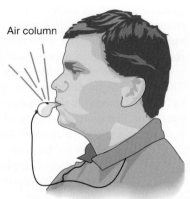

Air column

Figure 6.2 Vibrations
Examples of vibrational disturbances that produce sound waves. The vibrations of guitar strings produce waves that are propagated in the air. Blowing a whistle disturbs the small ball inside the whistle, causing it to vibrate and produce sound waves.

However, some waves can propagate without a medium (in vacuum), such as light from the Sun and radio waves from space probes. If light needed a medium to propagate, then the Earth would receive no sunlight.

After discussing the general properties of waves in the next section, light waves and sound waves will be considered in more detail.

Did You Learn?

- From an originating disturbance, energy is transmitted from one particle to another in a medium as the wave propagates outward.

- In general, energy is propagated by waves, not matter.

6.2   Wave Properties

Preview Questions

- What is the distinguishing difference between longitudinal and transverse waves?
- How are wave frequency and period related, and what is the unit of frequency?

A disturbance that generates a wave may be a simple pulse or shock, such as the clapping of hands or a book hitting the floor. A disturbance may also be periodic, repeated again and again at regular intervals. A vibrating guitar string or a whistle sets up periodic waves, and the waves are continuous as long as the disturbances are too (Fig. 6.2).

In general, waves may be classified as *longitudinal* or *transverse* based on particle motion and wave direction. In a **longitudinal wave**, the particle motion and the wave velocity are parallel to each other. For example, consider a stretched spring, as illustrated in ● Fig. 6.3. When several coils at one end are compressed and released, the disturbance is propagated along the length of the spring with a certain wave velocity. Notice that the displacements of the spring "particles" and the wave velocity vector are parallel to each other. The directions of the "particle" oscillations can be seen by tying a small piece of ribbon to the spring. The ribbon will oscillate similarly to the way the particles of the spring oscillate.

The single disturbance in the spring is an example of a longitudinal wave pulse. Periodic longitudinal waves are common. An example of a longitudinal wave is sound, as will be seen shortly. In a **transverse wave**, the particle motion is perpendicular to the direction of the wave velocity. A transverse wave may be generated by shaking one end of a stretched cord up and down or side to side (● Fig. 6.4). Notice how the cord "particles" oscillate perpendicularly (at an angle of 90°) to the direction of the wave velocity vector. The particle motion may again be demonstrated by tying a small piece of ribbon to the cord. Another example of a transverse wave is light. Recall that light and other such waves can propagate through the vacuum of space without a medium.

Certain wave characteristics are used in describing periodic wave motion (● Fig. 6.5). The wave velocity describes the speed and direction of the wave motion. The **wavelength** (λ, Greek lambda) is the distance from any point on the wave to the adjacent point with similar oscillation: the distance of one complete "wave," or where it starts to repeat itself. For example, the wavelength distance may be measured from one wave crest to an adjacent crest (or from one wave trough to the next wave trough).

The wave **amplitude** (A) is the maximum displacement of any part of the wave (or wave particle) from its equilibrium position. The energy transmitted by a wave is directly proportional to the square of its amplitude (A^2). However, the amplitude does not affect the wave speed. (See amplitude in Fig. 6.5.)

The oscillations of a wave may be characterized in terms of frequency. The wave **frequency** (f) is the number of oscillations or cycles that occur

Figure 6.3 Longitudinal Wave
In a longitudinal wave, as illustrated here for a stretched spring, the wave velocity, or direction of the wave propagation, is parallel to the (spring) particle displacements (back and forth). There are regions of compression and stretching (rarefaction) in the spring.

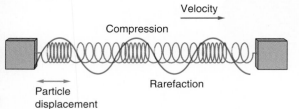

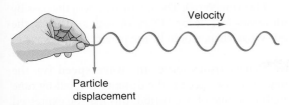

Figure 6.4 Transverse Wave
In a transverse wave as illustrated here for a stretched cord, the wave velocity (vector), or the direction of the wave propagation, is perpendicular to the (cord) particle displacements (up and down).

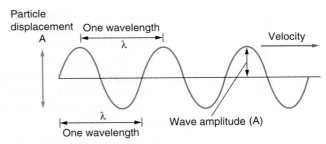

Figure 6.5 Wave Description
Some terms used to describe wave characteristics. (See text for description.)

during a given period of time, usually one second. Frequency is the number of cycles per second, but this unit is given the name **hertz** (Hz).* One hertz is one cycle per second. (In standard units, Hz = 1/s. The unitless "cycle" is carried along for descriptive convenience.)

For example, as illustrated in ● Fig. 6.6a, if four complete wavelengths pass a given point in 1 second, then the frequency of the wave is four cycles per second, or 4 Hz. The more "wiggles" or wavelengths per time period, the greater the frequency. A wave with a frequency of 8 Hz is illustrated in Fig. 6.6b.

There is another quantity used to characterize a wave. The wave **period** (T) is the time it takes the wave to travel a distance of one wavelength (Fig. 6.6a). Looking at the dashed-line portion, it can be seen that a particle in the medium makes one complete oscillation in a time of one period.

The frequency and period are inversely proportional. In equation form

$$\text{frequency} = \frac{1}{\text{period}}$$

or

$$f = \frac{1}{T}$$

6.1

Examine the units. The frequency is given in cycles per second, and the period in seconds per cycle.

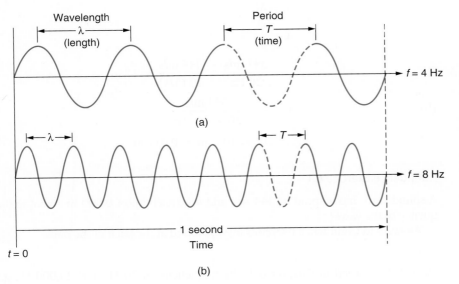

(a)

(b)

Figure 6.6 Wave Comparison
Wave (a) has a frequency of 4 Hz, which means that 4 wavelengths pass by a point in 1 second. With a wave of 8 Hz, there would be 8 wavelengths passing by in 1 second. Hence, the wavelength of wave (a) is twice as long as the wavelength of wave (b). The period (T) is the time it takes one wavelength to pass by, so the period of wave (a) is also twice as long as that of wave (b). The relationship between the frequency and the period is $f = 1/T$.

*In honor of Heinrich Hertz (1857–1894), a German scientist and an early investigator of electromagnetic waves.

Suppose a wave has a frequency of $f = 4$ Hz (Fig. 6.6a). Then, four wavelengths pass by a point in 1 second, and one wavelength passes in $\frac{1}{4}$ second ($T = 1/f = \frac{1}{4}$ s). That is, the period, or time for one cycle, is $\frac{1}{4}$ second. What, then, would be the period for the wave in Fig. 6.6b? (Right, $\frac{1}{8}$ s.)

Another simple relationship for wave characteristics relates the **wave speed** (v), the wavelength, and the period (or frequency). Because speed is the distance divided by time and because a wave moves one wavelength in a time of one period, this may be expressed in equation form as

$$\text{wave speed} = \frac{\text{wavelength}}{\text{period}}$$

$$v = \frac{\lambda}{T} \qquad\qquad 6.2$$

or, by Eq. 6.1 ($f = 1/T$),

$$\text{wave speed} = \text{wavelength} \times \text{frequency}$$
$$v = \lambda f \qquad\qquad 6.3$$

EXAMPLE 6.1   Calculating Wavelengths

Consider sound waves with a speed of 344 m/s and frequencies of (a) 20 Hz and (b) 20 kHz. Find the wavelength of each of these sound waves.

Solution

Step 1

Given: $v = 344$ m/s

(a) $f = 20$ Hz
(b) $f = 20$ kHz $= 20 \times 10^3$ Hz

(Note that kHz was converted to Hz, the standard unit, and recall that Hz $= 1/$s.)

Step 2

Wanted: λ (wavelength)

Step 3

(a) Rearrange Eq. 6.3 and solve for λ:

$$v = \lambda f$$

$$\lambda = \frac{v}{f}$$

$$= \frac{344 \text{ m/s}}{20 \text{ Hz}} = \frac{344 \text{ m/s}}{20 \ (1/s)} = 17 \text{ m}$$

(b)
$$\lambda = \frac{v}{f} = \frac{344 \text{ m/s}}{20 \times 10^3 \text{ Hz}}$$

$$= 17 \times 10^{-3} \text{ m} = 0.017 \text{ m}$$

Confidence Exercise 6.1

A sound wave has a speed of 344 m/s and a wavelength of 0.500 m. What is the frequency of the wave?

Answers to Confidence Exercises may be found at the back of the book.

As will be learned in Chapter 6.4, the frequencies of 20 Hz and 20,000 Hz given in Example 6.1 define the general range of audible sound wave frequencies. Thus, the wavelengths of audible sound cover the range from about 1.7 cm for the highest-frequency sound to about 17 m for the lowest-frequency sound. In British units sound waves range from wavelengths of approximately $\frac{1}{2}$ in. up to about 50 ft.

Did You Learn?

● Longitudinal and transverse waves are distinguished in terms of particle motion and wave velocity. They are parallel in longitudinal waves and perpendicular (90°) in transverse waves.

● The frequency and period are inversely related ($f = 1/T$), and the unit of frequency is 1/s or hertz (Hz).

6.3 Light Waves

Preview Questions

● How is the electromagnetic spectrum arranged?

● What is the speed of light in vacuum?

Light belongs to a family of waves that include radio waves, microwaves, and X-rays. Technically, these are *electromagnetic waves*. When charged particles such as electrons are accelerated, energy is radiated away in the form of waves. Electromagnetic waves consist of oscillating electric and magnetic fields (Chapter 8). For now, we will consider electromagnetic waves only in the context of waves.

Accelerated charged particles produce waves of various frequencies or wavelengths that form a continuous **electromagnetic (EM) spectrum** (● Fig. 6.7). Waves at one end (right) of the spectrum that have relatively low frequencies (10^4 Hz to 10^8 Hz) and long wavelengths are known as *radio* waves. Waves with frequencies greater than radio waves but less than visible light, from 10^{11} Hz to about 4.3×10^{14} Hz, include the *microwave* and *infrared* regions.

With increasing frequency come the visible and ultraviolet regions. Note the small portion of the spectrum that is visible to the human eye, 4.3×10^{14} Hz to 7.5×10^{14} Hz (or $\lambda = 700$ nm to 400 nm). It lies between the infrared (IR) and ultraviolet (UV) regions. It is the ultraviolet in sunlight that tans and burns our skin.

At still higher frequencies is the more energetic *X-ray* region. X-rays are widely used in medical and dental applications to take "pictures" of bones and teeth. Too much X-ray radiation can cause cell damage. Therefore, lead aprons are used when taking dental X-rays to protect other parts of the body. X-rays cannot penetrate lead. *Gamma rays* occupy a

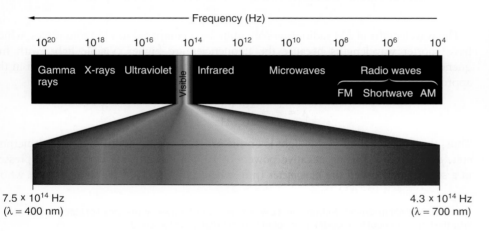

Figure 6.7 Electromagnetic (EM) Spectrum
Different frequency (or wavelength) regions are given names. Notice that the visible region forms only a very small part of the EM spectrum (much smaller than shown in the figure).

still higher frequency range. This energetic radiation is emitted in nuclear decay processes (discussed in Chapter 10.3).

The term *light* is commonly used for electromagnetic regions in or near the visible region; for example, we say *ultraviolet light*. Only the frequency (or wavelength) distinguishes visible light from the other portions of the spectrum. Our human eyes are sensitive only to certain frequencies or wavelengths, but other instruments can detect other portions of the spectrum. For example, a radio receiver can detect radio waves.

Keep in mind that radio waves are *not* sound waves. If they were, then you would "hear" many stations at once. Radio waves are detected and distinguished by frequency. Then, they are processed electronically and sent to the speaker system that produces sound waves.

Electromagnetic radiation consists of transverse waves. These waves can travel through a vacuum. For instance, light from the Sun travels through the vacuum of space before arriving at the Earth. This speed, which is called the **speed of light**, is designated by the letter c and has a value of

$$c = 3.00 \times 10^8 \text{ m/s}$$

(To a good approximation, this value is also the speed of light in air.*)

Equation 6.3 with $v = c$, that is, $c = \lambda f$, can be used to find the wavelength of light or any electromagnetic wave in a vacuum and to a good approximation in air. For example, let's calculate the wavelength of a typical radio wave.

EXAMPLE 6.2   Computing the Wavelength of a Radio Wave

What is the wavelength of the radio waves produced by an AM station with an assigned frequency of 600 kHz?

Solution

First, convert the frequency from kilohertz (kHz) into hertz. This conversion can be done directly, because *kilo-* is 10^3.

$$f = 600 \text{ kHz} = 600 \times 10^3 \text{ Hz} = 6.00 \times 10^5 \text{ Hz}$$

Then, using Eq. 6.3 in the form $c = \lambda f$ and rearranging for λ yields

$$\lambda = \frac{c}{f} = \frac{3.00 \times 10^8 \text{ m/s}}{6.00 \times 10^5 \text{ Hz}}$$

$$= 0.500 \times 10^3 \text{ m} = 500 \text{ m}$$

Confidence Exercise 6.2

The station in this example is an AM station, which generally uses kHz frequencies. FM stations have MHz frequencies. What is the wavelength of an FM station with an assigned frequency of 90.0 MHz?

The answers to Confidence Exercises may be found at the back of the book.

The wavelengths of AM radio waves are quite long compared to FM radio waves, which have shorter wavelengths because the frequencies are higher. Visible light, with frequencies on the order of 10^{14} Hz, has relatively short wavelengths, as can be seen in the approximation

$$\lambda = \frac{c}{f} \approx \frac{10^8 \text{ m/s}}{10^{14} \text{ Hz}} = 10^{-6} \text{ m}$$

Thus, the wavelength of visible light is on the order of one millionth of a meter (micrometer, μm). To avoid using negative powers of 10, wavelengths are commonly expressed in a smaller unit called the *nanometer* (nm, where 1 nm = 10^{-9} m) so as to have whole

---

*In this sense, *light* means all electromagnetic waves, all of which travels at the speed of light in vacuum. Why the letter *c* symbol for speed? It is adopted from *celeritas*, Latin for speed.

numbers with powers of 10. Using the values given in Fig. 6.7, you should be able to show that the approximate wavelength range for the visible region is between 4×10^{-7} m and 7×10^{-7} m. This range corresponds to a span of 400 nm to 700 nm.

For visible light, different frequencies or wavelengths are perceived by the eye as different colors, and the brightness depends on the energy of the wave (Chapter 7.4).

Did You Learn?

● The continuous electromagnetic spectrum is arranged in sequences of wave frequencies or wavelengths.

● The speed of light in vacuum is 3.00×10^8 m/s (about 186,000 mi/s).

6.4   Sound Waves

Preview Questions

● What is the frequency range of human hearing?

● When the decibel (dB) level is doubled, does the sound intensity double?

Technically, **sound** is the propagation of *longitudinal* waves through matter. Sound waves involve longitudinal particle displacements in all kinds of matter: solid, liquid, or gas.

Probably most familiar are sound waves in air, which affect our sense of hearing, but sound also travels in liquids and solids. When while swimming underwater someone clicks two rocks together also underwater, you can hear this disturbance. Also, sound can be heard through thin (but solid) walls.

The wave motion of sound depends on the elasticity of the medium. A longitudinal disturbance produces varying pressures and stresses in the medium. For example, consider a vibrating tuning fork, as illustrated in ● Fig. 6.8.

As an end of the fork moves outward, it compresses the air in front of it, and a *compression* is propagated outward. When the fork end moves back, it produces a region of decreased air pressure and density called a *rarefaction*. With continual vibration, a series of high- and low-pressure regions travels outward, forming a longitudinal sound wave. The waveform may be displayed electronically on an oscilloscope, as shown in ● Fig. 6.9.

Sound waves may have different frequencies and so form a spectrum analogous to the electromagnetic spectrum (● Fig. 6.10). However, the **sound spectrum** has much lower frequencies and is much simpler, with only three frequency regions. These regions are defined in terms of the audible range of human hearing, which is about 20 Hz to 20 kHz (20,000 Hz) and constitutes the *audible region* of the spectrum.

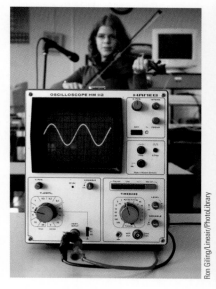

Figure 6.9 Waveform
The waveform of a tone from a violin is displayed on an oscilloscope by using a microphone to convert the sound wave into an electric signal.

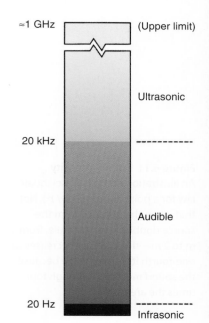

Figure 6.10 Sound Spectrum
The sound spectrum consists of three regions: the infrasonic region ($f < 20$ Hz), the audible region (20 Hz $< f <$ 20 kHz), and the ultrasonic region ($f > 20$ kHz).

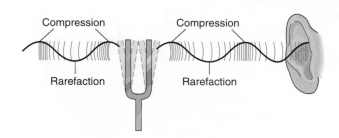

Figure 6.8 Sound Waves
Sound waves consist of a series of compressions (high-pressure regions) and rarefactions (low-pressure regions), as illustrated here for waves in air from a vibrating tuning fork. These regions can be described by a waveform.

Below the audible region is the *infrasonic region* and above is the *ultrasonic region*. (Note the analogy to infrared and ultraviolet light.) The sound spectrum has an upper limit of about a billion hertz (1 GHz, gigahertz) because of the elastic limitations of materials.

Waves in the infrasonic region, which humans cannot hear, are found in nature. Earthquakes produce infrasonic waves, and earthquakes and their locations are studied by using these waves (Chapter 21.5). Infrasound is also associated with tornados and weather patterns. Elephants and cattle have hearing response in the infrasonic region and may get advance warnings of earthquakes and weather disturbances. Aircraft, automobiles, and other rapidly moving objects produce infrasound.

The audible region is of prime importance in terms of hearing. Sound is sometimes defined as those disturbances perceived by the human ear, but as Fig. 6.10 shows, this definition would omit a majority of the sound spectrum. Indeed, ultrasound, which we cannot hear, has many practical applications, some of which are discussed shortly

We hear sound because propagating disturbances cause the eardrum to vibrate, and sensations are transmitted to the auditory nerve through the fluid and bones of the inner ear. The characteristics associated with human hearing are physiological and can differ from their physical counterparts.

For example, *loudness* is a relative term. One sound may be louder than another, and as you might guess, this property is associated with the energy of the wave. The measurable physical quantity is **intensity** (I), which is the rate of sound energy transfer through a given area. Intensity may be given as so many joules per second (J/s) through a square meter (m^2). Recall, though, that a joule per second is a watt (W), so sound intensity has units of W/m^2.

The loudness or intensity of sound decreases the farther one is from the source. As the sound is propagated outward, it is "spread" over a greater area and so has less energy per unit area. This characteristic is illustrated for a point source in ● Fig. 6.11. In this case the intensity is inversely proportional to the square of the distance from the source ($I \propto 1/r^2$); that is, it is an inverse-square relationship. This relationship is analogous to painting a larger room with the same amount of paint. The paint (energy) must be spread thinner and so is less "intense."

The minimum sound intensity that can be detected by the human ear (called the *threshold of hearing*) is about 10^{-12} W/m². At a greater intensity of about 1 W/m², sound becomes painful to the ear. Because of the wide range, the sound intensity level is commonly measured on a logarithmic scale, which conveniently compresses the linear scale. This logarithmic scale is called the decibel (dB) scale and is illustrated in ● Fig. 6.12. Notice that *sound intensity* is measured in W/m² and that *sound intensity level* is expressed in decibels (dB).

Figure 6.11 Sound Intensity
An illustration of the inverse-square law for a point source ($I \propto 1/r^2$). Note that when the distance from the source doubles—for example, from 1 m to 2 m—the intensity decreases to one-fourth its former value because the sound must pass through four times the area.

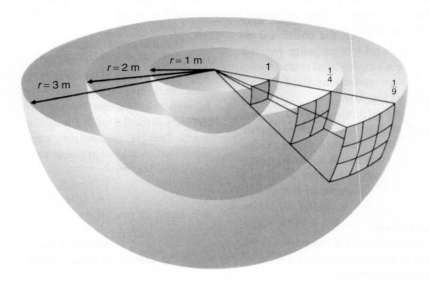

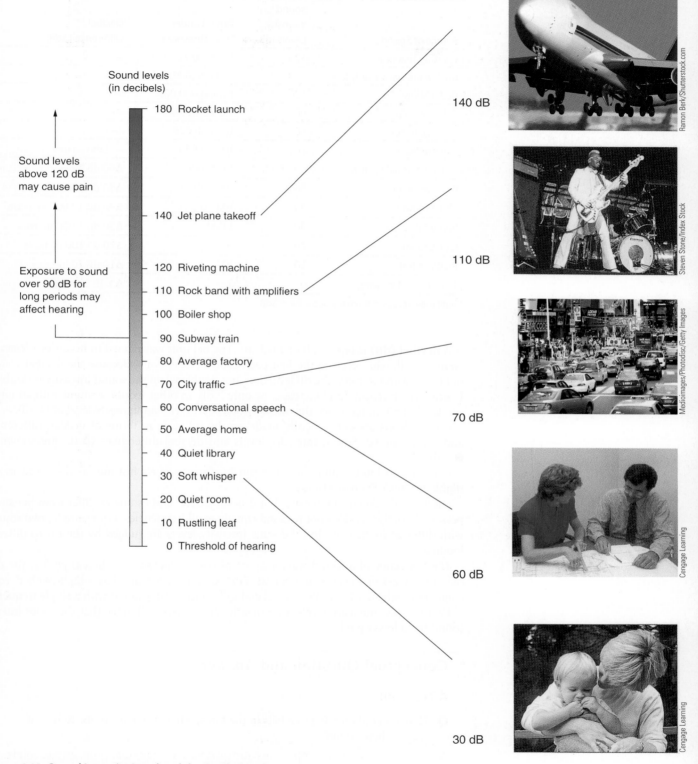

Figure 6.12 Sound Intensity Level and the Decibel Scale
The decibel scale of sound intensity levels, with examples of typical sources.

Table 6.1 Sound Intensity Levels and Decibel Differences

Source of Sound	Sound Intensity Levels (dB)	Times Louder Than Threshold	Decibel Difference (ΔdB)
Riveting machine	120	1,000,000,000,000	—
Rock band with amplifiers	110	100,000,000,000	—
Boiler shop	100	10,000,000,000	—
Subway train	90	1,000,000,000	—
Average factory	80	100,000,000	—
City traffic	70	10,000,000	— (and so on)
Conversational speech	60	1,000,000	Δ60 dB 1,000,000 increase*
Average home	50	100,000	Δ50 dB 100,000 increase
Quiet library	40	10,000	Δ40 dB 10,000 increase
Soft whisper	30	1,000	Δ30 dB 1,000 increase
Quiet room	20	100	Δ20 dB 100 increase
Rustling leaf	10	10	Δ10 dB 10 increase
Threshold of hearing	0	0	Δ3 dB 2 increase

*Similar decreases in intensity occur for −ΔdB.

A **decibel (dB)** is one-tenth of a bel (B). The bel unit was named in honor of Alexander Graham Bell, who received the first patent for the telephone. Because the decibel scale is not linear with intensity, the dB level does not double when the sound intensity is doubled. Instead, the intensity level increases by only 3 dB. In other words, a sound with an intensity level of 63 dB has twice the intensity of a sound with an intensity level of 60 dB.

Comparisons are conveniently made on the dB scale in terms of decibel differences and factors of 10. Sound intensity levels and decibel differences (**Δ**dB) are shown in
● Table 6.1.

Exposure to loud sounds or noise can be damage one's hearing, as discussed in the **Highlight: Noise Exposure Limits**.

Loudness is related to intensity, but it is subjective, and estimates differ from person to person. Also, the ear does not respond equally to all frequencies. For example, two sounds with different frequencies but the same intensity levels are judged by the ear to differ in loudness.

The frequency of a sound wave may be physically measured, whereas *pitch* is the *perceived* highness or lowness of a sound. For example, a soprano has a high-pitched voice compared with a baritone. Pitch is related to frequency. If a sound with a single frequency is heard at two intensity levels, then nearly all listeners will agree that the more intense sound has a lower pitch.

Conceptual Question and Answer

A Tree Fell

Q. Here's an old one. If a tree falls in the forest where there is no one to hear it, then is there sound?

A. Physically, sound is simply wave disturbances (energy) that propagate in solids, liquids, and gases. When perceived by our ears, sound is interpreted as speech, music, noise, and so forth. The answer to the question depends on the distinction between physical and sensory sound. The answer is no if thinking in terms of sensory hearing, but yes if considering physical waves.

Highlight Noise Exposure Limits

Sounds with intensity levels of 120 dB and higher can be painfully loud to the ear. Brief exposures to even higher sound intensity levels can rupture eardrums and cause permanent hearing loss. Long exposure to relatively lower sound (noise) levels can also cause hearing problems. (*Noise* is defined as unwanted sound.)

Examples of such loud sounds are motorcycles and rock bands with amplifiers (Fig. 1). Another more recent concern is a problem with loudness involving listening devices with earphones. Whether hearing is affected depends primarily on the loudness and the length of time one is exposed to the sound. (Pitch or frequency may also have a contributing effect.) Long exposure to loud sounds can damage the sensitive hair cells of the inner ear as well as the hearing nerve. Typical symptoms include feeling pressure in the ear, hearing speech as muffled, and hearing a ringing sound (tinnitus) in the ear. When the damage is not severe, these symptoms may go away in minutes or hours after the sound exposure ends.

Occupational noise hazards can also present problems. Workers in a noisy factory and members of an airplane ground crew, for example, may be affected. When danger to hearing exists on such jobs, ear protectors should be required (Fig. 2). Ear protectors are available at hardware stores, and people are wise to wear them when mowing grass or using a chain saw.

Federal standards now set permissible noise exposure limits for occupational loudness. These limits are listed in Table 1. Note that a person can safely work on a subway train (90 dB, Fig. 6.13) for 8 hours but should not play in (or listen to) an amplified rock band (110 dB) continuously for more than half an hour.

Table 1 Permissible Noise Exposure Limits

Maximum Duration per Day (h)	Intensity Level (dB)
8	90
6	92
4	95
3	97
2	100
$1\frac{1}{2}$	102
1	105
$\frac{1}{2}$	110
$\frac{1}{4}$ or less	115

Figure 1 A Lot of Decibels
Loud rock music may cause a ringing in the ears (tinnitus); long exposure could lead to permanent damage.

Figure 2 Sound Intensity Safety
An airport cargo worker wears ear protectors to prevent hearing damage from the high-intensity levels of jet plane engines.

Ultrasound is the term used for sound waves with frequencies greater than 20,000 Hz or 20 kHz. These waves cannot be detected by the human ear, but the audible frequency range for other animals includes ultrasound frequencies. For example, dogs can hear ultrasound, and ultrasonic whistles used to call dogs don't disturb humans. Bats use ultrasonic sonar to navigate at night and to locate and catch insects. This is called *echolocation* (● Fig. 6.13).

An important use of ultrasound is in examining parts of the body. Ultrasound is an alternative to potentially harmful X-rays. The ultrasonic waves allow different tissues, such as organs and bone, to be "seen" or distinguished by bouncing waves off the object examined. The reflected waves are detected, analyzed, and stored in a computer. An *echogram* is then reconstructed, such as the one of a fetus shown in ● Fig. 6.14. Energetic X-rays might

Figure 6.13 Ultrasonic Sonar
Bats use the reflections of ultrasound for navigation and to locate food (echolocation). The emitted sound waves (blue) are reflected, and the echoes (red) enable the bat to locate the wall and an insect.

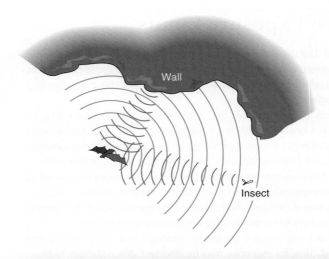

Figure 6.14 Echogram
An echogram in which the outline of a fetus at 21 weeks can be clearly seen.

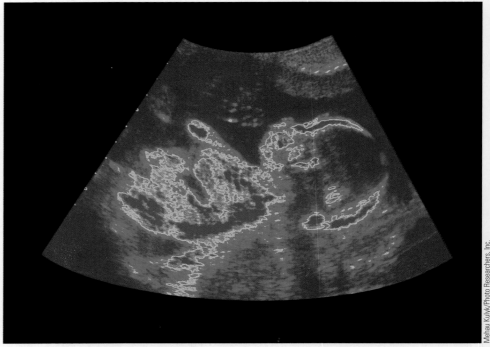

Mehau Kulyk/Photo Researchers, Inc.

harm the fetus and cause birth defects, but ultrasonic waves have less energetic vibrations and less chance of harming a fetus.

Ultrasound is also used as a cleaning technique. Minute foreign particles can be removed from objects placed in a liquid bath through which ultrasound is passed. The wavelength of ultrasound is on the same order of magnitude as the particle size, and the wave vibrations can get into small crevices and "scrub" particles free. Ultrasound is especially useful in cleaning objects with hard-to-reach recesses, such as rings and other jewelry. Ultrasonic cleaning baths for false teeth are also commercially available, as are ultrasonic toothbrushes. The latter transmit 1.6-MHz wave action to the teeth and gums to help remove bacterial plaque. There are also "sonic" toothbrushes that vibrate with a frequency of 18 kHz.

The **speed of sound** in a particular medium depends on the makeup of the material. A common medium is air. The speed of sound (v_s in air at 20°C) is

$$v_s = 344 \text{ m/s (770 mi/h)}$$

or approximately $\frac{1}{3}$ km/s, or $\frac{1}{5}$ mi/s.

The speed of sound increases with increasing temperature. For example, it is 331 m/s at 0°C and 344 m/s at 20°C. The speed of sound in air is much, much less than the speed of light.

The relatively slow speed of sound in air may be observed at a baseball game. A spectator sitting far from home plate may see a batter hit the ball but not hear the "crack" of the bat until slightly later. Similarly, a lightning flash is seen almost instantaneously, but the resulting thunder comes rumbling along afterward at a speed of about $\frac{1}{5}$ mi/s.

By counting the seconds between seeing a lightning flash and hearing the thunder, you can estimate your distance from the lightning or the storm's center (where lightning usually occurs). For example, if 5 seconds elapsed, then the storm's center is at a distance of approximately $\frac{1}{3}$ km/s × 5 s (= 1.6 km), or $\frac{1}{5}$ mi/s × 5 s (= 1.0 mi).

In general, as the density of the medium increases, the speed of sound increases. The speed of sound in water is about 4 times greater than in air, and in general, the speed of sound in solids is about 15 times greater than in air.

By using the speed of sound and frequency, the wavelength of a sound wave can easily be computed.

EXAMPLE 6.3   Computing the Wavelength of Ultrasound

What is the wavelength of a sound wave in air at 20°C with a frequency of 22 MHz?

Solution

The speed of sound at 20°C is v_s = 344 m/s (given previously), and the frequency is f = 22 MHz = 22 × 10^6 Hz, which is in the ultrasonic region.

To find the wavelength λ, Eq. 6.3 can be used with the speed of sound:

$$\lambda = \frac{v_s}{f}$$

$$= \frac{344 \text{ m/s}}{22 \times 10^6 \text{ Hz (1/s)}} = 1.6 \times 10^{-5} \text{ m}$$

This wavelength of ultrasound is on the order of particle size and can be used in ultrasonic cleaning baths, as described earlier.

Confidence Exercise 6.3

What is the wavelength of an infrasonic sound wave in air at 20°C with a frequency of 10.0 Hz? (How does this wavelength compare with ultrasound wavelengths?)

Did You Learn?

● The human hearing frequency range is 20 Hz to 20 kHz.

● The dB scale is nonlinear, and an increase of 3 dB doubles the sound intensity. For example, a sound with 63 dB has twice the intensity of a sound with 60 dB.

6.5 The Doppler Effect

Preview Questions

● What is the Doppler effect?

● What is necessary for a jet aircraft to generate a sonic boom?

When watching a race and a racing car with a loud engine approaches, one hears an increasing high-frequency "whee." When the car passes by, the frequency suddenly shifts

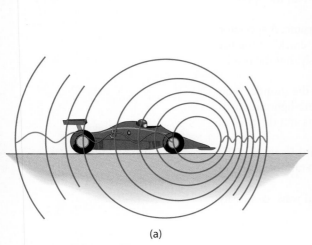

(a)

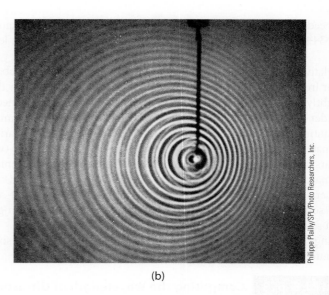

(b)

Philippe Plailly/SPL/Photo Researchers, Inc.

Figure 6.15 Doppler Effect
(a) Because of the motion of a sound source, illustrated here as a racing car, sound waves are "bunched up" in front and "spread out" in back. The result is shorter wavelengths (higher frequencies) in front of the sources and longer wavelengths (lower frequencies) behind the source. (b) The Doppler effect in water waves in a ripple tank. The source of the disturbance is moving to the right.

lower and a low-pitched "whoom" sound is heard. Similar frequency changes may be heard when a large truck passes by. The apparent change in the frequency of the moving source is called the **Doppler effect**.* The reason for the observed change in frequency (and wavelength) of a sound is illustrated in ● Fig. 6.15.

As a moving sound source approaches an observer, the waves are "bunched up" in front of the source. With the waves closer together (shorter wavelength), an observer perceives a higher frequency. Behind the source the waves are spread out, and with an increase in wavelength, a lower frequency is heard ($f = v/\lambda$). If the source is stationary and the observer moves toward and passes the source, then the shifts in frequency are also observed. Hence, the Doppler effect depends on the *relative* motion of the source and the observer.

Waves propagate outward in front of a source as long as the speed of sound, v_s, is greater than the speed of the source, v (● Fig. 6.16a). However, as the speed of the source approaches the speed of sound in a medium, the waves begin to bunch up closer and closer. When the speed of the source exceeds the speed of sound in the medium, a V-shaped bow wave is formed. Such a wave is readily observed for a motorboat traveling faster than the wave speed in water.

In air, when a jet aircraft travels at a supersonic speed (a speed greater than the speed of sound in air), a bow wave is in the form of a conical shock wave that trails out and downward from the aircraft. When this high-pressure, compressed wave front passes over an observer, a *sonic boom* is heard. The bow wave travels with the supersonic aircraft and does not occur only at the instant the aircraft "breaks the sound barrier" (first exceeds the speed of sound). There are actually two booms, because shock waves are formed at both the front and the tail of the plane (Fig. 6.16c).

Conceptual Question and Answer

Faster Than Sound

Q. If a jet pilot is flying faster than the speed of sound, is he or she able to hear sound?

A. Yes. The air in the cockpit is traveling with the pilot and is relatively stationary, so sound would be heard in the cockpit if not obstructed by communication headsets.

*Named after Christian Doppler (1803–1853), an Austrian physicist who first described the effect.

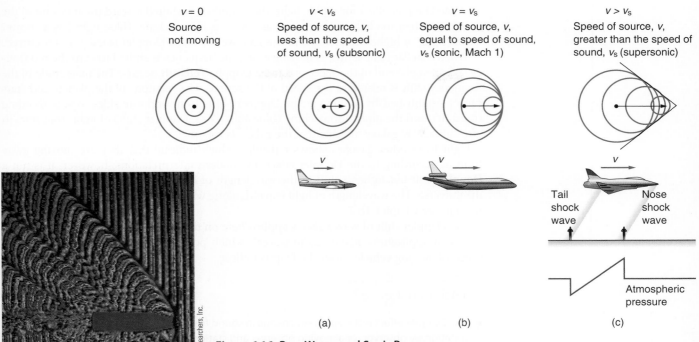

Figure 6.16 Bow Waves and Sonic Boom
Just as a moving boat forms a bow wave in water, a moving aircraft forms a bow wave in the air.
The sound waves bunch up in front of the airplane for increasing sonic speeds [(a) and (b)]. A
plane traveling at supersonic speeds forms a high-pressure shock wave in the air (c) that is heard
as a sonic boom when the plane passes over the observer. Actually, shock waves are formed
at both the nose and the tail of the aircraft. (d) This bullet is traveling at the speed of 500 m/s.
Notice the shock waves produced (and the turbulence behind the bullet).

You may hear jet aircraft speeds expressed as Mach 1 or Mach 2. The number Mach 1 is
equal to the speed of sound, Mach 2 is equal to twice the speed of sound, and so on. This
Mach number is named after Ernst Mach (1838–1916), an Austrian physicist who studied
supersonics.

On a smaller scale, you have probably heard a "mini" sonic boom, the crack of a whip.
When a whip is given a flick of the wrist, a wave pulse travels down the length of the whip.
Whips generally taper down from the handle to the tip, and the pulse speed increases the
thinner the whip. Traveling the length of the whip, the speed increases until it is greater
than the speed of sound. The "crack" is made by the air rushing back into the region of
reduced pressure created by the final supersonic flip of the whip's tip, much as the sonic
boom emanates from a shock trail behind a supersonic aircraft.

The Doppler effect is general and occurs for all kinds of waves, including water waves,
sound waves, and light waves. Because the Doppler effect can be used to detect and provide information on moving objects, it is used to examine blood flow in arteries and veins.
In this application ultrasound reflects from moving red blood cells with a change in frequency according to the speed of the cells. Information about the speed of blood flow helps
physicians to diagnose such things as blood clots and arterial closing.

For example, the Doppler effect can be used to assess the risk of stroke. Accumulations
of plaque deposits on the inner walls of blood vessels can restrict blood flow. A major cause
of stroke is obstruction of the carotid artery in the neck, which supplies blood to the brain.
The presence and severity of such obstructions may be detected by using ultrasound. An
ultrasonic generator (transducer), which generates high-frequency ultrasonic pulses, is
placed on the neck. Reflections from the red blood cells moving through the artery are
monitored to determine the rate of blood flow, providing an indication of and the severity
of any blockage.

In the Doppler effect for visible light, the frequency is shifted toward the blue end of the spectrum when the light source (such as a star) is approaching. (Blue light has a shorter wavelength, or higher frequency.) In this case we say that a Doppler *blueshift* has occurred.

When a stellar light source is moving away, the frequency is shifted toward the red (longer wavelength) end of the spectrum and a Doppler **redshift** occurs. The magnitude of the frequency shift is related to the speed of the source. The rotations of the planets and stars can be established by looking at the Doppler shifts from opposite sides; one is receding (redshift), and the other approaching (blueshift). Also, Doppler shifts of light from stars in our Milky Way galaxy indicate that the galaxy is rotating.

Light from other galaxies shows redshifts, which indicate that they are moving away from us according to the Doppler effect. By modern interpretations, however, it is not a Doppler shift but rather a shift in the wavelength of light influenced by the expansion of the universe. The wavelength of light expands along with the universe, giving a *cosmological redshift* (see Chapter 18.7).

The Doppler shift of waves also is applied here on the Earth. You may have experienced one such application. Radar (radio waves), which police officers use in determining the speed of moving vehicles, uses the Doppler effect.

Did You Learn?

- The Doppler effect is the apparent change in sound frequency of a moving source and a stationary observer (or a moving observer and stationary source).

- Jet aircraft with a speed greater than the speed of sound in air ($M > 1$) can generate a sonic boom.

6.6   Standing Waves and Resonance

Preview Questions

- Are the particles in a standing wave really "standing" or stationary?
- What does resonance mean in terms of a system's energy?

You may have shaken one end of a stretched cord or rope and observed wave patterns that seem to "stand" along the rope when it is shaken just right. These "stationary" waveforms are referred to as **standing waves** (● Fig. 6.17).

Standing waves are caused by the interference of waves traveling down and reflected back along the rope. When two waves meet, they interfere, and the combined waveform of the superimposed waves is the sum of the waveforms or particle displacements of the medium. Some points on the rope, called *nodes*, remain stationary at all times. At these points, the displacements of the interfering waves are equal and opposite and cancel each other completely such that the rope has zero displacement there. At other points, called *antinodes*, the individual amplitudes add to give the maximum amplitudes of the combined wave forms.

Notice that the string in Fig. 6.17 vibrates in standing wave modes only at *particular* frequencies (as evidenced by the number of loops or half wavelengths). These frequencies are referred to as the *characteristic*, or *natural*, *frequencies* of the stretched string.

When a stretched string or an object is acted on by a periodic driving force with a frequency equal to one of the natural frequencies, the oscillations have large amplitudes. This phenomenon is called **resonance**, and in this case there is maximum energy transfer to the system.

A common example of driving a system in resonance is pushing a swing. A swing is essentially a pendulum with only one natural frequency, which depends on the rope

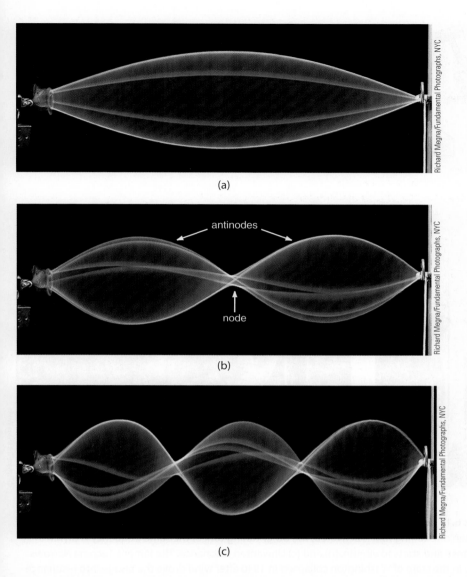

(a)

(b)

(c)

antinodes

node

Richard Megna/Fundamental Photographs, NYC

Figure 6.17 Standing Waves
Actual standing waves in a stretched rubber string. Standing waves are formed only when the string is vibrated at particular frequencies. Note the differences in wavelength; in (a), one-half wavelength ($\lambda/2$); in (b), one wavelength (λ); and in (c), a wavelength and a half ($3\lambda/2$).

length. When a swing is pushed periodically with a period of $T = 1/f$, energy is transferred to the swing and its amplitude gets larger (higher swings). If the swing is not pushed at its natural frequency, then the pushing force may be applied as the swing approaches or after it has reached its maximum amplitude. In either case the swing is not driven in resonance (at its natural frequency).

A stretched string has many natural frequencies, not just one like a pendulum. When the string is shaken, waves are generated, but when the driving frequency corresponds to one of the natural frequencies, the amplitude at the antinodes will be larger because of resonance.

There are many examples of resonance. The structures of the throat and nasal cavities give the human voice a particular tone as a result of resonances. Tuning forks of the same frequency can be made to resonate, as illustrated in ● Fig. 6.18a.

A steel bridge or most any structure is capable of vibrating at natural frequencies, sometimes with dire consequences (Fig. 6.18b). Soldiers marching in columns across bridges are told to break step and not march at a periodic cadence that might correspond to a natural frequency of the bridge and result in resonance and large oscillations that could cause structural damage. In 1850 in France, about 500 soldiers marching across a suspension bridge over a river caused a resonant vibration that rose to such a level that the bridge collapsed. More than 200 of the soldiers drowned.

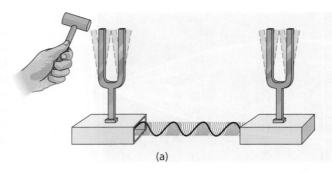

(a)

(b)

(c)

Figure 6.18 Resonance
(a) When one tuning fork is activated, the other tuning fork of the same frequency is driven in resonance and starts to vibrate. (b) and (c) Unwanted resonance. The famous Tacoma Narrows Bridge in the state of Washington collapsed in 1940 after wind drove the bridge into resonance vibrations.

Conceptual Question and Answer

It Can Be Shattering

Q. Opera singers are said to be able to shatter crystal glasses with their voices. How is this possible?

A. A few opera singers with powerful voices have been able to shatter glasses (● Fig. 6.19). If you wet your finger and move it around the rim of a crystal glass with a little pressure, you can get the glass to "sing" or vibrate at its natural frequency. The wavelength of the sound is the same as the distance around the rim of the glass. (If you ping the glass with your finger, then you'll hear the resonance frequency.)

  If a singer is able to sustain an intense tone with the proper frequency, then the resonance energy transfer may increase the amplitude of the vibrations of the glass to the point it shatters. (Try this resonance with your finger, not your singing.)

Musical instruments use standing waves and resonance to produce different tones. On stringed instruments such as the guitar, violin, and piano, standing waves are formed on strings fixed at both ends. When a stringed instrument is tuned, a string is tightened or loosened, which adjusts the tension and the wave speed in the string. This adjustment changes the frequency with the length of the string being fixed. Different musical notes (frequencies) on a guitar or violin are obtained by placing a finger on a string, which effectively shortens its length (● Fig. 6.20).

A vibrating string does not produce a great disturbance in air, but the body of a stringed instrument such as a violin acts as a sounding board and amplifies the sound. Thus, the body of such an instrument acts as a resonance cavity, and sound comes out through holes in the top surface.

In wind instruments standing waves are set up in air columns. Organ pipes have fixed lengths just as fixed strings do, so only a certain number of wavelengths can be fitted in the tube. However, the length of an air column and the frequency or tone can be varied in some instruments, such as a trombone, by varying the length of the column.

The *quality* (or timbre) of a sound depends on the waveform or the number of waveforms present. For example, you can sing the same note as a famous singer, but a different combination of waveforms gives the singer's voice a different quality, perhaps a pleasing "richness." It is the quality of our voices that gives them different sounds.

Figure 6.19 Shattering Glass
Some singers with the right frequency and intensity can cause a glass to vibrate in resonance and shatter.

Did You Learn?

● In a standing wave, opposite moving particles continually interfere, with the nodes being the only stationary points.

● At resonance frequencies there is maximum energy transfer to a system.

Figure 6.20 Different Notes
Placing the fingers on the strings at different locations effectively shortens the lengths and changes the musical notes (frequencies).

KEY TERMS

1. waves (6.1)
2. longitudinal wave (6.2)
3. transverse wave
4. wavelength
5. amplitude
6. frequency
7. hertz
8. period
9. wave speed
10. electromagnetic spectrum (6.3)
11. speed of light
12. sound (6.4)
13. sound spectrum
14. intensity
15. decibel
16. ultrasound
17. speed of sound
18. Doppler effect (6.5)
19. redshift
20. standing waves (6.6)
21. resonance

MATCHING

For each of the following items, fill in the number of the appropriate Key Word from the preceding list. Compare your answers with those at the back of the book.

a. _____ Particle motion and wave velocity parallel

b. _____ In air, its value is 344 m/s at 20°C

c. _____ A spectrum of waves, including visible light

d. _____ Maximum displacement of wave particle

e. _____ Indicates movement of a receding source

f. _____ Time to travel one wavelength

g. _____ Waveforms caused by wave interference

h. _____ Longitudinal waves that propagate through matter

i. _____ Propagation of energy after a disturbance

j. _____ Maximum energy transfer to a system

k. _____ Rate of transfer of sound energy through a given area

l. _____ Number of oscillations per time

m. _____ $f > 20,000$ Hz

n. _____ 3.00×10^8 m/s

o. _____ Particle motion perpendicular to wave velocity

p. _____ Equal to λ/T

q. _____ Regions of sound

r. _____ Unit of sound intensity level

s. _____ Apparent change of frequency because of relative motion

t. _____ Unit equivalent to 1/s

u. _____ Distance between two wave maxima

MULTIPLE CHOICE

Compare your answers with those at the back of the book.

1. A wave with particle oscillation parallel to the direction of propagation is a(n) _____ . (6.2)
   (a) transverse wave   (b) longitudinal wave
   (c) light wave   (d) none of the preceding

2. If a piece of ribbon were tied to a stretched string carrying a transverse wave, then how is the ribbon observed to oscillate? (6.2)
   (a) perpendicular to wave direction
   (b) parallel to wave direction
   (c) neither (a) nor (b)
   (d) both (a) and (b)

3. The energy of a wave is related to the square of which of the following? (6.2)
   (a) amplitude   (b) frequency
   (c) wavelength   (d) period

4. How fast do electromagnetic waves travel in vacuum? (6.3)
   (a) 3.00×10^8 m/s   (b) 9.8 m/s^2
   (c) 344 m/s   (d) 3.44×10^6 m/s

5. Which of the following is true for electromagnetic waves? (6.3)
   (a) They have different speeds in vacuum for different frequencies.
   (b) They are longitudinal waves.
   (c) They require a medium for propagation.
   (d) None of the preceding is true.

6. Which one of the following regions has frequencies just slightly less than the visible region in the electromagnetic frequency spectrum? (6.3)
   (a) radio wave   (b) ultraviolet
   (c) microwave   (d) infrared

7. The speed of sound is generally greatest in _____ . (6.4)
   (a) gases   (b) liquids   (c) solids   (d) vacuum

8. Which of the following sound frequencies would not be heard by the human ear? (6.4)
   (a) 25 Hz   (b) 900 Hz
   (c) 20 kHz   (d) 25 kHz

9. A sound with an intensity level of 30 dB is how many times louder than the threshold of hearing? (6.4)
   (a) 10   (b) 3000   (c) 100   (d) 1000

10. A moving observer approaches a stationary sound source. What does the observer hear? (6.5)
    (a) an increase in frequency
    (b) a decrease in frequency
    (c) the same frequency as the source

11. Which of the following properties does not change in the Doppler effect?
    (a) wavelength   (b) speed
    (c) frequency   (d) period

12. If an astronomical light source were moving toward us, then what would be observed? (6.5)
    (a) a blueshift
    (b) a shift toward longer wavelengths
    (c) a shift toward lower frequencies
    (d) a sonic boom

13. Which of the following occur(s) when a stretched string is shaken at one of its natural frequencies? (6.6)
    (a) standing waves   (b) resonance
    (c) maximum energy transfer   (d) all of the preceding

FILL IN THE BLANK

Compare your answers with those at the back of the book.

1. Waves involve the propagation of ___. (6.1)
2. Wave velocity and particle motion are ___ in transverse waves. (6.2)
3. The distance from one wave crest to an adjacent wave crest is called a(n) ___. (6.2)
4. Wave speed is equal to the wavelength times the ___. (6.2)
5. In vacuum electromagnetic waves travel at the speed of ___. (6.3)
6. Light waves are ___ waves. (6.3)
7. Sound waves are ___ waves. (6.4)
8. The audible region is above a frequency of ___ Hz. (6.4)
9. Decibels are used to measure the sound property of ___. (6.4)
10. To double the loudness, or sound intensity, a dB difference of ___ is needed. (6.4)
11. In the Doppler effect, when a moving sound source approaches a stationary observer, the apparent shift in frequency is ___. (6.5)
12. A Doppler blueshift in light from a star indicates that the star is ___. (6.5)
13. Resonance occurs at ___ frequencies. (6.6)

SHORT ANSWER

6.1 Waves and Energy Propagation

1. What is meant by a "wave"?
2. Do all waves require a medium to propagate? Explain.

6.2 Wave Properties

3. A wave travels upward in a medium (vertical wave velocity). What is the direction of particle oscillation for (a) a longitudinal wave and (b) a transverse wave?
4. What are the SI units for (a) wavelength, (b) frequency, (c) period, and (d) amplitude?
5. How many values of amplitude are there in one wavelength of a wave, and how is the amplitude related to the energy of a wave?
6. A displacement-versus-time graph for a wave form is shown in ● Fig. 6.21. What are the (a) amplitude and (b) frequency of the wave?

6.3 Light Waves

7. With what speed do electromagnetic waves propagate in vacuum?

8. Which end (blue or red) of the visible spectrum has the longer wavelength? Which has the higher frequency?
9. Are radio waves sound waves? Explain.
10. What is the range of wavelengths of visible light? How do these wavelengths compare with those of audible sound?

6.4 Sound Waves

11. What is a rarefaction?
12. What happens to the energy when a sound "dies out"?
13. Referring to Fig. 6.11, indicate over how many squares the sound waves would spread for $r = 5$ m. The sound intensity would decrease to what fraction in value?
14. What is the chief physical property that describes (a) pitch, (b) loudness, and (c) quality?
15. Why does the music coming from a band marching in a spread-out formation on a football field sometimes sound discordant?
16. What is the difference between sound wave energy and intensity?
17. Does doubling the decibels of a sound intensity level double the intensity? Explain.
18. Why lightning seen before thunder is heard?

6.5 The Doppler Effect

19. How is the wavelength of sound affected when (a) a sound source moves toward a stationary observer and (b) the observer moves away from a stationary sound source?
20. Under what circumstances would sound have (a) a Doppler "blueshift"? (b) a Doppler "redshift"?

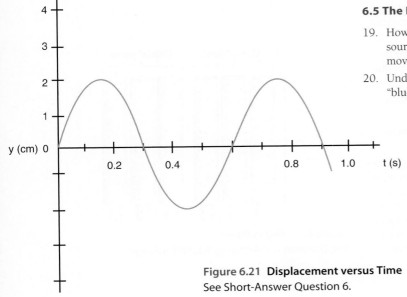

Figure 6.21 Displacement versus Time
See Short-Answer Question 6.

21. On a particular day the speed of sound in air is 340 m/s. If a plane flies at a speed of 680 m/s, is its Mach number (a) 1.5, (b) 2.0, (c) 2.5, or (d) 2.7?

22. Radar and sonar are based on similar principles. Sonar (which stands for *sound navigation and ranging*) uses ultrasound, and radar (which stands for *radio detecting and ranging*) uses radio waves. Explain the principle of detecting and ranging in these applications.

6.6 Standing Waves and Resonance

23. What is the effect when a system is driven in resonance? Is a particular frequency required? Explain.

24. Would you expect to find a node or an antinode at the end of a plucked guitar string? Explain.

25. What determines the pitch or frequency of a string on a violin or a guitar? How does a musician get a variety of notes from one string?

VISUAL CONNECTION

Visualize the connections and give answers for the blanks. Compare your answers with those at the back of the book.

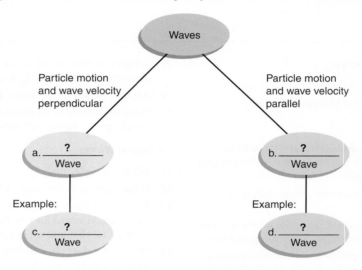

APPLYING YOUR KNOWLEDGE

1. The speed of sound in air is given for still air. How would wind affect the speed? What would happen if you shouted into the wind?

2. Were an astronaut on the Moon to drop a hammer, would there be sound? Explain. (*Follow-up*: How do astronauts communicate with one another and with mission control?)

3. We cannot see ultraviolet (UV) radiation, which can be dangerous to the eyes, but we can detect some UV radiations (without instruments). How is this done?

4. How fast would a "jet" fish have to swim to create an "aquatic" boom?

5. When one sings in the shower, the tones sound full and rich. Why is this?

6. Standing waves are set up in organ pipes. Consider an organ pipe with a fixed length, which may be open or closed. An open pipe is open at both ends, and a closed pipe is closed at one end and open at the other. A standing wave will have an antinode at an open end and a node at a closed end (● Fig. 6.22). In the figure determine (draw) the wavelengths of the first three characteristic frequencies for the pipes (that is, the first three wavelength segments that will "fit" into the pipes). Express your answers in terms of the length L of the pipe, such as $L = \lambda/3$ or $\lambda = 3L$ (not correct values).

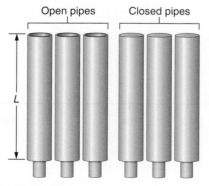

Figure 6.22 Organ Pipes
See Question 6 in Applying Your Knowledge.

IMPORTANT EQUATIONS

Frequency–Period Relationship: $f = \dfrac{1}{T}$ (6.1)   Wave Speed: $v = \dfrac{\lambda}{T} = \lambda f$ (6.2–6.3)

Speed of Light: $c = 3.00 \times 10^8$ m/s

EXERCISES

6.2 Wave Properties

1. A periodic wave has a frequency of 5.0 Hz. What is the wave period?

   Answer: 0.20 s

2. What is the period of the wave motion for a wave with a frequency of 0.25 kHz?

3. Waves moving on a lake have a speed of 2.0 m/s and a distance of 1.5 m between adjacent crests. (a) What is the frequency of the waves? (b) Find the period of the wave motion.

   Answer: (a) 1.3 Hz (b) 0.77 s

4. A sound wave has a frequency of 2000 Hz. What is the distance between crests or compressions of the wave? (Take the speed of sound to be 344 m/s.)

6.3 Light Waves

5. Compute the wavelength of the radio waves from (a) an AM station operating at a frequency of 650 kHz and (b) an FM station with a frequency of 95.1 MHz.

   Answer: (a) 4.62×10^2 m (b) 3.2 m

6. Compute the wavelength of an X-ray with a frequency of 10^{18} Hz.

7. What is the frequency of blue light that has a wavelength of 420 nm?

   Answer: 7.14×10^{14} Hz

8. An electromagnetic wave has a wavelength of 6.00×10^{-6} m. In what region of the electromagnetic spectrum is this radiation?

9. How far does light travel in 1 year? [This distance, known as a light-year (ly), is used in measuring astronomical distances (Ch. 18.1).]

   Answer: $9.4.8 \times 10^{12}$ km (about 6 trillion mi)

10. Approximately how long would it take a telephone signal to travel 3000 mi from coast to coast across the United States? (Telephone signals travel at about the speed of light.)

6.4 Sound Waves

11. Compute the wavelength in air of ultrasound with a frequency of 50 kHz if the speed of sound is 344 m/s.

    Answer: 6.9×10^{-3} m

12. What are the wavelength limits of the audible range of the sound spectrum? (Use the speed of sound in air.)

13. The speed of sound in a solid medium is 15 times greater than that in air. If the frequency of a wave in the solid is 20 kHz, then what is the wavelength?

    Answer: 0.26 m

14. A sound wave in a solid has a frequency of 15.0 kHz and a wavelength of 0.333 m. What would be the wave speed, and how much faster is this speed than the speed of sound in air?

15. During a thunderstorm, 4.5 s elapses between observing a lightning flash and hearing the resulting thunder. Approximately how far away, in kilometers and miles, was the lightning flash?

    Answer: 1.5 km or 0.90 mi

16. Picnickers see a lightning flash and hear the resulting thunder 9.0 s later. If the storm is traveling at a rate of 15 km/h, then how long, in minutes, do the picnickers have before the storm arrives at their location?

17. A subway train has a sound intensity level of 90 dB, and a rock band has a sound intensity level of about 110 dB. How many times greater is the sound intensity of the band than that of the train?

    Answer: 100 times

18. A loudspeaker has an output of 70 dB. If the volume of the sound is turned up so that the output intensity is 10,000 times greater, then what is the new sound intensity level?

ON THE WEB

1. Introduction to Waves

Do you now have a grasp of the fundamentals of waves? What is wave motion? Can you distinguish between a longitudinal wave and a transverse wave? What is the speed of light? Visit the student website at **www.cengagebrain.com/shop/ISBN/1133104096** and follow the recommended links to answer these questions. Also, use the worksheets on Vibration and Waveform Graph and Wave Vocabulary to reinforce what you know.

2. The Doppler Effect

Have you ever wondered about that shift in sound frequency as another vehicle is approaching and then passing yours? How does the speed of sound differ when the sound wave travels through the three different media of gas, liquid, and solid? How does the speed of an airplane affect the sound? How do stationary and moving sound sources differ? What creates the sonic boom as a plane breaks through the sound barrier? To explore the Doppler effect and sonic booms and to answer the questions above, follow the recommended links on the student website at **www.cengagebrain.com/shop/ISBN/1133104096**.

*Music is the arithmetic
of sound as optics is
the geometry of light.*

•

Claude Debussy
(1862–1918)

Because of refraction, the pencil >
appears to be severed.

Bill Beatty/Visuals Unlimited

PHYSICS FACTS

▶ Some emergency vehicles have AMBULANCE printed on the front. This is so that the word AMBULANCE can be read in the rearview mirrors of vehicles ahead ("right–left" reversal).

▶ The "right–left" reversal of a plane mirror is really a "front–back" reversal (Chapter 7.1).

You look into a mirror and see your image. Many of us wear eyeglasses (lenses) to be able to see more clearly. These common applications involve light and vision, which are the basis for the branch of physical science known as *optics*. To be able to describe light phenomena is of great importance because most of the information we receive about our physical environment involves light and sight (see Chapter 1.3). Optics is generally divided into two areas: *geometrical (ray) optics* and *physical (wave) optics*.

Geometrical optics uses lines, or "light rays," to explain phenomena such as reflection and refraction, which are the principles of mirrors and lenses, respectively. The majority of our mirrors are plane mirrors, like the flat mirrors used in bathrooms and dressing rooms. There are other types of mirrors as well, such as

Chapter Outline

cosmetic mirrors that produce magnified images. This type of mirror is curved, so geometry comes into play in describing mirrors.

The same goes for lenses. There are many different shapes of lenses that produce different effects. An optometrist must know these effects when prescribing lenses for eyeglasses (or contact lenses). And lenses are central components of a most important optical instrument: the human eye. Geometrical optics also explains such things as fiber optics and the brilliance of diamonds.

Physical optics, on the other hand, takes into account the wave effects that geometrical optics ignores. Wave theory leads to satisfactory explanations of such phenomena as polarization, interference, and diffraction. You may wear polarizing sunglasses to reduce glare. When you see a colorful display in a soap bubble, interference is occurring. When you speak loudly, a person out of sight around the corner of a doorway can hear you, indicating that sound waves "bend," or are diffracted around corners. You can be heard in the next room, but you are not seen. Light is diffracted also but not enough for us to observe in most cases.

Also discussed in this chapter are liquid crystal displays (LCDs), which you probably have on a calculator or watch and may have on a computer or TV monitor. So let's get started with the fascinating study of optics.

7.1 Reflection

Preview Questions

- What is reflection?
- Does the law of reflection apply to both specular (regular) and diffuse (irregular) reflections?

Light waves travel through space in a straight line and will continue to do so unless diverted from the original direction. A change in direction takes place when light strikes and rebounds from a surface. A change in direction by this method is called **reflection**.

Reflection may be thought of as light "bouncing off" a surface. However, it is much more complicated and involves the absorption and emission of complex atomic vibrations of the reflecting medium. To describe reflection simply, the reflection of rays is considered, which ignores the wave nature of light. A **ray** is a straight line that represents the path of light with a directional arrowhead.

An incident light ray is reflected from a surface in a particular way. As illustrated in ● Fig. 7.1, the angles of the incident and reflected rays (θ_i and θ_r) are measured relative to the *normal*, a line perpendicular to the reflecting surface. These angles are related by the **law of reflection:**

The angle of reflection θ_r is equal to the angle of incidence θ_i.

Also, the reflected and incident rays are in the same plane.

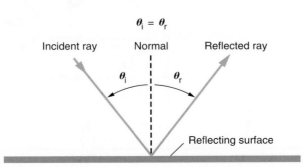

Figure 7.1 **Law of Reflection**
The angle of reflection θ_r is equal to the angle of incidence θ_i relative to the normal (a line perpendicular to the reflecting surface). The rays and the normal line lie in the same plane.

Regular reflection

(a)

Diffuse reflection

(b)

Figure 7.2 Reflection
(a) A smooth (mirror) surface produces specular (or regular) reflection. (b) A rough surface produces diffuse (or irregular) reflection. Both reflections obey the law of reflection.

The reflection from very smooth (mirror) surfaces is called **specular reflection** (or regular reflection, ● Fig. 7.2a). In specular reflection, incident parallel rays are parallel on reflection. In contrast, rays reflected from relatively rough surfaces are not parallel but scattered. This reflection is called **diffuse reflection** (or irregular reflection, Fig. 7.2b). The reflection from the pages of this book is diffuse. The law of reflection applies to both types of reflection, but the rough surface causes the incoming light rays to be reflected in different directions.

Conceptual Question and Answer

No Can See

Q. Some tractor-trailers have a sign on the back, "If you can't see my mirror, I can't see you." What does this mean?

A. For the trucker to see you in his rearview mirror, you must be in a position to see the mirror. The law of reflection works both ways; the rays are just reversed.

Rays may be used to determine the image formed by a mirror. A *ray diagram* for determining the apparent location of an image formed by a plane mirror is shown in ● Fig. 7.3. The image is located by drawing two rays emitted by the object and applying the law of reflection. Where the rays intersect, or appear to intersect, locates the image. For a plane mirror, the image is located behind, or "inside," the mirror at the same distance as the object is in front of the mirror.

Figure 7.3 Ray Diagram
By tracing the reflected rays, it is possible to locate a mirror image where the rays intersect, or appear to intersect, behind the mirror.

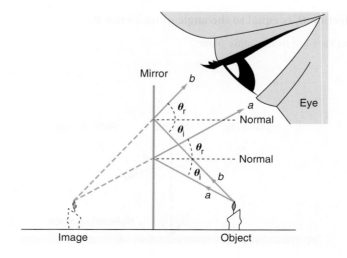

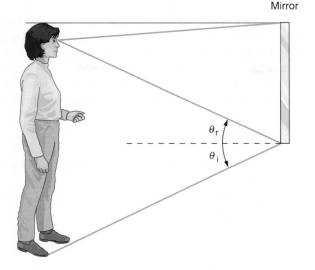

Mirror

Figure 7.4 Complete Figure
For a person to see his or her complete figure in a plane mirror, the height of the mirror must be at least one-half the height of the person, as can be demonstrated by ray tracing.

● Figure 7.4 shows a ray diagram for the light rays involved when a person sees a complete head-to-toe image. Applying the law of reflection, it can be shown that the total image is seen in a plane mirror that is only half the person's height. Also, the distance from the mirror is not a factor (see Exercise 3).

It is the reflection of light that enables us to see things. Look around you. What you see is light reflected from the walls, ceiling, floor, and other objects, which in general is diffuse reflection. Some beautiful specular reflections are seen in nature, as shown in ● Fig. 7.5.

Conceptual Question and Answer

Nighttime Mirror

Q. At night, a glass windowpane acts as a mirror viewed from the inside a lighted room. Why isn't it a mirror during the day?

A. When light strikes a transparent medium, most of it is transmitted but some is reflected. During the day, the light reflected from the inside of the window is overwhelmed by the light coming through the window from the outside. At night, though, when the light transmitted from the outside is greatly reduced, the inside reflections can be discerned and the windowpane acts as a mirror. (Can you now explain the principle of one-way mirrors and reflective sunglasses?)

Coco McCoy/Rainbow

Figure 7.5 Natural Reflection
Beautiful reflections, such as the one shown here on a still lake, are often seen in nature. Is the picture really printed right-side up? Turn it upside down and take a look. Without the tree limbs on the left, would you be able to tell?

Before leaving plane mirrors, let's consider another interesting aspect, commonly called a *right–left reversal*. When you raise your right hand when looking at a plane (bathroom-type) mirror, your image raises its left hand. This is really a *front–back reversal*. To understand, suppose you are facing north. Then your mirror image "faces" south. That is, your image has its front to the south and its back to the north: a front–back reversal. This reversal can be demonstrated by asking a friend to stand facing you (without a mirror). When your friend raises a right hand, you can see that the hand is actually on your left side.

Did You Learn?

● Reflection is a change in direction that takes place when light strikes a surface and rebounds.

● The law of reflection applies to both specular (parallel) reflection and diffuse (scattered) reflection.

7.2   Refraction and Dispersion

Preview Questions

● What causes light refraction, and what does the index of refraction (n) express?

● Why is white light separated into colors when passing through a prism?

Refraction

When light strikes a transparent medium, some light is reflected and some is transmitted. This transmission is illustrated in ● Fig. 7.6 for a beam of light incident on the surface of a body of water. Upon investigation, you will find that the transmitted light has changed direction in going from one medium to another. The deviation of light from its original path arises because of a change in speed in the second medium. This effect is called **refraction**. You have probably observed refraction effects for an object in a glass of water. For example, a spoon or pencil in a glass of water will appear to be displaced and perhaps severed (see the chapter-opening photo).

The directions of the incident and refracted rays are expressed in terms of the angle of incidence θ_1 and the angle of refraction θ_2, which are measured relative to the normal, a line perpendicular to the surface boundary of the medium (● Fig. 7.7).* The different

Figure 7.6 Refraction in Action
A beam of light is refracted—that is, its direction is changed—on entering the water.

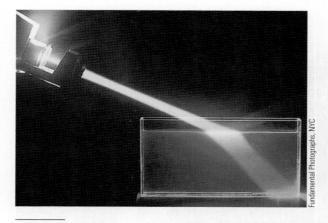

Fundamental Photographs, NYC

---

*For refraction, subscripts 1 and 2 are used for angles to distinguish from the i and r subscripts used for reflection.

speeds in the different media are expressed in terms of a ratio relative to the speed of light. This is known as the **index of refraction** n:

$$\text{index of refraction} = \frac{\text{speed of light in vacuum}}{\text{speed of light in medium}}$$

or

$$n = \frac{c}{c_m} \qquad\qquad 7.1$$

The index of refraction is a pure number (it has no units) because c and c_m are measured in the same units, which cancel. The indexes of refraction of some common substances are given in ● Table 7.1. Note that the index of refraction for air is close to that for vacuum.

When light passes obliquely $(0° < \theta_1 < 90°)$ into a denser medium—for example, from air into water or glass—the light rays are refracted, or bent toward the normal $(\theta_2 < \theta_1)$. It is the slowing of the light that causes this deviation. Complex processes are involved, but intuitively, we might expect the passage of light by atomic absorption and emission through a denser medium to take longer. For example, the speed of light in water is about 75% of its speed in air or vacuum, as shown in the following example.

EXAMPLE 7.1   **Finding the Speed of Light in a Medium**

What is the speed of light in water?

Solution

Step 1

Given: Nothing directly; therefore, quantities are known or available from tables.

Step 2

Wanted: Speed of light in a medium (water). This value may be found from Eq. 7.1. The speed of light c is known, $c = 3.00 \times 10^8$ m/s, and from Table 7.1, $n = 1.33$ for water.

Step 3

Rearranging Eq. 7.1 and doing the calculation,

$$c_m = \frac{c}{n} = \frac{3.00 \times 10^8 \text{ m/s}}{1.33}$$
$$= 2.26 \times 10^8 \text{ m/s}$$

This is about 75% of the speed of light in a vacuum (c), as can be seen by the ratio

$$\frac{c_m}{c} = \frac{1}{n} = \frac{1}{1.33} = 0.752 \ (= 75.2\%)$$

Confidence Exercise 7.1

According to Eq. 7.1, what is the speed of light in (a) a vacuum and (b) air, and how do they compare?

Answers to the Confidence Exercises may be found at the back of the book.

To help understand how light is bent, or refracted, when it passes into another medium, consider a band marching across a field and entering a wet, muddy region obliquely (at an angle), as illustrated in ● Fig. 7.8a. Those marchers who first enter the muddy region keep marching at the same cadence (frequency). Because they are slipping in the muddy earth, though, they don't cover as much ground and are slowed down (smaller wave speed).

The marchers in the same row on solid ground continue on with the same stride, and as a result, the direction of the marching column is changed as it enters the muddy region. This change in direction with change in marching speed is also seen when a marching band turns a corner and the inner members mark time.

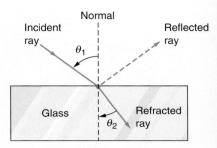

Figure 7.7 Refraction When light enters a transparent medium at an angle, it is deviated, or refracted, from its original path. As illustrated here, when light passes from air into a denser medium such as glass, the rays are refracted, or "bent," toward the normal $(\theta_2 < \theta_1$; that is, the angle of refraction is less than the angle of incidence). Some of the light is also reflected from the surface, as indicated by the dashed ray.

Table 7.1 Indexes of Refraction of Some Common Substances

Substance	n
Water	1.33
Crown glass	1.52
Diamond	2.42
Air (0°C, 1 atm)	1.00029
Vacuum	1.00000

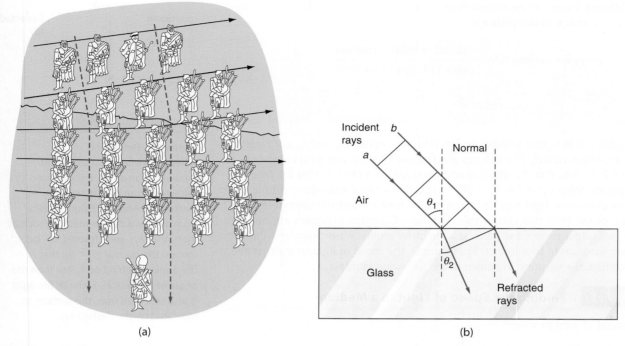

(a)   (b)

Figure 7.8 Refraction Analogy
(a) Marching obliquely into a muddy field causes a band column to change direction. The cadence (or frequency) remains the same, but the marchers in the mud slip and travel shorter distances (shorter wavelengths). This is analogous to the refraction of a wave front (b).

Wave fronts may be thought of as analogous to marching rows (Fig. 7.8b). In the case of light, the wave frequency (cadence) remains the same, but the wave speed is reduced, as is the wavelength ($c_m = \lambda_m f$, Eq. 6.3). The wavelength may be thought of as the distance covered in each step (shorter when slipping).

Conceptual Question and Answer

Twinkle, Twinkle

Q. On a clear night, stars are observed to "twinkle." What causes this?

A. The index of refraction of a gas varies with its density, which varies with temperature. At night, starlight passes through the atmosphere, which has temperature density variations and turbulence. As a result, the refraction causes the star's image to appear to move and vary in brightness, making the stars "twinkle."

A couple of other refraction effects are shown in ● Fig. 7.9. You probably have seen a "wet spot" mirage on a road on a hot day (Fig. 7.9a). No matter how long or how rapidly you travel toward the apparent water, the "spot" is never reached. As illustrated in the figure, the mirage is caused by refraction of light in the hot air near the road surface. This "water," which is the same illusion of thirst-quenching water that appears to desert travelers, is really a view of the sky via refracted sky light. Also, the variation in the density of the rising hot air causes refractive variations that allow hot air to be "seen" rising from the road surface. (Stop and think. You can't see air.)

Have you ever tried to catch a fish underwater and missed? Figure 7.9b shows why. We tend to think of our line of sight as a straight line, but light bends as a result of refraction at the air–water interface. Unless refraction is taken into account, the fish is not where it appears to be.

Finally, you may have noticed that the setting Sun appears flattened, as shown in ● Fig. 7.10a. This is a refractive effect. Light coming from the top and bottom portions is refracted differently as it passes through different atmospheric densities near the horizon, giving rise to a flattening effect. Light from the sides of the Sun is refracted the same, so there is no apparent side difference.

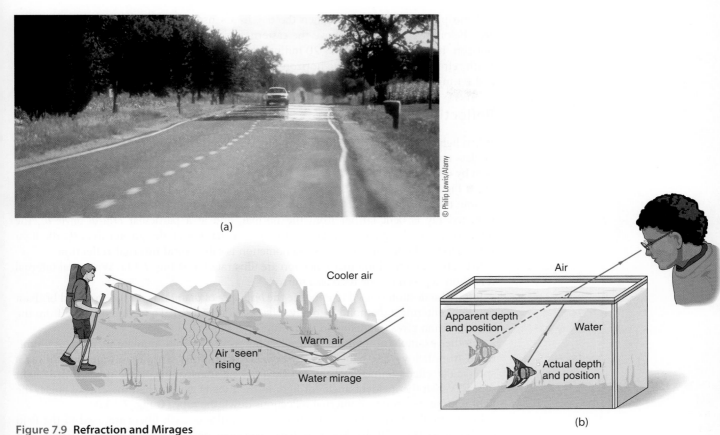

(a)

(b)

Figure 7.9 Refraction and Mirages
(a) A "wet spot" mirage is produced when light from the sky is refracted by warm air near the road surface (the index of refraction varies with temperature). Such refraction also enables us to perceive heated air "rising." Although air cannot be seen, the refraction in the turbulent updrafts causes variations in the light passing through. (b) Try to catch a fish. We tend to think of light as traveling in straight lines, but because light is refracted, the fish is not where it appears to be.

(a)

Figure 7.10 Refraction Effects
(a) The Sun appears flattened because light from the top and bottom portions is refracted as it passes through different atmospheric densities near the horizon. (b) The Sun is seen before it actually rises above the eastern horizon and after it sets below the western horizon because denser air near the Earth refracts the light over the horizon. (Drawing exaggerated for clarity.)

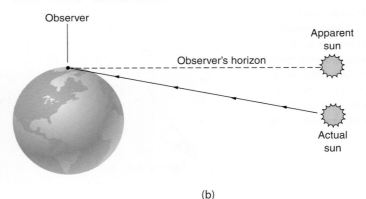

(b)

Atmospheric effects also lengthen the day in a sense. Because of refraction, the Sun is seen before it actually rises above the eastern horizon and after it sets below the western horizon. It may take as much as 20 minutes for rising and setting. The denser air near the Earth refracts the light over the horizon (Fig. 7.10b). The same effect occurs for the rising and setting of the Moon.

Reflection by Refraction

When light goes from a denser medium into a less dense medium (for example, from water or glass into air), the ray is refracted and bent away from the normal. This refraction can be seen by reverse ray tracing of the light shown in Fig. 7.7, this time as it goes from glass into air. ● Figure 7.11 shows this type of refraction for a light source in water.

Note that an interesting thing happens as the angle of incidence becomes larger. The refracted ray is bent farther from the normal, and at a particular *critical angle* θ_c, the refracted ray is along the boundary of the two media. For angles greater than θ_c, the light is reflected and not refracted. This phenomenon is called **total internal reflection**.

Refraction and total internal reflection are illustrated in ● Fig. 7.12a. With total internal reflection, a prism can be used as a mirror.

Internal reflection is used to enhance the *brilliance* of diamonds. In the so-called brilliant cut, light entering a diamond is totally reflected (Fig. 7.12b). The light emerging from the upper portion gives the diamond a beautiful sparkle.

Another example of total internal reflection occurs when a fountain of water is illuminated from below. The light is totally reflected within the streams of water, providing a spectacular effect. Similarly, light can travel along transparent plastic tubes called "light pipes." When the incident angle for light in the tube is greater than the critical angle, the light undergoes a series of internal reflections down the tube (● Fig. 7.13a).

Light can also travel along thin fibers, and bundles of such fibers are used in the field of *fiber optics* (Fig. 7.13b). You may have seen fiber optics used in decorative lamps. An important use of the flexible fiber bundle is to pipe light to hard-to-reach places. Light may also be transmitted down one set of fibers and reflected back through another so that an image of the illuminated area is seen. This illuminated area might be a person's stomach or heart in medical applications (Fig. 7.13c).

Fiber optics is also used in telephone communications. In this application electronic signals in wires are replaced by light (optical) signals in fibers. The fibers can be drawn out thinner than copper wire, and more fibers can be bundled in a cable for a greater number of calls.

Dispersion

The index of refraction for a material actually varies slightly with wavelength. When light is refracted, the different wavelengths of light are bent at slightly different angles. This

Figure 7.11 Internal Reflection
When light goes from a denser medium into a less dense medium, such as from water into air, as illustrated here, it is refracted away from the normal. At a certain critical angle θ_c, the angle of refraction is 90°. For incidence greater than the critical angle, the light is reflected internally.

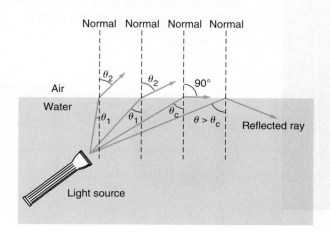

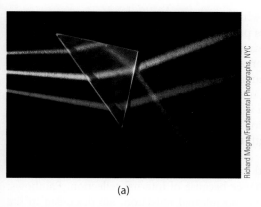

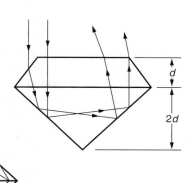

(a)

Figure 7.12 Refraction and Internal Reflection
(a) Beams of colored light are incident on a piece of glass from
the left. As light passes from air into the glass, the beams are
refracted. The incident angle of the blue beam at the glass–air
interface exceeds the critical angle θ_c, and the beam is internally
reflected. (b) Refraction and internal reflection give rise to the brilliance of a diamond. In the so-called brilliant cut, a diamond is cut
with a certain number of faces, or facets, along with the correct
depth to give the proper refraction and internal reflection.

(b)

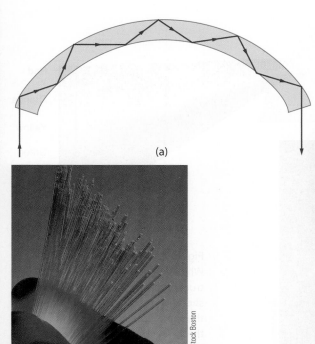

(a)

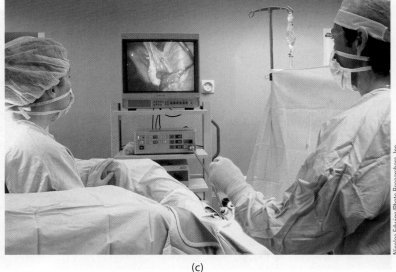

(b)

(c)

Figure 7.13 Fiber Optics
(a) When light that is incident on the end of a transparent tube exceeds the critical angle, it is
internally reflected along the tube, which acts as a "light pipe." (b) A fiber-optic bundle held
between a person's fingers. The ends of the fibers are lit up because of transmission of light by
multiple internal reflections. (c) A fiber-optic application. Endoscopes are used to view various
internal body parts. Light traveling down some fibers is reflected back through others, making it
possible to view otherwise inaccessible places on a monitor.

phenomenon is called **dispersion**. When white light (light containing all wavelengths of the visible spectrum) passes through a glass prism, the light rays are refracted upon entering the glass (● Fig. 7.14). With different wavelengths refracted at slightly different angles, the light is *dispersed* into a spectrum of colors (wavelengths).

That the amount of refraction is a function of wavelength can be seen by combining the two equations $n = c/c_m$ and $c_m = \lambda f$. Substituting the second into the first for c_m, we have $n = c/\lambda f$, and the index of refraction n varies inversely with wavelength λ. So, shorter wavelengths have greater indexes of refraction and are diverted from their path by a greater amount. Blue light has a shorter wavelength than red light; hence, blue light is refracted more than red light, as shown in Fig. 7.14.

As an example of dispersion, a diamond is said to have "fire" because of colorful dispersion. This is in addition to having brilliance because of internal reflection. Rainbows, a natural phenomenon involving dispersion and internal reflection, are discussed in the **Highlight: The Rainbow: Dispersion and Internal Reflection**.

The fact that light can be separated into its component wavelengths provides an important investigative tool. This process is illustrated in ● Fig. 7.15a. Light from a source goes through a narrow slit, and when the light is passed through a prism, the respective wavelengths are separated into "line" images of the slit. The line images, representing definite wavelengths, appear as bright lines. A scale is added for measurement of the wavelengths of the lines in the spectrum, providing an instrument called a *spectrometer*. The line spectra of four elements are shown in Fig. 7.15b.*

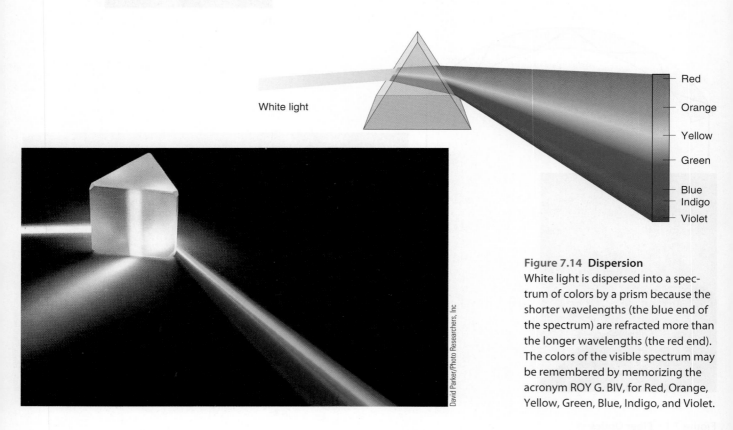

White light

Red
Orange
Yellow
Green
Blue
Indigo
Violet

David Parker/Photo Researchers, Inc

Figure 7.14 Dispersion
White light is dispersed into a spectrum of colors by a prism because the shorter wavelengths (the blue end of the spectrum) are refracted more than the longer wavelengths (the red end). The colors of the visible spectrum may be remembered by memorizing the acronym ROY G. BIV, for Red, Orange, Yellow, Green, Blue, Indigo, and Violet.

---

*In a spectrometer a diffraction grating (Chapter 7.6), which produces sharper lines, is commonly used instead of a prism.

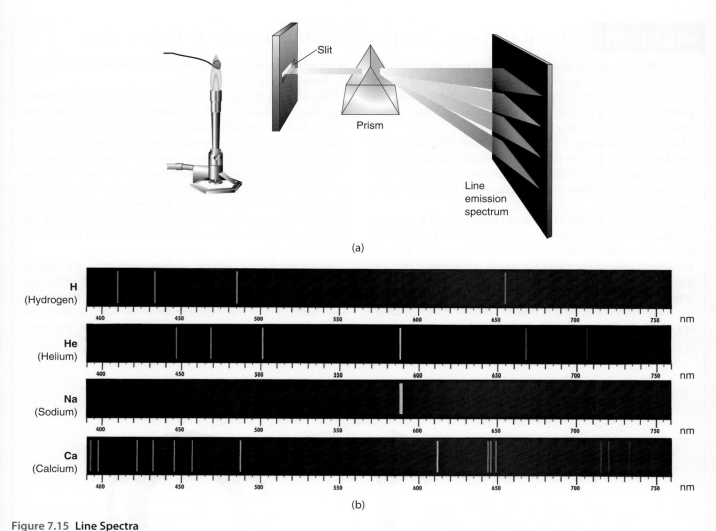

(a)

(b)

Figure 7.15 Line Spectra
(a) A line spectrum is generated when light from a heated source passes through a slit to produce a sharp beam that passes through a prism, which disperses the beam into line images of the slit. (b) Line spectra of various elements in the visible region. Note that each spectrum is unique to, or characteristic of, that element.

Notice in Fig. 7.15b that the spectra are different, or characteristic. Every substance, when sufficiently heated, gives off light of characteristic frequencies. Spectra can be studied and substances identified by means of spectrometers. Astronomers, chemists, physicists, and other scientists have acquired much basic information from the study of light. In fact, the element helium was first identified in the spectrum of sunlight (hence the name *helium* from *helios*, the Greek word for "Sun").

Did You Learn?

- Refraction occurs for transmitted light when the speeds are different in the different media. The index of refraction expresses the speed of light in a medium, relative to the speed of light in vacuum.

- The index of refraction varies with the wavelengths of light, and different wavelengths (colors) are refracted at different angles (dispersion).

Highlight   The Rainbow: Dispersion and Internal Reflection

A beautiful atmospheric phenomenon often seen after rain is the rainbow. The colorful arc across the sky is the result of several optical effects: refraction, internal reflection, and dispersion. The conditions must be just right. As is well known, a rainbow is seen after rain but not after *every* rain.

Following a rainstorm, the air contains many tiny water droplets. Sunlight incident on the droplets produces a rainbow, but whether a rainbow is visible depends on the relative positions of the Sun and the observer. The Sun is generally behind you when you see a rainbow.

To understand the formation and observation of a rainbow, consider what happens when sunlight is incident on a water droplet. On entering the droplet, the light is refracted and dispersed into component colors as it travels in the droplet (Fig. 1a). If the dispersed light strikes the water–air interface of the droplet at greater than the critical angle, then it is internally reflected and the component colors emerge from the droplet at slightly different angles. Because of the conditions for refraction and internal

reflection, the component colors lie in a narrow range of 40° to 42° for an observer on the ground.

Thus, a display of colors is seen only when the Sun is positioned such that the dispersed light is reflected to you through these angles. With this condition satisfied and an abundance of water droplets in the air, you see the colorful arc of a *primary rainbow,* with colors running vertically upward from violet to red (Fig. 1a and c).

Occasionally, conditions are such that sunlight undergoes *two* internal reflections in water droplets. The result is a vertical inversion of colors in a higher, fainter, and less frequently seen *secondary rainbow* (Fig. 1b and c). Note the bright region below the primary rainbow. Light from the rainbows combines to form this illuminated region.

The arc length of a rainbow you see depends on the altitude (angle above the horizon) of the Sun. As the altitude of the Sun increases, less of the rainbow is seen. On the ground, you cannot see a (primary) rainbow if the altitude of the Sun is greater than 42°. The rainbow is below the horizon in this case. However,

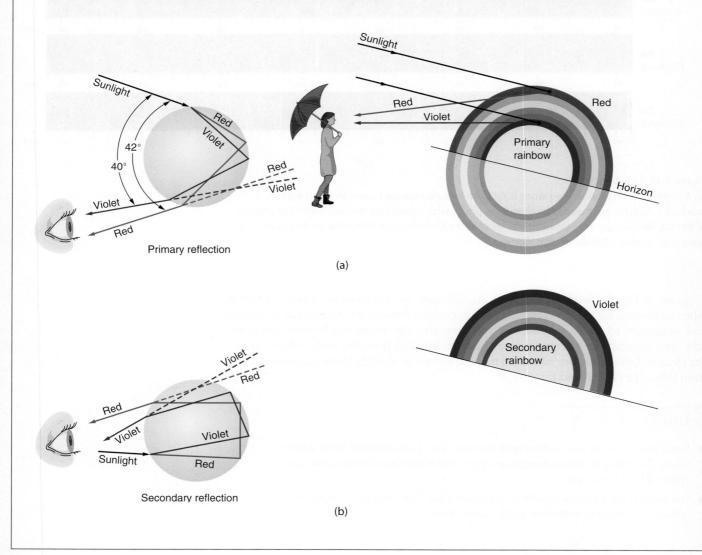

Highlight

if your elevation is increased, then more of the rainbow arc is seen. For instance, airplane passengers sometimes view a completely circular rainbow, similar to the miniature one that can be seen in the mist produced by a lawn sprayer. (No need for a pot of gold.)

(c)

Figure 1 Rainbow Formation
Sometimes two rainbows can be seen, a primary rainbow and a secondary rainbow. (a) For the more common primary rainbow, there are single internal reflections in the water droplets (top, previous page). Note that this separates the colors such that the red component appears above the violet component (dashed lines), and a primary rainbow's colors run sequentially upward from violet to red. (b) For the secondary rainbow, the sunlight enters the water droplets such that there are two internal reflections (bottom, previous page). This causes the sequence of colors in the secondary rainbow to be the reverse of that in the primary rainbow. Secondary rainbows are higher, fainter, and less frequently seen than primary rainbows. (c) Both the Sun and an observer must be properly positioned for the observer to see a rainbow. For the photo, the observer was positioned in such a way that both the primary and secondary rainbows were seen.

7.3 Spherical Mirrors

Preview Questions

● What are the shapes of converging and diverging spherical mirrors?

● What is the difference between real and virtual images?

Spherical surfaces can be used to make practical mirrors. The geometry of a spherical mirror is shown in ● Fig. 7.16. A spherical mirror is a section of a sphere of radius R. A line drawn through the center of curvature C perpendicular to the mirror surface is called the *principal axis*. The point where the principal axis meets the mirror surface is called the *vertex* (V in Fig. 7.16).

Another important point in spherical mirror geometry is *the focal point F*. The distance from the vertex to the focal point is called the **focal length** f. (What is "focal" about the focal point and the focal length will become evident shortly.) For a spherical mirror, the focal length is one-half the value of the radius of curvature of the spherical surface. Expressed in symbols, the *focal length of a spherical mirror* is

$$f = \frac{R}{2}$$

7.2

Figure 7.16 Spherical Mirror Geometry

A spherical mirror is a section of a sphere with a center of curvature C. The focal point F is halfway between C and the vertex V. The distance from V to F is called the *focal length f*. The distance from V to C is the radius of curvature R (the radius of the sphere). And $R = 2f$, or $f = R/2$.

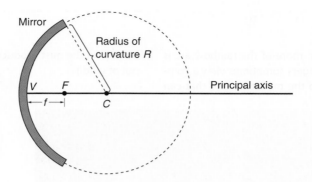

where f is the focal length and R is the radius of curvature for the spherical mirror. Equation 7.2 can be used to locate the focal point F or the center of the curvature C when f or R is known.

The inside surface of a spherical section is said to be *concave* (as though looking into a recess or cave), and when it has a mirrored surface, it is a **concave (converging) mirror**. The reason for "converging" is illustrated in ● Fig. 7.17a. Reflecting light rays parallel to the principal axis converge and pass through the focal point. The rays are "focused" at the focal point. (Off-axis parallel rays converge in the focal plane.)

Similarly, the outside surface of a spherical section is said to be *convex*, and when it has a mirrored surface, it is a **convex (diverging) mirror**. Parallel rays along the principal axis are reflected in such a way that they *appear* to diverge from the focal point (Fig. 7.17b).

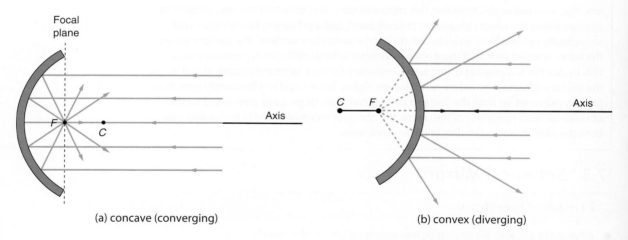

(a) concave (converging)

(b) convex (diverging)

Figure 7.17 Spherical Mirrors

(a) Rays parallel to the principal axis of a concave or converging spherical mirror converge at the focal point. Rays not parallel to the principal axis converge in the focal plane so as to form extended images. (b) Rays parallel to the axis of a convex or diverging spherical mirror are reflected so as to appear to diverge from the focal point inside the mirror. (c) The divergent property of a diverging mirror is used to give an expanded field of view, as shown here for a department store.

(c)

In regard to reverse ray tracing, light rays coming to the mirror from the surroundings are made parallel, and an expanded field of view is seen in the diverging mirror. Diverging mirrors are used on side mirrors of cars and trucks to give drivers a wider rear view of traffic and in stores to monitor aisles (Fig. 7.17c).

Ray Diagrams

The images formed by spherical mirrors can be found graphically using *ray diagrams*. An arrow is commonly used as the object, and the location and size of the image are determined by drawing two rays:

1. Draw a ray parallel to the principal axis that is reflected through the focal point.

2. Draw a ray through the center of curvature C that is perpendicular to the mirror surface and reflected back along the incident path.

The intersection of these rays (tip of arrow) locates the position of the image.

These rays are shown in ● Fig. 7.18 for an object at various positions in front of a concave mirror. In the ray diagrams, D_o is the *object distance* (distance of the object from the vertex) and D_i is the *image distance* (distance of the image from the vertex). The object distance in a ray diagram can be determined relative to the focal point (F) or the center of curvature (C), which is usually known from f or R.

The characteristics of an image are described as being (1) *real or virtual*, (2) *upright (erect) or inverted*, and (3) *magnified or reduced* (smaller than the object). If the diagram is drawn to scale, then the magnification (greater or less than 1) may be found by comparing the heights of the object and image arrows in Fig. 7.18. A **real image** is one for which the light rays converge so that an image can be formed on a screen. A **virtual image** is one for which

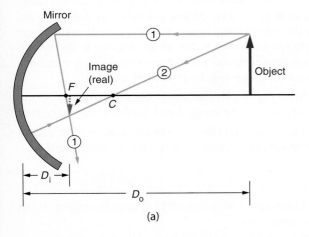

(a)

Figure 7.18 Ray Diagrams

Illustrations of rays 1 and 2 (see text) in ray diagrams. D_o and D_i are the object distance and image distance, respectively. (a) A ray diagram for an object beyond the center of curvature C for a concave spherical mirror shows where the image is formed. (b) A ray diagram for a concave mirror for an object located between F and C. In (a) and (b) the images are real and thus could be seen on a screen placed at the image distances. Note that the image moves out and grows larger as the object moves toward the mirror. (c) A ray diagram for a concave mirror with the object inside the focal point F. In this case, the image is virtual and is formed behind, or "inside," the mirror.

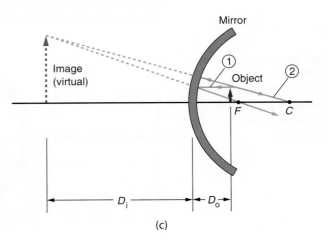

(b)

(c)

the light rays diverge and cannot be formed on a screen. Both real and virtual images are formed by a concave (converging) spherical mirror, depending on the object distance. An example of a virtual image is shown in ● Fig. 7.19, where magnification is put to use.

Note that the real images are formed in front of the mirror where a screen could be positioned. Virtual images are formed behind or "inside" the mirror where the light rays *appear* to converge. For a converging concave mirror, a virtual image always results when the object is inside the focal point. For a diverging mirror, a virtual image always results wherever the object is located. (What type of image is formed by a plane mirror?)

A convex mirror may also be treated by ray diagrams. The rays of a ray diagram are drawn by using the law of reflection, but they are extended through the focal point and the center of curvature inside or behind the mirror, as shown in ● Fig. 7.20. A virtual image is formed where these extended rays intersect. As Fig 7.20 suggests, even though the object distance may vary, the image of a diverging convex mirror is always virtual, upright, and smaller than the object.

Figure 7.19 Magnification
Concave cosmetic mirrors give magnification so that facial features can be seen better.

EXAMPLE 7.2   Finding the Images of Spherical Mirrors Using Ray Diagrams

A spherical concave mirror has a radius of curvature of 20 cm.

(a) An object is placed 25 cm in front of the concave mirror. Draw a ray diagram for this situation. Estimate the image distance and give the image characteristics.

(b) An object is placed 15 cm in front of the concave mirror. Draw a ray diagram, estimate the image distance, and give the image characteristics for this case.

Solution

(a) With $R = 20$ cm, then $f = R/2 = 20$ cm$/2 = 10$ cm, which gives the locations of C and F, respectively. Locating the object and drawing the two rays to locate the image gives the ray diagram shown in ● Fig. 7.21a. (When not asked to draw to scale, you may use a sketch to give the approximate image distance, as well as the image characteristics.) As can be seen from the sketch, the image distance is about midway between F and C, or 15 cm (mathematical calculations reveal that it is actually 16.7 cm), and the image characteristics are real, inverted, and reduced.

(b) Using the same procedure, from Fig. 7.21b the image distance is about 30 cm (mathematically it is actually 30 cm), and the image is real, inverted, and magnified.

The image is reduced when the object is beyond the center of curvature (C) but magnified when the object is inside the center of curvature. This result is true in general.

Confidence Exercise 7.2

Suppose the object in part (a) of Example 7.2 were placed 5 cm from the mirror. What would be the image characteristics in this case?

Answers to Confidence Exercises may be found at the back of the book.

Figure 7.20 Ray Diagram for a Diverging Mirror
A ray diagram for a convex spherical mirror with an object in front of the mirror. A convex mirror always forms a reduced, virtual image.

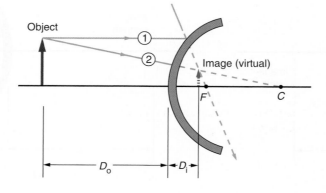

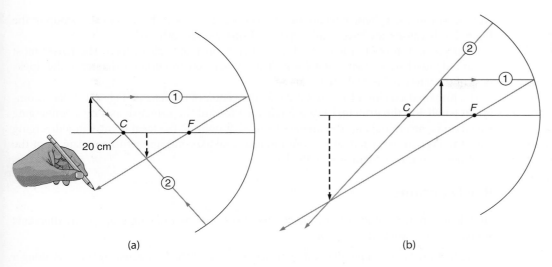

Figure 7.21 Ray Diagrams for Example 7.2
See text for description.

Conceptual Question and Answer

Up and Down

Q. When you look into the front side of a shiny spoon, you will see an inverted image of yourself. When you look at the back side of the spoon, your image is upright. Why?

A. You are alternately looking at concave and convex mirrors. Looking into the front of the spoon, or a concave mirror, as an object you are outside the focal length and the image is inverted. As you move the spoon away from you, the inverted image becomes smaller. [Compare with the ray diagrams in Fig. 7.18a and b.]

Looking at the back of the spoon, or a convex mirror, your image is upright as all images are for convex mirrors (see Fig. 7.20). Get a spoon and check it out.

Did You Learn?

● A converging mirror is concave, and a diverging mirror is convex.

● A real image is one for which light rays converge so that an image can be formed on a screen. For a virtual image, the light rays diverge and an image cannot be formed.

7.4 Lenses

Preview Questions

● What is the general difference in shapes between a converging lens and a diverging lens?

● What are the functions of the rods and cones in the retina of the human eye?

A lens consists of material such as a transparent piece of glass or plastic that refracts light waves to give an image of an object. Lenses are extremely useful and are found in eyeglasses, telescopes, magnifying glasses, cameras, and many other optical devices.

In general, there are two main types of lenses. A **converging lens** is thicker at the center than at the edges. A **diverging lens** is thinner at the center than at the edges. These two types and some of the possible shapes for each are illustrated in ● Fig. 7.22. In general, we

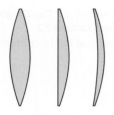
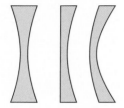

Converging, or
convex, lenses;
greatest thickness
at center

Diverging, or
concave, lenses;
greatest thickness
at edge

Figure 7.22 Lenses
Different types of converging and
diverging lenses. Note that converging lenses are thicker at the center
than at the edges, whereas diverging
lenses are thinner at the center and
thicker at the edges.

will investigate the spherical biconvex and biconcave lenses at the left of each group in the figure (*bi-* because they have similar spherical surfaces on both sides).

Light passing through a lens is refracted twice, once at each surface. The lenses most commonly used are known as *thin lenses*. Thus, when constructing ray diagrams, the thickness of the lens can be neglected.

The principal axis for a lens goes through the center of the lens (● Fig. 7.23). Rays coming in parallel to the principal axis are refracted toward the principal axis by a converging lens. For a converging lens, the rays are focused at point *F*, the focal point. For a diverging lens, the rays are refracted away from the principal axis and appear to emanate from the focal point on the incident side of the lens.

Ray Diagrams

How lenses refract light to form images can be shown by drawing graphic ray diagrams similar to those applied to mirrors.

1. The first ray is drawn parallel to the principal axis and then refracted by the lens along a line drawn through a focal point of the lens.

2. The second ray is drawn through the center of the lens without a change in direction.

The intersection of these rays (tips of arrows) locates the position of the image (tip of the image arrow).

Examples of this procedure are shown in ● Fig. 7.24. Only the focal points for the respective surfaces are shown—just focal points are needed. The lenses do have radii of curvature, but for spherical lenses, $f \neq R/2$ in contrast to $f = R/2$ for spherical mirrors. The characteristics of the images formed by a converging or convex lens change, similar to the way those of a converging mirror change as an object is brought toward the mirror from a distance. Beyond the focal point, an inverted, real image is formed, which becomes larger as the object approaches the focal point.

The magnification becomes greater than 1 when the object distance is less than $2f$. Once inside the focal point of a converging mirror, an object always forms a virtual image. For lenses, a *real image* is formed on the opposite side of a lens from the object and can be seen on a screen (Fig. 7.23a). A *virtual image* is formed on the object side of the lens (Fig. 7.24b).

For a diverging or concave lens, the image is always upright and reduced, or smaller than the object. When looking through a concave lens, one sees images as shown in ● Fig. 7.25. Also, a concave lens forms only virtual objects.

EXAMPLE 7.3   **Finding the Images of Converging Lenses Using Ray Diagrams**

A convex lens has a focal length of 12 cm. Draw ray diagrams for objects at (a) 18 cm and (b) 8 cm from the lens. Estimate the image distances and give the image characteristics for each case.

Figure 7.23 Lens Focal Points
For a converging spherical lens, rays parallel to the principal axis and incident on the lens converge at the focal point on the opposite side of the lens. Rays parallel to the axis of a diverging lens appear to diverge from a focal point on the incident side of the lens.

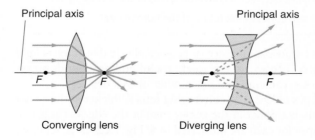

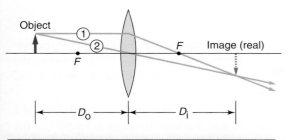

Figure 7.24 Ray Diagrams
(a) A ray diagram for a converging lens with the object outside the focal point. The image is real and inverted and can be seen on a screen placed at the image distance, as shown in the photo. (b) A ray diagram for a converging lens with the object inside the focal point. In this case, an upright, virtual image is formed on the object side of the lens.

(a)

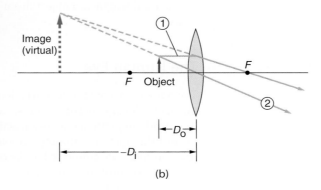

(b)

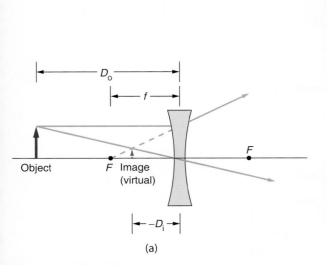

(a)

(b)

Figure 7.25 Diverging Lens
(a) A ray diagram for a diverging, concave lens. A virtual image is formed on the object side of the lens. Diverging lenses form only virtual images. (b) Like a diverging mirror, a diverging (concave) lens gives an expanded field of view.

Solution

(a) The focal length locates the focal point *F*. Locating the object and drawing the two rays to locate the image gives the ray diagram shown in ● Fig. 7.26a. It shows the image distance to be about twice (36 cm) that of the object distance (18 cm), and the image is real, inverted, and magnified.

(b) Using the same procedure, from Fig. 7.26b we see that the image is behind the object (with an image distance of about 24 cm) and that the image is virtual (on the object side of the lens), upright, and magnified.

Confidence Exercise 7.3

Suppose a diverging (concave) lens were used in part (b) of Example 7.3, with the same focal length and object distance. What would be the image characteristics in this case?

The Human Eye

The human eye contains a convex lens along with other refractive media in which most of the light refraction occurs. Even so, a great deal can be learned about the optics of the eye by considering only the focusing action of the lens. As illustrated in ● Fig. 7.27, the lens focuses the light entering the eye on the *retina*. The photoreceptors of the retina, called *rods* and *cones*, are connected to the optic nerve, which sends signals to the brain. The rods are more sensitive than the cones and are responsible for light and dark "twilight" vision; the cones are responsible for color vision. The retina contains about 120 million rods and 6 million cones. (Remember "c"ones for "c"olor.)

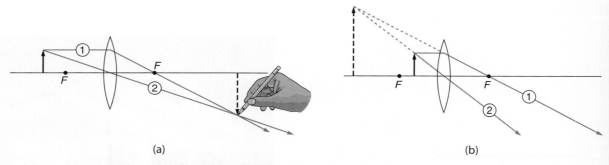

(a)   (b)

Figure 7.26 Ray Diagrams for Example 7.3
See text for description.

Figure 7.27 The Human Eye
The lens of the human eye forms an image on the retina, which contains rod and cone cells. The rods are more sensitive than the cones and are responsible for light and dark "twilight" vision; the cones are responsible for color vision. (The image is drawn vertically for clarity.)

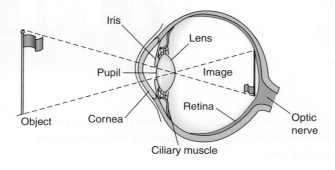

Right Side Up from Upside Down

Q. Note in Fig. 7.27 that an image focused on the retina is upside down. Why don't we see the world that way?

A. The brain learns early in life to interpret the inverted images of the world right side up. Experiments have been done with persons wearing special glasses that give them an inverted view of the world. After some initial run-ins, they become accustomed to and function quite well in their upside-down world.

Because the distance between the lens and retina does not vary, in this situation D_i is constant. Because D_o varies for different objects, the focal length of the lens of the eye must vary for the image to be on the retina. The lens is called the *crystalline lens* and consists of glassy fibers. By action of the attached ciliary muscles, the shape and focal length of the lens vary as the lens is made thinner and thicker. The optical adjustment of the eye is truly amazing. Objects can be seen quickly at distances that range from a few centimeters (the near point) to infinity (the far point).

Although the far point is infinity, objects can be resolved only for certain distances. When one is viewing distant objects, they appear smaller and eventually become indistinguishable (cannot be resolved). It is sometimes said that the Great Wall of China is the only human construction that can be seen by the unaided eye of an astronaut orbiting the Earth, but this statement is false. The Great Wall is on the order of 8.0 m (26 ft) wide at the base and 4.0 m (13 ft) wide at the top. The Los Angeles Freeway is much wider. Astronauts orbit the Earth at altitudes on the order of 400 km (250 mi). It can be shown that to see (visually resolve) the Great Wall, an astronaut would have to be at an altitude of 35 km (22 mi) or lower. This height is within the Earth's atmosphere. (See Chapter 19.1.)

Speaking of a "normal" eye implies that visual defects exist in some eyes, which is readily apparent from the number of people who wear glasses or contact lenses. Many people have trouble seeing objects at certain distances. These individuals have one of the two most common visual defects: nearsightedness and farsightedness.

Nearsightedness (myopia) is the condition of being able to see nearby objects clearly but not distant objects. This occurs when, for some reason, the distant image is focused in front of the retina (● Fig. 7.28a). Glasses with diverging lenses that move the image back to the retina can be used to correct this defect.

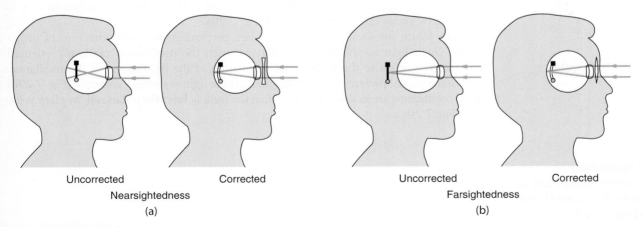

| Uncorrected | Corrected | | Uncorrected | Corrected |

Nearsightedness   Farsightedness

(a)   (b)

Figure 7.28 Vision Defects
Two common vision defects arise because the image is not focused on the retina. (a) Nearsightedness occurs when the image is formed in front of the retina. This condition is corrected by wearing glasses with diverging lenses. (b) Farsightedness occurs when the image is formed behind the retina. This condition is corrected by wearing glasses with converging lenses.

Farsightedness (hyperopia) is the condition of being able to see distant objects clearly but not nearby objects. The images of such objects are focused behind the retina (Fig. 7.28b). The near point is the position closest to the eye at which objects can be seen clearly. (Bring your finger toward your nose. The position where the tip of the finger goes out of focus is your near point.) For farsighted people, the near point is not at the normal position but at some point farther from the eye.

Children can see sharp images of objects as close as 10 cm (4 in.) to their eyes. The crystalline lens of the normal young-adult eye can be deformed to produce sharp images of objects as close as 12 to 15 cm (5 to 6 in.). However, at about the age of 40, the near point normally moves beyond 25 cm (10 in.).

You may have noticed older people holding reading material at some distance from their eyes so as to see it clearly. When the print is too small or the arm too short, reading glasses with converging lenses are the solution (Fig. 7.28b). The recession of the near point with age is not considered an abnormal defect of vision. It proceeds at about the same rate in all normal eyes. (You too may need reading glasses someday.)

Did You Learn?

- A converging (convex) lens is thicker at the center than at the edges. A diverging (concave) lens is thinner at the center than at the edges.

- The rods in the retina of your eye are responsible for light and dark "twilight" vision, and the cones are responsible for color vision.

7.5   Polarization

Preview Questions

- What does the polarization of light experimentally prove about light?
- What is the principle of polarizing sunglasses?

The wave nature of light gives rise to an interesting and practical optical phenomenon. Light waves are transverse waves with oscillations perpendicular to the direction of propagation (electromagnetic waves, see Figure 8.24). The atoms of a light source generally emit light waves that are randomly oriented, and a beam of light has transverse oscillations in all directions. Viewing a beam of light from the front, the transverse oscillations may be indicated by vector arrows as shown in ● Fig. 7.29a.

In the figure the oscillations are in planes perpendicular to the direction of propagation. Such light is said to be *unpolarized*, with the oscillations randomly oriented. **Polarization** refers to the preferential orientation of the oscillations. If the oscillations have some partial preferential orientation, then the light *is partially polarized* (Fig. 7.29b). If the oscillations are in a single plane, then the light is **linearly polarized**, or *plane polarized* (Fig. 7.29c).

Figure 7.29 Polarization
(a) When the electric field vectors are randomly oriented, as viewed in the direction of propagation, the light is unpolarized. (b) With preferential orientation, the light is partially polarized. (c) If the field vectors lie in a plane, then the light is linearly polarized.

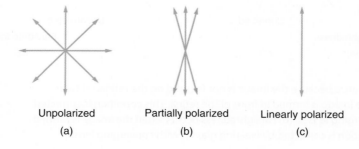

Unpolarized   Partially polarized   Linearly polarized
(a)   (b)   (c)

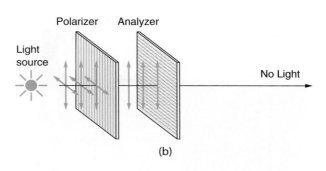

(a)   (b)

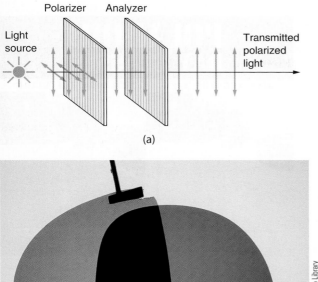

(c)

Leonard Lessin/Peter Arnold, Inc./Photo Library

Figure 7.30 Polarized Light
(a) Light is linearly polarized when it passes through a polarizer. (The lines on the polarizer indicate the direction of polarization.) The polarized light passes through the analyzer if it is similarly oriented. (b) When the polarization direction of the analyzer is perpendicular (90°) to that of the polarizer ("crossed Polaroids"), little or no light is transmitted. (c) A photo showing the condition of (b), "crossed Polaroids," using polarizing sunglass lenses.

A light wave can be polarized by several means. A common method uses a polymer sheet or "Polaroid."* Polaroid sheets have a polarization direction associated with long, oriented molecular chains of the polymer film. The *polarizer* allows only the components in a specific plane to pass through, as illustrated in ● Fig. 7.30a. The other field vectors are absorbed and do not pass through the polarizer.

The human eye cannot detect polarized light, so an *analyzer*, another polarizing sheet, is needed. When a second polarizer is placed in front of the first polarizer, as illustrated in Fig. 7.30b, little light (theoretically, no light) is transmitted and the sheets appear dark. In this case, the polarization directions of the sheets are at 90° and the polarizing sheets are said to be "crossed" (Fig. 7.30c).

The polarization of light is experimental proof that light is a transverse wave. Longitudinal waves, such as sound, cannot be polarized.

Sky light is partially polarized as a result of atmospheric scattering by air molecules. When unpolarized sunlight is incident on air molecules, the light waves set the electrons of the molecules into vibration. The accelerating charges emit radiation, similar to the vibrating charges in the antenna of a broadcast station. The radiated, or "scattered," sky light has polarized components, as may be observed with an analyzer. (The best direction to look to observe the polarization depends on the location of the Sun. At sunset and sunrise, the best direction is directly overhead.) It is believed that some insects, such as bees, use polarized sky light to determine navigational directions relative to the Sun.

A common application of polarization is in polarizing sunglasses. The lenses of these glasses are polarizing sheets oriented such that the polarization direction is vertical. When sunlight is reflected from a surface, such as water or a road, the light is partially polarized in the horizontal direction. Because the reflected light is scattered in a preferred direction, the intensity increases, which an observer sees as glare. Polarizing sunglasses allow only

*Named after the first commercial polarizing sheet, called Polaroid, developed by Edwin Land around 1930.

(a)   (b)

Figure 7.31 Polarizing Sunglasses
(a) Light reflected from a surface is partially polarized in the horizontal direction of the plane of the surface. Because the polarizing direction of the sunglasses is oriented vertically, the horizontally polarized component of the reflected light is blocked, thereby reducing the intensity or glare. (b) Old-time glare-reduction advertisement from the Polaroid Corporation Archives. Note the vintage of the cars and the price of the glasses.

the vertical component of light to pass through. The horizontal component is blocked out, which reduces the glare (● Fig. 7.31).

Another common but not as well-known application of polarized light is discussed in the **Highlight: Liquid Crystal Displays (LCDs)**.

Did You Learn?

● The polarization of light proves that light is a transverse wave.

● The lenses of polarizing sunglasses have the polarizing direction vertical so as to reduce the horizontally polarized reflective glare.

7.6   Diffraction and Interference

Preview Questions

● On what does diffraction depend?

● What is the difference between constructive interference and destructive interference?

Diffraction

Water waves passing through slits are shown in ● Fig. 7.32. Note how the waves are bent, or deviated, around the corners of the slit as they pass through. All waves (sound, light, and so on) show this type of bending as they go through relatively small slits or pass by the corners of objects. The deviation of waves in such cases is referred to as **diffraction**.

In Fig. 7.32 there are different degrees of bending, or diffraction. The degree of diffraction depends on the wavelength of the wave and the size of the opening or object. In general, the longer the wavelength compared to the width of the opening or object, the greater the diffraction.

Highlight Liquid Crystal Displays (LCDs)

When a crystalline solid melts, the resulting liquid generally has no orderly arrangement of atoms or molecules. However, some organic compounds have an intermediate state in which the liquid retains some orderly molecular arrangement, hence the name liquid crystal (LC).

Some liquid crystals are transparent and have an interesting property. When an electrical voltage is applied, the liquid crystal becomes opaque. The applied voltage upsets the orderly arrangement of the molecules, and light is scattered, making the LC opaque.

Another property of some liquid crystals is how they affect linearly polarized light by "twisting" or rotating the polarization direction 90°. This twisting, however, does not occur if a voltage is applied, causing molecular disorder.

A common application of these properties is in liquid crystal displays (LCDs), which are found on wristwatches, calculators, and TV and computer screens. How LCDs work is illustrated in Fig. 1.

Trace the incident light in the top diagram of Fig. 1. Unpolarized light is linearly polarized by the first polarizer. The LC then rotates the polarization direction, and the polarized light passes through the second polarizer (which is "crossed" with the first) and then is reflected by the mirror. On the reverse path, the rotation of the polarization direction in the LC allows the light to emerge from the LCD, which consequently appears bright or white.

However, if a voltage is applied to the LC such that it loses its rotational property, then light is not passed by the second polarizer. With no reflected light, the display appears dark. Thus, by applying voltages to segments of numeral and letter displays, it is possible to form dark regions on a white background (Fig. 2). The white background is the reflected, polarized light, which can be demonstrated by using an analyzer. The LCD display on your calculator may appear dark if you are wearing polarizing sunglasses.

(a)

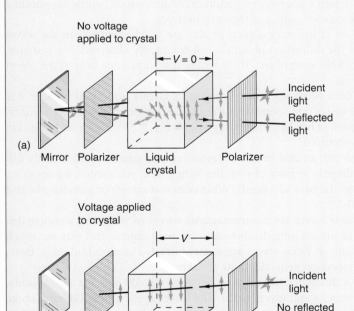

Figure 1 Liquid Crystal Display (LCD)
(a) An illustration of how a liquid crystal "twists" the light polarization through 90°. The light passes through the polarizer and is reflected back and out of the crystal with another twist.
(b) When a voltage is applied to the crystal, there is no twisting and light does not pass through the second polarizer. In this case, the light is absorbed and the crystal appears dark.

(a)

Figure 2 LCDs and Polarization
(a) The light from the bright regions of an LCD is polarized, as can be shown by using polarizing sunglasses as an analyzer. Here the numbers can still be seen, (b) but not when the glasses have been rotated 90°.

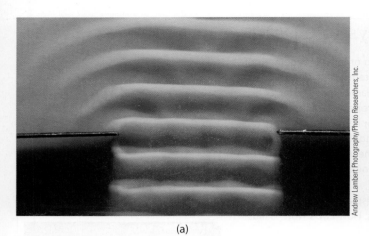

(a)

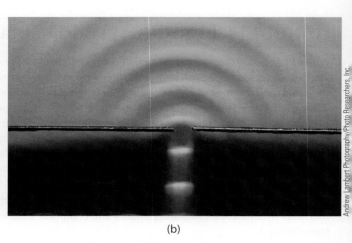

(b)

Andrew Lambert Photography/Photo Researchers, Inc.

Figure 7.32 Diffraction
(a) The diffraction, or bending, of the water waves passing through the slit can be seen in a ripple tank, with the bending at the edges of the waves. (b) When the slit is made smaller, the diffraction becomes greater. Note the greater bending of the waves.

As was shown in Example 6.1, audible sound waves have wavelengths on the order of centimeters to meters. Visible light waves, on the other hand, have wavelengths of about 10^{-6} m (a millionth of a meter). Ordinary objects (and slits) have dimensions of centimeters to meters. Thus, the wavelengths of sound are larger than or about the same size as objects, and diffraction readily occurs for sound. For example, when you are standing in one room, you can talk through a doorway into another room in which people are standing around the corner unseen on each side, and they can hear you.

However, the dimensions of ordinary objects or slits are much greater than the wavelengths of visible light, so the diffraction of light is not commonly observed. For instance, when you shine a beam of light at an object, there will be a shadow zone behind the object with very sharp boundaries.

Some light diffraction does occur at corners, but it goes largely unnoticed because it is difficult to see. Very close inspection reveals that the shadow boundary is blurred or fuzzy, and there is actually a pattern of bright and dark regions (● Fig. 7.33). This is an indication that some diffraction has occurred.

Think about this: When you sit in a lecture room or movie theater, sound is easily diffracted around a person directly in front of you, but light is not; you cannot see anything directly in front (other than the back of a head). What does that say about wavelengths and the size of people's heads?

As another example, radio waves are electromagnetic waves of very long wavelengths, in some cases hundreds of meters long. In this case, ordinary objects and slits are much smaller than the wavelength, so radio waves are easily diffracted around buildings, trees, and so on, making radio reception generally quite efficient.

You may have noticed a difference in reception between the AM and FM radio bands, which have different frequencies and wavelengths. The wavelengths of the AM band range from about 180 m to 570 m, whereas the wavelengths of the FM band range from 2.8 m to 3.4 m. Hence, the longer AM waves are easily diffracted around buildings and the like, whereas FM waves may not be. As a result, AM reception may be better than FM reception in some areas.

Interference

When two or more waves meet, they are said to *interfere*. For example, water waves from two disturbances on a lake or pond commonly interfere with each other. The resultant waveform of the interfering waves is a combination of the individual waves. Specifically, the waveform is given by the **principle of superposition**:

Ken Kay/Fundamental Photographs, NYC

Figure 7.33 Diffraction Pattern
Using special lighting, it is possible to see diffraction patterns clearly in the opening of a razor blade.

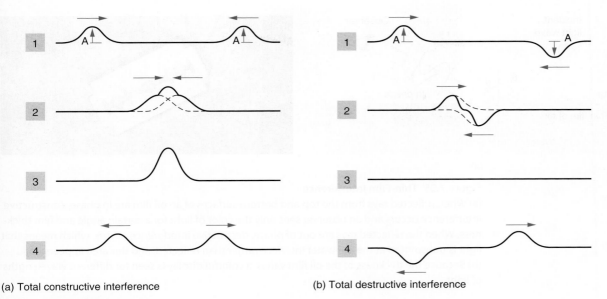

(a) Total constructive interference   (b) Total destructive interference

Figure 7.34 Interference
(a) When wave pulses of equal amplitude that are in phase meet and overlap, there is total constructive interference. At the instant of the overlap (a, 3), the amplitude of the combined pulse is twice that of the individual ones ($A + A = 2A$). (b) When two wave pulses of equal amplitude are out of phase, the waveform disappears for an instant when waves exactly overlap (b, 3); that is, the combined amplitude of the waveform is zero ($A - A = 0$).

At any time, the combined waveform of two or more interfering waves is given by the sum of the displacements of the individual waves at each point in the medium.

The displacement of the combined waveform of two waves at any point is given by $y = y_1 + y_2$, where the directions are indicated by plus and minus signs. The waveform of the interfering waves changes with time, and after interfering, the waves pass on with their original forms.

It is possible for the waves to reinforce one another when they overlap, or interfere, causing the amplitude of the combined waveform to be greater than either pulse. This is called **constructive interference**. On the other hand, if two waves tend to cancel each other when they overlap or interfere (that is, if one wave has a negative displacement), then the amplitude of the combined waveform is smaller than that of either pulse. This is called **destructive interference**.

Special cases of constructive and destructive interference are shown in ● Fig. 7.34 for pulses with the same amplitude A. When the interfering pulses are exactly in phase (crest coincides with crest when the pulses are overlapped), the amplitude of the combined waveform is twice that of either individual pulse ($y = A + A = 2A$), and this is referred to as *total constructive interference* (Fig. 7.34a). However, when two pulses are completely out of phase (crest coincides with trough when the pulses are overlapped), the waveforms disappear; that is, the amplitude of the combined waveform is zero ($y = A - A = 0$). This is referred to as *total destructive interference* (Fig. 7.34b).

The word *destructive* is misleading. Do not get the idea that the energy of the pulses is destroyed. The waveform is destroyed, but the propagating energy is still there in the medium, in the form of potential energy (conservation of energy). After interfering, the individual pulses continue on with their original waveforms.

The colorful displays seen in oil films and soap bubbles can be explained by interference. Consider light waves incident on a thin film of oil on the surface of water or on a wet road. Part of the light is reflected at the air–oil interface, and part is transmitted. The part of the light in the oil film is then reflected at the oil–water interface (● Fig. 7.35).

The two reflected waves may be in phase, totally out of phase, or somewhere in between. In Fig. 7.35a the waves are shown in phase, but this result will occur only for certain

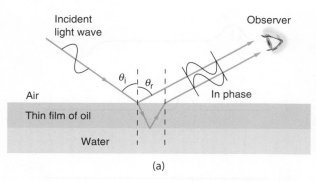

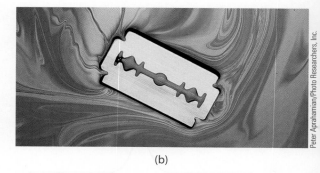

(a)

(b)

Figure 7.35 Thin-Film Interference
(a) When reflected rays from the top and bottom surfaces of an oil film are in phase, constructive interference occurs and an observer sees only the color of light for a certain angle and film thickness. When the reflected rays are out of phase, destructive interference occurs, which means that light is transmitted at the oil–water interface rather than reflected, and this area appears dark.
(b) Because the thickness of the oil film varies, a colorful display is seen for different wavelengths of light.

angles of observation, wavelengths of light (colors), and thicknesses of oil film. At certain angles and oil thicknesses, only one wavelength of light shows constructive interference. The other visible wavelengths interfere destructively, and these wavelengths are transmitted and not reflected.

Hence, different wavelengths interfere constructively for different thicknesses of oil film, and an array of colors is seen (Fig. 7.35b). In soap bubbles the thickness of the soap film moves and changes with time, and so does the array of colors.

Diffraction can also give rise to interference. This interference can arise from the bending of light around the corners of a single slit. An instructive technique employs two narrow double slits that can be considered point sources, as illustrated in ● Fig. 7.36. When the slits are illuminated with monochromatic light (light of only one wavelength), the diffracted light through the slits spreads out and interferes constructively and destructively at different points where crest meets crest and where crest meets trough, respectively. By placing a screen a distance from the slits, an observer can see an interference pattern of alternating bright and dark fringes. A double-slit experiment done in 1801 by English scientist Thomas Young demonstrated the wave nature of light. Such an experiment makes it possible to compute the wavelength of the light from the geometry of the experiment.

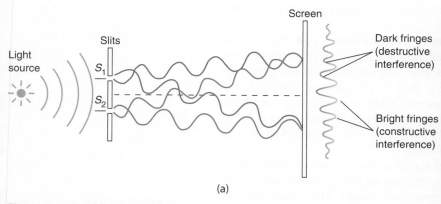

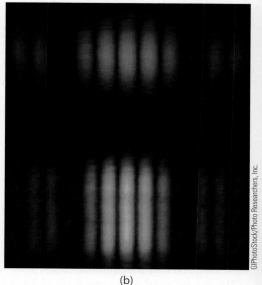

(a)

(b)

Figure 7.36 Double-Slit Interference
(a) Light waves interfere as they pass through two narrow slits that act as point sources, giving rise to regions of constructive interference, or bright fringes, and regions of destructive interference, or dark fringes. (b) Actual diffraction patterns of different colors of laser light through a double slit. Note that the fringe spacing is smaller for the shorter (green) wavelength.

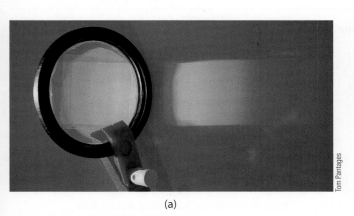

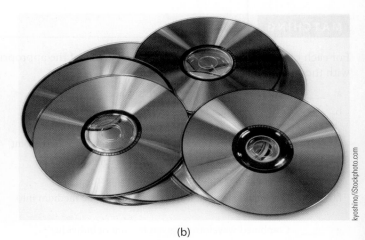

(a)   (b)

Figure 7.37 Diffraction Grating Interference
(a) The many slits of a diffraction grating produce a very sharp interference pattern compared with those of only two slits. The photo shows the colorful separation of colors (wavelengths) of white light passing through a transmission grating. (b) Diffraction is now readily observed. The grooves of a compact disc (CD) form a reflection diffraction grating, and the incident light is separated into a spectrum of colors.

This double-slit experiment may be extended. The intensity of the lines becomes less when the light has to pass through a number of narrow slits, but this produces sharp lines that are useful in the analysis of light sources and other applications. A *diffraction grating* consists of many narrow, parallel lines spaced very close together. When light is transmitted through a grating, it is called a *transmission grating*. Such gratings are made by using a laser to etch fine lines on a photosensitive material. The interference of waves passing through such a diffraction grating produces an interference pattern, as shown in ● Fig. 7.37a.

Reflection gratings (reflecting lines) are made by etching lines on a thin film of aluminum deposited on a flat surface. The narrow grooves of a compact disc (CD) act as a reflection diffraction grating, producing colorful displays (Fig. 7.37b).

Diffraction gratings are more effective than prisms for separating the component wavelengths of light emitted by stars (including our Sun) and other light sources (see Fig. 7.15).

Did You Learn?

● In general, the longer the wavelength compared to the size of the opening or object, the greater the diffraction (bending).

● In constructive interference, when two waves interfere, the combined wave form is greater in amplitude than either wave. In destructive interference the opposite occurs.

KEY TERMS

1. reflection (7.1)
2. ray
3. law of reflection
4. specular reflection
5. diffuse reflection
6. refraction (7.2)
7. index of refraction
8. total internal reflection
9. dispersion
10. focal length (7.3)
11. concave (converging) mirror
12. convex (diverging) mirror
13. real image
14. virtual image
15. converging lens (7.4)
16. diverging lens
17. polarization (7.5)
18. linearly polarized light
19. diffraction (7.6)
20. principle of superposition
21. constructive interference
22. destructive interference

MATCHING

For each of the following items, fill in the number of the appropriate Key Term from the preceding list. Compare your answers with those at the back of the book.

a. _____ Reflection from a very smooth surface

b. _____ Image for which light rays diverge and cannot form an image

c. _____ Parallel light rays appear to diverge from mirror focal point

d. _____ Amplitude of combined wave form is greater

e. _____ An image that can be formed on a screen

f. _____ A change in direction when going from one medium into another

g. _____ Combined waveform is given by sum of individual displacements

h. _____ A change in the direction of light at a surface

i. _____ Parallel light rays converge and pass through mirror focal point

j. _____ Amplitude of combined wave form is smaller

k. _____ Reflection from a relatively rough surface

l. _____ Lens thicker at the edge than at the center

m. _____ Distance from vertex to focal point

n. _____ Reflection back into same medium

o. _____ Preferential orientation of field vectors

p. _____ A straight line that represents the path of light

q. _____ Bending of light waves passing through slits and around corners

r. _____ Ratio of light speeds in vacuum and medium

s. _____ Refraction of wavelengths at slightly different angles

t. _____ Light that is plane polarized

u. _____ $\theta_i = \theta_r$

v. _____ Lens thicker at the center than at the edge

MULTIPLE CHOICE

Compare your answers with those at the back of the book.

1. For ray reflections from a surface, which statement is true? (7.1)
   (a) The angle of reflection is equal to the angle of incidence.
   (b) The reflection angle is measured from a line perpendicular to the reflecting surface.
   (c) The rays lie in the same plane.
   (d) All the preceding are true.

2. To what does the law of reflection apply? (7.1)
   (a) regular reflection
   (b) specular reflection
   (c) diffuse reflection
   (d) all the preceding

3. What is the case when the angle of refraction is smaller than the angle of incidence? (7.2)
   (a) The critical angle is exceeded.
   (b) The first medium is less dense.
   (c) The second medium has a smaller index of refraction.
   (d) The speed of light is greater in the second medium.

4. In refraction, which of the following wave properties is unchanged? (7.2)
   (a) frequency   (b) wavelength
   (c) speed   (d) both (a) and (b)

5. What is the unit of the index of refraction? (7.2)
   (a) m   (b) none; it is unitless
   (c) m/s   (d) l/s

6. Which is true of a convex mirror? (7.3)
   (a) It has a radius of curvature equal to f.
   (b) It is a converging mirror.
   (c) It forms only virtual images.
   (d) It forms magnified and reduced images.

7. Which is true for a real image? (7.3)
   (a) It is always magnified.
   (b) It is formed by converging light rays.

   (c) It is formed behind a mirror.
   (d) It occurs only for $D_i = D_o$.

8. Which of the following is true of a concave lens? (7.4)
   (a) It is a converging lens.
   (b) It is thicker at the center than at the edge.
   (c) It is a lens that forms virtual images for $D_o > f$.
   (d) It is a lens that forms real images for $D_o < f$.

9. Which is true of a virtual image? (7.4)
   (a) It is always formed by a convex lens.
   (b) It can be formed on a screen.
   (c) It is formed on the object side of a lens.
   (d) It cannot be formed by a concave lens.

10. What happens when the polarization directions of two polarizing sheets are at an angle of 90° to each other? (7.5)
   (a) No light gets through.
   (b) There is maximum transmission.
   (c) Maximum transmission is reduced by 50%.
   (d) None of the preceding.

11. Which is true of diffraction? (7.6)
   (a) It occurs best when the slit width is less than the wavelength of a wave.
   (b) It depends on refraction.
   (c) It is caused by interference.
   (d) It does not occur for light.

12. When does total constructive interference occur? (7.6)
   (a) when waves are in phase
   (b) at the same time as total destructive interference
   (c) when the waves are equal in amplitude and are completely out of phase
   (d) when total internal reflection occurs

FILL IN THE BLANK

Compare your answers with those at the back of the book.

1. Light rays are used in ___ optics. (Intro)
2. Reflection from a rough surface is referred to as ___ reflection. (7.1)
3. The index of refraction is the ratio of the speed of light in a medium to the speed of light in a(n) ___. (7.2)
4. When light passes obliquely into a denser medium, the light rays are bent ___ the normal. (7.2)
5. When light is reflected and none is refracted at an interface, it is called ___ reflection. (7.2)

6. A concave mirror is commonly called a ___ mirror. (7.3)
7. A virtual image ___ be formed on a screen. (7.3)
8. A diverging lens is ___ at the center than at the edge. (7.4)
9. A virtual image is always formed by a(n) ___ lens. (7.4)
10. Polarization is proof that light is a(n) ___ wave. (7.5)
11. The larger the wavelength compared to the size of an opening or object, the ___ the diffraction. (7.6)
12. The resultant waveform of combining waves is described by the ___. (7.6)

SHORT ANSWER

7.1 Reflection

1. For specular reflection, what is the situation with an angle of incidence of (a) 0° and (b) 90°?
2. Dutch painter Vincent van Gogh was emotionally troubled and once cut off part of his own ear. His *Self Portrait with Bandaged Ear* (1889) is shown in ● Fig. 7.38. Which ear did he cut? (*Hint:* How do you paint a self-portrait?)
3. When you walk toward a full-length plane mirror, what does your image do? How fast does the image move? Is the image in step with you?

4. How long does the image of a 12-in. ruler appear in a plane mirror? Does it depend on the distance the ruler is from the mirror?
5. Where would an observer see the image of the arrow shown in ● Fig. 7.39? (Draw in the image the observer would see.)

7.2 Refraction and Dispersion

6. Is there refraction for incident angles of (a) 0° and (b) 90°?
7. From the Earth, stars are seen to "twinkle." What does an astronaut see from the International Space Station (ISS) orbiting the Earth?
8. Explain why the pencil appears severed in the chapter-opening photo.
9. For any substance, the index of refraction is always greater than 1. Why?
10. Explain why cut diamonds have brilliance and why they have "fire."
11. Does atmospheric refraction affect the length of the day? Would the daylight hours be longer or shorter if the Earth had no atmosphere?

7.3 Spherical Mirrors

12. What relationships exist between the center of curvature, the focal point, the focal length, and the vertex of a spherical mirror?
13. Distinguish between real images and virtual images for spherical mirrors.
14. Explain when real and virtual images are formed by (a) a convex mirror and (b) a concave mirror.

Figure 7.38 *Self Portrait with Bandaged Ear* (1889) by Vincent Van Gogh
See Short-Answer Question 2.

Erich Lessing/Art Resource, NY

Mirror

Figure 7.39 Reflection and Image
See Short-Answer Question 5.

15. What happens to a light ray that passes through the focal point at an angle to the optic axis of a concave mirror?

16. When a light ray parallel to the optic axis is reflected from a concave mirror, where does it go?

17. Why are the back surfaces of automobile headlights curved?

18. What type of mirror would be used for the solar heating of water?

7.4 Lenses

19. Where is a diverging lens thickest?

20. Explain when real and virtual images are formed by (a) a convex lens and (b) a concave lens.

21. Why are slides put into a slide projector upside down, and where is the slide relative to the projector lens?

22. A magnifying glass is a convex lens. Sunlight can be focused to a small spot using such a lens. What is the small spot an image of? Why are holes burnt in pieces of paper or leaves when the small spot is focused on them?

23. Why do some people wear bifocal or trifocal eyeglasses?

7.5 Polarization

24. Give two examples of practical applications of polarization.

25. Is it possible for the human eye to detect polarized light? If not, why not?

26. How could you use polarization to distinguish between longitudinal and transverse waves?

27. While you are looking through two polarizing sheets, one of the sheets is rotated 180°. Will there be any change in what you observe? Explain.

7.6 Diffraction and Interference

28. How can it be shown or proved that light is diffracted?

29. Why do sound waves bend around everyday objects, whereas the bending of light is not generally observed?

30. Which are more easily diffracted by ordinary objects, AM radio waves or FM radio waves? Explain why.

31. Describe the interference of two wave pulses with different amplitudes if they are (a) in phase and (b) completely out of phase.

32. What optical phenomenon causes soap bubbles and oil slicks to show colorful displays?

VISUAL CONNECTION

Visualize the connections and give answers for the blanks. Compare your answers with those at the back of the book.

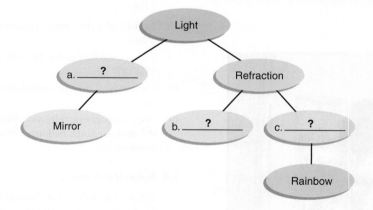

APPLYING YOUR KNOWLEDGE

1. If the Moon's spherical surface gave specular reflection, what would it resemble at full moon?

2. When you look at a window from the inside at night, two similar images, one behind the other, are often seen. Why?

3. On most automobile passenger-side rearview mirrors, a warning is printed: "Objects in mirror are closer than they appear." Why, and what makes the difference? (*Hint*: The mirrors are convex mirrors.)

4. How would a fish see the above-water world when looking up at various angles? (*Hint*: Think in terms of the critical angle and the "cone" of light coming in from above the water in reverse-ray tracing.)

5. You wish to buy a second pair of polarizing sunglasses. How can you check to make certain that the new glasses are indeed polarizing?

6. While you are looking through two polarizing sheets, one of the sheets is slowly rotated 180°. Describe what you will observe.

IMPORTANT EQUATIONS

Index of Refraction: $n = \dfrac{c}{c_m}$ (7.1)

Spherical Mirror Radius and Focal Length Equation: (7.2)

$$f = \frac{R}{2}$$

EXERCISES

7.1 Reflection

1. Light is incident on a plane mirror at an angle of 30° relative to the normal. What is the angle of reflection?

   Answer: 30°

2. Light is incident on a plane mirror at an angle of 30° relative to its surface. What is the angle of reflection?

3. Show that for a person to see his or her complete (head-to-toe) image in a plane mirror, the mirror must have a length (height) of at least one-half a person's height (see Fig. 7.4). Does the person's distance from the mirror make a difference? Explain.

   Answer: Bisecting triangles in the figure give one-half height. This is true for any distance.

4. How much longer must the minimum length of a plane mirror be for a 6-ft 4-in. man to see his complete head-to-toe image than for a 5-ft 2-in. woman to do so?

7.2 Refraction and Dispersion

5. What is the speed of light in a diamond?

   Answer: 1.24×10^8 m/s

6. The speed of light in a particular type of glass is 1.60×10^8 m/s. What is the index of refraction of the glass?

7. What percentage of the speed of light in vacuum is the speed of light in crown glass?

   Answer: 65.8%

8. The speed of light in a certain transparent material is 41.3% of the speed of light in vacuum. What is the index of refraction of the material? (Can you identify the material?)

7.3 Spherical Mirrors

(Assume significant figures to 0.1 cm.)

9. Sketch a ray diagram for a concave mirror with an object at $D_o = R$ and describe the image characteristics.

   Answer: Real, inverted, and same size

10. Sketch ray diagrams for a concave mirror showing objects at (a) $D_o > R$, (b) $D_o > f$, and (c) $D_o < f$. Describe how the image changes as the object is moved toward the mirror.

11. An object is placed 15 cm from a convex spherical mirror with a focal length of 10 cm. Estimate where the image is located and what its characteristics are.

    Answer: $D_i = 6.0$ cm, virtual, upright, and reduced

12. A reflecting, spherical Christmas tree ornament has a diameter of 8.0 cm. A child looks at the ornament from a distance of 15 cm. Describe the image she sees.

7.4 Lenses

13. Sketch a ray diagram for a spherical convex lens with an object at $D_o = 2f$ and describe the image characteristics.

    Answer: Real, inverted, and same size

14. Sketch ray diagrams for a spherical convex lens with objects at (a) $D_o > 2f$, (b) $2f > D_o > f$, and (c) $D_o < f$. Describe how the image changes as the object is moved closer to the lens.

15. An object is placed 45 cm in front of a converging lens with a focal length of 20 cm. Draw a ray diagram. Estimate the image distance and give the image characteristics.

    Answer: $D_i = 36$ cm, real, inverted, reduced

16. An object is placed in front of a converging lens at an object distance of twice the focal length of the lens. Sketch a ray diagram and compare the image and object distances. Repeat with two more ray diagrams, using different focal lengths and still making the object distance twice the focal length. Can you draw any conclusions by comparing the object distance and the image distance?

17. A particular convex lens has a focal length of 15 cm, and an object is placed at the focal point. Draw a ray diagram and comment on where the image is formed.

    Answer: Parallel rays never meet, or meet at infinity. (Thus, there really is no image.)

18. A spherical concave lens has a focal length of 20 cm, and an object is placed 15 cm from the lens. Draw a ray diagram. Estimate the image distance and give the image characteristics.

ON THE WEB

1. The Cause of Refraction

What is light? What happens when light hits an object? Why does light refract? What causes this behavior? Why is there one angle of incidence at which no refraction occurs? What is this angle? Does refractive behavior always occur? Explore answers to these questions by following the recommended links on the student website at **www.cengagebrain.com/shop/ISBN/1133104096**.

2. Let's Wish on a Rainbow

Have you ever wondered about the "physics" of a rainbow? Have you ever wondered exactly what a rainbow is? What will affect whether you see a rainbow (or two)? What do dispersion, refraction, and reflection have to do with rainbows? To answer these questions, follow the recommended links on the student website at **www.cengagebrain.com/shop/ISBN/1133104096**.

> Like charges repel, and unlike
> charges attract each other, with
> a force that varies inversely
> with the square of the distance
> between them.... Frictional
> forces, wind forces, chemical
> bonds, viscosity, magnetism,
> the forces that make the wheels
> of industry go round—all these
> are nothing but Coulomb's law.
>
> •
>
> J. R. Zacharias
> (1905–1986)

Electrical transmission lines >
transport electrical energy over
long distances. Here the towers
run through a field of sunflowers.

© Lester Lefkowitz/CORBIS

PHYSICS FACTS

▶ Electric eels can kill or stun
prey by producing voltages up
to 650 V, more than 50 times
the voltage of a car battery.

▶ A tooth hurts when aluminum
foil touches an amalgam
(metal) filling because a voltage is generated when two
different metals are separated
by a conducting liquid, in this
case saliva.

Ours is indeed an electrical society. Think of how your life might be without electricity. Some idea of this is obtained during extended power out-
ages. Yet when asked to define electricity, many people have difficulty.
The terms *electric charge* and *electric current* come to mind, but what are they?

You may recall from Chapter 1 that *electric charge* was mentioned as a fundamental quantity. That is, we really don't know what it is, so our chief concern is
what it does, which is the description of electrical phenomena.

As you will learn in this chapter, electric charge is associated with certain particles that have interacting forces. With a force, there is motion of electric charges
(current) as well as electrical energy and power. Understanding these principles

Chapter Outline

makes the benefits of electricity available to us. Electricity runs motors, heats food, provides lighting, powers our televisions and stereos, and so on.

But the *electric force* is even more basic than "electricity." It keeps atoms and molecules—even the ones that make up our bodies—together. It may be said that the electric force holds matter together, whereas the gravitational force (Chapter 3.5) holds our solar system and galaxies together.

Closely associated with electricity is *magnetism*. In fact, we refer to *electromagnetism* because these phenomena are basically inseparable. For example, without magnetism, there would be no generation of electrical power. As children (and perhaps as adults), most of us have been fascinated with the properties of small magnets. Have you ever wondered what causes magnets to attract and repel each other?

This chapter introduces the basic properties of electricity and magnetism. Examples of these exciting phenomena are everywhere around us.

8.1   Electric Charge, Electric Force, and Electric Field

Preview Questions

● What is the difference between the law of charges and Coulomb's law?

● What is static electricity?

Electric charge is a fundamental quantity. The property of electric charge is associated with certain subatomic particles, and experimental evidence leads to the conclusion that there are two types of charges, *positive* (+) and *negative* (−). In general, all matter is made up of small particles called *atoms*, which are composed in part of negatively charged particles called **electrons**, positively charged particles called **protons**, and particles called *neutrons* that have no electric charge (they are electrically neutral) and are slightly more massive than protons. ● Table 8.1 summarizes the fundamental properties of these atomic particles, which are discussed in more detail in Chapters 9 and 10.

As the table indicates, all three particles have certain masses, but only electrons and protons possess electric charges. The magnitudes of the electric charges on the electron and the proton are equal, but their natures are different, as expressed by the plus and minus signs. When there is the same number of electrons and protons, the *total* charge is zero (same number of positive and negative charges of equal magnitude), and the atom as a whole is electrically *neutral*.

The unit of electric charge is the *coulomb* (C), after Charles Coulomb (1736–1806), a French scientist who studied electrical effects. Electric charge is usually designated by the letter q. The symbol $+q$ indicates that an object has an excess number of positive charges, or fewer electrons than protons; and $-q$ indicates an excess of negative charges, or more electrons than protons.

Electric Force

An electric force exists between any two charged particles. On investigation, it is found that the mutual forces on the particles may be either attractive or repulsive, depending on the types of charges (+ or −). In fact, it is because of these different force interactions that

Table 8.1 Some Properties of Atomic Particles

Particle	Symbol	Mass	Charge
Electron	e^-	9.11×10^{-31} kg	-1.60×10^{-19} C
Proton	p^+	1.673×10^{-27} kg	$+1.60 \times 10^{-19}$ C
Neutron	n	1.675×10^{-27} kg	0

we know there are two different types of charges. Recall from Chapter 3.5 that for gravitation there is only one type of mass and that the force interaction between masses is always attractive.

The attraction and repulsion between different types of charges are described by the **law of charges**:

Like charges repel; unlike charges attract.

In other words, two negative charges (charged particles) or two positive charges experience repulsive electric forces: forces equal and opposite (Newton's third law). A positive charge and a negative charge experience attractive forces: forces toward each other. (Newton's third law still applies. Why?)

The law of charges gives the direction of an electric force, but what about its magnitude? In other words, how strong is the electric force between charged particles or bodies? Charles Coulomb derived a relationship for the magnitude of the electric force between two charged bodies that is appropriately known as **Coulomb's law**:

The force of attraction or repulsion between two charged bodies is directly proportional to the product of the two charges and inversely proportional to the square of the distance between them.

Written in equation form,

$$\text{force} = \frac{\text{constant} \times \text{charge 1} \times \text{charge 2}}{(\text{distance between charges})^2}$$

$$F = \frac{kq_1q_2}{r^2} \qquad \qquad 8.1$$

where F is the magnitude of the force in newtons, q_1 the magnitude of the first charge in coulombs, q_2 the magnitude of the second charge in coulombs, and r the distance between the charges in meters.

Here k is a proportionality constant with the value of

$$k = 9.0 \times 10^9 \text{ N} \cdot \text{m}^2/\text{C}^2$$

Coulomb's law is similar in form to Newton's law of universal gravitation (Chapter 3.5, $F = Gm_1m_2/r^2$). Both forces depend on the inverse square of the separation distance. One obvious difference between them is that Coulomb's law depends on charge, whereas Newton's law depends on mass.

Two other important differences exist. One is that Coulomb's law can have either an attractive or a repulsive force, depending on whether the two charges are different or the same (law of charges). The force of gravitation, on the other hand, is *always* attractive.

The other important difference is that the electric force is comparatively much stronger than the gravitational force. For example, an electron and a proton are attracted to each other both electrically and gravitationally. However, the gravitational force is so relatively weak that it can be ignored, and only the electric forces of attraction and repulsion are considered. (See Exercise 4.)

An object with an excess of electrons is said to be *negatively charged*, and an object with a deficiency of electrons is said to be *positively charged*. A negative charge can be placed on a rubber rod by stroking the rod with fur. (Electrons are transferred from the fur to the rod by friction. This process is called *charging by friction*.) In ● Fig. 8.1a, a rubber rod that has been stroked with fur and given a net charge is shown suspended by a thin thread that allows the rod to swing freely. The charge on the rod is negative. When another rubber rod that has been negatively charged is brought close to the suspended rod, the one that is free to move will swing away; the charged rods repel each other (like charges repel).

Doing the same thing with two glass rods that have been stroked with silk has similar results (Fig. 8.1b). Here electrons are transferred from the rods to the silk, leaving a positive charge on each rod.

The experiments show repulsion in both cases, but as shown in Fig. 8.1c, the charges on the stroked rubber rod and those on the glass rod attract one another (unlike charges

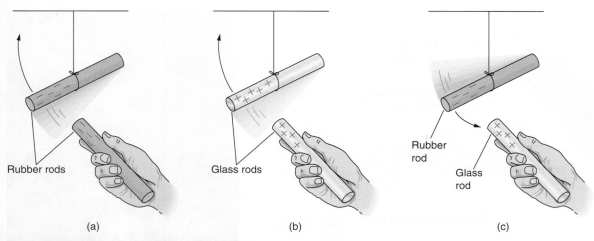

Figure 8.1   Repulsive and Attractive Electric Forces
(a) Two negatively charged objects repel each other. (b) Two positively charged objects repel each other. (c) A negatively charged object and a positively charged object attract each other.

attract). The charge on the glass rod is positive, and the charge on the rubber rod is negative. A charged object is said to have a static, or electrostatic, charge. *Electrostatics* is the study of charge at rest.

Static charge can be a problem. After walking across a carpet, you have probably been annoyingly zapped by a spark when reaching for a metal doorknob. You were charged by friction in crossing the carpet, and the electric force was strong enough to cause the air to ionize and conduct charge to the metal doorknob. This zapping is most likely to occur on a dry day. With high humidity (a lot of moisture in the air), there is a thin film of moisture on objects, and charge is conducted away before it can build up. Even so, such sparks are undesirable in the vicinity of flammable materials such as in an operating room with explosive gases or around gas pumps at a filling station (● Fig. 8.2).

From Coulomb's law (Eq. 8.1), it can be seen that as two charges get closer together, the force of attraction or repulsion increases. This effect can give rise to regions of charge, as illustrated in ● Fig. 8.3a. When a negatively charged rubber comb is brought near small pieces of paper, the charges in the paper molecules are acted on by electric forces—positive charges are attracted, negative charges repelled—and the result is an effective separation of charge. The molecules are then said to be *polarized*: they possess definite regions of charge.

Because the positive-charge regions are closer to the comb than the negative-charge regions, the attractive forces are stronger than the repulsive forces. Thus, a net attraction exists between the comb and the pieces of paper. Small bits of paper can be picked up by the comb, which indicates that the attractive electric force is greater than the paper's weight (the gravitational force on it).

Keep in mind, however, that overall the paper is uncharged; it is electrically neutral. Only molecular regions within the paper are charged. This procedure is termed *charging by induction*.

Conceptual Question and Answer

Defying Gravity

Q. Why does a balloon stick to a ceiling or wall after being rubbed on a person's hair or clothing (Fig. 8.3b)?

A. The balloon is charged by the frictional rubbing, which causes a transfer of charge. When the balloon is placed on a wall, the charge on the surface of the balloon induces regions of charge in the molecules of the wall material, attracting and holding the balloon the ceiling.

Figure 8.2   Static Danger
Warnings on gas pumps note the danger of static electric spark and how to prevent it.

© Jerry Wilson

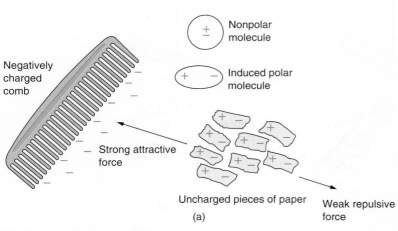

Figure 8.3 Polarization of Charge
(a) When a negatively charged comb is brought near small pieces of paper, the paper molecules are polarized with definite regions of charge, giving rise to a net attractive force. As a result, the bits of paper are attracted to and cling to the comb. (b) The force associated with electrical charges causes hair to stand on end and balloons to stick to the ceiling.

Another demonstration of electric force is shown in ● Fig. 8.4. When a charged rubber rod is brought close to a thin stream of water, the water is attracted toward the rod and the stream is bent. Water molecules have a permanent separation of charge, or regions of different charges. Such molecules are called *polar molecules* (Chapter 12.5).

Electric Field

The electric force, like the gravitational force, is an "action-at-a-distance" force. Since the electric force has an infinite range ($F \propto 1/r^2$) and approaches zero only as r approaches infinity, a charge can have an effect on any additional charge placed anywhere.

The idea of a force acting at a distance through space was difficult for early investigators to accept, and the concept of a *field* was introduced. In this approach, only the effect of the electrical interaction is considered, not the cause. We think of a charge interacting with an electric field rather than another charge responsible for it. An **electric field** surrounds a charge and represents the physical effect of a particular charge in nearby space. When another charge is placed in the field, the field will exert an electric force on that charge. This approach could have been used in Chapter 3.5 with the interaction of a mass with the gravitation field of another mass.

You can imagine determining or mapping out an electric field by using a small positive charge (a *test charge*) at a location near the charge of field interest. The force (magnitude and direction) on the test charge is recorded. When the electric force is determined at many locations, we have a vector "map" of the electric force field. The force is divided by a unit positive charge, and the electric field ($E = F/q_+$) is the force per unit charge. (Like force, the electric field E is a vector.) In this manner, if an arbitrary charge is placed in the field, then the magnitude of the force on it can be found by $F = q_+E$, with the direction depending on the sign of the charge or how it would react to a positive test charge.

The electric fields for some charges are illustrated in ● Fig. 8.5. For a single positive charge in Fig. 8.5a, the vectors point away from the charge. (Why?) Note that the vectors get shorter the farther from the charge as the force diminishes with distance.

Two configurations of charge are shown in Fig. 8.5b. When the field vectors are connected, we have *lines of force*, where the arrowheads indicate the force direction on a positive charge. If an arbitrary charge were put in a field and released, it would follow one of these lines, the field acting on the charge. The lines between the positive and negative charges begin and end on the charges, respectively. This indicates that the charges are

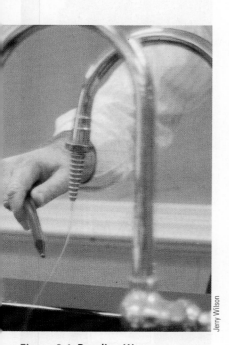

Figure 8.4 Bending Water
A charged rod brought close to a small stream of water will bend the stream because of the polarization of the water molecules.

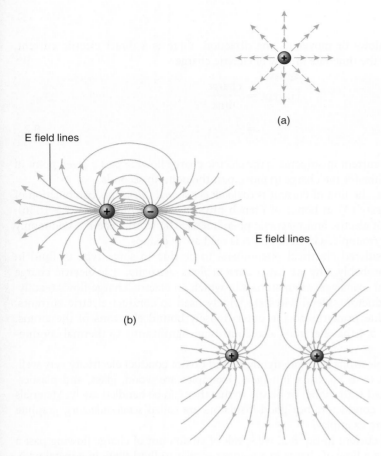

(a)

E field lines

(b)

E field lines

Figure 8.5 Electric Field Lines
(a) Electric field lines near a positive charge. (b) Electric field lines between unlike and like charges.

attractive, and the closer together the lines of force, the stronger the field. For the two positive charges (or two negative charges), there are no lines of force between, which indicates that the charges are repulsive.

Did You Learn?

● Coulomb's law gives the magnitude of the electrical forces between two charges, but not the direction. The law of charges indicates attraction or repulsion between different types of charges, giving the direction of the electric force.

● Static electricity, or electrostatics, is the study of charge at rest.

8.2 Current, Voltage, and Electrical Power

Preview Questions

● What is electric current, and how is it expressed?

● What is joule heat?

Current

When a net charge flows or moves in one direction, there is a direct electric current. **Current** is defined as the time rate of flow of electric charge:

$$\text{current} = \frac{\text{charge}}{\text{time}}$$

or

$$I = \frac{q}{t}$$

8.2

where I is the electric current in amperes, q the electric charge flowing past a given point in coulombs, and t the time for the charge to move past the point in seconds.

As Eq. 8.2 indicates, the unit of current is *coulomb per second* (q/t). This combination of units is called an *ampere* (A) in honor of French physicist André Ampère (1775–1836), an early investigator of electric and magnetic phenomena. The word *ampere* is commonly shortened to *amp*; for example, a current of 5 A is read as "five amps."

Early theories considered electrical phenomena to be due to some type of fluid in materials, which is probably why we say a current *flows*. Actually, it is electric charge that "flows." Electrical *conductors* are materials in which an electric charge flows readily. Metals are good conductors. Metal wires are widely used to conduct electric currents. This conduction is due primarily to the outer, loosely bound electrons of the atoms. (Recall from Chapter 5.4 that electrons also contribute significantly to thermal conduction in metals.)

Materials in which electrons are more tightly bound do not conduct electricity very well, and they are referred to as electrical *insulators*. Examples are wood, glass, and plastics. Electric cords are coated with rubber or plastic so that they can be handled safely. Materials that are neither good conductors nor good insulators are called *semiconductors;* graphite (carbon) and silicon are examples.

In the definition of current in Eq. 8.2, we speak of an amount of charge flowing past a given point. This is *not* a flow of charge in a manner similar to fluid flow. In a metal wire, for example, the electrons move randomly and chaotically, colliding with the metal atoms. Some go in one direction past a point, and others go in the opposite direction. An electric current exists when more electrons move in one direction than in the other. Thus, q is really a *net* charge in Eq. 8.2 (analogous to a *net* force in Chapter 3.1).

The net flow of charge is characterized by an average velocity called the *drift velocity*. The drift velocity is much smaller than the random velocities of the electrons themselves. Typically, the magnitude of the drift velocity is on the order of 1 mm/s. At this speed, it would take an electron about 17 min to travel 1 m in the wire.

You may be wondering how electrical signals in wires, such as telephone signals, can be transferred almost instantaneously across the country. The answer is that it is the electrical field that is transmitted at near the speed of light (in the wire), not the charge.

Voltage

The effects produced by moving charges give rise to what is generally called *electricity*. For charges to move, they must be acted on by other positive or negative charges. Consider the situation shown in ● Fig. 8.6. Start out with some unseparated charges and then begin to separate them. It takes very little work to pull the first negative charge to the left and the first positive charge to the right. When the next negative charge is moved to the left, it is repelled by the negative charge already there, so more work is needed. Similarly, it takes more work to move the second positive charge to the right. And as more and more charges are separated, it takes more and more work.

Because work is done in separating the charges, there is **electric potential energy**. If a separated charge were free to move, then it would move toward the charges of opposite sign. For example, a negative charge, as shown in Fig. 8.6, would move toward the positive charges. Electric potential energy would then be converted into kinetic energy as required by the conservation of energy.

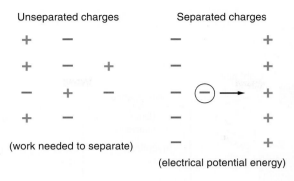

Unseparated charges   Separated charges

(work needed to separate)

(electrical potential energy)

Figure 8.6 Electric Potential Energy Work must be done to separate positive and negative charges. The work is done against the attractive electric force. When separated, the charges have electric potential energy and would move if free to do so.

Instead of electric potential energy, a related but different quantity called *potential difference*, or *voltage*, is most often considered. Voltage is defined as the amount of work it would take to move a charge between two points divided by the value of the charge. In other words, **voltage** (V) is the work (W) per unit charge (q), or the electric potential energy per unit charge.

$$\text{voltage} = \frac{\text{work}}{\text{charge}}$$

or
$$V = \frac{W}{q} \qquad\qquad 8.3$$

The *volt* (V) is the unit of voltage and is equal to one joule per coulomb (J/q). Voltage is caused by a separation of charge. When work is done in separating the charges, there is electric potential energy, which may be used to set up a current. The symbol for voltage is an italic "vee" (V), whereas the symbol for the volt unit is a roman "vee" (V).*

When there is a current, it meets with some opposition because of collisions within the conducting material. This opposition to the flow of charge is called **resistance** (R). The unit of resistance is the *ohm* (Ω, the Greek letter omega). A simple relationship involving voltage, current, and resistance was formulated by Georg Ohm (1787–1854), a German physicist, and applies to many materials. It is called **Ohm's law** and in equation form may be written

$$\text{voltage} = \text{current} \times \text{resistance}$$

or
$$V = IR \qquad\qquad 8.4$$

From this equation, it can be seen that one ohm resistance is one volt per ampere ($R = V/I$).

An example of a simple electric circuit is shown in ● Fig. 7.7a, together with a circuit diagram. The water circuit analogy given in Fig. 8.7b may help you better understand the components of the electric circuit. The battery provides the voltage to drive the circuit through chemical activity (chemical energy). This is analogous to the pump driving the water circuit. When the switch is *closed* (when the valve is opened in the water circuit), there is a current in the circuit. Electrons move away from the negative terminal of the battery toward the positive terminal.

The light bulb in the circuit offers resistance, and work is done in lighting it, with electrical energy being converted into heat and radiant energy. The waterwheel in the water circuit provides analogous resistance to the water flow and uses gravitational potential energy to do work. Note that there is a voltage, or potential, difference (drop) across the bulb, similar to the gravitational potential difference across the waterwheel. The components of an electric circuit are represented by symbols in a circuit diagram, as shown in the figure.

The switch in the circuit allows the path of the electrons to be open or closed. When the switch is open, there is not a complete path or circuit through which charge can flow and there is no current. (This is called an *open* circuit.) When the switch is closed, the circuit is completed, and there is a current. (The circuit is then said to be *closed*.) A sustained electric current requires a closed path or circuit.

---

*The volt unit is named in honor of Alessando Volta (1745–1827), an Italian scientist who constructed the first battery.

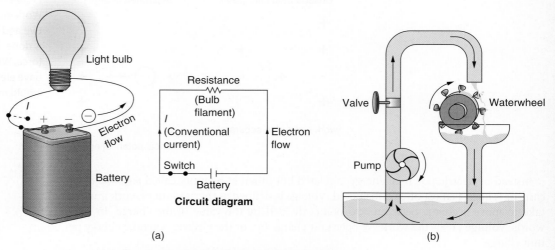

Figure 8.7 Simple Electric Circuit and a Water Analogy
(a) A simple electric circuit in which a battery supplies the voltage and a lightbulb supplies the resistance is shown. When the switch is closed, electrons flow from the negative terminal of the battery toward the positive terminal. Electrical energy is expended in heating the bulb filament. A circuit diagram with the component symbols is at the right. (b) In the water "circuit," the pump is analogous to the battery, the valve is analogous to the switch, and the waterwheel is analogous to the light bulb in furnishing resistance. Energy is expended, or work is done, in turning the waterwheel. (See text for more details.)

Note in the circuit diagram in Fig. 8.7a that the current (I) is in the opposite direction around the circuit to that of the electron flow. Even though electron charges are flowing in the circuit, it is customary to designate the *conventional current I* in the direction in which positive charges would flow. This designation is a historical remnant from Ben Franklin, who once advanced a fluid theory of electricity. All bodies supposedly contained a certain normal amount of this mysterious fluid, a surplus or deficit of which gave rise to electrical properties. With an excess resulting from a fluid flow, a body was positively "excited."

This theory later gave rise to the idea that it was the positive charges that flowed or moved. (Electrons were unknown at the time.) In any case, the current direction is still designated in the conventional sense or in the direction in which the positive charges would flow in the circuit, that is, away from the positive terminal of the battery and toward the negative terminal.

Electric Power

When current exists in a circuit, work is done to overcome resistance and power is expended. Recall from Eq. 4.8 that one definition of power (P) is

$$P = \frac{W}{t}$$

From Eq. 8.3, $W = qV$, and substituting for W yields

$$P = \frac{q}{t} V$$

Substituting $q/t = I$ gives an equation in terms of current and voltage for **electric power**:

$$\text{power} = \text{current} \times \text{voltage}$$
$$P = IV \qquad \qquad \text{8.5}$$

Using Ohm's law ($V = IR$) for V, we have $P = I(IR)$, and

$$\text{power} = (\text{current})^2 \times \text{resistance}$$
$$P = I^2R \qquad \qquad \text{8.6}$$

The power that is dissipated in an electric circuit is frequently in the form of heat. This heat is called *joule heat*, or I^2R *losses* (read I squared R losses), as given by Eq. 8.6. This heating effect is used in electric stoves, heaters, cooking ranges, hair dryers, and so on. Hair dryers have heating coils of low resistance so as to get a large current for large I^2R losses. When a light bulb is turned on, much of the power goes to produce heat as well as light. The unit of power is the watt, and light bulbs are rated in watts (● Fig. 8.8).

● Table 8.2 gives some typical power requirements for a few common household appliances.

(a)

EXAMPLE 8.1   Finding Current and Resistance

Find the current and resistance of a 60-W, 120-V light bulb in operation.

Solution

Step 1

Given: $P = 60$ W (power)
            $V = 120$ V (voltage)

Step 2

Wanted: I (current)
             R (resistance)

Step 3

The current is obtained using Eq. 8.5, $P = IV$. Rearranging yields

$$I = \frac{P}{V} = \frac{60 \text{ W}}{120 \text{ V}} = 0.50 \text{ A}$$

Equation 8.4 (Ohm's law) can be rearranged to solve for resistance:

$$R = \frac{V}{I} = \frac{120 \text{ V}}{0.50 \text{ A}} = 240 \ \Omega$$

Note that Eq. 8.6 could also be used to solve for R:

$$R = \frac{P}{I^2} = \frac{60 \text{ W}}{(0.50 \text{ A})^2} = 240 \ \Omega$$

(b)

Figure 8.8 Wattage (Power) Ratings
(a) A 60-W light bulb dissipates 60 J of electrical energy each second. (b) The curling iron uses 13 W at 120 V. Given the wattage and voltage ratings, you can find the current drawn by an appliance by using $I = P/V$.

Confidence Exercise 8.1

A coffeemaker draws 10 A of current operating at 120 V. How much romelectrical energy does the coffeemaker use each second?

Answers to Confidence Exercises may be found at the back of the book.

There are two principal forms of electric current and voltage. In a battery circuit, such as that shown in Fig. 8.7, the electron flow is always in one direction, away from the negative terminal and toward the positive terminal. This type of current is called **direct current**, or **dc**. Direct current is used in battery-powered devices such as flashlights, portable radios, and automobiles. Dc voltage usually has a steady, constant value. Batteries are rated in this voltage.

The other common type of current is **alternating current**, or **ac**, which is produced by a constantly changing (alternating) voltage from positive (+) to negative (−) to positive (+), and so on. (Although the usage is redundant, we commonly say "ac current" and "ac voltage.") Alternating current is produced by electric companies and is used in the home. (Alternating current and voltage generation are discussed in Chapter 8.5.)

The frequency of changing from positive to negative voltages is usually at the rate of 60 cycles per second (cps) or 60 Hz (see Fig. 8.8b). The average voltage varies from 110 V to 120 V, and household ac voltage is commonly listed as 110 V, 115 V, or 120 V. The equations for Ohm's law (Eq. 8.4) and power (Eqs. 8.5 and 8.6) apply to both dc and ac circuits containing only resistances.

Table 8.2 Typical Power Requirements of Some Household Appliances	
Appliance	**Power (W)**
Air conditioner	
Room	1500
Central	5000
Coffeemaker	1650
Dishwasher	1200
Water heater	4500
Microwave oven	1250
Refrigerator	500
Stove	
Range top	6000
Oven	4500
Television (color)	100

For the most part, we use 110-V ac voltage in household circuits. However, in Europe, the common household voltage is 220-V ac. To learn why the difference exists, see the **Highlight: United States and Europe: Different Voltages**.

Did You Learn?

● When a net charge flows in one direction, there is a direct electric current (I). Current is expressed as the time rate of flow of electric charge ($I = q/t$).

● Power is commonly dissipated in an electrical circuit in the form of heat, which is referred to as joule heat (or I^2R losses, where $P = IV = I^2R$).

8.3   Simple Electric Circuits and Electrical Safety

Preview Questions

● How do the currents in a series circuit and a parallel circuit differ?
● What happens when more resistance is added to (a) a series circuit and (b) a parallel circuit?

Once electricity enters the home or business, it is used in circuits to power various appliances and other items. Plugging appliances, lamps, and other electrical applications into an outlet places them in a circuit. There are two basic ways to connect elements in a circuit: in *series* and in *parallel*.

An example of a series circuit is shown in ● Fig. 8.9. The lamps are conveniently represented as resistances in the circuit diagram. In a **series circuit**, the same current passes through all the resistances. This is analogous to a liquid circuit with a single line connecting several components. The total resistance is simply the sum of the individual resistances. As with different height potentials, the total voltage is the sum of the individual voltage drops, and

$$V = V_1 + V_2 + V_3 + \cdots$$
$$V = IR_1 + IR_2 + IR_3 + \cdots$$

or
$$V = I(R_1 + R_2 + R_3 + \cdots)$$

where the equation is written for three or more resistances. Writing $V = IR_s$, where R_s is the *total equivalent series resistance*, then by comparison,

> total equivalent series resistance = summation of individual resistors
> $$R_s = R_1 + R_2 + R_3 + \cdots \qquad \text{8.7}$$
> resistances in series

Equation 8.7 means that all the resistances in series could be replaced with a single resistance R_s. The same current would flow, and the same power would be dissipated. For

Figure 8.9 Series Circuit
The light bulbs are connected in series, and the current is the same through each bulb.

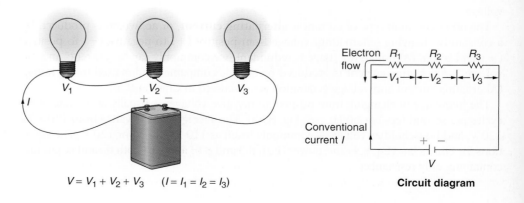

$V = V_1 + V_2 + V_3$ ($I = I_1 = I_2 = I_3$)

Electron flow R_1 R_2 R_3

Conventional current I

V

Circuit diagram

Highlight United States and Europe: Different Voltages

Many travelers to Europe have difficulty with their electrical appliances because the United States and a handful of other countries in the Americas use 110 V/60 Hz electricity. Europe and most other countries of the world use a 220 V/50 Hz system.* As a result, using appliances in Europe designed to operate on U.S. voltage can cause some real problems. For example, a 110-V hairdryer used in a 220-V European outlet would quickly burn up.

Why the different voltages? There is an historical explanation. In 1879 Thomas Edison invented an improved incandescent light bulb. He realized the need for an electrical distribution system to provide power for lighting and built a 110-V dc system that initially provided power in Manhattan. The dc system, with large wire conductors and big voltage drops, was somewhat cumbersome.

George Westinghouse introduced a distribution system based on 110-V alternating current (ac). Alternating current allows the voltage to be changed through the use of transformers. This allowed transmission at higher voltages and less current (see Chapter 8.5), thereby reducing line losses due to conductor resistance (joule heat) and making for greater transmission distances.

Alternating voltage generation took over from dc voltage generation, and power plants built in the early 1900s used 110 V/60 Hz voltage. There was some voltage variation, from 110 V to 115 V to 120 V, as there is today.

By the time most European countries got around to developing electrical distribution systems, engineers had figured out how to make 220-V bulbs. These bulbs did not burn out as quickly as 110-V bulbs, making them more economical. So, in Germany around the beginning of the twentieth century, 220-V/50 Hz (or 220 V–240 V) generation was adopted and spread throughout Europe. The United States stayed with 110 V because of the big investment in 110-V equipment. However, 220 V–240 V voltage is available on the U.S. three-wire system. (See Fig. 8.11 and text discussion there.) There are different plugs for 110-V and 220-V outlets, so the voltages cannot be mistaken.

Because of the voltage difference, travelers to Europe usually need to take a voltage converter with them. Nowadays, some devices, such as hair dryers, are designed to operate on either 110 V/60 Hz or 220 V/50 Hz by switching from one to the other. Equipment rated at 50 Hz or 60 Hz will usually operate on either cycle. However some devices, such as electric plug-in clocks that use the ac frequency for timing, may not function well.

One final note: Many countries use different plugs for normal outlets (Fig. 1). So, if you are going abroad, think about taking a plug adapter kit for connecting to foreign plugs.

---

*The 60 Hz and 50 Hz are the frequencies of the alternating voltages.

Stephen Kirschenmann/iStockphoto.com

Figure 1 Different Plugs
Different electrical plugs are used in different parts of the world. Going counterclockwise from the lower left; vertical prongs (North/South America), round prongs (Europe), three prongs (Great Britain), and slanted prongs (Australia).

---

example, $P = I^2R_s$ is the power used in the whole circuit. (The resistances of the connecting wires are considered negligible.)

The example of lamps or resistances in series in Fig. 8.9 could just as easily have been an early string of Christmas tree lights, which used to be connected in a simple series circuit. When a bulb burned out, the whole string of lights went out because there was no longer a complete path for the current and the circuit was "open." Having a bulb burn out was like opening a switch in the circuit to turn off the lights. However, in most strings of lights purchased today, one light can burn out but the others remain lit. Each bulb has a secondary "shunt" resistor that takes over if the main filament resistor burns out.

The other type of simple circuit is called *a parallel circuit*, as illustrated in ● Fig. 8.10. In a **parallel circuit**, the voltage across each resistance is the same, but the current through each resistance may vary (different resistances, different currents). Note that the current from the voltage source (battery) divides at the junction where all the resistances are connected. This arrangement is analogous to liquid flow in a large pipe coming to a junction where it divides into several smaller pipes.

Figure 8.10 Parallel Circuit
The light bulbs are connected in parallel, and the current from the battery divides at the junction (where the three bulbs are connected). The amount of current in each parallel branch is determined by the relative values of the resistance in the branches; the greatest current is in the path of least resistance.

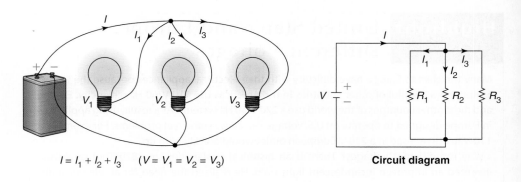

$I = I_1 + I_2 + I_3$ $(V = V_1 = V_2 = V_3)$

Circuit diagram

Because there is no buildup of charge at a junction, the charge leaving the junction must equal the charge entering the junction (law of conservation of charge), and in terms of current,

$$I = I_1 + I_2 + I_3 + \cdots$$

Using Ohm's law (in the form $I = V/R$), we have for the different resistances,

$$I = \frac{V}{R_1} + \frac{V}{R_2} + \frac{V}{R_3} + \cdots$$

or

$$I = V\left(\frac{1}{R_1} + \frac{1}{R_2} + \frac{1}{R_3} + \cdots\right)$$

The voltage V is the same across each resistance R because the voltage source is effectively connected "across" each resistance, and each gets the same voltage effect or drop.

If Ohm's law is written as $I = V/R_p$, where R_p is the *total equivalent parallel resistance*, then, by comparison,

reciprocal of total equivalent = summation of the reciprocals
parallel resistance   of the individual resistances

$$\frac{1}{R_p} = \frac{1}{R_1} + \frac{1}{R_2} + \frac{1}{R_3} + \cdots \qquad 8.8$$

resistances in parallel

For a circuit with only two resistances in parallel, this equation can be conveniently written as

$$R_p = \frac{R_1 R_2}{R_1 + R_2} \qquad 8.9$$

two resistances in parallel

As in the case of the series circuit, all the resistances could be replaced by a single resistance R_p without affecting the current from the battery or the power dissipation.

EXAMPLE 8.2   Resistances in Parallel

Three resistors have values of $R_1 = 6.0\ \Omega$, $R_2 = 6.0\ \Omega$, and $R_3 = 3.0\ \Omega$. What is their total resistance when connected in parallel, and how much current will be drawn from a 12-V battery if it is connected to the circuit?

Solution

Let's first combine R_1 and R_2 into a single equivalent resistance, using Eq. 8.9:

$$R_{p_1} = \frac{R_1 R_2}{R_1 + R_2} = \frac{(6.0\ \Omega)(6.0\ \Omega)}{6.0\ \Omega + 6.0\ \Omega} = 3.0\ \Omega$$

Hence, an equivalent circuit is a resistance R_{p_1} connected in parallel with R_3. Apply Eq. 8.9 to these parallel resistances to find the total resistance:

$$R_p = \frac{R_{p_1} R_3}{R_{p_1}} + R_3 = \frac{(3.0\ \Omega)(3.0\ \Omega)}{3.0\ \Omega + 3.0\ \Omega} = 1.5\ \Omega$$

The same current will be drawn from the source for a 1.5-Ω resistor as for the three resistances in parallel.

The problem also can be solved by using Eq. 8.8. In this case, R is found by using the lowest common denominator for the fractions (zeros and units initially omitted for clarity):

$$\frac{1}{R_p} = \frac{1}{R_1} + \frac{1}{R_2} + \frac{1}{R_3} = \frac{1}{6} + \frac{1}{6} + \frac{1}{3}$$

$$= \frac{1}{6} + \frac{1}{6} + \frac{2}{6} = \frac{4}{6\,\Omega}$$

or

$$R_p = \frac{6\,\Omega}{4} = 1.5\,\Omega$$

The current drawn from the source is then given by Ohm's law using R_p:

$$I = \frac{V}{R_p} = \frac{12\text{ V}}{1.5\,\Omega} = 8.0\text{ A}$$

Confidence Exercise 8.2

Suppose the resistances in Example 8.2 were wired in series and connected to the 12-V battery. Would the battery then supply more or less current than it would for the parallel arrangement? What would be the current in the circuit in this case?

Answers to Confidence Exercises may be found at the back of the book.

Conceptual Question and Answer

Series or Parallel

Q. Are automobile headlights wired in series or in parallel? How do you know?

A. Headlights are wired in parallel. When one headlight goes out, the other remains lit, which indicates a circuit path of a parallel circuit. You have probably seen a car approaching with only one headlight. If wired in series, then both headlights would go out.

An interesting fact:

> For resistances connected in parallel, the total resistance is always less than the smallest parallel resistance.

Such is the case in Example 8.2. Try to find a parallel circuit that proves otherwise. (Or better yet, forget it. You'd be wasting your time!)

Home appliances are wired in parallel (● Fig. 8.11). There are two major advantages of parallel circuits:

1. The same voltage (110–120 V) is available throughout the house, which makes it much easier to design appliances. (The 110–120 V voltage is obtained by connecting across the "hot," or high-voltage, side of the line to *ground*, or zero potential. This gives a voltage *difference* of 120 V, even if one of the "high" sides is at a potential of -120 V. The voltage for large appliances, such as central air conditioners and heaters, is 220–240 V, which is available by connecting across the two incoming potentials, as shown in Fig. 8.11. This potential is analogous to a height difference between two positions, one positive and one negative, for gravitational potential energy. See Fig. 4.8.)

2. If one appliance fails to operate, then the others in the circuit are not affected because their circuits are still complete. In a series circuit, when one component fails, none of the others will operate because the circuit is incomplete, or "open."

Figure 8.11 Household Circuits
As illustrated here, household circuits are wired in parallel. For small appliances, the circuit voltage is 120 V. Because there are independent branches, any particular circuit element can operate when others in the same circuit do not. For large appliances, such as a central air conditioner or electric stove, the connection is between the +120V and the −120V potential wires to give a voltage difference of 240 V.

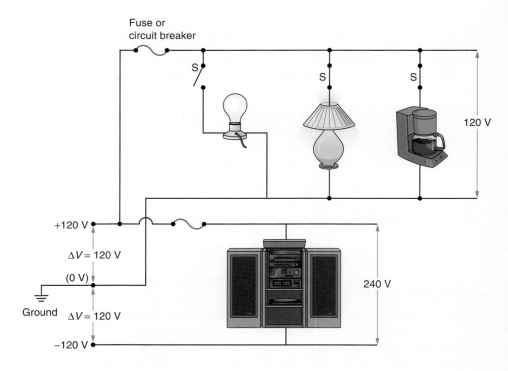

Resistances can be connected in *series-parallel circuits*, which give intermediate equivalent total resistances, but we will not examine these.

Conceptual Question and Answer

More Resistance, More Current

Q. When you turn on more lights and appliances in your home, the current demand in the circuit is greater. Why is this, given that you are adding more resistance with each component?

A. Household circuits are wired in parallel, and for resistances connected in parallel, the total resistance is always less than the smallest parallel resistance. Resistances may be added, but the total resistance is restricted to less than the smallest resistance, so there is more current.

Electrical Safety

Electrical safety for both people and property is an important consideration in using electricity. For example, in household circuits as more and more appliances are turned on, there is more and more current and the wires get hotter and hotter (joule heat). The fuse or circuit breaker shown in the circuit diagram in Fig. 8.11 is a safety device that prevents the wires from carrying too much current, getting too hot, and possibly starting a fire. When the preset amount of current is reached, the fuse filament gets so hot that it melts and opens the circuit. Fuses are primarily found in older homes. Circuit breakers (described below) are installed in newer homes.

Two types of fuses are generally used in household circuits. The *Edison-base fuse* has a base with threads similar to those on a light bulb (● Fig. 8.12a). Thus. they will fit into any socket, which can create a problem. For example, a 30-A fuse might be screwed into a socket that should have a 15-A fuse. Such a mix-up could be dangerous, so *type S fuses* are often used instead (Fig. 8.12b). With type S fuses, a threaded adapter specific to a particular fuse is put into the socket. Fuses that are rated differently have different threads, and a 30-A fuse cannot be screwed into a 15-A socket. Household fuses are being phased out, but small fuses are still used in automobile and other circuits.

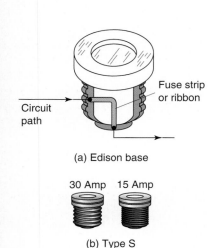

(a) Edison base

30 Amp   15 Amp

(b) Type S

Figure 8.12 Fuses
(a) An Edison-base fuse. If the current exceeds the fuse rating, then joule heat causes the fuse strip or ribbon to burn out and the circuit is opened. (b) Type S fuses. Edison-base fuses have the same screw thread for different ratings, so a 30-A fuse could be put into a 15-A circuit, which would be dangerous. (Why?) Type S fuses have different threads for different fuse ratings and cannot be interchanged.

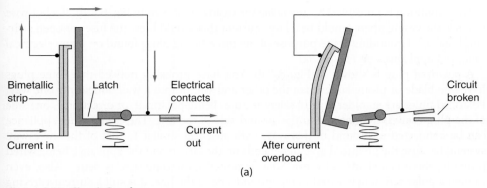

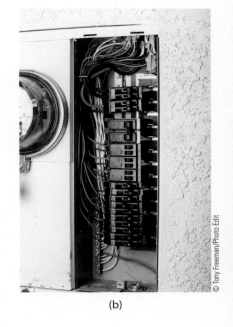

Figure 8.13 Circuit Breaker
(a) Thermal type. As the current through the bimetallic strip increases, it becomes warmer (joule heat) and bends. When the current-rated value is reached, the strip bends sufficiently to open the circuit. (b) Circuit breakers in a home electrical service entrance.

(b)

The more popular *circuit breaker* has generally replaced fuses and is required in newer homes. It serves the same function as fuses. A thermal type of circuit breaker, illustrated in ● Fig. 8.13a, uses a bimetallic strip (see Chapter 5.1). As the current through the strip increases, it becomes warmer (joule heat) and bends. When the current-rated value is reached, the strip bends sufficiently to open the circuit. The strip quickly cools, and the breaker can be reset. However, a blown fuse or a tripped circuit breaker indicates that the circuit is drawing or attempting to draw too much current. *You should find and correct the problem before replacing the fuse or resetting the circuit breaker.* Some circuit breakers operate on magnetic principles: the more current, the greater the magnetic attraction, and the circuit is opened at some preset current value. (See electromagnets in Chapter 8.4.)

Switches, fuses, and circuit breakers are always placed in the "hot," or high-voltage, side of the line. If they placed in the ground side, there would be no current when a circuit was opened. But there would still be a 120-V potential to the appliance, which could be dangerous if someone came in contact with it.

However, even when wired properly, fuses and circuit breakers may not always give protection from electrical shock. A hot wire inside an appliance or power tool may break loose and come into contact with its housing or casing, putting it at a high voltage. The fuse does not blow unless there is a large current. If a person touches a casing that is conductive, as illustrated in ● Fig. 8.14a, a path is provided to ground and the person receives an electric shock.

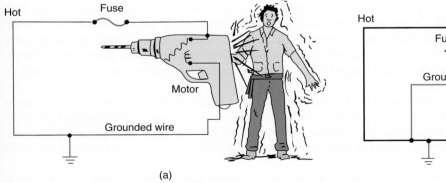

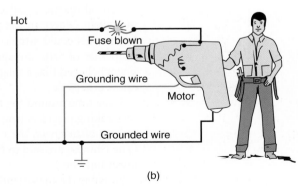

(a)   (b)

Figure 8.14 Electrical Safety by Use of Dedicated Grounding
(a) Suppose an internal "hot" wire broke and came in contact with the metal casing of an appliance. Without a dedicated ground wire, the casing would be at a high potential without a fuse being blown or a circuit breaker being tripped. If someone were to touch the casing, then a dangerous shock could result. (b) If the case were grounded with a dedicated ground wire through a third prong on the plug, then the circuit would be opened and the casing would be at zero potential.

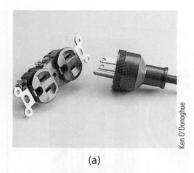

(a)

(b)

Figure 8.15 Electric Plugs
(a) A three-prong plug and socket. The third, rounded prong is connected to a dedicated grounding wire used for electrical safety. (b) A two-prong polarized plug and socket. Note that one blade, or prong, is larger than the other. The ground, or neutral (zero-potential) side of the line, is wired to the large-prong side of the socket. This distinction, or polarization, permits paths to ground for safety purposes.

This condition is prevented by *grounding* the casing, as shown in Fig. 8.14b. If a hot wire touches the casing, there would be a large current that would blow the fuse (or open a circuit breaker). Grounding is the purpose of the three-prong plugs found on many electrical tools and appliances (● Fig. 8.15a).

A *polarized* plug is shown in Fig. 8.15b. You have probably noticed that some plugs have one blade or prong larger than the other and will fit into a wall outlet only one way. Polarized plugs are an older type of safety feature. Being polarized, or directional, one side of the plug is always connected to the ground side of the line. The casing of an appliance can be connected to ground in this way, with an effect similar to that of the three-wire system. Because the polarized system depends on the circuit and the appliance being wired properly, there is a chance of error. So a dedicated grounding wire is better. Also, even though a polarized plug is wired to the ground side of the line, it is still a current-carrying wire, whereas the dedicated ground wire carries no current.

An electric shock can be very dangerous, and *touching exposed electric wires should always be avoided*. Many injuries and deaths occur from electric shock. The effects of electric shock are discussed in the **Highlight: Electrical Effects on Humans**.

Did You Learn?

● In a series circuit, the current is the same through all resistances. In a parallel circuit, the current through each resistance may vary (for different resistances).

● Resistance added to a series circuit increases the total resistance and less current flows for a given voltage. Resistance added to a parallel circuit reduces the total resistance and more current flows for a given voltage.

8.4   Magnetism

Preview Questions

● How are the law of poles and the law of charges similar?

● Where is the Earth's north magnetic pole?

Like most people, you have probably been fascinated by the attractive and repulsive forces between magnets: a hands-on example of force at a distance. Magnets are readily available today because we know how to make them, but they were once quite scarce and were found only as rocks in nature, or natural magnets.

Natural magnets, called lodestones, were discovered as early as the sixth century BCE in ancient Greece in the province of Magnesia, from which magnetism derives its name. Lodestones could attract pieces of iron and other lodestones. For centuries the attractive properties of natural magnets were attributed to supernatural forces. Early Greek philosophers believed that a magnet had a "soul" that caused it to attract pieces of iron. Now, we know otherwise.

Some time around the first century BCE, the Chinese learned to make artificial magnets by stroking pieces of iron with natural magnets. This led to one of the first practical applications of magnets, the compass, which implied that the Earth has magnetic properties. (The Chinese are said to have developed the compass, but several other peoples claim this invention, too.)

Probably the most familiar magnets are the common bar magnet and the horseshoe magnet (a bar magnet bent in the form of a horseshoe). One of the first things one notices when examining a bar magnet is that it has two regions of magnetic strength or concentration—one at each end of the magnet—which are called *poles*. One is designated as the north pole, N, and the other as the south pole, S. This is because the N pole of a magnet, when used as a compass, is the "north-seeking pole" (it points north) and the S pole is the "south-seeking pole."

Highlight   Electrical Effects on Humans

When working with electricity, common sense and knowledge of fundamental electrical principles are important. Electric shocks can be very dangerous, and they kill and injure many people every year. A major problem can be poor maintenance (Fig. 1).

The danger is proportional to the amount of electric current that goes through the body. The amount of current going through the body is given by Ohm's law as

$$I = \frac{V}{R_{body}} \tag{1}$$

where R_{body} is the resistance of the body.

A current of 5 mA (milliamp) can be felt as a shock (Table 1). A current of 100 mA is nearly always fatal.

The amount of current, as indicated in Eq. 1, depends critically on a person's body resistance. Human body resistance varies considerably, mainly as a result of whether the skin is wet or dry. Because our bodies are mostly water, skin resistance makes up most of the body's resistance.

A dry body can have a resistance as high as 500,000 Ω, and the current from a 110-V source would be only 0.00022 A, or 0.22 mA. Danger arises when the skin is moist or wet. Then, the resistance of the body can go as low as 100 Ω, and the current will rise to 1.1 A, or 1100 mA. Injuries and death from shocks usually occur

when the skin is wet. Therefore, appliances such as radios should not be used near a bathtub. If a plugged-in radio happened to fall into the bathtub, then the whole tub, including the person in it, might be plugged into 110 V.

Despite the availability of various electrical safety devices, it does not take much current to cause human injuries and fatalities. Only milliamps of current are needed. Were you to come into contact with a hot wire and become part of a circuit, it is not only your body resistance that is important (as discussed) but also how you are connected in the circuit. If the circuit is completed through your hand (finger to thumb), then a shock and a burn can result. However, if the circuit is completed through the body from hand to hand or hand to foot, then the resulting effects can be much more serious, depending on the amount of current.

Note in Table 1 that a current of 15 mA to 25 mA can cause muscular freeze, so the person affected may not be able to let go of a hot wire. Muscles are controlled by nerves, which in turn are controlled by electrical impulses. Slightly larger currents can cause breathing difficulties, and just slightly larger currents can cause ventricular fibrillation, or uncontrolled contractions of the heart. A current greater than 100 mA, or 0.10 A, generally results in death. Keep in mind, for your personal electrical safety, that a little current goes a long way.

Figure 1 Electrical Hazards
Electrical hazards, such as this frayed wire, can be dangerous and cause fire and injury.

Table 1	Effects of Electric Currents on Humans

Current (mA)	Effect*
1	Barely perceived
5–10	Mild shock
10–15	Difficulty in releasing
15–25	Muscular freeze, cannot release or let go
50–100	May stop breathing, ventricular fibrillation
100	Death

*Effects vary with individuals.

When examining two magnets, you will notice that there are attractive and repulsive forces between them that are specific to the poles. These forces are described by the **law of poles**:

Like poles repel; unlike poles attract.

In other words, N and S poles (N-S) attract, and N-N and S-S poles repel each other (● Fig. 8.16a). The strength of the attraction or repulsion depends on the strength of the magnetic poles. Also, in a manner similar to Coulomb's law, the strength of the magnetic

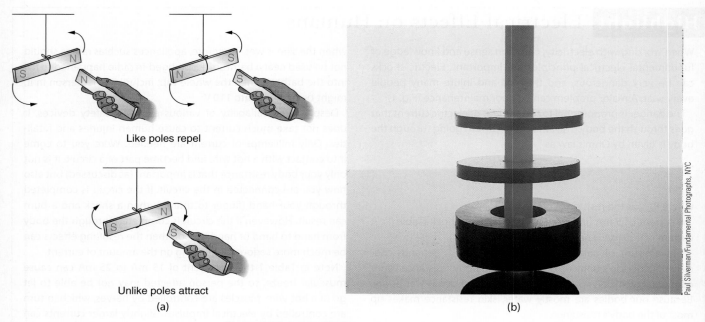

Figure 8.16 Laws of Poles
(a) Like poles repel, and unlike poles attract. (b) The adjacent poles of the circular magnets must be like poles. (Why?)

force is inversely proportional to the square of the distance between the poles. Figure 8.16b shows some toy magnets that seem to defy gravity as a result of their magnetic repulsion.

All magnets have two poles, so magnets are dipoles (*di-* means "two"). Unlike electric charge, which occurs in single charges, magnets are always dipoles. A *magnetic monopole* would consist of a single N or S pole without the other. There is no known physical reason for magnetic monopoles not to exist, but so far, their existence has not been confirmed experimentally. The discovery of a magnetic monopole would be an important fundamental development.

Every magnet produces a force on every other magnet. To discuss these effects, let's discuss the concept of a magnetic field, similar to an electric field in Chapter 8.1. A **magnetic field** (B) is a set of imaginary lines that indicates the direction in which a small compass needle would point if it were placed near a magnet. Hence, the field lines are indications of the magnetic force, or a force field. ● Figure 8.17a shows the magnetic field lines around a simple bar magnet. The arrows in the field lines indicate the direction in which the north pole of a compass needle would point. The closer together the field lines, the stronger the magnetic force.

Magnetic field patterns can be "seen" by using iron filings. The iron filings become magnetized and act as small compass needles. The outline of the magnetic field produced in this manner is shown for the bar magnet in Fig. 8.17b. The field concept is analogous to an *electric field* around charges, but with iron filings the magnetic field is more easily visualized. The electric and magnetic fields are vector quantities, and electromagnetic waves, as discussed in Chapter 6.3, are made up of electric and magnetic fields that vary with time.

Electricity and magnetism are generally discussed together because they are linked. (Electromagnetism is the topic of Chapter 8.5.) In fact, *the source of magnetism is moving and "spinning" electrons.* Hans Oersted, a Danish physicist, first discovered in 1820 that a compass needle is deflected by a wire carrying electric current. When a compass is placed near a wire in a simple battery circuit and the circuit is closed, there is current in the wire and the compass needle is deflected from its north-seeking direction. When the circuit is opened, the compass needle goes back to pointing north again.

The strength of the magnetic field is directly proportional to the magnitude of the current: the greater the current, the greater the strength of the magnetic field. Hence, a current produces a magnetic field that can be turned off and on at will.

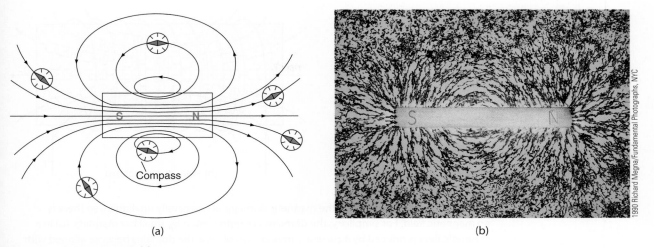

Figure 8.17 Magnetic Field
(a) Magnetic field lines may be plotted by using a small compass. The N pole of the compass needle (blue) points in the direction of the field at any point, (b) Iron filings become induced magnets and conveniently outline the pattern of the magnetic field.

Different configurations of current-carrying wires give different magnetic field configurations. For example, a straight, dc current–carrying wire produces a field in a circular pattern around the wire (● Fig. 8.18a). A single loop of wire gives a field comparable to that of a small bar magnet (Fig. 8.18b), and the field of a coil of wire with several loops is very similar to that of a bar magnet.

But what produces the magnetic field of a permanent magnet such as a bar magnet? In a basic model of the atom, electrons are pictured as going around the nucleus (Chapter 9.3). This is electric charge in motion, or a current loop, and it might be expected that it would be a source of a magnetic field. However, the magnetic field produced by orbiting atomic electrons is very small. Also, the atoms of a material are distributed such that the magnetic fields would be in various directions and would generally cancel each other, giving a zero net effect.

Modern theory predicts the magnetic field to be associated with electron "spin." This effect is pictured classically as an electron spinning on its axis in the same way that the

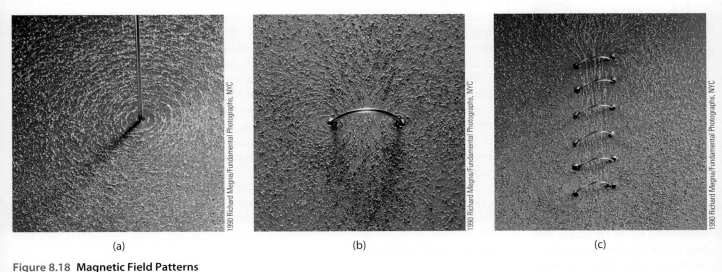

Figure 8.18 Magnetic Field Patterns
Iron filing patterns near current-carrying wires outline the magnetic fields for (a) a long, straight wire; (b) a single loop of wire; and (c) a coil of wire (a solenoid).

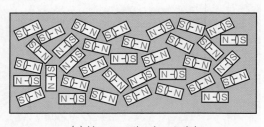

(a) Unmagnetized material

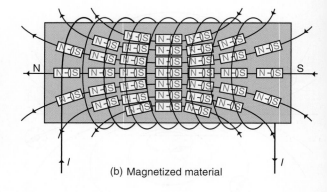

(b) Magnetized material

Figure 8.19 Magnetization
(a) In a ferromagnetic material, the magnetic domains are generally unaligned, so there is no magnetic field. For simplicity, the domains are represented by small bar magnets. (b) In a magnetic field produced by a current-carrying loop of wire, the domains become aligned with the field (the aligned domains may grow at the expense of others) and the material becomes magnetized.

Earth rotates on its axis.* A material has many atoms and electrons, and the magnetic spin effects of all these electrons usually cancel each other out. Therefore, most materials are not magnetic or are only slightly magnetic. In some instances, however, the magnetic effect can be quite strong.

Materials that are highly magnetic are called **ferromagnetic**. Ferromagnetic materials include the elements iron, nickel, and cobalt, as well as certain alloys of these and a few other elements. In ferromagnetic materials, the magnetic fields of many atoms combine to give rise to **magnetic domains**, or local regions of alignment. A single magnetic domain acts like a tiny bar magnet.

In iron the domains can be aligned or nonaligned. A piece of iron with the domains randomly oriented is not magnetic. This effect is illustrated in ● Fig. 8.19. When the iron is placed in a magnetic field, such as that produced by a current-carrying loop of wire, the domains line up or those parallel to the field grow at the expense of other domains, and the iron is magnetized. When the magnetic field is removed, the domains tend to return to a mostly random arrangement because of heat effects that cause disordering. The amount of domain alignment remaining after the field is removed depends on the strength of the applied magnetic field.

An application of this effect is an *electromagnet*, which consists of a coil of insulated wire wrapped around a piece of iron (● Fig. 8.20). Because a magnetic field can be turned on and off by turning an electric current on and off, it can be controlled whether or not the iron will be magnetized. When the current is on, the magnetic field of the coil magnetizes the iron. The aligned domains add to the field, making it about 2000 times stronger.

Electromagnets have many applications. Large ones are used routinely to pick up and transfer scrap iron, and small ones are used in magnetic relays and solenoids, which act as magnetic switches. Solenoids are used in automobiles to engage the starting motor. One type of circuit breaker uses an electromagnetic switch. The strength of an electromagnet is directly proportional to the current in its coils. When there is a certain amount of current in the breaker circuit, an electromagnet becomes strong enough to attract and "trip" a metallic conductor, thus opening the circuit.

The iron used in electromagnets is called "soft" iron. This does not mean that it is physically soft; rather, it means that this type of iron can be magnetized but quickly becomes demagnetized. Certain types of iron, along with nickel, cobalt, and a few other elements, are known as "hard" magnetic materials. Once magnetized, they retain their magnetic properties for a long time.

Switch

Soft iron

+ −

Voltage source   Iron filings

Figure 8.20 Electromagnet
A simple electromagnet consists of an insulated coil of wire wrapped around a piece of iron. When the switch is closed, there is a current in the wire, which gives rise to a magnetic field that magnetizes the iron and thus creates a magnet. When the switch is open, there is no current in the coil and the iron is not magnetized.

_____

* This is not actually the case. Electron spin is a quantum mechanical effect (Chapter 9) with no classical analog. However, the classical model is useful in understanding the effect.

Hard iron is used for permanent magnets such as bar magnets. When permanent magnets are heated or struck, the domains are shaken from their alignment and the magnet becomes weaker. Also, there is a temperature effect. In fact, above a certain temperature called the *Curie temperature*, a material ceases to be ferromagnetic. The Curie temperature of iron is 770°C.*

A permanent magnet is made by "permanently" aligning the domains inside the material. One way to do so is to heat a piece of hard ferromagnetic material above its Curie temperature and then apply a strong magnetic field. The domains line up with the field, and as the material cools, the domain alignment is frozen in, so to speak, producing a permanent magnet.

Conceptual Question and Answer

Coin Magnet

Q. Are coins (money) magnetic?

A. Some are, and some are not. It depends on the metal content. In general, U.S. "silver" coins are not magnetic, but Canadian coins are because Canadian coins contain nickel (a ferromagnetic material). Get a magnet and a few coins and see for yourself.

Have you ever put a Canadian coin in a coin-operated vending machine and had it refuse to drop down? This happens because the machines are equipped with magnets in the coin path to prevent odd-sized coins, metal slugs, or washers (usually iron) from entering the coin mechanism and causing damage.

The Earth's Magnetic Field

At the beginning of the seventeenth century, William Gilbert, an English scientist, suggested that the Earth acts as a huge magnet. Today we know that such a magnetic effect does exist for our planet. It is the Earth's magnetic field that causes compasses to point north. Experiments have shown that a magnetic field exists within the Earth and extends many hundreds of miles out into space. The aurora borealis and aurora australis (the northern lights and southern lights, respectively), common sights in higher latitudes near the poles, are associated with the Earth's magnetic field. This effect is discussed in Chapters 9.3 and 19.1.

The origin of the Earth's magnetic field is not known, but the most widely accepted theory is that it is caused by the Earth's rotation, which produces internal electrical currents in the liquid part of the core deep within the planet. It is not due to some huge mass of magnetized iron compound within the Earth. The Earth's interior is well above the Curie temperature, so materials are not ferromagnetic. Also, the magnetic poles slowly change their positions, a phenomenon that suggests changing currents.

The Earth's magnetic field does approximate that of a current loop or a huge imaginary bar magnet, as illustrated in ● Fig. 8.21. Note that the magnetic south pole is near the geographic North (N) Pole. For this reason, the north pole of a compass needle, which is a little magnet, points north (law of poles). Because the "north-seeking" pole of the compass needle points north along magnetic field lines, this direction is referred to as *magnetic north*. That is, magnetic north is in the direction of a magnetic "north" pole (actually a magnetic south pole), which is near the geographic North

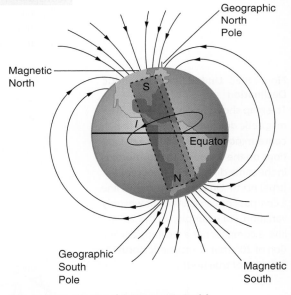

Figure 8.21 The Earth's Magnetic Field
The Earth's magnetic field is thought to be caused by internal currents in the liquid outer core, in association with the planet's rotation. The magnetic field is similar to that of a giant current loop or giant bar magnet within the Earth (such a bar magnet does not and could not really exist). Note that magnetic north (toward which the compass points) and the geographic North Pole (the Earth's axis of rotation) do not coincide.

---

* The Curie temperature is named after Pierre Curie (1859–1906), the French scientist who discovered the effect. Pierre Curie was the husband of Marie (Madame) Curie. They both did pioneering work in radioactivity (Chapter 10.3).

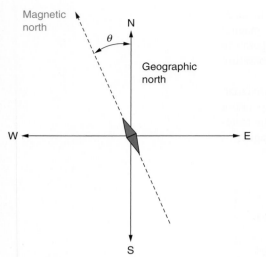

Figure 8.22 Magnetic Declination
The angle of magnetic declination is the angle between geographic (true) north and magnetic north (as indicated by a compass). The declination is measured in degrees east or west of geographic north.

Pole.* The direction of the geographic pole is called *true north*, or in the direction of the Earth's north spin axis. The magnetic and geographic poles do not coincide. The magnetic north pole is about 1000 km (620 mi) from the geographic North Pole. In the Southern Hemisphere the magnetic "south" pole (actually a magnetic north pole) is displaced even more from its corresponding geographic pole.

Hence, the compass does not point toward true north but toward magnetic north. The variation between the two directions is expressed in terms of **magnetic declination**, which is the angle between geographic (true) north and magnetic north (● Fig. 8.22). The declination may vary east or west of a geographic meridian (an imaginary line running from pole to pole).

It is important in navigation to know the magnetic declination at a particular location so that the magnetic compass direction can be corrected for true north. Magnetic declination is provided on navigational maps that show lines of declination expressed in degrees east and west, as illustrated in ● Fig. 8.23. Because the magnetic north pole moves, the magnetic declination varies with time. (See the **Highlight: Magnetic North Pole**.)

Notice that the magnetic field lines around the Earth are curved (Fig. 8.21). For north–south direction, a compass needle lines up with the horizontal components of the lines. As a result of being curved, however, there is a downward component giving rise to a *magnetic dip* or *inclination*, which is the angle made by a compass needle with the horizontal at any point on the Earth's surface. If a compass were held vertically, then the needle would dip downward in the Northern Hemisphere. What would be the inclination in the Southern Hemisphere?

The magnetic field of the Earth is relatively weak compared with that of magnets used in the laboratory, but the field is strong enough to be used by certain animals (including ourselves) for orientation and direction. For instance, it is believed that migratory birds and

Figure 8.23 United States Magnetic Declination
The map shows isogonic (same magnetic declination) lines for the conterminous United States. For locations on the 0° line, magnetic north is in the same direction as geographic (true) north. On either side of this line, a compass has an easterly or westerly variation. For example, on the 20°W line, a compass has a westerly declination of 20°; that is, magnetic north is 20° west of true north.

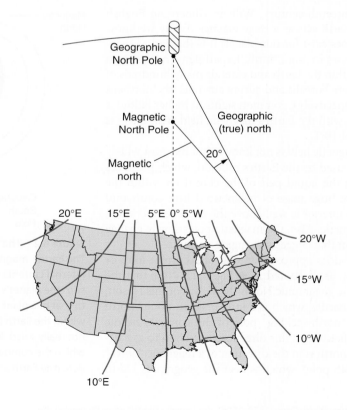

*These designations sometimes cause confusion. From the law of poles, the north pole of a compass points toward a south pole. However, it has become common to say that the magnetic north direction of a compass is toward "magnetic north" in the north polar regions, keeping everything north, particularly in navigation.

Highlight   Magnetic North Pole

The magnetic north pole is on the move. Its location was first determined in 1831 to be on the west coast of the Boothia Peninsula in northern Canada by British explorer James Clark Ross. The next determination was in 1904 by Norwegian explorer Roald Amundsen, who found that the magnetic pole had moved some 50 km (30 mi) from its first determined location (Fig. 1).

The magnetic pole's position was next determined by the Canadian government in 1948. This time it was located some 250 km (155 mi) northwest of where Amundsen determined. Other observations in 1962, 1972, 1984, and 1994 showed that the magnetic pole was continuing to move northwest with an average speed of 10 km (6.2 mi) per year. A 2001 measurement found the pole to be located in the Arctic Ocean. The movement of the magnetic north pole had sped up to about 40 km (25 mi) per year. The estimated position of the pole in 2005 is shown in Fig. 1 and has probably moved since then.

Where will the magnetic north pole be in the future? If the northwest path continues, then it will skirt south of the geo-graphic North Pole and be near or in Siberia later in this century. Of course, this is conjecture. The movement of the magnetic pole may change direction or become erratic because of changes within the Earth.

If the magnetic north pole *did* get to Siberia, then there would be notable changes. One would be that the aurora borealis ("northern lights") would not be seen predominantly in Alaska and Canada, as they are now. The auroras are caused by charged particles from the Sun, which are trapped in the Earth's magnetic field and deflected toward the poles (see Chapter 19.1). With the magnetic north pole in Siberia, the aurora would be observed predominantly in Siberia and northern Europe.

Another change would be in the magnetic declination, and this change would make compass navigation in the United States quite difficult. However, we now have the GPS (global position-ing system) that references directions to the fixed geographic North Pole. [See the Highlight: Global Positioning System (GPS) in Chapter 15.2.]

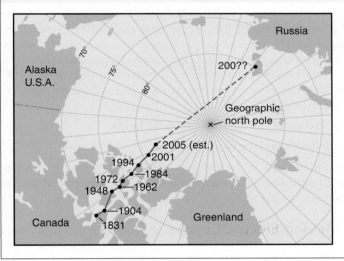

Figure 1 **Magnetic North Pole**
Measurements show that the magnetic north pole has been mov-ing to the northwest. If this northwest path continues, then the pole will skirt south of the geographic North Pole and will be near or in Siberia later in the century.

homing pigeons use the Earth's magnetic field to directionally orient themselves in their homeward flights. Iron compounds have been found in their brains.

Did You Learn?

- Like poles (charges) repel, and unlike poles (charges) attract.
- The Earth's magnetic north pole is near the geographic South Pole; the magnetic south pole is near the geographic North Pole, which is why compass needles point north. The direction the compass points is referred to as magnetic north.

8.5   Electromagnetism

Preview Questions

- What are the two basic principles of electromagnetism?
- What's the difference between a motor and a generator?

Figure 8.24 Electromagnetic Wave
An illustration of the vector components of an electromagnetic wave. The wave consists of two force fields, electric (*E*) and magnetic (*M*), oscillating perpendicularly to each other and to the direction of wave propagation (velocity vector).

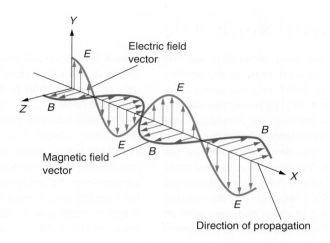

The interaction of electrical and magnetic effects is known as **electromagnetism**. One example of this intimate relationship is electromagnetic waves. When charged particles such as electrons are accelerated, energy is radiated away in the form of waves. *Electromagnetic waves* consist of oscillating electric and magnetic fields, and the field energy radiates outward at the speed of light, 3.00×10^8 m/s in vacuum.

An illustration of an electromagnetic wave is shown in ● Fig. 8.24. The wave is traveling in the *x* direction. The electric (*E*) and magnetic (*B*) field vectors are at angles of 90° to each other. Accelerated, oscillating charged particles produce electromagnetic waves of various frequencies or wavelengths. These waves form an *electromagnetic spectrum* as discussed in Chapter 6.3.

Electromagnetism is one of the most important aspects of physical science, and most of our current technology is directly related to this crucial interaction. Two basic principles of this interaction are as follows:

1. **Moving electric charges (current) give rise to magnetic fields.**

2. **A magnetic field may deflect a moving electric charge.**

The first principle forms the basis of an *electromagnet* considered previously. Electromagnets are found in a variety of applications, such as doorbells, telephones, and devices used to move magnetic materials (see Fig. 8.20).

Magnetic Force on Moving Electric Charge

The second of the electromagnetic principles may be described in a qualitative way: A magnetic field can be used to deflect moving electric charges. A stationary electric charge in a magnetic field experiences no force, but when a moving charge enters a magnetic field as shown in ● Fig. 8.25, it experiences a force. This magnetic force (F_{mag}) is perpendicular to the plane formed by the velocity vector (*v*) and the magnetic field (*B*).

In the figure, the force initially would be out of the page, and with an extended field, the negatively charged particle would follow a circular arc path. If the moving charge were positive, then it would be deflected in the opposite direction, or into the page. Also, if a charge, positive or negative, is moving parallel to a magnetic field, there is no force on the charge.

This effect can be demonstrated experimentally as shown in ● Fig. 8.26. A beam of electrons is traveling in the tube from left to right and is made visible by a piece of fluorescent paper in the tube. In Fig. 8.26a the beam is undeflected in the absence of a magnetic field. In Fig. 8.26b the magnetic field of a bar magnet causes the beam to be deflected downward. In Fig. 8.26c the opposite magnetic pole deflects the beam in the opposite direction.

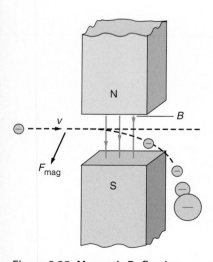

Figure 8.25 Magnetic Deflection
Electrons entering a vertical magnetic field as shown experience a force F_{mag} that deflects them out of the page. (See text for description.)

Motors and Generators

The electrons in a conducting wire also experience force effects caused by magnetic fields. Hence, a current-carrying wire in a magnetic field can experience a force. With such a force available, it might quickly come to mind that the force could be used to do work, and this

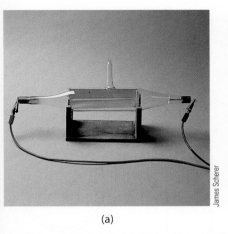

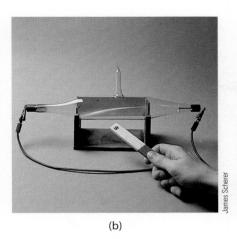

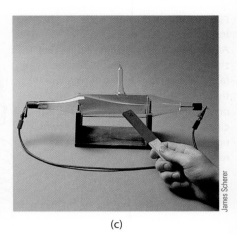

(a)   (b)   (c)

Figure 8.26 Magnetic Force on a Moving Charge
(a) The presence of a beam of electrons is made evident by a fluorescent strip in the tube, which allows the beam to be seen. (b) The magnetic field of a bar magnet gives rise to a force on the electrons, and the beam is deflected (downward). (c) The opposite pole of the bar magnet deflects the beam the other way.

is what is happens in electric motors. Basically, a **motor** is a device that converts electrical energy into mechanical energy. The mechanical rotation of a motor's shaft is used to do work. To help understand the electromagnetic-mechanical interaction of motors (of which there are many types), consider the diagram of a simple *dc motor* shown in ● Fig. 8.27a. Real motors have many loops or windings, but for simplicity only one is shown here. The battery supplies current to the loop, which is free to rotate in the magnetic field between the pole faces. The force on the current-carrying loop produces a torque, causing it to rotate.

Figure 8.27 A dc Motor
(a) An illustration of a loop of a coil in a dc motor. When carrying a current in a magnetic field, the coil experiences a torque and rotates the attached shaft. The split-ring commutator effectively reverses the loop current each half cycle so that the coil will rotate continuously. (b) The forces on the coil show why the reversal of current is necessary.

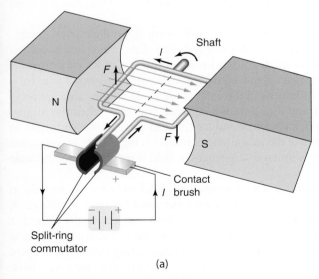

(a)

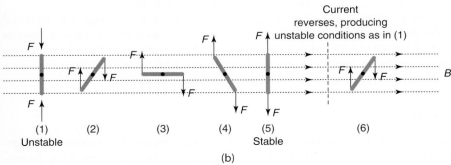

(b)

Figure 8.28 Electromagnetic Induction
An illustration of Faraday's experiment showing electromagnetic induction. (a) When the magnet is moved down through the coil of wire, the reading on the meter indicates a current in the circuit. (b) When the magnet is moved upward, the current in the circuit is reversed.

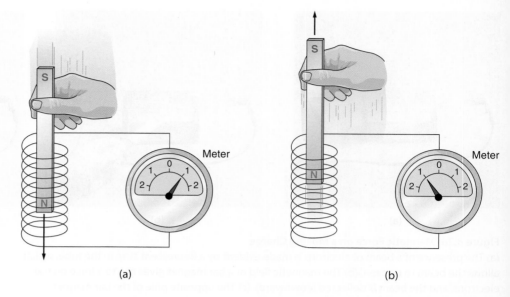

(a)   (b)

Continuous rotation requires a *split-ring commutator* that reverses the polarity and the current in the loop each half cycle so that the loop has the appropriate force to rotate continuously (Fig. 8.27b). The inertia of the loop carries it through the positions where unstable conditions exist. When a rotating armature has many windings (loops), the effect is enhanced. The rotating loops cause a connected shaft to rotate, and this motion is used to do mechanical work. The conversion of electrical energy into mechanical energy is enhanced by many loops of wire and stronger magnetic fields.

One might ask whether the reverse is possible. That is, is the conversion of mechanical energy into electrical energy possible? Indeed it is, and this principle is the basis of electrical generation. Have you ever wondered how electricity is generated? This crucial process is based on electromagnetic principles.

A **generator** is a device that converts mechanical work or energy into electrical energy. A generator operates on what is called *electromagnetic induction*. This principle was discovered in 1831 by Michael Faraday, an English scientist. An illustration of his experiment is shown in ● Fig. 8.28a. When a magnet is moved downward through a loop of wire (or a coil for enhancement), a current is induced in the wire, as indicated on the *galvanometer* (a meter that detects the magnitude and direction of a current). Similarly, when the magnet is moved upward through the coil, a current is induced, but in the opposite direction, as indicated by the opposite deflection of the galvanometer needle in Fig. 8.28b. Investigation shows that this effect is caused by a time-varying magnetic field through the loop because of the motion of the magnet.

The same effect is obtained by using a stationary magnetic field and rotating the loop in the field. The magnetic field through the loop varies with time, and a current is induced. A simple *ac generator* is illustrated in ● Fig. 8.29. When the loop is mechanically rotated, a voltage and current are induced in the loop that vary in magnitude and alternate back and forth, changing direction each half cycle. Hence, there is an alternating current (ac). There are also dc generators, which are essentially dc motors operated in reverse. However, most electricity is generated as ac and then converted, or *rectified*, to dc.

Generators are used in power plants to convert other forms of energy into electrical energy. For the most part, fossil fuels and nuclear energy are used to heat water to generate steam, which is used to turn turbines that supply mechanical energy in the generation process. The electricity is carried to homes and businesses, where it is either converted back into mechanical energy to do work or converted into heat energy.

Transformers

But how is electrical energy or power transmitted? You have probably seen towers with high-voltage (or high-tension) transmission lines running across the land, as shown in the chapter-

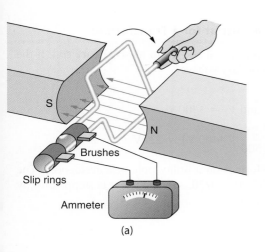

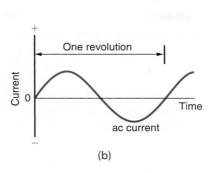

Figure 8.29 An ac Generator
(a) An illustration of a coil loop in an ac generator. When the loop is mechanically turned, a current is induced, as indicated by the ammeter. (b) The current varies in direction each half cycle and hence is called ac, or alternating current.

opening photo. The voltage for transmission is stepped up by means of **transformers**, simple devices based on electromagnetic induction (● Fig. 8.30). A transformer consists of two insulated coils of wire wrapped around an iron core, which concentrates the magnetic field when there is current in the input coil. With an ac current in the input or primary coil, there is a time-changing magnetic field as a result of the current going back and forth. The magnetic field goes through the secondary coil and induces a voltage and current.

Conceptual Question and Answer

No Transformation

Q. Will transformers operate on dc current? If not, why not?

A. Transformers operate on the induction of a time-changing magnetic field, which is obtained using ac current. Direct current produces a static magnetic field and so cannot be used for transformer operations (see Fig. 8.18).

Because the secondary coil has more windings than the primary coil, the induced ac voltage is greater than the input voltage, and this type of transformer is called a *step-up transformer*. However, when the voltage is stepped up, the secondary current is stepped down (by the conservation of energy, because $P = IV$). The factor of voltage step-up depends on the ratio of the numbers of windings on the two coils, which can be easily controlled.

So why step up the voltage? Actually, it is the step-down in current that is really of interest. Transmission lines have resistance and therefore I^2R losses. Stepping down the current reduces these losses, and energy is saved that would otherwise be lost as joule heat. If the voltage is stepped up by a factor of 2, then the current is reduced by a factor of 2, or by $\frac{1}{2}$. With half the current, there is only one-fourth the I^2R losses. (Why?) Thus, for power transmission, the voltage is stepped up to a very high voltage to get the corresponding current step-down and thereby avoid joule heat losses.

Of course, such high voltages cannot be used in our homes which, in general, have 220- to 240-V service entries. Therefore, to get the voltage back down (and the current up), a *step-down transformer* is used, which steps down the voltage and steps up the current. This is done by simply reversing the input and output coils. If the primary coil has more windings than the secondary coil, then the voltage is stepped down.

The voltage change for a transformer is given by

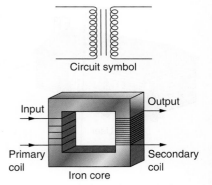

Circuit symbol

Input   Output

Primary coil   Secondary coil

Iron core

Figure 8.30 The Transformer
The basic features of a transformer and the circuit symbol for it are shown. A transformer consists of two coils of insulated wire wrapped around a piece of iron. Alternating current in the primary coil creates a time-varying magnetic field, which is concentrated by the iron core, and the field passes through the secondary coil. The varying magnetic field in the secondary coil produces an alternating-current output.

$$\text{secondary} = \left(\frac{\text{number of secondary coils}}{\text{number of rimary coils}}\right) \times \text{primary voltage}$$

$$V_2 = \left(\frac{N_2}{N_1}\right)V_1 \qquad\qquad 8.10$$

transformer voltage change

EXAMPLE 8.3   Finding Voltage Output for a Transformer

A transformer has 500 windings in its primary coil and 25 in its secondary coil. If the primary voltage is 4400 V, what is the secondary voltage?

Solution

Using Eq. 8.10 with $N_1 = 500$, $N_2 = 25$, and $V_1 = 4400$ V,

$$V_2 = \left(\frac{N_2}{N_1}\right)V_1 = \left(\frac{25}{500}\right)(4400 \text{ V}) = 220 \text{V}$$

This result is typical of a *step-down* transformer on a utility pole near residences. The voltage is stepped down by a factor of 25/500 = 1/20, so the current is stepped up by an inverse factor of 20 (that is, 500/25 = 20).

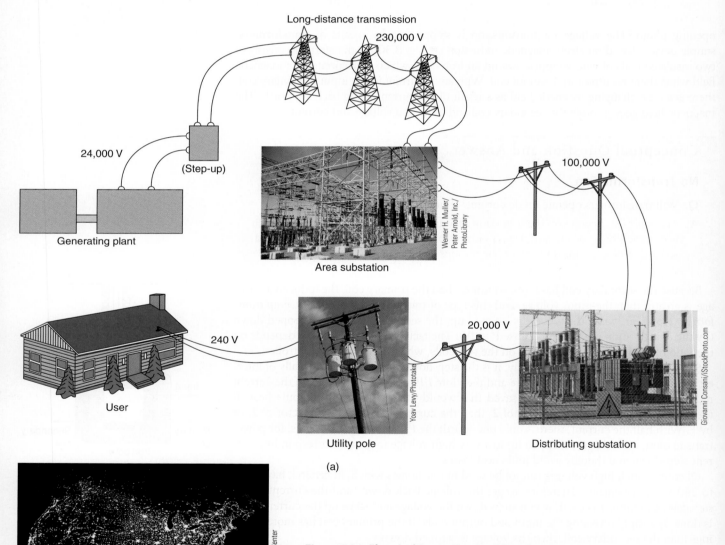

Figure 8.31 Electrical Power Transmission System
(a) At the generating plant, the voltage is stepped up with a corresponding current step-down to reduce the I^2R losses in the lines for long-distance transmission. The high voltage is then stepped down in substations and finally to 240 V by the common utility-pole transformer (sometimes on the ground for buried lines) for household usage. (b) All lit up. Can you identify the various large cities? Can you find your hometown?

Confidence Exercise 8.3

Suppose the transformer in Example 8.3 were reversed and used as a step-up transformer with a voltage input of 100 V. What would the voltage output be?

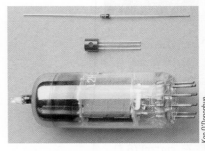

Figure 8.32 Solid-State Diode, Transistor, and Vacuum Tube
A diode (two leads, top) and a transistor (three leads) are shown above a vacuum tube. Solid-state diodes and transistors have all but replaced vacuum tubes in most applications.

An illustration of stepping up and stepping down the voltage in electrical transmission is shown in ● Fig. 8.31a. The voltage step-up and the corresponding current step-down, which reduces joule heat losses, are major reasons we use ac electricity in power transmission. Note how efficient electrical transmission is in Fig. 8.31b.

Indeed, we are now in an electrical age of high technology and electronics. *Electronics* is the branch of physics and engineering that deals with the emission and control of electrons. Our electronic instruments have become smaller and smaller, primarily because of the development of solid-state *diodes* and *transistors*. These devices control the direction of electron flow, and the transistor allows for the amplification of an input signal (as in a transistor radio). Solid-state diodes and transistors offer great advantages over the older vacuum tubes and have all but replaced them. Major advantages are smaller size, lower power consumption, and material economy (● Fig. 8.32).

Even further miniaturization has come about through *integrated circuits* (ICs). An integrated circuit may contain millions of transistors on a silicon *chip*. Current technology can produce transistors just 45 nm (10^{-9} m) wide and pack more than four hundred million transistors on a chip. Chips have the dimensions of only a few millimeters (called a *microchip or microprocessor*, ● Fig. 8.33).

Such chips can have many logic circuits and are the "brains" of computers. Microchips have many applications in processors that perform tasks almost instantaneously. For example, they are in our automobiles, computing the miles (or kilometers) per gallon of gasoline, applying antilock brakes, signaling the inflation of air bags when needed, and indicating location and direction to your destination with global positioning satellites. [See the Highlight: Global Positioning System (GPS) in Chapter 15.2.] What will the future bring? Think about it.

Did You Learn?

- Moving electric charges (current) give rise to a magnetic field, and a magnetic field may deflect moving electric charge.

- A motor converts electrical energy into mechanical energy; a generator converts mechanical energy or work into electrical energy.

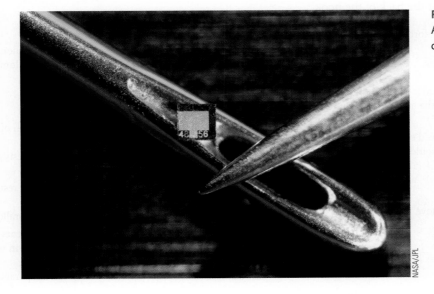

Figure 8.33 Integrated Circuits
A microprocessor integrated circuit, or chip, lies near the eye of a needle.

KEY TERMS

1. electric charge (8.1)
2. electrons
3. protons
4. law of charges
5. Coulomb's law
6. electric field
7. current (8.2)
8. electric potential energy
9. voltage
10. resistance
11. Ohm's law
12. electric power
13. direct current (dc) (8.3)
14. alternating current (ac)
15. series circuit
16. parallel circuit
17. law of poles (8.4)
18. magnetic field
19. ferromagnetic
20. magnetic domains
21. magnetic declination
22. electromagnetism (8.5)
23. motor
24. generator
25. transformer

MATCHING

For each of the following items, fill in the number of the appropriate Key Term from the preceding list. Compare your answers with those at the back of the book.

a. _____ Positively charged particles
b. _____ Angle between true north and magnetic north
c. _____ *IV*
d. _____ Unlike charges attract; like charges repel
e. _____ Interaction of electrical and magnetic effects
f. _____ A fundamental quantity
g. _____ Steps voltages up and down
h. _____ Relates voltage and current to resistance
i. _____ Converts electrical energy into mechanical energy
j. _____ Negatively charged particles
k. _____ Imaginary lines indicating magnetic direction
l. _____ Describes the force between charged particles
m. _____ Highly magnetic material

n. _____ Produced by a constantly changing voltage
o. _____ Time rate of flow of electric charge
p. _____ Unlike poles attract; like poles repel
q. _____ Equals W/q
r. _____ Same current through all resistances
s. _____ Opposition to charge flow
t. _____ Local regions of alignment
u. _____ Net electron flow in one direction
v. _____ Converts mechanical energy into electrical energy
w. _____ Results from separating electrical charges
x. _____ Voltage across each resistance is the same
y. _____ $E = F/q_+$ mapping

MULTIPLE CHOICE

Compare your answers with those at the back of the book.

1. What can be said about the electric force between two charged particles?
   (a) it is repulsive for unlike charges.
   (b) it varies as $1/r$.
   (c) it depends only on the magnitudes of the charges.
   (d) it is much, much greater than the attractive gravitational force.

2. Two equal positive charges are placed equidistant on either side of another positive charge. What would the middle positive charge experience? (8.1)
   (a) a net force to the right   (b) a net force to the left
   (c) a zero net force

3. In a dc circuit, how do electrons move? (8.2)
   (a) with a slow drift velocity.
   (b) in alternate directions.
   (c) near the speed of light.
   (d) none of the preceding.

4. What is a unit of voltage? (8.2)
   (a) joule   (b) joule/coulomb
   (c) amp-coulomb   (d) amp/coulomb

5. In electrical terms, power has what units? (8.2)
   (a) joule/coulomb   (b) amp/ohm
   (c) amp-coulomb   (d) amp-volt

6. Appliances with heating elements require which of the following? (8.3)
   (a) a large current   (b) a large resistance
   (c) a low joule heat

7. The greatest equivalent resistance occurs when resistances are connected in which type of arrangement? (8.3)
   (a) series   (b) parallel   (c) series–parallel

8. Given three resistances, the greatest current occurs in a battery circuit when the resistances are connected in what type of arrangement? (8.3)
   (a) series   (b) parallel   (c) series–parallel

9. When two bar magnets are near each other, the north pole of one of the magnets experiences what type of force from the other magnet? (8.4)
   (a) an attractive force
   (b) a repulsive force
   (c) a Coulomb force
   (d) both (a) and (b)

10. What is the variation in the location of the Earth's magnetic north pole from true north given by? (8.4)
   (a) the law of poles   (b) the magnetic field
   (c) magnetic domains   (d) the magnetic declination

11. What type of energy conversion does a motor perform? (8.5)
   (a) chemical energy into mechanical energy
   (b) mechanical energy into electrical energy
   (c) electrical energy into mechanical energy
   (d) mechanical energy into chemical energy

12. What type of energy conversion does a generator perform? (8.5)
   (a) chemical energy into mechanical energy
   (b) mechanical energy into electrical energy
   (c) electrical energy into mechanical energy
   (d) mechanical energy into chemical energy

13. Which of the following is true of a step-up transformer? (8.5)
   (a) It has an equal number of windings on the primary and secondary coils.
   (b) It has fewer windings on the secondary coil.
   (c) It has fewer windings on the primary coil.
   (d) None of the preceding statements is true.

14. A transformer with more windings on the primary coil than on the secondary coil does which of the following? (8.4)
   (a) Steps up the voltage.
   (b) Steps up the current.
   (c) Steps up both current and voltage.
   (d) Will operate off dc current.

FILL IN THE BLANK

Compare your answers with those at the back of the book.

1. An object with a deficiency of electrons is ___ charged. (8.1)

2. The unit of electric current is the___. (8.1)

3. ___ are neither good conductors nor good insulators. (8.1)

4. Voltage is defined as work per___. (8.2)

5. An electric circuit that is not a complete path is called a(n) ___ circuit. (8.2)

6. The unit of resistance is the ___. (8.2)

7. Another name for joule heat is ___ losses. (8.2)

8. A battery-powered device uses ___ current. (8.3)

9. In a circuit with resistances connected in parallel, the total resistance is always less than the ___ resistance. (8.3)

10. A material ceases to be ferromagnetic above the ___ temperature. (8.4)

11. Magnetic north is generally in the direction of the___ north pole. (8.4)

12. A step-up transformer has more windings on the ___ coil. (8.5)

SHORT ANSWER

8.1 Electric Charge, Electric Force, and Electric Field

1. Which two particles that make up atoms have about the same mass? Which two have the same magnitude of electric charge?

2. A large charge $+Q$ and a small charge $-q$ are a short distance apart. How do the electric forces on each charge compare? Is this comparison described by another physical law? (*Hint*: See Chapter 3.4.)

3. Explain how a charged rubber comb attracts bits of paper and how a charged balloon sticks to a wall or ceiling.

4. Why do clothes sometimes stick together when removed from a dryer?

8.2 Current, Voltage, and Electrical Power

5. Distinguish between electric potential energy and voltage.

6. What are two things that are required for there to be a current in a circuit?

7. How does joule heat vary with increasing and decreasing resistances?

8. If the drift velocity in a conductor is so small, then why does an auto battery influence the starter as soon as you turn the ignition switch?

8.3 Simple Electric Circuits and Electrical Safety

9. Distinguish between alternating current and direct current.

10. Why are home appliances connected in parallel rather than in series?

11. Compare the safety features of (a) fuses, (b) circuit breakers, (c) three-prong plugs, and (d) polarized plugs.

12. Is it safe to stay inside a car during a lightning storm (● Fig. 8.34)? Explain.

13. Sometimes resistances in a circuit are described as being connected "head to tail" and "all heads and all tails" connected together. What is being described?

8.4 Magnetism

14. Why do iron filings show magnetic field patterns?

15. Compare the law of charges and the law of poles.

Figure 8.34 Safe Inside a Car?
See Short-Answer Question 12.

16. (a) What is a ferromagnetic material? (b) Why does a permanent magnet attract pieces of ferromagnetic materials? What would happen if the pieces were above their Curie temperature?

17. What is the principle of an electromagnet?

18. (a) What does the Earth's magnetic field resemble, and where are its poles? (b) Why do airline pilots and ship navigators guided by compasses have to make corrections to stay on a course charted on a map?

8.5 Electromagnetism

19. Describe the basic principle of a dc electric motor.

20. What happens (a) when a proton moves parallel to a magnetic field and (b) when a proton moves perpendicular to a magnetic field?

21. What is the principle of a transformer, and how are transformers used?

Figure 8.35 High Voltage or High Current?
See Short-Answer Question 24.

22. What would happen if electric power were transmitted from the generating plant to your home at 120 V?

23. Why can birds perch on high-voltage power lines and not get hurt?

24. Body injury from electricity depends on the magnitude of the current and its path (see the Highlight: Electrical Effects on Humans, Chapter 8.4). However, signs warning "Danger. High Voltage" are commonly seen (● Fig. 8.35). Shouldn't the signs refer to high *current*? Explain.

VISUAL CONNECTION

Visualize the connections and give answers for the blanks. Compare your answers with those at the back of the book.

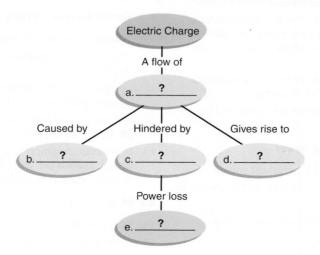

APPLYING YOUR KNOWLEDGE

1. What is the cause of "static cling" in clothes, and what is an economical way to get rid of it?

2. Two negative charges of -1 C each are placed at opposite ends of a meterstick. (a) Could a free electron be placed somewhere on the meterstick so that it would be in static equilibrium (zero net force)? How about a proton? (b) Could an electron or a proton be placed anywhere beyond the ends of the meterstick so that it would be in static equilibrium? Explain.

3. Answer both parts of Question 2 for a charge of $+1$ C placed at one end of the meterstick and a charge of -1 C placed at the other.

4. An old saying about electrical safety states that you should keep one hand in your pocket when working with high voltage electricity. What does this mean?

5. The following are incandescent light bulb questions. (Several billion bulbs are used in the United States each year.)
   (a) The gas in a light bulb is not air, but is a mixture of argon and nitrogen gases at low pressure. Why isn't air used? Wouldn't it be cheaper?

   (b) After long periods of use, a gray spot develops on the inside of a bulb. What is this gray spot? (*Hint:* It is metallic.)

6. Show that the resistance that is equivalent to two resistances in parallel can be written

$$R_p = \frac{R_1 R_2}{R_1 + R_2}$$

7. What happens when you cut a bar magnet in half? If it were continually cut in half, then would it finally yield two magnetic monopoles? Explain.

8. Suppose you are on an expedition to locate the magnetic north pole. (Assume it is still on land to make it easier to plant a flag.) How would you go about locating it? (*Hint:* Think of inclination.)

IMPORTANT EQUATIONS

Coulomb's Law: $F = \dfrac{kq_1q_2}{r_2}$ (8.1)

$(k = 9.0 \times 10^9 \text{ N} \cdot \text{m}^2/\text{C}^2)$

Current: $I = \dfrac{q}{t}$ (8.2)

Voltage: $V = \dfrac{W}{q}$ (8.3)

Ohm's Law: $V = IR$ (8.4)

Electric Power: $P = IV = I^2R$ (8.5–8.6)

Resistance in Series: $R_s = R_1 + R_2 + R_3 + \cdots$ (8.7)

Resistances in Parallel: $\dfrac{1}{R_p} = \dfrac{1}{R_1} + \dfrac{1}{R_2} + \dfrac{1}{R_3} \cdots$ (8.8)

Two Resistances in Parallel: $R_p = \dfrac{R_1R_2}{R_1 + R_2}$ (8.9)

Transformer (Voltages and Turns): $V_2 = \left(\dfrac{N_2}{N_1}\right)V_1$ (8.10)

EXERCISES

8.1 Electric Charge, Electric Force, and Electric Field

1. How many electrons make up one coulomb of charge? (*Hint:* $q = ne$.)

   Answer: 6.25×10^{18}

2. An object has one million more electrons than protons. What is the net charge of the object?

3. What are the forces on two charges of $+0.60$ C and $+2.0$ C, respectively, if they are separated by a distance of 3.0 m?

   Answer: 1.0×10^9 N, mutually repulsive

4. Find the force of electrical attraction between a proton and an electron that are 5.3×10^{-11} m apart (the arrangement in the hydrogen atom). Compare this force to the gravitational force between these particles (see Chapter 3.5).

5. There is a net passage of 4.8×10^{18} electrons by a point in a wire conductor in 0.25 s. What is the current in the wire?

   Answer: 3.1 A

6. A current of 1.50 A flows in a conductor for 6.5 s. How much charge passes a given point in the conductor during this time?

8.2 Current, Voltage, and Electrical Power

7. To separate a 0.25-C charge from another charge, 30 J of work is done. What is the electric potential energy of the charge?

   Answer: 30 J

8. What is the voltage of the 0.25-C charge in Exercise 7?

9. If an electrical component with a resistance of 50 Ω is connected to a 120-V source, then how much current flows through the component?

   Answer: 2.4 A

10. What battery voltage is necessary to supply 0.50 A of current to a circuit with a resistance of 20 Ω?

11. A car radio draws 0.25 A of current in the auto's 12-V electrical system.
    (a) How much electric power does the radio use?
    (b) What is the effective resistance of the radio?

    Answer: (a) 3.0 W (b) 48 Ω

12. A flashlight uses batteries that add up to 3.0 V and has a power output of 0.50 W.
    (a) How much current is drawn from the batteries?
    (b) What is the effective resistance of the flashlight?

13. How much does it cost to run a 1500-W hair dryer 30 minutes each day for a month (30 days) at a cost of 12¢ per kWh?

    Answer: $2.70

14. A refrigerator using 1000 W runs one-eighth of the time. How much does the electricity cost to run the refrigerator each month at 10¢ per kWh?

15. A 24-Ω component is connected to a 12-V battery. How much energy is expended per second?

    Answer: 6.0 W

16. In Exercise 15, using the equation given in the chapter, you probably found the power in two steps. Show that $P = V^2/R$, which requires only one step.

17. The heating element of an iron operates at 110 V with a current of 10 A.
    (a) What is the resistance of the iron?
    (b) What is the power dissipated by the iron?

    Answer: (a) 11 Ω (b) 1100 W

18. A 100-W light bulb is turned on. It has an operating voltage of 120 V.
    (a) How much current flows through the bulb?
    (b) What is the resistance of the bulb?
    (c) How much energy is used each second?

19. Two resistors with values of 25 Ω and 35 Ω, respectively, are connected in series and hooked to a 12-V battery.
    (a) How much current is in the circuit?
    (b) How much power is expended in the circuit?

    Answer: (a) 0.20 A (b) 2.4 W

20. Suppose the two resistors in Exercise 19 were connected in parallel. What would be (a) the current and (b) the power in this case?

21. A student in the laboratory connects a 10-Ω resistor, a 15-Ω resistor, and a 20-Ω resistor in series and then connects the arrangement to a 50-V dc source.
    (a) How much current is in the circuit?
    (b) How much power is expended in the circuit?

    Answer: (a) 1.1 A (b) 55 W

22. The student in Exercise 21 repeats the experiment but with the resistors connected in parallel.
    (a) What is the current?
    (b) What is the power?

23. A 30.0-Ω resistor and a 60.0-Ω resistor in series are connected to a 120-V dc source.
    (a) What is (are) the current(s) through the resistors?
    (b) What is the voltage drop across each resistor?

    Answer: (a) 1.33 A (b) 40 V and 80 V

24. A 30.0-Ω resistor and a 60.0-Ω resistor in parallel are connected to a 120-V dc source.
    (a) What is (are) the current(s) thorough the resistors?
    (b) What is the voltage drop across each resistor?

8.5 Electromagnetism

25. A transformer has 300 turns on its secondary and 100 turns on its primary. The primary is connected to a 12-V source.
    (a) What is the voltage output of the secondary?
    (b) If 2.0 A flows in the primary coil, then how much current is there in the secondary coil?

    Answer: (a) 36 V (b) 0.67 A

26. A transformer has 500 turns on its primary and 200 turns on its secondary.
    (a) Is it a step-up or a step-down transformer?
    (b) If a voltage of 100 V is applied to the primary and a current of 0.25 A flows in these windings, then what are the voltage output of the secondary and the current in the secondary?

27. A transformer with 1000 turns in its primary coil has to decrease the voltage from 4400 V to 220 V for home use. How many turns should there be on the secondary coil?

    Answer: 50

28. A power company transmits current through a 240,000-V transmission line. This voltage is stepped down at an area substation to 40,000 V by a transformer that has 900 turns on the primary coil. How many turns are on the secondary of the transformer?

ON THE WEB

1. Static Electricity

In winter, why do you get a shock when you touch a light switch or even another person or pet? Why do balloons cling to the wall at birthday parties? Describe the process called "induction" and explain how it is related to static electricity. Explain briefly how knowing about static electricity can help you understand other aspects of electricity. Visit the student website at **www.cengagebrain.com/shop/ISBN/1133104096** to answer these questions.

2. Electromagnetic Waves

What are force fields? What role do vibrating charges play in electromagnetic processes? Can you visualize classical and electromagnetic waves? What do you know about lines of force? Follow the recommended links on the student website at **www.cengagebrain.com/shop/ISBN/1133104096** to better understand the various terms and components of electromagnetic waves and how electromagnetism works.

Atomic Physics

Courtesy IBM Corporation, Research Division, Almaden Research Center, Comp.

All things are made of atoms—little particles that move around in perpetual motion, attracting each other when they are a little distance apart, but repelling upon being squeezed into one another.

•

Richard Feynman,
physics Nobel Laureate
(1918–1988)

< Individual atoms in the "stadium corral"—iron (Fe) and copper (Cu).

T he development of physics prior to about 1900 is termed *classical physics* or *Newtonian physics*. It was generally concerned with the *macrocosm*, that is, with the description and explanation of large-scale observable phenomena such as the movements of projectiles and planets.

As the year 1900 approached, scientists thought the field of physics was in fairly good order. The principles of mechanics, wave motion, sound, and optics were reasonably well understood. Electricity and magnetism had been combined into electromagnetism, and light had been shown to be electromagnetic waves. Certainly some rough edges remained, but it seemed that only a few refinements were needed.

PHYSICS FACTS

▶ Theoretically, a sample of hot hydrogen gas can give off many different wavelengths, but only four are in the visible range.

▶ The basis of the microwave oven was discovered by a scientist working with radar

Chapter Outline

As scientists probed deeper into the submicroscopic world of the atom (the *microcosm*), however, they observed strange things, strange in the sense that they could not be explained by the classical principles of physics. These discoveries were unsettling because they made clear that physicists would need radical new approaches to describe and explain submicroscopic phenomena. One of these new approaches was *quantum mechanics*, which describes the behavior of matter and interactions on the atomic and subatomic levels.

The development of physics since about 1900 is called *modern physics*. This chapter is concerned with *atomic physics*, the part of modern physics that deals mainly with phenomena involving the electrons in atoms. Chapter 10 will then examine *nuclear physics*, which deals with the central core, or nucleus, of the atom.

An appropriate way to start the examination of atomic physics is with a brief history of the concept of the atom. How that concept has changed provides an excellent example of how scientific theories adapt as new experimental evidence is gathered.

9.1   Early Concepts of the Atom

Preview Questions

● What was John Dalton's hypothesis about the make-up of matter?
● How did Rutherford's nuclear model picture the atom?

Around 400 BCE, Greek philosophers were debating whether matter was continuous or discrete (particulate). For instance, if one could repeatedly cut a sample of gold in half, would an ultimate particle of gold theoretically be reached that could not be divided further? If an ultimate particle could be reached, matter would be discrete; if not, matter would be continuous.

Most of these philosophers, including the renowned Aristotle, decided that matter was continuous and could be divided again and again, indefinitely. A few philosophers thought that an ultimate, *indivisible* (Greek: *atomos*) particle would indeed be reached. The question was purely philosophical, since neither side could present scientific evidence to support its viewpoint. Modern science differs from the approach of the ancient Greeks by relying not only on logic but also on the scientific method (Chapter 1.2): the systematic gathering of facts by observation and experimentation and the rigorous testing of hypotheses.

The "continuous" model of matter postulated by Aristotle and his followers prevailed for about 2200 years until an English scientist, John Dalton, in 1807 presented evidence that matter is discrete and exists as particles. Dalton's evidence for the atomic theory will be examined in Chapter 12.3. For now, it is sufficient to point out that Dalton's major hypothesis was that each chemical element is composed of tiny, indivisible particles called **atoms**, which are identical for that element but different (particularly in masses and chemical properties) from atoms of other elements. Dalton's concept of the atom has been called the "billiard ball model," because he thought of atoms as essentially featureless, indivisible spheres of uniform density (● Fig. 9.1a).

Dalton's model had to be refined about 90 years later when the electron was discovered by J. J. Thomson at Cambridge University in England in 1897. Thomson studied electrical discharges in tubes of low-pressure gas called *gas-discharge tubes* or *cathode-ray tubes*. He discovered that when high voltage was applied to the tube, a "ray" was produced at the negative electrode (the cathode) and sped toward the positive electrode (the anode). Unlike electromagnetic radiation, the ray was deflected by electric and magnetic fields. Thomson concluded that the ray consisted of a stream of negatively charged particles, which are now called **electrons**. (See Chapter 8.5, Fig. 8.26.)

Further experiments by Thomson and others showed that an electron has a mass of 9.11×10^{-31} kg and a charge of -1.60×10^{-19} C and that the electrons were being produced by the voltage "tearing" them away from atoms of gas in the tube. Because identical electrons were being produced regardless of what gas was in the tube, it became apparent that atoms of all types contain electrons.

Dalton's model

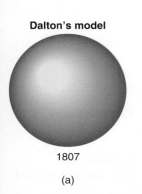

1807

(a)

Thomson's model

Spherical cloud
of positive
charge

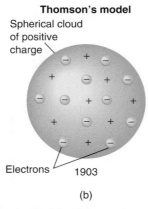

Electrons   1903

(b)

Rutherford's model

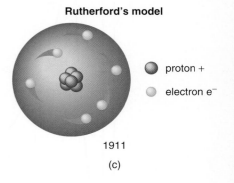

proton +

electron e⁻

1911

(c)

Figure 9.1 Dalton's, Thomson's, and Rutherford's Models of the Atom
(a) John Dalton's 1807 "billiard ball model" pictured the atom as a tiny, indivisible, uniformly dense, solid sphere. (b) J. J. Thomson's 1903 "plum pudding model" of the atom was a sphere of positive charge in which negatively charged electrons were embedded. (c) Ernest Rutherford's 1911 "nuclear model" depicted the atom as having a dense center of positive charge, called the *nucleus*, around which electrons orbited. (The sizes of the internal particles relative to the atom are *greatly* exaggerated in the figure.)

As a whole, an atom is electrically neutral. Therefore, some other part of the atom must be positively charged. Indeed, further experiments detected positively charged particles (now called *positive ions*) as they sped to and passed through holes in the negative electrode of a cathode-ray tube. In 1903, Thomson concluded that an atom was much like a sphere of plum pudding; electrons were the raisins stuck randomly in an otherwise homogeneous mass of positively charged pudding (Fig. 9.1b).

Thomson's "plum pudding model" of the atom was modified only 8 years later in 1911. Ernest Rutherford discovered that 99.97% of the mass of an atom is concentrated in a very tiny core which he called the *nucleus*. (The classic experiment that Rutherford performed to discover the nucleus is discussed in Chapter 10.2.)

Rutherford's nuclear model of the atom pictured the electrons as circulating in some way in the otherwise empty space around this very tiny, positively charged core (Fig. 9.1c). However, as will be discussed in the following sections, even Rutherford's model has undergone modification.

Did You Learn?

- John Dalton proposed that each chemical element was composed of tiny, indivisible particles called "atoms."

- Rutherford's model of the atom pictured electrons circulating around a tiny, positively charged core which he called the nucleus.

9.2 The Dual Nature of Light

Preview Questions

- What is a photon, and on what does its energy depend?
- What is meant by the "dual nature of light"?

Before discussing the next improvement in the model of the atom, a radical development about the nature of light should be considered. Even before the turn of the twentieth century, scientists knew that visible light of all frequencies was emitted by the atoms of an incandescent (glowing hot) solid, such as the filament of a light bulb. For example, ● Fig. 9.2

Figure 9.2 Red-Hot Steel
The radiation component of maximum intensity determines a hot solid's color, as shown here by orange-red hot steel coming out of a furnace.

Stacy Pick/Stock Boston

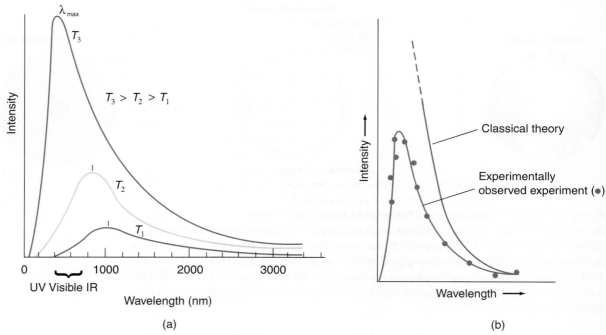

Figure 9.3 Thermal Radiation
(a) Intensity versus wavelength curves for thermal radiation. The wavelength associated with the maximum intensity (λ_{max}) becomes shorter with increasing temperature. (b) Classical theory predicts that the intensity of thermal radiation should be inversely related to the wavelength of the emitted radiation. If that were true, then the intensity would be much greater for shorter wavelengths than is actually observed.

Figure 9.4 Max Planck (1858–1947)
While a professor of physics at the University of Berlin in 1900, Planck proposed that the energy of thermal oscillators exists in only discrete amounts, or quanta. The important small constant *h* is called *Planck's constant*. Planck was awarded the Nobel Prize in physics in 1918 for his contributions to quantum physics. Planck's second son was executed by the Nazis for conspiring to assassinate Adolf Hitler.

shows that the radiation emitted by a hot ingot of steel as it comes from the furnace has its maximum intensity in the orange-red region of the visible spectrum.

Although there is a dominant orange-red color perceived by our eyes, in actuality there is a continuous spectrum. As illustrated in ● Fig. 9.3a, the intensity of the emitted radiation depends on the wavelength (λ). Practically all wavelengths are present, but there is a dominant color (wavelength), which depends on temperature. Consequently, a hot solid heated to a higher and higher temperature appears to go from a dull red to a bluish white. This outcome is expected because the hotter the solid, the greater the vibrations in the atoms and the higher frequency (shorter wavelength) of the emitted radiation. The wavelength of the maximum intensity component (λ_{max}) becomes shorter.

According to classical wave theory, the intensity (I) of the radiation spectrum is inversely related to the wavelength (actually, $I \propto 1/\lambda^4$). This relationship predicts that the intensity should increase without limit as the wavelengths get shorter, as illustrated in Fig. 9.3b. This prediction is sometimes called the *ultraviolet catastrophe*: *ultraviolet* because the difficulty occurs with wavelengths shorter than the ultraviolet end of the spectrum and *catastrophe* because it predicts emitted energy growing without bounds at these wavelengths.

The dilemma was resolved in 1900 by Max Planck (pronounced "plonck"), a German physicist (● Fig. 9.4). He introduced a radical idea that explained the observed distribution of thermal radiation intensity. In doing so, Planck took the first step toward a new theory called *quantum physics*. Classically, an electron oscillator may vibrate at any frequency or have any energy up to some maximum value, but *Planck's hypothesis* stated that the energy is *quantized*. That is, an oscillator can have only discrete, or specific, amounts of energy. Moreover, Planck concluded that the energy (E) of an oscillator depends on its frequency (f) in accordance with the following equation:

$$\text{energy} = \text{Planck's constant} \times \text{frequency}$$
$$E = hf \qquad \qquad 9.1$$

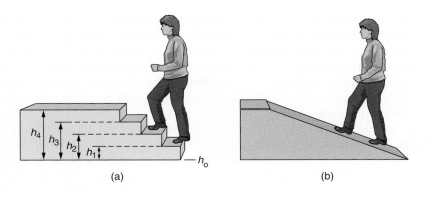

Figure 9.5 The Concept of Quantized Energy
(a) The woman on the staircase can stop only on one of the steps, so she can have only four potential-energy values. (b) When on the ramp, she can be at any height and thus can have a continuous range of potential-energy values. (See Conceptual Question and Answer.)

where h is a constant, called *Planck's constant*, that has the very small value of 6.63×10^{-34} J·s.

Planck's hypothesis correctly accounted for the observed radiation curve shown in Fig. 9.3b. Thus, Planck introduced the idea of a **quantum**, a discrete amount of energy (or a "packet" of energy).

Conceptual Question and Answer

Step Right Up

Q. Can mechanical energy be quantized?

A. Quantized energy in quantum physics is analogous to the potential energy of a person on a staircase who can have only discrete potential-energy values determined by the height of each particular step (● Fig. 9.5a). Continuous energy, on the other hand, is like the potential energy of a person on a ramp who can stand at any height and thus can have any value of potential energy (Fig. 9.5b).

In the latter part of the nineteenth century, scientists observed that electrons are emitted when certain metals are exposed to light. The phenomenon was called the **photoelectric effect**. This direct conversion of light (radiant energy) into electrical energy now forms the basis of photocells used in calculators, in the automatic door openers at your supermarket, and in the "electric eye" beam used in many automatic garage door openers to protect children and pets from a descending door, as in ● Fig. 9.6.

As in the case of the ultraviolet catastrophe, certain aspects of the photoelectric effect could not be explained by classical theory. For example, the amount of energy necessary to

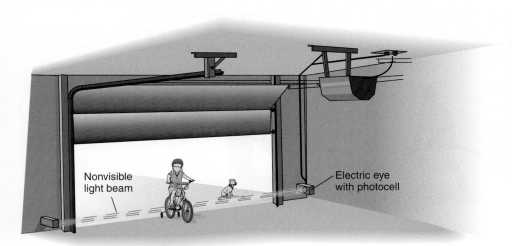

Nonvisible light beam

Electric eye with photocell

Figure 9.6 Photoelectric Effect Application: The Electric Eye
When light strikes a photocell, electrons are freed from the atoms and a current is set up in an "electric eye" circuit. When the garage door starts to move downward, any interruption of the electric eye beam (usually infrared, IR), which affects the circuit current and signals the door to stop, protects anything that might be under it.

free an electron from a photomaterial could be calculated. According to classical theory, in which light is considered a wave with a continuous flow of energy, it would take an appreciable time for electromagnetic waves to supply the energy needed for an electron to be emitted. However, electrons flow from photocells almost immediately upon being exposed to light. Also, it was observed that only light above a certain frequency would cause electrons to be emitted. According to classical theory, light of any frequency should be able to provide the needed energy.

In 1905, Albert Einstein solved the problems of the photoelectric effect. Applying Planck's hypothesis, Einstein postulated that light (and, in fact, all electromagnetic radiation) was quantized and consisted of "particles," or "packets," of energy, rather than waves. Einstein coined the term **photon** to refer to such a quantum of electromagnetic radiation. He used Planck's relationship ($E = hf$) and stated that a quantum, or photon, of light contains a discrete amount of energy (E) equal to Planck's constant (h) times the frequency (f) of the light. The higher the frequency of the light, the greater the energy of its photons. For example, because blue light has a higher frequency (shorter wavelength) than red light, photons of blue light have more energy than photons of red light. Example 9.1 illustrates how photon energy can be determined.

EXAMPLE 9.1   Determining Photon Energy from the Frequency

Find the energy in joules of the photons of red light of frequency 5.00×10^{14} Hz. (Recall from Chapter 6.2 that the unit hertz is equivalent to reciprocal second, 1/s.)

Solution

Given the frequency, the energy can be found directly by using Eq. 9.1.

$$E = hf = (6.63 \times 10^{-34} \, \text{J} \cdot \text{s})(5.00 \times 10^{14} \, \text{1/s})$$
$$= 33.2 \times 10^{-20} \, \text{J} = 3.32 \times 10^{-19} \, \text{J}$$

Confidence Exercise 9.1

Find the energy in joules of the photons of blue light of frequency 7.50×10^{14} Hz.
Answers to Confidence Exercises may be found at the back of the book.

By considering light to be composed of photons, Einstein was able to explain the photoelectric effect. The classical time delay necessary to get enough energy to free an electron is not a problem when using the concept of photons of energy. A photon with the proper amount of energy could deliver the release energy instantaneously in a "packet." (An analogy to illustrate the difference between the delivery of wave energy and that of quantum energy is shown in ● Fig. 9.7.) The concept of the photon also explains why light with greater than a certain minimum frequency is required for emission of an electron. Because $E = hf$, a photon of light with a frequency smaller than this minimum value would not have enough energy to free an electron. (See the **Highlight: Albert Einstein**.)

How can light be composed of photons (discrete packets of energy) when it shows wave phenomena such as polarization, diffraction, and interference (Chapters 7.5 and

Figure 9.7 Wave and Quantum Analogy
A wave supplies a continuous flow of energy, somewhat analogous to the stream of water from the garden hose. A quantum supplies its energy all at once in a "packet" or "bundle," somewhat like each bucketful of water thrown on the fire.

Wave nature   Quantum nature

Highlight   Albert Einstein

Isaac Newton's only rival for the accolade of "greatest scientist of all time" is Albert Einstein, who was born in Ulm, Germany, in 1879 (Fig. 1). In high school, Einstein did poorly in Latin and Greek and was interested only in mathematics. His teacher told him, "You will never amount to anything, Einstein."

Einstein attended college in Switzerland, graduated in 1901, and accepted a job as a junior official at the patent office in Berne, Switzerland. He spent his spare time working in theoretical physics. In 1905, five of his papers were published in the *German Yearbook of Physics*, and in that same year he earned his Ph.D. at the age of 26. One paper explained the photoelectric effect (Chapter 9.2), and he was awarded the 1921 Nobel Prize in physics for that contribution.

Another of Einstein's 1905 papers put forth his ideas on what came to be called the *special theory of relativity*. This paper dealt with what would happen to an object as it approached the speed of light. Einstein asserted that to an outside observer, the object would get shorter in the direction of motion, it would become more massive, and a clock would run more slowly in the object's system. These predictions are against "common sense," but common sense is based on limited experience with objects of ordinary size moving at ordinary speeds. All three of Einstein's predictions have now been verified experimentally.

One other important result came from the special theory of relativity: Energy and matter are related by what has become one of the most famous equations in scientific history: $E = mc^2$. This relationship and its use will be discussed in Chapter 10.6.

In 1915, Einstein published his *general theory of relativity*, which deals mainly with the effect of a gravitational field on the behavior of light and has profound implications with regard to the structure of the universe. Once again, Einstein's predictions were verified experimentally, and the general theory of relativity is a cornerstone of modern physics and astronomy.

Of course, Einstein was not infallible. He thought quantum mechanics bordered on the absurd, and throughout the 1930s he fought a friendly battle with Niels Bohr on the subject. (See Chapter 9.3 for information on Bohr.) Bohr won. Predictions of quantum mechanics are demonstrated by experiments.

One famous exchange between Einstein and Bohr went like this:

Einstein: "God doesn't play dice with the cosmos."

Bohr: "Einstein, don't tell God what to do."

AFP/Newscom

Figure 1 **Albert Einstein (1879–1955)** Einstein is shown here during a visit to Caltech in the 1930s.

7.6)? Such behavior is explained by assuming the wave nature of light, but it cannot be explained by the photon (particle) concept. On the other hand, the photoelectric effect cannot be explained by invoking the wave nature of light; for this effect, the photon concept is necessary. Hence, there is a confusing situation. Is light a wave, or is it a particle? The situation is expressed by the term **dual nature of light**, which means that to explain various phenomena, light must be described sometimes as a wave and sometimes as a particle (● Fig. 9.8).

Our idea that something is *either* a wave *or* a particle breaks down here. Light is not really a wave, nor is it really a particle. It has characteristics of both, and we simply have no good, single, macroscopic analogy that fits the combination. Therefore, scientists (renowned for being pragmatic) use whichever model of light works in a specific type of experiment. In

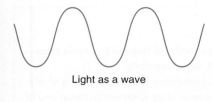

Light as a wave

Light as a stream of photons
(packets of energy)

Figure 9.8 The Wave-Particle Duality of Light
Electromagnetic radiation (a beam of light) can be pictured in two ways: as a wave (top) or as a stream of individual packets of energy called *photons* (bottom).

some experiments the wave model does the job; in other experiments the particle model is necessary.

The concept of the dual nature of light has been around for almost a century now. It actually does an excellent job of explaining both known and newly discovered phenomena and of making valid predictions that have served as the basis of new technologies. But it is still puzzling.

Did You Learn?

● A photon is a quantum or "packet" of electromagnetic energy (light), and its energy depends on the frequency, $E = hf$.

● In explaining phenomena, light sometimes behaves as a wave and sometimes as a particle, giving it a dual nature.

9.3 Bohr Theory of the Hydrogen Atom

Preview Questions

● What does the principal quantum number n in the Bohr theory designate?

● When does a hydrogen atom emit or absorb radiant energy?

Now that you have an idea of what is meant by quantum theory and photons, it is time to discuss the next advance in the understanding of the atom. Recall from Chapter 7.2 that when light from incandescent sources, such as light bulb filaments, is analyzed with a spectrometer, a *continuous spectrum* (continuous colors) is observed (● Fig. 9.9a).

In addition to continuous spectra, there are two types of *line spectra*. In the late 1800s much experimental work was being done with gas-discharge tubes, which contain a little neon (or another element) and emit light when subjected to a high voltage. When the light from a gas-discharge tube is analyzed with a spectrometer, a **line emission spectrum**, rather than a continuous spectrum, is observed (Fig. 9.9b). In other words, only spectral lines of certain frequencies or wavelengths are found, and each element gives a different set of lines (see Fig. 7.15). Spectroscopists at that time did not understand why only discrete, characteristic wavelengths of light were emitted by atoms in various excited gases.

The second type of line spectrum is found when visible light of all wavelengths is passed through a sample of a cool, gaseous element before entering the spectrometer. The **line absorption spectrum** that results has dark lines of missing colors (Fig. 9.9c). The dark lines are at exactly the same wavelengths as the bright lines of the *line emission spectrum* for that particular element. Compare, for instance, the wavelengths of the lines in the emission and absorption spectra of hydrogen in Fig. 9.9b and c.

An explanation of the spectral lines observed for hydrogen was advanced in 1913 by Danish physicist Niels Bohr. The hydrogen atom is the simplest atom, which is no doubt why Bohr chose it for study. Its nucleus is a single proton, and Bohr's theory assumes that its one electron revolves around the nuclear proton in a circular orbit in much the same way a satellite orbits the Earth or a planet orbits the Sun. (In fact, Bohr's model is often called *the planetary model* of the atom.)

However, in the atom, the electric force instead of the gravitational force supplies the necessary centripetal force. The revolutionary part of the theory is that Bohr assumed that the angular momentum (Chapter 3.7) of the electron is quantized. As a result, an electron can have only specific energy values in an atom. He correctly reasoned that a discrete line spectrum must be the result of a quantum effect. This assumption led to the prediction that the hydrogen electron could exist only in discrete (specific) orbits with particular radii. (This is not the case for Earth satellites. With proper maneuvering, a satellite can have any orbital radius.)

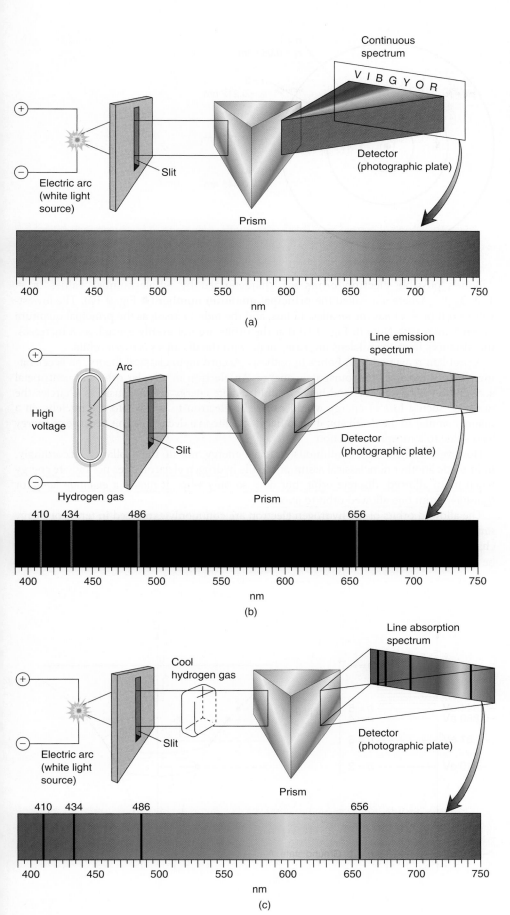

Figure 9.9 Three Types of Spectra
(a) A continuous spectrum containing all wavelengths of visible light (indicated by the initial letters of the colors of the rainbow). (b) The line emission spectrum for hydrogen consists of four discrete wavelengths of visible radiation. (c) The line absorption spectrum for hydrogen consists of four discrete "missing" wavelengths that appear as dark lines against a rainbow-colored background.

Figure 9.10 Bohr Electron Orbits
The Bohr hypothesis predicts only certain discrete orbits for the hydrogen electron. Each orbit is indicated by a principal quantum number n. The orbit shown in blue is the ground state ($n = 1$). The orbits move outward and get farther apart with increasing values of n.

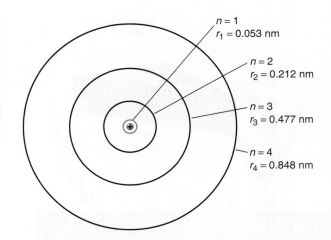

$n = 1$
$r_1 = 0.053$ nm

$n = 2$
$r_2 = 0.212$ nm

$n = 3$
$r_3 = 0.477$ nm

$n = 4$
$r_4 = 0.848$ nm

Bohr's possible electron orbits are characterized by whole-number values, $n = 1, 2, 3, \ldots$, where n is called the **principal quantum number** (● Fig. 9.10). The lowest-value orbit ($n = 1$) has the smallest radius, and the radii increase as the principal quantum number increases. Note in Fig. 9.10 that the orbits are not evenly spaced; as n increases, the distances from the nucleus increase, along with the distances *between* orbits.

A problem remained with Bohr's hypothesis. According to classical theory, an accelerating electron radiates electromagnetic energy. An electron in circular orbit has centripetal acceleration (Chapter 2.4) and hence should radiate energy continuously as it circles the nucleus. Such a loss of energy would cause the electron to spiral into the nucleus, in a manner similar to the death spiral of an Earth satellite in a decaying orbit because of energy losses due to atmospheric friction.

However, atoms do not continuously radiate energy, nor do they collapse. Accordingly, Bohr made another nonclassical assumption: the hydrogen electron does not radiate energy when in an allowed, discrete orbit, but does so only when it makes a *quantum jump*, or *transition*, from one allowed orbit to another.

The allowed orbits of the hydrogen electron are commonly expressed in terms of *energy states*, or *energy levels*, with each state corresponding to a specific orbit (● Fig. 9.11). We characterize the energy levels as states in *a potential well* (Chapter 4.2). Just as energy must be expended to lift a bucket in a water well, energy is necessary to lift the electron to a

Figure 9.11 Orbits and Energy Levels of the Hydrogen Atom
The Bohr theory predicts that the hydrogen electron can occupy only certain orbits having discrete radii. Each orbit has a particular energy value, or energy level. The lowest level, which has the quantum number $n = 1$, is called the *ground state*. The higher energy levels, which have n values greater than 1, are called *excited states*.

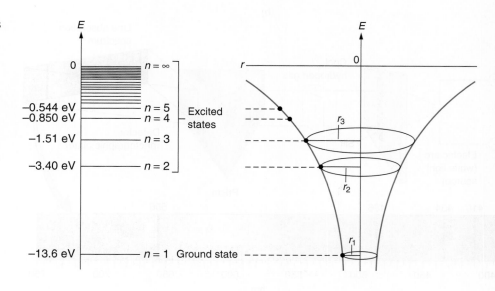

E

0    $n = \infty$

-0.544 eV $n = 5$ Excited
-0.850 eV $n = 4$ states

-1.51 eV $n = 3$

-3.40 eV $n = 2$

-13.6 eV $n = 1$ Ground state

E

0

r

r_3

r_2

r_1

higher level. If the top of the potential well is taken as the zero reference level, then the energy levels in the well all have negative values.

In a hydrogen atom, the electron is normally at the bottom of the "well," or in the **ground state** ($n = 1$) and must be given energy, or "excited," to raise it up in the well to a higher energy level, or orbit. The states above the ground state ($n = 2, 3, 4, \ldots$) are called **excited states**. The level for $n = 2$ is the *first excited state*, the level for $n = 3$ is the *second excited state*, and so on.

The levels in the energy well resemble the rungs of a ladder except that the energy level "rungs" are not evenly spaced. Just as a person going up and down a ladder must do so in discrete steps on the ladder rungs, so a hydrogen electron must be excited (or de-excited) from one energy level to another by discrete amounts. If enough energy is applied to excite the electron to the top of the well, then the electron is no longer bound to the nucleus and the atom is *ionized*, becoming a positive ion (H^+).

A mathematical development of Bohr's theory is beyond the scope of this textbook. However, the important results are its prediction of the radii and the energies of the allowed orbits. The radius of a particular orbit is given by

Table 9.1	Allowed Values of the Hydrogen Electron's Radius and Energy for Low Values of n	
n	r_n	E_n
1	0.053 nm	−13.60 eV
2	0.212 nm	−3.40 eV
3	0.477 nm	−1.51 eV
4	0.848 nm	−0.85 eV

Bohr radius = 0.053 × the square of the principal quantum number n

$$r_n = 0.053\, n^2 \text{ nm} \qquad\qquad 9.2$$

where r is the orbit radius, measured in nanometers (1 nm = 10^{-9} m), and n is the principal quantum number of an orbit ($n = 1, 2, 3, \ldots$).

Allowed values of r are listed in ● Table 9.1 for some low values of n. Note that the radii indeed get farther apart with increasing n, as indicated in Fig. 9.10.

EXAMPLE 9.2   Determining the Radius of an Orbit in a Hydrogen Atom

Determine the radius in nanometers (nm) of the first orbit ($n = 1$, the ground state) in a hydrogen atom.

Solution

The principal quantum number is given, so the orbital radius can be found directly using Eq. 9.2.

$$r_1 = 0.053\, n^2 \text{ nm} = 0.053\,(1)^2 \text{ nm} = 0.053 \text{ nm}$$

Confidence Exercise 9.2

Determine the radii in nm of the second and third orbits ($n = 2, 3$, the first and second excited states) in a hydrogen atom. Compare the values you compute with those in Table 9.1.

Answers to Confidence Exercises may be found at the back of the book.

The total energy (in eV) of an electron in an allowed orbit is given by

$$E_n = \frac{-13.60}{n^2} \text{ eV} \qquad\qquad 9.3$$

where E is energy measured in electron volts (eV) and n is the orbit's principal quantum number.*

---

*An *electron volt* is the amount of energy an electron acquires when it is accelerated through an electric potential of 1 volt. The eV is a small, common, nonstandard unit of energy in atomic and nuclear physics, and 1 eV = 1.60 × 10^{-19} J. Its size makes it an appropriate unit on these levels.

EXAMPLE 9.3   Determining the Energy of an Orbit
in the Hydrogen Atom

Determine the energy of an electron in the first orbit ($n = 1$, the ground state) in a hydrogen atom.

Solution

The energy of a particular orbit, or energy level, in a hydrogen atom is calculated by using Eq. 9.3 and the n value for that orbit. For $n = 1$, then,

$$E_1 = \frac{-13.60}{(1)^2} \text{ eV} = -13.60 \text{ eV}$$

Confidence Exercise 9.3

Determine the energies of an electron in the second and third orbits ($n = 2, 3$, the first and second excited states) in a hydrogen atom. Compare your answers with the values given in Table 9.1.

Table 9.1 shows the energies for the hydrogen electron for low values of n (orbits nearest the nucleus). These values correspond to the energy levels shown in Fig. 9.11. Note that, unlike the distances between orbits, the energy levels get *closer* together as n increases. Recall that the minus signs, indicating negative energy values, show that the electron is in a potential-energy well. Because the energy value is -13.60 eV for the ground state, it would require that much energy input to ionize a hydrogen atom. Thus, we say that the hydrogen electron's *binding energy* is 13.60 eV.

How did the hypothesis stand up to experimental verification? Recall that Bohr was trying to explain discrete line spectra. According to his hypothesis, an electron can make transitions only between two allowed orbits, or energy levels. In these transitions, the total energy must be conserved. If the electron is initially in an excited state, then it will lose energy when it "jumps down" to a less excited (lower n) state. In this case, the electron's energy loss will be carried away by a photon, or a quantum of light.

By the conservation of energy, the total initial energy (E_{n_i}) must equal the total final energy ($E_{n_f} + E_{\text{photon}}$):

$$E_{n_i} = E_{n_f} + E_{\text{photon}}$$
(energy before = energy after)

Or, rearranging, the energy of the emitted photon (E_{photon}) is the difference between the energies of the initial and final states:

photon energy = energy of initial orbit minus energy of final orbit

$$E_{\text{photon}} = E_{n_i} - E_{n_f}$$ **9.4**

A schematic diagram of the process of *photon emission* is shown in ● Fig. 9.12a. Hydrogen's line emission spectrum results from the relatively few allowed energy transitions as the electron de-excites. Figure 9.12b illustrates the reverse process of *photon absorption* to excite the electron. Hydrogen's line absorption spectrum results from exposing hydrogen atoms in the ground state to visible light of all wavelengths (or frequencies). The hydrogen electrons absorb only those wavelengths that can cause electron transitions "up." These wavelengths are taken out of the incoming light, whereas the other, inappropriate wavelengths pass through to produce a spectrum of color containing dark lines.

Of course, in a hydrogen atom, a photon of the same energy emitted in a "down" transition will have been absorbed in an "up" transition between the same two levels. Therefore, the dark lines in the hydrogen absorption spectrum exactly match up with the bright lines in the hydrogen emission spectrum (see Figs. 9.9b and 9.9c).

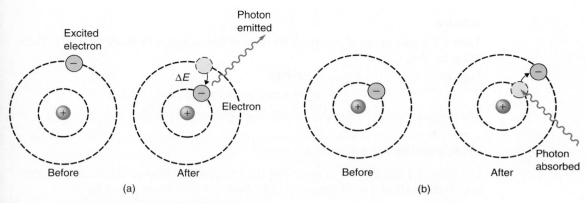

Figure 9.12 Photon Emission and Absorption
(a) When an electron in an excited hydrogen atom makes a transition to a lower energy level, or orbit, the atom loses energy by emitting a photon. (b) When a hydrogen atom absorbs a photon, the electron is excited into a higher energy level, or orbit.

The transitions for photon emissions in the hydrogen atom are shown on an energy level diagram in ● Fig. 9.13. The electron may "jump down" one or more energy levels in becoming de-excited. That is, the electron may go down the energy "ladder" using adjacent "rungs," or it may skip "rungs." (To show photon absorption and jumps to higher energy levels, the arrows in Fig. 9.13 would point up.)

EXAMPLE 9.4   Determining the Energy of a Transition in a Hydrogen Atom

Use Table 9.1 and Eq. 9.4 to determine the energy of the photon emitted as an electron in the hydrogen atom jumps down from the $n = 2$ level to the $n = 1$ level.

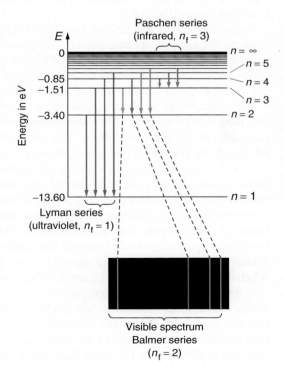

Figure 9.13 Spectral Lines for Hydrogen
The transitions among discrete energy levels by the electron in the hydrogen atom give rise to discrete spectral lines. For example, transitions down to $n = 2$ from $n = 3$, 4, 5, and 6 give the four spectral lines in the visible region that form the Balmer series. Bohr correctly predicted the existence of both the Lyman series and the Paschen series.

Solution

Table 9.1 shows values of -3.40 eV for the $n = 2$ level and -13.60 eV for $n = 1$. Then, using Eq. 9.4,

$$E_{\text{photon}} = E_2 - E_1$$
$$= -3.40 \text{ eV} - (-13.60 \text{ eV}) = 10.20 \text{ eV}$$

The positive value indicates that the 10.20-eV photon is *emitted*.

Confidence Exercise 9.4

Use Table 9.1 and Eq. 9.4 to determine the energy of the photon absorbed as an electron in the hydrogen atom jumps up from the $n = 1$ level to the $n = 3$ level.

Thus, the Bohr hypothesis predicts that an excited hydrogen atom will emit light with discrete frequencies (and hence wavelengths) corresponding to discrete "down" transitions. Conversely, a hydrogen atom in the ground state will absorb light with discrete frequencies corresponding to discrete "up" transitions. The theoretical frequencies for the four allowed transitions that give lines in the visible region were computed using the energy values for the various initial and final energy levels. These were compared with the frequencies of the lines of the hydrogen emission and absorption spectra. The theoretical and the experimental values were identical, a triumph for the Bohr theory.

Transitions to a particular lower level form a *transition series*. These series were named in honor of early spectroscopists who discovered or experimented with the hydrogen atom's spectral lines that belonged to particular regions of the electromagnetic spectrum. For example, the series of lines in the *visible* spectrum of hydrogen—which corresponds to transitions from $n = 3, 4, 5$, and 6 down to $n = 2$—is called the *Balmer series* (Fig. 9.13).

Bohr's calculations predicted the existence of a series of lines of specific energies in the *ultraviolet* (UV) region of the hydrogen spectrum and another series of lines in the *infrared* (IR) region. Lyman and Paschen, who like Balmer were spectroscopists, discovered these series, the lines of which were exactly at the wavelengths Bohr had predicted. These series bear their names (Fig. 9.13).

So quantum theory and the quantum nature of light scored another success. As you might imagine, the energy level arrangements for atoms other than hydrogen—those with more than one electron—are more complex. Even so, the line spectra for atoms of various elements are indicative of their energy level spacings and provide characteristic line emission and line absorption "fingerprints" by which atoms may be identified using spectroscopy.

The compositions of distant stars can be determined via analysis of the dark absorption lines in their spectra. In fact, the element helium was discovered in the Sun before it was found on the Earth. In 1868 a dark line was detected in the solar spectrum that did not match the absorption line of any known element. It was concluded that the line must be that of a new element. The element was named *helium* (after the Greek word for Sun, *helios*). Twenty-seven years later, helium was found on the Earth, trapped in a uranium mineral. The major source of helium today is from natural gas.

Another interesting quantum phenomenon is *auroras*, or what are often called the *northern lights* and *southern lights*. Auroras are caused by charged particles from the Sun entering the Earth's atmosphere close to the magnetic north and south poles (see Fig. 19.6). These particles interact with molecules in the air and excite some of their electrons to higher energy levels. When the electrons fall back down, some of the absorbed energy is emitted as visible radiation.

A similar transition phenomenon occurs in the production of light by fluorescent lamps—those long, white tubes that probably light your classroom—or by the relatively new compact fluorescent bulbs (Chapter 4.6). The primary radiation emitted by electrically excited mercury atoms in a fluorescent tube is in the ultraviolet (UV) region. The UV radiation is absorbed by the white fluorescent material that coats the inside of the tube. This material reradiates at frequencies in the visible region from various "down" transitions of lesser energy, providing white light for reading and other purposes.

Did You Learn?

● The principal quantum number (*n*) designates the possible electron orbits (energy levels or states) in the Bohr theory, $n = 1, 2, 3, \ldots$.

● Photons are emitted and absorbed by a hydrogen atom when its electron changes energy levels, "down" and "up" transitions, respectively.

9.4 Microwave Ovens, X-Rays, and Lasers

Preview Questions

● What is the main reason foods heat up in microwave ovens?

● What does the acronym "laser" stand for?

In this section three important technological applications that involve quantum theory will be considered: microwave ovens, X-rays, and lasers.

Microwave Ovens

Large parts of modern physics and chemistry are based on the study of energy levels of various atomic and molecular systems. When light is emitted or absorbed, scientists study the emission or absorption spectrum to learn about the energy levels of the system, as shown in Fig. 9.13 for the hydrogen atom.

Some scientists do research in *molecular spectroscopy*, the study of the spectra and energy levels of molecules (combinations of atoms). Molecules of one substance produce a spectrum different from that produced by molecules of another substance. Molecules can have quantized energy levels because of molecular vibrations or rotations or because they contain excited atoms.

The water molecule has some rotational energy levels spaced very closely together. The energy differences are such that microwaves, which have relatively low frequencies and energies (see Figure 6.7), are absorbed by the water molecules. This principle forms the basis of the *microwave oven*.* Because all foods contain moisture, their water molecules absorb microwave radiation, thereby gaining energy and rotating more rapidly; thus, the food is heated and cooked. Molecules of fats and oils in a food also are excited by microwave radiation, so they, too, contribute to the cooking. The interior metal sides of the oven reflect the radiation and remain cool.

Because it is the water content of foods that is crucial in microwave heating, objects such as paper plates and ceramic or glass dishes do not get hot immediately in a microwave oven. However, they often become warm or hot after being in contact with hot food (heat transfer by conduction, Chapter 5.4).

Some people assume that the microwaves penetrate the food and heat it throughout, but that is not the case. Microwaves penetrate only a few centimeters before being completely absorbed, so the interior of a large mass of food must be heated by conduction as in a regular oven. For this reason, microwave oven users are advised to let foods sit for a short time after microwaving. Otherwise, the center may be disagreeably cool even though the outside of the food is quite hot.

---

*"Percy Spencer didn't know better than to bring candy with him into his microwave lab in 1946. When the American engineer, who was developing radar components for the Raytheon Corp., let his chocolate bar get too close to a piece of equipment, it turned into chocolate goo. Cooking would never be the same. Within a year, Raytheon had introduced the first commercial microwave oven."—*Time,* March 29, 1999

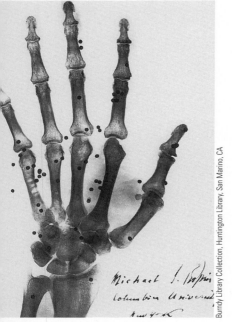

Figure 9.14 X-Rays Quickly Found Practical Use
Roentgen discovered X-rays in December 1895. By February 1896 they were being put to practical use. X-rays can penetrate flesh relatively easily and leave a skeletal image on film. The black spots in this "X-ray," or radiograph, are bird shot embedded in the subject's hand from a hunting accident.

Burndy Library Collection, Huntington Library, San Marino, CA

Conceptual Question and Answer

Can't Get Through

Q. Microwave oven glass doors have a metal mesh with holes. What is the purpose of this mesh?

A. The oven door glass window is for easy viewing, but the window has a perforated metal mesh over it for safety. Because of the size of the perforations (holes) in the mesh are much less than microwave wavelengths [on the order of 12 cm (4.7 in.)], most of the microwave radiation cannot pass through the door, whereas light with wavelengths on the order of 10^{-11} cm can. For microwaves, the mesh behaves as a continuous metal sheet that reflects the radiation back into the oven.

X-Rays

X-rays are another example of the technological use of quantum phenomena. **X-rays** are high-frequency, high-energy electromagnetic radiation (Chapter 6.3). These rays were discovered accidentally in 1895 by German physicist Wilhelm Roentgen (pronounced "RUNT-gin"). While working with a gas-discharge tube, Roentgen noticed that a piece of fluorescent paper across the lab was glowing, apparently from being exposed to some unknown radiation emitted from the tube. He called it *X-radiation*, with the X standing for "unknown." X-rays are now widely used in industrial and medical fields (● Fig. 9.14).

In a modern X-ray tube, electrons are accelerated through a large electrical voltage toward a metal target (● Fig. 9.15). When the electrons strike the target, they interact with the electrons in the target material and the electrical repulsion decelerates the incident electrons. The result is an emission of high-frequency X-ray photons (quanta). In keeping with their mode of production, X-rays are called *Bremsstrahlung* ("braking rays") in German.

The wise use of X-rays wasn't always the rule. Large doses of X-rays can cause skin "burns," cancer, and other conditions. Chest and dental X-rays once exposed patients to large doses of X-rays. These X-rays are now less intense and are monitored for appropriate safety levels.

X-ray imagery, along with magnetic resonance imagery, is discussed in the Highlight: **X-Ray CAT Scan and MRI**.

Lasers

Another device based on energy levels is the *laser*, the development of which was a great success for modern science. Scientific discoveries, such as X-rays and microwave heating, have often been made accidentally. X-rays were put to practical use before anyone understood the how or why of the X-ray phenomenon. Similarly, early investigators often applied a trial-and-error approach until they found something that worked. Edison's improvement of the incandescent light is a good example of this approach. He tried various materials before settling on a carbonized filament. In contrast to X-rays and the light bulb, the idea of the laser was first developed "on paper" from theory around 1965. The laser was then built with the full expectation that it would work as predicted.

The word **laser** is an acronym for *light amplification by stimulated emission of radiation*. The amplification of light provides an intense beam. Ordinarily, when an electron in an atom is excited by a photon, it emits a photon and then returns to its ground state immediately. In this process, which is called *spontaneous emission*, one photon goes in and one photon comes out (● Fig. 9.16a and b).

However, some substances, such as ruby crystals and carbon dioxide gas, and some combinations of substances, such as a mixture of the gases helium and neon, have *metastable* excited states. That is, some of their electrons can jump up into these excited energy levels and remain there briefly.

When many of the atoms or molecules of a substance have been excited into a metastable state by the input of the appropriate energy, we say that a *population inversion* has occurred

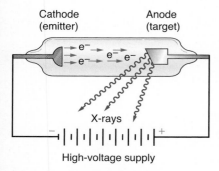

Figure 9.15 X-Ray Production
X-rays are produced in a tube in which electrons from the cathode are accelerated toward the anode. Upon interacting with the atoms of the anode material, the electrons are slowed down, and the atoms emit energy in the form of X-rays.

Cathode (emitter)   Anode (target)

X-rays

High-voltage supply

Highlight   X-Ray CAT Scan and MRI

CAT scan refers to an X-ray medical imaging method, not a feline glance. In conventional medical and dental X-ray photography, the rays emerging from an X-ray tube are detected on film. The X-rays themselves may expose the film or excite some fluorescent material that produces light for the film exposure. The latter method reduces the amount of X-rays needed. The difference in the absorption by different structures in the body gives rise to the image production: the less the absorption, the greater the transmission and darker the film. In a sense, the image is a "shadow" of what the rays have passed through.

In the 1970s a new technique called computer tomography (CT) was developed. In conventional X-ray images, the entire thickness of the body is projected on the film. As a result, one structure may obscure the view of another. A tomographic image, on the other hand, is an image of a "slice" through the body. (*Tomography* comes from the Greek words *tomo*, meaning "slice," and *graphon*, meaning "written.")

Together, an X-ray source and detector rotate around the body, scanning it at a great number of points to produce an image slice. Obtaining data for a complete picture would take some time, but fan beams and multiple digital detectors for a computerized image speed up the process (Fig. 1). Dental X-rays are now digitized and can be viewed almost instantaneously.

What does *CAT* stand for? Because the image of slice is perpendicular to the body axis, CAT stands for *computerized axial tomography* or *computer-assisted tomography*, but it is usually shortened to just CT for a CT scan. The computer assists in reconstructing the angular slices with resolution that cannot be achieved by conventional X-ray photographs.

Like CT scans, MRI (magnetic resonance imaging) is a medical imagery technique used to view detailed internal body structures. The good contrast it provides between soft tissues make it particularly useful in brain, heart, spinal cord, and cancer imaging.

Unlike CT scans or regular X-rays, which use potentially dangerous radiation, MRI uses magnets and radio waves as the patient passes through a chamber, much like a CT chamber. The human body is largely composed of water molecules (H_2O), with each molecule having two protons (hydrogen nuclei). A magnet creates a powerful magnetic field that aligns the protons of the hydrogen atoms, which are then exposed to radio waves. When the radio waves have just the right frequency (resonance), the protons "flip" in alignment and energy (a photon) is emitted.* This energy is detected by the scanner and sent to a computer. With multiple scans, a slice image of an organ or part of the body is formed, and these slices can be combined into a three-dimensional image (Fig. 2).

*Resonance is discussed in Chapter 6.6.

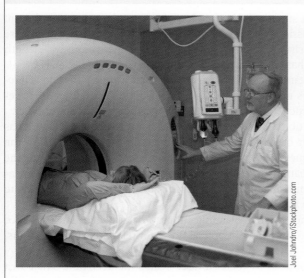

Figure 1   CAT (CT) Scan
A patient entering the scanning chamber.

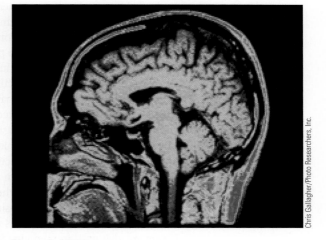

Figure 2   MRI Image
A color-enhanced MRI scan of a 38-year-old male showing the cranial anatomy. (Can you identify any of the organs?)

(● Fig. 9.17a). In such a condition, an excited atom can be stimulated to emit a photon (Fig. 9.16c and b). In a **stimulated emission**, the key process in a laser, an excited atom is struck by a photon of the same energy as the allowed transition and two photons are emitted (one in, two out: amplification). Of course, in this process, the laser is not giving something for nothing; energy is needed to excite the atom initially.

The light intensity is amplified because the emitted photon is in phase with the stimulating photon and thus interferes constructively to produce maximum intensity (Chapter 7.6).

Figure 9.16 Spontaneous and Stimulated Emissions
(a) An atom absorbs a photon and becomes excited. (b) The excited atom may return spontaneously to its ground state almost instantaneously with the emission of a photon, or (c) if the excited atom is struck by a photon with the same energy as the initially absorbed photon, then the atom is stimulated to emit a photon and both photons leave the atom.

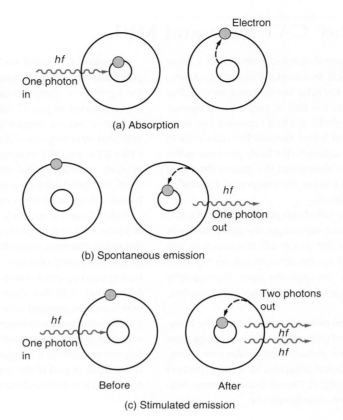

(a) Absorption

(b) Spontaneous emission

(c) Stimulated emission

Each of the two photons can then stimulate the emission of yet another identical photon. The result of many stimulated emissions and reflections in a laser tube is a narrow, intense beam of laser light. The beam consists of photons having the same energy and wavelength (*monochromatic*) and traveling in phase in the same direction (*coherent*). See Fig. 9.17c.

Light from sources such as an incandescent bulb consists of many wavelengths and is *incoherent* because the excitation occurs randomly. The atoms emit randomly at different wavelengths, and the waves have no particular directional or phase relationships to one another.

Because a laser beam is so directional, it spreads very little as it travels. This feature has enabled scientists to reflect a laser beam back to the Earth from a mirror placed on the Moon by astronauts. This technique makes accurate measurements of the distance to the Moon possible so that small fluctuations in the Moon's orbit can be studied. Similar measurements of light reflected from mirrors on the Moon are used to help determine the rate of plate tectonic movement on the Earth (see Chapter 21.3).

Lasers are used in an increasing number of applications. For instance, long-distance communications use laser beams in space and in optical fibers for telephone conversations. Lasers are also used in medicine as diagnostic and surgical tools (● Fig. 9.18).

In industry the intense heat produced by focused laser beams incident on a small area can drill tiny holes in metals and can weld machine parts. Laser "scissors" cut cloth in the garment industry. Laser printers produce computer printouts. Other applications occur in surveying, weapons systems, chemical processing, photography, and holography (the process of making three-dimensional images).

Another common laser application is found at supermarket checkout counters. You have probably noticed the reddish glow that is produced by a helium–neon laser in an optical scanner used for reading the product codes on items in supermarkets and other stores.

You may own a laser in a compact disc (CD) player. A laser "needle" is used to read the information (sound) stored on the disc in small dot patterns. The dots produce reflection patterns that are read by photocells and converted into electronic signals, which are changed to sound waves by a speaker system.

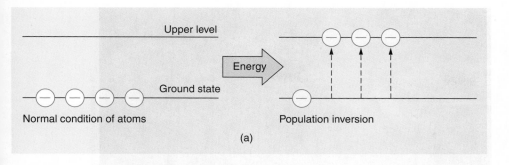

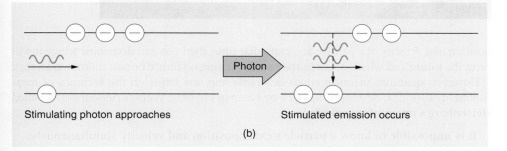

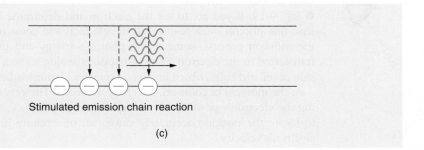

Upper level

Energy

Ground state

Normal condition of atoms

Population inversion

(a)

Stimulating photon approaches

Photon

Stimulated emission occurs

(b)

Stimulated emission chain reaction

(c)

Figure 9.17 Steps in the Action of a Laser
(a) Atoms absorb energy and move to a higher energy level (a population inversion). (b) A photon approaches, and stimulated emission occurs. (c) The photons that are emitted cause other stimulated emissions in a chain reaction. The photons are of the same wavelength, are in phase, and are all moving in the same direction.

Did You Learn?

- The absorption of microwaves mainly by water molecules in food causes it to heat up.

- Laser is an acronym for *l*ight *a*mplification by *s*timulated *e*mission of *r*adiation.

9.5 Heisenberg's Uncertainty Principle

Preview Questions

- How does Heisenberg's uncertainty principle affect the determination of a particle's location and velocity?

- Where does Heisenberg's uncertainty principle have practical importance in measurement?

There is another important aspect of quantum mechanics. According to classical mechanics, there is no limit to the accuracy of a measurement. Theoretically, accuracy can be continually improved by refinement of the measuring instrument or procedure to the point where the measurement contains no uncertainty. This notion resulted in a deterministic view of nature. For example, it implied that if you either know or measure the exact

Figure 9.18 Eye Surgery by Laser
A laser beam can be used to "weld" a detached retina into its proper place. In other surgical operations, a laser beam can serve as a scalpel, and the immediate cauterization prevents excessive bleeding.

Will & Deni McIntyre/Photo Researchers, Inc.

position and velocity of a particle at a particular time, then you can determine where it will be in the future and where it was in the past (assuming no future or past unknown forces).

However, quantum theory predicts otherwise and sets limits on the accuracy of measurement. This idea, developed in 1927 by German physicist Werner Heisenberg, is called **Heisenberg's uncertainty principle**:

It is impossible to know a particle's exact position and velocity simultaneously.

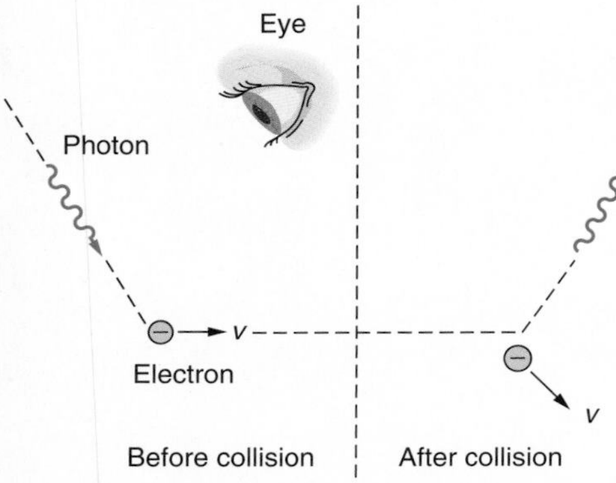

This concept is often illustrated with a simple example. Suppose you want to measure the position and velocity of an electron, as illustrated in ● Fig. 9.19. If you are to see the electron and determine its location, at least one photon must bounce off the electron and come to your eye. In the collision process, some of the photon's energy and momentum are transferred to the electron. (This situation is analogous to a classical collision of billiard balls, which involves a transfer of momentum and energy.)

At the moment of collision, the electron recoils. The very act of measuring the electron's position has altered its velocity. Hence, the very effort to locate the position accurately causes an uncertainty in knowing the electron's velocity.

Further investigation led to the conclusion that when the mass (m) of the particle, the minimum uncertainty in velocity (Δv), and the minimum uncertainty in position (Δx) are multiplied, a value on the order of Planck's constant ($h = 6.63 \times 10^{-34}$ J·s) is obtained;

$$m(\Delta v)(\Delta x) \approx h$$

The bottom line of Heisenberg's uncertainty principle: <u>There is a limit on measurement accuracy that is philosophically significant, but it is of practical importance only when dealing with particles of atomic or subatomic size.</u> As long as the mass is relatively large, Δv and Δx will be very small.

Figure 9.19 Uncertainty
Imagine trying to determine accurately the location of an electron with a single photon, which must strike the electron and come to the detector. The electron recoils at the moment of collision, which introduces a great deal of uncertainty in knowing the electron's velocity or momentum.

Eye

Photon

Electron

v

Before collision

After collision

v

Did You Learn?

● If you know the position of a moving particle, then there is uncertainty in knowing its velocity and vice versa.

● The act of microscopic measurement causes uncertainty.

9.6 Matter Waves

Preview Questions

● What are matter waves or de Broglie waves?

● How do mass and speed affect the wavelength of matter waves?

As the concept of the dual nature of light developed, what was thought to be a wave was sometimes found to act as a particle. Can the reverse be true? In other words, can particles have a wave nature? This question was considered by French physicist Louis de Broglie, who in 1925 hypothesized that matter, as well as light, has properties of both waves and particles.

According to de Broglie's hypothesis, any moving particle has a wave associated with it whose wavelength is given by

$$\text{wavelength} = \frac{\text{Planck's constant}}{\text{mass} \times \text{speed}}$$

$$\lambda = \frac{h}{mv} \qquad \qquad 9.5$$

where λ is the wavelength of the moving particle, m the mass of the particle, v its speed, and h is Planck's constant (6.63×10^{-34} J·s). The waves associated with moving particles are called **matter waves** or **de Broglie waves**.

In Eq. 9.5, the wavelength (λ) of a matter wave is inversely proportional to the mass of the particle or object; that is, the smaller the mass, the larger (longer) the wavelength. Thus, the longest wavelengths are generally for particles with little mass. (Speed is also a factor, but particle masses have more effect because they can vary over a much wider range than speeds can.) However, Planck's constant is such a small number (6.63×10^{-34} J·s) that *any* wavelengths of matter waves are quite small. Let's use an example to see how small.

EXAMPLE 9.5   Finding the de Broglie Wavelength

Find the de Broglie wavelength for an electron ($m = 9.11 \times 10^{-31}$ kg) moving at 7.30×10^5 m/s.

Solution

The mass and speed are given, so the wavelength can be found by using Eq. 9.5.

$$\lambda = \frac{h}{mv}$$

$$= \frac{6.63 \times 10^{-34}\,\text{J·s}}{(9.11 \times 10^{-31}\,\text{kg})(7.30 \times 10^5\,\text{m/s})}$$

$$= 1.0 \times 10^{-9}\,\text{m} = 1.0\,\text{nm (nanometer)}$$

This wavelength is several times larger than the diameter of the average atom, so although small, it is certainly significant relative to the size of an electron. (See whether the units in the equation are correct and actually cancel to give meters.)

Confidence Exercise 9.5

Find the de Broglie wavelength for a 1000-kg car traveling at 25 m/s (about 56 mi/h).

Conceptual Question and Answer

A Bit Too Small

Q. If moving masses have wave properties, why aren't the waves normally observed?

A. For normal objects and speeds, the wavelengths are so small that the wave properties go unnoticed. Your answer to Confidence Exercise 9.5 should

Highlight Electron Microscopes

Can atoms and molecules be seen? You bet. They can even be moved around. Welcome to the world of electron microscopy. Electron microscopes use the wavelike properties of electrons to image objects that are difficult or impossible to see with the unaided eye or with ordinary microscopes, which rely on beams of light (Fig. 1).

Unlike light photons, electrons are charged particles and so can be focused by the use of electric and magnetic fields. Such focusing was done routinely to form images on TV screens using older cathode ray tubes. By accelerating electrons to very high speeds, wavelengths as small as 0.004 nm (nanometer, 10^{-9} m) can be obtained. According to the laws of physics, it would be theoretically possible to image objects as small as 0.002 nm. Compare this value

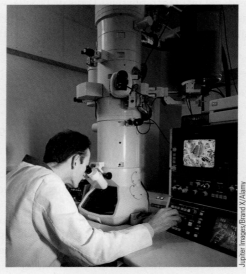

Figure 1 Observing through an electron microscope.

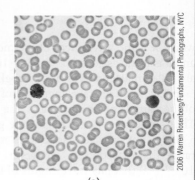

(a)

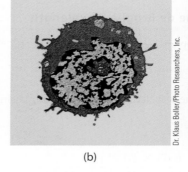

(b)

(c)

Figure 2 (a) Two white blood cells in a field of red blood cells seen under an optical (light) microscope. (The white blood cells are stained for distinction.) (b) A lymphocyte (type of white blood cell) seen under a tunneling electron microscope (TEM). (c) A lymphocyte seen under a scanning electron microscope (SEM). Note the distinct surface features.

confirm that a moving, relatively massive object has a short wavelength. The 1000-kg car traveling at 56 mi/h has a wavelength on the order of 10^{-38} m, which is certainly not significant relative to the size of the car.

Recall that wave properties, such as diffraction (Chapter 7.6), are observed when the wavelength is on the same order as the size of an object or opening. A wavelength of 10^{-38} m is just too small for wave effects to be observed.

De Broglie's hypothesis was met with skepticism at first, but it was verified experimentally in 1927 by G. Davisson and L. H. Germer in the United States. They showed that a beam of electrons exhibits a diffraction pattern. Because diffraction is a wave phenomenon, a beam of electrons must have wave-like properties.

For appreciable diffraction to occur, a wave must pass through a slit with a width smaller than the wavelength (Chapter 7.6). Visible light has wavelengths from about 400 nm to 700 nm, and slits with widths of these sizes can be made quite easily. As Example 9.5 showed, however, a fast-moving electron has a wavelength of about 1 nm. Slits of this width cannot be manufactured.

Fortunately, nature has provided suitably small slits in the form of crystal lattices. The atoms in these crystals are arranged in rows (or some other orderly arrangement), and spaces

Highlight

with the imaging power of visible light, where the limit on the smallest object that can be seen is a relatively whopping 200 nm.

The first two types of electron microscopes developed were the transmission electron microscope (TEM) and the scanning electron microscope (SEM). In TEMs the electron beam passes through a very thin slice of material and probes its interior structure. In SEMs the beam reflects off the surface of the material and reveals its exterior details (Fig. 2).

A more recent development, the scanning tunneling microscope (STM), probes surfaces with a tungsten needle that is only a few atoms wide at its tip. At very short distances, electrons "tunnel" (a quantum phenomenon) from the needle across the gap and through the surface being examined, which produces a tiny current that can be converted into images of individual atoms. Incredibly, IBM scientists then found that STMs could apply a voltage to the needle tip that would allow the atoms (or small molecules) on the surface to be moved around (see the chapter-opening photo).

Figure 3 shows a stunning image of the 5-nm-tall "molecular man," which is formed from 28 carbon monoxide (CO) molecules on a platinum surface. Chemists have even been able to take two molecules, break the appropriate chemical bonds, and rearrange the parts into new molecules. The various types of electron microscopes are among today's most powerful tools in scientific research and have led to the development of the field called *nanotechnology* (any technology done on a nanometer scale). There is no question that exciting discoveries involving "nanotech" lie in our future.

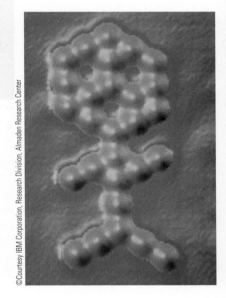

©Courtesy IBM Corporation, Research Division, Almaden Research Center

Figure 3 Molecular Man
This "molecular man" was crafted by moving 28 individual molecules, one at a time. Each of the gold-colored peaks is the image of a carbon monoxide (CO) molecule. The molecules rest on a single-crystal platinum surface (represented in blue).

between the rows provide natural "slits." Davisson and Germer bombarded nickel (Ni) crystals with electrons and obtained a diffraction pattern on a photographic plate. A diffraction pattern made by X-rays (electromagnetic radiation) and one made by an electron beam incident on a thin aluminum (Al) foil are shown in ● Fig. 9.20. The similarity in the diffraction patterns from the electromagnetic *waves* and from the electron *particles* is evident.

Electron diffraction demonstrates that moving matter has not only particle characteristics but also wave characteristics. Remember that the wave nature of ordinary-size moving particles is too small to be measurable. The wave nature of matter becomes of practical importance only with small particles such as electrons and atoms.

The *electron microscope* is based on the theory of matter waves. This instrument uses a beam of electrons, rather than a beam of light, to view an object. See the **Highlight: Electron Microscopes**.

Did You Learn?

- De Broglie or matter waves are waves associated with moving particles (moving particles have a wave nature).

- The wavelength of a matter or de Broglie wave of a moving particle is inversely proportional to its mass and speed.

Figure 9.20 Diffraction Patterns
(a) The diffraction pattern produced by X-rays can be explained using a wave model of the X-rays. (b) The appearance of the diffraction pattern made by a beam of electrons shows that electrons have a wave nature, which can be explained using de Broglie's concept of matter waves.

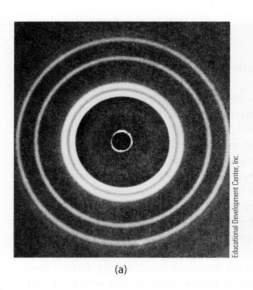

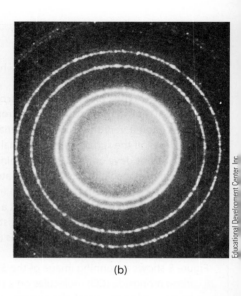

(a)   (b)

9.7   The Electron Cloud Model of the Atom

Preview Questions

● In quantum mechanics, what replaces the classical view of mechanics?

● What is the principle of the electron cloud model?

Niels Bohr chose to analyze the hydrogen atom because it's the simplest atom (Chapter 9.3). It is increasingly difficult to analyze atoms with two or more electrons (*multielectron atoms*) and determine their electron energy levels. The difficulty arises because in multielectron atoms, more electrical interactions exist than in the hydrogen atom. Forces exist among the various electrons, and in large atoms, electrons in outer orbits are partially shielded from the attractive force of the nucleus by electrons in inner orbits. Bohr's theory, so successful for the hydrogen atom, did not give the correct results when applied to multielectron atoms.

Recall from Chapter 9.3 that Bohr deduced from the small number of lines in the hydrogen emission spectra that electron energy levels are quantized. But he was unable to say *why* they are quantized. Bohr also stated that although classical physics says that the electron should radiate energy as it travels in its orbit, that does not occur. Here, too, he could not offer an explanation. A better model of the atom was needed.

As a result of the discovery of the dual nature of waves and particles, a new kind of physics called **quantum mechanics** or *wave mechanics*, based on the synthesis of wave and quantum ideas, was born in the 1920s and 1930s. In accordance with Heisenberg's uncertainty principle, the concept of *probability* replaced the view of classical mechanics that everything moves according to *exact* laws of nature.

De Broglie's hypothesis showed that waves are associated with moving particles and somehow govern or describe the particle behavior. In 1926 Erwin Schrödinger, an Austrian physicist, presented a widely applicable mathematical equation that gave new meaning to de Broglie's matter waves. Schrödinger's equation is a formulation of the conservation of energy. The detailed form of the equation is quite complex, but it is written in simple form as

$$(E_k + E_p)\Psi = E\Psi$$

where E_k, E_p, and E are the kinetic energy, potential energy, and total energy, respectively, and Ψ (the Greek letter psi) is a wave function.

Schrödinger's *electron cloud model* (or *quantum model*) of the atom focuses on the wave nature of the electron and treats it as a spread-out wave, its energy levels being a consequence of the wave, requiring a *whole number* of wavelengths to form standing waves (Chapter 6.6) in orbits around the nucleus (● Fig. 9.21a and b). Any orbit between two adjacent permissible orbits would require a fractional number of wavelengths and would not produce a standing wave (Fig. 9.21c).

This requirement of a whole number of wavelengths explains the quantization that Bohr had to assume. Furthermore, standing waves do not move from one place to another, so an electron in a standing wave is not accelerating and would not have to radiate light, which explains why Bohr's second assumption was correct.

In Schrödinger's equation the symbol Ψ is called the *wave function* and mathematically represents the wave associated with a particle. At first, scientists were not sure how Ψ should be interpreted. For the hydrogen atom, they concluded that Ψ^2 (the wave function squared, psi squared), when multiplied by the square of the radius r, represents the *probability* that the hydrogen electron will be at a certain distance r from the nucleus. (In Bohr's theory, the electron can be only in circular orbits with discrete radii given by $r = 0.053\ n^2$ nm.)

A plot *of* $r^2\Psi^2$ versus r for the hydrogen electron (● Fig. 9.22a) shows that the most probable radius for the hydrogen electron is $r = 0.053$ nm, which is the same value Bohr calculated in 1913 for the ground state orbit of the hydrogen atom. (In fact, all the energy levels for the hydrogen atom were found to be exactly the same as those Bohr had calculated.) The electron might be found at other radii, but with less likelihood, that is, with lower probability. This idea gave rise to the model of an *electron cloud* around the nucleus, where the cloud's density reflects the probability that the electron is in that region (Fig. 9.22b).

Thus, Bohr's simple planetary model was replaced by a more sophisticated, highly mathematical model that treats the electron as a wave and can explain more data and predict more accurately. The electron cloud model, or quantum model, of the atom is more difficult to visualize than the Bohr model. The location of a specific electron becomes more vague than in the Bohr model and can be expressed only in terms of probability. The important point is that the quantum mechanical model enables us to determine the energy of the electrons in multielectron atoms. For scientists, knowing the electron's energy is much more important than knowing its exact location.

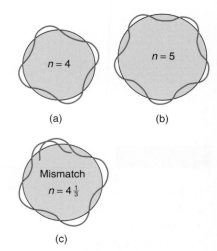

Figure 9.21 The Electron as a Standing Wave
The hydrogen electron can be treated as a standing wave in a circular orbit around the nucleus. For the wave to be stable, however, the circumference must accommodate a *whole number* of wavelengths, as shown in (a) and (b). In (c), the wave would destructively interfere with itself, so this orbit is forbidden. This restriction on the orbits, or energies, explains why the atom is quantized.

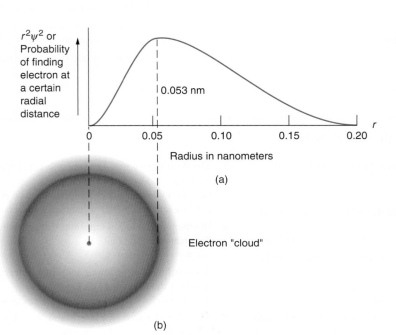

$r^2\psi^2$ or Probability of finding electron at a certain radial distance

0.053 nm

Radius in nanometers

(a)

Electron "cloud"

(b)

Figure 9.22 $r^2\Psi^2$ Probability
The square of the wave function (Ψ^2) multiplied by the square of the radius (r^2) gives the probability of finding the electron at that particular radius. As shown here, the radius of a hydrogen atom with the greatest probability of containing the electron is 0.053 nm, which corresponds to the first Bohr radius. (b) The probability of finding the electron at other radii gives rise to the concept of an "electron cloud," or probability distribution.

Did You Learn?

● The concept of probability replaced the classical view that everything moves according to *exact* laws of nature.

● The density of an electron cloud around the nucleus reflects the probability that an electron will be in that region.

KEY TERMS

1. atoms (9.1)
2. electrons
3. quantum (9.2)
4. photoelectric effect
5. photon
6. dual nature of light

7. line emission spectrum (9.3)
8. line absorption spectrum
9. principal quantum number
10. ground state
11. excited states
12. X-rays (9.4)

13. laser
14. stimulated emission
15. Heisenberg's uncertainty principle (9.5)
16. matter (de Broglie) waves (9.6)
17. quantum mechanics (9.7)

MATCHING

For each of the following items, fill in the number of the appropriate Key Term from the preceding list. Compare your answers with those at the back of the book.

a. _____ The electron level of lowest energy in an atom

b. _____ Type of spectrum given by light from a gas-discharge tube

c. _____ A discrete amount, or packet, of energy

d. _____ A device based on light amplification by stimulated emission of radiation

e. _____ Type of spectrum obtained when white light is passed through a cool gas

f. _____ Branch of physics based on synthesis of wave and quantum ideas

g. _____ The basic particles of elements

h. _____ It is impossible to know a particle's exact position and velocity simultaneously

i. _____ Electron emission by some metals when exposed to light

j. _____ Negatively charged particles that are components of all atoms

k. _____ High-frequency electromagnetic radiation produced when high-speed electrons strike a metal target

l. _____ Light has both wave-like and particle-like characteristics

m. _____ Integer that identifies a Bohr orbit

n. _____ Waves associated with moving particles

o. _____ A quantum of electromagnetic radiation

p. _____ Process wherein an excited atom is struck by a photon and emits additional photons

q. _____ Electron levels of higher-than-normal energy

MULTIPLE CHOICE

Compare your answers with those at the back of the book.

1. Who championed the idea of the atom about 400 BCE? (9.1)
(a) Aristotle   (b) Plato
(c) Democritus   (d) Archimedes

2. Which scientist is associated with the "plum pudding model" of the atom? (9.1)
(a) Thomson   (b) Rutherford   (c) Bohr   (d) Dalton

3. Planck developed his quantum hypothesis to explain which of these phenomena? (9.2)
(a) the ultraviolet catastrophe   (b) line spectra
(c) the photoelectric effect   (d) uncertainty

4. Light of which of the following colors has the greatest photon energy? (9.2)
(a) red   (b) orange   (c) yellow   (d) violet

5. The Bohr theory was developed to explain which of these phenomena? (9.3)
(a) energy levels   (b) the photoelectric effect
(c) line spectra   (d) quantum numbers

6. In which of the following states does a hydrogen electron have the greatest energy? (9.3)
(a) $n = 1$ (b) $n = 3$ (c) $n = 5$ (d) $n = 7.5$

7. Bombarding a metal anode with high-energy electrons produces which of the following? (9.4)
(a) laser light   (b) X-rays   (c) microwaves   (d) neutrons

8. The "s" in the acronym laser stands for (9.4)
(a) simple   (b) specific
(c) spontaneous (d) stimulated

9. Which of the following does a laser do?
   (a) amplifies light
   (b) produces monochromatic light
   (c) produces coherent light
   (d) all the preceding

10. Limitations on measurements are described by which of the following? (9.5)
   (a) Heisenberg's uncertainty principle
   (b) de Broglie's hypothesis
   (c) Schrödinger's equation
   (d) Einstein's special theory of relativity

11. Which of the following pairs of particle properties is it impossible to determine exactly and simultaneously? (9.5)
   (a) charge and mass   (b) position and velocity
   (c) charge and position   (d) velocity and momentum

12. What scientist first hypothesized matter waves? (9.6)
   (a) Schrödinger   (b) de Broglie
   (c) Heisenberg   (d) Einstein

13. According to the de Broglie hypothesis, how is the wavelength associated with a moving particle?
   (a) It is independent of mass.
   (b) It is longer the greater the speed of the particle.
   (c) It easily shows diffraction effects.
   (d) None of the preceding.

14. Why did the Bohr model need improvement? (9.7)
   (a) It worked only for the hydrogen atom.
   (b) It did not explain why the atom is quantized.
   (c) It did not explain why an electron does not emit radiation as it orbits.
   (d) All these answers are correct.

FILL IN THE BLANK

Compare your answers with those at the back of the book.

1. The subatomic particle called the ___ was discovered by J. J. Thomson. (9.1)

2. The scientist associated with the "nuclear model" of the atom is ___. (9.1)

3. In the equation $E = hf$, the h is called ___. (9.2)

4. A quantum of electromagnetic radiation is commonly called a(n) ___. (9.2)

5. In the Bohr model, as n increases, the distance of the electron from the nucleus ___. (9.3)

6. When analyzed with a spectrometer, light from an incandescent source produces a(n) ___ spectrum. (9.3)

7. A photon is absorbed when an electron makes a transition from one energy level to a(n) ___ one. (9.3)

8. Microwave ovens heat substances mainly by exciting molecules of ___. (9.4)

9. The X in X-ray stands for ___. (9.4)

10. Heisenberg's ___ principle is of practical importance only with particles of atomic or subatomic size. (9.5)

11. According to de Broglie's hypothesis, a moving particle has a(n) ___ associated with it. (9.6)

12. In the electron cloud model of the atom, the electron's location is stated in terms of ___. (9.7)

SHORT ANSWER

9.1 Early Concepts of the Atom

1. What is the basic difference between classical mechanics and quantum mechanics?

2. How did Thomson know that electrons are negatively charged?

3. What major change was made in Thomson's model of the atom after Rutherford's discovery?

9.2 The Dual Nature of Light

4. How does the radiation from a hot object change with temperature?

5. Name a phenomenon that can be explained only by light having a wave nature and one that can be explained only by light having a particle nature.

6. If electromagnetic radiation is made up of quanta, then why don't we hear a radio intermittently as discrete packets of energy arrive?

7. Distinguish between a proton and a photon.

8. How are the frequency and wavelength of an electromagnetic wave related?

9. Explain the difference between a photon of red light and one of violet light in terms of energy, frequency, and wavelength.

10. Light shining on the surface of a photomaterial causes the ejection of electrons if the frequency of the light is above a certain minimum value. Why is there a certain minimum value?

11. What scientist won the Nobel Prize for explaining the photoelectric effect? Name another theory for which that scientist is famous.

9.3 Bohr Theory of the Hydrogen Atom

12. How does the number of lines in the emission spectrum for an element compare with the number of lines in the absorption spectrum?

13. Does light from a neon sign have a continuous spectrum? Explain.

14. In the Bohr theory, principal quantum numbers are denoted by what letter?

15. Why was it necessary for Bohr to assume that a bound electron in orbit did not emit radiation?

16. Distinguish between a *ground state* for an electron and an *excited state*.

17. How many visible lines make up the emission spectrum of hydrogen? What are their colors?

18. How does the Bohr theory explain the discrete lines in the *emission* spectrum of hydrogen?

19. How does the Bohr theory explain the discrete lines in the *absorption* spectrum of hydrogen?

20. In which transition is the photon of greater energy emitted, $n = 3$ to $n = 1$ or $n = 2$ to $n = 1$?

21. A hydrogen electron is in the excited state $n = 3$. How many photons of different frequencies could possibly be emitted in the electron's return to the ground state?

9.4 Microwave Ovens, X-Rays, and Lasers

22. Why does a microwave oven heat a potato but not a ceramic plate?

23. What does the acronym *laser* stand for?

24. What is unique about light from a laser source?

25. Why should you never look directly into a laser beam or into its reflection?

26. Why are X-rays called "braking rays" in German?

9.5 Heisenberg's Uncertainty Principle

27. State Heisenberg's uncertainty principle.

28. Why isn't Heisenberg's uncertainty principle relevant to everyday observations?

9.6 Matter Waves

29. What is a matter wave, and when is the associated wavelength significant?

30. Niels Bohr was never able to actually explain why a hydrogen electron is limited to certain orbits. How did de Broglie explain it?

31. How was a beam of electrons shown to have wave-like properties?

32. What useful instrument takes advantage of the wave properties of electrons?

9.7 The Electron Cloud Model of the Atom

33. What scientist is primarily associated with the electron cloud model of the atom?

34. What other name is often used to refer to the electron cloud model of the atom?

VISUAL CONNECTION

Visualize the connections and give answers for the blanks. Compare your answers with those at the back of the book.

Models of the Atom

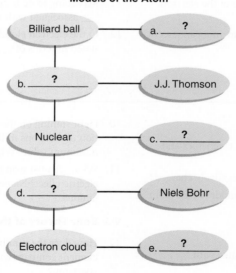

APPLYING YOUR KNOWLEDGE

1. Why are microwave ovens constructed so that they will not operate when the door is open?

2. While you are shopping for a new car, a salesperson tells you that the newest technology is a *quantized* cruise control. What might this statement mean?

3. Your friend says that atoms do not exist because no one has ever seen an atom. What would be your reply?

4. Why at night, under the mercury or sodium vapor lights in a mall parking lot, do cars seem to be peculiar colors?

5. Explain why Heisenberg's uncertainty principle wouldn't pose a problem for police officers using radar to determine a car's speed.

IMPORTANT EQUATIONS

Photon Energy:
$$E = hf$$
$$(h = 6.63 \times 10^{-34}\,\text{J}\cdot\text{s}) \qquad (9.1)$$

Hydrogen Electron Orbit Radii:
$$r_n = 0.053\,n^2\,\text{nm} \quad (n = 1, 2, 3, \dots) \qquad (9.2)$$

Hydrogen Electron Energy:
$$E_n = \frac{-13.60}{n^2}\,\text{eV} \quad (n = 1, 2, 3, \dots) \qquad (9.3)$$

Photon Energy for Transition: $E_{\text{photon}} = E_{n_i} - E_{n_f}$ (9.4)

de Broglie Wavelength: $\lambda = \dfrac{h}{mv}$ (9.5)

EXERCISES

9.2 The Dual Nature of Light

1. The human eye is most sensitive to yellow-green light having a frequency of about 5.45×10^{14} Hz (a wavelength of about 550 nm). What is the energy in joules of the photons associated with this light?

   Answer: 3.61×10^{-19} J

2. Light that has a frequency of about 5.00×10^{14} Hz (a wavelength of about 600 nm) appears orange to our eyes. What is the energy in joules of the photons associated with this light?

3. Photons of a certain ultraviolet light have an energy of 6.63×10^{-19} J. (a) What is the frequency of this UV light? (b) Use $\lambda = c/f$ to calculate its wavelength in nanometers (nm).

   Answer: (a) 1.00×10^{15} Hz (b) 300 nm

4. Photons of a certain infrared light have an energy of 1.50×10^{-19} J. (a) What is the frequency of this IR light? (b) Use $\lambda = c/f$ to calculate its wavelength in nanometers (nm).

9.3 Bohr Theory of the Hydrogen Atom

5. What is the radius in nm of the electron orbit of a hydrogen atom for $n = 3$?

   Answer: 0.48 nm

6. What is the radius in nm of the electron orbit of a hydrogen atom for $n = 4$?

7. What is the energy in eV of the electron of a hydrogen atom for the orbit designated $n = 3$?

   Answer: -1.51 eV

8. What is the energy in eV of the electron of a hydrogen atom for the orbit designated $n = 4$?

9. Use Table 9.1 to determine the energy in eV of the photon emitted when an electron jumps down from the $n = 4$ orbit to the $n = 2$ orbit of a hydrogen atom.

   Answer: 2.55 eV

10. Use Table 9.1 to determine the energy in eV of the photon absorbed when an electron jumps up from the $n = 1$ orbit to the $n = 4$ orbit of a hydrogen atom.

9.6 Matter Waves

11. Calculate the de Broglie wavelength of a 0.50-kg ball moving with a constant velocity of 26 m/s (about 60 mi/h).

    Answer: 5.1×10^{-35} m

12. Estimate your de Broglie wavelength when you are running. (Recall that $h \sim 10^{-34}$ in SI units and 1 lb is equivalent to 0.45 kg.) For the computation, estimate how fast you can run in meters per second.

ON THE WEB

1. Atoms with Attitude

What does the earliest model of the atom look like? What quandary does it present? What do you know about the quantum atom and spectral lines? What can you say about Niels Bohr and Bohr's atom? Where does the term *quantum leap* come from, and how has its real meaning changed? Explore answers to these questions by following the links at **www.cengagebrain.com/shop/ISBN/1133104096.**

2. You're Cookin' with Gas? Nope, the Microwave.

How do microwaves work? Are they dangerous? Can you explain the relationship between water and microwave cooking? What happens when you cook frozen foods in the microwave, and why don't such foods always cook evenly? What might you do to deal with that? Why do microwave manufacturers warn the user about the dangers of heating *only* water in the microwave oven? Visit the student website at **www.cengagebrain.com/shop/ISBN/1133104096** and follow the links to learn more about cooking with microwaves and answer the above questions.

Nuclear Physics

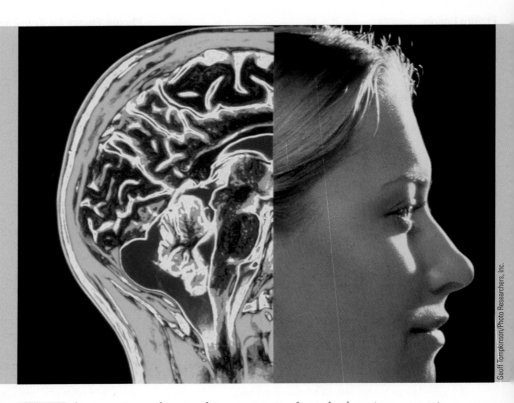

Geoff Tompkinson/Photo Researchers, Inc.

*It is a source of grati-
fication to us all that
we have been able
to contribute a little
to an understanding
of the nucleus of the
atom.*

•

Ernest Lawrence,
physics Nobel Laureate
(1901–1958)

Technetium-99, a laboratory-   >
produced radioactive isotope, is
often used in brain scans. Here,
a color-enhanced scan has been
superimposed on the back of a
woman's head.

PHYSICS FACTS

▶ The elements technetium (Tc)
and promethium (Pm) are
not found in nature, but they
can be artificially made. They
don't exist naturally because
their half-lives are on the order
of hours and minutes, and if
originally present, they would
have decayed away.

The atomic nucleus and its properties have had an important impact on
our society. For example, the nucleus is involved with archeological
dating, diagnosis and treatment of cancer and other diseases, chemical
analysis, radiation damage and nuclear bombs, and the generation of electricity.
This chapter discusses these topics and includes Highlights on The Discovery of
Radioactivity and Nuclear Power and Waste Disposal.

An appropriate way to begin the study of nuclear physics is with a brief history
of how the concept of the element arose and how elements and their nuclei are
expressed by symbols.

Chapter Outline

10.1 Symbols of the Elements

Preview Questions

- What original "elements" did Aristotle think composed all matter on the Earth?
- Why are some element symbols very different from their names? For example, carbon is C, but silver is Ag.

The Greek philosophers who lived during the period from about 600 to 200 BCE were apparently the first people to speculate about what basic substance or substances make up matter. In the fourth century BCE, the Greek philosopher Aristotle developed the idea that all matter on the Earth is composed of four "elements": earth, air, fire, and water. He was wrong on all four counts, and in Chapter 11 the discovery and properties of true elements will be discussed. We will consider some of these elements in terms of their atomic nuclei.

The symbol notation used to designate the different elements was first introduced in the early 1800s by Swedish chemist Jöns Jakob Berzelius ("bur-ZEE-lee-us"). He used one or two letters of the Latin name to represent each element. For example, sodium was designated Na for *natrium* and silver Ag for *argentum* (● Table 10.1).

Since Berzelius' time, most elements have been symbolized by the first one or two letters of the English name. Examples include C for carbon, O for oxygen, and Ca for calcium. The first letter of a chemical symbol is always capitalized, and the second is lowercase. Inside the front cover of this book, you will find a periodic table of the elements showing the positions, names, and symbols of the elements presently known. There are 112 officially named elements. Elements 113 through 118 have designations but are unnamed. (An international committee assigns new element names. For more on the elements and periodic table, see Chapter 11.4.)

Although you are not expected to learn the names and symbols of all the elements, you should become familiar with most of the names and symbols of the elements listed in ● Table 10.2.

Did You Learn?

- Aristotle's first "periodic table" consisted of earth, air, fire, and water.
- Some chemical symbols are derived from their Latin names, for example, silver, Ag (argentum) or sodium, Na (natrium).

PHYSICS FACTS *cont.*

- You are radioactive because your body contains carbon-14.
- A lengthy plane flight at high altitude can expose passengers to an amount of radiation energy (from cosmic rays) comparable to that of a chest X-ray.
- "Moonshine! Pure moonshine!!" That's what Ernest Rutherford, the discoverer of the proton and the atomic nucleus, said about the possibility of atomic (nuclear) energy.
- Spent nuclear fuel rods from nuclear reactors contain many radioactive isotopes. The disposal of this waste is a problem. (See the Highlight: Nuclear Power and Waste Disposal.)
- More radioactive isotopes are released into the atmosphere from power plants burning coal and oil than from nuclear power plants.

Table 10.1 Some Chemical Symbols from Latin Names		
Modern Name	Symbol	Latin Name
Copper	Cu	*Cuprum*
Gold	Au	*Aurum*
Iron	Fe	*Ferrum*
Lead	Pb	*Plumbum*
Mercury	Hg	*Hydrargyrum*
Potassium	K	*Kalium*

Table 10.2 Names and Symbols of Some Common Elements

Name	Symbol	Name	Symbol	Name	Symbol
Aluminum	Al	Gold	Au	Phosphorus	P
Argon	Ar	Helium	He	Platinum	Pt
Barium	Ba	Hydrogen	H	Potassium	K
Boron	B	Iodine	I	Radium	Ra
Bromine	Br	Iron	Fe	Silicon	Si
Calcium	Ca	Lead	Pb	Silver	Ag
Carbon	C	Magnesium	Mg	Sodium	Na
Chlorine	Cl	Mercury	Hg	Sulfur	S
Chromium	Cr	Neon	Ne	Tin	Sn
Cobalt	Co	Nickel	Ni	Uranium	U
Copper	Cu	Nitrogen	N	Zinc	Zn
Fluorine	F	Oxygen	O		

10.2 The Atomic Nucleus

Preview Questions

● How was it determined that atoms have nuclei?

● What is the atomic number, and how is it related to an element?

Matter is made up of atoms. An atom is composed of negatively charged particles, called **electrons**, which surround a positively charged nucleus. The **nucleus** is the central core of an atom. It consists of positively charged **protons** and electrically neutral **neutrons**. An electron and a proton have the same magnitude of electric charge, but the charges are different. The charge on the electron is designated negative ($-$) and that on the proton positive ($+$). (See Chapter 8 1.)

Protons and neutrons have almost the same mass and are about 2000 times more massive than an electron. Nuclear protons and neutrons are collectively called **nucleons**. ● Table 10.3 summarizes the basic properties of electrons, protons, and neutrons.

In 1911, British scientist Ernest Rutherford discovered that the atom consists of a nucleus surrounded by orbiting electrons. He was curious about what would happen when energetic alpha particles (helium nuclei) bombarded a very thin sheet of gold.* J. J. Thomson's "plum pudding model" (Fig. 9.1b) predicted that the alpha particles would pass through the evenly distributed positive charges in the gold atoms with little or no deflection from their original paths.

Rutherford's experiment was conducted using a setup such as that illustrated in ● Fig. 10.1. The behavior of the alpha particles was determined by using a movable screen coated with zinc sulfide. When an alpha particle hit the screen, a small flash of light was emitted that could be observed with a low-power microscope. (A similar phenomenon causes cathode-ray TV screens to glow when hit by moving electrons.) Rutherford found that the vast

Table 10.3 Major Constituents of an Atom

Particle (symbol)	Charge (C)	Electronic Charge	Mass (kg)	Location
Electron (e)	-1.60×10^{-19}	-1	9.109×10^{-31}	Outside nucleus
Proton (p)	$+1.60 \times 10^{-19}$	$+1$	1.673×10^{-27}	Nucleus
Neutron (n)	0	0	1.675×10^{-27}	Nucleus

*Alpha particles (doubly positively charged helium nuclei) come from the radioactive decay of certain elements, as will be discussed in Chapter 10.3.

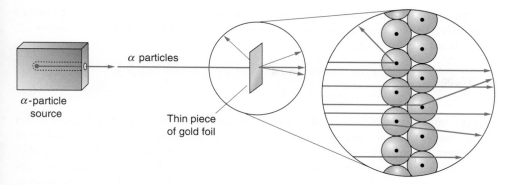

Figure 10.1 **Rutherford's Alpha-Scattering Experiment**
Nearly all the alpha particles striking the gold foil went through. A few were deflected, and some bounced back. These results led to the discovery of the nucleus. (The zinc sulfide screen used to monitor the alpha particles is not shown.)

majority of the alpha particles went through the gold foil as though it were not even there. A few of the positively charged alpha particles were deflected, however, and about 1 out of 20,000 actually bounced back. Rutherford could only explain this behavior by assuming that each gold atom had its positive charge concentrated in a small core rather than distributed throughout the atom. He called the core the atomic *nucleus* and assumed that electrons move around the nucleus "like bees around a hive."*

The alpha-scattering experiment showed that a nucleus has a diameter of about 10^{-14} m (● Fig. 10.2). In contrast, the atom's outer electrons have orbits with diameters of about 10^{-10} m (Chapter 9.3). Thus, the diameter of an atom is approximately 10,000 times the diameter of its nucleus, and most of an atom's volume consists of empty space. Imagine that the nucleus of an atom were the size of a peanut. If you place the nut in the middle of a baseball stadium, then the stadium itself would be about the relative size of the atom.

The electrical repulsion between an atom's electrons and those of adjacent atoms keeps matter from collapsing. Electron orbits determine the size (volume) of atoms, but the nucleus contributes more than 99.97% of the mass.

The particles in an atom are designated by certain numbers. The **atomic number**, symbolized by the letter Z, is the number of protons in the nucleus of each atom of that element.

An **element** is a substance in which all the atoms have the same number of protons (the same atomic number, Z). For an atom to be electrically neutral (have a total net charge of zero), the numbers of electrons and protons must be the same. Therefore, the atomic number also indicates the number of electrons in a neutral atom.

Electrons may be gained or lost by an atom, and the resulting particle, called an *ion*, will be electrically charged. However, because the number of protons has not changed, the particle is a positively charged ion of that same element. For instance, if a *sodium atom* (Na) loses an electron, then it becomes a *sodium ion* (Na^+), not an atom or ion of some other element. The sodium ion still has the same number of protons (11) as the sodium atom.

▶ The **neutron number** (N) is the number of neutrons in a nucleus.

▶ The **mass number** (A) is the number of protons plus neutrons in the nucleus: the total number of nucleons.

The general designation for a specific nucleus places the mass number (A) to the upper left of the chemical symbol (shown here as X for generality), and the atomic number (Z) goes at the lower left.†

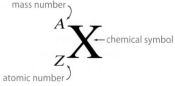

mass number
$$^{A}_{Z}X$$ ←chemical symbol
atomic number

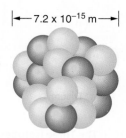

|←— 7.2×10^{-15} m —→|

Figure 10.2 **A Representation of the Nucleus**
The nucleus of an aluminum-27 atom consists of 13 protons (blue) and 14 neutrons (yellow), for a total of 27 nucleons. The diameter of this nucleus is 7.2×10^{-15} m, close to the 10^{-14}-m diameter of an average nucleus.

_____

*Rutherford described the backscattering as "almost as incredible as if you had fired a 15-inch shell at a piece of tissue paper, and it came back and hit you."

†Why are the letters Z and A used? "Atomic number" in German is *"Atomzahl,"* so the Z probably comes from *zahl* (number). M is sometimes used for mass number (*Massenzahl* in German), but the symbol A is recommended by the American Chemical Society (ACS) Style Guide.

Sometimes the neutron number N is placed at the lower right ($^A_Z X_N$). However, the number of neutrons (N) in a nucleus is easily determined by subtracting the atomic number (Z) from the mass number (A).

$$\text{neutron number} = \text{mass number} - \text{atomic number}$$

$$N = A - Z \hspace{4cm} \text{10.1}$$

It is common to write the symbol for a uranium nucleus as $^{238}_{92}U$. But because it is a simple matter to obtain an element's atomic number from the periodic table, a nucleus of an element is sometimes represented by just the mass number and the chemical symbol (for example, ^{238}U) or by the name of the element followed by a hyphen and the mass number (uranium-238). The chemical symbols and names for all the elements are given in the periodic table inside the front cover of this book.

EXAMPLE 10.1   Determining the Composition of an Atom

Determine the number of protons, electrons, and neutrons in the fluorine atom $^{19}_9F$.

Solution

The atomic number Z is 9, so the number of protons is 9 (as is the number of electrons for a neutral atom). The mass number A is 19, so the number of neutrons is $N = A - Z = 19 - 9 = 10$. The answer is 9 protons, 9 electrons, and 10 neutrons.

Confidence Exercise 10.1

Determine the number of protons, electrons, and neutrons in the carbon atom ^{131}I (iodine-131), a radioactive nucleus used in the treatment of thyroid cancer.

The answers to Confidence Exercises may be found at the back of the book.

Atoms of the same element can be different because of different numbers of neutrons in their nuclei. Atoms that have the same number of protons (same Z, same element) but differ in their numbers of neutrons (different N, and therefore different A) are known as the **isotopes** of that element. *Isotope* literally means "same place" (*iso-*, Greek for same, and *tropos*, meaning place), and it designates atoms that occupy the same place in the periodic table of elements. Isotopes are like members of a family. They all have the same atomic number (Z) and the same element name (surname), but they are distinguishable by the number of neutrons (N) in their nuclei (the equivalent of their given name). For example, three isotopes of carbon are $^{12}_6C_6$, $^{13}_6C_7$, and $^{14}_6C_8$: carbon-12, carbon-13, and carbon-14, respectively.

The isotopes of an element have the same chemical properties because they have the same number of electrons, which determines chemical activity and reactions. But they differ somewhat in physical properties because they have different masses. ● Figure 10.3 illustrates the atomic composition of the three isotopes of hydrogen. They even have their own names: ^1_1H is *protium* (or just *hydrogen*); ^2_1H is *deuterium* (D); and ^3_1H is *tritium* (T). The atomic nuclei in these cases are referred to as *protons*, *deuterons*, and *tritons*, respectively. That is, the proton is the nucleus of a protium atom, and so on.

In a given sample of naturally occurring hydrogen, about 1 atom in 6000 is deuterium and about 1 atom in 10,000,000 is tritium. Protium and deuterium are stable atoms, whereas tritium is unstable (that is, radioactive; Chapter 10.3). Deuterium is sometimes called heavy hydrogen. It combines with oxygen to form *heavy water* (D_2O).

The Atomic Mass

Generally, each element occurs naturally as a combination of its isotopes. The weighted average mass of an atom of the element in a naturally occurring sample is called the

Protium
^1_1H

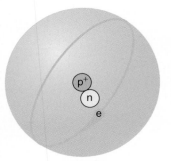

Deuterium
^2_1H

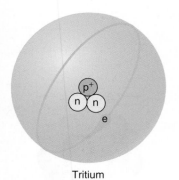

Tritium
^3_1H

Figure 10.3 The Three Isotopes of Hydrogen
Each atom has one proton and one electron, but they differ in the number of neutrons in the nucleus. (*Note:* This figure is not drawn to scale; the nucleus is shown much too large relative to the size of the whole atom.)

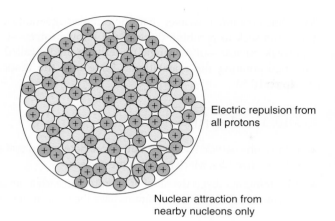

Electric repulsion from
all protons

Nuclear attraction from
nearby nucleons only

Figure 10.4 A Multinucleon Nucleus
The protons on the surface of the
nucleus, such as those shown in the
red semicircle, are attracted by the
strong nuclear force of only the six or
seven closest nucleons, but they are
electrically repelled by all the other
protons. When the number of protons
exceeds 83, the electrical repulsion
overcomes the nucleon attraction and
the nucleus is unstable.

atomic mass and is given under its symbol in the periodic table (in *atomic mass units*,
symbolized u).*

All atomic masses are based on the ^{12}C atom, which is assigned a relative atomic mass of
exactly 12 u. Naturally occurring carbon has an atomic mass slightly greater than 12.0000 u
because it contains not only ^{12}C but also a little ^{13}C and a trace of ^{14}C. An isotope's mass
number closely approximates its atomic mass (its actual mass in u).

The Strong Nuclear Force

In previous chapters, two fundamental forces were considered: the electric force and gravitational force. The electric force between a proton and an electron in an atom is about
10^{39} times the corresponding gravitational force. The electric force is the only important
force on the electrons in an atom and is responsible for the structure of atoms, molecules,
and matter in general. In a nucleus the positively charged protons are packed closely
together. According to Coulomb's law (Chapter 8.1), like charges repel each other, so the
repulsive electric forces in a nucleus are huge. Then, why doesn't the nucleus fly apart?

Obviously, because nuclei generally remain intact, there must be something else: a
third fundamental force. This **strong nuclear force** (or just *strong force* or *nuclear force*)
acts between nucleons: between two protons, between two neutrons, and between a
proton and a neutron. It holds the nucleus together. The exact equation describing the
nucleon–nucleon interaction is unknown. However, for very short nuclear distances of
less than about 10^{-14} m, the interaction is strongly attractive; in fact, it is the strongest
fundamental force known. At distances greater than about 10^{-14} m, however, the nuclear
force is zero.

A multinucleon nucleus is illustrated in ● Fig. 10.4. A proton on the surface of the
nucleus is attracted only by the six or seven nearest nucleons. Because the strong nuclear
force is a short-range force, only the nearby nucleons contribute to the attractive force.

On the other hand, the repulsive electric force is a long-range force and acts between
any two protons, no matter how far apart they are in the nucleus. As nuclei of different
elements contain more and more protons, the electric repulsive forces increase, yet the
attractive nuclear forces remain constant because they are determined by nearest neigh-
bors only.

When the nucleus has more than 83 protons, the electric forces of repulsion overcome
the nuclear attractive forces and the nucleus is subject to spontaneous disintegration, or
decay. That is, particles are emitted to adjust the neutron–proton imbalance.

There is also a *weak nuclear force*. It is a short-range force that reveals itself principally
in beta decay (Chapter 10.3). The weak nuclear force is stronger than the gravitational

*Because the masses are so small in relation to the SI standard kilogram, another unit of appropriate size, the
atomic mass unit (u), is used, where 1 u = 1.66054 × 10^{-27} kg.

force but very much weaker than the electromagnetic force and the strong nuclear force. Physicists seek to combine three of the known forces—electromagnetic, strong nuclear, and weak nuclear—into a single underlying theory called the *grand unified model* (*GUT*), but incorporating the gravitational force into the model has yet to be accomplished (Chapter 10.8).

Did You Learn?

● Using alpha particle scattering, Rutherford determined that atoms have a small electrically positive core, which he called the nucleus.

● The atomic number is the number of protons in each atom of an element. An element is a substance in which all the atoms have the same atomic number (Z).

10.3   Radioactivity and Half-Life

Preview Questions

● What are the three common processes of radioactive decay, and what is emitted in each?

● What is half-life?

A particular species or isotope of any element is called a *nuclide*. A nuclide is a nucleus characterized by a definite atomic number and mass number, such as $^1_1$H, $^{14}_6$C, and $^{238}_{92}$U. Nuclides whose nuclei undergo spontaneous decay (disintegration) are called **radioactive isotopes** (or radioisotopes for short, or radionuclides). The spontaneous process of nuclei undergoing a change by emitting particles or rays is called *radioactive decay*, or **radioactivity**. Substances that give off such radiation are said to be *radioactive*. (The **Highlight: The Discovery of Radioactivity** discusses the discovery of radioactivity by Becquerel and the discovery of two new radioactive elements by the Curies.)

Radioactive nuclei can disintegrate in three common ways: *alpha decay*, *beta decay*, and *gamma decay*; see ● Fig. 10.5. (Fission, another important decay process, will be discussed in Chapter 10.5.) In all decay processes, energy is given off, usually in the form of energetic particles that produce heat. Equations for radioactive decay are generally written in the form

$$A \rightarrow B + b$$

The original nucleus (A) is sometimes called the *parent* nucleus, and the resulting nucleus (B) is referred to as the *daughter* nucleus. The b in the equation represents the emitted particle or ray.

Figure 10.5 The Three Components of Radiation from Radioactive Isotopes
An electric field separates the rays from a sample of a heavy radioisotope, such as uranium, into alpha (α) particles (positively charged helium nuclei), beta (β) particles (negatively charged electrons), and neutral gamma (γ) rays (high-energy electromagnetic radiation). The electrically charged particles are deflected toward oppositely charged plates.

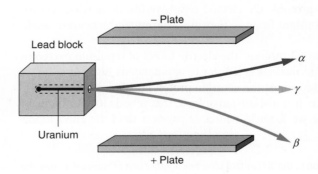

Highlight   The Discovery of Radioactivity

In Paris in 1896, Henri Becquerel ("beh-KREL") heard of Wilhelm Roentgen's recent discovery of X-rays (Chapter 9.4). While experimenting with photographic plates to determine whether any of the fluorescent materials he was investigating might emit X-rays, Becquerel discovered that a mineral containing the element uranium was emitting radiation that had nothing to do with fluorescence. What he discovered was a new type of radiation resulting from radioactivity.

In 1897, also in Paris, Marie Curie began a search for naturally radioactive elements. In 1898, she and her husband, physicist Pierre Curie (discoverer of the magnetic Curie temperature, Chapter 8.4), isolated a minute amount of a new element from tons of uranium ore. Named *polonium* (Po) after Marie's native country, Poland, it was hundreds of times more radioactive than uranium. Later, they found an even more radioactive element, which they named *radium* (Ra) because of the intense radiation it emitted (Fig. 1).

In 1903, the Curies shared the Nobel Prize in physics with Becquerel for their work on radioactivity. Marie Curie was also awarded the Nobel Prize in chemistry in 1911 for further work on radium and the study of its properties. (Pierre was killed in a horse-drawn carriage accident in 1906.) Madame Curie (as she is commonly known) was the first person to win two Nobel Prizes in two different fields, being one of only two persons to do so. The other was American chemist Linus Pauling, who won Nobel prizes in chemistry (1954) and peace (1962).

The rest of her career was dedicated to establishing and supervising laboratories for research on radioactivity and the use of radium in the treatment of cancer. In 1921, Madame Curie toured the United States, and President Warren Harding, on behalf of the women of the United States, presented her with a gram of radium (a relatively large and expensive amount) in recognition of her services to science.

Madame Curie died in 1934 of leukemia, probably caused by overexposure to radioactive substances. She carried test tubes containing radioactive isotopes in her pocket and stored them in a desk drawer. Her death came shortly before an event that would no doubt have made her very proud. In 1935, the Curies' daughter Irene Joliot-Curie and her husband, Frederic Joliot, were awarded the Nobel Prize in chemistry.

Time & Life Pictures/Getty Images

Figure 1 The Curies
Marie (1867–1934) and Pierre (1859–1906) Curie discovered polonium and radium in 1898. They were awarded the Nobel Prize in physics in 1903 for their work on radioactivity. (The prize was shared with Henri Becquerel.)

Alpha decay is the disintegration of a nucleus into a nucleus of another element with the emission of an *alpha particle*, which is a helium nucleus ($^{4}_{2}\text{He}$). An alpha particle with two protons has a positive charge of $+2e$. Alpha decay is common for elements with atomic numbers greater than 83. An example of alpha decay is that of thorium (Th) into radium (Ra):

$$^{232}_{90}\text{Th} \rightarrow {}^{228}_{88}\text{Ra} + {}^{4}_{2}\text{He}$$

In this decay equation, the sum of the mass numbers is the same on each side of the arrow; that is, $232 = 228 + 4$. Also, the sum of the atomic numbers is the same on each side; that is, $90 = 88 + 2$. This principle holds for all nuclear decays and involves the conservation of nucleons and the conservation of charge, respectively.

In a nuclear decay equation, the sum of the mass numbers will be the same on both sides of the arrow, as will the sum of the atomic numbers.

> **EXAMPLE 10.2**   **Finding the Products of Alpha Decay**
>
> $^{238}_{92}U$ undergoes alpha decay. Write the equation for the process.
>
> **Solution**
>
> **Step 1**
>
> Write the symbol for the parent nucleus followed by an arrow.
>
> $$^{238}_{92}U \rightarrow$$
>
> **Step 2**
>
> Because alpha decay involves the emission of ^4_2He, this symbol can be written to the right of the arrow and preceded by a plus sign, leaving space for the symbol for the daughter nucleus.
>
> $$^{238}_{92}U \rightarrow \underline{} + {^4_2He}$$
>
> **Step 3**
>
> Determine the mass number, atomic number, and chemical symbol for the daughter nucleus. The sum of the mass numbers on the left is 238. The sum on the right must also be 238, and so far, only the 4 for the alpha particle shows. Thus, the daughter must have a mass number of $238 - 4 = 234$. By similar reasoning, the atomic number of the daughter must be $92 - 2 = 90$. From the periodic table (see inside front cover), it can be seen that the element with atomic number 90 is Th (thorium). The complete equation for the decay is
>
> $$^{238}_{92}U \rightarrow {^{234}_{90}Th} + {^4_2He}$$

> **Confidence Exercise 10.2**
>
> Write the equation for the alpha decay of the radium isotope $^{226}_{88}Ra$.
>
> Answers to the Confidence Exercises may be found at the back of the book.

Beta decay is the disintegration of a nucleus into a nucleus of another element with the emission of a *beta particle*, which is an electron $(_{-1}^{0}e)$. An example of beta decay is

$$^{14}_6C \rightarrow {^{14}_7N} + {^0_{-1}e}$$

A beta particle, or electron, is assigned a mass number of 0 (because it contains no nucleons) and an atomic number of -1 (because its electric charge is opposite that of a proton's $+1$ charge). The sums of the mass numbers and atomic numbers on both sides of the arrow are equal: $14 = 14 + 0$ and $6 = 7 - 1$. In beta decay, with a decrease in the neutron number, a neutron $(_0^1n)$ is transformed into a proton and an electron $(_0^1n \rightarrow {^1_1p} + {^0_{-1}e})$. The proton remains in the nucleus, and the electron is emitted.

Gamma decay occurs when a nucleus emits a *gamma ray* (γ) and becomes a less energetic form of the same nucleus. A gamma ray is a photon of high-energy electromagnetic radiation and has no mass number and no atomic number. Gamma rays are similar to X-rays but are more energetic. An example of gamma decay is

$$^{204}_{82}Pb^* \rightarrow {^{204}_{82}Pb} + \gamma$$

The asterisk (*) following the lead (Pb) symbol means that the nucleus is in an excited state, analogous to an atom being in an excited state with an electron in a higher energy level (Chapter 9.3). When the nucleus de-excites, one or more gamma rays are emitted. The nucleus is left in a state of lower excitation and ultimately in the "ground (stable) state" of the same nuclide. Gamma decay generally occurs when a nucleus is formed in an excited state, as a product of alpha or beta decay.

Table 10.4 Nuclear Radiations

Name	Symbol	Charge	Mass Number
Alpha	$_2^4\text{He}$	2+	4
Beta	$_{-1}^{0}\text{e}$	1−	0
Gamma	γ	0	0
Positron	$_{+1}^{0}\text{e}$	1+	0
Neutron	$_0^1\text{n}$	0	1

In addition to alpha, beta, and gamma radiation, certain nuclear processes (generally involving artificial radioisotopes) emit *positrons* $\left(_{+1}^{0}\text{e}\right)$. For example,

$$_9^{17}\text{F} \rightarrow {_8^{17}}\text{O} + {_{+1}^{0}}\text{e}$$

Positrons are sometimes referred to as *beta-plus* particles because they are the *antiparticle* of the electron, having the same mass but an electric charge of +1. ● Table 10.4 lists five common forms of nuclear radiation. (Neutrons are also the product of some nuclear reactions.)

A nucleus with atomic number greater than 83 is always radioactive and commonly undergoes a series of alpha, beta, and gamma decays until a stable nucleus is produced. For example, the series of decays beginning with uranium-238 and ending with stable $_{82}^{206}\text{Pb}$ is illustrated in ● Fig. 10.6. Note how the alpha (α) and beta (β) transitions are indicated in Fig. 10.6. The gamma decays that accompany the alpha and beta decays in the series are not apparent on the diagram because the neutron and proton numbers do not change in gamma decay.

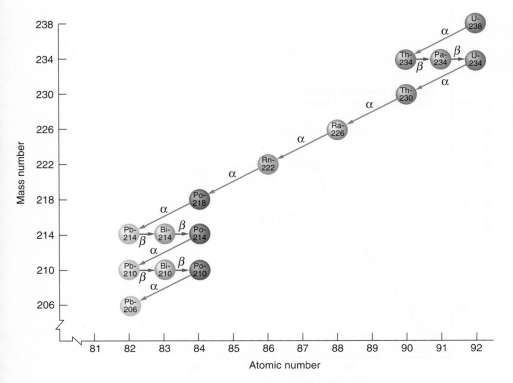

Figure 10.6 The Decay of Uranium-238 to Lead-206
Each radioactive nucleus in the series undergoes either alpha (α) decay or beta (β) decay. Finally, stable lead-206 is formed as the end product. The gamma decays, which change only the energy of nuclei, are not shown.

Conceptual Question and Answer

A Misprint?

Q. Suppose you picked up a newspaper and saw a story reporting the discovery of a new radioactive element. The story states that the element was formed from radioactive decay: $^{274}_{120}X \rightarrow \, ^{276}_{121}Y$. Did the newspaper make a misprint?

A. Yes. The increase in the proton number in the decay (120 to 121) would imply beta decay with an additional proton. However, in beta decay, the mass number does not change, so if the proton number is correct, then the daughter element should be $^{274}_{121}Y$.

Identifying Radioactive Nuclei

Which nuclei are unstable (radioactive) and which are stable? When the number of protons (Z) versus the number of neutrons (N) for each stable nucleus is plotted, the points (red dots) form a narrow band called the *band of stability* (● Fig. 10.7). For comparison, the straight red line in the figure represents equal numbers of protons and neutrons. The increasing divergence of the band from the $N = Z$ line shows that there are more neutrons than protons.

The blue dots in Fig. 10.7 represent known radioactive nuclei. Note that the nuclei cluster on each side of the band of stability and sometimes are found within it. No stable nuclides (red dots) are found past $Z = 83$, but numerous radioactive nuclei with more than 83 protons are known.

An inventory of the number of protons and the number of neutrons in stable nuclei reveals an interesting pattern (● Table 10.5). Most of the stable nuclides have both an even

Figure 10.7 A Plot of Number of Neutrons (N) versus Number of Protons (Z) for Nuclei
The red dots representing stable nuclei trace out a *band of stability*. It begins on a line where the number of *neutrons* (N) and the number of *protons* (Z) are equal and gradually diverges from the line as the *number of protons* gets greater. Because all nuclei with more than 83 protons are radioactive, the band ends at this number of protons. The blue dots represent known radioisotopes.

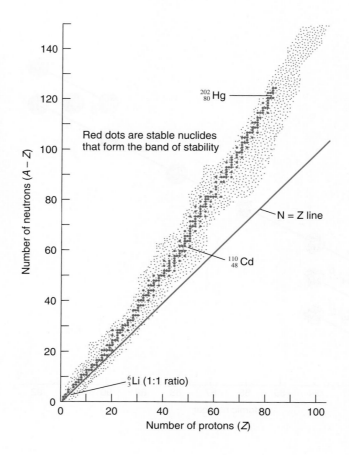

Table 10.5 The Pairing Effect in Stabilizing Nuclei

Proton Number, Z	Neutron Number, N	Number of Stable Nuclides	Example
Even	Even	160	$^{24}_{12}Mg$
Even	Odd	52	$^{13}_{6}C$
Odd	Even	52	$^{6}_{5}Be$
Odd	Odd	4	$^{14}_{7}N$

number of protons (Z) and an even number of neutrons (N) in their nuclei and are referred to as *even–even* nuclei. Practically all the other stable nuclei are either *even–odd* or *odd–even*. Nature dislikes *odd–odd* nuclei (only four stable ones exist) apparently because of the existence of energy levels in the nucleus that favor the pairing of two protons or two neutrons.

Such descriptions as *odd–odd* refer to the number of protons and neutrons, respectively, not to the atomic number and mass number. For example, because $N = A - Z$, an *odd* atomic number (say, 9) coupled with an *even* mass number (say, 20) means an *odd* number of protons (9) but also an *odd* number of neutrons (11).

A nucleus will be radioactive if it meets any of the following criteria.

1. Its atomic number is greater than 83.

2. It has fewer neutrons, n, than protons, p (except for $^{1}_{1}H$ and $^{3}_{2}He$).

3. It is an odd–odd nucleus (except for $^{2}_{1}H$, $^{6}_{3}Li$, $^{10}_{5}B$, and $^{14}_{7}N$).*

EXAMPLE 10.3   **Identifying Radioactive Isotopes**

Identify the radioactive nucleus in each pair and state your reasoning.

(a) $^{208}_{82}Pb$ and $^{222}_{86}Rn$

(b) $^{19}_{10}Ne$ and $^{20}_{10}Ne$

(c) $^{63}_{29}Cu$ and $^{64}_{29}Cu$

Solution

(a) $^{222}_{86}Rn$ (Z above 83)

(b) $^{19}_{10}Ne$ (fewer n than p)

(c) $^{64}_{29}Cu$ (odd–odd)

Confidence Exercise 10.3

Predict which two of the following nuclei are radioactive.

$$^{232}_{90}Th \quad ^{24}_{12}M \quad ^{40}_{19}K \quad ^{31}_{15}P$$

Half-Life

Some samples of radioisotopes take a long time to decay; others decay very rapidly. In a sample of a given isotope, the decay of an individual nucleus is a random event. It is impossible to predict which nucleus will be the next to undergo a nuclear change. However, given a large number of nuclei, it is possible to predict how many will decay in a certain length of time. The rate of decay of a given radioisotope is described by the term **half-life**,

---

*A fourth criterion, which will not be used because it is difficult to apply, is that unless the mass number of a nucleus is relatively close to the element's atomic mass, the nucleus will be radioactive.

Figure 10.8 Radioactive Decay and Half-Life
Starting with the number of nuclei N_o of a radioactive sample, after one half-life has elapsed, only one-half $(\frac{1}{2} N_o)$ of the original nuclei will remain un-decayed (as indicated by the shading in the box above the curve). The other half of the sample consists of nuclei of the decay product (white portion of the box). After two half-lives, only one-quarter of the original nuclei will remain, and so on.

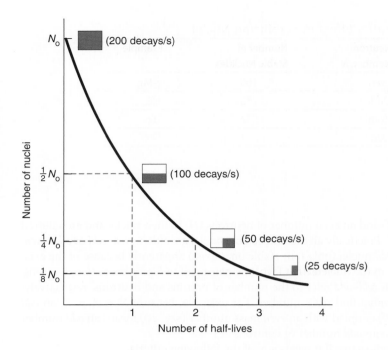

which is the time it takes for half of the nuclei of a given radioactive sample to decay. In other words, after one half-life has gone by, one-half of the original amount of isotope remains undecayed; after two half-lives $(\frac{1}{2} \times \frac{1}{2}) =$ one-fourth $(\frac{1}{4})$ of the original amount is undecayed; and so on (● Fig. 10.8).*

To determine the half-life of a radioisotope, the *activity* (the rate of emission of decay particles) is monitored. The activity is commonly measured in counts per minute (cpm). This measurement may be done with an instrument such as a *Geiger counter* (● Fig. 10.9). Hans Geiger, who developed the counter in 1913, was one of Rutherford's assistants. If half

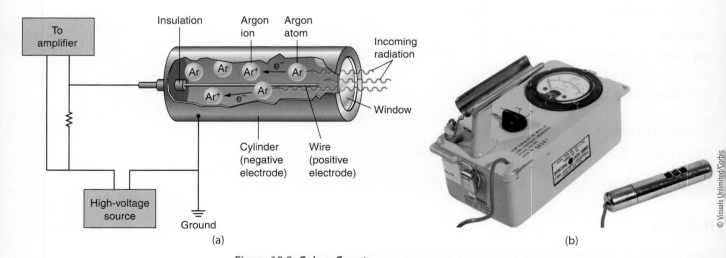

Figure 10.9 Geiger Counter
(a) A Geiger counter detects ions formed as a result of a high-energy particle from a radioactive source entering the window and ionizing argon atoms along its path. The ions and electrons formed produce a pulse of current, which is amplified and counted. (b) A portable (battery-operated) Geiger counter.

*A radioactive isotope's half-life can be measured without waiting throughout the duration of one half-life. The half-life can be calculated by measuring the rate of decay of a known quantity of the isotope.

of the original nuclei of sample decay in one half-life, then the activity decreases to one-half of its original counts during that time.

If a radio isotope's half-life is, say, 12 y, then keep the units straight by putting that information into your calculations as 12 y/half-life (12 years per half-life).

For simplicity, we will work with only a number of half-lives that are a small whole number. In a given exercise, the quantity solved for will be one of the following: the number of half-lives, the final sample amount, or the elapsed time.

EXAMPLE 10.4   Finding the Number of Half-Lives and the Final Amount

What fraction and mass of a 40-mg sample of iodine-131 (half-life = 8 d) will remain after 24 days?

Solution

Step 1

Find the number of half-lives that have passed in 24 d.

$$\frac{24 \text{ d}}{8 \text{ d/half-life}} = 3 \text{ half-lives}$$

Step 2

Starting with the defined original amount N_o, halve it three times (because three half-lives have passed).

$$N_o \xrightarrow{\text{first half-life}} \frac{N_o}{2} \xrightarrow{\text{second half-life}} \frac{N_o}{4} \xrightarrow{\text{third half-life}} \frac{N_o}{8}$$

Thus, three half-lives have passed, and with $N_o/8$ remaining, the final amount of iodine-131 is $\frac{1}{8}$ of 40 mg, or 5 mg.

Confidence Exercise 10.4

Strontium-90 (half-life = 29 y) is one of the worst components of fallout from atmospheric testing of nuclear bombs because it concentrates in the bones. The last such bomb was tested in 1963. In the year 2021, how many half-lives will have gone by for the strontium-90 produced in the blast? What fraction of the strontium-90 will remain in that year?

EXAMPLE 10.5   Finding the Elapsed Time

How long would it take a sample of ^{14}C to decay to one-fourth of its original activity? The half-life of ^{14}C is 5730 y.

Solution

The ^{14}C will decay for a time period equal to two half-lives, as shown by the number of arrows in the sequence

$$N_o \rightarrow \frac{N_o}{2} \rightarrow \frac{N_o}{4}$$

To find the elapsed time, multiply the number of half-lives by the half-life.

$$(2 \text{ half-lives})(5730 \text{ y/half-life}) = 11{,}460 \text{ y}$$

Confidence Exercise 10.5

Technetium-99 is often used as a radioactive tracer to assess heart damage. Its half-life is 6.0 h. How long would it take a sample of technetium-99 to decay to one-sixteenth of its original amount?

Carbon-14 Dating

Because their decay rates are constant, radioisotopes can be used as nuclear "clocks." Half-life can be used to determine how much of a radioactive sample will exist in the future (see Fig. 10.8). Similarly, by using the half-life to calculate backward in time, scientists can determine the ages of objects that contain known radioisotopes. Of course, some idea of the initial amount of the isotope must be known.

An important dating procedure commonly used in archeology involves the radioisotope ^{14}C. **Carbon-14 dating** is used on materials that were once part of living things, such as wood, bone, and parchment. The process depends on the fact that living things (including you) contain a known amount of radioactive ^{14}C, which has a half-life of 5730 years.

The ^{14}C nuclei exist in living things because the isotope is continually being produced in the atmosphere by cosmic rays. *Cosmic rays* are high-speed charged particles that reach the Earth from various sources, like the Sun. The "rays" are primarily protons, and on entering the upper atmosphere, they can cause reactions that produce neutrons (● Fig. 10.10). These neutrons react with the nuclei of nitrogen atoms in the atmosphere to produce ^{14}C and a proton ($^{1}_{1}H$):

$$^{14}_{7}N + {}^{1}_{0}n \rightarrow {}^{14}_{6}C + {}^{1}_{1}H$$

It is assumed that the intensity of incident cosmic rays has been relatively constant over thousands of years because of atmospheric mixing. Changes in solar activity and the

Figure 10.10 Carbon-14 Dating
An illustration of how carbon-14 forms in the atmosphere and enters the biosphere. See text for description.

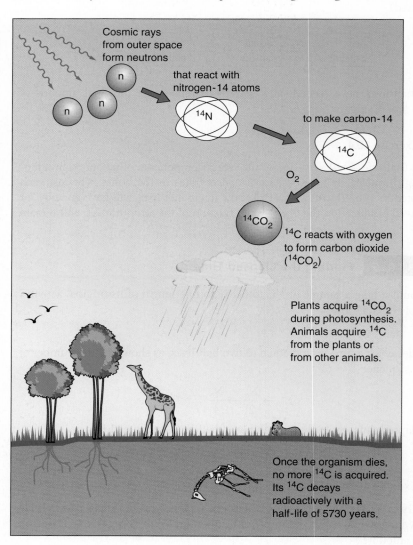

Cosmic rays from outer space form neutrons

that react with nitrogen-14 atoms

to make carbon-14

O_2

$^{14}CO_2$

^{14}C reacts with oxygen to form carbon dioxide ($^{14}CO_2$)

Plants acquire $^{14}CO_2$ during photosynthesis. Animals acquire ^{14}C from the plants or from other animals.

Once the organism dies, no more ^{14}C is acquired. Its ^{14}C decays radioactively with a half-life of 5730 years.

Earth's magnetic field may have caused it to vary somewhat, but the dating is a good approximation.

The newly formed ^{14}C reacts with oxygen in the air to form radioactive carbon dioxide, $^{14}CO_2$ (Fig. 10.10). This, along with ordinary carbon dioxide, $^{12}CO_2$, is used by plants in photosynthesis (Chapter 19.1). About one out of every trillion (10^{12}) carbon atoms in plants is ^{14}C. Animals eat the plants containing ^{14}C, and animals eat the animals that ate the plants.

Thus, all living matter has about the same level of radioactivity due to ^{14}C, an activity of about 16 counts (beta emissions) per minute per gram of total carbon ($^{14}_{6}C \rightarrow ^{14}_{7}N + ^{0}_{-1}e$). Once an organism dies, it ceases to take in ^{14}C, but the original amount of ^{14}C continues to undergo radioactive decay. The longer an organism has been dead, the lower the radioactivity is of each gram of carbon in its remains.

The limit of radioactive carbon dating depends on the ability to measure the very low activity in old samples. Current techniques give an age-dating limit of about 40,000–50,000 years, depending on the size of the sample. After about ten half-lives, the radioactivity is barely measurable.

EXAMPLE 10.6   Carbon-14 Dating

An old scroll (like the Dead Sea Scrolls) is found in a cave that has a carbon-14 activity of 4 counts/min per gram of total carbon. Approximately how old is the scroll?

Solution

First the number of half-lives of ^{14}C that have passed is determined. The plant, from which the parchment was made, originally had an activity of 16 counts/min per gram of carbon. Then, to get the current 4 counts:

$$16 \text{ counts} \rightarrow (t_{\frac{1}{2}}) \ 8 \text{ counts} \rightarrow (t_{\frac{1}{2}}) \ 4 \text{ counts}$$

so two half-lives have elapsed.

Knowing that the half-life of ^{14}C is 5730 years,

$$2 \times 5730 \text{ years} = 11{,}460 \text{ years}$$

so the parchment is between approximately 11,000 and 12,000 years old.

Confidence Exercise 10.6

An archeology dig unearths a skeleton. Analysis shows that there is a ^{14}C activity of 1 count/min per gram of total carbon. Approximately how old is the skeleton?

Did You Learn?

- Radioactivity is the spontaneous decay of nuclei undergoing a change by emitting particles or rays: alpha decay (alpha particle or helium nucleus), beta decay (beta particle or electron), or gamma decay (gamma ray or photon).

- Half-life is the time it takes for one-half of a given radioactive sample to decay.

10.4   Nuclear Reactions

Preview Questions

- What quantities are conserved in nuclear reactions?
- What are transuranium elements?

Through the emission of alpha and beta particles, radioactive nuclei spontaneously change (undergo *transmutation*) into nuclei of other elements. Scientists wondered whether the reverse process was possible. Could a particle be added to a nucleus to change it into that of another element? The answer is yes.

Rutherford produced the first *nuclear reaction* in 1919 by bombarding nitrogen (^{14}N) gas with alpha particles from a radioactive source. Other particles were observed coming from the gas and were identified as protons. Rutherford reasoned that an alpha particle colliding with a nitrogen nucleus can occasionally knock out a proton. The result is an *artificial transmutation* of a nitrogen nucleus into an oxygen nucleus. The equation for the reaction is

$$^{4}_{2}\text{He} + ^{14}_{7}\text{N} \rightarrow ^{17}_{8}\text{O} + ^{1}_{1}\text{H}$$

The conservation of mass number and the conservation of atomic number hold in nuclear reactions, just as in nuclear decay.

The general form of a nuclear reaction is

$$a + A \rightarrow B + b$$

where a is the particle that bombards nucleus A to form nucleus B and an emitted particle b. In addition to the particles listed in Table 10.4, the particles commonly encountered in nuclear reactions are protons ($^{1}_{1}\text{H}$), deuterons ($^{2}_{1}\text{H}$), and tritons ($^{3}_{1}\text{H}$).

EXAMPLE 10.7   Completing an Equation for a Nuclear Reaction

Complete the equation for the proton bombardment of lithium-7.

$$^{1}_{1}\text{H} + ^{7}_{3}\text{Li} \rightarrow \underline{} + ^{1}_{0}\text{n}$$

Solution

The sum of the mass numbers on the left is 8. So far, only a mass number of 1 shows on the right, so the missing particle must have a mass number of $8 - 1 = 7$.

The sum of the atomic numbers on the left is 4. The total showing on the right is 0. Thus, the missing particle must have an atomic number of $4 - 0 = 4$. The atom with mass number 7 and atomic number 4 is an isotope of Be (beryllium, Z = 4; see the periodic table inside the front cover). The completed equation is

$$^{1}_{1}\text{H} + ^{7}_{3}\text{Li} \rightarrow ^{7}_{4}\text{Be} + ^{1}_{0}\text{n}$$

Confidence Exercise 10.7

Complete the equation for the deuteron bombardment of aluminum-27.

$$^{2}_{1}\text{H} + ^{27}_{13}\text{Al} \rightarrow \underline{} + ^{4}_{2}\text{He}$$

The reaction in Rutherford's experiment was discovered almost by accident because it took place so infrequently. One proton is produced for about every one million alpha particles that shoot through the nitrogen gas. Consider the implications of its discovery: One element had been changed into another. It was the age-old dream of the alchemists, the original researchers into transmutation, although their main concern was to change common metals, such as lead, into gold.

Such artificial transmutations are now common. Large machines called *particle accelerators* use electric fields to accelerate charged particles to very high energies. The energetic particles are used to bombard nuclei and initiate nuclear reactions. Different reactions require different particles and different bombarding energies. One nuclear reaction that occurs when a proton strikes a nucleus of mercury-200 is

$$^{1}_{1}\text{H} + ^{200}_{80}\text{Hg} \rightarrow ^{197}_{79}\text{Au} + ^{4}_{2}\text{He}$$

Highlight   Number of Naturally Occurring Elements: A Quandary

We currently have 118 known elements. (See the periodic table inside the front cover.) Each element has nuclei with the same atomic number Z (same number of protons). As noted, some of the elements do not occur naturally and are made artificially by nuclear reactions. The question then arises, how many *naturally* occurring elements are there? That is, how many of the 118 known elements are found in nature?

The transuranium elements ($Z > 92$) are all artificially made, so that eliminates 16 elements. It would seem logical that the first 92 elements in the periodic table, from hydrogen ($_1$H) to uranium ($_{92}$U), would be naturally occurring, but a couple of elements, technetium ($_{43}$Tc) and promethium ($_{61}$Pm), have only been created artificially. Technetium (Tc) was the first synthetic element produced (in 1937) by nuclear bombardment of the element molybdenum (Mo) with deuterons, $_1^2$H:

$$_{42}^{96}\text{Mo} + _{1}^{2}\text{H} \rightarrow _{43}^{98}\text{Tc}$$

The Tc and Pm natural absence can be understood from their half-lives, which are about 8 hours and about 20 minutes, respectively. If formed at the beginning of the universe, these elements would have long since decayed away and not occur in nature today.

So, we are down to 90 elements. It is commonly said that there are 88 naturally occurring elements. The difference involves element 85, astatine ($_{85}$At), and element 87, francium ($_{87}$Fr). These elements do appear in nature, but only briefly and in trace amounts. They are found in radioactive decay series (see Exercise 10), and their half-lives are on the order of 2 seconds and 20 minutes, respectively.

Some people believe that even though only small amounts of astatine and francium are present at any given time, they are "naturally occurring" because they occur spontaneously in nature, making the total 90 elements. Others argue that such elements should not really be considered "naturally occurring" since they are not in nature in the sense of other elements (thereby making the total 88 elements).

What do you think? Are there 88 or 90 naturally occurring elements? (Most go with 88.)

Gold (Au) can indeed be made from another element. Unfortunately, making gold by this process would cost millions of dollars an ounce, much more than the gold is worth.

Neutrons produced in nuclear reactions can be used to induce other nuclear reactions. Because they have no electric charge, neutrons do not experience repulsive electrical interactions with nuclear protons as would alpha particle and proton projectiles, both of which have positive charges. As a result, neutrons are especially effective at penetrating the nucleus and inducing a reaction. For example,

$$_{0}^{1}\text{n} + _{21}^{45}\text{Sc} \rightarrow _{19}^{42}\text{K} + _{2}^{4}\text{He}$$

The *transuranium elements*, which have an atomic number greater than uranium-92, are all artificially made as a result of induced reactions, as are Tc (43) and Pm (61). The elements At (85) and Fr (87) can also be made artificially, but there is some question about their occurring naturally. (See the **Highlight: Number of Naturally Occurring Elements.**) Elements 93 (neptunium, Np) to 101 (mendelevium, Md) can be made by bombarding a lighter nucleus with alpha particles or neutrons. For example,

$$_{0}^{1}\text{n} + _{92}^{238}\text{U} \rightarrow _{93}^{239}\text{Np} + _{-1}^{0}\text{e}$$

Beyond mendelevium, heavier bombarding particles are required. For example, element 109, meitnerium (Mt), is made by bombarding bismuth-209 with iron-58 nuclei.

$$_{26}^{58}\text{Fe} + _{83}^{209}\text{Bi} \rightarrow _{109}^{266}\text{Mt} + _{0}^{1}\text{n}$$

Figure 10.11 A Smoke Detector
In most smoke detectors, a weak radioactive source ionizes the air and sets up a small current. If smoke particles enter the detector, then the current is reduced, causing an alarm to sound.

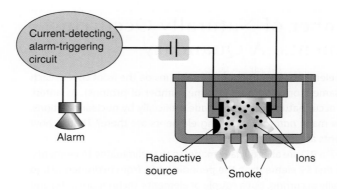

Atoms of hydrogen ($_1$H), helium ($_2$He), and lithium ($_3$Li) are thought to have been formed in the Big Bang theory of the universe (Chapter 18.7), whereas atoms of beryllium ($_4$Be) up through iron ($_{26}$Fe) are made in the cores of stars by nuclear reactions (Chapter 18.4). Atoms of elements heavier than iron are believed to be formed during supernova explosions of stars, when neutrons are in abundance and can enter into nuclear reactions with medium-size atoms to form larger ones (Chapter 18.5).

Some Uses of Radioactive Isotopes

Conceptual Question and Answer

Around the House

Q. Do you have any radioactive sources in your residence?

A. Probably so, if you are prudent enough to have a smoke detector. Americium-241, an artificial transuranium radioactive isotope (half-life = 432 y), is used in the most common type of residential smoke detector. As the americium-241 decays, the alpha particles that are emitted ionize the air inside part of the detector (● Fig. 10.11).
   The ions form a small current that allows a battery (or house voltage) to power a closed circuit. If smoke enters the detector, then the ions become attached to the smoke particles and slow down, causing the current in the circuit to decrease and an alarm to sound. (An older model of smoke detector uses a light path and photocell. When smoke dims the light path and less current is supplied by the photocell, an alarm is sounded.)

Radioactive isotopes have many uses in medicine, chemistry, biology, agriculture, and industry. For example, a radioactive isotope of iodine, ^{123}I, is used in a diagnostic measurement connected with the thyroid gland. The patient is administered a prescribed amount of ^{123}I, which, like regular iodine in the diet, is absorbed by the thyroid gland. Doctors can monitor the iodine uptake of the thyroid by measuring the absorbed radioactive iodine.

Radiation is used in many other types of medical diagnoses, like the brain scans pictured in the chapter-opening photo. Plutonium-238 powers a tiny battery used in heart pacemakers. Nuclear radiation also can be used to treat diseased cells, which generally can be destroyed by radiation more easily than healthy cells. For example, focusing an intense beam of radiation from cobalt-60 on a cancerous tumor destroys its cells and thus impairs or halts its growth.

In chemistry and biology, radioactive "tracers," such as ^{14}C (radiocarbon) and ^{3}H (tritium), are used to tag an atom in a certain part of a molecule so that it can be followed through a series of reactions. In this way, the reaction pathways of hormones, drugs, and other substances can be determined.

In industry, tracer radioisotopes help manufacturers test the durability of mechanical components and identify structural weaknesses in equipment. In environmental studies,

© Justin Sullivan/ Getty Images

Figure 10.12 Is It Safe?
Airport baggage being screened using neutron activation analysis. Almost all explosives contain nitrogen, which when bombarded with neutrons gives off gamma rays that can be detected. Note the radiation caution sign over the opening.

small amounts of radioisotopes help detect groundwater movement through soil and trace the paths of industrial air and water pollutants.

In agriculture, food is irradiated. Meat, poultry, and egg products are irradiated with gamma rays to reduce the number of harmful bacteria and parasites present. The Food and Drug Administration (FDA) found irradiation to be safe and approved the process in the 1960s. Irradiation is an important food safety tool.

Neutron activation analysis is one of the most sensitive analytical methods in science. A beam of neutrons irradiates the sample, and each constituent element forms a specific radioisotope that can be identified by the characteristic energies of the gamma rays it emits. Neutron activation analysis has the advantage over chemical and spectral identification of elements because it needs only minute samples. It can be used to identify and measure 50 different elements in amounts as small as 1 picogram (10^{-12} g).

Neutron activation analysis is used as an antiterrorist tool in airports. Virtually all explosives contain nitrogen. By using neutron activation analysis and analyzing the energy of any emission of gamma rays from airport baggage, it is possible to detect the presence of nitrogen and then check the baggage manually to investigate any suspicious finding (● Fig. 10.12).

The next two sections address the controlled and uncontrolled release of nuclear energy.

Did You Learn?

● The mass number (*A*) and the atomic number (*Z*) are conserved in nuclear reactions.

● Transuranium elements are those with atomic numbers greater than 92, and all are artificially made.

10.5 Nuclear Fission

Preview Questions

● Is mass conserved in fission reactions?

● What is a self-sustaining chain reaction, and how can it grow in energy release?

Figure 10.13 Fission and Chain Reaction
(a) In a fission reaction such as that shown for uranium-235, a neutron is absorbed and the unstable ^{236}U nucleus splits into two lighter nuclei with the emission of energy and two or more neutrons. (b) If the emitted neutrons cause increasing numbers of fission reactions, then an expanding *chain reaction* occurs.

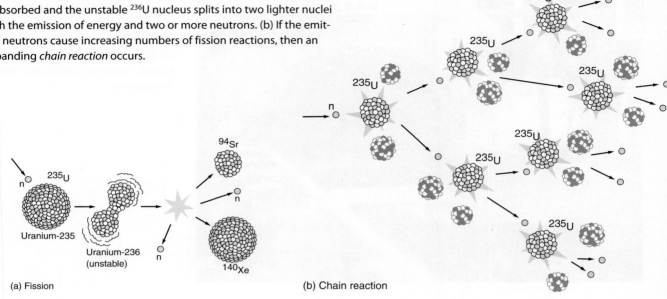

(a) Fission   (b) Chain reaction

Fission is the process in which a large nucleus "splits" (fissions) into two intermediate-size nuclei, with the emission of neutrons and the conversion of mass into energy. For example, consider the fission decay of ^{236}U. If ^{235}U is bombarded with low-energy neutrons, then ^{236}U is formed:

$$^{1}_{0}n + ^{235}_{92}U \rightarrow ^{236}_{92}U$$

The ^{236}U immediately fissions into two smaller nuclei, emits several neutrons, and releases energy. ● Figure 10.13a illustrates the following typical fission of ^{236}U:

$$^{236}_{92}U \rightarrow ^{140}_{54}Xe + ^{94}_{38}Sr + 2^{1}_{0}n$$

This is just one of many possible fission decays of ^{236}U. Another is

$$^{236}_{92}U \rightarrow ^{132}_{50}Sn + ^{101}_{42}Mo + 3^{1}_{0}n$$

EXAMPLE 10.8   Completing an Equation for Fission

Complete the following equation for fission.

$$^{236}_{92}U \rightarrow ^{88}_{36}Kr + ^{144}_{56}Ba + \underline{\ \ }$$

Solution

The atomic numbers are balanced ($92 = 36 + 56$), so the other particle must have an atomic number of 0. The mass number on the left is 236, and the sum of the mass numbers on the right is $88 + 144 = 232$. Hence, if the mass numbers are to balance, then there must be four additional units of mass on the right-hand side of the equation. Because no particle with an atomic number of 0 and a mass number of 4 exists, the missing "particle" is actually four neutrons. The reaction is then

$$^{236}_{92}U \rightarrow ^{88}_{36}Kr + ^{144}_{56}Ba + 4^{1}_{0}n$$

Both the atomic numbers and the mass numbers are now balanced or conserved.

Confidence Exercise 10.8

Complete the following equation for fission.

$$^{236}_{92}U \rightarrow ^{90}_{38}Sr + \underline{\ \ } + 2^{1}_{0}n$$

The fast-fissioning ^{236}U is an intermediate nucleus and is often left out of the equation for the neutron-induced fission of ^{235}U; the equation for the reaction in Example 10.8 is usually written

$$^{1}_{0}n + ^{235}_{92}U \rightarrow ^{88}_{36}Kr + ^{144}_{56}Ba + 4^{1}_{0}n$$

Nuclear fission reactions have three important features:

1. The fission products are always radioactive. Some have half-lives of thousands of years, which lead to major problems in the disposal of nuclear waste.

2. Relatively large amounts of energy are produced.

3. Neutrons are released.

In an *expanding* **chain reaction**, one initial reaction triggers a growing number of subsequent reactions. In the case of fission, one neutron hits a nucleus of ^{235}U and forms ^{236}U, which can fission and emit two (or more) neutrons. These two neutrons can then hit another two ^{235}U nuclei, causing them to fission and release energy and four neutrons. These four neutrons can cause four more fissions, releasing energy and eight neutrons, and so on (Fig. 10.13b). Each time a nucleus fissions, energy is released; as the chain expands, the energy output increases.

For a *self-sustaining* chain reaction, each fission event needs to cause only one more fission event, which leads to a steady release of energy, not a growing release. The process of energy production by fission is not as simple as just described. For a self-sustaining chain reaction to proceed, a sufficient amount and concentration of fissionable material (^{235}U) must be present. Otherwise, too many neutrons would escape from the sample before reaction with a ^{235}U nucleus. The chain would be broken. The minimum amount of fissionable material necessary to sustain a chain reaction is called the **critical mass**. The critical mass for pure ^{235}U is about 4 kg, which is approximately the size of a baseball. With a *subcritical mass*, no chain reaction occurs. With a *supercritical mass*, the chain reaction grows, and under certain conditions an explosion occurs.

Natural uranium is 99.3% ^{238}U, which does not undergo fission. Only the remaining 0.7% is the fissionable ^{235}U isotope. So that more fissionable ^{235}U nuclei will be present in a sample, the ^{235}U is concentrated, or "enriched." The enriched uranium used in U.S. nuclear reactors for the production of electricity is about 3% ^{235}U. Weapons-grade uranium is enriched to 90% or more; this percentage provides many fissionable nuclei for a large and sudden release of energy.

In a fission bomb, or "atomic bomb," a supercritical mass of highly enriched fissionable material must be formed and held together for a short time to get an explosive release of energy. Subcritical segments of the fissionable material in a fission bomb are kept separated before detonation so that a critical mass does not exist for the chain reaction. A chemical explosive is used to bring the segments together in an interlocking, supercritical configuration that holds them long enough for a large fraction of the material to undergo fission. The result is an explosive release of energy.

Nuclear Reactors

A nuclear (atomic) bomb is an example of *uncontrolled* fission. A nuclear reactor is an example *of controlled* fission, in which the growth of the chain reaction and the release of energy are controlled. The first commercial fission reactor for generating electricity went into operation in 1957 at Shippingport, Pennsylvania. That reactor was shut down in 1982 after 25 years of operation.

The basic design of a nuclear reactor vessel is shown in ● Fig. 10.14. Enriched uranium oxide fuel pellets are placed in metal tubes to form long *fuel rods*, which are placed in the reactor core where fission takes place. Also in the core are *control rods* made of neutron-absorbing materials such as boron (B) and cadmium (Cd). The control rods are adjusted (inserted or withdrawn) so that only a certain number of neutrons are absorbed, ensuring that the chain reaction releases energy at the rate desired. For a steady rate of energy release, one neutron from each fission event should initiate only one additional fission event. If more energy is needed, then the rods are withdrawn farther. When fully inserted

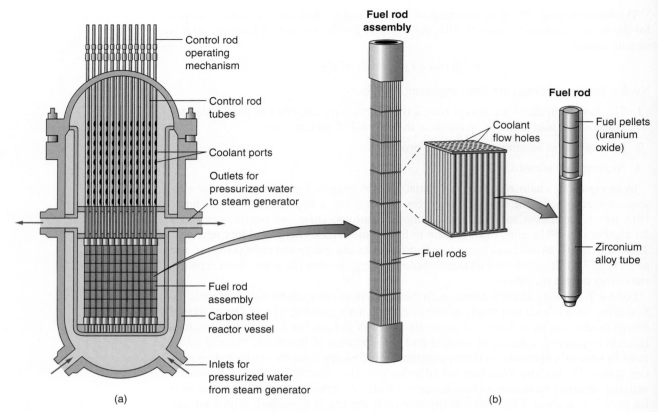

Figure 10.14 Nuclear Reactor Diagram
(a) A schematic diagram of a reactor vessel. (b) A fuel rod and its assembly. A typical reactor contains fuel rod assemblies of approximately 200 rods each, and the fuel core can have up to 3000 fuel assemblies. One of the uranium nuclear fuel pellets the size of the tip of your little finger inside a rod can provide energy equivalent to 1780 lb of coal or 149 gallons of oil. That's quite a bit of energy.

into the core, the control rods absorb enough neutrons to stop the chain reaction, and the reactor shuts down.

A reactor's core is a heat source, and the heat energy is removed by a coolant flowing through the core. Reactors in the United States are light-water reactors in which the coolant is commonly H_2O (light water, as opposed to heavy water, D_2O, which is used in some Canadian reactors and requires lower uranium fuel enrichment). The coolant flowing through the hot fuel assemblies removes heat that is used to produce steam to drive a turbogenerator, which produces electricity. ● Fig. 10.15 shows a *pressurized water reactor* (PWR). Pressure prevents the reactor water from boiling (giving it a higher temperature, Chapter 5.3), and the hot water is sent to a steam generator that produces steam to drive a turbine. The generation of steam is accomplished without radioactive water coolant reaching the turbine. In the United States, 78% of the reactors are PWRs. An older type, the *boiling water reactor* (BWR), uses boiling water in the reactor to produce steam that directly drives the turbine. The water is then cooled, condensed, and returned to the reactor.

In addition, the coolant acts as a *moderator*. The ^{235}U nuclei react best with "slow" neutrons. The neutrons emitted from the fission reactions are relatively "fast," with energies that are not best suited for ^{235}U fission. The fast neutrons are slowed down, or moderated, by transferring energy to the water molecules in collision processes. After only a few collisions, the neutrons are slowed down to the point at which they efficiently induce fission in the ^{235}U nuclei.

With a continuous-fission chain reaction, the possibility of a nuclear accident is always present. The word *meltdown* is commonly used when discussing such accidents. The

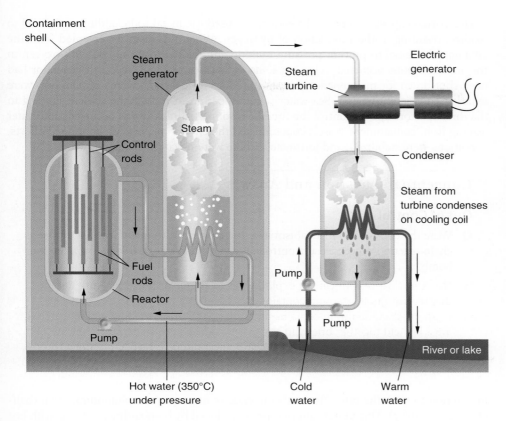

Containment shell

Steam generator

Steam

Control rods

Fuel rods

Reactor

Pump

Steam turbine

Electric generator

Condenser

Steam from turbine condenses on cooling coil

Pump

Pump

River or lake

Hot water (350°C) under pressure

Cold water

Warm water

Figure 10.15 Diagram of a Nuclear Reactor
The nuclear reactor consists of fuel rods with interspersed control rods. By raising or lowering the control rods, an operator can increase or decrease the rate of energy release from the fuel rods. Heat from the fuel rods raises the temperature of the liquid water in the reactor. A pump circulates the hot water to a steam generator, and the resulting steam passes through a turbine that operates an electric generator. The steam leaves the turbine and goes into the condenser, where it liquefies on the cooling coil. A nearby river or lake provides the cold water for the condenser.

coolant must be maintained. If heat energy is not removed continuously and the core becomes partially exposed, then some of the fuel rods may "melt," or fuse. This is called a *partial meltdown*. With the loss of more coolant and the exposure of more of the fuel rods, there is a fissioning mass of fuel pellets becoming extremely hot, fusing, dropping down, melting, and breaching the containing vessel. At this stage, there is a *total meltdown* and radioactive material enters the environment. (This situation is sometimes called the *China Syndrome* because the "melt" is heading downward through the center of the Earth "toward China." Of course, this description is inaccurate because China is not on the other side of the Earth from the United States; both countries are in the Northern Hemisphere).

Well-known accidents occurred in 1979 at the Three Mile Island nuclear plant in Pennsylvania, in 1986 with the reactor at Chernobyl in the Ukraine in Russia, and in 2011 at the Fukushima Daiichi nuclear plant in Japan. At Three Mile Island, a partial meltdown occurred as the result of an accidental shutdown of cooling water. There was a slight fusing of the fuel pellets and the release of large amounts of radioactive material inside the containment building. However, only a small amount of radioactive gases escaped into the environment. At Chernobyl, poor human judgment, including the disconnection of several emergency safety systems, led first to a meltdown, then to an explosion in the reactor core, and finally to a fire. This particular type of reactor used graphite (carbon) blocks for a moderator. Gas explosions caused the carbon to catch fire, radioactive material escaped with the smoke, and weather conditions caused radioactive fallout to spread over many European countries. Several hundred deaths occurred in the immediate region, and it is estimated that as many as 50,000 additional cancer deaths will occur from the long-term effects of the radioactive fallout.

In March 2011, a severe earthquake and tsunami occurred off the northeast coast of Japan (see Chapter 21.5). The boiling water nuclear reactors at the Fukushima Daiichi generating facility were affected when external electrical power was lost in the earthquake and the tsunami waves disabled the backup generators that were to keep the water coolant flowing in the reactors. Without sufficient water, three reactor cores were partially exposed.

This partial exposure generated steam and caused the metal rod cladding of the fuel to oxidize, resulting in the production of hydrogen. When the gases were vented from the containment vessel to prevent pressure buildup and the hydrogen united with oxygen in the air, explosions occurred, releasing some radioactive material. A fourth generator had been shut down for maintenance, but its stored spent fuel rods, which remain hot, were exposed and caught on fire. Sea water was pumped in to replace the coolant flowing in the three reactors and to control the fire. Even so, partial meltdowns occurred, and water leaking from containment vessels contaminated the environment. With continued efforts, conditions were stabilized, and fortunately, there were no complete meltdowns.

Conceptual Question and Answer

Out of Control

Q. Were the control-rod mechanism in a nuclear reactor to malfunction and the chain reaction proceeded uncontrolled, could the reactor explode like a nuclear bomb?

A. No. A nuclear reactor cannot explode like an atomic or nuclear bomb. Recall that reactor-grade uranium contains only about 3% fissionable U-235, whereas weapons-grade uranium contains more than 90%. Also, the high-grade material must be held together briefly in critical mass to achieve an explosive release of energy. A meltdown and gaseous explosions could be possible, but not a tremendous explosion like a nuclear bomb.

In addition to ^{235}U, the other fissionable nuclide of importance is plutonium, ^{239}Pu (half-life of 2.4×10^4 y). This plutonium isotope is produced by bombardment of ^{238}U with fast neutrons, meaning that ^{239}Pu is produced as nuclear reactors operate because not all the neutrons are moderated or slowed down. Being fissionable, ^{239}Pu extends the time before the refueling of a reactor is necessary.

In a *breeder reactor*, the process of producing fissionable ^{239}Pu from ^{238}U is promoted. ^{238}U is otherwise useless for energy production. Breeder reactors are currently being operated in France and Germany, but not in the United States. The ^{239}Pu can be chemically separated from the fission by-products and used as the fuel in an ordinary nuclear reactor.

In addition to concerns about the safety of operating nuclear fission power plants, the other major problem is what to do with the radioactive waste generated. This subject is discussed later after some other considerations.

Did You Learn?

- In nuclear fission, some mass is converted to energy.
- In a self-sustaining chain reaction, each fission event causes one or more fission events, leading to a steady release of energy, and the reaction may grow with sufficient amounts and concentration of fissionable material (supercritical mass).

10.6 Nuclear Fusion

Preview Questions

- Where does nuclear fusion occur "naturally"?
- What are the major advantages of fusion energy production over fission energy production?

Fusion is the process in which smaller nuclei combine to form larger ones with the release of energy. Fusion is the source of energy of the Sun and other stars. In the Sun, the fusion process produces a helium nucleus from four protons (hydrogen nuclei). Also produced are two positrons. The thermonuclear process takes place in several steps (see Chapter 18.2), the net result being

$$4{}_1^1\text{H} \rightarrow {}_2^4\text{He} + 2({}_{+1}^0e) + \text{energy}$$

In the Sun, about 600 million tons of hydrogen is converted into 596 million tons of helium *every second*. The other 4 million tons of matter are converted into energy. Fortunately, the Sun has enough hydrogen to produce energy at its present rate for several billion more years.

Two other examples of fusion reactions are

$$ {}_1^2\text{H} + {}_1^2\text{H} \rightarrow {}_1^3\text{H} + {}_1^1\text{H}$$

and

$$ {}_1^2\text{H} + {}_1^3\text{H} \rightarrow {}_2^4\text{He} + {}_0^1\text{n}$$

In the first reaction, two deuterons fuse to form a triton and a proton. This is termed a D-D (deuteron–deuteron) reaction. In the second example (a D-T reaction), a deuteron and a triton form an alpha particle and a neutron (● Fig. 10.16).

Fusion involves no critical mass or size because there is no chain reaction to maintain. However, the repulsive force between two positively charged nuclei opposes fusing. This force is smallest for hydrogen fusion because the nuclei contain only one proton. To overcome the repulsive forces and initiate fusion, the kinetic energies of the particles must be increased by raising the temperature to about 100 million kelvins. At such high temperatures, the hydrogen atoms are stripped of their electrons and a **plasma** (a gas of free electrons and positively charged ions) results. To achieve fusion, a high temperature is necessary, and the plasma must be confined at a high enough density for the protons (or other nuclei) to collide frequently.

Large amounts of fusion energy have been released in an uncontrolled manner in a hydrogen bomb (H-bomb), where a fission bomb is used to supply the energy needed to initiate the fusion reaction (● Fig. 10.17). Unfortunately, controlled fusion for commercial use remains elusive. Controlled fusion might be accomplished by steadily adding fuel

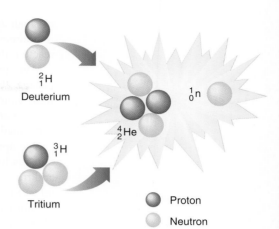

Figure 10.16 A D-T Fusion Reaction
The combination of a deuteron (D) and a triton (T) to produce an alpha particle and a neutron is one example of fusion. Nuclei of other elements of low atomic mass also can undergo fusion to produce heavier, more stable nuclei and release energy in the process.

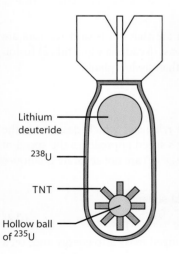

Figure 10.17 H-Bomb
The diagram shows the basic elements of a hydrogen bomb. To detonate an H-bomb, the TNT is exploded, forcing the ${}^{235}\text{U}$ together to get a supercritical mass and a fission explosion (a small atomic bomb, so to speak). The fusionable material is deuterium in the lithium deuteride (LiD). When it is heated to a plasma, D-D fusion reactions occur. Neutrons from the fission explosion react with the lithium to give tritium (${}^3\text{H}$), and then D-T fusion reactions also take place. The bomb is surrounded with ${}^{238}\text{U}$, which tops off the explosion with a fission reaction. The result is shown in the photo.

in small amounts to a fusion reactor. Since the D-T reaction has the lowest temperature requirement (about 100 million K) of any fusion reaction, it is likely to be the first fusion reaction developed as an energy source.

Major problems arise in reaching such temperatures and in confining the high-temperature plasma. If the plasma were to touch the reactor walls, then it would cool rapidly, but the walls would not melt. Even though the plasma is nearly 100 million K above the melting point of any material, the total quantity of heat that could be transferred from the plasma is very small because the plasma's concentration is extremely low.

One approach to controlled fusion is *inertial confinement*, a technique in which simultaneous high-energy laser pulses from all sides cause a fuel pellet containing deuterium and tritium to implode, resulting in compression and high temperatures. If the pellet stays intact for a sufficient time, then fusion is initiated.

Another approach to controlled fusion is *magnetic confinement*. Because a plasma is a gas of charged particles, it can be controlled and manipulated with electric and magnetic fields. A nuclear fusion reactor called a *tokomak* uses a doughnut-shaped magnetic field to hold the plasma away from any material. Electric fields produce currents that raise the temperature of the plasma.

Plasma temperatures, densities, and confinement times have been problems with magnetic and inertial confinements, and no one knows when commercial energy production via nuclear fusion can be expected. Even so, fusion is a promising energy source because of three advantages over fission:

1. The low cost and abundance of deuterium, which can be extracted inexpensively from water. Scientists estimate that the deuterium in the top 2 inches of water in Lake Erie could provide fusion energy equal to the combustion energy in all the world's oil reserves. On the other hand, uranium for fission is scarce, expensive, and hazardous to mine.

2. Dramatically reduced nuclear waste disposal problems. Some fusion by-products are radioactive because of nuclear reactions involving the neutrons that are formed in the D-T reactions, but they have relatively short half-lives compared with those of fission wastes.

3. Fusion reactors could not get out of control. In the event of a system failure in a fusion plant, the reaction chamber would immediately cool down and energy production would halt.

The two disadvantages of fusion compared with fission are that (1) fission reactors are presently operational (commercial fusion reactors are at least decades away) and (2) fusion plants will probably be more costly to build and operate than fission plants.

Nuclear Reactions and Energy

In 1905, Albert Einstein published his *special theory of relativity*, which deals with the changes that occur in mass, length, and time as an object's speed approaches the speed of light (c). The theory also predicted that mass (m) and energy (E) are not separate quantities but are related by the equation

$$\text{energy} = \text{mass} \times \text{the speed of light squared}$$
$$E = mc^2 \tag{10.2}$$

The prediction proved correct. Scientists have indeed changed mass into energy and, on a very small scale, have converted energy into mass.

For example, a mass of 1.0 g (0.0010 kg) has an equivalent energy of

$$E = mc^2 = (0.0010 \text{ kg})(3.00 \times 10^8 \text{ m/s})^2$$
$$= 90 \times 10^{12} \text{ J}$$

This 90 *trillion* joules is the same amount of energy that is released by the explosion of about 20,000 *tons* of TNT. Such calculations convinced scientists that nuclear reactions, in which just a very small amount of mass was "lost," were a potential source of vast amounts of energy.

The units of mass and energy commonly used in nuclear physics differ from those discussed in preceding chapters. Mass is usually given in atomic mass units (u), and energy is usually given in mega electron volts, MeV (1 MeV $= 1.60 \times 10^{-13}$ J). With these units, Einstein's equation reveals that 1 u of mass has the energy equivalent of 931 MeV, so there are 931 MeV/u (931 MeV per atomic mass unit).

To determine the change in mass and hence the energy released or absorbed in any nuclear process, just add up the masses of all reactant particles and from that sum subtract the total mass of all product particles. If an increase in mass has taken place, then the reaction is *endoergic* (absorbs energy) by that number of atomic mass units times 931 MeV/u. As is more common, if a decrease in mass has resulted, then the reaction is *exoergic* (releases energy) by that number of atomic mass units times 931 MeV/u. The decrease in mass in a nuclear reaction is called the **mass defect**.

EXAMPLE 10.9 Calculating Mass and Energy Changes in Nuclear Reactions

Calculate the mass defect and the corresponding energy released during this typical fission reaction:*

$$^{236}_{92}\text{U} \rightarrow \ ^{88}_{36}\text{Kr} \ + \ ^{144}_{56}\text{U} \ + \ 4^{1}_{0}\text{n}$$
$$(236.04556 \text{ u}) \quad (87.91445 \text{ u}) \quad (143.92284 \text{ u}) \quad (4 \times 1.00867 \text{ u})$$

Solution

The total mass on the left of the arrow is 236.04556 u. Adding the masses of the particles on the right gives 235.87197 u. The difference (0.17359 u) is the mass defect, which has been converted to

$$(0.17359 \text{ u})(931 \text{ MeV/u}) = 162 \text{ MeV of energy}$$

Thus, during the reaction 0.17359 u of mass is converted to 162 MeV of energy.

Confidence Exercise 10.9

Calculate the mass defect and the corresponding energy released during a D-T fusion reaction:

$$^{2}_{1}\text{H} \ + \ ^{3}_{1}\text{H} \ \rightarrow \ ^{4}_{2}\text{He} \ + \ ^{1}_{0}\text{n}$$
$$(2.0140 \text{ u}) \quad (3.0161 \text{ u}) \quad (4.0026 \text{ u}) \quad (1.0087 \text{ u})$$

When nuclear fuels are compared, it is apparent that *kilogram for kilogram*, more energy is available from fusion than from fission. Comparing fission and fusion with energy production by ordinary chemical reactions, the fission of 1 kg of uranium-235 provides energy equal to burning 2 million kg of coal, whereas the fusion of 1 kg of deuterium releases the same amount of energy as burning of 40 million kg of coal.

● Figure 10.18 plots the relative stability of various nuclei as a function of the mass number (the number of nucleons) and shows that energy can be released in both nuclear fission *and* nuclear fusion. Note that fission of heavy nuclei at the far right of the curve to intermediate-size nuclei in the middle leads upward on the curve. Fusion of small nuclei on the left to larger nuclei farther to the right also leads upward on the curve. Any reaction that leads *upward* on the curve in Fig. 10.18 releases energy because such a reaction is accompanied by a mass defect. Basically, each nucleon in the reactant nucleus (or nuclei) loses a little mass in the process.

Any nuclear reaction in which the products are lower on the curve than the reactants can proceed only with a net increase in mass and a corresponding net absorption of energy.

---

*Because we are dealing with *differences* in mass, either the masses of the atoms or the masses of just their nuclei can be used. The number of electrons is the same on each side of the equation and thus does not affect the mass difference. The masses of the atoms are used because they are more easily found in handbooks.

Figure 10.18 The Relative Stability of Nuclei

To obtain more stability (with the release of energy), the fission of more massive nuclei (right) to less massive nuclei is upward on the curve. The fusion of less massive nuclei into more massive nuclei (left) is upward on the curve. Any reaction that leads upward on the curve releases energy.

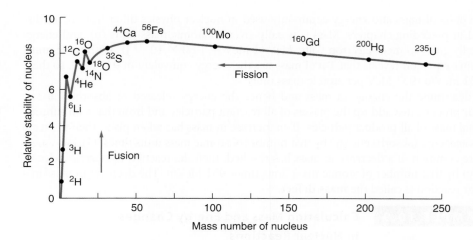

One type of nucleus cannot give a net release of nuclear energy either by fission or by fusion. Of course, it is the one at the top of the curve, ^{56}Fe (iron-56). You cannot go higher than the top, so no net energy will be released either by splitting ^{56}Fe into smaller nuclei or by fusing several ^{56}Fe into a larger nucleus.

Did You Learn?

● The Sun's energy results from the fusion process of converting hydrogen nuclei into helium nuclei.

● Fusion advantages over fission: (1) low cost and abundance of fuel (deuterium), (2) reduced nuclear waste, and (3) little chance of reaction going out of control.

10.7 Effects of Radiation

Preview Questions

● What is "ionizing" radiation, and why is it harmful?

● How do particles and rays rate in protective shielding?

It is a common misconception that radioactivity is something new in the environment. Radioactivity has been around far longer than humans as a natural part of the environment. Still, we must be aware of the dangers associated with radiation.

Radiation that is energetic enough to knock electrons out of atoms or molecules and form ions is classified as *ionizing radiation*. Alpha particles, beta particles, neutrons, gamma rays, and X-rays all fall into this category. Such radiation can damage or even kill living cells, and it is particularly harmful when it affects protein and DNA molecules involved in cell reproduction. Ionizing radiation is especially dangerous because you cannot see, smell, taste, or feel it.

Radiation doses are measured in *rads* (short for radiation *a*bsorbed *d*ose), where 1 rad corresponds to 0.01 joule of energy deposited per kilogram of tissue. Because alpha, beta, and gamma radiations differ in penetrating ability and ionizing capabilities, both the energy dose of the radiation *and* its effectiveness in causing human tissue damage must be considered. The *rem* (short for *r*oentgen *e*quivalent for *m*an), which takes into account both the dosage and its relative biological effectiveness, is the unit we generally use when discussing biological effects of radiation.*

---

*The SI unit of radiation biological effectiveness is the sievert (Sv), where 1 Sv = 100 rem (named after Rolf Sievert, a Swedish medical physicist).

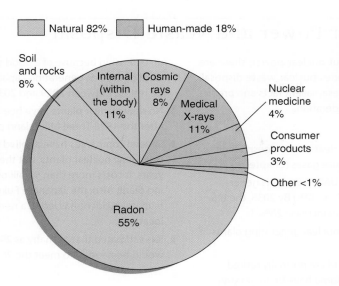

Natural 82%   Human-made 18%

Soil and rocks 8%

Internal (within the body) 11%

Cosmic rays 8%

Medical X-rays 11%

Nuclear medicine 4%

Consumer products 3%

Other <1%

Radon 55%

Figure 10.19 Sources of Exposure to Radiation
On average, each person in the United States receives a yearly radiation exposure of 0.2 rem, of which 82% is from the natural sources. The other 18% is from human-made sources.

The average U.S. citizen receives about 0.2 rem of natural and human-made background radiation each year. ● Figure 10.19 shows that about 82% of this background radiation comes from natural sources and about 18% from human activities. However, individual exposures vary widely, depending on location, occupation, and personal habits.

Sources of natural radiation include cosmic rays from outer space. Travel in high-flying jetliners and living in high-altitude cities, such as Denver, Colorado, entail more exposure to this part of the background radiation. Other sources of natural background radiation include radionuclides in the rocks and minerals in our environment. One of the decay products of ^{238}U is radon-222, an inert noble gas that quickly alpha decays (half-life = 3.8 days) into an isotope of polonium (^{218}Po). Uranium-238 occurs naturally in the environment, as does its by-product radon-222. As a gas, radon can seep from the ground into the air and into a building, primarily thorough the foundation with cracks in the basement floor and drains.

Radon-laden air breathed into the lungs can decay into polonium-218. This isotope can settle in the lungs, where it begins (half-life = 3 min) a relatively short decay series with a sequence of alpha, beta, and gamma emissions, leading to mutations in the lung tissue and causing cancer.

The Environmental Protection Agency estimates that nearly 1 out of 15 homes in the United States has radon at or above the recommended levels. There are relatively inexpensive, do-it-yourself kits to check on radon levels in a residence.

Human-made sources of radiation include X-rays and radioisotopes used in medical procedures, fallout from nuclear testing, tobacco smoke, nuclear wastes, and emissions from power plants. Ironically, because fossil fuels contain traces of uranium, thorium, and their daughter nuclei, more radioactive isotopes are released into the atmosphere from power plants burning coal and oil than from nuclear power plants.

Shielding is used to decrease radiation exposure. Clothing and our skin are sufficient protection against alpha particles, unless the particles are ingested or inhaled. Beta particles can burn the skin and penetrate into body tissue, but not far enough to affect internal organs. Heavy clothing can shield against beta particles. Gamma rays, X-rays, and neutrons are more difficult to stop (● Fig. 10.20). Protective shielding from these rays requires thick lead, concrete, or earth.

So, with the knowledge gained in this chapter, let's consider a final, but very important, nuclear topic. See the **Highlight: Nuclear Power and Waste Disposal**.

Did You Learn?

● Ionizing radiation is radiation energetic enough to knock electrons out of atoms or molecules and form ions. Such radiation can damage cells and produce harmful health hazards.

Highlight Nuclear Power and Waste Disposal

In making reasoned judgments about nuclear power, there are many aspects to consider. This includes nuclear waste disposal. Rather than present a narrative on these, salient facts and predictions will be presented for your consideration.

Nuclear Power

▶ Unlike coal, oil, and natural gas, nuclear power doesn't emit carbon dioxide and other greenhouse gases (Chapter 19.2).

▶ About 20% of the electricity in the United States is generated by nuclear power. (In France, it is 80%.) By 2035, the U.S. demand for electricity is expected to increase 28%.

▶ In the United States, there are 104 nuclear generating plants at 65 locations in 31 states (Fig. 1).

▶ Existing nuclear plants are aging and are normally retired after 40 to 60 years of service, but some have been granted

an extension because of a good safety record. More than one-third of the U.S. generating capacity of nuclear plants should be retired between 2029 and 2035.

▶ No new nuclear plants have been built in the United States after the 1978 Three Mile Island partial meltdown.

▶ Several companies have applied for regulatory approval to build new nuclear plants, but the process and building takes years. It costs more than $2 billion to build a nuclear generating plant. Also, the Japanese Fukushima Daiichi earthquake-tsunami incident has led to a re-evaluation of safe building locations.

▶ It is estimated that as many as 29 new generating plants would be needed to meet the 2035 electricity demand.

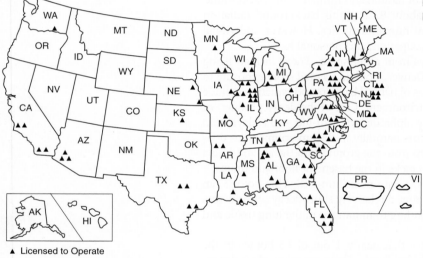

Figure 1 Location of Nuclear Power Reactors in the U.S.

▲ Licensed to Operate

● Alpha particles and beta particles are easily shielded, but gamma rays, X-rays, and neutrons are not. Alpha particles can be shielded by clothing and skin, and beta particles can be shielded by heavy clothing.

10.8 Elementary Particles

Preview Questions

● Why are some subatomic particles called "elementary" particles?

● What are "exchange" particles?

The search for the *fundamental* "building blocks" of nature is as old as science itself. The simple picture of indivisible atoms gave way to a model of the atom with subatomic particles. By the 1930s, scientists had identified four of these particles: the electron, proton,

Highlight

Nuclear Waste

▶ Nuclear generating plants generate nuclear wastes classified as "low level" and "high level."

▶ Low-level nuclear waste usually comes from material used to handle highly radioactive parts of a nuclear reactor, such as cooling water pipes. Waste from medical procedures involving radioactive treatment is also low level.

▶ High-level radioactive waste is generally material from nuclear reactor cores and nuclear weapons. The waste includes uranium, plutonium, and other highly radioactive isotopes made during fission. These isotopes have extremely long half-lives, sometimes longer than 100,000 years.

▶ Generating plants in the United States produce on the order of 32,000 tons of nuclear waste annually.

How do we get rid of or dispose of nuclear waste?

▶ The most promising disposal method at this time is a geologic repository. In this process, waste is packaged and is stored deep below the Earth's surface in underground tunnels or chambers.

▶ The location of such a repository must be geologically "safe," without the possibility of groundwater seepage and with low earthquake probability.

▶ A proposed site for a deep geological repository was Yucca Mountain in southwest Nevada, 100 miles from Las Vegas. It was scheduled to accept waste in 1998. However, the opening was delayed for more than a decade, and in 2010, after more than $10 million was spent, the project was cancelled.

▶ There is one deep geological repository in the United States, the Waste Isolation Pilot Plant (or WIPP), 26 miles east of Carlsbad, New Mexico. It uses tunnels in salt formations. WIPP began operation in 1999 and is expected to continue disposal until 2070. Most of the waste comes from government storage sites.

Some Alternatives?

▶ Because of delays with adequate underground repositories, a number of power plants in the United States have resorted to onsite "dry cast storage" where waste is stored in steel and concrete aboveground casts.

▶ Weapons-grade plutonium destined for disposal can be mixed with uranium, producing a fuel that can be used in nuclear reactors.

▶ Nuclear waste could be stored in large salt domes. Once the waste is stored, the salt oozes around it, becoming geologically stable for 50 million to 100 million years, but there is no further access to the waste.

▶ It has even been suggested to load the waste on a rocket and shoot it into deep space. However, what would happen if the rocket malfunctioned and exploded in the Earth's atmosphere?

▶ More realistic is a subductive waste disposal method. Subduction refers to a process in which one tectonic plate slides underneath another and is absorbed in the Earth's mantle (see Chapter 21.1). Were a repository located on a subducting plate, both the waste and the plate would be absorbed into the mantle. The best site for a plate repository would be on the ocean floor where plate subduction occurs. However, the waste would have to be packaged for a long stay because subduction progresses at only a few centimeters per year.

Have you got any ideas about possibilities for nuclear waste disposal?

---

neutron, and photon. Since then, more than 200 various particles have been discovered coming from the nucleus. They are called **elementary particles** because it is not certain that they are fundamental. You may have heard of some of them, such as neutrinos, mesons, bosons, lambda particles, and others. (Only a few particles and theories will be considered here.)

Scientists believe that most elementary particles do not exist outside the nucleus but rather are created when the nucleus is disrupted. Some elementary particles are thought to be the *exchange particles* responsible for the four fundamental interactions: electromagnetic, strong, weak, and gravitational. For example, in one theory the "exchange" particle of the strong nuclear interaction is the pi meson, or pion. Nuclear particles with a strong interaction are viewed as interacting by exchanging pions back and forth (analogous to the way you interact with someone by tossing a beach ball back and forth). All strongly interacting particles, which include the nuclear protons and neutrons, are called *hadrons*.

In 1964, Murray Gell-Mann at the California Institute of Technology and George Zweig in Switzerland independently suggested that all hadrons, the elementary particles with the strong interaction, were made up of no more than three subatomic particles with fractional

Figure 10.20 Penetration of Radiation
Alpha particles cannot penetrate clothing or skin. Beta particles can slightly penetrate body tissue. However, gamma rays, X-rays, and neutrons can penetrate an arm easily.

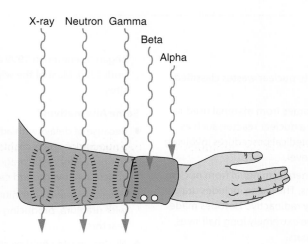

X-ray   Neutron   Gamma
Beta
Alpha

electronic charges, called *quarks*.* For instance, a nuclear proton is thought to consist of three quarks (two with a $+\frac{2}{3}$ and one with $-\frac{1}{3}$ electronic charge).

Quarks apparently do not exist as free particles but are permanently bound inside hadrons, so we never see these fractional electronic charges in nature. However, there is indirect experimental evidence for their existence.

Other exchange particles, W and Z bosons, were discovered for the nuclear weak force that is important in governing the stability of basic matter particles. This discovery generated an *electroweak theory* that unified the electromagnetic and weak interactions. The electroweak theory and the strong force hadron theory then combined into a *grand unified theory* (GUT) or *standard model*. Thus, three forces (electromagnetic, strong, and weak) have been combined into a single theory. The gravitational force is not included in this theory. Scientists would like to believe that all forces could be combined and manifest a single *superforce*.

Elementary particles are currently studied in the Large Hadron Collider (LHC), a huge particle accelerator built on the French–Swiss border (● Fig. 10.21). It became operational in 2010, after almost 20 years of building its 10-km-diameter, 27-km-circumference circular tunnels. Scientists build particle accelerators to collide particles at high energies in hope of releasing elementary particles from the nucleus, and the LHC is the biggest particle accelerator built so far. Two counterorbiting proton beams make 11,000 round trips per second at speeds close to the speed of light, and more than 1200 superconducting magnets provide the centripetal magnetic force.

An inconsistency exists in the standard model due to a large mass difference between the exchange particles. This inconsistency led to the proposal of the *Higgs boson* particle by British physicist Peter Higgs in the 1960s. If the Higgs boson exists, then it would explain why particles have mass and would resolve the wide differences in the mass of the standard model's exchange particles. If the energy of the LHC is enough to produce a free Higgs boson particle, then it could provide the fundamental knowledge about the basic makeup of matter. The Higgs boson is often popularized as the "God particle."

In Chapter 10.3, it was mentioned that the positron ($_{+1}^{0}e$) was the *antiparticle* of the electron. *Antimatter* is believed to be composed of antiparticles in the same way that normal matter is composed of particles. For example, a positron and an antiproton can form an antihydrogen atom in the same way that an electron and a proton form a normal hydrogen atom. The mixing of particles and their antiparticles or matter–antimatter causes an annihilation of the particles with a release of energy.

Antiparticles have been created and quickly annihilated in particle accelerators, but they tend to disappear so fast that scientists do not have time to study them. Antihydrogen atoms

---

*The name is from a line in James Joyce's novel *Finnegans Wake*, "Three quarks for Muster Mark!" The "three quarks" denote the children of Mr. Finn, who sometimes appear as Mister (Muster) Mark. It is a bit strange, but there are also strange quarks.

Figure 10.21 Large Hadron Collider (LHC)
(a) A safety inspector riding a bicycle along the LHC tunnel at CERN (the European particle physics laboratory) near Geneva, Switzerland. The LHC is a 27-kilometer (17 mile) -long-underground ring of superconducting magnets housed in a pipe-like structure. (b) Aerial view of countryside outside Geneva, Switzerland. Beneath the fields lies a 27-kilometer-circumference tunnel that houses the large particle accelerator used to study elementary particles.

have been created in the LHC that may be able to stay around long enough for possible study. Such study would be an exciting new field for energy with antimatter–matter propulsion.

Conceptual Question and Answer

Star Trek Adventure

Q. When antimatter comes in contact with regular matter, annihilation occurs with the release of energy. In the science fiction series *Star Trek*, antimatter–matter energy was used as propulsion for the starship *Enterprise*, with the antimatter being stored on board in antimatter pods. Since antimatter reacts with matter, what could be used to contain the antimatter?

A. Obviously the container couldn't be a regular matter container or tank. What is a container without ordinary walls? Plasma is contained by magnetic fields (magnetic confinement) (Chapter 10.6). Charged antiparticles might be contained in a magnetic field "container."

The study of elementary particles may yield unknown information about forces and matter. In addition to exploring the Higgs boson theory, others theories predict that the LHC has the potential to provide information on other forms of matter, such as dark matter (Chapter 18.7), black holes (Chapter 18.8), and magnetic monopoles (Chapter 8.4). Stay tuned for some interesting results.

Did You Learn?

- Particles are called elementary when it is not certain if they are fundamental.

- Exchange particles are believed to be responsible for the interaction of fundamental forces. Some theoretical exchange particles are the pi meson (pion) for the strong nuclear force, and W and Z bosons for the nuclear weak force.

KEY TERMS

1. electrons (10.2)
2. nucleus
3. protons
4. neutrons
5. nucleons
6. atomic number
7. element
8. neutron number
9. mass number
10. isotopes
11. atomic mass
12. strong nuclear force
13. radioactive isotope (10.3)
14. radioactivity
15. alpha decay
16. beta decay
17. gamma decay
18. half-life
19. carbon-14 dating
20. fission (10.5)
21. chain reaction
22. critical mass
23. fusion (10.6)
24. plasma
25. mass defect
26. elementary particle

MATCHING

For each of the following items, fill in the number of the appropriate Key Term from the preceding list. Compare your answers with those at the back of the book.

a. _____ Fundamental force that holds the nucleus together

b. _____ Process in which smaller nuclei combine to form larger ones

c. _____ Neutral particles in atoms

d. _____ Spontaneous process of nuclei changing by emitting particles or rays

e. _____ Negatively charged particles in atoms

f. _____ Radioactive decay in which electrons are emitted

g. _____ Specific types of nuclei that are unstable

h. _____ A, the number of protons plus neutrons in a nucleus

i. _____ The central core of an atom

j. _____ Process in which a large nucleus splits and emits neutrons

k. _____ Used to date organic objects

l. _____ Positively charged particles in atoms

m. _____ A hot gas of electrons and ions

n. _____ Z, the number of protons in an atom

o. _____ The minimum amount of fissionable material needed to sustain a chain reaction

p. _____ N, the number of neutrons in a nucleus

q. _____ The weighted average mass of atoms of an element in a naturally occurring sample

r. _____ Disintegration of a nucleus, with the emission of a helium nucleus

s. _____ A substance in which all the atoms have the same number of protons

t. _____ The time it takes for the decay of half the atoms in a sample

u. _____ Process in which one initial reaction triggers a growing number of subsequent reactions

v. _____ Collective term for nuclear protons and neutrons

w. _____ Forms of atoms having the same number of protons but differing in number of neutrons

x. _____ The decrease in mass during a nuclear reaction

y. _____ Disintegration of a nucleus, with the emission of a high-energy photon

z. _____ Do not exist outside of the nucleus

MULTIPLE CHOICE

Compare your answers with those at the back of the book.

1. Which scientist devised the symbol notation we now use for elements? (10.1)
   (a) Newton
   (b) Berzelius
   (c) Dalton
   (d) Einstein

2. What is the symbol notation for the element potassium? (10.1)
   (a) P   (b) Po   (c) Pt   (d) K

3. How many neutrons are in the nucleus of the atom $^{35}_{17}Cl$? (10.2)
   (a) 35   (b) 17   (c) 18   (d) 52

4. Is a nucleon (a) a proton, (b) a neutron, (c) an electron, or (d) both a proton and a neutron? (10.2)

5. Which radioactive decay mode does not result in a different nuclide? (10.3)
   (a) alpha   (b) beta
   (c) gamma   (d) all the preceding

6. What is the missing particle in the nuclear decay $^{179}_{79}Au \rightarrow {}^{175}_{77}Ir + \underline{\quad}$? (10.3)
   (a) deuteron
   (b) neutron
   (c) beta particle
   (d) alpha particle

7. The majority of stable isotopes belong to which category? (10.3)
   (a) odd–odd
   (b) even–even
   (c) even–odd
   (d) odd–even

8. Which of the following scientists discovered radioactivity? (10.3)
   (a) Rutherford
   (b) Heisenberg
   (c) Becquerel
   (d) Pierre Curie

9. How many half-lives would it take for a sample of a radioactive isotope to decrease its activity to $\frac{1}{32}$ of the original amount? (10.3)
   (a) 5   (b) 16   (c) 6   (d) 32

10. Which of the following is not conserved in all nuclear reactions?
    (a) nucleons
    (b) mass number,
    (c) atomic number
    (d) neutron number

11. Which of the following completes the reaction
    $^{2}_{1}H + ^{98}_{42}Mo \rightarrow$ ___ $+ ^{1}_{0}n$? (10.4)
    (a) $^{97}_{42}Mo$ (b) $^{100}_{44}Ru$
    (c) $^{99}_{43}Tc$ (d) $^{93}_{41}Nb$

12. What is the appropriate procedure to decrease the heat output of a fission reactor core during a crisis? (10.5)
    (a) Insert the control rods farther.
    (b) Remove fuel rods.
    (c) Increase the level of coolant.
    (d) Decrease the amount of moderator.

13. What is a very hot gas of nuclei and electrons called? (10.6)
    (a) tokomak
    (b) laser
    (c) plasma
    (d) ideal gas

14. Which unit is most closely associated with the biological effects of radiation? (10.7)
    (a) the curie
    (b) the rem
    (c) the becquerel
    (d) the cpm

15. What is the theoretical exchange particle for the nuclear weak force? (10.8)
    (a) Z particle
    (b) pion
    (c) graviton
    (d) gluon

FILL IN THE BLANK

Compare your answers with those at the back of the book.

1. K is the symbol for the element ___. (10.1)

2. All atomic masses are based on an atom of ___. (10.2)

3. The collective name for neutrons and protons in a nucleus is ___. (10.2)

4. Carbon-12, carbon-13, and carbon-14 are ___. (10.2)

5. No stable nuclides exist that have Z greater than ___. (10.3)

6. The nuclear notation $^{0}_{-1}e$ refers to a(n) ___. (10.3)

7. The amount of a radioactive isotope will have dropped to 12.5% of what it was originally after ___ half-lives have elapsed. (10.3)

8. The proton number of the daughter nucleus in beta decay is ___ than that of the parent nucleus. (10.3)

9. In nuclear reactions, both atomic number and ___ are conserved. (10.4)

10. For an atomic bomb to explode, a(n) ___ mass is necessary. (10.5)

11. In discussions of nuclear fusion reactions, the letter D stands for ___. (10.6)

12. Of the average amount of radiation received by a person in the United States, ___% comes from natural sources. (10.7)

13. All hadrons are believed to be made up of ___.

SHORT ANSWER

10.1 Symbols of the Elements

1. What are the chemical symbols for (a) carbon, (b) chlorine, and (c) lead?

2. What are the names of the elements with the symbols (a) N, (b) He, and (c) Fe?

3. Why is the symbol for the transuranic element Rutherfordium Rf instead of Ru?

10.2 The Atomic Nucleus

4. Why is the neutron number N equal to the mass number A minus the atomic number Z?

5. What is the collective name of the two particles that make up a nucleus?

6. What evidence is there to support the idea that the strong nuclear force is stronger than the electric force?

7. The diameter of the uranium atom is about the same as that of a hydrogen atom. What does that imply about the structure of the atom?

8. About what percentage of the mass of an atom is contained in the nucleus?

9. What do the letters Z, A, and N in nuclear notation stand for?

10. State the special names by which the isotopes ^{1}H, ^{2}H, and ^{3}H are known.

11. What are the nuclear notations for the isotopes of hydrogen, using H, D, and T? What names are given to these nuclei?

12. On which atom are all atomic masses based? What mass is assigned to that atom?

13. Name the force that holds a nucleus together. At what distance does this force drop to zero?

10.3 Radioactivity and Half-Life

14. What convincing evidence is there that radioactivity is a nuclear effect and not an atomic effect?

15. How does the charge of a nucleus change with beta decay?

16. How does the mass of a nucleus change with alpha decay?

17. Indicate which of the three types of radiation—alpha, beta, or gamma—each of the following phrases describes.
    (a) is not deflected by a magnet
    (b) has a negative charge
    (c) consists of ions
    (d) is similar to X-rays
    (e) has a positive charge

18. After three half-lives have gone by, what fraction of a sample of a radioactive isotope remains?

19. Why can't carbon-14 dating be used for ages 50,000 years and older?

10.4 Nuclear Reactions

20. Use the letters a, A, B, and b to write the general form of a nuclear reaction.

21. How does the common household smoke alarm detect smoke?

22. What is the principle of neutron activation analysis, and how is it used?

10.5 Nuclear Fission

23. What subatomic particle is emitted when a nucleus fissions?

24. In terms of a chain reaction, explain what is meant by critical mass, subcritical mass, and supercritical mass.

25. What percentage of natural uranium is fissionable ^{235}U? To what percentage must it be enriched for use in a U.S. nuclear reactor? For use in nuclear weapons?

26. What is a "meltdown?" How is this related to the "China syndrome"?

27. Both control rods and moderators are involved with neutrons in a nuclear reactor. What is the role of each?

28. Why can't nuclear reactors accidentally cause a nuclear explosion like an atomic bomb?

29. Fission was once referred to as "splitting the atom." Is this terminology correct?

30. During operation, breeder reactors make fissionable fuel from nonfissionable material. What is the fuel made, and what is the nonfissionable material used?

10.6 Nuclear Fusion

31. The fusion of what element allows the Sun to emit such enormous amounts of energy?

32. In discussions of nuclear fusion, what do the letters D and T stand for?

33. What is a plasma? Distinguish between magnetic and inertial confinements. Why is confinement such a problem for fusion?

34. Briefly list three advantages and two disadvantages of energy production by fusion compared with by fission.

35. The equation $E = mc^2$ was developed by which scientist? Identify what each of the letters in the equation stands for.

36. Why is an atomic bomb needed to start a hydrogen bomb?

37. What term is applied to a nuclear reaction if the products have less mass than the reactants? What term is applied to the difference in mass in such a case?

38. Show by means of sketches the nuclear processes by which energy can be released by both fission and fusion.

10.7 Effects of Radiation

39. What is ionizing radiation, and what problems can it cause?

40. How do nuclear radiations vary in terms of shielding?

10.8 Elementary Particles

41. What are exchange particles, and how do they relate to the fundamental forces?

42. How many quarks are believed to make up a proton?

VISUAL CONNECTION

Visualize the connections and give answers for the blanks. Compare your answers with those given at the back of the book.

Constituents of the Atom

APPLYING YOUR KNOWLEDGE

1. Suppose a magnetic field instead of an electric field were used in Fig. 10.5 to distinguish nuclear radiations. What would be observed?

2. The technique of carbon-14 dating relies on the assumption that the cosmic-ray intensity has been constant for at least the last 50,000 years. Suppose it was discovered that the cosmic-ray intensity was much greater 10,000 years ago. How would this discovery affect the ages of samples that have already been dated?

3. Would you rather live downwind of a nuclear power plant or downwind of a coal-burning power plant?

4. What steps might you take to lower your exposure to ionizing radiation?

5. If the Higgs boson were confirmed, what effect would this have on the theory of matter?

IMPORTANT EQUATIONS

Neutron Number = Mass Number − Atomic Number:

$$N = A - Z \tag{10.1}$$

Mass–Energy: $E = mc^2$ (10.2)

EXERCISES

10.2 The Atomic Nucleus

1. Fill in the nine gaps in this table.

Element symbol	B		
Protons		9	
Neutrons		10	
Electrons			18
Mass number	11		40

Answer: First col.: 5, 6, 5; second col.: F, 9, 19; third col.: Ar, 18, 22

2. Fill in the nine gaps in this table.

Element symbol	Ga		
Protons		15	
Neutrons	39		20
Electrons			17
Mass number		31	

3. Oxygen ($_8$O) has three stable isotopes with consecutive mass numbers. Write the complete nuclear symbol (with neutron number) for each.

Answer: $^{16}_{8}$O$_8$, $^{17}_{8}$O$_9$, $^{18}_{8}$O$_{10}$

4. Show that the neutron number for the following nuclides generally exceeds the atomic number for nuclei with atomic numbers greater than 20: lithium-6, bromine-80, silicon-28, titanium-48, fluorine-19, and platinum-179.

10.3 Radioactivity and Half-Life

5. Complete the following equations for nuclear decay, and state whether each process is alpha decay, beta decay, or gamma decay.
   (a) $^{46}_{21}$Sc* → $^{46}_{21}$Sc + ___
   (b) $^{232}_{90}$Th → ___ + $^{4}_{2}$He
   (c) $^{47}_{21}$Sc → $^{47}_{22}$Ti + ___

Answer: (a) γ, gamma (b) $^{228}_{88}$Ra, alpha (c) $^{0}_{-1}$e, b, beta

6. Complete the following equations for nuclear decay, and state whether each process is alpha decay, beta decay, or gamma decay.
   (a) $^{8}_{5}$B → ___ + $^{0}_{-1}$e
   (b) $^{210}_{84}$Po → $^{206}_{82}$Pb + ___
   (c) $^{207}_{84}$Po* → $^{207}_{84}$Po + ___

7. Write the equation for each of the following.
   (a) alpha decay of $^{226}_{88}$Ra
   (b) beta decay of $^{60}_{27}$Co

Answer: (a) $^{226}_{88}$Ra → $^{222}_{86}$Rn + $^{4}_{2}$He (b) $^{60}_{27}$Co → $^{60}_{28}$Ni + $^{0}_{-1}$e

8. Actinium-225 ($^{225}_{89}$Ac) undergoes alpha decay.
   (a) Write the equation.
   (b) The daughter formed in part (a) undergoes beta decay. Write the equation.

9. Radon-222 ($^{222}_{86}$Rn), a radioactive gas, undergoes alpha decay. (a) What is the daughter nucleus in this process? (b) The daughter nucleus undergoes both beta and alpha decay. What is the "granddaughter" nucleus in each case?

Answer: (a) $^{218}_{84}$Po, (b) $^{218}_{85}$At and $^{214}_{82}$Pb

10. A radioactive decay series called the neptunium-237 series is shown in ● Fig. 10.22. (a) What is the decay mode for each of the sequential decays? Notice the double decay mode toward the end of the series. (b) Determine the daughter nucleus at the end of each decay. (You can find information on astatine and francium given in the Highlight: Number of Naturally Occurring Elements.)

11. Pick the radioactive isotope in each set. Explain your choice.
   (a) $^{249}_{98}$Cf $^{12}_{6}$C
   (b) $^{79}_{35}$Br $^{76}_{33}$As
   (c) $^{15}_{8}$O $^{17}_{8}$O

Answer: (a) $^{249}_{98}$Cf (Z > 83), (b) $^{76}_{33}$As (odd-odd), (c) $^{15}_{8}$O (fewer n than p)

12. Pick the radioactive isotope in each set. Explain your choice.
   (a) $^{17}_{9}$F $^{32}_{16}$S
   (b) $^{209}_{83}$Bi $^{226}_{88}$Ra
   (c) $^{23}_{11}$Na $^{20}_{9}$F

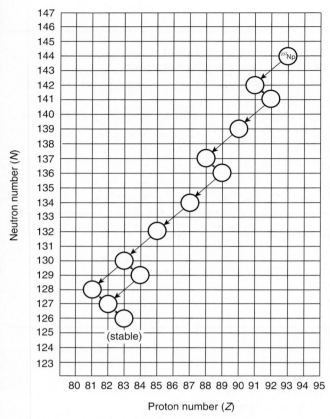

Figure 10.22 The neptunium-237 series. See Exercise 10.

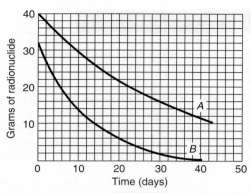

Figure 10.23 See Exercise 15.

13. Technetium-99 (half-life = 6.0 h) is used in medical imaging. How many half-lives would go by in 36 h?

Answer: six half-lives

14. How many half-lives would have to elapse for a sample of a radioactive isotope to decrease from an activity of 160 cpm to an activity of 5 cpm?

15. A thyroid cancer patient is given a dosage of ^{131}I (half-life = 8.1 d). What fraction of the dosage of ^{131}I will still be in the patient's thyroid after 24.3 days?

Answer: $\frac{1}{8}$

16. A clinical technician finds that the activity of a sodium-24 sample is 480 cpm. What will be the activity of the sample 75 h later if the half-life of sodium-24 is 15 h?

17. Tritium (half-life = 12.3 y) is used to verify the age of expensive brandies. If an old brandy contains only $\frac{1}{16}$ of the tritium present in new brandy, then how long ago was it produced?

Answer: 49 y

18. What is the half-life of thallium-206 if the activity of a sample drops from 2000 cpm to 250 cpm in 21.0 min?

19. Use the graph in ● Fig. 10.23 to find the half-life of isotope A. All you need is a sound understanding of the definition of half-life.

Answer: For A, half-life = 22 d, because half of 40 g is 20 g, and 20 g is reached after 22 d.

20. Use the graph in Exercise 15 to find the half-life of isotope B.

21. Use the graph in Exercise 15 to find how long it would take the original sample of isotope A to decrease to 12 g.

Answer: 38 days

22. Use the graph in Exercise 15 to find how long it would take the original sample of isotope B to decrease to 2 g.

10.4 Nuclear Reactions

23. Complete the following nuclear reaction equations.
    (a) $^{4}_{2}\text{He} + ^{14}_{7}\text{N} \rightarrow ^{17}_{8}\text{O} + \underline{\quad}$
    (b) $^{4}_{2}\text{He} + ^{27}_{13}\text{Al} \rightarrow ^{30}_{15}\text{P} + \underline{\quad}$
    (c) $\underline{\quad} + ^{66}_{29}\text{Cu} \rightarrow ^{67}_{30}\text{Zn} + ^{1}_{0}\text{n}$
    (d) $^{1}_{0}\text{n} + ^{235}_{92}\text{U} \rightarrow ^{138}_{54}\text{Xe} + \underline{\quad} + 5^{1}_{0}\text{n}$

Answer: (a) $^{1}_{1}\text{H}$ (b) $^{1}_{0}\text{n}$ (c) $^{2}_{1}\text{H}$ (d) $^{93}_{38}\text{H}$

24. Complete the following nuclear reaction equations.
    (a) $^{16}_{8}\text{O} + ^{20}_{10}\text{Ne} \rightarrow \underline{\quad} + ^{12}_{6}\text{C}$
    (b) $^{1}_{0}\text{n} + ^{28}_{14}\text{Si} \rightarrow \underline{\quad} + ^{1}_{1}\text{H}$
    (c) $\underline{\quad} + ^{230}_{90}\text{Th} \rightarrow ^{223}_{87}\text{Fr} + 2^{4}_{2}\text{He}$
    (d) $^{246}_{96}\text{Cm} + ^{12}_{6}\text{C} \rightarrow \underline{\quad} + 4^{1}_{0}\text{n}$

10.5 Nuclear Fission

25. Complete the following equation for fission.

$$^{240}_{94}\text{Pu} \rightarrow ^{97}_{38}\text{Sr} + ^{140}_{56}\text{Ba} + \underline{\quad}$$

Answer: 3^{1}_{0}n

26. Complete the following equation for fission.

$$^{252}_{98}\text{Cf} \rightarrow \underline{\quad} + ^{142}_{55}\text{Cs} + 4^{1}_{0}\text{n}$$

10.6 Nuclear Fusion

27. One of the fusion reactions that takes place as a star ages is called the triple alpha process.

$$3^{4}_{2}\text{He} \rightarrow ^{12}_{6}\text{C}$$

Calculate the mass defect (in u) and the energy produced (in MeV) each time the reaction takes place. (Atomic mass of ^{4}He = 4.00260 u; atomic mass of ^{12}C = 12.00000 u.)

Answer: 0.00780 u, 7.26 MeV

28. Calculate the mass defect (in u) and the energy produced (in MeV) in the D-D reaction shown.

$$\underset{(2.0140\ \text{u})}{^{2}_{1}\text{H}} + \underset{(2.0140\ \text{u})}{^{2}_{1}\text{H}} \rightarrow \underset{(3.0161\ \text{u})}{^{3}_{1}\text{H}} + \underset{(1.0078\ \text{u})}{^{1}_{1}\text{H}}$$

ON THE WEB

1. It's All Quite Elemental, Dear Hydrogen Atom

Follow the recommended links on the student website at **www.cengagebrain.com/shop/ISBN/1133104096** to "interact" with the periodic table. What basic information about hydrogen are you given there? Notice that hydrogen is a nonmetal. Describe the characteristics of nonmetals and compare them with metals. What other elements are considered to be nonmetallic?

2. Beam Me Up, EBIT

Commercial use of controlled fusion is presently elusive. Have you heard of the Electron Beam Ion Trap (EBIT)? How close are we really to being able to control production of those highly charged ions necessary for commercial use? What exactly is the EBIT, and what are its practical applications? If you were to become a physicist interested in nuclear fusion, then how might you be able to use this device? What future applications can you see in the field of nuclear fusion, and how could you develop them? Explore answers to these questions by following the recommended links on the student website at **www.cengagebrain.com/shop/ISBN/1133104096**.

Appendixes

Appendix I | The Seven Base Units of the International System of Units (SI)

1. **meter, m (length):** The meter is defined in reference to the standard unit of time. One meter is the length of the path traveled by light in a vacuum during a time interval of 1/299,792,458 of a second. That is, the speed of light is a universal constant of nature whose value is defined to be 299,792,458 meters per second.
2. **kilogram, kg (mass):** The kilogram is a cylinder of platinum-iridium alloy kept by the International Bureau of Weights and Measures in Paris. A duplicate in the custody of the National Institute of Standards and Technology serves as the mass standard for the United States. This is the only base unit still defined by an artifact.
3. **second, s (time):** The second is defined as the duration of 9,192,631,770 cycles of the radiation associated with a specified transition of the cesium-133 atom.
4. **ampere, A (electric current):** The ampere is defined as that current that, if maintained in each of two long parallel wires separated by one meter in free space, would produce a force between the two wires (due to their magnetic fields) of 2×10^{-7} newtons for each meter of length.
5. **kelvin, K (temperature):** The kelvin is defined as the fraction 1/273.16 of the thermodynamic temperature of the triple point of water. The temperature 0 K is called *absolute zero*.

Table I.1 Prefixes Representing Powers of 10*

Multiple	Prefix	Abbreviation
10^{18}	exa-	E
10^{15}	peta-	P
10^{12}	tera-	T
10^{9}	giga-	G
10^{6}	mega-	M
10^{3}	kilo-	k
10^{2}	hecto-	h
10	deka-	da
10^{-1}	deci-	d
10^{-2}	centi-	c
10^{-3}	milli-	m
10^{-6}	micro-	μ**
10^{-9}	nano-	n
10^{-12}	pico-	p
10^{-15}	femto-	f
10^{-18}	atto-	a

*The most commonly used prefixes are highlighted in color.

**This is the Greek letter mu.

6. **mole, mol (amount of substance):** The mole is the amount of substance of a system that contains as many elementary entities as there are atoms in 0.012 kilogram of carbon-12.
7. **candela, cd (luminous intensity):** The candela is defined as the luminous intensity of 1/600,000 of a square meter of a black body at the temperature of freezing platinum (2045 K).

Appendix II   Solving Mathematical Problems in Science

When taking a science course, some students worry unduly about their ability to handle exercises involving mathematics. Any such apprehension should be replaced with a sense of confidence that they can handle *any* exercise presented in this textbook if they will just learn, *early on,* the few fundamental skills presented in Chapter 1 and these appendixes.

Mathematics is fundamental in the physical sciences, and it is difficult to understand or appreciate these sciences without certain basic mathematical abilities. Dealing with the quantitative side of science gives the student a chance to review and gain confidence in the use of basic mathematical skills, to learn to analyze problems and reason them through, and to see the importance and power of a systematic approach to problems. We recommend the following approach to solving mathematical problems in science.

1. Read the exercise and list what you are given and what is wanted (unknown). Include all units—not just the numbers. Sometimes, making a rough sketch of the situation is helpful.
2. From that information, decide the type of problem with which you are dealing, and select the appropriate equation. (A brief list of **Important Equations** is provided near the end of any chapter that contains mathematical exercises.) *Occasionally,* you may need to use conversion factors (Chapter 1.6) to change, say, 66 g to kg. In general, all quantities should be in the same system of units (generally, the mks system).
3. If necessary, rearrange the equation for the unknown. (Appendix III discusses equation rearrangement.)
4. Substitute the known numbers *and their units* into the rearranged equation.
5. See whether the units combine to give you the appropriate unit for the unknown. (Appendix IV discusses the analysis of units.)
6. Once you have determined that the units are correct, do the math, being sure to express the answer to the proper number of significant figures and to include the unit. (Appendixes V, VI, and VII describe how to use positive and negative numbers, powers-of-10 notation, and significant figures.)
7. Evaluate the answer for reasonableness. (For example, it would not be *reasonable* for a car to be traveling 800 mi/h.)

Appendix III   Equation Rearrangement

An important skill for solving mathematical problems in science is the ability to rearrange an equation for the unknown quantity. Basically, we want to get the unknown

1. into the numerator
2. positive in sign
3. to the first power (not squared, cubed, etc.)
4. alone on one side of the equals sign ($=$)

Addition or Subtraction to Both Sides of an Equation

The equation $X - 4 = 12$ states that the numbers $X - 4$ and 12 are equal. To solve for X, use this rule: Whatever is added to (or subtracted from) one side can be added to (or subtracted from) the other side, and equality will be maintained. We want to get X, the unknown in this case, alone on one side of the equation, so we add 4 to both sides (so that $-4 + 4 = 0$ on the left side). Example III.1 illustrates this procedure.

EXAMPLE III.1

$$X - 4 = 12$$
$$X - 4 + 4 = 12 + 4 \quad \text{(4 added to both sides)}$$
$$X = 16$$

EXAMPLE III.2

Suppose in the scientific equation $T_K = T_C + 273$ we wish to solve for T_C. All we need to do is to get T_C alone on one side, so we subtract 273 from each side. The procedure is

$$T_K = T_C + 273$$
$$T_K - 273 = T_C + 273 - 273 \quad \text{(273 subtracted from both sides)}$$
$$T_K - 273 = T_C \text{ (or } T_C = T_K - 273)$$

Shortcut After you understand the principle of adding or subtracting the same number or symbol from each side, you may wish to use a shortcut for this type of problem: To move a number or symbol added to (or subtracted from) the unknown, take it to the other side but change its sign. See how Examples III.1 and III.2 are solved using the shortcut.

Change sign

$$X \left(- 4\right) = 12 \quad \text{gives } X = 12 + 4$$

Change sign

$$T_K = T_C \left(+ 273\right) \quad \text{gives } T_K - 273 = T_C$$

PRACTICE PROBLEMS

Solve each equation for the unknown. As you proceed, check your answers against those given at the end of this appendix.

(a) $X + 9 = 11; X = ?$

(b) $T_f - T_i = \Delta T; T_f = ?$

(c) $\lambda f = E_i - E_f; E_i = ?$

(d) $H = \Delta E_i + W; W = ?$

(e) $\dfrac{\Delta E_p}{mg} = h_2 - h_1; h_2 = ?$

(f) $H = E_p - \dfrac{mv^2}{2}; E_p = ?$

Multiplication or Division to Both Sides of an Equation

For equations such as $\frac{X}{4} = 6$, the rule is: Multiply (or divide) both sides by the number or symbol that will leave the unknown alone on one side of the equation. Thus, in the equation $\frac{X}{4} = 6$, we multiply both sides by 4, as shown in Example III.3.

EXAMPLE III.3

$$\frac{X}{4} = 6$$

$$\frac{4X}{4} = 6 \times 4 \quad \text{(both sides multiplied by 4)}$$

$$X = 24$$

EXAMPLE III.4

In the scientific equation $F = ma$, solve for a. The unknown is already in the numerator, so all we do is move the m by dividing both sides by m.

$$F = ma$$

$$\frac{F}{m} = \frac{ma}{m} \quad \text{(both sides divided by m)}$$

$$\frac{F}{m} = a \left(\text{or } a = \frac{F}{m} \right)$$

EXAMPLE III.5

Suppose the unknown is in the denominator to start with; for example, solving for t in $P = \frac{W}{t}$. Multiply both sides by t to get t in the numerator, and then divide both sides by P to move P to the other side. The procedure is

$$P = \frac{W}{t}$$

$$tP = \frac{tW}{t} \quad \text{(both sides multiplied by t)}$$

$$tP = W$$

$$\frac{tP}{P} = \frac{W}{P} \quad \text{(both sides divided by P)}$$

$$t = \frac{W}{P}$$

Shortcut After you understand the principle of multiplying or dividing both sides of the equation by the same number or symbol, you may wish to use a shortcut to move the number or symbol: Whatever is multiplying (or dividing) the whole of one side winds up dividing (or multiplying) the whole other side. See how Examples III.3, III.4, and III.5 are solved using the shortcut.

$$\frac{X}{4} = 6 \quad \text{gives } X = 4 \times 6 \text{ (or 24)}$$

$$F = ma \quad \text{gives } \frac{F}{m} = a$$

$$P = \frac{W}{t} \quad \text{gives } t = \frac{W}{P}$$

(The shortcut saves many steps when an unknown is in the denominator.)

You can see that the number of zeros in the answers above is just equal to the exponent, or power of 10. As an example, 10^{23} is a 1 followed by 23 zeros.

Negative powers of 10 also can be used. For example,

$$10^{-2} = \frac{1}{10^2} = \frac{1}{100} = 0.01$$

We see that if a number has a negative exponent, we shift the decimal place to the left once for each power of 10. For example, 1 centimeter (cm) is 1/100 m or 10^{-2} m, which is 0.01 m.

We also can multiply numbers by powers of 10. Table VI.1 shows examples of various large and small numbers expressed in powers-of-10 notation.

We can represent a number in powers-of-10 notation in many different ways—all correct. For example, the distance from the Earth to the Sun is 93 million miles. This value can be represented as 93,000,000 miles, or 93×10^6 miles, or 9.3×10^7 miles, or 0.93×10^8 miles. Any of the given representations of 93 million miles is correct, although 9.3×10^7 is preferred. (In expressing powers-of-10 notation, it is customary to have one digit to the left of the decimal point. This is called *conventional* or *standard form*.)

TABLE VI.1 Numbers Expressed in Powers-of-10 Notation

Number	Powers-of-10 Notation*
247	2.47×10^2
186,000	1.86×10^5
4,705,000	4.705×10^6
0.025	2.5×10^{-2}
0.0000408	4.08×10^{-5}
0.00000010	1.0×10^{-7}

*Note: The exponent (power of 10) is increased by 1 for every place the decimal point is shifted to the left and is decreased by 1 for every place the decimal point is shifted to the right.

Thus it can be seen that the exponent, or power of 10, changes when the decimal point of the prefix number is shifted. General rules for this are as follows:

1. The exponent, or power of 10, is *increased* by 1 for every place the decimal point is shifted to the *left*.
2. The exponent, or power of 10, is *decreased* by 1 for every place the decimal point is shifted to the *right*.

This is simply a way of saying that if the coefficient (prefix number) gets smaller, the exponent gets correspondingly larger, and vice versa. Overall, the number is the same.

Try the following practice problems.

PRACTICE PROBLEMS

Put parts (a) through (d) in standard powers-of-10 form, and parts (e) through (h) in decimal form. The answers are given at the end of this appendix.

(a) 2500
(b) 870,000
(c) 0.0000008
(d) 0.0357

(e) 6×10^4
(f) 5.6×10^3
(g) 5.6×10^{-6}
(h) 7.9×10^{-2}

Changing Between Powers-of-10 Forms

When changing from one powers-of-10 form to another, you must ensure that the final number is equal to the number with which you started. Thus, if the exponential is made larger, the decimal in the prefix becomes correspondingly smaller, and vice versa.

EXAMPLE VI.1

Change 83×10^5 to the 10^6 form.
Going from 10^5 to 10^6 is an *increase* by a factor of 10. Therefore, the prefix part must *decrease* by a factor of 10. Because 83 divided by 10 is 8.3, the answer is 8.3×10^6.

Change 4.5×10^{-9} to the 10^{-10} form.
Going from 10^{-9} to 10^{-10} is a decrease by a factor of 10. Therefore, the decimal prefix must *increase* by a factor of 10. Because 4.5 multiplied by 10 is 45, the answer is 45×10^{-10}.

PRACTICE PROBLEMS

Determine the value required in place of the question mark for the equation to be true. Check your answers.

(i) $3.02 \times 10^7 = ? \times 10^6$
(j) $126 \times 10^{-3} = ? \times 10^{-2}$
(k) $896 \times 10^4 = ? \times 10^6$
(l) $32.7 \times 10^5 = 3.27 \times 10^?$

Addition and Subtraction of Powers of 10

In addition or subtraction, the exponents of 10 must be the same value.

EXAMPLE VI.2

$$\begin{array}{r} 4.6 \times 10^{-8} \\ +\ 1.2 \times 10^{-8} \\ \hline 5.8 \times 10^{-8} \end{array} \qquad \text{and} \qquad \begin{array}{r} 4.8 \times 10^{7} \\ -2.5 \times 10^{7} \\ \hline 2.3 \times 10^{7} \end{array}$$

PRACTICE PROBLEMS

Perform the designated arithmetical operations. Check your answers.

(m) $\begin{array}{r} 4.5 \times 10^5 \\ +\ 3.2 \times 10^5 \\ \hline ? \end{array}$ (n) $\begin{array}{r} 5.66 \times 10^{-3} \\ -3.24 \times 10^{-3} \\ \hline ? \end{array}$

Multiplication of Powers of 10

In multiplication, the exponents are added.

EXAMPLE VI.3

$(2 \times 10^4)(4 \times 10^3) = 8 \times 10^7$ and $(1.2 \times 10^{-2})(3 \times 10^6) = 3.6 \times 10^4$

PRACTICE PROBLEMS

Perform the designated arithmetical operations.

(o) $(7 \times 10^5)(3 \times 10^4) = ?$
(p) $(2 \times 10^{-3})(4 \times 10^6) = ?$

Division of Powers of 10

In division, the exponents are subtracted.

EXAMPLE VI.4

$$\frac{4.8 \times 10^8}{2.4 \times 10^2} = 2.0 \times 10^6 \qquad \text{and} \qquad \frac{3.4 \times 10^{-8}}{1.7 \times 10^{-2}} = 2.0 \times 10^{-6}$$

An alternative method for division is to transfer all powers of 10 from the denominator to the numerator by changing the sign of the exponent. Then, the exponents of the powers of 10 may be added, because they are now multiplying. **The decimal parts are not transferred; they are divided in the usual manner.** This method requires an additional step, but many students find it leads to the correct answer more consistently. Thus,

$$\frac{4.8 \times 10^8}{2.4 \times 10^2} = \frac{4.8 \times 10^8 \times 10^{-2}}{2.4} = 2.0 \times 10^6$$

PRACTICE PROBLEMS

Perform the designated arithmetical operations.

(q) $\dfrac{18 \times 10^7}{3 \times 10^4}$

(r) $\dfrac{(3 \times 10^{17})(4 \times 10^{-8})}{6 \times 10^{-11}} = ?$

Squaring Powers of 10

When squaring exponential numbers, multiply the exponent by 2. The decimal part is multiplied by itself.

EXAMPLE VI.5

$$(3 \times 10^4)^2 = 9 \times 10^8$$
$$(4 \times 10^{-7})^2 = 16 \times 10^{-14}$$

PRACTICE PROBLEMS

Perform the designated algebraic operations. Check your answers.

(s) $(8 \times 10^{-5})^2$

(t) $(4 \times 10^3)^2$

(u) $(3 \times 10^{-8})^2$

Finding the Square Root of Powers of 10

To find the square root of an exponential number, follow the rule $\sqrt{10^a} = 10^{\left(\frac{a}{2}\right)}$. Note that the exponent must be an even number. If it is not, change to a power-of-10 form that gives an even exponent. Find the square root of the decimal part by determining what number multiplied by itself gives that number.

EXAMPLE VI.6   (Two Examples)

$$\sqrt{9 \times 10^8} = 3 \times 10^4$$
$$\sqrt{2.5 \times 10^{-17}} = \sqrt{25 \times 10^{-18}} = 5 \times 10^{-9}$$

PRACTICE PROBLEMS

Perform the designated algebraic operations. Check your answers.

(v) $\sqrt{4 \times 10^8}$

(w) $\sqrt{16 \times 10^{-10}}$

(x) $\sqrt{78 \times 10^{-11}}$

ANSWERS

(a)	2.5×10^3	(m)	7.7×10^5
(b)	8.7×10^5	(n)	2.42×10^{-3}
(c)	8×10^{-7}	(o)	21×10^9
(d)	3.57×10^{-2}	(p)	8×10^3
(e)	60,000	(q)	6×10^3
(f)	5600	(r)	2×10^{20}
(g)	0.0000056	(s)	64×10^{-10}
(h)	0.079	(t)	16×10^6
(i)	30.2×10^6	(u)	9×10^{-16}
(j)	12.6×10^{-2}	(v)	2×10^4
(k)	8.96×10^6	(w)	4×10^{-5}
(l)	3.27×10^6	(x)	2.8×10^{-5}

Appendix VII   Significant Figures

Chapter 1 introduced the concept of significant figures (Chapter 1.7). Let's expand on what you learned there and get some practice.

In scientific work, most numbers are *measured* quantities and thus are not exact. All measured quantities are limited in significant figures (abbreviated s.f.) by the precision of the instrument used to make the measurement. The measurement must be recorded in such a way as to show the degree of precision to which it was made—no more, no less. Furthermore, calculations based on the measured quantities can have no more (or no less) precision than the measurements themselves. Thus the answers to the calculations must be recorded to the proper number of significant figures. To do otherwise is misleading and improper.

Counting Significant Figures

Measured Quantities

Rule 1:   **Nonzero integers** are always significant (for example, both 23.4 g and 234 g have 3 s.f.).

Rule 2:   **Captive zeros,** those bounded on both sides by nonzero integers, are always significant (e.g., 20.05 g has 4 s.f.; 407 g has 3 s.f.).

Rule 3:   **Leading zeros,** those *not bounded* on the *left* by nonzero integers, are never significant (e.g., 0.04 g has 1 s.f.; 0.00035 has 2 s.f.). Such zeros just set the decimal point; they always disappear if the number is converted to powers-of-10 notation.

Rule 4:   **Trailing zeros,** those bounded *only on the left* by nonzero integers, are probably not significant *unless a decimal point is shown,* in which case they are always significant. For example, 45.0 L has 3 s.f. but 450 L probably has only 2 s.f.; 21.00 kg has 4 s.f. but 2100 kg probably has only 2 s.f.; 55.20 mm has 4 s.f.; 151.10 cal has 5 s.f.; 3.0×10^4 J has 2 s.f. If you wish to show *for sure* that, say, 150 m is to be interpreted as having 3 s.f., change to powers-of-10 notation and show it as 1.50×10^2 m.

Exact Numbers

Rule 5: Exact numbers are those obtained not by measurement but by definition or by counting small numbers of objects. They are assumed to have an unlimited number of significant figures. For example, in the equation $c = 2\pi r$, the "2" is a defined quantity, not a measured one, so it has no effect on the number of significant figures to which the answer can be reported. In counting, say, 15 pennies, you can see that the number is exact because you cannot have 14.9 pennies or 15.13 pennies. The $\frac{9}{5}$ and 1.8 found in temperature conversion equations are exact numbers based on definitions.

PRACTICE PROBLEMS

Using Rules 1–5, determine the number of significant figures in the following measurements. As you proceed, check your answers against those given at the end of the appendix.

(a) 4853 g

(b) 36.200 km

(c) 0.088 s

(d) 30.003 J

(e) 6 dogs

(f) 74.0 m

(g) 340 cm

(h) 40 mi

(i) 8.9 L

(j) 1.30×10^2 cal

(k) 0.002710 ft

(l) 4000 mi

(m) 0.0507 mL

(n) the 2 in $E_k = \dfrac{mv^2}{2}$

Multiplication and Division Involving Significant Figures

Rule 6: In calculations involving only multiplication and/or division of measured quantities, the answer shall have the same number of significant figures as the *fewest* possessed by any measured quantity in the calculation.

EXAMPLE VII.1

A calculator gives 4572.768 cm^3 when 130.8 cm is multiplied by 15.2 cm and then by 2.3 cm. However, this answer would be rounded and reported as 4.6×10^3 cm^3, because 2.3 cm has the fewest significant figures (two). The reasoning behind this is that the measured 2.3 cm could easily be wrong by 0.1 cm.

Suppose it were really 2.4 cm. What difference would this make in the answer on the calculator? You would get 4771.584 cm^3! Comparing this to what the calculator originally gave, you see that the uncertainty in the answer is in the hundreds place, so the answer is properly reported only to the hundreds place—that is, to 2 s.f.

The measured quantity with the fewest significant figures will have the greatest effect on the answer because of percentage effects (a miss of 1 out of 23 is more damaging than a miss of 1 out of 1308, for example).

PRACTICE PROBLEMS

Rewrite the following calculator-given answers so that the proper number of significant figures is shown in each case. When necessary, use exponential notation to avoid ambiguity in the answer. Refer to the rounding rules given in Section 1.7 of the textbook.

(o) $7.7 \dfrac{m}{s^2} \times 3.222\ s \times 2.4423\ s = 60.59199762\ m$

(p) $93.0067\ g \div 35\ mL = 2.65733428571\ \dfrac{g}{mL}$

(q) $7.43 \dfrac{kg}{L} \times 15\ L = 111.45\ kg$

(r) $5766 \dfrac{m}{s} \times 322\ s = 1,856,652\ m$

The Evening Sky in September (Adapted from tclescope.com)

Answers to Selected Questions

CHAPTER 1 ANSWERS

Answers to Matching Questions
a. 5, b. 17, c. 23, d. 7, e. 22, f. 16, g. 10, h. 2, i. 12, j. 1, k. 9, l. 4, m. 18, n. 6, o. 11, p. 3, q. 20, r. 8, s. 15, t. 14, u. 22, v. 13. w. 19

Answers to Multiple-Choice Questions
1. c, 2. b, 3. c, 4. b, 5. b, 6. b, 7. d, 8. c, 9. d, 10. c, 11. d, 12. d. 13. a

Answers to Fill-in-the-Blank Questions
1. biological 2. experiment 3. scientific method 4. sight 5. limitations 6. greater 7. shorter 8. fundamental 9. time or second 10. 10^6 or 1,000,000 (million) 11. liter 12. mass

Answers to Visual Connection
a. kilogram (kg) b. meter (m) c. second (s) d. pound (lb) e. foot (ft) f. second (s)

CHAPTER 2 ANSWERS

Answers to Matching Questions
a. 9, b. 4, c. 11, d. 17, e. 7, f. 10, g. 3, h. 12, i. 5, j. 15, k. 18, l. 8, m. 2, n. 14, o. 6, p. 1, q. 13, r. 16

Answers to Multiple-Choice Questions
1. d, 2. c, 3. d, 4. c, 5. d, 6. b, 7. c, 8. d, 9. d, 10. d, 11. c, 12. c

Answers to Fill-in-the-Blank Questions
1. position 2. scalar 3. vector 4. distance 5. speed 6. constant or uniform 7. time· t^2 8. free-fall 9. m/s^2 10. speed 11. 4 12. acceleration (due to gravity)

Answers to Visual Connection
a. acceleration b. distance c. displacement d. velocity e. m/s f. m/s g. m/s²

CHAPTER 3 ANSWERS

Answers to Matching Questions
a. 3, b. 18, c. 8, d. 13, e. 17, f. 4, g. 15, h. 6, i. 19, j. 10, k. 1, l. 12, m. 7, n. 9, o. 2, p. 16, q. 11, r. 5, s. 14

Answers to Multiple-Choice Questions
1. d, 2. d, 3. c, 4. b, 5. a, 6. d, 7. d, 8. b, 9. c, 10. a, 11. c, 12. a, 13. b, 14. d, 15. c

Answers to Fill-in-the-Blank Questions
1. capable 2. vector 3. could 4. net or unbalanced 5. mass 6. inversely 7. kg·m/s² 8. static, kinetic or sliding 9. different 10. everywhere 11. greater 12. more 13. net or unbalanced 14. torque

Answers to Visual Connection
a. action b. inertia c. acceleration

CHAPTER 4 ANSWERS

Answers to Matching Questions
a. 4, b. 10, c. 2, d. 12, e. 7, f. 6, g. 1, h. 3, i. 15, j. 11, k. 9, l. 5, m. 13, n. 8, o. 14

Answers to Multiple-Choice Questions
1. a, 2. d, 3. d, 4. c, 5. b, 6. d, 7. c, 8. a, 9. b, 10. a, 11. a, 12. c, 13. b, 14. c

Answers to Fill-in-the-Blank Questions
1. parallel 2. scalar 3. joule 4. work 5. kinetic 6. square 7. transferring 8. isolated 9. work 10. 0.75 11. energy 12. coal 13. exhausted 14. ethanol (alcohol)

Answers to Visual Connection
a. power b. kinetic energy c. potential energy d. conservation of mechanical energy

CHAPTER 5 ANSWERS

Answers to Matching Questions
a. 10, b. 8, c. 14, d. 23, e. 12, f. 1, g. 15, h. 25, i. 4, j. 11, k. 2, l. 16, m. 7, n. 5, o. 13, p. 20, q. 18, r. 3, s. 24, t. 9, u. 17, v. 22, w. 6, x. 19, y. 21

Answers to Multiple-Choice Questions
1. b, 2. a, 3. a, 4. c, 5. b, 6. c, 7. a, 8. b, 9. d, 10. c, 11. c, 12. b

Answers to Fill-in-the-Blank Questions
1. smaller 2. temperature 3. 1000 4. J/kg·°C 5. seven 6. pressure 7. conduction 8. gas 9. area 10. inversely 11. direction 12. pump

Answers to Visual Connection
a. melting b. freezing c. vaporization d. deposition e. condensation

CHAPTER 6 ANSWERS

Answers to Matching Questions
a. 2, b. 17, c. 10, d. 5, e. 19, f. 8, g. 20, h. 12, i. 1, j. 21, k. 14, l. 6, m. 16, n. 11, o. 3, p. 9, q. 13, r. 15, s. 18, t. 7, u. 4

Answers to Multiple-Choice Questions
1. b, 2. a, 3. a, 4. a, 5. d, 6. d, 7. c, 8. a, 9. d, 10. a, 11. b, 12. a, 13. d

Answers to Fill-in-the-Blank Questions
1. energy 2. perpendicular 3. wavelength 4. frequency 5. light or 3.00×10^8 m/s 6. electromagnetic 7. longitudinal 8. 20 9. intensity 10. 3 11. higher 12. approaching 13. natural or characteristic

Answers to Visual Connection
a. transverse b. longitudinal c. light or electromagnetic d. sound

CHAPTER 7 ANSWERS

Answers to Matching Questions
a. 4, b. 14, c. 12, d. 21, e. 13, f. 6, g. 20, h. 1, i. 11, j. 22, k. 5, l. 16, m. 10, n. 8, o. 17, p. 2, q. 19, r. 7, s. 9, t. 18, u. 3, v. 15

Answers to Multiple-Choice Questions
1. d, 2. d, 3. b, 4. a, 5. b, 6. c, 7. b, 8. c, 9. c, 10. a, 11. a, 12. a

Answers to Fill-in-the-Blank Questions
1. geometrical or ray 2. diffuse 3. vacuum 4. toward 5. total internal 6. converging 7. cannot 8. thinner 9. concave or diverging 10. transverse 11. greater 12. principle of superposition

Answers to Visual Connection
a. reflection b. total internal reflection c. dispersion

CHAPTER 8 ANSWERS

Answers to Matching Questions
a. 3, b. 21, c. 12, d. 4, e. 22, f. 1, g. 25, h. 11, i. 23, j. 2, k. 18, l. 5, m. 19, n. 14, o. 7, p. 17, q. 9, r. 15, s. 10, t. 20, u. 13, v. 24, w. 8, x. 16, y. 6

Answers to Multiple-Choice Questions
1. d, 2. c, 3. a, 4. b, 5. d, 6. a, 7. a, 8. b, 9. d, 10. d, 11. c, 12. b, 13. c, 14. b

Answers to Fill-in-the-Blank Questions
1. positively 2. ampere (amp) 3. Semiconductors 4. charge 5. open 6. ohm 7. I^2R 8. direct or dc 9. smallest 10. Curie 11. geographic 12. secondary

Answers to Visual Connection

a. electrons b. voltage (potential difference) c. resistance d. current e. I^2R or joule heat

CHAPTER 9 ANSWERS

Answers to Matching Questions

a. 10, b. 7, c. 3, d. 14, e. 8, f. 18, g. 1, h. 16, i. 4, j. 2, k. 13, l. 6, m. 9, n. 17, o. 5, p. 15, q. 11

Answers to Multiple-Choice Questions

1. c, 2. a, 3. a, 4. d, 5. c, 6. c, 7. b, 8. d, 9. d, 10. a, 11. b, 12. b, 13. b, 14. d

Answers to Fill-in-the-Blank Questions

1. electron 2. Rutherford 3. Planck's constant 4. photon 5. increases 6. continuous 7. higher 8. water 9. unknown 10. uncertainty 11. wave 12. probability

Answers to Visual Connection

a. Dalton b. Plum pudding c. Rutherford d. Planetary e. Schrödinger

CHAPTER 10 ANSWERS

Answers to Matching Questions

a. 12, b. 23, c. 4, d. 14, e. 1, f. 16, g. 13, h. 9, i. 2, j. 20, k. 19, l. 3, m. 24, n. 6, o. 22, p. 8, q. 11, r. 15, s. 7, t. 18, u. 21, v. 5, w. 10, x. 25, y. 17, z. 26

Answers to Multiple-Choice Questions

1. b, 2. d, 3. c, 4. d, 5. c, 6. d, 7. b, 8. c, 9. a, 10. c, 11. c, 12. a, 13. c, 14. b, 15. d

Answers to Fill-in-the-Blank Questions

1. potassium 2. ^{12}C 3. nucleons 4. isotopes 5. 83 6. beta particle (electron) 7. three 8. one more 9. mass number 10. critical 11. deuteron (or deuterium)12. 82%, 13. quarks

Answers to Visual Connection

a. electrons b. neutrons c. + 1 d. 0 (zero)

CHAPTER 11 ANSWERS

Answers to Matching Questions

a. 12, b. 14 c. 13, d. 21, e. 18, f. 1, g. 7, h. 10, i. 2, j. 3, k. 23, l. 25, m. 24, n. 22, o. 4, p. 8, q. 16, r. 15, s. 6, t. 5, u. 19, v. 11, w. 9, x. 17, y. 20

Answers to Multiple-Choice Questions

1. b, 2. c, 3. a, 4. b, 5. d, 6. c, 7. c, 8. c, 9. b, 10. d, 11. a, 12. c

Answers to Fill-in-the-Blank Questions

1. Organic chemistry 2. solvent 3. more 4. experimentation 5. molecules 6. aluminum 7. O_3 8. Mendeleev 9. four 10. increases 11. nitrate 12. sodium hydroxide

Answers to Visual Connection

a. Li b. K c. Br d. I e. Zn f. V g. Mg h. Ca i. Ne j. Ar

CHAPTER 12 ANSWERS

Answers to Matching Questions

a. 10, b. 18, c. 6, d. 14, e. 4, f. 17, g. 15, h. 8, i. 11, j. 19, k. 1, l. 5, m. 12 n. 3, o. 13, p. 9, q. 2, r. 16, s. 7

Answers to Multiple-Choice Questions

1. b, 2. a, 3. d, 4. c, 5. c, 6. d 7. c, 8. c, 9. d, 10. a, 11. c, 12. b 13. a 14. b

Answers to Fill-in-the-Blank Questions

1. mass 2. CO_2 3. definite proportions 4. chemistry 5. CuO 6. anion 7. two 8. M_2X 9. ionic 10. double 11. decreases 12. nitrogen

Answers to Visual Connection

a. electron sharing b. ionic bonding c. unequal sharing d. nonpolar covalent bonding

CHAPTER 13 ANSWERS

Answers to Matching Questions

a. 13, b. 9, c. 1, d. 14, e. 22, f. 19, g. 4, h. 20, i. 6, j. 23, k. 3, l. 21, m. 8 n. 16, o. 10, p. 25, q. 17, r. 11, s. 5, t. 2, u. 7, v. 12, w. 15, x. 18, y. 24, z. 26

Answers to Multiple-Choice Questions

1. d, 2. c, 3. b, 4. b, 5. d, 6. a, 7. c, 8. a, 9. c, 10. a, 11. a, 12. d

Answers to Fill-in-the-Blank Questions

1. physical, 2. the same, 3. *AB*, 4. enzymes, 5. lower, 6. catalyst, 7. OH^-, 8. neutral, 9. acid–carbonate, 10. redox, 11. will not, 12. two

Answers to Visual Connection

a. combination, b. $AB \rightarrow A + B$, c. single replacement, d. $AB + CD \rightarrow AD + CB$, e. hydrocarbon combustion

CHAPTER 14 ANSWERS

Answers to Matching Questions

a. 2, b. 21, c. 12, d. 9, e. 4, f. 22, g. 6, h. 1, i. 8, j. 19, k. 9, l. 18, m. 11, n. 14, o. 25, p. 5, q. 26, r. 24, s. 3, t. 20, u. 15, v. 16, w. 23, x. 13, y. 17, z. 7

Answers to Multiple-Choice Questions

1. b, 2. c, 3. d, 4. c, 5. b, 6. b, 7. a, 8. b, 9. a, 10. c, 11. c, 12. b

Answers to Fill-in-the-Blank Questions

1. carbon	7. alkyne
2. three	8. alcohols
3. Covalent	9. amide
4. aliphatic	10. condensation
5. Benzene	11. nylon
6. cycloalkane	12. carbohydrate

Answers to Visual Connection

a. aromatic

b. alkenes

c. cycloalkanes

d. $-C \equiv C-$

CHAPTER 15 ANSWERS

Answers to Matching Questions

a. 2, b. 17, c. 13, d. 7, e. 19, f. 6, g. 15, h. 21, i. 1, j. 14, k. 9, l. 4, m. 16, n. 11, o. 5, p. 18, q. 12, r. 20, s. 3, t. 8, u. 22, v. 23, w. 10

Answers to Multiple-Choice Questions

1. d, 2. d, 3. c, 4. b, 5. b, 6. b, 7. d, 8. c, 9. d, 10. b, 11. c, 12. b 13. c, 14. b, 15. b, 16. c, 17. b, 18. c, 19. c, 20. d

Answers to Fill-in-the-Blank Questions

1. rectangular 2. origin 3. parallels 4. great circle 5. latitude 6. longitude 7. solar 8. twenty-four 9. four 10. International Date Line 11. altitude 12. date 13. 30°E 14. spring 15. Cancer 16. seasons 17. zodiac 18. three 19. Common Era 20. top

Answers to Visual Connection

a. latitude b. meridians c. parallels d. north–south e. east–west

CHAPTER 16 ANSWERS

Answers to Matching Questions

a. 12, b. 3, c. 18, d. 14, e. 9, f. 23, g. 1, h. 17, i. 20, j. 7, k. 19, l. 13, m. 2, n. 11, o. 16, p. 5, q. 10, r. 21, s. 4, t. 15, u. 8, v. 24, w. 6, x. 22

Answers to Multiple-Choice Questions

1. d, 2. b, 3. c, 4. b, 5. d, 6. b, 7. b, 8. c, 9. c, 10. a, 11. b, 12. b, 13. c, 14. c, 15. b, 16. c, 17. d, 18. c

Answers to Fill-in-the-Blank Questions

1. Astronomy	10. Mercury
2. geocentric	11. greenhouse effect
3. major axis	12. iron oxide
4. period	13. Uranus
5. superior	14. Ceres
6. prograde	15. Eris
7. opposition	16. condensation
8. albedo	17. deviations (wobbles)
9. Foucault pendulum	

Answers to Visual Connection

a. Mercury h. Neptune
b. Venus   i. Ceres
c. Earth   j. Pluto
d. Mars   k. Eris
e. Jupiter   l. Haumea
f. Saturn   m. Makemake
g. Uranus

CHAPTER 17 ANSWERS

Answers to Matching Questions

a. 3, b. 11, c. 21, d. 9, e. 15, f. 14, g. 7, h. 20, i. 4, j. 1, k. 13, l. 18, m. 14, n. 6, o. 8, p. 25, q. 10, r. 5, s. 17, t. 22, u. 24, v. 23, w. 19, x. 2, y. 12

Answers to Multiple-Choice Questions

1. b, 2. c, 3. b, 4. b, 5. a, 6. c, 7. a, 8. b, 9. c, 10. d, 11. a, 12. c, 13. b, 14. c, 15. a, 16. d, 17. b, 18. d, 19. d, 20. c, 21. c, 22. a, 23. a, 24. b, 25. c, 26. e

Answers to Fill-in-the-Blank Questions

1. maria, 2. rays, 3. later, 4. 6 A.M., 5. full, 6. waning, 7. lunar, 8. umbra, 9. spring, 10. twelve, 11. zero, 12. two, 13. Ganymede, 14. Io, 15. Titan, 16. Charon, Nix, and Hydra, 17. Water, 18. asteroids, 19. meteorite, 20. coma

Answers to Visual Connection

a. Moon, b. Phobos (Deimos), c. Deimos (Phobos), d. Ganymede, e. Io, f. Titan, g. Miranda, h. Triton, i. Charon, j. Dysnomia, k. Hi'iaka, j. Namaka

CHAPTER 18 ANSWERS

Answers to Matching Questions

a. 9, b. 19, c. 26, d. 10, e. 14, f. 24, g. 7, h. 2, i. 23, j. 17, k. 12, l. 5, m. 8, n. 22, o. 27, p. 4, q. 16, r. 20, s. 11, t. 15, u. 6, v. 25, w. 18, x. 13, y. 1, z. 21, aa. 3

Answers to Multiple-Choice Questions

1. a, 2. a, 3. d, 4. b, 5. d, 6. a, 7. a, 8. b, 9. d, 10. a, 11. b, 12. d, 13. b, 14. b, 15. a, 16. d, 17. b, 18. a, 19. c, 20. a

Answers to Fill-in-the-Blank Questions

1. parallax 2. celestial equator 3. right ascension 4. 23.5° 5. sunspot 6. helium 7. Flares 8. constellations 9. red 10. spectrum 11. brightness 12. main sequence 13. red giant 14. contract 15. Nebula 16. nova 17. pulsar 18. supernova 19. supermassive 20. 13.7

Answers to Visual Connection

a. Nuclear reactions b. Photosphere c. Chromosphere d. Solar wind

CHAPTER 19 ANSWERS

Answers to Matching Questions

a. 5, b. 12, c. 26, d. 8, e. 19, f. 23, g. 4, h. 27, i. 10, j. 28, k. 1, l. 30, m. 15, n. 6, o. 25, p. 16, q. 9, r. 17, s. 21, t. 2, u. 20, v. 11, w. 24, x. 13, y. 29, z. 3, aa. 22, bb. 18, cc. 14, dd. 7

Answers to Multiple-Choice Questions

1. a, 2. c, 3. a, 4. b, 5. c, 6. d, 7. b, 8. a, 9. b, 10. d, 11. d, 12. b

Answers to Fill-in-the-Blank Questions

1. Meteorology 2. stratosphere 3. stratosphere 4. carbon dioxide, CO_2 5. 14.7 6. 76 cm, 30 in. 7. maximum 8. opposite 9. isobar 10. land 11. counterclockwise 12. low

Answers to Visual Connection

a. cumulonimbus b. cumulus c. cirrus d. cirrocumulus e. cirrostratus f. altostratus g. altocumulus h. stratus i. stratocumulus j. nimbostratus k. advection l. radiation

CHAPTER 20 ANSWERS

Answers to Matching Questions

a. 5, b. 18, c. 8, d. 15, e. 2, f. 13, g. 21, h. 3, i. 16, j. 7, k. 25, l. 11, m.19, n. 1, o. 14, p. 22, q. 6, r. 24, s. 12, t. 20, u. 4, v. 17, w. 10, x. 23, y. 9

Answers to Multiple-Choice Questions

1. b, 2. a, 3. d, 4. d, 5. a, 6. c, 7. b, 8. d, 9. a, 10. b, 11. d, 12. c

Answers to Fill-in-the-Blank Questions

1. coalescence 2. rain 3. temperature 4. cP 5. warm 6. occlusion 7. heat 8. warning 9. 24 10. subsidence 11. photochemical 12. CFCs

Answers to Visual Connection

a. rain b. snow c. sleet d. hail e. dew f. frost

CHAPTER 21 ANSWERS

Answers to Matching Questions

a. 20, b. 4, c. 21, d. 23, e. 24, f. 5, g. 14, h. 27, i. 10, j. 28, k. 7, l. 9, m. 8, n. 15, o. 18, p. 26, q. 22, r. 13, s. 17, t. 2, u. 3, v. 6, w. 16, x. 12, y. 11, z. 25, aa. 19, bb. 1

Answers to Multiple-Choice Questions

1. b, 2. d, 3. c, 4. d, 5. a, 6. d, 7. c, 8. c, 9. c, 10. c, 11. a, 12. b

Answers to Fill-in-the-Blank Questions

1. Geology 2. surface waves 3. asthenosphere 4. outer core 5. deep sea trenches 6. mid-ocean 7. asthenosphere 8. transform 9. Ring of Fire 10. earthquakes 11. volcanic 12. reverse

Answers to Visual Connection

a. Divergent Boundaries b. Red Sea c. Cascade Range d. Continental Collision e. Himalayas f. Transform Boundaries

CHAPTER 22 ANSWERS

Answers to Matching Questions

a. 25, b. 4, c. 13, d. 11, e. 8, f. 3, g. 23, h. 5, i. 14, j. 6, k. 10, l. 12, m. 7, n. 20, o. 22, p. 1, q. 19, r. 18, s. 2, t. 9, u. 17, v. 21, w. 16, x. 15, y. 24

Answers to Multiple-Choice Questions

1. d, 2. b, 3. a, 4. c, 5. b, 6. b, 7. b, 8. a, 9. b, 10. b 11. c, 12. a, 13. d, 14. c, 15. d, 16. d, 17. a, 18. a, 19. d, 20. b

Answers to Fill-in-the-Blank Questions

1. silicon 2. feldspars 3. luster 4. gem 5. igneous 6. uniformitarianism 7. sedimentary 8. basalt 9. stalactites 10. viscosity 11. cinder cone 12. concordant 13. hot spot 14. pluton 15. discordant 16. coal 17. bedding 18. slate 19. Foliation 20. hydrothermal

Answers to Visual Connection

a. Sedimentary b. sandstone, limestone, etc. c. Melting, cooling, solidification d. Metamorphic e. marble, gneiss, etc.

CHAPTER 23 ANSWERS

Answers to Matching Questions

a. 5, b. 12, c. 22, d. 2, e. 19, f. 15, g. 7, h. 13, i. 11, j. 3, k. 21, l. 4, m. 24, n. 8, o. 1, p. 10, q. 16, r. 23, s. 9, t. 18, u. 6, v. 20, w. 14, x. 17

Answers to Multiple-Choice Questions

1. a, 2. c, 3. c, 4. c, 5. d, 6. b, 7. b, 8. c, 9. d, 10. b, 11. b, 12. a

Answers to Fill-in-the-Blank Questions

1. mechanical 2. permafrost 3. moisture 4. stream 5. bed 6. continental glaciers 7. mudflows 8. moraines 9. Subsidence 10. aquifer 11. tides 12. continental slopes

Answers to Visual Connection

a. precipitation b. evaporation c. Land d. streams e. glacier flow

CHAPTER 24 ANSWERS

Answers to Matching Questions

a. 12, b. 25, c. 14, d. 11, e. 3, f. 18, g. 20, h. 1, i. 26, j. 19, k. 6, l. 23, m. 7, n. 5, o. 4, p. 10, q. 13, r. 16, s. 17, t. 2, u. 9, v. 8, w. 21, x. 22, y. 24, z.15

Answers to Multiple-Choice Questions

1. d, 2. c, 3. c, 4. b, 5. a, 6. b, 7. d, 8. b, 9. a, 10. d, 11. d, 12. a 13. c, 14. c, 15. d, 16. d, 17. c, 18. a, 19. b, 20. c

Answers to Fill-in-the-Blank Questions

1. paleontology 2. replacement fossil 3. algae 4. Cenozoic 5. unconformity 6. younger 7. relative time 8. Correlation 9. eons 10. trilobite 11. superposition 12. carbon-14 13. larger 14. primordial 15. 4.56 16. younger 17. Rhodinia 18. K-T event 19. explosion 20. epoch

Answers to Visual Connection

a. one-celled (or multicelled) organisms b. Silurian c. amphibians d. Triassic e. primates

Glossary

The number in parentheses following each definition refers to the section in which the term is discussed.

aberration of starlight The apparent displacement in the direction of light coming from a star because of the orbital motion of the Earth. (16.3)

absolute (numerical) geologic time The actual age of geologic events, established on the basis of the radioactive decay of certain atomic nuclei. (24.3)

absolute magnitude The brightness a star would have if it were placed 10 pc (32.6 ly) from the Earth. (18.3)

acceleration The time rate of change of velocity; $a = \Delta v/\Delta t$ (2.3)

acceleration due to gravity Usually given as the symbol g; equal to 9.80 m/s², or 32 ft/s². (2.3, 3.5)

acid A substance that gives hydrogen ions, H^+ (or hydronium ions, H_3O^+) in water (Arrhenius definition). (13.3)

acid-base reaction The H^+ of an acid unites with the OH^- of a base to form water, while the cation of the base combines with the anion of the acid to form a salt. (13.3)

acid-carbonate reaction An acid and a carbonate (or hydrogen carbonate) react to give carbon dioxide, water, and a salt. (13.3)

acid rain Rain that has a relatively low pH (i.e., relatively high acidity) because of air pollution. (20.4)

activation energy The energy necessary to start a chemical reaction; a measure of the minimum kinetic energy that colliding molecules must possess in order to react chemically. (13.2)

activity series A list of elements in order of relative tendency to lose electrons to ions of another metal or to hydrogen ions.. (13.4)

addition polymers Polymers formed when molecules of an alkene monomer add to one another. (14.5)

air current Vertical air motions. (19.4)

air mass A large body of air with physical characteristics that distinguish it from the surrounding air. (20.2)

albedo The fraction of incident sunlight reflected by a celestial object. (16.3)

alcohols Organic compounds containing a hydroxyl group, —OH, attached to an alkyl group. The general formula for an alcohol is R—OH, or just ROH, and the IUPAC names of alcohols end in -ol. (14.4)

aliphatic hydrocarbon Hydrocarbons having no benzene rings. (14.3)

alkali metals The elements in Group 1A of the periodic table, except for hydrogen (Li, Na, K, Rb, Cs, Fr). (11.6)

alkaline earth metals The elements in Group 2A of the periodic table (Be, Mg, Ca, Sr, Ba, Ra). (11.6)

alkanes Hydrocarbons that contain only single bonds; general formula, C_nH_{2n+2}. (14.3)

alkenes Hydrocarbons that have a double bond between two carbon atoms; general formula, C_nH_{2n}. (14.3)

alkyl group A substituent that contains one less hydrogen atom than the corresponding alkane; given the general symbol R. (14.3)

alkyl halide An alkane derivative in which one or more of the hydrogen atoms have been replaced by halogen atoms; general formula, RX, where X is a halogen atom and R is an alkyl group. (14.4)

alkynes Hydrocarbons that have a triple bond between two carbon atoms; general formula, C_nH_{2n-2}. (14.3)

allotropes Two or more forms of the same element that have different bonding structures in the same physical phase. (11.3)

alpha decay The disintegration of a nucleus into a nucleus of another element with the emission of an *alpha particle*, which is a helium nucleus. (10.3)

alternating current (ac) Electric current produced by a constantly changing (alternating) voltage from positive (+) to negative (−) to positive (+), and so on. (8.2)

alternative energy sources Energy sources that are not based on the burning of fossil fuels and nuclear processes. (4.6)

altitude The angle measured from the horizon to a celestial object. (15.4)

amber Fossilized tree resin. (24.1)

amides Nitrogen-containing organic compounds that have the general formula RCONHR′. (14.4)

amine Organic compound that contains nitrogen and is basic (alkaline); general formula, R—NH₂, or just RNH₂. (14.4)

amino acids Organic compounds that contain both an amino group and a carboxyl group. (14.6)

ampere (A) The unit of electric current. (8.2)

amplitude The maximum displacement of any part of the wave (or wave particle) from its equilibrium position. (6.2)

anemometer An instrument used to measure wind speed. (19.3)

angular momentum mvr for a mass m going at a speed v in a circle of radius r. (3.7)

anions Negative ions; so called because they move toward the anode (the positive electrode) of an electrochemical cell. (12.4)

annular eclipse A solar eclipse in which the Moon blocks out all of the Sun except for a ring around the Sun's outer edge. (17.2)

ante meridiem (A.M.) Pertaining to time from 12 midnight to 12 noon. (15.3)

aphelion The point when Earth (or another orbiting object) is farthest from the Sun. (15.5)

apparent magnitude The brightness of a star (or other celestial object) as observed from the Earth. (18.3)

aquifer A body of permeable rock that both stores and transports groundwater. (23.3)

Archimedes' principle An object immersed wholly or partially in a fluid experiences a buoyant force equal in magnitude to the weight of the *volume of fluid* that is displaced. (3.6)

aromatic hydrocarbon A hydrocarbon that possesses one or more benzene rings. (14.2)

asteroids Large and small chunks of matter that orbit the Sun (usually between Mars and Jupiter), sometimes called minor planets. (17.6)

asthenosphere The part of the mantle that lies beneath the lithosphere and is essentially solid rock, but is so close to its melting temperature that it contains pockets of thick, molten rock and is relatively plastic. (21.1)

astronomical unit (AU) The average distance between the Earth and the Sun, which is 1.5×10^8 km (93 million miles). (16.1)

astronomy The scientific study of the universe, which is the totality of all matter, energy, space, and time. (16.Intro)

atmospheric science The investigation of every aspect of the atmosphere. (19.Intro)

atom The smallest particle of an element that can enter into a chemical combination. (9.1)

atomic mass The weighed average mass of an atom of the element in naturally occurring samples; given under its symbol in the period table (in *atomic mass units,* symbolized u). (10.2)

atomic number Symbolized by the letter Z, it is equal to the number of protons in the nucleus of each atom of that element. (10.2)

autumnal equinox The point where the Sun crosses the celestial equator from north to south, around September 22. The beginning of fall. (15.5)

average acceleration The change in velocity divided by the time for the change to occur. (2.3)

average speed The total distance traveled divided by the time spent in traveling the total distance; $\bar{v} = \Delta d/\Delta t$. (2.2)

average velocity The displacement divided by the total travel time. (2.2)

Avogadro's number 6.02×10^{23}, symbolized N_A; the number of entities in a mole. (13.5)

barometer A device used to measure atmospheric pressure. (19.3)

base A substance that produces hydroxide ions, OH^-, in water (Arrhenius definition). (13.3)

bedding The layering that develops at the time sediment is deposited; stratification of sedimentary rock formations. (22.5)

Bergeron process The process by which precipitation is formed in clouds. (20.1)

beta decay The disintegration of a nucleus into a nucleus of another element with the emission of a *beta particle*, which is an electron. (10.3)

Big Bang Theory of the beginning of the universe that states that the known universe was smaller, hotter, and denser in the past, and that it began rapidly expanding 13.7 billion years ago. (18.7)

black hole An object so dense that even light cannot escape from its surface because of the object's intense gravitational field. (18.5)

British system The system of units still often employed in the United States, wherein the foot, pound, and second are the standards of length, weight, and time, respectively. The system is sometimes referred to as the *fps* (foot-pound-second) *system*. (1.4)

brown dwarfs Low-mass objects that are larger than a typical planet but do not have enough mass to begin fusion in their cores. Also called "failed stars." (18.4)

Btu (British thermal unit) The amount of heat necessary to raise one *pound* of water one Fahrenheit degree at normal atmospheric pressure. (5.2)

buoyant force The upward force resulting from an object being wholly or partially immersed in a fluid. (3.6)

caldera A roughly circular, steep-walled depression formed primarily from the collapse of the chamber at a volcano's summit. (22.4)

calorie (cal) The amount of heat necessary to raise one *gram* of pure water one Celsius degree at normal atmospheric pressure. (5.2)

Cambrian explosion The great proliferation of life forms that followed the extinction event at the beginning of the Paleozoic era. (24.5)

carbohydrates An important class of compounds that contain multiple hydroxyl groups in their molecular structures. (14.6)

carbon-14 dating A procedure used to establish the age of ancient organic remains by measuring the amount of ^{14}C in an ancient sample. (10.3, 24.3)

carboxylic acids A class of organic compounds that contain a *carboxyl group* and have thegeneral formula, RCOOH. (14.4)

carcinogen A cancer-causing agent. (14.2)

Cartesian coordinate system A two-dimensional coordinate system in which two number lines (x, y) are drawn perpendicular to each other and the *origin* is assigned at the point of intersection. A third dimension may be taken in the z direction. (15.1)

cast Fossil formed when new mineral material fills a mold and hardens. (24.1)

catalyst A substance that increases the rate of reaction but is not itself consumed in the reaction. (13.2)

cations Positive ions; so called because they move toward the cathode (the negative electrode) of an electrochemical cell. (12.4)

celestial prime meridian An imaginary half-circle running from the north celestial pole to the south celestial pole and crossing perpendicular to the celestial equator at the point of the vernal equinox. (18.1)

celestial sphere The apparent sphere of the sky on which all the stars seem to appear. (18.1)

Celsius scale A temperature scale based on an ice point of 0° and a steam point of 100° with 100 equal units or divisions between these points. (5.1)

centi- The metric prefix meaning 1/100, or 0.01. (1.5)

centripetal acceleration The "center-seeking" acceleration necessary for circular motion; $a = v^2/r$. (2.4)

centripetal force The "center-seeking" force that causes an object to travel in a circle. (3.3)

CFCs Chlorofluorocarbons, such as dichlorodifluoromethane (Freon-12), which have been used commonly in air conditioners, refrigerators, and heat pumps, and which helped deplete the ozone layer. (14.4, 20.5)

chain reaction Occurs when each fission event causes at least one or more fission events. (10.5)

charges, law of Like charges repel; unlike charges attract. (8.1)

chemical properties Characteristics that describe the chemical reactivity of a substance—that is, its ability to transform into another substance. (13.1)

chemical reaction A change that alters the chemical composition of a substance and hence forms one or more new substances. (13.1)

chemistry The study of the composition and structure of matter (anything that has mass) and the chemical reactions by which substances are changed into other substances. (11.Intro)

cleavage The tendency of some minerals to break along definite smooth planes. (22.1)

climate The long-term average weather conditions of a region. (20.5)

cloud A buoyant mass of visible droplets of water and ice crystals. (19.5)

coalescence The formation of drops by the collision of droplets, the result being that larger droplets grow at the expense of smaller ones. (20.1)

combination reaction A reaction in which at least two reactants combine to form just one product: $A + B = AB$. (13.1)

combustion reaction A reaction in which a substance reacts with oxygen to burst into flame and form an oxide. (13.2)

comet A relatively small object that is composed of dust and ice and that revolves about the Sun in a highly elliptical orbit. (17.6)

compound A pure substance composed of two or more elements chemically bonded in a definite, fixed ratio by mass. (11.1)

concave mirror A mirror shaped like the inside (concave side) of a small section of a sphere. (7.3)

condensation polymers Large molecules constructed from smaller molecules that have two or more reactive groups. Generally, one molecule attaches to another by an ester or amide linkage, and water is the other product. (14.5)

condensation theory A process of solar system formation in which interstellar dust grains act as condensation nuclei. (16.7)

conduction (thermal) The transfer of heat by molecular collisions. (5.4)

conjunction When two planets are lined up with respect to the Sun. (16.2)

conservation of angular momentum, law of The angular momentum of an object remains constant if there is no external, unbalanced torque acting on it. (3.7)

conservation of linear momentum, law of The total linear momentum of an isolated system remains the same if there is no external, unbalanced force acting on the system. (3.7)

conservation of mass, law of No detectable change in the total mass occurs during a chemical reaction. (12.1)

conservation of mechanical energy, law of In an ideal system, the sum of the kinetic and potential energies is constant: $E_k + E_p = E$ (a constant). (4.3)

conservation of total energy, law of The total energy of an isolated system remains constant. (4.3)

constellation Prominent groups of stars appearing as patterns in each section of the night sky. (15.5, 18.3)

constitutional (structural) isomers Compounds that have the same *molecular* formula but different *structural* formulas. (14.3)

constructive interference A superposition of waves for which the combined waveform has a greater amplitude. (7.6)

contact metamorphism A change in rock brought about primarily by heat, with very little than pressure involved. (22.6)

continental drift The theory that continents move, drifting apart or together. (21.2)

continental shelf A gently sloping, relatively shallow submerged area that borders a continental landmass. (23.4)

continental slope The seaward slope beyond the continental shelf. It extends downward to the ocean basin. (23.4)

convection The transfer of heat by the movement of a substance, or mass, from one place to another. (5.4)

convection cycle The cyclic movement of matter (such as air) as a result of localized heating and convectional heat transfer. (19.4)

convergent boundary A region where moving plates of the lithosphere are driven together, causing one of the plates to be consumed into the mantle as it descends beneath an overriding plate. (21.3)

converging lens A lens that is thicker at the center than at the edges. (7.4)

conversion factor An equivalence statement expressed as a ratio. (1.6)

convex mirror A mirror shaped like the outside (convex side) of a spherical section. (7.3)

Coordinated Universal Time (UTC) The international time standard based on time kept by atomic clocks. (15.3)

Coriolis force A pseudoforce that results because an observer on the Earth is in a rotating frame of reference. (19.4)

correlation The process of matching rock layers in different localities by the use of fossils or other means. (24.2)

cosmic microwave background The microwave radiation that fills all space and is believed to be the redshifted glow from the Big Bang. (18.7)

cosmological redshift The shift toward longer wavelengths caused by the expansion of the universe. (18.7)

cosmology The branch of astronomy that is the study of the structure and evolution of the universe. (18.7)

coulomb (C) The unit of electric charge, equal to one ampere-second (A·s). (8.1)

Coulomb's law The force of attraction or repulsion between two charged bodies is directly proportional to the product of the two charges and inversely proportional to the square of the distance between them. (8.1)

covalent bond The force of attraction caused by a pair of electrons being shared by two atoms. (12.5)

covalent compounds Those in which the atoms share pairs of electrons to form molecules. (12.5)

crater (lunar) A circular depression on the surface of the Moon caused by the impact of a meteoroid. (17.1)

creep A type of slow mass wasting that involves the particle-by-particle movement of weathered debris down a slope. (23.2)

crescent moon The Moon viewed when less than one-half of its observed surface is illuminated. (17.2)

critical mass The minimum amount of fissionable material necessary to sustain a chain reaction. (10.5)

cross-cutting relationships, principle of An igneous rock or fault is younger than the rock layers it has intruded (cut into or across). (24.2)

crust The thin, rocky, outer layer of the Earth. (21.1)

Curie temperature The temperature above which a material ceases to be ferromagnetic. (8.4)

current (electrical) The time rate of flow of electric charge; $I = q/t$. (8.2)

cycloalkanes Members of a series of saturated hydrocarbons that have the general molecular formula C_nH_{2n} and possess rings of carbon atoms, each carbon atom bonded to a total of four carbon or hydrogen atoms. (14.3)

dark energy A mysterious energy that seems to be causing the expansion of the universe to accelerate. (18.7)

dark matter The as-yet-unidentified nonluminous matter in the universe. (18.6)

Daylight Saving Time (DST) Time advanced one hour from standard time, adopted during the spring and summer months to take advantage of longer evening daylight hours and save electricity. (15.3)

decibel (dB) A unit of sound intensity level; one-tenth of a bel (B). (6.4)

declination The angular measure in degrees, minutes, and seconds north or south of the celestial equator. (18.1)

decomposition reaction One in which only one reactant is present and decomposes into two (or more) products: $AB = A + B$. (13.1)

definite proportions, law of Different samples of a pure compound always contain the same elements in the same proportion by mass. (12.2)

delta The accumulation of sediment formed where running water enters a large body of water such as a lake or ocean. (23.2)

density A measure of the compactness of the matter or mass of a substance using a ratio of mass to volume; $\rho = m/V$. (1.6)

derived units Multiples or combinations of units. (1.6)

desert An area on the Earth's surface that has a severe lack of precipitation. (23.2)

destructive interference A superposition of waves for which the combined waveform has a smaller amplitude. (7.6)

dew point The temperature to which a sample of air must be cooled to become saturated—that is, has a relative humidity of 100%. (19.3)

diffraction The bending of waves as they go through relatively small slits or pass by the corners of objects. (7.6)

direct current (dc) Electric current in which the electrons flow directionally from the negative (−) terminal toward the positive (+) terminal. (8.2)

dispersion Different frequencies of light refracted at slightly different angles, giving rise to a spectrum. (7.2)

displacement The straight-line distance between the initial and final positions, with direction toward the final position, and is a vector quantity. (2.2)

distance The actual length of the path that is traveled. (2.2)

divergent boundary A region where one plate of the lithosphere is moving away from one another and new oceanic rock is formed. (21.3)

diverging lens A lens that is thinner at the center than at the edges. (7.4)

Doppler effect The apparent change in frequency of a moving sound source. (6.5)

Doppler radar Radar that uses the Doppler effect on water droplets in clouds to measure the wind speed and direction. (19.3)

double-replacement reactions Reactions in which the positive and negative components of the two compounds "change partners." The general format is $AB + CD \rightarrow AD + CB$. (13.3)

dual nature of light Light must be described sometimes as a wave and sometimes as a particle. (9.2)

dwarf planet A new class of planets including Pluto, Ceres, Eris Haumea, and Makemake. (16.6)

earthquake The tremendous release of energy accompanying the rupture or repositioning of underground rock and is manifested by the vibrating and sometimes violent movement of the Earth's surface. (21.5)

eclipse The blocking of the light of one celestial body by another. (17.2)

ecliptic The apparent path the Sun traces annually along the celestial sphere. (18.1)

electric charge A fundamental property of matter that can be either positive or negative and gives rise to electric forces. (8.1)

electric field A force field of imaginary lines surrounding a charge representing the electrical effect a positive unit charge would experience. (8.1)

electric potential energy The potential energy that results from work done in separating electric charges. (8.2)

electric power The expenditure of electrical work divided by time; $P = W/t = IV$. (8.2)

electromagnetic wave A transverse wave consisting of oscillating electric and magnetic fields. (8.5)

electromagnetism The interaction of electrical and magnetic effects. (8.5)

electron configuration The order of electrons in the energy levels of their atoms. (11.4)

electronegativity A measure of the ability of an atom in a molecule to draw bonding electrons to itself. (12.5)

electrons Negatively charged subatomic particles. (8.1, 9.1, 10.2)

element A substance in which all the atoms have the same number of protons (the same atomic number, Z). (10.2, 11.1)

elliptical orbits, law of (Kepler's first law) All planets move in elliptical orbits around the Sun, with the Sun at one focus of the ellipse. (16.1)

endothermic reaction A reaction that causes a net absorption of energy from the surroundings to occur. (13.2)

energy The ability to do work. (4.2)

entropy A mathematical quantity; thermodynamically speaking, its change tells whether or not a process can take place naturally. (5.7)

eon The largest unit of geologic time. Eons are divided into eras. (24.2)

epicenter The point on the surface of the Earth directly above the focus of an earthquake. (21.5)

epoch An interval of geologic time that is a subdivision of a period. (24.5)

equal areas, law of (Kepler's second law) An imaginary line (radial vector) joining a planet to the Sun sweeps out equal areas in equal periods of time. (16.1)

equilibrium In chemistry, a dynamic process in which the reactants are combining to form the products at the same rate at which the products are combining to form the reactants. (13.3)

equinox The two points where the ecliptic and the celestial equator intersect (18.1)

era An interval of geologic time that is a subdivision of an eon and is made up of periods and epochs. (24.2)

erosion The downslope movement of soil and rock fragments under the influence of gravity (mass wasting) or by agents such as streams, glaciers, wind, and waves. (23.2)

ester An organic compound that has the general formula RCOOR' where R and R' are any alkyl groups. (14.4)

excess reactant A starting material that is only partially used up in a chemical reaction. (12.2)

excited states The energy levels above the ground state in an atom. *See ground state.* (9.3)

exoplanets (extrasolar planets) Planets orbiting stars other than our own Sun. (16.8)

exothermic reaction A reaction that has a net release of energy to the surroundings. (13.2)

experiment The testing of a hypothesis under controlled conditions to see whether the test results confirm the hypothetical assumptions, can be duplicated, and are consistent. (1.2)

Fahrenheit scale A temperature scale with and ice point of 32° and a steam point of 212° with 180 equal units or divisions between these points. (5.1)

fats Esters composed of the trialcohol named glycerol, $C_3H_5(OH)_3$, and long-chain carboxylic acids known as fatty acids. (14.4)

fault A break or fracture in the surface of a planet or moon along which movement has occurred. (17.1, 21.5)

   normal The result of expansive forces that cause the fault's overlying side to move downward relative to the side beneath. (21.6)

   reverse The result of compressional stress forces that cause the overlying side of the fault to move upward relative to the side beneath. (21.6)

   transform (or strike-slip) The result of stresses that are parallel to the fault boundary such that the fault slip is horizontal. (21.6)

fault-block mountains Mountains that are built by normal faulting in which giant pieces of the Earth's crust were faulted and uplifted at the same time. (21.6)

ferromagnetic Characteristic of substances such as iron, nickel, and cobalt that exhibit the ability to acquire high magnetization. (8.4)

first law of thermodynamics The heat added to a system must go into increasing the internal energy of the system, or any work done by the system, or both. The law, which is based on the conservation of energy, also states that heat energy removed from a system must produce a decrease in the internal energy of the system, or any work done on the system, or both. (5.7)

first-quarter phase The Moon when it is 90° east of the Sun and appears as a quarter moon on an observer's meridian at 6 P.M. (17.2)

fission The process in which a large nucleus "splits" (fissions) into two intermediate-size nuclei, with the emission of neutrons and the conversion of mass into energy. (10.5)

floodplain The low adjacent land to a river or stream that can become inundated when the river or stream overflows. (23.2)

focal length The distance from the vertex of a mirror or lens to the focal point. (7.3)

focus (earthquake) The point within the Earth at which the initial energy release or slippage of an earthquake occurs. (21.5)

fold A folded rock layer that can form an arch (anticline) or a trough (syncline) as a result of compressional forces. (21.6)

fold mountains Mountains characterized by folded rock strata, with external evidence of faulting and internal evidence of high temperature and pressure changes. Fold mountains are believed to be formed at convergent plate boundaries. (21.6)

foliation The parallel alignment of minerals characteristic of some metamorphic rocks that results from directional pressures during transformation. (22.6)

foot-pound (ft·lb) The unit of work (and energy) in the British system. (4.1)

force A vector quantity capable of producing motion or a change in motion, that is, a change in velocity or an acceleration. (3.1)

formula mass The sum of the atomic masses given in the formula of a substance. (12.2)

formula unit The smallest combination of ions that gives the formula of the compound. (12.4)

fossil Any remnant or indication of prehistoric life preserved in rock. (24.1)

Foucault pendulum A pendulum that is used to demonstrate the rotation of the Earth. (16.3)

free fall A state of motion solely under the influence of gravity. (2.3)

frequency The number of oscillations or cycles of a wave that occur during a given period of time, usually one second. (6.2)

friction The ever-present resistance to relative motion that occurs whenever two materials are in contact with each other, whether they are solids, liquids, or gases. (3.3)

front The boundary between two air masses. (20.2)

full moon The phase of the Moon that occurs when the Moon is 180° east of the Sun and appears on the observer's meridian at 12 midnight local solar time. (17.2)

functional group Any atom, group of atoms, or organization of bonds that determines specific properties of a molecule. (14.4)

fusion The process in which smaller nuclei combine to form larger ones with the release of energy. (10.6)

G The universal gravitational constant; $G = 6.67 \times 10^{-11}$ N·m^2/kg^2. (3.5)

galaxy An extremely large collection of stars bound together by mutual gravitational attraction. Galaxies have a spiral, elliptical, or irregular structure. (18.6)

gamma decay An event in which a nucleus emits a *gamma ray* and becomes a less energetic form of the same nucleus. (10.3)

gas Matter that is made up of rapidly moving molecules and assumes the shape and size of its container; has no definite volume or shape. (5.5)

generator A device that converts mechanical work or energy into electrical energy. (8.5)

geocentric model The old false theory of the solar system, which placed the Earth at its center. (16.1)

geologic time The time span that covers the long history of the Earth. (24.Intro)

geologic time scale A relative time scale based on the fossil contents of rock strata and the principles of superposition and cross-cutting relationships. (24.5)

geology The study of the planet Earth: its composition, structure, and history. Also, the study of the chemical and physical properties of other solar system bodies. (21.Intro)

gibbous moon The Moon viewed when more than one-half of its illuminated surface is observed from the Earth. (17.2)

glacial drift General term for rock material that is transported and deposited by ice. (23.2)

glacier A large, thick mass of "permanent" ice that consists of recrystallized snow and that flows on a land surface under the influence of gravity. (23.2)

globular cluster A spherical collection of hundreds of thousands of gravitationally bound stars, usually found in the outlying regions of a galaxy. (18.6)

gravitational potential energy The potential energy resulting from an object's position in a gravitational field—in other words, the stored energy that comes from doing work against gravity. (4.2)

great circle Any circle on the surface of a sphere whose center is at the center of the sphere. It applies especially to imaginary circles on the Earth's surface that pass through both the North Pole and the South Pole. (15.2)

Great Dying The most devastating extinction known to geologists; it marked the end of the Paleozoic era and the beginning of the Mesozoic era. (24.5)

greenhouse effect The heat-retaining process of atmospheric gases, such as water vapor (H_2O) and carbon dioxide (CO_2), that results from the selective absorption of terrestrial radiation. (19.2)

Greenwich Mean Time (GMT) The time at the central prime meridian, or Greenwich meridian (0° longitude). (15.3)

Greenwich (prime) meridian The reference meridian of longitude, which passes through the old Royal Greenwich Observatory near London. (15.2)

Gregorian calendar The reformed Julian calendar—our present-day calendar. (15.5)

ground state The lowest energy level of an atom. (9.3)

groundwater Water that soaks into the soil down into the subsurface. (23.3)

groups The vertical columns in the periodic table. (11.4)

half-life The time it takes for half the nuclei in a given radioactive sample to decay. (10.3)

halogens The elements in Group 7A of the periodic table (F_2, Cl_2, Br_2, I_2). (11.6)

harmonic law (Kepler's third law) The square of the sidereal period of a planet is proportional to the cube of its semimajor axis (one-half the major axis). (16.1)

heat The net energy transferred from one object to another because of a temperature difference; energy in transit because of a temperature difference. (5.2)

heat engine A device that uses converts heat into work. (5.7)

heat pump A device that uses work input to transfer heat from a low-temperature reservoir to a high-temperature reservoir. (5.7)

Heisenberg's uncertainty principle It is impossible to know a particle's exact position and velocity simultaneously. (9.5)

heliocentric model The model of the solar system that places the Sun at its center. (16.1)

hertz (Hz) One cycle per second or 1/s. The SI unit of frequency. (6.2)

horsepower (hp) A unit of power equal to 550 f·lb/s. (746 W); commonly used to rate the power of motors and engines. (4.4)

H-R diagram A plot of the absolute magnitude of stars versus the temperature of their photospheres. (18.3)

Hubble's law The greater the recessional velocity of a galaxy, the farther away the galaxy, $V_r = H \times d$. (18.7)

Hubble's constant The proportionality constant for Hubble's law, currently believed to be 73 km/s/Mpc; also the average rate of expansion of the universe. (18.7)

humidity A measure of the moisture, or water vapor, in the air. (19.3)

hurricane A tropical storm with winds of 119km/h (74 mi/h or 64 knots) or greater. (20.3)

hurricane warning An alert that hurricane conditions are expected within 24 hours. (20.3)

hurricane watch An advisory alert that hurricane conditions are a threat within 24 to 36 hours. (20.3)

hydrocarbons The simplest organic compounds which contain only carbon and hydrogen. (14.2)

hydrogen bond A special kind of dipole–dipole interaction that can occur whenever a compound contains hydrogen atoms covalently bonded to small, highly electronegative atoms (only O, F, and N meet these criteria). (12.6)

hydrothermal metamorphism The chemical alteration of preexisting rocks by chemically reactive, hot-water solutions, which dissolve some ions from the original minerals and replace them with other ions, thus changing the mineral composition of the rock. (22.6)

hydrologic cycle The cyclic movement of the Earth's water supply from the oceans to the mountains and back again to the oceans. (23.3)

hypothesis A possible explanation for observations; tentative answer or an educated guess. (1.2)

ice storm A storm with accumulations of ice as a result of the surface temperature being below the freezing point. (20.3)

ideal gas law Relates the pressure, volume, and absolute temperature of a gas; $p_1V_1/T_1 = p_2V_2/T_2$. (5.6)

igneous rock Rock formed by the solidification of magma. (22.2)

index fossil A fossil that is widespread, numerous, easily identified, and typical of a particular limited time segment of the Earth's history. (24.2)

index of refraction The ratio of the speed of light in a vacuum to the speed of light in a medium. (7.2)

inertia The natural tendency of an object to remain in a state of rest or in uniform motion in a straight line. (3.2)

inner core The innermost region of the Earth, which is solid and probably composed of about 85% iron and 15% nickel. (21.1)

inner transition elements The *lanthanides* and *actinides*, the two rows at the bottom of the periodic table, make up the inner transition elements. (11.4)

insolation The solar radiation received by the Earth and its atmosphere; **in**coming **sol**ar radi**a**tion. (19.2)

instantaneous speed An object's speed at a particular instant of time. (2.2)

instantaneous velocity The velocity at a particular instant of time. (2.2)

intensity (of sound wave) The rate of sound energy transfer through a given area, with units of watts per square meter (W/m^2). (6.4)

interference, constructive A superposition of waves for which the combined waveform has a greater amplitude. (7.6)

interference, destructive A superposition of waves for which the combined waveform has a smaller amplitude. (7.6)

International Date Line (IDL) The meridian that is 180° E or W of the prime meridian. (15.3)

interplanetary dust Very small solid particles known as *micrometeoroids* that exist in the space between the planets. (17.6)

ion An atom, or chemical combination of atoms, that has a net electric charge because of a gain or loss of electrons. (11.5)

ionic bonds Electrical forces that hold the ions together in the crystal lattice of an ionic compound. (12.4)

ionic compounds Compounds formed by an electron transfer process in which one or more atoms lose their valence electrons, and other atoms gain these same electrons to achieve noble gas configurations. (12.4)

ionization energy The amount of energy it takes to remove an electron from an atom. (11.4)

ionosphere The region of the atmosphere between about 70 km (43 mi) and several hundred kilometers in altitude. It is characterized by a high concentration of ions. (19.1)

isobar A line on a weather map drawn through the locations (points) of equal pressure. (19.4)

isostasy The depth to which a floating object sinks into underlying material depends on the objects density and thickness; the state of buoyancy between the Earth's lithosphere and asthenosphere. (21.3)

isotopes Forms of nuclei of an element that have the same numbers of protons but differ in their numbers of neutrons. (10.2)

jet streams Rapidly moving "rivers" of air in the upper troposphere. (19.4)

joule (J) A unit of energy equivalent to 1 N·m or 1 kg·m^2/s^2. (4.1)

Jovian planets The four outer planets—Saturn, Jupiter, Uranus, and Neptune. All have characteristics resembling those of Jupiter, having gaseous outer layers. (16.2)

kelvin (K) The unit of temperature on the Kelvin (absolute) temperature scale. A kelvin is equal in magnitude to a degree Celsius. (5.1)

Kelvin scale The "absolute" temperature scale that takes absolute zero as 0 K. (5.1)

kilo- Metric prefix that means 10^3, or one thousand. (1.5)

kilocalorie (kcal) The amount of heat necessary to raise the temperature of one *kilogram* of water one Celsius degree. (5.2)

kilogram (kg) The standard metric unit of mass; 1 kilogram has an equivalent weight of 2.2 pounds. (1.4)

kilowatt-hour (kWh) A unit of energy (power × time); $P = E/t$, and $E = Pt$. (4.4)

kinetic energy Energy of an object's motion, equal to $\frac{1}{2}mv^2$. (4.2)

kinetic theory A gas consists of molecules moving independently in all directions at high speeds (the higher the temperature, the higher the average speed), colliding with one another and the walls of the container, and having a distance between molecules that is large, on average, compared with the size of the molecules themselves. (5.6)

K-T Event The extinction episode that marks the transition from the Cretaceous period (K) to the Tertiary period (T). (24.5)

Kuiper belt A doughnut-shaped ring of space around the Sun beyond the orbit of Neptune and that extends to well beyond the orbit of Pluto and Eris, containing many short-period comets. (17.5)

land breeze A local wind from land to sea resulting from a convection cycle. (19.4)

lapse rate The rate at which the temperature of the air in the troposphere decreases with altitude. The normal lapse rate is −6.5 C°/km, or −3.5 F°/1000 ft. (19.5)

laser An acronym for **l**ight **a**mplification by **s**timulated **e**mission of **r**adiation; it produces coherent, monochromatic light. (9.4)

last-quarter (third quarter) phase The phase that occurs when the Moon is 270° east of the Sun and appears on the observer's meridian at 6 A.M. local solar time. (17.2)

latent heat The heat associated with a phase change. (5.3)

    of fusion The amount of heat necessary to change one kilogram of a solid into a liquid. (5.3)

    of vaporization The amount of heat required to change one kilogram of a liquid to a gas . (5.3)

latitude The angular measurement in degrees north or south of the equator for a point on the surface of the Earth. (15.2)

lava Magma that reaches the Earth's surface through a volcanic vent. (22.3)

law A concise statement in words or a mathematical equation that describes a fundamental relationship of nature. (1.2)

law of:

    charges Like charges repel; unlike charges attract. (8.1)

    elliptical orbits All planets move in elliptical orbits around the Sun, with the Sun at one focus of the ellipse. (16.1)

    equal areas An imaginary line (radial vector) joining a planet to the Sun sweeps out equal areas in equal periods of time. (16.1)

    poles (magnetic) Like poles repel; unlike poles attract. (8.4)

    reflection The angle of incidence is equal to the angle of reflection, $\theta_i = \theta_r$, as measured relative to the normal, a line perpendicular to the reflecting surface. (7.1)

length The measurement of space in any direction. (1.4)

Lewis structures "Electron dot" symbols used to show valence electrons in molecules and ions of compounds. (12.4)

Lewis symbol The element's symbol represents the nucleus and inner electrons of an atom, and the valence electrons are shown as dots arranged around the symbol. (12.4)

lightning A huge discharge of electrical energy in the atmosphere. (20.3)

light-year The distance traveled by light in one year (9.5×10^{12} km or 6 trillion mi). (18.1)

limiting reactant A starting material that is used up completely in a chemical reaction. (12.2)

line absorption spectrum A set of dark spectral lines of certain frequencies or wavelengths, formed by dispersion of light that has come from an incandescent source and has then passed through a sample of cool gas. (9.3)

line emission spectrum A set of bright spectral lines of certain frequencies or wavelengths formed by dispersion of light from a gas discharge tube. Each element gives a different set of lines. (9.3)

linear momentum The product of an object's mass and its velocity. (3.7)

linearly polarized light The condition of transverse light waves that vibrate in only one plane. (7.5)

liquid An arrangement of molecules that may move and assume the shape of the container; has a definite volume but no definite shape. (5.5)

liter (L) A metric unit of volume or capacity; $1 \text{ L} = 1000 \text{ cm}^3$. (1.5)

lithification The process of transforming a sediment into a sedimentary rock; also called consolidation. (22.5)

lithosphere The outermost solid portion of the Earth, which includes the crust and part of the upper mantle. (21.1)

Local Group The cluster of galaxies that includes our own Milky Way. (18.6)

longitude The angular measurement in degrees east or west of the reference meridian, known as the Greenwich (prime) meridian for a point on the surface of the Earth. (15.2)

longitudinal wave A wave in which the particle motion and the wave velocity are parallel to each other. (6.2)

long-shore current A current along a shore that results from waves that break at an angle to the shoreline. (23.4)

lunar eclipse An eclipse of the Moon caused by the Earth's blocking the Sun's rays to the Moon. (17.4)

    partial lunar eclipse The Earth's umbral (dark) shadow does not completely cover the Moon. (17.4)

    total lunar eclipse The Earth's umbral (dark) shadow completely covers the Moon. (17.4)

luster The appearance of a mineral's surface in reflected light. (22.1)

magma The molten material beneath the Earth's surface. (22.3)

magnetic declination The angle between geographic (true) north and magnetic north. (8.4)

magnetic domains Local regions of alignment of the magnetic fields of numerous atoms in ferromagnetic materials. (8.4)

magnetic field A magnetic force field represented by a set of imaginary lines that indicate the direction in which a small compass needle would point if it were placed near a magnet. (8.4)

magnitude (absolute) The brightness that a star would have if it were placed 10 parsecs from the Earth. (18.3)

magnitude (apparent) The brightness of a star as observed from the Earth. (18.3)

main sequence The narrow band going from the lower right to the upper left on the H-R diagram; most stars fall into this category. (18.3)

mantle The interior region of the Earth between the core and the crust. (21.1)

maria Large, dark, flat areas on the Moon believed to be craters formed by large impacts from space that then filled with volcanic lava. (17.1)

mass A quantity of matter and a measure of the amount of inertia that an object possesses. (1.4, 3.2)

mass defect The decrease in mass in a nuclear reaction. (10.6)

mass number The number of protons plus neutrons in a nucleus; the total number of nucleons. (10.2)

mass wasting The general geologic term for the downslope movement of soil and rock under the influence of gravity. (23.2)

matter (de Broglie) waves The waves associated with moving particles. (9.6)

meander A loop-like bend in a stream channel influenced by gravity and the rotating Earth. (23.2)

measurement A quantitative observation, one involving numbers. (1.2)

mega- Prefix that means 10^6, or one million. (1.5)

meridians Imaginary lines drawn along the surface of the Earth running from the geographic North Pole to the geographic South Pole perpendicular to the equator. (15.2)

mesosphere The region of the Earth's atmosphere that lies between approximately 50 and 80 km (30 and 50 mi) in altitude. (19.1)

metal An element whose atoms tend to lose valence electrons during chemical reactions. (11.4)

metamorphic rock Rock that is formed by the alteration of preexisting rock in response to the effects of pressure, temperature, or the gain or loss of chemical components. (22.2)

metamorphism The process by which the structure, mineral content, or both of a rock is changed while the rock remains a solid. (22.6)

meteor A metallic or stony object that burns up as it passes through the Earth's atmosphere and appears to be a "shooting star." (17.6)

meteorite A metallic or stony object from the solar system that strikes the Earth's surface. (17.6)

meteoroids Small, interplanetary metallic and stony objects in space before they encounter the Earth. (17.6)

meteorology The study of the lower atmosphere. (19.Intro)

meter (m) The standard unit of length in the metric system. It is equal to 39.37 inches, or 3.28 feet. (1.4)

metric system The decimal (base-10) system of units employed predominantly throughout the world. (1.4)

mid-ocean ridge A series of mountain ranges on the ocean floor, more than 84,000 km (52,000 mi) in length, extending through the North and South Atlantic, the Indian Ocean, and the South Pacific. (21.2)

milli- The metric prefix that means 10^{-3}, or 1 one-thousandth. (1.5)

mineral A naturally occurring, crystalline inorganic element or compound that possesses a fairly definite chemical composition and a distinctive set of physical properties. (22.1)

mixture A type of matter composed of varying proportions of two or more substances that are just physically mixed, *not* chemically bonded. (11.1)

mks system The metric system that has the *meter*, *kilogram*, *second*, and *coulomb* as the standard units of length, mass, time, and electric charge, respectively. (1.4)

Moho (Mohorovicic discontinuity) The sharply defined boundary that separates the Earth's crust from the upper mantle. (21.1)

Mohs scale A list of 10 minerals used to measure the hardness of other minerals. (22.1)

molarity (M) A measure of solution concentration in terms of moles of solute per liter of solution. (13.5)

mold A hollow depression formed when an embedded shell or bone is dissolved out of a rock. (24.1)

mole (mol) The quantity of a substance that contains as many elementary units as there are atoms in exactly 12 g of carbon-12; 6.02×10^{23} formula units. (13.5)

molecule An electrically neutral particle composed of two or more atoms chemically bonded. (11.3)

monomer A fundamental repeating unit of a polymer (14.5)

moraine A ridge of glacial drift. (23.2)

motion The undergoing of a continuous change in position. (2.1)

motor A device that converts electrical energy into mechanical energy. (8.5)

mountain range A series of mountains. (21.6)

neap tides Moderate tides with the least variation between high and low. They occur at the first- and last-quarter phases of the Moon. (17.2)

nebulae Cool, dense clouds of interstellar gas and dust. (18.4)

neutron number N, the number of neutrons in the nucleus of an atom. (10.2)

neutrons Neutral particles found in the nuclei of atoms. (10.2)

neutron star An extremely high-density star composed almost entirely of neutrons. (18.5)

new moon The phase of the Moon that occurs when the Moon is on the same meridian as the Sun at 12 noon local solar time. (17.2)

newton (N) The unit of force in the metric system; $1 \, kg \cdot m/s^2$. (3.3)

Newton's first law of motion An object will remain at rest or in uniform motion in a straight line unless acted on by an external, unbalanced force. (3.2)

Newton's law of universal gravitation Every particle in the universe attracts every other particle with a force that is directly proportional to the product of their masses and inversely proportional to the square of the distance between them; $F = Gm_1m_2/r^2$. (3.5)

Newton's second law of motion The acceleration of an object is equal to the net force on the object divided by the mass of the object; $a = F/m$. (3.3)

Newton's third law of motion For every action there is an equal and opposite reaction; for every force there is an equal and opposite force, acting on different bodies. (3.4)

nitrogen oxides (NO_x) Chemical combinations of nitrogen and oxygen, such as NO and NO_2. (20.4)

noble gases The elements of Group 8A of the periodic table (He, Ne, Ar, Kr, Xe, Rn). (11.6)

nonmetal An element whose atoms tend to gain (or share) electrons during chemical reactions. (11.4)

nova A white dwarf star that suddenly increases dramatically in brightness for a brief period of time. (18.5)

nucleons A collective term for neutrons and protons (particles in the nucleus). (10.2)

nucleosynthesis The creation of the nuclei of elements inside stars. (18.4)

nucleus The central core of an atom; composed of protons and neutrons. (10.2)

nuclide A particular species or isotope of any element, characterized by a definite atomic number and mass number. (10.3)

octet rule In forming compounds, atoms tend to gain, lose, or share valence electrons to achieve electron configurations of the noble gases; that is, they tend to get eight electrons (an octet) in the outer shell. Hydrogen is the main exception; it tends to get two electrons in the outer shell, like the configuration of the noble gas helium. (12.4)

ohm (Ω) The unit of resistance; equal to one volt per ampere. (8.2)

Ohm's law The voltage across two points is equal to the current flowing between the points times the resistance between the points; $V = IR$. (8.2)

Oort cloud The cloud of cometary objects believed to be orbiting the Sun far beyond the orbit of Neptune at 50,000 astronomical units and from which the majority of comets originate. (17.6)

opposition The time at which one of the superior planets is on the opposite side of the Earth from the Sun. (16.2)

organic chemistry The study of carbon compounds. (14.Intro)

original horizontality, principle of The principle that sediments and lava flows are deposited as horizontal layers. (24.2)

outer core Part of the innermost region of the Earth, which is composed of iron and nickel in two parts: a solid inner core and a molten, highly viscous outer core. (21.1)

oxidation Occurs when oxygen combines with a substance or when an atom or ion loses electrons. (13.4)

ozone O_3, a form of oxygen found naturally in the atmosphere in the ozonosphere. It is also a constituent of photochemical smog. (19.1, 20.4)

ozonosphere A region of the atmosphere, below 70 km (45 mi) in altitude, characterized by ozone concentration. (19.1)

paleontology The systematic study of fossils and prehistoric life forms. (24.1)

Pangaea The giant supercontinent that is believed to have existed over 200 million years ago. (21.2)

parallax The apparent motion, or shift, that occurs between two fixed objects when the observer changes position. (16.3, 18.1)

parallel circuit A circuit in which the voltage across each resistance is the same, but the current through each resistance may vary (different resistances, different currents). (8.3)

parallels Imaginary lines encircling the Earth parallel to the plane of the equator. (15.2)

parsec (pc) The distance to a star when the star exhibits a parallax of one second of arc, where 1 second of arc is defined to be 1/3,600 of 1°. This distance is equal to 3.26 light-years or 206,265 astronomical units. (18.1)

partial lunar eclipse The Earth's umbral (dark) shadow does not completely cover the Moon. (17.2)

partial solar eclipse Partial blocking of the Sun, seen by an observer in the penumbra. (17.2)

penumbra A semidark region of the Moon's shadow. During an eclipse, an observer in the penumbra sees only a partial eclipse. (17.2)

perihelion The point when Earth (or another orbiting object) is closest to the Sun. (15.5)

period In physics, the time for a complete cycle of motion. In chemistry, one of the seven horizontal rows of the periodic table. In geology, an interval of geologic time that is a subdivision of an era and is made up of epochs. (6.2, 11.4, 24.2)

periodic law The properties of elements are periodic functions of their atomic numbers. (11.4)

periodic table Organization of the elements on the basis of atomic numbers into seven rows called periods. (11.4)

permafrost Ground that is permanently frozen. (23.1)

permeability A material's capacity to transmit fluids. (23.3)

pH A measure (on a logarithmic scale) of the hydrogen ion (or hydronium ion) concentration in a solution. (13.3)

phases of matter The physical forms of matter—most commonly, solid, liquid, and gas. (5.5)

photochemical smog Air pollution resulting from the chemical reactions of hydrocarbons with oxygen in the air and other pollutants in the presence of sunlight. (20.4)

photoelectric effect The emission of electrons that occurs when certain metals are exposed to light. (9.2)

photon A "particle" of electromagnetic energy. (9.2)

photosphere The bright, visible "surface" of the Sun. (18.2)

photosynthesis The process by which plants convert CO_2 and H_2O into carbohydrates (needed for plant life) and O_2, using energy from the Sun. (19.1)

physics The most fundamental physical science; concerned with the basic principles and concepts that describe the workings of the universe. It deals with matter, motion, force, and energy. (2.Intro)

planetary nebula A luminous shell of gas ejected from an old, low-mass star. (18.4)

plasma A high-temperature gas of free electrons and positively charged ions. (10.6)

plate tectonics The theory that the Earth's lithosphere is made up of a series of solid sections or segments called *plates* that are constantly interating with one another in very slow motion. (21.3)

plutons Intrusive igneous rocks, formed below the surface of the Earth by solidification of magma. (22.4)

polar covalent bond One in which the pair of bonding electrons is unequally shared, leading to the bond's having a slightly positive end and a slightly negative end. (12.5)

polar molecule A molecule that has a positive end and a negative end—that is, one that has a dipole. (12.5)

polarization The preferential orientation of the electric vector of a light wave. (7.5)

poles, law of (magnetic) Like poles repel; unlike poles attract. (8.4)

pollution Any atypical contribution to the environment resulting from the activities of humans. (20.4)

polymer A compound of very high molecular mass whose chain-like molecules are made up of repeating units called monomers. (14.5)

position The location of an object with respect to a reference point. (2.1)

post meridiem (P.M.) Pertaining to time from 12 noon to 12 midnight. (15.3)

potential energy The energy an object has because of its position or location; the energy of position. (4.2)

power The time rate of doing work. (4.4)

powers-of-10 notation Notation in which numbers are expressed by a coefficient and a power of 10; for example, $2500 = 2.5 \times 10^3$. Also called *scientific notation*. (1.7)

precession The slow rotation of the axis of spin of the Earth around an axis perpendicular to the ecliptic plane. The rotation is clockwise as observed from the north celestial pole. (15.6)

precipitate An insoluble solid that appears when two liquids (usually aqueous solutions) are mixed. (13.3)

pressure The force per unit area; $p = F/A$. (5.6)

principal quantum number The numbers $n = 1, 2, 3, \ldots$ used to designate the various principal energy levels that an electron may occupy in a hydrogen atom. (9.3)

principle of

　cross-cutting relationships An igneous rock is younger than the rock layers it has intruded (cut into or across). (24.2)

　original horizontality Sediments and lava flows are deposited as horizontal layers. (24.2)

　superposition (geology) The principle that in a sequence of undisturbed sedimentary rocks, lavas, or ash, each layer is younger than the layer beneath it and older than the layer above it. (24.2)

　superposition (wave) At any time, the combined waveform of two or more interfering waves is given by the sum of the displacements of the individual waves at each point in the medium. (7.6)

products The substances formed during a chemical reaction. (13.1)

prograde motion Orbital or rotational motion in the forward direction. In the solar system, this is west-to-east, or counterclockwise, as viewed from above the Earth's North Pole. (16.2)

projectile motion The motion of a projected or thrown object under the influence of gravity. (2.5)

proteins Biological polymers and extremely long-chain polyamides formed by the enzyme-catalyzed condensation of *amino acids* under the direction of nucleic acids in the cell (or the biochemist in the lab). (14.6)

proton-proton chain A series of stellar nuclear reactions in which four hydrogen nuclei (protons) combine to form one helium nucleus and release energy. (18.2)

protons Positively charged particles in the nuclei of atoms. (8.1, 10.2)

psychrometer An instrument used to measure relative humidity. (19.3)

pyroclastics (tephra) Solid material emitted by volcanoes; range in size from fine dust to large boulders. (22.4)

quantum A discrete amount of energy. (9.2)

quantum mechanics The branch of physics that replaced the classical-mechanical view (that everything moved according to exact laws of nature) with the concept of probability. Schrödinger's equation forms the basis of quantum wave mechanics. (9.7)

quasar Shortened from quasi-stellar radio sources, these are extremely distant objects emitting a tremendous amount of energy. (18.6)

radar An instrument that sends out electromagnetic (radio) waves, monitors the returning waves that are reflected by some object, and thereby locates the object. Radar stands for **ra**dio **d**etecting **an**d **r**anging. Radar is used to detect and monitor precipitation and severe storms. (19.3)

radiation A method of heat transfer by means of electromagnetic waves. (5.4)

radioactive isotope A nuclide whose nucleotide undergoes spontaneous decay (disintegration). (10.3)

radioactivity The spontaneous process of nuclei undergoing a change by the emitting particles or rays. (10.3)

radiometric dating The determination of age by using radioactivity; geology's best tool for establishing absolute geologic time. (24.3)

radionuclides Types of nuclei that undergo radioactive decay. (10.3)

rain gauge An open, calibrated container used to measure amounts of precipitation. (19.3)

ray A straight line that represents the path of light with a directional arrowhead. (7.1)

Rayleigh scattering The preferential scattering of light by air molecules and particles that accounts for the blueness of the sky. The scattering is proportional to $1/\lambda^4$. (19.2)

rays (lunar) Streaks of light-colored material extending outward from craters on the Moon. (17.1)

reactants The original substances in a chemical reaction. (13.1)

real image An image from a mirror or lens for which the light rays converge so that an image can be formed on a screen. (7.3)

red giant A relatively cool, very bright star that has a diameter much larger than average. (18.3)

redshift A Doppler effect caused when a light source, such as a galaxy, moves away from the observer and shifts the light frequencies lower, or toward the red end of the electromagnetic spectrum. (6.5)

reduction Occurs when oxygen is removed from a compound or when an atom or ion gains electrons. (13.4)

reflection The change in the direction of a wave when it strikes and rebounds from a surface or the boundary between two media. (7.1)

reflection

　diffuse Reflection from a rough surface in which reflected rays are not parallel but scattered. (7.1)

　law of The angle of reflection equals the angle of incidence, $\theta_i = \theta_r$ as measured relative to the normal, a line perpendicular to the reflecting surface. (7.1)

　specular Reflection from very smooth (mirror) surfaces in which the reflected rays are parallel. (7.1)

　total internal A phenomenon in which light is totally reflected in a medium because of refraction. (7.2)

refraction The deviation of light from its original path caused by a change in speed in the second medium. (7.2)

regional metamorphism A change in rock over a large area, brought about by both heat and pressure. (22.6)

relative geologic time A time scale obtained when rocks and the geologic events they record are placed in chronologic order without regard to actual dates. (24.2)

relative humidity The ratio of the actual moisture content to the maximum moisture capacity of a volume of air at a given temperature. (19.3)

remanent magnetism The magnetization of rocks that form in the presence of an external magnetic field. (21.2)

renewable energy sources Energy sources from natural processes that are constantly replenished, such as wind and hydro power (4.6)

replacement fossil Fossil formed when a mineral slowly replaces parts of a buried organism. (24.1)

representative elements Those in Groups 1A through 8A in the periodic table. (11.4)

resistance (electrical) The opposition to the flow of electric charge. (8.2)

resonance A wave effect that occurs when an object has a natural frequency that corresponds to an external frequency. (6.6)

retrograde rotation Orbital or rotational motion in the backward direction. In the solar system, this is east to west, or clockwise, as viewed from above the Earth's North Pole. (16.2)

revolution The movement of one object around another. (16.3)

Richter scale The severity of an earthquake as an absolute measure of the energy released. (21.5)

right ascension A coordinate for measuring the east-west positions of celestial objects. The angle is measured eastward from the vernal equinox in hours, minutes, and seconds. (18.1)

rill A narrow trench or valley on the Moon. (17.1)

Ring of Fire The plate boundaries of the Pacific Ocean where volcanoes and earthquakes are common. (21.4)

rock A solid, cohesive natural aggregate of one or more minerals. (22.2)

rock cycle A series of events through which a rock changes over time between igneous, sedimentary, and metamorphic forms. (22.2)

rotation The turning (spinning) of an object about an internal axis. (16.3)

salt An ionic compound composed of any cation except H^+ and any anion except OH^-. (13.3)

saturated solution A solution that has the maximum amount of solute dissolved in the solvent at a given temperature. (11.1)

scalar A quantity that has a magnitude but has no direction associated with it. (2.2)

science An organized body of knowledge about the natural universe and the processes by which that knowledge is acquired and tested. (1.1)

scientific method An investigative process that holds that no concept or model of nature is valid unless the predictions it generates agree with experimental results. That is, all hypotheses should be based on as much relevant data as possible and then should be tested and verified. (1.2)

sea breeze A local wind blowing from the sea to land as a result of a convection cycle. (19.4)

seafloor spreading The theory that the seafloor slowly spreads and moves sideways away from mid-ocean ridges. The spreading is believed to be due to convection cycles of subterranean molten material that cause the formation of the ridges and a surface motion in a lateral direction from the ridges. (21.2)

seamount An isolated submarine volcanic mountain that may extend to heights of more than 1.6 km (1 mi) above the seafloor. (23.4)

second The standard unit of time. It is now defined in terms of the frequency of a certain transition in the cesium atom. (1.4)

second law of thermodynamics It is impossible for heat to flow spontaneously from a colder body to a hotter body. (5.7)

sedimentary rock Rock formed at the Earth's surface by compaction of layers of sediment. (22.2)

sediment Sand, mud, precipitated material, or rock fragments that have been transported or deposited by water, air, or ice. (22.5)

seismic waves The waves generated by the energy release of an earthquake. (21.1)

series circuit A circuit in which an entering current flows individually through all the circuit elements. (8.3)

shear metamorphism A change in rock brought about primarily by pressure rather than heat. (22.6)

SI (International System of Units) A modernized version of the metric system that contains seven base units. (1.4)

sidereal day The elapsed time between two successive crossings of the same meridian by a star other than the Sun. One sidereal day is 23 h, 56 min, 4.091 s. (15.3)

sidereal month The time it takes for the Moon to make one complete cycle relative to the stars, 27.3 days. (17.2)

sidereal period The time it takes a planet (or other object) to make one full orbit around the Sun relative to a fixed star. (16.2)

sidereal year The time interval for the Earth to make one complete revolution around the Sun with respect to any particular star other than the Sun. (15.5)

significant figures A method of expressing measured numbers properly; involves the accuracy of measurement and mathematical operations. (1.7)

silicate Any one of numerous minerals that have the oxygen and silicon tetrahedron as their basic structure. (22.1)

single-replacement reactions Reactions in which one element replaces another that is in a compound: $A + BC \rightarrow B + AC$. (13.4)

sinkhole A depression on the land surface where soluble rock (limestone) has been removed by groundwater. (23.1)

snowstorm An appreciable accumulation of snow. When accompanied by high winds and low temperatures, it is referred to as a *blizzard*. (20.3)

smog A contraction of **sm**oke-**fo**g, used to describe the combination of these conditions. (20.4)

solar day The elapsed time between two successive crossings of the same meridian by the Sun. (15.3)

solar eclipse An eclipse of the Sun caused by the Moon blocking the Sun's rays to an observer on the Earth. (17.2)

    partial Partial blocking of the Sun, seen by an observer in the penumbra. (17.2)

    total Complete blocking of the Sun, seen by an observer in the umbra. (17.2)

solar nebula A large, spherical cloud of cold gases and dust that contracted under the influence of its own gravity, began rotating, and then flattened into a swirling disk of gas and dust. (16.7)

solar system A complex system of moving masses held together by gravitational forces, consisting of the Sun, eight major planets and their satellites, dwarf planets, the asteroids, comets, meteoroids, and interplanetary dust. (16.1)

solid Matter that has relatively fixed molecules and a definite shape and volume. (5.5)

solstice The point where the Sun is farthest north (or south) from the equator, approximately on June 21 (or December 22). (18.1)

solubility The amount of solute that will dissolve in a specified volume or mass of solvent (at a given temperature) to produce a saturated solution. (11.1)

solute The substance(s) present in a smaller amount in a solution. (11.1)

solution A mixture that is uniform throughout, also called a homogeneous mixture. (11.1)

solvent The substance present in the larger amount in a solution. (11.1)

sound The propagation of *longitudinal* waves through matter. (6.4)

sound spectrum An ordered arrangement of various frequencies or wavelengths of sound. The three main regions of the sound spectrum are the infrasonic, the audible, and the ultrasonic. (6.4)

source region The region from which an air mass derives its physical characteristics. (20.2)

specific gravity The ratio of a sample?s mass to the mass of an equal volume of water. (1.6, 22.1)

specific heat The amount of heat energy in kilocalories necessary to raise the temperature of one kilogram of the substance one Celsius degree. (5.3)

speed, average The total distance traveled divided by the time spent in traveling the total distance. (2.2)

speed, instantaneous An object's speed at a particular instant of time (Δt becoming extremely small). (2.2)

speed of light (c) How fast light travels. In air or a vacuum, $c = 3.00 \times 10^8$ m/s, or 186,000 mi/s. (6.3)

speed of sound How fast sound travels in a medium; for example, $v_s = 344$ m/s (770 mi/h) in air at room temperature. (6.4)

spring tides The tides of greatest variation between high and low. They occur at the new and full phases of the Moon. (17.2)

standard time zones The division of the surface of the Earth into 24 time zones, each containing about 15° of longitude. (15.3)

standard unit A fixed and reproducible value for the purpose of taking accurate measurements. (1.4)

standing wave A "stationary" waveform arising from the interference of waves traveling in opposite directions. (6.6)

steam point The temperature at which water boils at normal atmospheric pressure, 100 °C or 212 °F. (5.1)

stimulated emission Process in which an excited atom is caused to emit a photon. (9.4)

Stock system A system of nomenclature for compounds of metals that form more than one ion. A Roman numeral placed in parentheses directly after the name of the metal denotes its ionic charge in the compound being named. (12.4)

storm surge The great dome of water associated with a hurricane when it makes landfall. (20.3)

stratosphere The region of the Earth's atmosphere from approximately 16 to 50 km (10 to 30 mi) in altitude. (19.1)

streak The color of the powder of a mineral on a streak plate (unglazed porcelain). (22.1)

stream Any flow of water occurring between well-defined banks. (23.2)

strong nuclear force The short-range force of attraction that acts between two nucleons and holds the nucleus together. (10.2)

structural formula A graphical representation of the way the atoms are connected to one another in a molecule. (14.3)

subduction The process in which one plate is deflected downward beneath another plate into the asthenosphere. (21.3, 22.3)

subsidence The sinking of the land surface due to the excessive extraction of groundwater. (23.3)

sulfur dioxide (SO_2) An atmospheric pollutant formed by the oxidation of sulfur; it contributes to acid rain. (20.4)

summer solstice The farthest point of the Sun's latitude north of the equator (for the Northern Hemisphere), around June 21. The beginning of summer. (15.5)

sunspot Huge regions of cooler gas on the surface of the Sun where the magnetic field is very strong. (18.2)

sunspot cycle The 11-year variation of the number and location of the sunspots on the Sun. (18.2)

supernova An exploding star. (18.5)

superposition, principle of (geology) In a sequence of undisturbed sedimentary rocks, lavas, or ash, each layer is younger than the layer beneath it and older than the layer above it. (24.2)

superposition, principle of (wave) At any time, the combined waveform of two or more interfering waves is given by the sum of the displacements of the individual waves at each point in the medium. (7.6)

supersaturated solution A solution that contains more than the normal maximum amount of dissolved solute at a given temperature and hence is unstable. (11.1)

synodic month The time it takes the Moon to go through one complete cycle of phases (a month of phases), 29.5 days. (17.2)

synthetics Materials whose molecules have no duplicates in nature. (14.5)

system of units A group of standard units and their combinations. The two major systems of units in use today are the metric system and the British system. (1.4)

temperature A measure of the average kinetic energy of the molecules of a substance. (5.1)

temperature inversion A condition characterized by an inverted lapse rate. (20.4)

terminal velocity The maximum velocity reached by a falling object because of air resistance. (2.3)

terminator The boundary of the circle of illumination between daylight and dark. (15.5)

terrestrial planets The four inner planets—Mercury, Venus, Earth, and Mars. All are similar to the Earth in general chemical and physical properties. (16.2)

theory A well-tested explanation of observed natural phenomena. (1.2)

thermodynamics The science dealing with the production of heat, the flow of heat, and the conversion of heat to work. (5.7)

thermodynamics, first law of The heat energy added to a system must go into increasing the internal energy of the system, or any work done by the system, or both. The law, which is based on the conservation of energy, also states that heat energy removed from a system must produce a decrease in the internal energy of the system, or any work done on the system, or both. (5.7)

thermodynamics, second law of It is impossible for heat to flow spontaneously from a colder body to a hotter body. (5.7)

thermodynamics, third law of It is impossible to attain a temperature of absolute zero. (5.7)

thermosphere The region of the Earth's atmosphere extending from about 80 km (50 mi) in altitude to the outer reaches of the atmosphere. (19.1)

thunder The sound associated with lightning; it arises from the explosive release of electrical energy. (20.3)

tides The periodic rise and fall of the water level along the shores of large bodies of water. (17.2, 23.4)

time The continuous forward flow of events. (1.4, 15.3)

tornado The most violent of storms, characterized by a whirling, funnel-shaped cloud and high winds. (20.3)

tornado warning The alert issued when a tornado has actually been sighted or is indicated on radar. (20.3)

tornado watch The alert issued when atmospheric conditions indicate that tornadoes may form. (20.3)

torque A twisting action that produces rotational motion or a change in rotational motion. (3.7)

total internal reflection A phenomenon in which light is totally reflected in a medium because of refraction. (7.2)

total lunar eclipse The Earth's umbral (dark) shadow completely covers the Moon. (17.2)

total solar eclipse Complete blocking of the Sun, seen by an observer in the umbra. (17.2)

trace fossil A fossil imprint made by the movement of an animal. (24.1)

transform boundary A region of the lithosphere where a moving plate slides along one side of another without creating or destroying rock. (21.3)

transformer A device based on electromagnetic induction that increases or decreases the voltage or alternating current. (8.5)

transition elements The B group of elements in the periodic table. (11.4)

trans-Neptunian object (TNO) Large collection of comet-like objects orbiting the Sun beyond the orbit of Neptune. (17.6)

transverse wave A wave in which the particle motion is perpendicular to the direction of the wave velocity. (6.2)

tropical year The time interval from one vernal equinox to the next; the elapsed time between two successive northward crossings of the Sun above the equator (vernal equinox). (15.5)

troposphere The region of the Earth's atmosphere from the ground up to about 16 km (10 mi). (19.1)

tsunami A Japanese word for a "harbor" wave—an unusually large sea wave produced by a seaquake or undersea volcanic eruption. (21.5)

ultrasound Sound with frequency greater than 20,000 Hz or 20 kHz. (6.4)

umbra A region of total darkness in a shadow. During an eclipse, an observer in the umbra sees a total eclipse. (17.2)

unbalanced (net) force The sum of vector forces with a nonzero result. A force capable of producing motion. (3.1)

unconformity A break in the geologic rock record. (24.2)

uniformitarianism The principle that the same processes operate on and within the Earth today as in the past. Hence the present is considered the key to the past. (22.2)

universe The totality of all matter, energy, and space. (18.Intro)

unsaturated solution A solution in which more solute can be dissolved at the same temperature. (11.1)

valence electrons The electrons that are involved in bond formation, usually those in an atom's outer shell. (11.4)

valence shell An atom's outer shell, which contains the valence electrons. (11.4)

vector A quantity that has both magnitude and direction. (2.1)

velocity, average The displacement divided by the total travel time; $\bar{v} = \Delta d/\Delta t$. (2.2)

velocity, instantaneous The velocity at any instant of time. (2.2)

velocity, terminal The maximum velocity reached by a falling object because of air resistance. (2.3)

vernal equinox The point where the Sun crosses the celestial equator from south to north, around March 21. The beginning of spring. (15.5)

virtual image An image from a lens or mirror for which the light rays diverge and cannot be formed on a screen. (7.3)

viscosity The internal property of a substance that offers resistance to flow. (22.4)

volcanic mountains Mountains that have been built by material ejected during volcanic eruptions. (21.6)

volcano A vent from which hot molten rock (lava), ash, and gases escape from deep below the Earth's surface, or the mountain or elevation created by solidified lava and volcanic debris that accumulates near the vent. (21.4, 22.4)

volt (V) The unit of voltage equal to one joule per coulomb. (8.2)

voltage The amount of work it would take to move a charge between two points divided by the value of the charge—that is, work per unit charge $V = W/q$ or the electric potential energy per unit charge. (8.2)

waning phase The illuminated portion of the Moon is getting smaller each day as observed from the Earth. (17.2)

water table The boundary between the zone of aeration and the zone of saturation. (23.3)

watt (W) A unit of power equivalent to $1 \text{ kg·m}^2/\text{s}^3$, or 1 J/s. (4.4)

wave The propagation of energy in media from a disturbance. (6.1)

wavelength The distance from any point on a wave to an adjacent point with similar oscillation: the distance of one complete "wave," or where it starts to repeat itself. (6.2)

wave speed The distance a wave travels divided by the time of travel. (6.2)

waxing phase The illuminated portion of the Moon is getting larger each day as observed from the Earth. (17.2)

weather The conditions of the lower atmosphere. (19.1)

weathering The process of breaking down rock on or near the Earth's surface. (23.1)

weight A measure of the force due to gravitational attraction ($w = mg$, on the Earth's surface). (3.3)

white dwarf A hot white star that has a much smaller diameter and much higher density than average. It is believed to be the final stage of a low-mass star. (18.3)

wind The horizontal movement of air or air motion along the Earth's surface. (19.4)

wind vane A freely-rotating device that, because of its shape, lines up with the wind and indicates the direction from which the wind is blowing. (19.3)

winter solstice The farthest point of the Sun's latitude south of the equator (for the Northern Hemisphere), around December 22. The beginning of winter. (15.5)

work The product of the magnitude of a force (or a parallel component of a force) and the parallel distance through which the object moves while the force is applied. (4.1)

X-rays High-frequency, high-energy electromagnetic radiation formed when high-speed electrons strike a metallic target. (9.4)

zenith The position directly overhead for an observer on the Earth. (15.4)

zenith angle The complementary angle of the altitude; it is the angle between the zenith and an object in the sky (the Sun for example). (15.4)

Index